Lady CHARLOTTE BURY

Lady CHARLOTTE BURY

Notorious Diarist, Renowned Novelist and Celebrated Beauty

MARGARET STORRIE

FONTHILL

Front cover: *Lady Charlotte Campbell as a child* by John Opie, 1784, Inveraray Castle. (*Argyll Estates, by kind permission of the Duke of Argyll*)

First published in Great Britain in 2025 by
Fonthill
An imprint of
Pen & Sword Books Ltd
Yorkshire – Philadelphia
www.fonthill.media

ISBN 978-1-03615-146-1

A CIP catalogue record for this book
is available from the British Library.

Typeset in Sabon LT Std 10.5/13
Printed and bound in the UK by CPI Group (UK) Ltd, Croydon, CR0 4YY

The Publisher's authorised representative in the EU for product
safety is Authorised Rep Compliance Ltd., Ground Floor,
71 Lower Baggot Street, Dublin D02 P593, Ireland.
www.arccompliance.com

For a complete list of Pen & Sword titles please contact

PEN & SWORD BOOKS LIMITED
47 Church Street, Barnsley, South Yorkshire, S70 2AS, England
E-mail: enquiries@pen-and-sword.co.uk
Website: www.pen-and-sword.co.uk

Or

PEN AND SWORD BOOKS
1950 Lawrence Rd, Havertown, PA 19083, USA
E-mail: Uspen-and-sword@casematepublishers.com

Acknowledgements

The inspiration to follow Lady Charlotte was not the 'showy' village of Port Charlotte on the Hebridean island of Islay, but the lively 9-year-old girl and her dog in John Opie's portrait hanging in Inveraray Castle that is reproduced as the dustjacket of this book. I am grateful to the Duke of Argyll for permission to include this and other images, as well as for granting access to the Argyll Papers at Inveraray. The ever-enabling Murdo MacDonald, inaugural chair of the Friends of the Argyll Papers and former archivist of Argyll and Bute Council, has pointed me in the direction of many relevant sources throughout my research life. While information on Lady Charlotte's haphazard financial affairs has proved unsatisfyingly elusive, as a biographer, I also have to acknowledge serendipity—it was perhaps unexpected for an account of a moonlit fishing expedition on Loch Fyne in 1799 to turn up in the archival collection of the Scottish Mountaineering Club.

Among the various repositories and archives consulted, especial thanks are due to the staff of the National Library of Scotland in which I transcribed millions of words from manuscripts, particularly those letters deposited by the Gordon-Cumming family. The equally helpful staff in the literally cool Rare Books Room of Cambridge University Library enabled me to read millions of published words written by Lady Charlotte and others, wishing I could turn the page just as the library had to close. Librarians and archivists based in North America have, without exception, been unfailingly helpful and expeditious. Another indispensable resource that has assisted with dating, or correcting misdated letters and journal entries, has been C. R. Cheney's *Handbook of Dates for Students of British History*.

Further afield, visits to Switzerland, Genoa and the Ligurian coast, Florence, Milan, Lombardy and the Veneto, Rome and the Bay of Naples and its islands, have been accompanied by the thoughts of Lady Charlotte, her families and others. Reading Lady Charlotte's diary, sitting among the rooftop pinnacles on Milan Cathedral in April sunshine was definitely more inspiring than deciphering old microfilm on an antiquated machine in London.

Given Lady Charlotte's connections with Islay House and its estate lands, it is especially fitting that her biography is being published by Fonthill Media, perpetuating a local connection to Alastair Morrison, Baron Margadale, and his family. I am grateful to Jane Carswell, Clare Jackson, Rose Sanguinetti and the late Margaret Staniforth for generously devoting many hours to reading the draft manuscript, and to Alasdair Scouller for earlier discussions. I owe an especial debt to Charlène Busalli for her indispensable assistance in preparing the final manuscript for publication, and to Kenny Millar for introducing us. Thank you also to Ishbel Capper for her valuable help with proofreading, arranging photographs of some of the plates, and for many useful conversations. For granting access and permission to reproduce illustrations of Lady Charlotte I would like to thank Alastair Morrison, Baron Margadale, and the Abercorn Heirlooms Settlement Trustees. On Islay, I am indebted to Margaret Aird, Sally Christie, Dorothy Dennis, Cathy Hodges, Oscar Goldsmith, Angus MacTaggart, Bob Newcombe, Richard Russell, Sheena Stevenson and Sandy Taylor for their ongoing kind support. Thanks are likewise due to Myrtle and Richard Pont for hospitality in Edinburgh. Any errors or misconceptions remain mine alone.

Contents

Prologue

Winters were often fierce; over Christmas in 1836, a snowstorm raged for five days in the south of England, and an avalanche killed eight people in Lewes in Sussex. Likewise, in 1838 the frost set in on 7 January and over the next fortnight it deepened until on 20 January the thermometer in Hyde Park registered 3 degrees Fahrenheit (minus 16 Celsius) at 6.30 a.m., with a maximum that day of only 18 (minus 8) and the Thames was frozen over. The 'savagery' of the cold at the start of January 1838 and of the violent reception of the two volumes comprising *The Diary of the Times of George the Fourth* were to be remembered for many years to come.[1] On 3 January Sydney, Lady Morgan, penned the observation in her journal that 'nothing has been thought of or talked of but the *Diary*', continuing: 'The murder is out! There is the *Diary* in everybody's hands … a scandal; a libel on the queen, people, and court of that day; such a book has not been seen, written or read.'[2] The full title read *Diary illustrative of the Times of George the Fourth, interspersed with original letters from the late Queen Caroline, and from various other distinguished persons*.[3] No author's name appeared on the title page which titillated the reader with Maintenon's words: 'Tôt ou tard, tout se sçait' ('sooner or later all is known').

Even the title was misleading. Although George III had long been ailing, and a regency had been in place from 5 February 1811, it was only when he died on 29 January 1820 that George IV became king. The first of the two volumes started with an entry in 1810 and was mainly concerned with the next five years; so at best the title was indicative of the publisher Henry Colburn's over-egging, at worst, deceitful. The diary and letters related not to George IV, but to the establishment around Caroline, the Princess of

Wales. Through the later eighteenth and earlier nineteenth centuries, as George III became increasingly incapacitated, the Court revolved around his wife, Queen Charlotte and the Prince of Wales. The latter and his wife had been estranged since the birth of their daughter Princess Charlotte on 7 January 1796. The king, fond uncle to the Princess of Wales had normally supported her against the increasing machinations of his wife and son to be rid of her. But after the regency was declared, relationships became more poisonous and corrosive, and finally in 1814 the princess, against all advice, left England to wander on the continent for six years.

Always on the ball, and with memoirs in demand, Henry Colburn recognised that the time was perhaps right to revisit the events and people of about quarter of a century before. A new and different Victorian age was just beginning, yet interest in the Regency and George IV was still very much alive. 5,000 copies of Colburn's *Literary Gazette* were rushed out to encourage sales when the notices of this 'abominable' book appeared. The volumes had been 'scored with our pencil from beginning to end', claimed *The Athenæum* of 6 January.[4] In *The Times* of 11 January, William Makepeace Thackeray reviewed the supposedly anonymous, allegedly scurrilous, *Diary*.[5] Lambasting the diarist for letting down a thousand years of family history with disloyalty, Thackeray thundered, 'We never met with a book more pernicious or more mean', comparing it in genre to Harriette Wilson's memoirs. On 12 January 1838 the diarist Charles Greville noted:

> Read in the newspapers that Colburn gave Lady Charlotte Bury £1,000 for the wretched catchpenny trash called 'Memoirs of the Time of George IV', which may well set all the world what Scott calls 'gurnelising' [sharing or gossiping], for nobody could by any possibility compile anything more vile and despicable.[6]

In the Tory *Quarterly Review*, the critic John Wilson Croker strenuously denounced the work, concluding: 'We have no doubt that the unhappy Princess was really insane—and it would be consolatory to have even the same melancholy excuse for the Lady-in-Waiting.'[7] Another noted that strong condemnation of the author and the *Diary* by 'the leading journals and the public did not, however, prevent—may, rather have helped—it to run through several editions' in London, Paris, Philadelphia and New York.[8] Colburn's undeniable skill at advertising was hardly needed to produce an immense sale, although the author, unlike the publisher who held the copyright, presumably did not profit any further financially.[9] As the *Idler and Breakfast Table-Companion* put it, however, 'We need hardly add that this book, disgusting as it is, will produce Mr. Colburn some thousands of pounds. Of this the crafty bibliophile was aware, when he tendered ... the £1000' for the copyright.[10]

The two volumes that caused such a fuss were published anonymously, and publicly denied by both author and publisher. The crude device of attempting to present the work as written by a male, with the insertion of decoy entries to a lady-in-waiting was unlikely to have fooled many. Moreover the authorship had been none too subtly hinted at by Colburn in his *Literary Gazette*. Bizarrely, a letter was published in the *Morning Post* of 18 April 1838, about the claim in the *Edinburgh Review* regarding the authorship of the *Diary.*[11] Thomas Nettleship wrote that he, as the former lady-in-waiting's solicitor, had been directed by her again, to deny this, and 'also to deny that Mr. Colburn has ever "ransacked" or had in his possession any of Lady Charlotte Bury's private papers or letters' (which would seem to be at odds with a subsequent Colburn claim).[12] Almost a hundred years later, the Nettleship letter was quoted in a letter to the Editor of *The Times* in February 1930: 'Nothing could be more authoritative than this contradiction, which, curiously, appears to have escaped the notice of the commentators on the Diary and its supposed writer.' The cleverly crafted wording, however, seems to have eluded his understanding; it was probably the Scots writer John Galt who had to wade through what Walter Scott called the diarist's 'elephantine' handwriting (see plate 1). In his 1851 account of Gillray's caricatures of Lady Charlotte Bury, née Campbell, Thomas Wright's view was that 'the Vox Populi, however, will make her un auteur malgré lui, and pertinaciously persists in ascribing to her pen' the diary, continuing:

> Her Ladyship repudiates this production, and assured a noble poet She did not write it; he replied, 'he felt confident she did not, as no lady of any delicacy of mind could have written it'. No answer being returned, we do not know whether [the lady] received the remark as sarcasm or a compliment.[13]

No other person, however, ever claimed authorship. It could only have been written by one of the women of the bedchamber or one of the ladies-in-waiting at the time, of whom there was less than a handful, all known. They were three North sisters of the Guildford family, Lady Glenbervie and her sister, Lady Charlotte Lindsay, both of whose styles read very differently. Lady Charlotte's husband, son of the 5th Earl of Balcarres, had incidentally sold his wife's correspondence regarding Queen Caroline's affair to the Solicitor to the Treasury.[14] The third, Lady Sheffield, was replaced in 1810 by Lady Charlotte Campbell, recently widowed daughter of the 5th Duke of Argyll, and the fourth position was taken up by others as available. The main criterion was a title, but stamina was also a requirement of those chosen, as well as the diplomacy required when having to act as court go-between.

In 1789 the 14-year-old Lady Charlotte had studiously written up her travel journey of seventy-seven days and nights spent on a journey to Naples for the health of her mother, the Duchess of Argyll. In 1804 she had not only copied out this journal, but had also composed a family memoir which may have stimulated her to continue 'keeping' a diary of her life henceforth.[15] Covering the years 1805 to 1810 this manuscript journal is now in the Huntington Library in California. Despite often being written up in arrear, it exhibits a stream of consciousness in a highly personal narrative. The published *Diary* concerned the years 1810 to 1815, with some subsequent entries relating to 1819; the selections and extracts are similar in style but exhibit a deliberately different approach and only a few references to Charlotte's family life. All of the people involved had probably at the least, been party to dissembling. Author of the Regency Lewis Melville went as far as to suggest: 'It is believed that John Galt … who did a good deal of literary hack-work, was responsible for seeing the first two volumes of the *Diary* through the press.'[16] The letters received, the obfuscatory and descriptive input by John Galt, and possibly even some of the narrative or extended footnotes and commentaries could have been written a quarter of a century after, and could be regarded, strictly speaking, as not being her diary authorship.

At the distance of almost two centuries it is perhaps difficult to understand the furore caused by this *succès de scandale*. By the time it was published many of the persons referred to were already dead. Perhaps the very persons of *ton* felt betrayed more by one of their kind publishing hypocritical reality in a journal, as opposed to betraying their mores in many of her works of fiction. As with such volumes through time, it was the scandalous or even scurrilous references on which attention then focussed. On 17 January 1838, Lady Louisa Molyneux wrote:

> Papa has found some amusement in a book that occupies everybody now—more, it appears, from the atrocity than from any merit it has—*Mémoires et Correspondence* of Queen Caroline, edited by Lady Charlotte Bury, in which there are so many bad stories ill told, and so many personal remarks on living people, that I cannot imagine anybody ever speaking to her again. Her name is not to the book, but everybody knows it is hers.[17]

All her enemies, and many of her friends apparently joined in the chase. The poet, Thomas Hood, 'on reading a diary lately published', was inspired to compose the tendentious lines:

When I resign this world so briery
To have across the Styx my ferrying,
O may I die without a DIARY!
And be interr'd without a BURY-ing!
The poor dear dead have been laid out in vain.
Turn'd into cash, they are laid out again![18]

Charlotte hinted in a letter to aspiring authoress Harriet Pigott in July 1838 that it was not perhaps the optimum time to use her name or be associated with it.[19] Writing to her eldest daughter at the beginning of March 1838, she also claimed that 'very many of my soi-disant old friends have cut me', adding however, that she had made 'many new ones'.[20] Somewhat disingenuously she declared: 'Everybody says that abominable book is mine ... it is unwarrantable to affix my name to an anonymous work.' Theresa Villiers gossiped cattily to the Countess of Morley on 17 April that the author got 'well cut', adding:

> She was at a christening at her son's, where the Duke of Sussex was and placed herself directly in his way meaning he should speak to her ... he made a very slight bow and passed on. She has been seen no where but at Sebastiani's and they say (I hope truly) that the D. of Devonshire too had cut her and turned his back.

She went on to recount that when arriving to visit another of Charlotte's daughters, Lady Euston 'instantly got up and went away without noticing' her mother.[21]

Charlotte's views and justifications of diaries or journals were notably ambivalent. While at court she claimed on 10 February 1811 that of the many times in which she had started writing a journal, 'some reason or other has prevented its continuance, or at least thrown upon it that check, which diminishes the pleasure of writing, and renders the matter less interesting'.[22] So she had decided that it would not be a journal that she would write, 'but brief notes of such things as I conceive may be amusing, without incurring danger to myself or others'.

How can the appearance of the *Diary* more than quarter of a century after Charlotte had penned her entries be explained? In the 1830s she had sundry money-making projects in the air other than her novels (which at times she ambivalently considered as hack work for money). But why 1838? Why did she not make or take time to write a memoir rather than hand over her journal and letters to John Galt and/or Henry Colburn, producing two apparently rushed and deliberately obfuscatory volumes, followed in 1839 by two others with little direct relation to the first two apart from the late Georgian context? New Yorkers over breakfast on Saturday 10 August 1839 reading the 'Jottings from London' discovered that 'Lady Charlotte Bury has, as they say in London, got herself into a precious mess with her Life and Times of George IV' and was being shunned by all but a few of her friends. The correspondent expressed regret at her being so unwise, but went on:

> A lady of some celebrity present objected to such a phrase, and said 'Lady Charlotte was starving in the midst of these 500 friends, who would not have lent her a guinea to save her life. She had the opportunity of choosing between these friends and a thousand pounds. Who would hesitate?' You see there is a practical way of looking at things even in high life.[23]

Perhaps *The Athenæum* had been near the mark in January 1838 when asking the following question:

> Was the publication a reluctant sacrifice to pecuniary necessity? Can it be possible that one so elevated in rank and station ... should be so abandoned by her noble relations, as to be reduced to such a necessity or, being so, is it possible that she should sink under the temptation, for filthy lucre?

In its notoriety, however, it is unfortunately and perhaps unfairly almost the only work for which its author has been remembered, as it has all the characteristics of the proverbial curate's egg. Melville, however, summarised the venture:

> The Book has an historical and biographical value that cannot be gainsaid. It gives an intimate picture of the private, as well as the public, life of the Princess of Wales that is to be found nowhere else; but its immediate success arose from its indiscretions.

Charlotte may have had the last word, however, when composing her introduction to Harriet Pigott's *Records of Real Life* in June 1839, by which time she herself thought that at least her name was back 'in repute in the Publishers estimation, as a marquetable article'.[24] Perhaps she had not foreseen the furore ahead, and she desperately needed the £1,000 from the less than scrupulous Henry Colburn, who soon went on to make much more from subsequent editions.

Charlotte may have sat in her writing room shuddering at the denunciation being poured on her and the *Diary*. But it is possible that, by then in her sixties and a hardened writer of *ton*, having scandalised society twenty years before when choosing to marry her son's tutor, she was probably at least inured to some of the notoriety, and may not even have overly cared. The rather naïve view of Susan Ferrier's biographer, Aline Grant, was that Charlotte could hardly have realised the effect the book would have since her nature was 'blithe, careless and fun-loving. She was not ever sensitive herself and had always lived among people like Jane Austen's Mr Bennet.'[25] While she had excoriated that very society in her fiction, the *Diary* would prove that she was not just a writer of fashionable novels but would also find her place in history at the hub of real events. It illustrated that when she exposed the morals of royalty and aristocracy she knew what she was writing about. She had endured five years in an establishment or minicourt of increasingly dubious reputation which resulted in her cynical views of such society. Despite its deficiencies the work has been cited and used by scores of writers of the regency period right up to the present. Voices such as that of Percy Fitzgerald in 1884 not only castigated Croker's mauling of Charlotte's 'vivacious Diary … full of piquant incidents, traits of manners and "characteristical letters"', but then added that it was 'extraordinary to what an extent the innumerable books of memoirs since published support all that is set out in it, though it was so impugned at the time'.[26]

The *Diary* notwithstanding, Charlotte lived on for another quarter of a century. John Opie's captivating portrait in Inveraray Castle of the 9-year-old Charlotte Campbell in her pink sash and rakish hat, with flashing eyes and lips that forebode trouble (see front cover), has long involved this biographer in Charlotte's long life. The 'normal' trajectory for such a ducal daughter was not to be. This book chronicles its many vicissitudes and ambivalences, from the fashionable beauty of Argyll celebrated in over fifty likenesses, through millions of words in her journals, poems and novels of *ton*, charting a woman's life at the private and public interface during almost nine decades of enormous social, economic and technical change from mid-Georgian to mid-Victorian times. King George IV and Sir Thomas Lawrence adjudged her the most beautiful woman either had ever seen. A daughter of the House of Argyll, dozens of likenesses (and exaggerated caricatures) of her were created in oils, pastels, chalks and pencil during her long lifetime. She became the muse of Walter Scott, 'Monk' Lewis and others, while the Irish Tommy Moore said that of all those who sang his melodies no one gave him such pleasure. The manager of Drury Lane Theatre, Alfred Munn, averred that the vocal talent of Charlotte and Scottish music would long be talked of together. Niel Gow, the renowned Scots fiddler, included 'Lady Charlotte Campbell's Medley, Strathspey and Reel' in his collections, and she danced easily and elegantly. She imbibed poetry from her nanny, was fluent in French and Italian from an early age, and became a lifelong Italophile. With two marriages and widowhoods and up to a dozen children, nine of whom survived infancy and exchanged hundreds of letters, Charlotte wrote millions of words in prose, poetry and letters, although she is chiefly and notoriously remembered as Lady Charlotte Bury[27] for her much consulted but infamous *Diary of a Lady-in-Waiting* at the court of the strange and estranged wife of the equally notorious prince of Wales.

It is almost a *sine qua non* for a biographer to have some liking or empathy with their chosen subject. But while pondering which of Lady Charlotte's 1,600 recipes might be tried, readers will hopefully become absorbed in the long and varied life of an Argyll ducal beauty and courtier, musical and multilingual, one who twice married for love rather than rank. She had journeyed to her beloved Continent by sail and coach at least by the time she was 9, but was also to travel faster and more directly later in life by rail and steamship, as far afield as the bay of Naples and the Hebrides of Scotland. The five-guinea entry for 'aqua' given to the pipers assembled to receive Charlotte jumped out of the large leatherbound folio of 1828 embossed 'Islay Estate'. Despite a lifelong dislike of sailships, the sea and equinoctial gales, Charlotte did venture several times to the Hebridean island of Islay, almost all of which was owned by her first husband's family. In another large rental volume, cleared agricultural tenants were listed as building houses that year in a new village. Not every woman, not even a beautiful ducal daughter, had her name commemorated in what Lord Teignmouth described a few years later as 'the showy village of Port Charlotte', which this Georgian planned village remains to this day.

More usually, she remained on the mainland at Inveraray Castle. She also stayed at Ardencaple Castle, the home of her younger brother, Lord John Campbell, before heading south via Edinburgh and coach to Argyll House in London. This seasonal migration and progress would have formed the expected annual life cycle for the family of one of the premier dukes of Scotland and the United Kingdom. Parliament and the Grand Tour, the Edinburgh and London seasons and the landed estates continued despite the Jacobite rebellion in which her father had played a prominent role, and despite the subsequent American and European wars in which many of her male relatives wore uniform. For ducal and other aristocratic daughters, however, titled marriage was normally the destination. In this Charlotte was not to conform. Her main passions became love, religion, music, *belles lettres* and Italy, and it was on her unconventional choice of love before status that the entire outcome of her life revolved, taking her biographer to unexpected locations, whether geographic, archival or literary. In the same year as Jane Austen was born, the *Times* recorded the 'birth of a little girl' to the 41-year-old 'double duchess', renowned for her Gunning beauty and strong intellect. The *Times* also recorded Charlotte's death aged 86, as it claimed, alone and forgotten. Even the notorious *Diary* for which she is almost solely remembered, was omitted in the *Times* obituary. But her genes of both beauty and writing have carried on through her descendants both male and female. She experienced a full, colourful and long life spanning very different eras and involving aristocratic life, indebtedness, continental travel, as well as unexpectedly proving a major figure in the silver fork genre of commercial publishing.

[illegible] renowned for his cunning, bravery and strong intellect. The [illegible] [illegible] [illegible] [illegible] [illegible] [illegible] [illegible] [illegible] [illegible] [illegible]

1

Aristocratic Mobility

London's Argyll Street today links the busy shopping thoroughfare of Oxford Street and Liberty's store opened in 1875. Over two centuries ago one of the foremost dukes in Britain, 52-year-old John, 5th Duke of Argyll (see plate 2), lived in the eponymous Argyll House (see plate 3).[1] 'That capital, that magnificent, and extensive town residence' was situated on the east side of Argyll Street, but also had a separate entrance from Queen Street and Marlborough Mews.[2] Behind a screen wall, iron railings and gates, the courtyard surrounded a large *porte cochère*; inside, a grand staircase led to the piano nobile with its eight 'capital apartments, all with lofty ceilings'.

The duke's beautiful, tall duchess, Elizabeth, was regarded by all as one of the great European beauties of her time (see plate 4).[3] The second eldest of four Irish Gunning sisters and one brother, she became the wife of two dukes, a duchess in her own right, mother to seven sons (of whom four inherited dukedoms) and she had three daughters. It was in Argyll House on 28 January 1775 that the duchess, by then in her forty-second year, gave birth to her youngest daughter.[4] The newborn girl was given three forenames, Charlotte Susan Maria, although she was rarely to use the second. Her mother had escorted the future queen, Princess Charlotte of Mecklenburg-Strelitz, to England on the eve of her marriage to George III in 1761, and was one of the new queen's women of the bedchamber until resigning in 1784. The name Susan was perhaps after maternal and paternal grand aunts, a Gunning aunt-in-law, or several of her mother's closest friends and confidantes. Maria was chosen in memory of the infant's late aunt, Maria Gunning, the eldest Gunning sister, perhaps even more renowned for her beauty.[5] The duchess had been the widowed

Duchess of Hamilton when she remarried in 1759; by the time Lady Charlotte was born, her surviving half-brother, Douglas, 8th Duke of Hamilton was 18 years of age, his sister, Lady Elizabeth (Betty) Hamilton, 17. Surviving Campbell siblings were Lady Augusta, aged 14 and Lord Lorne, 7. Another brother, Lord John, was to follow when Charlotte was almost 3 years old.

In the western world today, most people accumulate photographs throughout their lives. Some may be sketched, caricatured, or have their likeness portrayed in pastels. But only a few are committed to canvas or paper for posterity. In the past, beauty, fashion, rank, wealth and even notoriety were among the influences that led to portraiture. The factor of chance, however, influences greatly the number of portraits that remain after the sitter has gone. Of oils, pastels, chalks, sketches, lithographs, etchings, caricatures, miniatures, sculptures and the like that were produced during Charlotte's long lifetime, over fifty are known to remain today. While these are mostly by professional artists, some were also created by friends and female members of the family. Her mother and aunt had earlier been portrayed by Cotes, Gainsborough, Reynolds and Romney. Charlotte was in turn to sit for many well-known artists of her day including Kauffman, Tischbein, Hoppner, Lawrence and others. Except during her first widowhood and remarriage, when she had no wealthy financial backer to commission portraits in the 1810s and 1820s, she was assiduously captured during almost every decade. Most of the images that remain are of Charlotte alone, and many are formal in approach; several were painted specifically for particular rooms such as the Tapestry Drawing Room in Inveraray Castle.

The earliest sight of the younger Argyll daughter is in a formal oil painting by Swiss-born Angelica Kauffman (see plate 5).The artist had arrived in England in 1766 and was a founder member of the Royal Academy of Arts two years later, becoming one of the most successful women portraitists and historical-allegorical artists as well as a leading figure in the art world of late-eighteenth century London.[6] During her first year in the capital, she had painted an Argyll niece, Anne Seymour Conway (later Damer).[7] In 1775, the infant Charlotte is sitting on her mother's lap, with her sister, Augusta, standing nearby. The portrait is one of many of the beautiful tall duchess, but tells very little about Charlotte. The next image is a pastel, formerly thought to be by Francis Cotes; he had, however, died in 1770. It has subsequently been attributed to Catherine or Katherine Read, but this is also unlikely.[8] The pastel of Charlotte, however, is of an assured girl who appears to be older than could have been depicted by Read since, by February 1777, Charlotte had just celebrated her second birthday. Assuming the portrait is of Charlotte,[9] whoever the artist may have been, the little girl is seen sitting, facing the onlooker's left, with her head and eyes slightly looking to the right. She wears a necklace and hair ornament and a dove is cradled in her hands on her lap. Indeed, a dove formed part of her grandfather Gunning's coat of arms and crest, and was to feature in several future portraits.[10]

While the younger Argylls were growing up, the courtier duchess was often in London, launching Betty Hamilton and Augusta Campbell into society, but she was also pursuing one of the longest court cases in eighteenth-century Scotland, the Douglas case, on behalf of her Hamilton son and his succession. During the 1780s the duke and duchess were also much involved in creating their chateau or castle in the burgeoning wooded policies around Inveraray on the shore of Loch Fyne in Argyll. In the grounds of the castle the river Aray flows between banks that are covered in springtime with a succession of snowdrops, wild daffodils and bluebells; the path through them is still called Lady Charlotte's Walk. The drawing and dining rooms, decorated in French style, were to be the backdrop of many early scenes in Charlotte's eventful life. Formerly hanging in the Salon at Inveraray Castle are four matching oil portraits (50 x 40 inches) of the four Argyll children painted by John Opie, all with magnificent matching gilded frames.[11] That year, 1784, John Opie had eight pictures hung at the Academy, all portraits.[12] His particular gift for child portraiture was demonstrated in these paintings of the Argyll children, the seated Augusta playing her trademark guitar, George (afterwards 6th Duke) in the act of drawing a statue, Charlotte, and, leading a favourite dog, the youngest, John Campbell (afterwards 7th Duke), who was then a boy of 6.[13] Nine-year-old Charlotte is delightfully portrayed in a flowing, off-white, three-quarters dress, with a broad pink sash at waist level echoing the extravagant ribbon in her rakishly angled hat. The first of her iconic pet dogs to appear in her portraits is being held rather precariously on her lap.

In the opinion of one of her mother's biographers, and of most people, the radiant beauty of Elizabeth Gunning was 'destined to live again in her youngest daughter, Lady Charlotte Campbell, a golden-haired girl in her tenth year, strong-limbed and buxom, a true daughter of the house of Argyll'.[14] Since her earliest childhood she had 'led a free open-air life, spending many of her days on the banks of the Clyde' at Rosneath and Ardencaple,[15] and was 'as wild as an untamed colt, having suffered little restraint from pastor or master. Yet the rigour of her intellect concealed any defects of education, for even at this early stage of her career she was beginning to show evidence of true genius', it was claimed.

When she was 11, harpsichord lessons were being arranged for her during the summer at Inveraray, albeit with some difficulty. In Edinburgh, the duke's agent, John Ferrier, 'had eventually found one Stuart ... a tolerable teacher, tho' a very indifferent performer' who would 'eat at the second table and expect from three half crowns to ten shillings a day'.[16] Charlotte, however, later underlined the 'defects' of her education in a memoir.[17] With hindsight, she wrote that her consumptive mother's increasing ill health and her father's anxiety about his duchess made her lose 'many precious moments that never can be recover'd'. She admitted that she was left to do whatever she wanted: 'My Mind like My Will was allow'd to run riot and has grown up into a Sad Wilderness.' It was to her maid, 'Lewis', that she owed her lifelong pleasure to read and recite poetry, before she could read very well or spell. Lewis was deemed 'the first being I ever remember to have loved passionately'. The 'handsome' daughter of a clergyman, Lewis was described in the memoir as a 'Woman of violent uncontrouled [*sic*] Passions, and devoid of Chastity or Principle', who was nevertheless 'adored rather than lov'd'. When Charlotte was 9, however, some misdemeanour on Lewis's part was to remove this loving childhood support. From the time her maid knew that she was to be dismissed:

> Her Temper even to me whom she lov'd became Insufferably Cruel and at Night well do I remember when I used to be Eating My Supper of Bread and Milk instead of Singing to me or repeating Verses (which were her favourite Amusements), she sat Sullenly Silent. My poor little Heart swelld to Bursting and I drank the Tears I scorn'd to shed, if after having said My Prayers too I did not receive Her blessing.

Charlotte thought her heart would break, but did not have the courage even to enquire when Lewis was to leave, nor could she 'bear to bid Her adieu', throwing instead 'a sort of black arm of despair over a Circumstance I could neither remedy or prevent'.

In the autumn of 1784, doctors declared that the duchess should spend the winter in a warmer climate.[18] Owing partly to the Queen's having refused to receive her Hamilton daughter, Lady Elizabeth Derby, after she had left her husband, and also to the state of her own health, the duchess had resigned her position at Court. A biographer would write later: 'It was evident that she was very ill, and a message of death seemed written in her careworn features. Yet, although her beauty had fled, the lines of her figure were as perfect as old.'[19] On 22 October Lady Louisa Stuart[20] paid 'a most formal awkward visit where we were not welcome, and I am sure had no business. It was to the Duchess of Argyll, who is going to the south of France in a day or two for her health and Lady Augusta's—both looking very ill.'[21] Neither London's fogs nor Scotland's mists and rains were kind to those with ailing lungs, and towards the end of October 1784 the duchess and her retinue set out in three carriages on their long journey to the Mediterranean coast, accompanied by their physician, Dr Robertson.[22] This was perhaps the first of Charlotte's travels abroad, and while she was subsequently to recall in her memoir that her 9-year-old's 'remembrance of the different Countries we pass'd through is faint and like a Dream, yet even then the Coliseum at Nismes, and the Pont de Garde in its Vicinity is impress'd in indelible Characters on my reccolection [*sic*]'.[23] She also claimed even then 'to have felt their Beauties, for Beauty in Animate or Inanimate Objects must be understood before it is tasted must be felt as well as seen, and that intuitive sensation of what was Great or fair, I must say even in Infancy was an Inmate of My Breast'. While she enjoyed the renowned Dessins Hotel in Calais, what she mainly remembered of Paris was the dirtiness and business of the city's streets. All the same, she was 'not insensible to Luxury and Voluptuousness a white satin Quilt that cover'd My Bed was an Object of My great Veneration, and I fancied Myself some Princess of Consequence while lieing beneath it'.

The party spent two months on the way and only reached Marseille, where they had arranged to spend the winter, a few days before Christmas on 19 December 1784.[24] Although the busy seaport of Marseille was perhaps not optimal for anyone with pulmonary illness, there was the 'warm sunlit promenade screened from the northern winds in the open corso around the harbour'.[25] The duchess avoided most social engagements and apparently only appeared once in public at the English colony's Pic Nic Ball. The cultivated Leicestershire squire Joseph Cradock, to whose family the Argylls were 'best friends', described the duchess coming down to coffee after dinner 'dressed in all her splendour; everyone was struck with astonishment'.[26] He continued, 'Her Grace looked as well as when I first saw her in the Court-Room in England, as Duchess of Hamilton', to which the duke rather ungallantly replied, albeit with a smile, 'less aided then, perhaps, than now, Sir'. The Lieutenant of Police rescued the situation, exclaiming that he had never before seen anyone 'so completely beautiful'. The duchess frequently invited small parties from the little English colony to her rooms in the evening. Cradock, a Classical and dramatic enthusiast, enjoyed their frequent concerts and noted that 'their own family could always supply excellent catches and glees'. On these occasions the card-table was never brought out, for although the duke loved a game of cribbage with his daughters:

> the poor mother ... wished no doubt to prevent her younger Argyll children from becoming imbued with a taste for play. Music-making and conversation replaced quinze [a card game whose object was to score as close to fifteen as possible without going above it] and commerce.

While her three daughters entertained the company with Scottish airs and 'excellent catches and glees', 'the courtly old duke moved among his guests, and his stately wife held a little court of delighted gentlemen'. This six-month journey and sojourn helped develop Charlotte's proficiency in French.[27]

Cradock reported that the Argylls had intended moving along the coast to Montpellier, but 'some business suddenly occurred, and they finally resolved to return to England again, by the route of Lyons'.[28] It was on 28 June 1785 that a somewhat revived duchess arrived back in London.[29] The family did not loiter long in the metropolis, staying at Ealing Grove, a small estate 6 miles west of London,[30] which her husband had purchased, the 40-acre grounds being 'arranged with great taste'.[31] A few weeks later the family set out for Inveraray Castle, where as of wont they remained until late in the autumn of 1785.[32]

From late 1779 to 1782 the young Prince of Wales had pursued Augusta.[33] The Hon. Robert Fulke Greville, Equerry to King George III, described a sultry summer evening on the terrace at Windsor Castle in August 1781, with the duchess and Augusta 'both in Riding Habits—the former in a striped Buff & white [cotton] Manchester, the other attired in a light spotted Manchester'.[34] A couple of nights later at a ball in the St George's Hall given to celebrate his nineteenth birthday, 'the Prince of Wales Table was on the Right of His Majesty's. It was jocosely surmised that on this occasion it was not quite accident which had placed HRH next to Lady Augusta Campbell.'[35] But although Augusta's 'youth, her rank, and her face, which was very charming, though not intelligent, compensated for the defects of her shape and figure', as American traveller Sir Nathaniel William Wraxall opined, 'the "Ophelia" of the court of George III ... possessed neither accomplishments nor mental qualifications to retain her "Hamlet" and the Prince soon transferred his affections to Lady Melbourne'.[36]

Charlotte elaborated on the subsequent years and affairs of her sister Augusta in her memoir. Since all her ambitious mother's 'Romantic Hopes' with regard to the Prince of Wales and Augusta had been 'blown over', Lord Graham, son of the Duke of Montrose, was the next prospect 'Her Eyes were turn'd upon—as a Proper and Elligible [*sic*] Husband for Sister Augusta'. The idea pleased her father, 'who tho' never addicted to plans or intrigues in their most innocent Sense still thought such a Match desirable for the Daughter he adored, as County Interest and every other would be the Consequences of such an Union'. The duchess used a Hamilton relative, the future Lord Abercorn, 'to bring this Matter to bear, but whatever might once have been Lord Grahames Intentions with respect to Augusta Her undisguised Passion for the Prince had check'd every favourable Opinion he Might have entertain'd for Her, and all the means that could be devised by Lord Abercorn or My Mother proved fruitless'.

While the family was wintering in France in 1784-5, however, Augusta seemingly formed an 'Unfortunate Attachment with a Mr Nisbet' of Dirleton, brother of the then Mrs Campbell of Shawfield.[37] Charlotte used the pejorative adjective, which was in reality somewhat unfair; it was not a 'Match her Parents could Consent to, as the young Man had neither Family or Connection or Fortune tho of an Amiable Disposition'.[38] As matters turned out, Charlotte deemed it 'a sad Pity she was not united to the Man who Seem'd really to possess her Heart, for all her other Loves were those of Pleasure Vanity or Ambition'. Mr. Nisbet 'behaved very handsomely with respect to not taking advantage of Augusta's attachment to him, as she would have run away with Him, anything to be his Wife'. He declined 'any such methods of procuring what might have been Supposed an Interested Match. And Augusta had not that Energy of Mind, which Makes a person Act for themselves in Spite of Difficulties'. After their return to England, Augusta sank into a 'Torpid State and was only roused now and then from that Lethargy when Her Temper was Irritated. Her whole Intellectual Powers seem'd to have faded away and with them also her Person alter'd sadly and scarcely left a Wreck of Her former Self.' When they subsequently stayed at Rosneath and Inveraray she became ill-tempered, and 'ill mannered to Her Parents', frequently remaining for whole days in her room, rendering herself 'in every respect disagreeable'.

Augusta 'still fancied Herself in Love with Nisbet', but after only a fortnight's acquaintance in the Highlands, this 'transferable passion was all she bestowed on the new Object of her Unoccupied Ennui, a poor promise for future Bliss'. By February 1788 when the Duke of York was visiting his mother, Queen Charlotte, 'the subject of his talk was Lady Augusta Campbell's elopement from the masquerade'.[39] Without the consent of the duke or duchess, Augusta had eloped from the Duchess of Ancaster's masquerade ball to become the wife of Lieutenant Henry Clavering.[40] Charlotte declared the latter 'a 2d Brother who tho an Honourable Man in the Worlds Acceptation was of a Character little likely to make a Womans happiness and fortune and Splendour cast no brilliant Light to Gloss over the rude Surface with illusion'.[41] Horace Walpole remarked 'there was no great occasion for Lady Augusta to be married'.[42] The Argylls, however, accepted the marriage as a *fait accompli*.

The duchess had likewise not been taken into the confidence of her eldest daughter, Charlotte's half-sister Betty Hamilton, over her marital fancies.[43] Charlotte recounted how the Duke of Dorset had won the heart of Betty:

> A Captivating Amiable Woman, but a Natural want of Solidity of Character joined to an Artless and Tender Disposition left Her an Easy Prey to Folly, and to Vice—The Duke of Dorset then a Gallant Gay Lothario talk'd but never dreamt of Marriage. He went over Ambassador to Paris Carried with Him My Unhappy Sisters Affections, and ... never wrote to Her as he had promis'd.[44]

According to Charlotte, Betty buried her mortification 'in Dissipation and Admiration' and, in the memoirist's view, 'Among the Number of Her profess'd Lovers', the aforementioned Mr. Nisbet of Dirleton[45], was one of Betty's best conquests. But the young woman's 'Heart was barr'd against His Addresses for ever' and her mother and a Hamilton relative, Lady Charlotte Edwin, instead dreamed up marriage with the latter's nephew, Lord Derby. The duchess saw wealth, title and grandeur ahead for her daughter and spared no effort until the reluctant bride-to-be gave in:

> No Blandishments that Power and Splendour and Passion could bestow were spared to Dazzle the Unhappy Victim—a great Fête was given in Honor of their approaching Nuptials, Music and Masks, and all fine arts which Vice perverted to its own detestable uses were at this Fête put in Action to deceive My Unhappy Sister.

During this over-extravagant *fête champêtre* at The Oaks in Epsom in June 1774, and as Charlotte was to say of her family memoir—'it read like a novel'—the Duke of Dorset suddenly reappeared and 'Happiness from that instant forsook Her'. Her half-sister did marry Lord Derby, but, after having two children, left him for the duke who subsequently deserted her, pregnant with his daughter. Despite the scandal, the Duchess of Argyll had tried to have Betty received at court, and resigned from her post after falling out with Queen Charlotte over the affair. The Duke of Dorset's daughter, Elizabeth[46], was born to Lady Derby in Nice and three years later they returned to England, her health impaired. After suffering a stroke in the 1780s, she became an invalid member of the Argyll household. By the time her daughter was 15, Betty had lost her speech and was unable to move, and on 14 March 1797 she died, aged 44.[47] Although only very young at the time, Charlotte had been deeply impressed by her half-sister's 'Sad Story'.

As Charlotte grew into her teens, it would have been surprising if her mother's marital ambitions had not then been transferred to her youngest daughter. Less has been written of the duke's influence on his daughters. Charlotte termed herself, even at almost 15 years old, a 'Chambermaid Scribe', having been taught by her maid Lewis. When she heard her brother learning Latin, her ambition tempted her to follow, and she claimed in her memoir to have 'succeeded quicker and I am told as thoroughly as any Boy of my Age could have done'. But 'of this I also grew tired and having read Cesar's Commentaries, flung the Book at My Unfortunate Teachers Head and never more thought of Latin'. Despite the well-stocked libraries of Argyll House, Inveraray Castle and other homes of the extended Argyll family, Charlotte admitted: 'What I read ... only did Me harm and never was I taught to peruse useful Books or follow any regular Mode of Education.' Nevertheless, she could lose herself in poetry and plays, as well as, from time to time, papers in *The Spectator* and other essays. But she confessed to hating history and not understanding Shakespeare. By this time she rather 'fancied Myself and indeed was in My Intellectual faculties a Woman', but also 'Loath'd the Company of Girls of My Own Age devour'd Novels and Trash and was completely Romantick and Silly'.

Charlotte recalled a restricted family circle, constrained by her mother's frailty, and since 'My Fathers affections bound Him to her society alone—a certain number of Elderly Persons came constantly to Argyll House with a slight sprinkling of Young Ones'.[48] She was very fond of her paternal uncles and aunts, Lord and Lady Frederick Campbell, Field Marshall Conway and Lady Ailesbury, as well as General and Lady Cecilia Johnston. Other kin or close acquaintances included the Duchess of Richmond, Mrs Grenville (mother to Lady Stanhope), an 'Old' Mrs French, Lady Dillon of Mount Edgecumbe, Lady Mary Betty McKenzie and Lady Greenwich, who 'formd the principal part. The more formal Visitors were of course innumerable and every now and then an old Mouser of Quality droppd in to seek what it could devour at the Card Table before the Hours of wider and more fashionable ravage began.'

Charlotte's cousin, the sculptress, Anne Seymour Conway Damer, at about 40 'scarcely to be calld young', the two Miss Berrys ('I verily believe worthy and sensible but a Love of the fine Arts and the Attention they met with in Consequence of Cultivating them exclusively to the Detriment of the Slighter Attentions of Society, together with their success in so doing got them a great deal of Envy and made them Enemys'), two Miss Gunnings ('cousins and protegees of My Mothers the Eldest was a Maid of Honor And a Maid rather withering on the Virgin Thorn but a very worthy well inform'd tho' rather prudish pragmatical Woman Her Sister an Echo to Her with a Handsome Woman Emperor Head on a Dwarfs Body'), a Mrs Anderson ('as Clever as Uncultivated Genius can make Anyone, but as Heartless as Fashion and intrigue and want of principle can induce a Person to be') and two or three unnamed others were among the 'only Young Women who ever enter'd the Coterie of Cats'. The picture was completed by 'a few old Gentleman [*sic*] Among which let me select

Lord Orford then Sir Horace Walpole Andrew Stewart Sir Robert Keith and Gen[l] Ohara, Skeene, Murray and some others', who 'made up the Group of pairs like twos and twos walking beside a Canal in the old Print of some Vauxhall Garden view'd in a Camera Obscura'. As she later wistfully observed, 'these were all I knew of the World or its Inhabitants'. She added that Lord and Lady Abercorn (his first wife) and his Hamilton family and relatives were perpetual visitors who,

> With the Young Women I Have mention'd some times talkd of that World I wish'd so much to be old enough to enter into, but in Lord Abercorn, tho' he affected a Sort of Charge of me and My Education and tho' I look'd up to Him as something very Superior I certainly thought I Saw a Superiorly old and Ugly Man who was Consequently very fit for a Friend, but I now believe My every Thought on that Score was perfectly false.

In 1788 her maternal cousin, Betty or Betsey (Elizabeth) Gunning, younger daughter of the duchess's only brother, John, and six years older than Charlotte, joined the household to be brought up by her aunt, the duchess, and to be 'Introduced to the great World'.[49] She had grown up in Edinburgh when her father was in the military in America, then moved to London (St James Palace and Twickenham) and into the Argyll family. Charlotte described Betsey as follows:

> Far from handsome or clever but she had aparent [*sic*] goodness and gentleness and fascinated me so much I thought Her pretty. As My Heart was really form'd to love some thing exclusively and My Novel turn'd brain heated it with Fictitious fires, I form'd a friendship with this Girl which in spite of the disparity of our years [was] lasting and never to be forgotten.

Lady Stafford, a close friend of the duchess, described an evening at Lord Hawkesbury's 'where we found the Duke and Duchess of Argyll, Lady Augusta and Lady Charlotte Campbell and Miss Gunning. We had a great deal of Musick after Dinner. Lady Augusta has a wonderful fine voice and sings with great taste.'[50] In her memoir, however, Charlotte unkindly adjudged Betsey as 'having worm'd herself into My affections'. This friendship had been jeopardised during the winter of 1790-1 when Charlotte encouraged her cousin to 'fancying Herself in Love with My Brother George'. To make the latter jealous, Betsey announced her imagined betrothal to the Marquis of Blandford, but it backfired and she was banished from the Argyll household.[51] Betsey's mother, Susannah

Minifie or Gunning had produced half a dozen novels in the 1760s, and, after this episode in 1791, she launched a pamphlet war involving the Duke of Argyll in an unsuccessful attempt to clear her daughter's name,[52] the affair being termed the 'Gunningiad' by Horace Walpole, and occupying columns in the newspapers as well as being caricatured by Gillray.[53] In the last decade of the eighteenth century her literary career was reanimated after this major scandal, her novels being thinly disguised references to this matchmaking scheme gone wrong. John Gunning meanwhile had thrown his wife and daughter out, and had then eloped with his mistress to Naples where he died on 2 September 1799. Susannah died the following year on 28 August. Betsey also became a novelist, publishing a collection of fairy tales for children and translating other works.[54]

Consumption continued to affect the duchess and Charlotte noted in 1789 that her mother 'should once more try the Effects of Foreign Air, a last and generally Hopeless Tryal made only to Amuse and Despair'.[55] 'With lamentable ignorance of climate', doctors advised her to spend the winter of 1789-90 in southern Italy.[56] On 4 June she attended the Drawing-Room held in honour of the King's birthday and even visited the Assembly Rooms at Hampton Court on 18 August just before her departure.[57] Sadly, she did not manage to pay her usual visit to Scotland; at Inveraray the 22 September would celebrate the coming of age of her son, George, the Marquis of Lorne. On 6 September, the evening before she left London all her family came to Argyll House 'to say good-bye, for no doubt most of them imagined that they would never look upon her face again'.[58] Horace Walpole informed Mary Berry that the Duchess of Argyll was 'very ill indeed'.[59] Augusta by this time had a little boy, whom she left with her widowed mother-in-law, Lady Clavering, while she and her husband accompanied the Argylls on their journey south to Italy.[60] Lady Derby was now 'unable to follow us': although only 36 years old, 'she could not walk without assistance and even her Arms and Speech were evidently Affected'. She was to go to the sea coast of Devon at Sidmouth, a base also for 11-year-old John and his tutor, Dr W. F. Cumming.

2

Neapolitan Adventure

On 7 September 1789 the duke, duchess and Charlotte, accompanied by George as far as Dover, set out in one coach, the Claverings in another, and the servants and the duchess's doctor, Halliday, in a third. Instead of venturing near Paris that year they proceeded east to their destination, Naples, through the low countries, Rhineland, Bavaria, Tirol and Switzerland.[1] Whose idea the journal was is not known, and at the end of her memoir, Charlotte later tells of her decision to copy her journal of the journey.[2] She even inserted a disclaimer:

> Such was the little insight I had in the Affairs of the world so warm was my heart so Uninform'd My Brain and in this Uncultivated State of growing Womanhood was written My following Journal no further alter'd from its original form than in being I hope better Spelt and a few And as and tautologies ommitted.

Perhaps spelling was not one of her strong points. Her granddaughter, Lady Constance Russell, subsequently claimed that her journal showed 'for one so young, a very remarkable and true appreciation of all that is most elevating in nature and art'.[3] The journey related was the outward one only; there was a writing desk and ink on their coach, though, given its movement, it must have been hard to write legibly. At other times the 14-year-old Charlotte retreated to her inn room to compose perhaps 1,500 words; sometimes she was too fatigued by the rigours of travel to write much at all. What becomes clear when reading the copied journal is that her father appears more often, leading his daughters' 'grand tour'.

At the start of the gilded, leather-bound and buckled volume is a detailed listing of the 'Route of His Grace The Duke of Argyll from Ostend to Naples Begun Saturday the 12 September 1789'. Every overnight stop at an inn or hotel, and some meal stops, are recorded. The last entry just before arriving in Naples is written after seventy-six days of travelling, having spent more than one night in only eight places—Augsburg (2), Bolzano (2), Verona (2), Bologna (2), Venice (2), Florence (3), Perugia (2) and Rome (3). The year being 1789, the nearer Mediterranean was out of bounds, therefore, despite being subject to cold rainstorms and sometimes bitter winds in winter, Naples had been chosen as their place of residence for the winter, which seems somewhat unsuitable for a consumptive patient.[4] The choice may also have been influenced, however, by the presence of the British minister, Sir William Hamilton, cousin of the duchess's first husband. But whether such a long journey with both political and physical hazards was ideal for an ill 56-year-old is at least arguable. Charlotte refers to her mother's late starts each day, or to plans changed on account of her mother's fatigue.

The first entry is stark: 'We left London this morning to go abroad. I need not say how sorry I was to leave London and My dear Friend Betty [Gunning].' They got as far as Frederick Campbell's 'vastly pretty Place' at Coomb Park[5] and three days later Charlotte left her uncle and aunt with 'real regret'. When George had seen them 'all safe stowed' on Captain Rey's vessel at Dover, ready to sail at midnight on Friday 10 September, Charlotte's 'heart grew very tight and I burst into tears'. They were on board for fourteen hours, the last four of which were wild, leaving Charlotte squeamish and, on landing, sick. On Saturday they followed a 'good' road to Bruges while the following day they boarded a fraxcoot on the canal from Bruges to Ghent built in the seventeenth century when the Schelde was closed by war. But before they set off at nine o'clock, what was to become habitual was that Charlotte and her 'Papa' got up at seven 'to see some fine Churches, with tomb stones, fonts, statues and paintings'. She wrote down many of the titles and attributions but also honestly admitted to forgetting some. She described Bruges as 'formerly one of the greatest trading Towns in Europe but ... the Civil Wars put an End to that and it is now only famous for Churches and Monasteries'. Even after this quick tour, they managed to 'stuff down a little Breakfast' before going on the fraxcoot. In the evening in the St Sebastian Hotel at Ghent, Charlotte wrote up almost a thousand words of her impressions of fellow passengers 'Stinking like Polecats', local dignitaries including the following:

> A short fat Man with a Blue Silk Coat two watch Chains a Round Hat a L'Anglois as he flattered himself and to render the Whole Complete a bag

> and sword his Manner of inclining his Head for he did not deign to Bow Seem'd as if he thought he was doing a thing much below his Dignity.

There was also a 'great Fat Fryar'. Everything at the dining table was 'Stinking: Oil, and Guts, and Garbage so I eat little tho' hungry which gave me more time to See and Smell the People round me'. There was a contretemps involving rank between the duchess and the blue-coated baron which silenced the table, after which an afternoon's ennui ensued since the high banks of the canal meant that little could be observed. 'A tiresome Conveyance' and 'no variety' was Charlotte's verdict.

Before leaving Ghent the following day, the doctor, Charlotte, Augusta and Henry Clavering did more sightseeing, including the 'very fine' churches of St Bavo and St Peters with their renowned interiors and paintings by Rubens, Vandyke and others 'which from the hurried Manner of viewing them have escaped My Immediate recollection'. The rest of the day was spent in the carriage till, at six in the evening, they reached Allost, 'a dirty looking place' and a 'bad Inn and bad beds'. On Wednesday 16 September, they left at noon to cross what she described as follows:

> A striped, flat but fertile Country, as most of the Austrian Netherlands are, the last three or four Miles the general appearance of the Scenery enlivens a little and there is some inequality in the Ground which the Inhabitants call Hills, and where English Horses would Gallop theirs creep like Snails.

On reaching Brussels, Charlotte was struck by its cleanliness and beauty. The Hotel Belle Vue passed muster, being 'large and good in every respect'. Between arrival and 11.30 the following morning, assiduous sightseeing managed to encompass the archduke's palace as well as his country seat, Chateau du Lac, 'magnificently furnished throughout'. After dining they drove through the streets to the Grande Place where they even found time to shop, the formidable duchess haggling down by half, a 'beautiful Suit of Lace' for Betty Gunning 'which shews what Cheats the Trades People in this Country are'. Charlotte also recorded that the famous tapestry manufactory was 'gone much into disrepute and [went] on very Ill'.

The countryside beyond Brussels was deemed one of the finest she had ever seen: 'it is as rich as our Yorkshire and I think in some places the view is prettier than any I have seen in that County'. With Brookes's *Gazetteer*[6] to hand, they passed through Louvain, noting the beautiful building of its 'celebrated' university. But 'while stopping at the Poste to eat something— we observed a Sort of Confusion among the People and the Hote informed us there was Something en l'air which in eight or ten days would break forth—this Alarmed us a good deal'. So they hastened on to Firlemont only to find it overrun with soldiers while the 'patriots Had broke into all the Houses of the principal people and had pillaged and Plunder'd' and 'had torn up the very Trees by their roots'. The accommodation was the worst so far encountered, and early next morning they made haste into their carriages after breakfast. In 'very fine weather' they finally reached the Hotel du Moulin in Maestrick at seven in the evening. The following day dawned very cold and wet, the gloomy atmosphere not helped by passing 'Six Men hanging close to the publick Road, evidently lately executed from the freshness of their Cloaths'. Charlotte was under-impressed by the few remains of Charlemagne's tomb in Aix-la-Chapelle, adding that so far she had 'seen nothing which delighted me half as much as the Pictures at Ghent'.

Although it was sometimes possible to use the writing desk in the carriage 'the Coach shook so violently yesterday I could not write any more'. By this time they had reached the Rhine at Cologne but 'I can never express how ruinous how dirty and how stinking it is'. Charlotte's spirits were low and she wrote introspectively. Sunday 22 was 'dear Georges Birth Day' and she was perhaps pining to participate in her brother's coming-of-age celebrations at Inveraray. She confided: 'How little did I dream of spending it here how little one ought to depend on future Hopes. I thought last year that this one would be a very happy one to me but I do not find it so.' She mused as to who her family would now try marrying George to, hoping that he was not more involved with that 'Horrid Crocodile Mrs Anderson': 'I do believe she has the blackest of all Hearts with a semblance of everything that is perfect.' Charlotte would like to have used her time in Cologne looking at the many churches and their 'fine Pictures', this being Reuben's birthplace as well as the Capital of the Electorate of Cologne, but 'we have not seen them Mama is so unwell'. Only leaving after one o'clock, by the time they reached the 'excellent' Hotel de la Cour Imperiale in Bonn, Charlotte was 'so sleepy and the Beds look so Tempting I can add no more'.

The justly renowned Rhine valley made a huge impression on the young diarist, as on most others over time. 'I never made any Journey that Amused me so much as this Days', she wrote on 23 September, describing the steep-sided valley, 'cover'd with woods and vines and orchards' and 'on the summits of the Hills there are Old Castles or towers or fortresses of the finest and most Picturesque Forms', with scattered villages. The postilions took no notice of the female fears caused by the road being 'made on an amazing steep Bank hanging over the river very narrow and not the smallest Fence to prevent one from breaking ones Neck, tho' apparently few accidents were heard of'. Continuing on through Andernach and Limbourg with 'scarcely two Miles of flat Ground' they stopped on 26 September at the Hotel de la Rose in the spa town of Wiesbaden, the duchess so fatigued that they didn't carry on to Mainz until the following day. Just before reaching the latter, they crossed the Rhine, quarter of a mile wide, 'on a bridge made of Boats which are chain'd together and surmounted by a wooden Plat form with a rail upon each side'. Having dined, they had a quick look round Mannheim before arriving at yet another 'bad Inn, with imbecil[e] people and Exorbitant Charges'.

From Stuttgart, which she described as pretty but melancholy, they reached Geisengen where their servants were to experience a sleepless night at the 'Hotel du Cigne Blanche' [*sic*]. The duchess's maid, Humberstone, told them next morning that a German had used a ladder to get in through her window during the night and she had run for help to the courier's room. Connor was her saviour, and they discovered next morning it was the innkeeper who had intruded on a trumped-up pretext. Later in their travels Charlotte was to note that the same Humberstone 'chooses to fancy herself in Love with Connor and he cannot bear her'. They left this 'horrid Place with Pleasure', continued via the cathedral city of Ulm on the Danube and reached Augsburg on 4 October. There they caught up with Augusta and her husband who had been travelling ahead. As well as writing up her journal, Charlotte had also been writing letters to her brother John, her cousin Betsey Gunning, and others. At last, after nearly a month of spending almost every night in a different place and bed, they spent two nights at Augsburg where Charlotte was delighted to receive two letters from Betsey, among others. Approaching Reitz on 7 October in fine weather the Tirol alps were covered with snow, which 'scene had to me the additional beauty of Novelty' and the day's travel 'was more beautiful than any thing can be Imagin'd ... this Magnificent scenery ... surpasses everything for sublime Beauty that I can conceive'. The steep hills and dangerous roads became a constant refrain. Innsbruck, the capital of the Tirol, she deemed impressive, with its wide streets and well-built houses, but she was upset by the understandably melancholy look on the faces of convicts drawing carts from the gold, silver and copper mines. The host at the inn had amassed a collection of 500 different Tirol marbles, while Charlotte recorded the 'Hottest and most extraordinary wind to Day I ever in My Lifetime felt it is call'd the Shiroc [Sirocco] and reckon'd very unwholesome'. The weather in the mountains was variable but the same could hardly be said of the inns—almost all 'bad'.

Floods and the rising waters of the river Inn caused problems for the travellers. Though admitting that 'some of the views [were] quite sublime', Charlotte seemed more concerned with the dangers posed by the floods and roads than impressed with crossing the Alps. But on 12 October they left the north behind, reaching Bolzano via the Brenner Pass. At 1370 metres or 4495 feet it was the oldest and lowest pass used, the 19-kilometre [12-mile] road having been finished in 1772. They still had to contend with swollen rivers in the Adige valley, driving through a metre or over 3 feet of water, and encountering 'violent' rains. There were often hiatuses when they had to wait for horses, and while delayed by the rains at Trento, Charlotte wrote five letters to England and Scotland, before carrying on to Roveredo, where silk was made 'in finer Colours ... than anywhere else'. Despite the servants' carriage being overturned near Alla, they reached Peri in fine weather ('disagreeably warm') on 15 October where 'the people cheated poor Papa sadly'. Two nights were spent in Verona's 'good but dear inn'. In the morning they visited the amphitheatre 'which tho' fine is not so perfect as the one at Nismes', before enthusing about the beautiful Ponte Nuove and the 'still more so' Porte de Paille. Pliny's birthplace, the Cathedral, new palazzi and other sights were noted and presumably relayed in letters to her younger brother John and her cousin Louisa Campbell.[7] Passing Caldo and Montebello Charlotte noted that 'the Grapes for the first time I have seen them do so look beautiful they are trained up to the Tops of high Mulberry Trees and hang in rich festoons from one Tree to another'. In Vicenza, Palladio's Palazza della Regina was deemed 'a most Beautiful Building', while in the church of St Antonia di Padua she was overwhelmed by 'some of the finest Carving (sculpture I believe I should say) in white marble that can be imagin'd'. She looked forward to exploring more of Padua on their return from Venice.

Continuing down the Lombardy plain of the Po valley into the Veneto, they went on the Brenta, which she thought looked more like a canal than a river, reminding her of the passage from Bruges to Ghent, but 'its sides are still gayer and more cover'd with houses'—villas such as the Palladian Villa Foscari. The intention was to spend four days in Venice, the first sight of which burst 'with all its Wonders in the view'.

> Amazement is the only Distinct Sensation one can be said to Experience to behold an Immense City on the Bosom of the Ocean (for the Lagunnes [*sic*] as they are call'd have that appearance) creates a sort of Doubt and admiration that Words or at least My words can convey no Just idea of.

But she also noted the mismatch where the well-known scenes of 'Marble Pallaces and Gay Gondolas crowded with splendours and Beauty' were in reality 'converted into very Dark narrow stinking Canals ... on whose surface glided a few melancholy Gondolas being cover'd with Black', which brought to mind 'more the Idea of floating Hearses than any Vehicle for the living'.

The duchess herself 'conceived so strong a prejudice' against Venice that she resolved they would only stay for two of the four planned days. After again meeting up with Augusta, and devouring letters from Betsey, cousin Louisa and uncle Frederick, Charlotte's spirits flagged since Betsey had been ill, and she went to bed, sleeping only fitfully. Next morning, the family party headed for St Mark's Piazza which did indeed 'Compensate for the narrow Dreary Canals and fully exceeded My expectation'. The beautiful buildings, the gay concourse of people, the brilliancy of the shops and the coffee houses in the arcades 'to which the Women as well as the men resort' all dazzled Charlotte's eyes. Best of all she liked the large 'Brass Doors brought from Constantinople and the four Brazen Horses outside the Cathedral'. However, the Rialto bridge on the Grand Canal did not quite live up to her high expectations; she disputed the height of its famous arch recorded in Brookes's *Gazetteer*. Like all visitors, she appraised and listed the paintings, not shy to note which she particularly admired. Indefatigable—'to My Excessive sorrow we could see nothing more that Day owing to the lateness of the Hour'—she regretted having to leave the next morning, since 'Mama had so determined'. They returned by the Brenta to Padua, 'where alas we did not stop as it was previously determin'd we should do'. By Sunday 25 October Charlotte was once more noting that her mother was very ill.

Oxen were being used to take the carriages through the deep thick mud; rivers including the Po had to be crossed on large boats or on bridges without parapets. Two nights were to be spent in Bologna on Thursday 29 and Friday 30 October, which meant that Bologna also had to be 'done' in one day. But one filled with wonders, as Charlotte was to record: 'We saw this Day so many fine things that my head quite turns with it.' Guides or guidebooks must have helped her notice and note many of the paintings and drawings in St Peter's Cathedral, including Raphael's picture of Saint Cecilia 'as beautiful as it is famous', then other churches, palazzi and the Galeria Zampieri and Lampieri. The wistful 14-year-old 'left this Place with regret and could have staid Days admiring the beauty of the Pictures and Statue of Andromeda which appear'd to me wonderfully fine'. She declared this town 'the finest I have seen except Bruxells—wide regular Streets Handsome Buildings Piazzas and Palaces with an appearance of Gayety and Clenliness [*sic*] that charms me', but was to leave it the next Morning.

The roads, inns and beds deteriorated again as they climbed out of the Po valley into the foothills of the Apennines, before descending some days later and on 2 November reaching the 'very fine' gated entry into the city of Florence, where they stayed in the equally renowned Vaninis Hotel. Charlotte enthused of Florence: 'This Town does indeed deserve its Fame surpassing all I have yet seen—The Galeries are wonderful such a variety and Quantity of Pictures and Statues it is quite Confusing.' This time luck was on her side since 'Papa is persuaded to stay another day—I shall go again to that delightful gallery and mark down what most pleases me altho' such a Hasty view of them leaves but an imperfect impression'. Perceptively she wondered whether it was worth writing down all such impressions 'since that is so much better done in all the Books one can buy'. But on the following evening she still had the energy to write 1,500 words, noting those statues and paintings 'which I shall never forget', many of 'improper subjects'.

In the end it was not until the morning of Wednesday 4 November that they left Florence, 'sorry to quit so agreeable and so famous a City'. As in many parts of their journeyings, Charlotte bemoaned the lack of trees, or the ways in which they were managed and cut. She wondered why the 'Thrasimene' Lake, though beautiful, looked very green. At Perugia it was once again raining and their heavy carriage could not venture over the fords until the river waters had fallen. A visit to the convent at St Angelo elicited the view that 'that Horrid Grate' deprived the twenty-five nuns 'forever of Liberty which is dearer far than Life': 'we took our leave of this Hospitable Sisterhood and for the first time I felt the full Delight of Liberty'. In another church on the way to Spoleto the 'Superior Monk seem'd quite Drunk I conclude He had been making some of their Liqueurs'. While Spoleto had boasted a fine inn, that at Monte Rosi on 14 November was 'a horrid Ale House, but the Letters are come (by courier sent to collect them from Rome) and I can think of nothing else'. Correspondents of Charlotte and her parents included Betsey and Catherine or Kitty Gunning [the duchess' sister], Lord Frederick, 'Sidmouth' [Lady Betty] and George, Marquis of Lorne.

By the evening of Monday 16 November, Charlotte was confessing that she was 'now in Love with Rome with regard to the things there are to be seen of Antique Curiosity, but if one may judge by the appearance of the Town in driving through it is Dull and melancholy in Comparison to Florence'. From the Trinità dei Monte at the head of the Spanish Steps they viewed the city before exploring, treasuring the Porta del Popolo and obelisk before venturing into St Peters 'which surpass'd every idea I had formed of it—never was there or will there be any thing to exceed it'. One wonders how long it took the 14-year-old to pen several thousand words on St Peter's, before she then continued to describe other churches, the Trajan and Antonius columns, Constantine's arch, the Pantheon and the Coliseum. Abruptly either her muse or her later copying of her journal ceases, still in Rome and still a few days from Naples, which they finally reached on 22 November 1789, seventy-six days after setting out.

Sir William Hamilton, cousin of the duchess' first husband, had been Britain's chief diplomatic representative at the Court of Ferdinand IV and Maria Carolina when Naples was second in size only to Paris in continental Europe. From 1764, first as envoy extraordinary, then from 1767 as minister plenipotentiary, he served the kingdom of the Two Sicilies until 1800. When younger, he had acted as aide-de-camp to the Duke of Argyll's brother-in-law, General Conway. Apart from attending court and participating in the king's only real passion, hunting, Sir William occupied much of his time and energies in collecting (and selling) art and artefacts, as well as studying the abundant natural phenomena around the bay of Naples. The keyboard skills of his wife, Catherine, were admired by Mozart's father, Leopold, and many musical evenings were held at their various residences. The main one was the Villa or Palazzo Sessa, a spacious, three-storey set of apartments (still extant) in a former monastery in the Pizzofalcone district of Naples, that had recently been acquired by the Marchese di Sessa. For about £150 a year Sir William rented the entire southern length of the building and half of the adjoining western portion above the entrance.[8] Under the English-style Adamesque ceilings, Old Master paintings covered the walls, and every surface in both public and private salons was adorned with Etruscan vases, terracotta heads, relics from Pompeii and Herculaneum then being excavated, cabinets of gems, medals, lava specimens, cameos, atlases and books, all much admired by visitors such as the writer Johann Wolfgang von Goethe and the artist Johann Heinrich Wilhelm Tischbein in 1787. Sir William had a circular balcony room or observatory constructed on the south-western upper corner of his apartments, the view from which encompassed the enormous sweep of land, sea and islands, as well as Mount Posillipo, the Villa Reale promenade and the Sorrento coastline, all reflected in the inside half of the room in enormous mirrors. A cushioned seat the whole way round was particularly enticing in winter. To escape the summer afternoon heat of Naples a carriage drive would take them to what subsequently became known as Villa Emma, a three-roomed summer house (No 27 Via Russo) near Posilippo just north of Naples.

Another of Sir William's passions was Vesuvius and telescopes in his observatory were trained on the fiery mountain. Some of his paintings showed the volcano before its top had been blown away in 1767 (other major eruptions occurred in 1779 and 1794). He was so entranced by the steaming and sulphurous Vesuvius that he often ventured out when it was stirring, to collect rock and soil samples for his collection and writings, which he then despatched to the Royal Society in London.[9] To be nearer his researches, he rented another house, the Villa Angelici near the royal palace at Portici. This villa became one of his wife's favourite homes, in which she entertained the likes of William Beckford of Fonthill. To enable Sir William's participation in King Ferdinand's hunting they also stayed in a 'cabin' of fifty rooms in the grounds of the royal palace north-east of Naples at Caserta, the palace built between 1738 and 1742 intended to rival Versailles in grandeur. From 1785 Sir William and Lady Hamilton, with Banks and Grafer, supervised the design and layout of the English gardens there.

In most of these homes, Sir William welcomed kin such as Anne Damer, who stayed in 1782 and again in 1786. Almost every evening English visitors doing the Grand Tour or wintering in the south were entertained, along with continentals. As the fourth son of a seventh ducal son, Sir William was not a wealthy man, his initial salary as minister plenipotentiary being only £8 per day (£2,920 per annum), but his wife was an heiress. Scores of servants, including musicians, were employed to look after all these residences, belongings, guests and wine cellars of the local Montechristo Lacryma. His collection of paintings expanded into several hundreds, while his first collection of over 1,000 'rescued' Greek vases was sold to the British Museum in 1772. With the help of an elderly monk, Antonio Piaggio, he had also produced beautifully coloured illustrations of the vases which Wedgwood copied for his celebrated Etruscan ware. A successor collection, begun in 1789, was similarly destined, but unfortunately lost when HMS *Colossus* was wrecked on a reef in the Isles of Scilly on 10 December 1798.

Sir William's asthmatic wife died in 1782, and by the time the Argylls arrived in Naples in November 1789 the musical evenings had been replaced by the theatrical 'attitudes' of Emma Lyon or Hart, in which Sir William had coached her to adopt poses from his paintings. Even after her marriage to Sir William in 1791 Emma was never to be accepted at the English Court. However, the Duchess of Argyll and her family not only looked favourably on her, but, as Sir William wrote to his niece, Mary Hamilton or Dickenson, they 'doat upon Emma'.[10] On her part Emma avowed that she 'never had such a friend' as the duchess who had shown her so many acts of kindness. The latter had asked Sir William to find a villa for the Argyll family, and like many of the other English visitors this was in the Chaia. Other residents that winter included their friends, Lord and Lady Elcho of the Wemyss family. The Argylls, Claverings, Elchos and Hamiltons frequently intervisited and the ladies enjoyed walks in the formal gardens of the royal palace, the Villa Reale. The duchess was easily fatigued, and Augusta was again pregnant, so it is likely that Charlotte's own grand tour continued with outings accompanying her father to the architectural and art treasures of Naples while she also acquired 'a very considerable knowledge of Italian, art and a real love of literature and music', by now having a 'pleasant singing voice'.[11] Perhaps what her granddaughter was to write was already becoming a truism for this young daughter of Argyll: Charlotte's 'love for Italy was then, as it continued to be throughout her long life, a veritable passion'.[12]

Like others of her gender, Charlotte was an observer of, rather than a participant in, royal hunts in the oak forests around Naples. At the end of one such hunt, when the carriages were approaching from all directions to collect participants, Charlotte panicked and fled to avoid them. Every way she ran she seemed to be in danger from another vehicle. The artist Wilhelm Tischbein was amazed by her grace and fluid movement and wrote of seeing what he had only 'admired before in art the lovely youthful fleeting figures on bas-reliefs, and the swaying dancers of the paintings at Herculaneum ... this exquisite, slender, boyish figure fleeing like a frightened deer running through trees'.[13] He was captivated by her and thought she was 'more perfect than the best artist could have imagined ... like a muse or goddess in total harmony with the natural world around her'.

Now belonging to the Scottish National Portrait Gallery, the large canvas (77 x 52 inches; 197 x 134cm—see plate 6) depicted the larger than life but graceful form of the 15-year-old Charlotte as Aurora, the Roman goddess of dawn. Wilhelm Tischbein was the best known of a family of painters and a frequent guest of Sir William; friend and painter of Goethe, he had by 1789 become director of the Naples Academy.[14] Skirving thought the painting 'unusually composed'.[15] Facing not quite fully to the onlooker's right, she is in a simple clinging robe of white, a long scarf of pale gold echoing the tint of her hair, the curls and ringlets crowned with a wreath of pink roses. The 'wondrously small foot', with its arched instep, is encased in a white and gold shoe. One of the 'beautifully moulded arms' is uplifted to bend down a branch of the oak tree under which she sits, to enable a fawn to nibble the leaves. Her right hand (whose length appears somewhat exaggerated) rests on a scroll of music. In the background there is a dawn tinge to the clouds in the lightening sky. Her granddaughter, Lady Constance Russell, described the painting as giving 'a good idea of her dawning beauty when she was about 16, although the colour has somewhat faded from the face',[16] the picture having hung for many years on the staircase of 29 Upper Brook Street (later 'Brook House'), 'exactly' facing a window.[17]

Leaving Naples after their six-month sojourn, about the middle of May, there were many anxieties for the Argylls and the Claverings on their homeward journey, but no journal was to record the adventures of this return.[18] Soon after arrival in Florence on 24 May, Lady Augusta

Clavering gave birth to her second child, Charlotte. Thereafter they may have travelled by the St Bernard Pass to reach Lyon, where the whole party ran the gauntlet of a savage mob, their coaches being pelted with mud and stones.[19] At last, on the evening of Sunday 25 July 1790, over two months after leaving Naples, the weary duchess reached London where all were 'shocked by her appearance, for it was evident that she was sick unto death'.[20] Her biographer catalogued the duchess' longstanding woes over all her older children but trusted that:

> In these last sad days the mother's eyes must have rested wistfully upon her two younger children, for the pretty Lady Charlotte, now a graceful girl of fifteen, and the little Lord John Campbell, a modest twelve-year old boy, were revealing a strength of character that promised well for the future.

During the rest of the summer the sick duchess remained at Ealing Grove with her husband and two younger daughters, visited by her closest friends. She moved to Argyll House on 5 November but before the end of the month 'her pulse was 110, and the doctors believed that her lungs were partly gone'.[21] On Monday 20 December 1790, just after her 57th birthday, 'while a wintry tempest was howling through the London streets' Elizabeth Gunning died,[22] 'her grief-stricken daughters and the duke in an agony of tears'.[23] The 67-year-old bereaved duke took his daughters back to Ealing Grove.[24]

> [On 29 December] the remains of the Duchess of Argyll were carried in a hearse and Six Horses, attended by four Mourning Coaches and Six on their way to the Family Burying-Place in the county of Argyll in Scotland. The Hearse and all the Horses were decorated with Escutcheons of her Rank and Titles in all the Funeral pomp becoming her elevated station.[25]

No friend or relative followed the bier. Proceeding from London through Edinburgh to Glasgow, the hearse finally came to rest a week later at Kilmun on the shores of Holy Loch in Argyll. The sole mourner, the only one of her children to attend her last resting place in the Argyll mausoleum,[26] was her surviving Hamilton son, Douglas, the 8th Duke of Hamilton.[27]

Charlotte was not quite 16 when her 'Mama' died, and for much of her life her mother's illness had been in both background and foreground. In her memoir she recalled that 'Nature had already sown the Seeds of that fatal and hereditary Disorder, a Consumption'.[28] Not only had her mother's sister, Maria, Countess of Coventry, succumbed to the same disease at the much earlier age of 28 (although some were also to suggest that she died of lead poisoning from facial makeup), but the duchess had also lost her similarly afflicted first and second Hamilton sons and an Argyll son. 'Considering the Dazzling brightness of her Morn of Life, its Noon was scarcely to be envied, suffering an additional share of Gloom by the contrast of its former brilliancy.'[29]

Charlotte recounted the births in 1733 and 1734 of the two elder Gunning sisters, Maria or Mollie and Elizabeth or Betty, at Hemingford Grey near Huntingdon. They had returned to their father's family estate at Castle Coote in Roscommon.[30] Their mother, Bridget, a daughter of the 6th Viscount Burke of Mayo, had presented them at Court in Dublin, before launching them in London to 'universal admiration'. 'Without the aid of heels that Women then wore', her mother Betty was 'at least five foot seven', an inch or so taller than her sister.

> [Maria's] Form was faultless and the Jet Black of Her Eyes and hair ... more Dazzlingly attractive than the Mild dignified Air which characterised my Mother's beauty ... I have always heard that the soft beam of her Blue Eye never was known to give one Glance in favour of Coquetry.[31]

Charlotte further illustrated the difference between the two when they were preparing for Lord Chesterfield's Grand Masked Ball in February 1752. Betty 'had ordered a Magnificent Sutanas [*sic*] Dress sparkling with Gold and jewels ... her sister ... the Habit of a Quaker'. Maria was so dissatisfied with her choice, that her sister had offered to exchange. It was thus to a Quaker that a besotted, if dissolute, 6th Duke of Hamilton proposed, and the couple had run off to be married two days later on St Valentine's Day at the Rev. Alexander Keith's chapel in Curzon Street, Mayfair, using a curtain ring. Maria's marriage to the 6th Earl of Coventry had followed on 5 March. Widowed in January 1758, at the age of 24 and already with three surviving children and an annual jointure of £3,000, on 3 March 1759 Elizabeth married John Campbell, who succeeded as 5th Duke of Argyll in 1770. The duchess illustrated her formidable talents when she went to Scottish law in 1761 on behalf of her Hamilton son's substantial inheritance in what became the infamous Douglas Cause. After five years of litigation against the Douglas family, the Court of Session voted in favour of Hamilton by one vote, but it was subsequently overturned on appeal to the House of Lords two years later.[32] With the death of the duchess in 1790 the Gunning connection almost disappeared from Charlotte's world, except when she wrote it up in her memoir, and in its consumptive shadow. It was the extended Campbell family that then enveloped and concerned Charlotte.

3

Celebrated Beauty

Either Augusta or Charlotte, just turned 16, acted as chatelaine for their father at Argyll House in London or Edinburgh and, increasingly, at Inveraray Castle where the duke spent more and more time.[1] Georgian Inveraray had become more accessible after the mid-century completion of the military road from Dumbarton, and in summer and autumn became a regular destination for visitors. Horace Walpole, writing in January 1791 to Miss Mary Berry, opined that 'everybody admires the youngest daughter's person and understanding'.[2] But a more cynical view of the family during the sad time after the duchess's death is given by the duke's niece and Charlotte's cousin, the sculptress Anne Damer, in a letter to Mary Berry in the summer of 1791:

> The Campbells are at Inveraray—my uncle what people call *thinking* himself ill, that is, *being* so, for otherwise, I am convinced, it is a subject no one *thinks* about. His spirits are low—cause or consequence of the first: Lady Augusta, no doubt, dawdling away her time with that most *indifferent* sposo ... and hanging on his arm when she can catch hold of it. But he is sick to death of her.[3]

She also observed that Charlotte was probably 'carving *some* name on *some* tree and lolling on the arm of a confidante, in the form of Miss [Louisa] Campbell', while regretting 'the most unfortunate education of this cousin and the dangers that now surround her'.

> 'Tis really a pity this *optima indoles* will, from what I hear, make a sad figure. Lady Frederick, whom we agree in thinking perfectly clear

> sighted, tho' she does sometimes use a magnifier, gave me an account of her dress and manner that hurt me, and that *you* will easily guess, without my attempting to describe.

Anne Damer confided to Mary Berry in August:

> What you say of Lady Charlotte puts me in mind (tho' I know not if justly) of Miss Boil [Boyle], now Lady H[enry] F[itzgerald]. Would to God! That half that instruction, which has been lavished on her, and seems now jumbling, jolting and filtering away, in rides, drives, balls and a round of dull, empty amusements, had been bestowed on my poor cousin. I think she would have profited by it, and now, in a '*worldly way*', the best thing one can hope for her is some hurried marriage, with a thousand chances, even in that, against her.[4]

When she was about 17, Charlotte was presented at Court[5] and Lady Hester Stanhope remembered how it unfolded:

> The effect was very much what she describes of Miss Mordaunt [a character in one of Lady Charlotte Campbell's edited novels, *Marriage in High Life*] that is, somebody said, 'She is too thin, very, handsome to be sure, but too thin'; and somebody else observed that in a year's time, when she filled out, she would be remarkably beautiful, which turned out to be the case ... She had such a hand and arm and such a leg! She had beautiful hair too, gold colour, and a finely-shaped nose and fine complexion.[6]

The reputed beauty that she had inherited from both father and mother was now about to be portrayed in oils, pastels and chalks. She was painted in fancy dress on several occasions; a miniature of her in 1793 as Beatrice Cenci (best known subsequently from Shelley's tragedy of the parricide, *The Cenci*, in 1819), was produced by Jane Ferrier, sister of Susan, and daughter of the duke's agent, John Ferrier.[7] In 1794 John Russell completed a fairly large pastel (37.75 x 29.75 inches) of Charlotte, then 19 years old, with her dog.[8] Russell had been a pupil of the pastellist, Francis Cotes (who had himself earlier portrayed the Gunning sisters), and had set up independently in London by 1767.[9]

Around the same time Anna Tonelli (née Nistri)[10] exhibited an oval portrait of Charlotte at the Royal Academy (see plate 7). Seated beside a classical column and facing three-quarters left, Charlotte's curls of hair cascaded to her hips, her headdress was fashionable, the waist high below a well-endowed bosom, sleeves covered her upper arms, and she was depicted holding an iconic book in her right hand which was resting on her thigh. Some of the most sympathetic likenesses and images of Charlotte were created at this period by Thomas, later Sir Thomas, Lawrence in his trademark charcoal or pencil, red and chalk (like Titian);[11] some being subsequently lithographed for inclusion in Charlotte's publications or in ladies' magazines.

In the aftermath of the French Revolution, Europe's re-interest in classicism appeared in many guises. Charlotte, though probably as tall as her mother or father, had a tendency at this time towards plumpness, particularly in her full cheeks and in the tops of her arms. The rather plump lady, almost flowing out of the flimsy and revealing classical dress, was captured by some of the leading caricaturists of the day. *Modern Elegance* is the first of James Gillray's satirisations of the high-spirited leader of society and fashionable celebrity that Charlotte became during the 1790s (see plate 8). There was a huge demand for new single sheet caricatures in Ackermann's shop; they were never intended to be put on a wall, but to be studied at arm's length. It was on 22 May 1795 that Charlotte appeared in ink and colour dressed in the extreme of the 'mode' with clinging transparent draperies showing every line of her figure.[12] The by now celebrated beauty is drawn in profile, a voluptuous figure seated in a reclining posture, a mirror giving back the reflection of her full face. Charlotte is dressed in a loose high-waisted gown in the new French style. In his annotations on his copy of the print Horace Walpole wrote: 'Lady Charlotte Campbell is universally allowed to have been one of the most celebrated beauties of the period, to have possessed considerable intellectual acquirements, and the most fascinating manners.'[13] The loose indoor dresses in the French style, with their high waists were upstaged by lofty ostrich feathers, 'one, two, three' or, as here, 'four surmounting a muslin turban from which a few strands and locks of hair escape'.[14] A fan is in her right hand, pointing downwards on her left knee ('you are too willing'). Lady Elizabeth Stanley was reported as being 'dressed exactly like Lady Charlotte Campbell, with diamonds and loads of fair hair and feathers higher than herself, no waist and white beads'.[15] Henry Bate Dudley, notorious newspaper proprietor and editor, and himself frequently featured in contemporary satirical prints, parodied Gillray's caricature of Charlotte in a highly-coloured description in his *Vortigern and Rowena*:

> Looke what a shape!
> Limbes fondly fashioned in the wanton moulde
> of Nature! Warm in Love's slie- flie- Wytcheries
> And scorning all the draperies of Arte

A spider's loome nowe weaves her thinne attire,
Through which the rogueish tell-tale windes
Do frolicke as they lifte![16]

Lady Stafford, a long-standing friend of her mother's, had tellingly come to Charlotte's defence on 3 February 1794, writing to her husband: 'Lady Charlotte Campbell is sadly abused about her dress. I think it very bad, but her beauty makes the women severe.'[17] During the 1790 season it was the same person who had suggested that her son, Lord Granville Leveson-Gower, should attend an assembly at Augusta Clavering's. 'I want you to see Lady Charlotte Campbell, for I think you have so much Taste that will admire her, although she is *fair* and *FULL*.'[18] At a ball on 30 May 1793, Lady Stafford observed that 'Lady Charlotte Campbell was not there, as she had set out for Scotland with her father, adding that 'there were many pretty Girls, but none so pretty as she is'.[19] The Duke of Argyll had taken her away from London 'and all the sighing swains', including Lord Boringdon, the future Earl of Morley, reportedly 'desperately in love' with her.[20]

Gillray's second sendup was to appear just as Charlotte came of age early in 1796. It was entitled *Ladies dress, as it soon will be*. This was an altered impression of the earlier one; she is standing, with a closed fan in her left hand resting across her right hand, while her profile has been altered with a thickening of her arms, and more curls allowed to escape.[21] The high-waisted and extremely *décolleté* flowing garment is slit at the left side to show her thigh and leg with gartered stocking. At the very time it was put up in Humphry's window the weather was cold and the pavements slippery, and the *Morning Chronicle* of 26 February 1794 suggested that 'the ladies of the present day, without waists, do not perhaps know that they copy that fashion from Madame Talheu, who copied it from the Greeks'. This style was particularly associated with Charlotte Campbell; one has to wonder how she kept warm.[22]

I. C. Cruikshank had probably also satirised the fashionable Charlotte in May 1793 in *Frailties of Fashion*.[23] This depicted the Prince of Wales, Mrs Fitzherbert and the Duke of York walking in the park, with various other people; the one right of centre is probably Charlotte. The ladies all had high waists, pads on the stomach and great bosom display. The introduction of the pad was attributed to Charlotte and was ridiculed on stage at Covent Garden that April in an epilogue to Frederic Reynolds' comedy, *How to grow Rich*, and in May in a farce by Robert Woodbridge called *The Pad*.[24] (She would scarcely have needed one after 1796). Following a ball at Lady Anstruther's on 24 April, Lady Malmesbury described 'the modern fashion of dress for young ladies, by which they are made to appear five or six months gone with child', and went on to mention pads and 'a complete display of bosom'. She continued: 'I am giving you a faithful description of Lady Charlotte Campbell as she was at the ball last night. She is the most exaggerated in this fashion, but is followed in considerable degree by many others.' According to another observer in January 1793 gowns were so high-waisted 'that every woman looked as though she was within a week of lying in'.[25] Nor did Augusta escape being excoriated: she 'literally goes so naked, that at a ball the other day all the men swear she had nothing on but a thin calico dress over her shift, and the whole clung like wet drapery'. The same diarist noted Charlotte as the 'inventress of the high waist', and recorded that she had been seen in Kensington Gardens in the winter of 1794 'with only one thin petticoat ... short enough to discover a pair of very fine Muslin Drawers, trimmed with lace'. A subsequent Cruikshank may also have caricatured Charlotte.[26] In *Too much and too little, or summer cloathing for 1556 & 1796*, which appeared in February 1796, two ladies, one in Elizabethan dress and the other scantily draped, gaze at each other in astonishment; on the wall are parodied portraits of men in corresponding outfits. A still later Cruikshank of 1799 perhaps also involved Charlotte; *Savoyards of Fashion—or the musical mania* shows five ladies playing instruments; the central figure playing cymbals 'with graceful energy, her head turned to the left to show her best classical profile, may perhaps be of Lady Charlotte'.[27]

Almost as different as possible from Gillray and Cruikshank is John Hoppner's large oil painting (93 x 55.5 inches, see plate 9)—one of the largest in Inveraray Castle—commissioned by the Duke of Argyll and designed to be placed over the fireplace in the Tapestry Drawing Room in 1796. Entitled 'Portrait of a lady of quality', it depicted Charlotte as 'Flora' (sometimes mistitled 'Aurora').[28] Viewed from below, the full-length figure is standing facing to our right, the head slightly turned and looking at the spectator three-quarter face. Barefoot, she is wearing a classical low-cut but high-waisted white dress, and a long robe flows in an interesting shape at her back. Her hair is knotted on top with a band of white ribbon, long tresses flowing over her shoulder. Against a background of tinted clouds, flowers are being scattered with both hands. On the whole John Hoppner did not do preliminary drawings and sketches but began his portraits directly on to the final canvas. However, he probably first depicted Charlotte in a study completed before the better known full-length picture. The earlier one (30 x 25 inches) is captivating and shows a serene young woman with simple hair style, in a white muslin V-necked dress with short sleeves, and a pink cloak lined with fur.[29] His portraits were frequently thought to be very good likenesses, even when the composition as a whole was less satisfactory. His style wasn't as flamboyant as that of Lawrence, and while some deemed his male portraits best, those of beautiful young women were particularly esteemed for their sweetness and tenderness.

On 16 February 1796 the artist Joseph Farington recorded in his diary: 'Hoppner spoke in raptures of the fine face and form of Lady Charlotte Campbell, who is now sitting to him for a whole length. He says she has more of the *antique beauty* than any woman He ever saw; and her neck is exquisitely formed.'[30] By 9 April Farington noted that he 'had gone early to Hoppner and found his whole length of Lady Charlotte Campbell in a bad state. I gave my opinion freely.' Fortunately a few days later he deemed 'Lady C. Campbell's picture much improved'. Next day it was the turn of academician Richard Westall, who thought Charlotte's head 'not well turned'.[31] The large painting was, however, hung at the Royal Academy's 28th exhibition in the early summer of 1796. According to editor Greig's note in Farington's *Diary*, Hoppner's portrait 'did not win much favour at the time it was painted'.[32] The notoriously critical Anthony Pasquin also wrote in his Royal Academy notice:

> [Hoppner] had not been very kind to the lady, there being but little of the chaste simplicity of the blushing Aurora; the ruddy figure is inanimate. The background is misty, and the effect of the whole is too sombre; in the purple hue there is a muddiness that excites different sensations from those which arise from a felicitous view of the allegory. The right arm is injudiciously foreshortened, which gives it the appearance of a defective limb. Upon the whole we do not think the lady very eminently obliged to the artist.[33]

The Times' critic, however, took a different view:

> We persist in our opinion, that there is a depth of science, and firmness of colouring throughout the whole of the piece, which defies the most minute inspection. We certainly do not admire the plan, and we confine our observations to the execution, which, with very few exceptions, (and what work has ever been completely unobjectionable) is very masterly.[34]

Although Hoppner's earlier study now appears more sympathetic than the somewhat inanimate large oil, nevertheless it was the latter on which Wilkin's much reproduced and more lively engraving was based. Wilkin manipulated the portrait to fit in with other portraits in his 1799 series *Bygone Beauties*, and Charlotte's arms are only partly seen, with her hair long, waved and flowing over her shoulders.[35] Further engravings and mezzotints based on the Hoppner were produced in 1830 by Burke, Richard and Hart and Wright.[36]

Perhaps one of the reasons for the Hoppner commission can be explained by the notice that had been given in *The Times* of 30 January 1796 that 'a marriage had been arranged between Captain Campbell and Lady Charlotte Campbell'.[37] The banns were subsequently proclaimed on Saturday 18 June 1796 by the parish minister of Inveraray, the Rev. Paul Fraser, when 'John Campbell Esq of Shawfield Captain of the third Regt Guards and the Right Honourable Lady Charlotte Campbell lawl Daur of His Grace the Duke of Argyll gave in their monies in order for proclamation of marriage'.[38] Within days a marriage contract was drawn up by her father and elder brother and a dowry of £15,000 arranged.[39] It was thus at a midsummer Inveraray Castle on Friday 24 June 1796, in sight of Hoppner's painting, that the talented and beautiful, perhaps romantic rather than wise or ambitious, 21-year-old Charlotte entered a phase in her life that family and friends viewed less than wholeheartedly. She was marrying a distant kinsman three years older than herself, 'Jack' or John Campbell, son and heir to Walter Campbell of Shawfield and Islay. 'Long John' was a very tall, strong and handsome man, of whom it was said: 'When Campbell walks the street/The paviours cry/"God bless your legs!"/And lay their rammers by.'[40] Born on 8 December 1772, John or Jack Campbell of Shawfield and Islay was described as follows:

> A remarkably goodlooking person, upwards of six feet high, and possessed of a fine figure, with the commanding military carriage of a soldier. At the time of his marriage ... he was well known in London, in the circle of its bucks by the name of 'handsome Jack of the Guards'.[41]

An ensign (1789), lieutenant and then captain (1793) in the 3rd Regiment of Foot (Scots) Guards, he subsequently served in the Argyllshire Militia, founded in 1798, ending up as colonel in the Argyll and Bute Militia formed in 1802. From 1807 he sat in Parliament as member for the constituency of Ayr Burghs which comprised the Ayrshire burghs of Ayr and Irvine, Rothesay in Buteshire and Campbeltown and Inveraray in Argyllshire.[42]

Despite landed prospects, Jack Campbell was the eldest of fourteen children and regarded by many as a poor catch for the beautiful Charlotte—for both, however, it seems to have been a love match. While Charlotte had been accustomed to the grandeur of Inveraray Castle, as well as staying at Rosneath and Ardencaple Castles, in apartments in Holyrood Palace and other houses in Edinburgh and at Argyll House in London, her relatives, friends and subsequent family biographers were perhaps less than fair to the Campbells of Shawfield, successful entrepreneurs and innovative landlords. Daniel Campbell of Shawfield had awarded the first commission to his nephew Colen Campbell to design the Palladian style Shawfield Mansion in the Trongate in Glasgow in 1711; Daniel then became a subscriber to the first two volumes of Colen Campbell's *Vitruvius Britannicus*.[43] The façade of another home, Woodhall House, near Holytown, Bothwell in Lanarkshire was also 'heavily dependent' on Colen Campbell's design, and may have been added to an earlier house by Daniel's grandson.[44] Of this second Daniel Campbell, also a parliamentarian, it was said that 'Taste and elegance seemed natural to him' and that the 'fine arts were his favourite amusements'.[45] The house had 'noble apartments, and a good library', and had been visited by Princess of Darchoff or Daschow,[46] to whom the younger Daniel was reputed to have given the Shawfield pearls. When this Daniel died in 1777 aged only 40, the landscape around the house 'received a complete melioration' for his brother, Walter. 'Few places in the west of Scotland are upon a more liberal scale; few gentlemen ... have done more than he upon his several seats.' Walter Campbell's heir, young Jack Campbell and his bride could thus enjoy Woodhall's drives, belvederes, ha-has, extensive gardens, pleasure walks, greenhouses and the lake. Daniel Campbell the Elder had also acquired the island of Islay and Islay House in 1726, and both he and his grandson Daniel extended the tower house, so that by the time Jack Campbell's father, Walter Campbell, became laird of the island in 1777, Hebridean visitors were surprised by the sight of a handsome Georgian mansion house, with another, Eallabus, nearby.[47] Today's magnificent beech tree at the latter, with a girth of over six metres, would already have been 70 years old when Jack Campbell was born.[48] Just as Daniel Campbell had been ahead of his time, so his brother, Walter, was renowned as the 'greatest of the Hebridean improvers'. It was assumed by all that Jack Campbell and Charlotte would become the laird and chatelaine of Woodhall House and Islay House in due course: not aristocratic, but perhaps with better landed gentry prospects than their detractors allowed.

Hester Stanhope observed, however, that three years after being presented at Court, Charlotte 'all at once' disappeared from the *beau monde* when 'she married her cousin and was still Lady Charlotte Campbell, but always in uneasy circumstances'.[49] This was perhaps an overstatement, although she was less often in London. Charlotte was said to possess the handsomest limbs of any lady at court, 'and she was not sparing of exhibiting them'.[50] Like her mother before her, she was mobbed as a celebrity of her time. One Glasgow reminiscer recalled that Lord Lorne was frequently in Glasgow with his sisters, visiting haberdashers and the like. Such was Charlotte's 'transcendant [*sic*] beauty that crowds ran after her to get a glimpse of her and to tell that they had really seen her ... "For ne'er did Grecian chisel trace/A Nymph, a Naiad, or a Grace/

of finer form or lovelier face."'[51] One day soon after her marriage she was walking in the Candleriggs with another young couple—probably her in-laws, the Jenkinsons—'dressed in the height of the then Parisian fashion, with petticoats almost as short as a Highlandman's philabeg [kilt]. The mob ran down … King Street, Candleriggs and Gallowgate to get a sight of the celebrated beauty.' Such was the crush that Charlotte and her companions had to rush into a shop opposite the Tron church. The owner put up the shutters before leaping out of the back window to summon a sergeant and soldiers. In turn, Charlotte also jumped out at the back, fled to a nearby house and was taken by carriage to the Black Bull Inn where she was staying.

As Shawfield heir, no house or estate were provided for Jack and Charlotte. Their life was peripatetic, partly aristocratic and partly military. With forays to Argyll House in London for the early summer season, the later summer and autumn usually found them at Inveraray, staying en route at Woodhall,[52] Rosneath or Ardencaple. The Edinburgh 'season' then enveloped them from before New Year until Easter. Her husband was variously stationed near Edinburgh when they stayed at Woodburn House near Dalkeith, or in the Argyll House at 11 Queen Street, Edinburgh, next door to her brother, Lord John at No. 12. The duke also rented the grand Adam Bellevue House in the centre of Drummond Place. When in the Argyll—later Argyll and Bute—militia, they were to be found at Inveraray or Campbeltown.

Charlotte had acquired a large number of in-laws, with many of whom she maintained longstanding friendship and contact. Her father-in-law had eleven children by his first wife, and three by his second. His four surviving sons from the first marriage were Jack, his heir; Robert of Skipness, an apparently reluctant advocate; Walter, ship's captain in the East Indies Company and later of Sunderland in Islay; and Colin, who became an admiral in the royal navy, and later of Ardpatrick. Of the seven daughters of this first marriage, Harriet married Daniel Hamilton of Gilkerscleugh in Lanarkshire, Glencairn became the wife of Thomas Carter of Edgcott in Northamptonshire, Margaret married Francis Charteris, 8th Earl of Wemyss, Katherine espoused (Sir) Charles Jenkinson, cousin of the second Lord Liverpool, prime minister from 1812 to 1827, and Elizabeth became the wife of Stuart Thriepland of Middleton. Two daughters of the second marriage were Hamilton, who married Lord Belhaven, and Mary who became Lady Ruthven; their brother, William Campbell of Winton and Pencaitland was unmarried. Many of these Shawfield in-laws appear in the following pages either as friends of Charlotte, or as involved aunts and uncles to her sons and daughters.

4

Salonnière

Compiled around the time of her marriage was a small, 48-page volume, *Poems on Several Occasions*, 'by a Lady', privately printed in Edinburgh in 1797.[1] Charlotte was very much a British aristocrat, of a generation that was shaped partly in Argyll and Edinburgh, but also in London, France and Italy before the Continent mostly became off-limits for British travellers. Her outlook and output were thus cosmopolitan but often included Scottish references (echoing Burns who had died in 1796). In her poetry and novels she sometimes used Lallans in conversations or epistolary episodes; although as a child in Argyll hearing Gaelic speakers, like them she would not have known how to write it. She experimented with tone and style—aristocratic raciness, melancholy sensibility and severe piety. Stimulated by, or perhaps even composed during her walks in the policies along the river Aray, the slim volume was typical of the feminine fashions of the day and the intuitive sensations she expressed in the sublime (particularly in descriptions of scenery and the natural world) as well as in arguments for and against sensibility.[2] Her sister-in-law, Glencairn Carter, suggested manuscript alterations on her copy, and another was in Elizabeth Thriepland's library.[3] A copy was sent to Walter Scott,[4] while several decades later, on December 28, 1831, Charlotte presented one to her friend, Viscountess Kirkwall, in which she wrote: 'Printed but not published—The Girlish Lays of one who has sung since but almost always to a Lyre of Sorrow.'[5]

Few of Charlotte's poems have survived in manuscript, so those printed in the volume may represent but a selection. She was 22 years old when they were printed: they are professionally and technically structured, with oppositional themes, images and words, varied numbers and lengths of line and varied rhythm patterns. The lyric poet's themes are all included: youthful passion, evening and death, happiness and unhappiness, dreams and reality, transient love and nature's calm, swallows and seasons, sensibility and insensibility, the city throng and rural tranquillity, angst and peace, unrequited love and religious devotion. Perhaps by this time, marriage, first pregnancy and motherhood had intensified her experience of life, but the poems often seem to be those of an older, serious person, not the famed salonnière organising music, amateur theatricals and dancing in Edinburgh and at Inveraray. While each poem has oppositional lighter phrases and words, there is little let up, apart from one song in which the chorus exults:

Sound the lyre in mirthful strain;
Let music fill the air;
The nectar draught of Bacchus drain:
Drink deep, and banish care.

It is doubtful if she would have composed such a carefree poem a decade later, but one more recent reviewer has deemed the little volume 'charmingly feminine and extremely fashionable "occasions" revealing a woman's capacity for refined emotion as well as the sublime', with echoes of Burns in the 'Shepherd of the Glen' and of Gray's *Elegy*.[6]

From winter to early summer her salon in 'New Athens', as Charles Kirkpatrick Sharpe headed his letters,[7] at Queen Street or in Bellevue House, was graced by many of her near contemporaries, the literati of both Edinburgh and London. She frequently entertained the young Walter Scott, who, 'sitting at her feet', used to repeat to her the Border Ballads such as the 'Eve of St John' and some of his other compositions of verse including 'Glenfinlas' that 'were later to find their way into the Waverley novels'.[8] Scott showed his regard for her literary abilities by placing four of her lines, albeit anonymous (all the others were attributed), from her volume of poems, 'To the Shepherd of the Glen', as a chapter heading in the *Heart of Midlothian*: 'Happy thou art! then happy be,/ Nor envy me my lot;/ Thy happy state I envy thee./ And peaceful cot.'[9] On 1 November 1799 he penned four verses to her:

Of old tis said, in ?Ilium's battling days
Ere Friendship knew a price or Faith was sold
The Chief high minded, famed in Homers Lays
For meanest brass ex changed his arms of gold

Say, lovely lady, know you not of one
Who with the Lycian heroes generous fire
Grave lays might rival Graeca's sweetest ?tone
For in rude numbers of a Northern Lyre?

Yet—tho' unequal all to match my debt-
Yet take these lines to thy protecting hand
Nor needless hear a Gothick bard repeat
The wizard harpings of thy native land

For each (forgive the vaunt) a wreath may grow,
At distance due as my rude verse from thine,
The Classic Laurel crowns thy lovely brow.
The fruids 'Magic Mistletoe' be mine.[10]

The following year Charlotte was in turn to inscribe a manuscript copy of Scott's drama, 'House of Aspen' with the words 'Charlotte Maria from Walter Scott'.[11] Perhaps this 'Drama of Chivalry', based on a German story, might even have been enacted in the amateur dramatics at Inveraray that summer. She must also have been very gratified when in January 1801 he sent her a signed and dated copy of his songs.[12] In early 1802 Walter Scott gossiped that 'Lady Charlotte Campbell, Lord John and Col: Campbell were so good as to scramble for bread and cheese with us and between reading, reciting and music the time glided very pleasantly away'.[13] He also referred to 'the Marquess of Lorn, whom I have frequently met at the house of his charming sister, Lady Charlotte Campbell, whom, I am sure, if you are acquainted with her, you must admire as much as I do'.[14] Scott wrote on 21 April 1803 from London to his Edinburgh printer, James Ballantyne, that the publishers, Longman and Rees, were 'delighted with the printing' of *The Minstrelsy* and he also asked for one of ten presentation copies on large 'fine paper to be sent to Lady Charlotte ... by Inveraray carrier'.[15] Scott later sent her copies of further works, including presentation copies of the *Lady of the Lake*, *Rokeby* and his *Transcendent Poem*.[16]

'The two leaders of society in Edinburgh, in the winter of 1801-02' were deemed by Elizabeth Grant of Rothiemurchus to be 'the celebrated duchess of Gordon, and Lady Charlotte Campbell, the lovely daughter of the lovelier Gunning'.[17]

Iridescent and sentimental, [Charlotte] was a creature of impulse, but always of sympathetic impulse: herself a wit and dabbler in literature, she could overlook uncouthness in a man of genius. She was at this time

> the centre of a society so overflowing with poetry, painting, music, love, and philanthropy.[18]

As 'Monk' Lewis wrote to Moore: 'The angels might come down and beg Lady Charlotte Campbell to take them to sup with us.'[19] In that society John Leyden was content to describe himself as Charlotte's 'dancing bear'.[20] Then a zealous young preacher, Leyden had accompanied two young foreigners who had studied in Edinburgh the previous winter on their grand tour of the Highlands and Islands in the autumn of 1800. To Charlotte he dedicated his ballad founded on the romantic legend concerning MacPhail of Colonsay and the Mermaid of Corryvreckan, and included by Scott in his *Border Minstrelsy*:[21]

> To brighter charms depart my simple lay,
> Though pour'd diffusive o'er the silver sea.
> Than graced of old the maid of Colonsay,
> Go boldy forth—but, ah! the listening throng,
> When her fond lover lessening her view,
> Rapt by the siren, would forget the song!
> With eyes reverted, o'er the surge withdrew;
> Lo! While they pause nor dare to gaze around.
> But happier still, should *lovely Campbell* sing
> Afraid to break the soft enchanting sound,
> Thy plaintive numbers to the trembling string.
> While swells to sympathy each flattering hear
> The mermaid's melting strains would yield to thee,
> 'Tis not the poet's, but the Siren's art, &c.[22]

Before long, Leyden left these shores for the Indian ocean where he played an influential medical and linguistic role in the colourful and adventurous East India Company activities of Stamford Raffles and his wife, Olivia.[23]

It was at one of her parties in Edinburgh that the antiquarian Charles Kirkpatrick Sharpe, sometimes referred to as the Scots Walpole, reputedly introduced Walter Scott to Matthew Lewis whose 'Divinity' or muse she was alleged to be.[24] She was also Lewis' heroine in *The Monk* (1796).

> When Lewis reached Edinburgh, Lady Charlotte Campbell, always distinguished by her passion for elegant letters, was ready, 'in pride of rank, in beauty's bloom', to do the honours of Scotland to the 'Lion of Mayfair', and I believe Scott's first introduction to Lewis took place at one of her Ladyship's parties.[25]

Scott himself always recalled that he had never felt such elation as when the 'Monk' invited him to dine with him for the first time at his hotel.[26] Since he had gazed on Burns in his seventeenth year, Scott had seen no one enjoying the fame of a poet by general consent, and Lewis, whatever Scott might on more mature consideration think of his title to such fame, had certainly done him no small service; for the ballads of "Slonzo the Brave" and "The Fair Imogine" and "Durandarte", had rekindled effectually in his breast the spark of poetical ambition. Scott, however, added:

> Lewis was fonder of great people than he ought to have been, either as a man of talent or as a man of fashion. He always had dukes and duchesses in his mouth, and was pathetically fond of anyone who had a title. You would have sworn he had been a *parvenu* of yesterday, yet he had lived all his life in good society ... Matt had queerish eyes—they projected like those of some insects, and were flattish on the orbit. His person was extremely small and boyish—he was indeed the least man I ever saw, to be strictly well and neatly made ... This boyishness went through life with him. He was a child, and a spoiled child, but a child of high imagination; and so he wasted himself on ghost-stories and German romances. He had the finest ear for rhythm I ever met with—finer than Byron's.[27]

'Lady Charlotte was the bright particular star which held a powerful influence over the life of Matthew Lewis', and he celebrated her charms in his lyrical effusions on 'Amoret'.[28,29] In his Introduction to the *Monk* Anderson tells of the sensational success of 'Monk' Lewis in 1796, which enabled him to indulge his penchant for high society: 'he dines everywhere, spent fortnights at ducal country homes, and developed friendships with Scott (and later Byron)'.[30] Born the same year as Charlotte, into a rich and influential family, he was educated at Westminster and Christ Church before going to Weimar and as an attaché in the Hague in 1794 composed *The Monk*, still deemed 'a stunning read' by Simon Brett in 1996.[31] Matthew Lewis was also a frequent visitor at Inveraray from at least 1795. His visits were notable for the musical evenings or night-long billiard matches with Lord Lorne and Tom Sheridan, son of the Irish Richard, rehearsals of amateur theatricals, and the composition of much fantastical poetry and doggerel. But often Lewis passed weeks at the castle in deliberate solitude and melancholy, reading books and writing to his mother or to an absent Charlotte, to whom he dedicated his four-volume *Romantic Tales* in 1802.[32] From Inveraray Castle on 27 October 1804, Lewis's translation from the German of *The Bravo of Venice* was dedicated to another Irishman and Argyll habitué, Lord Moira. Some of Lewis's verses for the weekly Inveraray jottings in 'The Bugle' and his letters to Charlotte clearly testify to his passion. One poem surely refers to this unrequited love.[33] 'Lines written on a Journey' devotes its ten quatrains of rhyming couplets to his longings for Amoret's possible bestowal of a smile.[34]

Even one of Charlotte's habitual dogs was honoured with lines for its collar: 'Stranger! If other dogs beguile/Me from my mistress fair to stray,/ Restore me; she'll vouchsafe a smile,/ Which might e'en Avarice repay!'[35] On one of their walks in the policies of Inveraray Castle, Charlotte had been alarmed on meeting a 'poor mad woman' known locally as 'Crazy Jane'. Lewis's slip-song, 'Why, fair maid, in ev'ry feature', was set to music 'for a high voice with an accompaniment for harp or pianoforte by Miss Abrams'.[36] Long after he was dead, Charlotte, who did not scruple to publish private letters from her friends, noted maliciously that while Lewis had 'talents and good qualities', 'one of his mistakes was trying to be witty, for which nature had never designed him'.[37]

Year after year the Argyll family spent long periods at Inveraray, especially in summer and autumn, involving a long and somewhat arduous land journey. Describing the route from Edinburgh to Inveraray in her novel *Conduct is Fate*, Charlotte had the paterfamilias of the story making the 'usual tour taken by all tourists to the Highlands'.[38] After the 'dreary' Kirk o' Shotts, the carriages arrived in Glasgow to allow the ladies to shop, then the Clyde and its villas gave way to the grandeur of Lochs Gair [*sic*], Goil and Long with steep precipitous roads.

> The mountain-side of the road was chiefly composed of micaceous schists and slate stone, forming a dark back-ground to the bright purple heath and setting off the scarlet rowan, which slanted its irregular branches far athwart the sky, pendant with clustering berries.

Just as at the present day, the mountain streams tumbled down as 'snowy torrents of foam'. Equally evocative is the storm around the Arrochar hotel where the party stayed. 'The night became stormy and some heavy squalls announced an approaching tempest.' They were the more appreciative of the blazing fires and good supper of 'lovely broiled and devilled herring', washed down with claret. 'The night grew every moment worse, and the tempest raved wildly around; it did indeed seem as if all the elements were at war, for between the showers vivid flashes of lightning poured down the mountainside.' The following morning 'the rushing of the mountain cataracts was the only remains of the storm', while 'thick impenetrable mist and a fine soft drizzling rain eventually gave way to a gleam of sun'. Thereafter they 'entered the narrow pass of Glencroe ... wild and barren pass a few sheep straggled from rock to rock'. This was enough to give one of the characters the 'blue, black or green devils'. By the time they reached

Loch Fyne 'how refreshing was the first view of its bright glittering waves, with Ardkinglas and its luxuriant larches and beeches'. They turned Strone Point with its sudden view of Inveraray, the town and massive imposing form of the castle, but 'they paused not to consider whether or not it transgressed the laws of architecture ... art seemed to combine with nature to render the scene one of the most magnificently beautiful that fancy could paint'. As portrayed by Charlotte, the autumnal colours contrasted with the great long avenues of beeches and limes, and the lawns sloping to the river Aray.

Also annually, the house parties consisted mostly of the young and gay friends of the duke's children, gathered there with the charming but reckless and somewhat feckless George, Marquis of Lorne, the sickly, disappointed Lady Augusta, the fecund Lady Charlotte and their studious brother, Lord John. 'By all accounts they were a happy, devoted family, and whatever their failings, at home in Inveraray they appear their gayest and best.'[39] Names in the visitors' books included Thomas Campbell, Joseph Farington, James Hogg, William Lamb, the Palmerstons, Lachlan MacQuarrie, Tommy Moore, Tom Sheridan, Lady Louisa Stuart, J. M. W. Turner, Dr Thomas Young and others such as the 11th Duke of Somerset and the 5th Duke of Rutland. One visitor to Inveraray in 1795 was Peter Mark Roget, polymath and later compiler of *The Thesaurus*.[40] 'Immediately upon our arrival having ordered dinner, we visited the Duke's castle, having previously given in our names. On approaching the house, Lady Charlotte Campbell rode by us.' After succinctly describing the exterior, he observed the 'richly decorated and ornamented and very highly finished' interior rooms and pictures. Another visitor with a pen was a medical man, Thomas Young who described riding out after breakfast with Augusta and Charlotte. They went down by the side of the loch, where Charlotte showed him 'a new style of barn for drying corn'. After an evening of music and cards he recorded his impression of the two sisters (fifteen years apart):

> Lady Charlotte is handsomer than Lady Augusta, she sings better, but she has less good sense, and less sweetness; an innocent giddiness sometimes gives her the appearance of a little affectation: she is to Lady Augusta what Venus is to Minerva; I suppose she wishes for no more. Both are goddesses.[41]

The duke's agent, John Ferrier, described the celebrations at Rosneath for the naval victory of the Nile in a letter of 12 October 1798 to his daughter, Susan. Walter Campbell of Shawfield and Islay was visiting with his wife en route to Woodhall and 'Lady Augusta took the hint and lighted up

Ardencaple', potatoes and turnips being gouged out for lights. She was there 'with her whole family', as well as the Mures of Caldwell.[42]

The honours of launching a 45- or 48-foot cutter built by Scotts of Greenock for 'Col. Campbell an Argyllshire soldier' were bestowed on Charlotte, despite her oft-professed dislike of the sea.[43] This was put to use on Loch Fyne for fishing and other expeditions. One such was described by James Hook, the husband of one of Charlotte's lifelong friends. Anne Hook was the daughter of the royal physician, Sir Walter Farquhar, and, like Charlotte was a frequent feature of, and participant in, both Edinburgh and London society. On 8 June 1797 she married a young multi-talented clergyman, James Hook, son of the renowned musician, organist and impresario of the same name and his artistic wife, Elizabeth Madden. Many years later Lady Louisa Stuart asked her sister: 'Do you not see her still with her fair locks, dressed after Lady Charlotte?'[44] During their tour of the Highlands in 1799 the Hooks joined the house party at Inveraray Castle. His journal describes a moonlit expedition on Loch Fyne in the cutter; the herring or 'silver darlings' were always pursued at night, and whisky was bartered by the ducal party for their fish supper.[45] James Hook also joined in the roe-buck shooting by day which provided tasty lunch 'as joints larded with sauce piquante'. Noteworthy were the obligatory Argyll jacket instead of a coat and 'a sort of pantaloon' which was *de rigueur* for the future Dean of Worcester and fellow guests. Salmon and trout fishing were recalled in *Conduct is Fate*.[46]

William Lamb, the future prime minister as Lord Melbourne, was one of the guests at Inveraray Castle in October 1802, Matt Lewis reporting amusedly to Lamb's mother, Lady Melbourne.[47] He had travelled with George, 8th Baron Kinnaird, a man known for his taste in art and his sympathy with the early views of the French Revolution. The castle was overflowing:

> Bed-rooms are in great request and William and Kinnaird being the last comers, are moved about from chamber to chamber, never knowing one night where they are to sleep the next. Whoever passes a few hours out of the Castle is certain of finding one of the two new-comers established in his room when he returns.

A formal complaint had been lodged by a great Russian count that he had only stepped out for half an hour, and 'the first things which He saw lying on his bed, when He came back, were a dozen pair of Kinnaird's leather breeches'. Lewis later added a postscript to the effect that 'William's Newspaper has just appeared, in which He informs the Public that he is at Length stationary in Lady Augusta's dressing-room'.

The Ettrick Shepherd, James Hogg, stayed at the Inn at Inveraray on 1 and 2 June 1803 and was shown round the castle, policies and the rest of the estate by Colonel [Jack] Campbell, whom he described as having 'unaffected simplicity of manner'.[48] He was immediately introduced to Charlotte; as Hogg confessed to Walter Scott, he protested himself overcome at the thought of meeting this celebrated beauty.

> Shawfield bolted into a circular room in one of the turrets, where her ladyship was sitting with some others, closely engaged with something, but I cannot tell what it was were I to die for it, and I am vexed to this hour that I had not noted what they were employed in when alone.

The turrets were ideal for small pleasant little libraries and parlours for tête-à-têtes. Charlotte greeted him 'with the greatest familiarity', and took him on a tour of the principal rooms in the castle, leading her little daughter by the hand, a 'most beautiful stem of the noble bough'. Hogg was hugely impressed with the duke's Highland cattle: 'Campbell of Shawfield and Islay—and he only—hath long disputed the field with Argyll for the best breed of Highland cattle'. While being 'truly ashamed' of the attention paid to him by Colonel Campbell, who was 'indefatigable in his endeavour to make me understand ... everything, both within and without the castle', he felt intimidated, and embarrassed, by 'blunders every hour', especially when engaging with Charlotte and Augusta.

Another tourist that year was, however, distinctly underwhelmed by Inveraray. At the end of August Dorothy Wordsworth stayed at the Inn with her brother and friends, and on the evening of their arrival walked in the policies where she noted the tallest trees that she had ever seen. The Castle itself she did not think worth visiting, 'there being no pictures, and the house ... is fitted up in the modern style. If there had been any reliques of the ancient costume of the castle of a Highland chieftain, we should have been sorry to have passed it'.[49] She recollected the town itself as 'but a doleful example of Scotch filth', and while enjoying the moonlight views of the 'lake', Loch Fyne and Duniquaich, considered the church spire less beautiful than English ones.

More appreciative was Lachlan MacQuarrie, on military leave and future Governor of New South Wales, who recorded a kindlier impression as a guest in August 1804.[50] After breakfast on 29 August he had gone to the castle where he was welcomed by the Marquis of Lorne, his younger brother, Lord John Campbell, and the duke's 'son in law John Campbell Yr of Shawfield', who conversed with him for some time 'in a very frank and friendly manner'. His afternoon was spent on a ride through the 'beautiful and extensive grounds' with the parish minister, the Rev. Paul Fraser. Lorne had introduced a new fashionable hour for dinner, at 6.30pm. The duke 'ate and drank heartily and was very sociable and attentive to everyone, sitting at the head of the table, with Lady Augusta and Lady Charlotte on either side of him'. The other diners included Lord Lorne and Lord John, Colonel Campbell and his eldest daughter, Eliza and the governess, Mlle de la Chaux, Mrs Campbell of Carrick, Mr Lachlan of Maclachlan from across Loch Fyne, and 'Monk' Lewis .[51] 'Mr Sheridan sung two or three most Excellent Songs after Dinner, and then the Duke left us to take his usual Evening's Ride in his Carriage accompanied by his favourite Daughter Lady Charlotte.' The rest of the guests remained at table for some time, then adjourned to the drawing room 'to drink Tea with the Ladies', until the party broke up at nine o'clock. Walter Scott described another presence in the dining room at Inveraray.[52] 'There was hardly a great house in Scotland where there was not an all-licensed fool—half crazy and half knavish—many of whose bon mots are still recited and preserved.' He told of the Duke of Argyll having a jester like this 'who stood at the sideboard among the servants, and was a great favourite, until he got into disgrace by rising up in the Kirk before the sermon, and proclaiming the bans of marriage between himself and my friend Lady Charlotte Campbell'.

Matt Lewis regaled his correspondents with tales of the 'flourishing theatricals' pursued at the castle. 'We played The Rivals last Monday and though I say it, that should not say it, it was really very well acted.' The pregnant Charlotte played Julia, 'allowing for a worshipper's blindness', as Monk Lewis put it, 'as well as I ever saw it performed'.

> William Campbell[53] was a capital Sir Anthony; and my Sister made a very good Mrs. Malaprop, only her wig not being properly fastened, the strangest interest which the Audience seemed to take in the performance while she was on the stage, seemed to rest upon the single doubt, whether her perruque would fall off or not.

Inveraray's theatricals were performed in Robert Mylne's riding stables in the nearby Maltland, which witnessed many a high-flown speech and dramatic gesture even though the audience was pretty sparse. The theatre's interior design and fittings were Colonel Jack Campbell's own work according to James Hogg.[54] On 2 November 1796 one MacNeal wrote to another Captain Campbell:

> This evening we are to perform a play translated from the French by Lady Charlotte and her man in which I play the part of Champaigne a pretty long one the Lord send me well over it—the rest of the actors

> are Lady Charlotte, her husband, Lord John and young [Campbell of] Asknish—who are all play mad.[55]

In 1797 Monk Lewis wrote an epilogue for Charlotte to declaim at the end of one such dramatic performance of Barbarossa, which gives something of the flavour of these evenings.[56] Other dramatic schemes attempted a 'walking' ballet, and a machine was contrived in which Lewis's sister was to fly up into the clouds in the character of the Queen of the Fairies.

> Unluckily the want of an Orchestra put a stop to this daring attempt, to the great mortification of the Authoress, who had taken infinite pains in instructing her performers, though her exertions had been repaid with very little success, and very great ingratitude; for the story was voted extremely dull, and the actors made no scruple of wounding her feelings by telling her, that they thought it so.

Eventually, at the conclusion of one rehearsal, Lord Lorne, being ordered to present his sister to the Queen of the Fairies, in order to be punished for her crimes, made her offence sufficiently clear by saying 'She composed this Pantomime', which gave it 'a death-blow'. Other projects included *The Citizen* and Fielding's *The Mock Doctor*, in which Lewis persuaded William Lamb to play the part of Leander, 'but he obstinately refuses to be dressed as a shepherd with a wreath of roses and a bunch of cherry coloured ribband ornamenting his hat'.

Another venture, 'The Bugle', launched in 1802, was not only a collection of sentimental ballads.[57] The 'Monk' recounted to Lady Melbourne that he was now busily employed as that week's editor of 'a Domestic Newspaper which has been lately established at Inveraray'. With different guest editors, 'The Bugle' appeared on Saturday's breakfast-table. Facetious news and abuse of the house party and reams of satirical verses, freely based on trivial domestic events, filled its handwritten columns. That autumn's assembly was particularly gay and the house was even fuller than usual. The Monk told Tom Moore that they had kept up 'such a continued riot' that he had changed the name of Inveraray to that of 'Confusion Castle with universal approbation'.[58] He continued: 'I purpose leaving this place with [the Comte de] Beaujolois on Wednesday next; William and Kinnaird stay two days longer, when they set out in company with Lady Charlotte and her suite.'

As always in Scotland, music and dancing featured in the evening entertainments. Walpole had noted that by the time she was a young woman, Charlotte had acquired a 'very considerable knowledge of art and a real love of literature and music with a pleasant singing voice', and

Augusta was also an accomplished amateur musician.[59] The younger sister was apparently celebrated for the grace and agility of her dancing, and she played the harp and sang with great delicacy and expression.[60] The Duke of Rutland was bowled over:

> The noble ladies entertained us by dancing reels, in a style of ease and elegance which I never before saw, and increased our pleasure by playing on the organ ... which gratified me far beyond my expectations, when accompanied by the sweet voice of the amiable sisters.[61]

He continued:

> The fascinating melodies of Lady Charlotte Campbell were intended so to occupy the attention of our clerical tourists, that they were not to suspect that any other amusement but that derived from the 'concord of sweet sounds' was going on in the House. After dinner we were entertained by some excellent catches and glees, from Lord Lorne and his sister, Lady Charlotte Campbell, in which they were assisted by the duke himself. During the evening the two former sung duets from Italian operas, in a superior style of tone, taste and exertion.

The Irish Tommy Moore, a protégé of Lord Moira, said that of all those who sang his melodies no one gave him such pleasure as Charlotte,[62] and describing a party at Barnes cottage in 1805, wrote: 'Ah! and there was music, since *she* was prevailed upon to sing; and the high-born and fairest of Caledonia's daughters breathed the simple melodies of her native hills to many a spellbound heart.' Alfred Bunn, the manager of Drury Lane Theatre thought that 'the vocal talent of Lady Charlotte Campbell and Scotch music will be long spoken of together'.[63] The renowned Scots fiddler, Niel Gow, included 'Lady Charlotte Campbell's Medley, Strathspey and Reel' in his collections (see plate 10),[64] while 'Colonel Campbell of Shawfield's March and Quickstep' were included in the Finch *Marches*.[65] The handsome and charismatic Hamilton Paul also composed a ballad in Charlotte's honour, 'the Maid of Inveraray', which was then set to music for her by a young Campbeltown man.[66] Charlotte is also said to have composed a plaintive air to one of Matt Lewis' poems, 'The Banks of Allan Water', which became a popular aria in the opera *Rich and Poor*.[67]

A relative of the duke's, Lady Louisa Stuart, youngest daughter of the 3rd Earl of Bute, had 'always longed to see' Inveraray and was a guest in September 1804, deeming it 'the finest place I ever saw in my Life'.[68] Writing to her sister, Lady Portarlington, she was, however, censorious of the heir, George, Marquis of Lorne. Astutely forecasting that the death of the ageing duke would be likely to 'break up the whole comfort, if not being, of his family, which is a thousand pities', she reckoned, using strong words, that although his heir had 'a thousand pleasing qualities … between his attachment to Lady William Russell and his madness for deep play all are to no avail … he will ruin himself and everyone belonging to him'. One of his earlier amours had been the courtesan Harriette Wilson, and his father was remonstrating with his 34-year-old son that he should extricate himself from all his difficulties and settle down and marry. Louisa found the duke 'a charming old man, with all his faculties, but of course not very attentive to his household concerns, though very much to his farm and estate'. In her memoir, Charlotte depicted her younger brother John's 'unhappy marriage', and her sister's 'total nonentity of Existence'.[69] Louisa likewise censured 'the dejected and indolent' Augusta, who would not help with managing anything, but Charlotte was exonerated as the younger sister and visitor who felt she should not meddle. 'Lady Charlotte is a sweet creature and her character as well as her beauty improves on a nearer view. I wish she were better bestowed than on that great fellow her husband, but she loves him tenderly and he is after his fashion fond of her.' She continued:

> The servants do exactly as they think proper, and it is Confusion Castle … the dinner is abominably addressed, but nobody cares. Sometimes Lord Lorne goes into the kitchen and bustles to get the potatoes well boiled, but he relapses into indolence and the next day 'tis just the same.

As the duke grew older, he left Inveraray less and less, only to visit Rosneath or Ardencaple or attend to business in Edinburgh.[70] After a fire at Rosneath in 1802, the duke had started to replace it with a new castle, nay palazzo, there, although it was mainly his ambitious heir, along with Joseph Bonomi who was involved in what became a ruinously expensive scheme. His father warned Lorne: 'Taste without prudence and Economy, is a mill-stone about a man's neck And therefore I hope you will not associate too much with Bonomis and Naismith. You will find them expensive Pets … they will not consult your Pecuniary interest.'[71]

The duke's younger son, Lord John, had married Elizabeth Campbell of Fairfield on 31 August 1802, but realised quite quickly that the marriage would not be a happy one. By early the following summer he had joined the thousands of British who flocked to Paris and other parts of the continental mainland during the fourteen-month interlude in the Napoleonic Wars after the Peace of Amiens in March 1802. With his companion, Dr Robertson, he was staying at Madame de Staël's small Coppet estate on Lake Geneva. While Germaine de Staël's 'Neville' in her semi-autobiographical novel *Corinne* has been thought by some to be based on Lord John, it is more likely that his attributes and associations were welded on to those of de Staël's lover, Benjamin Constant, or others. It has also been hinted that it was Dr Robertson rather than Lord John who was the object of her attention around this time. With war on France once again declared by Britain on 17 May 1803, it was imperative that the two young men remove themselves rapidly and safely. Lord John disguised himself in the clothes of a maid to accompany Mlle de la Chaux back across the Channel, Robertson following subsequently.[72] It was from the latter that Charlotte heard of their safe return to London and she welcomed her 'dear Johny' back 'once more to Britain's shore' in 'Rhyme and Prose', incorporating her only poetry on the topic of war.[73] Writing from Lord Ancram's great house of Newbattle, she asked him to come soon to visit her and her husband at Dalkeith. By the autumn of 1803 Inveraray Castle was 'tranquillity personified'—Charlotte and her family were in Edinburgh.

M. G. Lewis 'Epilogue to Barbarossa'

Till now, all who glow'd with theatrical flame,
Love of money inspir'd, or else love of fame;
But non of these motives, 'tis clearer than light,
Have produced the dramatic attempt of to-night:
No shillings for entrance were dropt at the door,
No voices, applauding, bawl "Bravo!" "Encore"
And our ardour for glory it surely must quench,
To think that we play to three chairs and a bench.
When Selim, the tyrant, presumed to rebuke,
All he wish'd was obtaining a smile from the Duke;
And when the Queen said the King's cruelty shock'd her,
She hoped for some little applause from the Doctor.
But our utmost ambition was stretch'd to its tether,
If the Duke and the Doctor cried "Bravo!" together.
Yet the fame of our mirth confined shall not be
To a circle so small as the one I now see:
No, I'll tell all the world, in the "Times" and the "Sun,"
How much we have dared, and how much we have done;
And inform the whole kingdom, by means of the papers,
That we've just had an access of tragical vapours.
In fancy already I see, with delight,
"Inveraray Theatricals," full in my sight:
"Barbarossa was lately (they cannot say less)

Perform'd at the Duke's with the greatest success;
The scenes were well painted, the dresses were fine,
The orchestra well fill'd, and the acting—divine.
In truth, such perfection in women and men
Was ne'er seen before, nor will e'er be again;
Captain Campbell gave Othman with strength and effect,
Mr Traffors was graceful—Lord John was correct;
Lord Lorne's easy air, when he got in a passion,
Proved a tyrant must needs be a person of fashion;
He seem'd much at home the whole of the play,—
He died in a style which was quite degage;
All his orders for murder, declared by their tone,
Was the same if he gave them, or let them alone.
The worst (we are sorry to say, but it true is)
Was the epilogue, written, we hear, by one Lewis;
'Twas terrible trash, but in justice we tell,
It was thought to be *spoken* uncommonly well.
Indeed Lady Charlotte, all own'd with delight,
Outdid all her former outdoings that night.
When she got her high prancing theatrical pony on,
Her voice, air, and action, how truly Sidonian!
How wisely she said she'd not marry her brother,
And having one spouse, not just then take another.
And when, in the midst of her griefs and vexations,
'Twas needful to rap out a few execrations,
Her oaths were as truly deserving of praise,
As she had done nothing but swear all her days.
Perhaps some may think, but the fact I deny,
My own merits are rated a little too high.
But if in our play any merit is shown,
I assure you, my friends, that the whole is my own.
I made up the dresses, I painted the scenes—
For constructing the playhouse, invented machines:
And made all the actors rehearse, which I swear,
Was without great exertion no easy affair.
For when to rehearse the fifth act I was wishing
I was told Barbarossa was just gone a fishing
Out of tune, while Irene was straining at her throat,
That Othman was busy in building a boat.
However, I scolded, and bustled, and storm'd,
Till the parts were all learnt and the play was perform'd.

And now Barbarossa's heroics are o'er,
Should you chance, as is likely, to vote him a bore,—
Should you think our performance deserving no praise,
And our play the worst thing you e'er saw in your days,
As your judgments must err, and an audience is scarce,
We condemn you for penance to sit out the farce.

5

Peregrinations

Paterfamilias Walter Campbell of Shawfield had acquired estates in Argyll to give to each of his younger sons on their marriage: Skipness to Robert, Sunderland on Islay to Walter and Ardpatrick to Colin. As his heir, Jack expected to inherit Woodhall and Islay. All four had professions, Jack in the military, Robert a reluctant advocate, Walter an East Indies captain and Colin in the Royal Navy. Lady Hester Stanhope's view that Charlotte was always in uneasy circumstances turned out to be a gross understatement. The Shawfields never provided a home for the heir, and for the first ten years of their marriage, Charlotte and her husband moved among Argyll and Shawfield houses in Inveraray, Woodhall, Edinburgh and London, occasionally renting or being loaned grand houses as required to be near Jack's regimental activities. Charlotte confessed in her journal that she had long wanted a home of her own.[1] Late summer and autumn in Inveraray (occasionally Islay), winter in Edinburgh and spring and early summer in London involved days of challenging travel by coach. From London at least four nights were normally involved, sometimes even continuing by moonlight. Travel in Scotland was broken by staying with widely extended family at Pencaitland or Gosford in Lothian, Woodhall and Ardencaple, or with other friends.

Colonel Jack and Charlotte produced children annually—nine in the same number of years. *The Times* of 27 April 1797 noted their firstborn who arrived less than ten months after the marriage and was baptised with the maternal family names Eliza Maria after her beautiful Gunning grandmother and grandaunt.[2] She was followed less than a year later on 10 April 1798 by a first son and heir, Walter Frederick, named after his paternal grandfather and maternal uncle. Just under another year later on

25 March 1799, Eleanora arrived and, also following Scottish custom, was named after her paternal grandmother. Staying at Woodhall on Thursday 21 November 1799, Charlotte opened a large padlock on a leather-bound volume, picked up her pen and dedicated:

> This Book to my Husband Alone, and when we are dead it must be Eliza Marias, if it should for that long space of time continue in Existance [*sic*]. I write it for my own private Amusement and at the same time from a faint Hope that my Thoughts and Sentiments may be of use to a Daughter and keep up the remembrance of me when I am gone; the History of our Family is like a little novel. I have often turn'd it in my head and now commit it to paper.[3]

Over eighty sides later, with many changes of pen and ink, the memoir was finished at Woodburn House near Dalkeith on Tuesday 8 July 1800. John George arrived that year, named after his father and his Argyll uncles George and John, and was followed on 15 October 1801 by another brother, (Edward) Henry Carter—after a paternal granduncle. Of this third son, little more is known except that he died on 9 February 1803 and is never referred to.[4] On 22 October 1802 Louisa Stuart noted that Charlotte Campbell had left Inveraray in mid-October since she was 'due to lie in in November'.[5] Her third daughter was 'Beaujolois'. Also given a Shawfield family name of Harriet (which her mother called her when younger) and her mother's name, Charlotte, her godfather was Louis-Charles d'Orléans, Comte de Beaujolois, youngest brother of Louis-Philippe, Duc d'Orléans, the future French king. After returning from America the brothers spent much time in London, Twickenham and Scotland, often with the Argyll Campbells, and Louis Charles asked Charlotte to name after him the child she was then expecting.[6] Beaujolois' birth took place at the grand Dalkeith House south of Edinburgh on 4 December 1802[7], not 1801 as often reported, the name Beaujolois, perhaps more appropriate for a boy, still being endowed on the new baby girl. Dalkeith House or Palace, modelled on William of Orange's early eighteenth-century Dutch palace, and Woodburn House standing in their parks on opposite sides of the Esk valley, near to several barracks for Colonel Jack, were lent by or rented from the Marquis of Lothian to the Campbells.[8] Then on Wednesday 16 March 1803 Charlotte picked up her leather volume again while at Inveraray awaiting yet another 'approaching Hour of Tryal ... my Convalescent Hours when I am become Mother of four children'. Charlotte seemed to have lost count—even though Henry had just died, she still had five children, the last born in the previous December. Perhaps the date should have read 1804. She began to copy the journal which she had kept while travelling to Naples in the autumn of 1789. Both in real life when advising her daughters during their child-rearing times, and in her fictions, Charlotte always stuck firmly to her belief that women, for the sake of their appearance, should not nurse their own children, which was probably the main factor in her own annual productions. As she put it, Charlotte was pregnant 'in perpetuity'. After slow physical recovery from each birth, and presumably not nursing herself, she was usually soon again pregnant within months. Even though she was mainly still in her twenties it was presumably hard for her body ever to recover fully before another life was draining her resources, and even when it came to her last parturitions she still described the process of childbirth in cataclysmic terms. Understandably depression also dogged her at times during pregnancy, confinement or post-natally. She was dismayed to be 'a girl-maker', which meant repeating it all for her daughters in future, although since her eldest may have fed her children herself, she managed to stretch childbearing at two yearly intervals over a quarter of a century.

The annually increasing number of children were mostly left in Inveraray or Edinburgh in the charge of the Swiss Mlle Marie-Charlotte de la Chaux (Mamie or Tiranna) and nursemaids. But on occasion Mamselle had to travel south with several of the children to stay with their aunt and uncle, the Carters, at Edgcott, Northamptonshire. A combination of aristocratic upbringing and army or militia life is disclosed by Charlotte in a letter written from Inveraray Castle earlier in 1803 to her two eldest children who were staying at the Argyll House in Queen Street, Edinburgh.[9] It is perhaps hard to realise that Eliza was not quite 6 years old, her brother Walter a year younger. Presumably it was read to them by Mlle de la Chaux, who must have been delighted with the contents. After telling them that their aunt, Augusta, and their 12-year-old cousin, Charlotte Clavering, would be seeing them in a few days' time when they passed through Edinburgh en route for London, Charlotte wrote that she was having to send her maid, Fanny, to 'pack up the things at Woodburn as I am afraid I shall not see you for a good while—your Father's Regiment is at Campbelltown [*sic*] and he will most likely be obliged to go there'. She hoped that Eliza would remember to read 'all the Books I desired—The Sacred History and the History of England' and that she would practise writing twice a day. Eliza was admonished for not having tried hard enough to learn French, and her mother hoped that she 'was doing better now—remember I shall be very anxious to know this and very angry too if you are not diligent'. Unlike Lady Charlotte's own childhood, war was one factor preventing continental travel for her own children. Nor did 5-year-old Walter escape, since his mother hoped he 'could read well by this time for I shall be quite ashamed of you if you are an ignorant little boy'.

Edinburgh relatives, the Misses Johnstone, wanted very much to have the children to 'drink Tea' with them, and Charlotte asked Eliza to get 'Nurse or somebody to take you there in the morning and then if they chuse [*sic*] it they will invite you to Tea'. She added the rider that although they could go to tea once, they should not do so very often because 'Children must be very regular in their hours or else they cannot learn their lessons properly and will never grow up to be strong healthy people'. She told them both 'and you Eliza in particular who are a bit of a Chatter Box' not to talk too much when visiting for without intending it things might be said 'that hurt or affront people'. She added:

> It is a terrible thing for any body a little girl in particular to be call'd impudent—not that I want you to be always grave and silent to me you may talk all the nonsense that come in your head first because I would tell you when you were speaking or thinking what was wrong and secondly because as I like you better than any body else I could find more excuse for all the huff you may talk.

Then she signed herself off with 'God bless you Loves Beleive [*sic*] me to be your Affec Mother C:M:C'. A prosaic postscript asked 'Nanny to order two pairs white Evening kid Shoes for me and two of yellow … and two pairs strong black walking morning Shoes—very large'. Then she cheerfully sent the news that Edinburgh was 'never so gay', or having 'so much good society in it before'.

On another occasion when her husband was colonel in the Argyll Militia, Charlotte was glad that he had not been despatched to 'Sunderland or Port Patrick, as two Thousand men are sent away'.[10] Instead, her husband was rising 'at six every morning, not a transient revolution' since there was to be a 'a Great Field Day on Friday at which all the troops thereabout are to be present'. She continued:

> As Jack must be constantly at Dalkeith and that I cannot bear to be absent from him, we shall avail ourselves in part of a very kind offer Lord Ancram made us, and sleep at Newbattle,[11] the remainder of this week, when I intend to pass my time between that and Dalkeith House. I have not found my séjour here so unpleasant as I expected for My Infants now with opening charms display fresh joys, fresh duties for the coming day.[12]

Somehow, sitting for sketches and paintings had also to be fitted in. Henry Edridge drew many members of the Argyll family about 1801, including Charlotte and Colonel Campbell (see plate 11). While it is possible to imagine the wooded Inveraray policies which frame the tall young couple, such a background was an Edridge trademark. Her appearance is both à la mode but also probably pregnant. There are several other charming and unpretentious portraits of Charlotte and her husband about this time. In one oil, artist unknown, Charlotte is portrayed in near half profile, unusually turned to the viewer's left, in a red dress and fur stole, her long flowing hair beribboned in teal, and she is reading an octavo volume. Her husband's portrait, also unattributed but possibly by George Sanders (Saunders), is very romantic in style, the face half in shadow, a simple coat and necktie, the Shawfield traits clearly captured (see plate 12). There is another similarly unadorned portrait of Lady Charlotte in the Scottish National Portrait Gallery.

Archibald Skirving, described by Scott after an Italian sojourn as 'an unrivalled ... painter in crayons' and one of its few Scottish exponents, had been employing his highly worked crayon or pastel technique on companion portraits of Charlotte and her husband in Edinburgh in about 1802.[13] Sitters whom he did accept had to know that 'it was on strict terms and only as a favour'. Charlotte Campbell had nevertheless managed to persuade him. But she altered her dress and headdress between sittings at which the artist remonstrated: 'Can't stand the like of this, Madam!' He was temporarily overruled, then she tried it again and arrived for her third sitting, headdress slightly altered once more. In addition, she always arrived accompanied by her husband and her pet dog, which contributed to her distracted behaviour. Skirving had put up with this for two sittings; 'at last, losing all patience, he said to her ladyship, "Lady Charlotte, if you wish me to complete your portrait, I beg you will leave your husband and lap-dog at home."'[14] Another biographer writes that 'Skirving threw down his brush; inexorable to apologies, persuasions, and entreaties'.[15] This ultimatum, a serious breach of decorum, gave offence to Charlotte and she never returned. After the lapse of many years, one of her family applied to Mr Skirving for the portrait, unfinished as it was, and offered to give any price he chose to ask. This, however, he positively refused, as he thought he had been ill treated.[16] The unfinished portrait of Charlotte (see plate 13), perhaps understandably somewhat unflattering, was in Skirving's studio, along with her husband's, at the painter's death in 1819 and was then valued at £106 4*s*.[17]

Charlotte had not, however, completely deserted London and Argyll House and some of the more sympathetic portraits of her were by Thomas Lawrence, who was perhaps less abrasive than Skirving. He made several drawings of her from 1795 onwards, in his characteristic charcoal or pencil, red pastel and white chalk highlighting, before being commissioned by her long-time elderly admirer, the Duke of Abercorn, to paint a full-length oil, for £126, in 1802-3 (see plate 14). Lawrence exhibited only five works in the 1803 exhibition of the Royal Academy, all of them portraits and including Charlotte, Lady Derby (as the actress Elizabeth Farren had now become, replacing Charlotte's half-sister) and Emma Hamilton. At this time his prices ranged from thirty-five guineas for a half-length to 140 for a whole-length. Charlotte's portrait (96 x 60 inches) was hung in the library or dining room at Stanmore Priory beside 'the equally exquisite full-length' of Emma Hamilton, also by Lawrence.[18] The 28-year-old mother of six Charlotte was painted in a theatrical classical pose from a low viewpoint, enhancing her height and stature. In one of the obituaries of the artist, it was referred to as 'one of the most graceful and elegant figures ever painted'.[19] About the same time, Tommy Moore recalled seeing her waltzing in 1802 at Argyll House with her husband; Lawrence was looking on, and, studying her upturned eyes, exclaimed to Moore: 'Oh, if I could but catch that look!' Moore recounts how he had seen the picture a few days before, but 'on seeing it again found that he had profited by that night's study of her and turned the eyes upward'.[20] Visitors to the Royal Academy that year could marvel at Charlotte in her short-sleeved white dress, gold scarf and a draped brown cloak lined in red. Behind were a classical urn on a pedestal with framing classical columns, and in front, a low stool on which there was a pile of books. Her hair appeared dark, her eyes looked up to our far right, and the whole appearance is solemn, perhaps even fashionably melancholy. Today it hangs in the Abercorn home.

When it was shown at the 2010–11 Lawrence exhibition in the National Portrait Gallery, the curators' revisionist take on the portrait would perhaps have startled the nineteenth-century onlookers, suggesting that:

> The divide between sitter and portraitist had been bridged and that Lawrence had in fact violated a professional code, the very appearance of the portrait of Lady Charlotte Campbell, its 'showy' taste—the oversized, flaunting body, the arm thrown back casually—opened up the artist to the charge of having trespassed his sitter's morals. Lady Charlotte was showing off or acting out her desires, and the artist rendered them with a bravura technique that attracted the eye to the canvas.[21]

The politician and essayist, J. W. Croker, made the following entry in his journal on July 23, 1828:

> Dined at Sir Henry Hardinge's ... Talking of beautiful women, I told the anecdote that I had separately asked the King [George IV] and Sir Thomas Lawrence, whom they thought the most beautiful woman they had ever seen, and before I gave their answer I asked the present

> company to guess whom they had named. Sir Herbert Taylor and Holmes both agreed in saying Lady Charlotte Campbell, and it was Lady Charlotte that both his Majesty and Sir Thomas selected ... I have never met any one except the Duke of York who had known her in their youth who did not represent her as the most beautiful creature they had ever seen.[22]

He added: 'I saw her in 1801, still magnificent, whole theatres turning round to look at her.' Charles Kirkpatrick Sharpe went even further, judging her as 'handsomer than either mother or aunt', while adding that 'no picture did her common justice'.[23] Joseph Farington recorded in his diary on 17 April that West had told him that the Royal Academy Exhibition looked 'all portraits' but that he had picked out Lawrence's Lady Charlotte Campbell as looking 'very well ... and above them all', while Opie liked it also, Fuseli less so.[24] A later commentator mused:

> What an enchanting Gallery might be formed of the beauties of George the Third's Reign [especially Lawrence's Lady Charlotte Campbell] if these could be taken from their scattered stations over pianos and chimney-pieces, and assembled together for one spring in the British Gallery, an exhibition more interesting, more attractive, more dazzlingly beautiful, can scarcely be imagined.[25]

The portrait was subsequently engraved by both Richard Lane and Thomas Wright.[26]

Not only do family letters amplify the comings and goings of the Argyll Campbells, but pages in Charlotte's own hand disclose much more between 1805 and 1810. Today in The Huntington Library at San Marino in California, the journal was acquired from a London antiquarian bookdealer. The volume started in Edinburgh on Saturday 15 June 1805. Five months' pregnant, Charlotte had 'enjoyed the Ball last night ... after supper I danced with great delight till past five in the morning'. Lord Moira, then in Scotland, had been the host and a few days later was guest of honour at another 'great dinner' at the home of Colonel and Mrs Duff. The latter was criticised by Charlotte for her naivety:

> She does nor understand a party of Twenty or Thirty Persons—she is used to the great Assemblys where Curtseys and a word of Nonsense to everybody is all that is required ... she does not understand Cards are a necessary requisite in that sort of society which is not large enough to be Publick or small enough to be private.

Charlotte had 'endeavord last night to draw [Count Piper] into Conversation':

> But tho' Lady Charlotte Rawdon sat next to me ... she cannot enter into any conversation that exceeds a Tete a Tete—this Defect is very common to British Woman—they are taught to think of themselves as men—they ... seldom converse with the Male sex for the sake of information and the pure enjoyment of intellectual gratification ... The remembrance of this Defect in the Common Education of Girls may be of service to my own.

There was more satisfactory gratification the following evening when Mr and Mrs Dugald Stewart were fellow guests at another dinner: 'To converse with them is truly to converse.' But there was frustration there too:

> I had only the pleasure of seeing Mr Stewart during dinner—as is usually the case in this country he was detained at the table till obligd to go home—What a ruin to the Pleasures of Society. Fortunately Mrs Dugald Stewart is so sensible her observations do one so much good.

It is to be wondered whether the next evening lived up to her expectations when Charlotte and her husband had 'quantities of people to dinner'. After the ladies left to go on to another assembly, her husband and his military companions not only became very drunk, but his brother, Robert, subsequently became involved in a brawl.

'Glad to escape from the unprofitable bustle of an Edin[r] life', they soon set off in 'the finest weather imaginable' for Inveraray, dining en route with the Stirlings of Drumpellier where they met the actress, Mrs Siddons, greatly admired by the host's toadying daughter. Inveraray by now seemed less socially frenetic. Charlotte employed herself 'regularly with the children, diverted myself reading and Drawing ... and never found the day sufficient for occupations'. The 'only company' at the castle that summer of 1805 included Lord and Lady Glenbervie ('as ugly as it is possible for the Human form to be ... yet all agree in saying her person is totally forgot in the charms of her society') and Brownlow North; her favourite aunt and uncle Lord and Lady Frederick, 'eccentric' cousin Anne Damer, Miss Berry and a few others. Even so, she was concerned at her father's physical decline, though mentally as alert as ever and worrying over his various children, Charlotte even going so far as suggesting that Augusta was affected by 'the madness in Argyll family'. Charlotte did not accompany her husband and the Carters to Islay and left Inveraray on 24 September for Edinburgh—not enjoying the last month of another pregnancy.

Adelaide Constance had been added to the family in Scotland in June 1804,[27] Emma arrived in October 1805 and Julia Seymour Buccleuch would follow in December 1806. Charlotte received lots of visitors during her confinement and by December was recovering her energies. Lord John Campbell in Inveraray with his father, brother George, Lord Lorne, and sister Augusta, gave family news to his cousin Anne Damer in a letter of 14 January 1806.[28]

> From Queen St Edin[r] I heard yesterday from Lady Charlotte. She is well, happy and Chearful [*sic*] round her social hospitable fire with a sensible society of Friends and some of these agreeable companions and even kindred souls one of these is soon expected to return, Ld Moira, and though my lady is in confinement she sees her friends in the Evening.

He contended that 'Col. Campbell has had a desided [*sic*] fit of the Gout which his friends are pleased has taken place as the Gout is considered as a vortex that sweeps off its opponents in the Human frame', and also described 'their last little girl but one' as being 'still very sickly and they fear much it is with her a regular decline which La. Charlotte seems much to feel but makes a sensible reflection in such a prospect like her good sense'.

Anne Damer received more news from her cousin Charlotte herself a fortnight later, when the latter wrote to thank her for the cast she had sent to Lord John and which he had brought to Edinburgh, saying: 'I shall now put an Additional Value upon my Head since you have thought it worth while to make a copy of it.'[29] She also thanked Mrs Damer for 'the materials you have been kind enough to send me for work', adding that if she were to 'give up the pursuit, I shall return the box and its contents to you with the feeling which such a loan deserves, for I think I know how to appreciate the value you must put on it'. Anne Damer's mother was an enthusiastic needlewoman of 'worsteds', which Charlotte emulated. She also hoped her father could spare her brother to spend a fortnight with them 'for our family is now often separated and affection loses its lively warmth, if the friendly intercourse of society and its enjoyment do not assist and keep it alive'. After commenting on her secondhand views on the death of Pitt, saying she has 'not one single sentiment on the subject, perhaps this is giving you a very poor opinion of my intellect but truth is best', she tells her cousin that in Edinburgh 'private amusement and pleasure ceases not to hold its sway and here in this little London are Balls and parties and all the etcs of dissipation'. While she was 'very fond of dancing and no enemy to gayety I find some pleasure in partaking of them, but should feel no loss in their deprivation'. She expressed her delight in the thought that one day she might see *The Lady of the Rock* 'imortalized [*sic*] by Miss Baillie',[30] and hoped that 'some day or other perhaps you will introduce me to her acquaintance, an acquaintance which I should be proud and pleased to obtain'. She imparted gossip about the marriage of Mr Tommy Sheridan and the pregnant Miss Callander.

Charlotte and five of her 'infantry' were at Inveraray in April 1806 although, pregnant once more, she could not mount the 'high stairs and attend to the childrens lessons which a few weeks before they arrived would have delighted me'. She had read 'Teignmouth's Life of Sir William Jones[31] and other desultory readings—never but once did the fit of Poesy come upon me, and then it was a very poor low fit'. Jack's brothers Walter and Colin were on leave and joined them for a time, and in mid-May the family were back in Edinburgh en route for London, Jack again unwell, being 'a little Goutish here and there'.[32] His father Walter Campbell had received them at Woodhall 'with great kindness. Would to heaven his kindness was more substantial ... Alas! that Vile Money.' As ever the London scene raised her spirits. 'At last my wishes gratified and I am to see once more the people and the place that I like and where the habit of my young days fix'd my first tastes.' They reached London on 21 May: 'I never felt so happy as I did to see London—this old house where I pass'd so many happy days.' Staying in Argyll House, they caught up with friends and relatives (although relations amongst her Shawfield in-laws were not always cordial: 'life is too short to embitter it by enmities, family enmities particularly ... one does not want family parties in London'), and she was quite happy when Mrs Carter graciously took them to the Opera. Shopping every morning, a visit to Saunders 'who owes his present fame' to the patronage of the Shawfield family elicited her claim: 'I believe I am to sit for him again.'

A few days later on Monday 25 May, when 'in the midst of gay thoughts', word suddenly arrived that the Duke of Argyll was 'very Ill'—George, Lord Lorne had even told Jack that 'perhaps by this time all is over'. Letters had come from Lord John describing the serious stroke that his father had had the day after the Campbells had reached London, and detailed the futile remedies. Charlotte felt that she would never forget that Monday—'it was the saddest I ever pass'd in my life'; she wanted solitude although Anne Damer and Anne Hook both came to Argyll House. Anne Hook's father, physician Sir Walter Farquhar, advised waiting for news, but George and she decided to set off next morning. Jack was incapacitated by a 'severe fit of gout' and was unable to go north with them. They set off next morning at eleven but at Borough Bridge found a letter informing them of the death of the duke on Saturday 24 May/Sunday 25, aged 82. They carried on, up the west coast route, breaking for six hours' rest at Penrith that night, but delayed next day for three hours at Carlisle with a broken carriage wheel. It was 8pm on Thursday 29 May when they reached Inveraray.

Even for wordsmith Charlotte words could not 'convey her emotions on seeing her father's empty seat in the Yellow Drawing Room'. Mlle de la Chaux comforted her and when 'tolerably composed' Charlotte was reunited with her children. On the Saturday morning she lifted the coffin lid and wept over the wrapped body of her father mulling over mixed regrets and affections. He had died with George still unmarried and heirless, John still unhappily married and Augusta having 'lost all'. As to herself:

> The Duke had heap'd so many kindnesses on me and mine, had showed such a very great portion of affection to me that I cannot but feel a double share of affliction and a Grief. A main consolation was her own 'Lordy's letters—Thank God first—there is yet much Joy in store for me.

There was a delay for 'some of the mournful pomp being sent for from London'. *The Gentleman's Magazine* reported his funeral on Tuesday 6 June, the ceremony itself allegedly being performed 'in the most private manner possible'.[33] About ten o'clock the revenue brig *Princess Elizabeth* sailed from Rosneath, with the corpse of his Grace. It was accompanied by the revenue cutters, the *Prince William-Henry* and the *Prince of Wales*, while the Campbeltown packet, *Henrietta*, had on board his Grace George, the new 6th Duke of Argyll, Lord John Campbell, Lady Augusta Clavering and her daughter Charlotte, Lady Charlotte Campbell, Sir Alexander Campbell of Ardkinglas, other friends, and the late duke's servants. His Grace's remains were to be deposited beside those of his duchess in the burying-place of the family beside the Collegiate Church at Kilmun. The small flotilla anchored in Holy Loch between twelve and one o'clock, nearly opposite Kilmun, and the body of his Grace was towed in his barge by the crew of the *Princess Elizabeth*:

> Dressed in nankeen, with crapes round their hats, and received on a platform, near which the present Duke, Lord John etc. were landed ... The outer coffin was covered with crimson velvet, and had two coronets, one at the head, and another at the foot ... At a small distance, Lady Clavering and the other ladies came on shore, accompanied by Sir Alexander Campbell, etc. and proceeded to the vault, where they waited for the procession.

Part of the *Prince William-Henry*'s crew was placed on each side of the path leading to it, 'dressed in white frocks, with black velvet caps trimmed with silver ... The mourners wore sashes, with a large knot upon the right shoulder, and another on the left thigh'. The revenue cruiser started to fire minute-guns when the corpse left the brig, and continued so to do for about an hour, and sixty or more vessels in the loch all had their colours hoisted at half-mast, watched by spectators from Greenock, Port Glasgow, and Gourock. The Kilmun Volunteers carried the corpse of his Grace shoulder-high to the tomb, and it was then laid next to his duchess in the new mausoleum.[34] The family remained for a few minutes, then went on board the *Prince-William-Henry* cutter and proceeded to Ardencaple. A salute of nine guns was fired on their going ashore and the brig and the other cutter also fired a salute upon leaving Holy Loch.

As 'Colonel Jack' the 5th Duke had commanded the Argyll Militia in the 1745 rebellion, playing a notable role at the Battle of Culloden the following year.[35] He served as member of Parliament for Glasgow burghs between 1744 and 1761, and for Dover in 1765, having been appointed Commander in Chief of H.M. Forces in Scotland in 1762. Created a Peer of Great Britain in 1766 as Baron Sundridge of Coombank, in Kent, he then sat in the House of Lords. Apart from all the agrarian, economic and social changes instigated on mainland and insular Argyll, he and his beautiful 'double duchess' had been much occupied with the rebuilding of their castle and the burgh of Inveraray. But he was also an enthusiast for many new Scottish institutions, acting as first president in 1784 of what became the Royal Highland and Agricultural Society of Scotland and as first governor of the British Fisheries Society in 1786. As Louisa Stuart had foreseen, however, his death was the harbinger of difficult and disruptive times for his family and their homes.

Charlotte's own version of these events was not committed to her journal until the end of the year. Her sister had held herself together throughout, despite worrying over the illness of her eldest son George. Augusta and her daughter Charlotte, together with Lady Charlotte, had been in Captain Hamilton's brig and in hindsight deemed the sombre flotilla 'the most beautiful and impressive sight that could be conceived'. After all the mourners had left they went into the mausoleum to shed private tears for their parents before returning to Rosneath. The following weeks proved a great trial for Charlotte. Moving between Rosneath, Ardencaple and Inveraray 'with many unsupportable days', she admitted that 'only Mlle de la Chaux knows what I went through'. Without wherewithal arrangements for her return south were seemingly low on her brothers' priorities, and it was almost the end of the month before she set off, 'with an aching heart' parting with her two sons, Walter, aged 8, and John, who were going to a tutor, Mr Wemyss, but 'they had already forgotten the melancholy event'. The girls were left behind even when the ever supportive Mamselle got into the carriage with Charlotte, holding an umbrella over their heads. After four days they reached London, her joy at being reunited with Jack being short lived since for the whole of July she was feverish and 'in a confused dream'. Her husband had 'opened the state of his affairs to his father who had given him no further hope of aiding him out of our difficulties than by giving security for my portion by taking the principle. This scheme remained unpursued ... and God knows what is finally to become of us'. Mlle returned north by sea, but had to turn round quite quickly again as Charlotte continued to feel poorly—she was once more five months' pregnant—and it was decided to bring the girls south to Edgcott.

6

Accumulating Problems

In August 1806 Charlotte and her family were staying, along with the new duke and Lord John, in Argyll House in London. Although the Argylls were in mourning, two of Colonel Jack's brothers, 31-year-old Robert and 28-year-old Walter, were in London for the season.[1] The former was conducting a swift courtship of Eugenia Wynne of Falkingham; the diaries of Eugenia and her older sister, Elizabeth, bring to life the breathless pace of the social whirl, as well as the colossal anxieties of whether a second son's income was sufficiently attractive to an heiress (Robert had reluctantly followed his father to train as an advocate). There were breakfast meetings, opera rehearsals, walks in the park, preparations for successive masquerades, theatre outings, and so on. In the late afternoon of Wednesday 11 June Eugenia and Robert Campbell dined at Argyll House where she thought 'Col. Campbell the most good humoured Creature in the world'. Various relatives and friends were involved—Mr and Mrs Jenkinson, Mr Hook, Mr Carter and Lady Elizabeth Cole and Mr Cole ('couple peu aimable, elle est belle et soufre sa jonte avec beaucoup de philosphie').[2] Several of them left as soon as dessert was on the table to go to the play—they had Lady Hawkesbury's box for *School for Scandal* and *High Life below Stairs*—before returning to Argyll House for supper. This schedule was repeated on the following Saturday, with chariots to Sadlers Wells. After sundry ups and downs, father Walter Campbell finally consented to his son Robert's marriage, giving him the estate of Skipness in Argyll, with an allowance of just £600 a year. Within days the wedding was arranged, although the new duke, Charlotte and John could not attend since they were in 'deep' mourning. The day before there was a large Argyll and Shawfield family gathering at Argyll House (like Charlotte, Eugenia was acquiring the large number of Shawfield Campbell in-laws). That evening she and Robert went off to the lawyers after dinner and she signed the papers without reading them—then Robert told her of their 'disgraceful contents'. Early on the morning of the next day, 22 June 1806, she went to her own catholic priest for confession and a first marriage before breakfast, but then changed into her white satin dress and long veil, for a second marriage at noon in St George's Church, Hanover Square, recalling: 'I shall never forget Jack's kindness to me before we left the vestry.' Other guests included her sister, Elizabeth, the Charterises,[3] the Jenkinsons, Walter Frederick Campbell, the Coles, Theodore Hook and the Comte de Beaujolois who gave her a 'very handsome amethyst and diamond Maltese cross'. After a 'cold collation' at Argyll House, the newly-wed pair were off to stay at Elizabeth Cole's house in Twickenham. When they shortly afterwards reached her sister's home at Swanbourne in Berkshire, the village church bells pealed and the house had been specially decorated.

Their prolonged honeymoon found them in Islay by late August 1806. On the morning of Tuesday 26 August, Eugenia recorded that she had taken a walk with her new husband on 'a delightful day only now and then interrupted by partial showers—the View of the Sea, from the House is quite beautiful and this country altho' destitute of trees seems to lay claim to a high degree of picturesque beauty'.[4] A percipient and informative diarist, she was 'diverted by the Sight of barefooted and barelegg'd poor people who apparently enjoy themselves much thus unencumbered with too much attire'. She continued: 'Female beauty does not seem to abound, or at least they lose it early from the hard life they lead and the constant exposure of their complexions to the sea and air. They wear no bonnets.' They had come across a wedding party, 'all on foot, and bare legg'd, attended with bagpipes and flags'. She felt herself to be 'an object of curiosity to the inhabitants with whom Robert seems a great favourite. They crowd round us wishing us joy, and shake hands with him after kissing him then their own hand.' She added: 'They chiefly talk Gaelic, which I do not understand.'

Back in Swanbourne, Elizabeth Fremantle wrote in her diary that Colonel Jack, Charlotte and 'Miss' Campbell arrived there on the afternoon of Monday 1 September 1806, Charlotte 'looking very pretty altho' she is now getting quite large. They are most anxious to get a House, and are almost determined to take Hartwell.'[5] Since their marriage Charlotte and her husband were alleged to have 'paid many visits and then in 1803 [*sic*], took up residence by renting Hartwell House' in Buckinghamshire, subsequently the residence of the exiled Louis XVIII of France. But from her journal, 'having no longer a house for nothing', they rented Hartwell

House from 1 October 1806, which Charlotte described to Walter Scott as an 'Excellent place for Ghosts and Horrors'.[6] Situated in the Berkshire Vale of Aylesbury near her in-laws, the Carters at Edgcott, and the Fremantles at Swanbourne, in a hollow with a lake, Hartwell House was by then a somewhat awkward double house, part Jacobean and part eighteenth-century.[7] The rooms were grand, including a Soane dining room (copied from the one in 11 Downing Street), but the house was not overly large for their increasing family and retinue.[8]

Possibly in reaction to her father's death, Charlotte suffered 'a severe illness brought on by fatigue of Mind and Body', but she was also advanced in pregnancy. Calling their last daughter 'it', Julia Seymour Buccleuch was born on 26 November 1806 and baptised in the Hartwell chapel on New Year's Day 1807, with Anne Damer and the Duke of Buccleuch as godparents. Today it is hard to imagine the relentlessness of nine years of annual pregnancies and births with virtually no time for the body to recover. For Charlotte this last parturition was as traumatic as ever. She wrote in her journal:

> It is now four weeks since undergoing all of pain that the Human Frame is capable of enduring. I was brought to Bed of another Child—it is really something beyond barbarous to torment a poor Woman about the Sex of the child Alas! Alas! What does any Man know, impossible is it for him to conceive what the racking Tortures are that produce a child not to mention previous and long and lasting pains and uneasiness and subsequent Languor and Depression or I do not think they could be so totally devoid of feeling of Humanity.[9]

Recovery cannot have been helped by 'all our dreadful distress about money', while the two boys and Beaujolois caught scarlet fever, Walter almost succumbing, the news being kept from Charlotte, in isolation with her new infant.

In a letter to Walter Scott on 9 November 1806 Charlotte had described their leading a 'very retired life' since she had returned from Scotland.[10] Her severe illness' had forced her to stay in England. She continued:

> We then determin'd to remove our Family for a time Here in order to avoid two Establishments but we have never had the smallest Thought of forsaking Scotland—all the obliging things they say about our absence I am willing to attribute to the partiality of Friendship, and thus escape the Imputation of Vanity tho I accept them all and believe them as Gospel.

She added that they hoped to see the Scotts when in Edinburgh in the New Year of 1807. Scott had written enlisting her help in getting subscribers for a new work of James Hogg's, and she in turn had asked her friend, Anne Hook, who had drummed up 'a decent number'.[11] When in London they now stayed at 13 Upper Brook Street, neighbours to the duke at 19 (Brook House) and Anne Damer at 9.

A delightful and amusing 'cartoon' of the patriarch, Walter Campbell of Shawfield and his large family is still in Islay today (see plate 15). The date and artist are unknown and it is to some extent a work of the imagination, but depicts Walter Campbell's five sons and nine daughters, many of them with spouses and offspring. His eldest son, Colonel Jack, is resplendent in scarlet uniform, marshalling his three sons and six daughters, with his statuesque wife, Charlotte, looking on. Walter Frederick has an iron hoop; all the girls have cotton pantaloons below their high-waisted dresses. Only dogs are missing amongst the numerous aunts, uncles and cousins.

Unlike his Shawfield brothers, Jack Campbell had been dependent on income from his father's encumbered estates which had also to support the rest of Walter Campbell's large family. As a militia colonel and subsequently an MP, a ducal daughter as his wife and eight surviving children, Jack Campbell's expenses were likely to be large. Particularly after her father's death Charlotte's journal often exhibited a litany of worry and stress over lack of wherewithal. 'What is to become of us?' became a regular refrain. Despite pleas to Walter Campbell for an allowance of even £100 per month—meeting him had become 'the Inquisition'—by 1807 Jack already owed a lot of money. Charlotte was fretting about living beyond their slender means, worrying about daily increasing debts with 'not a farthing to pay old or current debts'. Jack even asked his father if they could live at Woodhall, and was prepared to stand as a Member of Parliament for nearby Lanark. Walter Campbell flatly refused, and father and son concocted a scheme whereby Walter Campbell promised to look after Charlotte and the children in the event of her husband's death, using Charlotte's dowry of £15,000 as surety.[12] Perhaps the prospect of this had the opposite effect to that intended, for extravagant spending escalated, though the dowry plan was not acted upon.

As well as an increasing degree of desperation about money there were continuing concerns over health. The family had stayed in Hartwell House during the winter of 1806-7, with Charlotte still fragile: 'depression such as I have hardly ever endured has constantly overpowered me'. But her husband was also increasingly ill or incapacitated; based at Warners Hotel in London, after dining at the Jenkinsons' grand house on 16 January, 'the two husbands got very drunk' along with Comte de Beaujolois and the duke (now with Lady William Russell—'I wish he would marry and get an heir'). The next day, 'Jack was of course extremely Ill'. Other dinners were enjoyed at the duke's, the Berry sisters, the Farquhars or with Anne Damer, to whom she showed a 'head I had worked in worsted' which was much admired. They were 'every day plunging deeper in debt—we can enjoy nothing. The idea of our debts presses upon us and weighs us down.' By the 22nd of the month, Jack was so ill all day that Sir Walter Farquhar visited three times. Next day a long letter came from the royal physician strongly advising them not to travel as planned to Scotland, but instead to spend two months in Bath. A 'certificate' was dispatched to Jack's regiment, and on Wednesday 4 February they set out, having just received a letter from Jack's father 'positively refusing to do anything for him'. In Bath, 'we imagin'd we were not spending any money but alas it proved a very different story before we left', since there was much socialising among 'heaps' of friends and acquaintances also visiting the spa. Charlotte herself had 'great faith in natural remedys' [*sic*] and in the two-month sojourn recovered her health and strength, as well as indulging in a dozen singing lessons. Strangely, she noted little of her husband's health, and at a cold and snowy start to April they joined forces with the Comte de Beaujolois and others trying to be April Fool revellers and romantic sightseers in Clifton and various other places en route home.

Jack had meanwhile been encouraged to cultivate the burghs of Ayr and Irvine, Inveraray and Campbeltown in Argyll, and Rothesay in Bute. Despite his continuing health problems, May 1807 was to be spent in a tour of the constituency; perhaps the main benefit for Charlotte was to observe and store up characters for her future novels. Leaving Hartwell House on Monday 4 May Charlotte, her husband, his brother Robert and his sister-in-law Harriet Wynne were in the carriage and dicky, and stopped at Wellingborough, Doncaster, Darlington and Morpeth where they were detained, waiting six hours for replacement horses. They carried on through the Dukeries in moonlight before reaching Edinburgh at 8 a.m. on the Friday, where they checked in to Dumbrecks Hotel for a busy round of social get-togethers. They reached Ayr via Glasgow on Wednesday 14 May and 'stayed in the same room where five years ago I had been with Jack upon account of the disbandment of the regiment'. Jack gave his Election Dinner and after a sleep, Charlotte recorded that she danced till midnight without ceasing, partnered by 'all these drunken men—Jack who always knows when he is Drunk would only Dance one Dance'. She and Miss Wynne had to sing for their supper, after which there were 'reels with those who could still stand—at length I had literally not one man left to Dance with ... I was as yet only a Noviciate in Electioneering.' The scene at Irvine was far worse 'with a still higher degree of blackguardism'. While she claimed to love dancing, she thought 'one of the Expences should be

Gloves for the dancers'. Continuing up the coast the sight of Arran inspired poetry in her head, and dining at Fairlie Inn she considered it 'one of the most romantic spots I ever saw, reminding her of the Mold di Gaeta in Italy, while the 'tenderest Holiest feelings are inspired by the Contemplation of the Moon'. In cutter and brig visiting family, they set sail on Tuesday for Bute. Jack was 'extremely Ill with the vile Gout' and could not get up. 'Poor Lordy', she wrote. She admitted 'I am Romantic' but did not appreciate the evening of 'Bawling and Balling' and was very glad next morning to see the brig that was to take her overnight to Inveraray, her 'sea terrors ... much lessen'd by being in a large vessel'. By the end of the month they were in deluged Campbeltown, before returning to Inveraray where John had organised a Ball in the Great Drawing Room. Thanks to the patronage of the new Duke of Argyll, Jack Campbell did become Member of Parliament in 1807 for the Ayr Burghs.[13] Dumbrecks Hotel in Edinburgh was their base for the whole of June, both worrying about shortage of funds and Jack's health, before returning to London. But by August they were on their way to Hertingfordbury to enjoy being with the Hooks in their elegant parsonage before returning with them to Hartwell House.

Charlotte and her husband travelled in a barouche through Oxfordshire and Hampshire, taking time to explore Winchester Cathedral and staying with his sister Katherine and her husband Charles Jenkinson at Beech House on the Southampton Inns which reminded Charlotte of the Clyde. They then returned to Hartwell before she was to set off for London and Gravesend. But, surprisingly, Charlotte was somehow persuaded by her neurotic, even neurasthenic, sister Augusta, to return to Scotland by sea up the east coast, although she had strong misgivings both regarding her sailing aversion and her husband's continuing ill health. By this time, 'Augusta's Mind was in a sad state of derangement'. She was 'mad, or at least in such a melancholy state of absence of intellect that is the same thing'. Augusta's daughter Charlotte and her ailing brother George were of the party, along with the family maid, Fanny. What was to transpire had probably been beyond even Lady Charlotte's vivid imagination. In the southern North Sea basin, on board their brig, a huge sea developed from a 'universal storm' (a late September equinoctial gale) and they had to anchor on a sandbank off the east Anglian coast. They had 'only avoided Death for a few hours' and Charlotte even confessed to a 'lack of confidence in Heaven'. A pilot had to rescue them, and they were eventually landed, dishevelled, on the shore at Yarmouth. Going to church there on the Sunday, 'on the first tones of the organ her heart melted'. Spending four days there, the party might well have considered abandoning not only the ship but the whole project. But one gallant Captain Bureton offered to take them to Scotland in his 74-ton *Resolution*. This 'spectacle of the

Line' had been on watch at the mouth of Texel. They were on board for three and a half days with the complement of 700 men, some of whom had served Lord Nelson. Every evening entertainment was provided—a band, 'flutes', a puppet show, plays and concerts seemingly including a production of 'Il Figlio Prodigo'. Instead of going as far as Leith, Captain Bureton proceeded to Berwick where they were met by Jack, thence in a small smack being tossed about before reaching Leith, fourteen days after setting out from Gravesend.

After deliverance from this adventure they once again stayed at Dumbrecks for ten days, but 'no sooner had we recovered than the Difficulties and Embarrassments of our pecuniary affairs again rose up with Hydra Head to overcome our Spirits and blast our Happiness ... debts increasing, our creditors more troublesome'. She continued in her journal that she could write 'volumes' regarding her husband's health, but decided to 'hope for a better day'. This seems to have arrived quite suddenly. After leaving Inveraray in the autumn of 1807, Charlotte rejoiced in spending three weeks of happiness in Edinburgh, with Jack's health restored by the combination of a quiet life, early hours and a strict medical régime. 'I passed happier weeks than I have known for a long time. There was no ennui' and 'thank God that My Health alone is a source of great and inestimable pleasure. God grant I may be duly thankful for Jack's health.' He was 'better than he had been for years'; 'peace restored to my mind its native tone', she continued. 'I read several books of Improvement (Watts on the Mind) and proceeded with some Verses I had begun raised my imagination ... read Shakespeare plays and copied a head of Adonis in worsteds.' Their two sons, Walter and John, were in the apparently acceptable hands of tutor Wemyss, newly married to a kind and affectionate woman (this arrangement, however, fell apart a few months later when the Wemyss couple moved to York). The girls were at Hartwell although Charlotte 'felt the Gloom of Hartwell was more striking than ever' and 'I truly felt for Mlle de la Chaux who had been under its influence for six or eight weeks'. Water was pouring down the Hartwell walls, the children looked pale and ill, so as John and Jack had to be in London for parliament, they decided to give up Hartwell House and take a London one instead, which required some hunting. It took until the start of May 1808 to find a suitably large house, No 50 Upper Brook Street, where the children joined them.

From March until August 1808 Charlotte was once more in her element. She described being out constantly, taking part in 'gayeties', as well as 'the grandest Dinners I ever saw at Lady Kinnaird's house—Taste and magnificence, gold plate finer than any I ever beheld'. She was asked to dinner at three o'clock at the home of Augusta, Duchess of Brunswick, mother of Caroline, Princess of Wales. The duchess' son, the Duke of Brunswick, had rather ungallantly briefed his mother, in Charlotte's words, 'that I was very little like my parents and far from inheriting their Beauty'.

The autumn of 1808 saw them again in Argyll via Skipness where Charlotte was surprised by the elegance and refinement achieved so quickly by Robert and Eugenia Campbell. Sailing in sundry cutters, and the Islay packet, they spent the first fortnight of October in Islay. Amongst other amusements Charlotte found time to read and write, as well as experiencing an autumn storm that caused the shipwreck of a sloop which dragged anchor and ended up without mast or rigging at the head of Loch Indaal in full view of the windows of Islay House, fortunately without loss of life. 'It was all we could do to stand or rather crawl along the beach to witness this tremendous scene ... every body in the island declared the storm to be greater than any they had ever witnessed.' It had scarcely abated when they set out on their return journey from Port Askaig, Charlotte experiencing her usual fears transferring between vessels and suffering her accustomed 'extreme Giddiness which the sea always gives me'. Her journal is silent for the next few months, but after Inveraray and Edinburgh, they returned to London life, as the manifold bills from suppliers detailed.

Some idea of the family's new parliamentarian life and expenditure emerges in the invoices delivered to Jack Campbell from suppliers in Scotland (mainly Edinburgh), Aylesbury (for Hartwell), Stoke Newington and London.[14] Grocers, butchers, bakers, cheesemongers, confectioners, fishmongers, poulterers and wax makers supplied goods alongside booksellers, clothiers, glovemakers, haberdashers, hatters, linen and woollen drapers, milliners, perfumers, shoemakers and silk mercers. Jewellers were sought, candlesticks and other household goods were crested and music sellers patronised while printers produced visiting cards, invitations and the like. Despite being financially straitened, crested silver plate was ordered on 8 July 1808.[15] Others submitting bills included chandlers, coal merchants, glaziers, gunsmiths, painters, coachmakers, innkeepers, post horse suppliers and so on. There is one bill from John Broadwood and Sons—was this for an upright or a grand piano?

The colonel was also still part of the Prince of Wales' fashionable London set, and the September 1808 bill for his wardrobe purchases amounted to £587 1*s*.[16] Post horses were hired from William Shepherd 'Hackneyman and Postmaster' in Edward Street, Cavendish Square to visit Lord and Lady Frederick Campbell at Coome [*sic*] Park in Kent on 8 September 1807,[17] and pairs of horses were often hired to ride out for the day to Blackheath, Hounslow and elsewhere. A chaise and pair were ordered on another day for an excursion to Barnett (*sic*). But a major extravagance was a 'best finished light Phaeton' ordered by Colonel Campbell on 11 August 1808 from Chamberlayne and Williams in Cumberland Street, Portman Square.[18] Detailed instructions for the 'yellow, pick'd black and thrice varnished circular phaeton', with embossed crest on the back, blue morocco leather cushions and silk and lace interior also included uniforms for the grooms; with various running costs, the bill over the next nine months amounted to £258 18*s.* 6*d.*[19]

Rather startling in their quantities were the bills for alcohol ordered from brewers, spirit dealers, vintners, Schweppes and others. In 1806 from 23 May to 15 December Gledstones and Nisbett of Salisbury Street delivered port, sherry, madeira, claret, beer and ale to a total of £132 1*s.* (there was no entry for September when presumably the family were in Scotland).[20] The bill for several months in 1807 amounted to £299 4*s.* Orders continued without payment of bills rendered; from 6 February to 9 December 1808 for example (and the family were in Scotland for part of the time) Nisbett supplied, to a total of £488 9*s.* 8*d.* 696 bottles of port, 366 of sherry, 330 of Madeira, 180 of claret and 2,022 of beer and ale, as well as nineteen 'hampers'.[21] Jack's visiting younger brothers may have accounted for some of this imbibing, but averaged over perhaps eight months, and excluding 'hampers', daily consumption in the household amounted to several bottles of port, sherry, and madeira as well as beer, porter and ale. The most expensive, claret, was drunk more moderately, while whisky may have been consumed only in Islay and Argyll.

It is perhaps unsurprising to find surgeons' and apothecaries' bills. These suggest different ailments for husband and wife (few for the eight children under 10 often staying elsewhere). In one month alone, July 1806, forty-six separate prescriptions were dispensed for Colonel Campbell and his family by S. Chilver and M Tupper, 5 New Burlington St, amounting to £8 6s.[22] Apart from 'stomach drops' and a large box of 'opening pills' for the colonel at the end of June, there were also large phials of stomach drops, stopper phials, and daily stomach draughts for him, while draughts for nervous ailments and night-time sleeping were required for Charlotte. The supply of medicines in London continued through August and resumed in November, and by January of 1807 large bottles of 'nervous Mixture' were arriving while seven dozen powders were supplied in July 'for the Country' and other remedies included large phials of 'drops', twenty-eight boluses (large pills) and three plasters as well as the recurrent 'opening pills'. By 1808 the Chilver and Tupper bill reached £60 14*s.* 3*d.*

They were once again staying in Dumbrecks Hotel in Edinburgh in early March 1809, before renting Cameron's Lodgings in St David's Street, to be in the vicinity of the senior Campbells and Jack's eldest sister, Eleanor or

'Elly', in Shawfield House, and 'above all to medical skill'. By this time, Charlotte was bluntly terming the search for these lodgings 'looking for a place in which our Beloved was to die'. At such stressful times a journal comes into its own, but it sometimes feels prurient as well as distressing for later readers. For months Jack had been in sleepy torpor; not only 'his Dear and Glorious mind had long been much altered', but his temper flashed, and sadly, his wife's presence 'made him worse'. Dreadful as this was for Charlotte, Jack's parents, Elly, and other relatives were also sadly involved in caring for Charlotte's 'dieing Love'. Elly became 'quite worn out' sitting up until 3 a.m. with her sister-in-law and all were frightened and violently abused when his thirst for brandy overcame them all. 'Forgetting all my fears to be alone with Him, Determined at all Risks to sleep with Him', Charlotte confided to her diary that it was the last time she 'ever lay by his Dear side', but next day he was as delusional as ever, constantly calling for brandy and 'fancied himself haranguing his Regiment'. The doctors absolutely forbade giving him alcohol, even considering him in 'no immediate danger', but Charlotte recognised the 'rattle in his throat'. Her journal became silent for nine months after his death on 15 March 1809.

While all this alcoholic tragedy had been unfolding in Edinburgh of a young son, brother, husband and father, on 4 March 1809 Louisa Stuart relayed to the Duchess of Buccleuch the charges made in the House of Commons against the Duke of York in which Mrs Mary Ann Clarke was stated to have taken money from officers to procure advancement through her influence with the duke. Mrs Clarke mentioned Brigadier General Henry Clavering as having offered her a bribe to obtain promotion. Although he denied this, she produced his incriminating letters and he was therefore accused of prevarication and committed to Newgate. Not only was he caricatured there by Gillray, but his promotion to General was cancelled.[23] His silence could perhaps have prevented him getting into such a fix and disgracing his family and rank. Louisa insinuated:

> Amongst the respectable figures made in this business, what say you to our cousin [by marriage] General Clavering? Who went and ran himself up to the neck in the puddle of his own accord, without the smallest necessity, or any reason upon earth, unless the admirable one he gave, his extreme dread of being supposed connected with a naughty woman, which to be sure, would have been a sad stain on the character of such an attentive, kind husband, and a terrible blow to the peace of the poor Lady Augusta. She would almost be tempted to laugh at this apprehension of his, I should think, if he did not take care she should usually be more inclined to cry. I pity her very much for this new cause of misery.

John rose to Clavering's defence in the House of Lords. At one time, index cards in the National Library of Scotland deemed this General Clavering's suicide of 4 March 1809[24] but, although long separated from Augusta, he lived on until 1850.

Only a few days after this commotion, however, it was Augusta's sister, Charlotte, who was having to arrange *her* husband's funeral. He was buried at Bothwell Collegiate Church near his mother, Eleanor Kerr.[25] The parish register for Bothwell records that ten shillings was paid for the 'best mortcloth' for Colonel John Campbell of Shawfield.[26] A memorial tablet with his name is today partly hidden, with others of the Shawfield/Woodhall family, beside the organ in the church.[27] Eight years on, the bill was still unpaid for some of the 'mourning articles' supplied to Charlotte back in London a month after the funeral by Matthew Wood, Mayor of London and his partner:

Apr 12	difference in exchange of 2 pair of silk hose @ 5/-	£15
May 17	9 yards of fine flannel @ 5/6 and	
	24 yards calico [*sic*] @ 2/8	5 13 6
	25 yards 4/4 Irish linen @ 3/6	4 7 6
	5 pairs girls black @ 2/6	12 6
	3 ditto @ 3/- and 1 @ 3/6	12 6
	4 pairs girls Habits @ 2/- and 2 @ 2/9	13 6
	2 yds Black Silk 3/- and 3 yds black crepe @ 6/6	1 5 6
	12 yds black finest 3d,12 yds ribbon 3d, 2 yds ribbon 6d	12 0
	20 yds black bombazeen @4/-	4 0 0
	14 pairs black cotton hose @ 2.4	1 12 8
	14 pairs ditto @ 3/6 and 14 @ 5/- 5 19 0	
	Total	£25 13*s.* 8*d.*[28]

Written up on the last day of the year 1809 in Inveraray, Charlotte's journal recorded that 'nine months have passed since I have become a widow'. While ascribing 'God as the Arbiter of Life and Death' she had accepted that 'the warmest and truest Love may end', also reflecting that 'the alteration in her husband's temper had gradually increased for years'. Nowadays it would be said that she had begun to move on, and her end of year prayer was that 'God grant I may make a good use of the portion of Life he still designs for me'. She had remained at Woodhall for the rest of March, but was relieved when her 'kind brother George' took her for a few days to Inveraray, then to London for some days with her younger brother John to meet mourning in-laws and other friends. She was subsequently reunited with her children, by then at Edgcott, and was once more enveloped in the arms of Mlle de la Chaux and the Carters. However, the gloom of the countryside did little for her spirits, and for some months she suffered from tremors, also requiring laudanum to help her sleep. Nevertheless she had courageously 'determined to take the boys to Islay to see their grandfather', but after detailing another unpleasant voyage, her journal is unfortunately silent as she decided 'to pass over the ten days spent in Islay'.

In August that year, 1809, Walter Scott recalled an 'agreeable evening society at poor dear Lady Charlotte's', and continued:

> I can never think on her without deep emotion, with talents, rank, beauty, accomplishments, above all the best of human hearts how much she has had to suffer in her passage through this valley of sorrow. Petty paltry calumny, pecuniary embarrassment, the long lingering and cruel illness of poor Jack Campbell whom her attentions alone could soothe and gratify at last his death for whom I may say she lived almost exclusively and all this distress accumulated on a mind peculiarly sensitive makes up a bitter cup indeed.[29]

Just how bitter was revealed in a letter written to her eldest daughter almost a decade later.[30] After asking Eliza to 'lay aside for a while the tie of filial connection and read me as a Friend', Charlotte bravely admitted that, although she had married her father for love, she 'was made the most wretched of human Beings—and never to Mortal Ear, did I breathe his disgrace or my wretchedness till heaven had parted us—how I conducted myself through twelve years of perpetual suffering is well known to the whole World'. She recalled how she recoiled 'from the nature of the treatment I received—while I was pregnant—and from the disgust of forced Embraces—when frequently, too frequently inebriety render'd those embraces loathsome even to my tender and adoring Nature'. She then explained that while she perhaps did not feel that 'exquisite maternal love for my young Children which it is the fortunate privilege of most Mothers to feel':

> I thought of those children of their education—of their welfare—and well knowing that the more they saw of *our life* and the modes of going on in a very disorderly House—disorderly from Drink, and low company—and the debauchery of your Uncles, with maids under my own Eyes—all of which pass'd as good Jokes for the drunken wassalers, that infested us, wherever we went—well knowing all this I say—I wish'd from principle to separate your lives and habits as much as possible from all which disgraced ours—and this it was which divided all your young years from those intimacies and tenderness's which generally exist between Parents and Children.

She told of one occasion on which she had taken Eliza with her to Ayrshire and Inveraray and tried a different approach, but by her husband 'was accused of loving you better than all my other Children spoiling and making you detestable'. The net result had been that to prevent all the children's 'tempers' suffering, 'with a foresight which was dictated by prudence as well as by real affection I set you all more than ever aside'. Charlotte continued: 'ask Mrs Hook if this is not true. She knew my Sentiments. She knew my Motives of Action. Although I never expressd the one—or shewed the other openly—but what was passing under her eyes—she could not but see and understand.' Little wonder the children were moved about so often.

Charlotte described:

> Watching over your Father with the solicitude of a Wife—with the love of a Mistress—with the care of a nurse—performing the most menial and disgusting offices—entreating Him to spare His health—and save his Life if not for my sake for his Childrens' ... entreating in vain—constantly with child—constantly ill used personally—and disgraced mentally.

She admitted that her father, brothers, sister and friends had also all been abused in terms of the 'grossest reproach' and she had even been accused of 'intrigues with My own Brother' although 'I never spoke or lookd at another man'. From all this suffering and experience she explained that her 'heart became at length seared to the softer affections and from my own Mind alone I drew that firmness and those resources which enabled me to battle with the storm. When it ceased—I sunk to a calm my own approving conscience gave me peace'.

While the soldierly binge drinking episodes and subsequent effects on health were recorded by Charlotte, it was to take over a century and a half before anyone put Jack Campbell's addiction into print. In 1961 Auda Prucher averred that he had died an alcoholic, 'à force de s'enivrer et l'a battue pendant près de quinze ans sans qu'elle n'ait jamais rien dit à personne'.[31] The poem which Charlotte included in her novel, *The Devoted*, could well have been composed at this time:

> Yes! I have loved thee long and well,
> How well thou dost not know;
> For thou art stranger to the spell
> Of my impassioned woe:
> But there's a time, that time is near,
> When I may cease to feel;
> The altered mien I see thee wear,

Has cased my heart with steel;
This numbing power, this deadly chill,
Is now a welcome guest,—
It is my wish, it is my will,
To nurse it in my breast.[32]

A biographer of Susan Ferrier's considered that Charlotte's 'devotion to her husband had been genuine and complete, but with all her sentimental softness she was of an energetic, forward looking nature'.[33] Her poetic quill had been busy. In what must have seemed a somewhat doleful and perhaps even unsuitable contribution to Susan Ferrier's autograph album in October 1809, Charlotte composed a poem of sixteen quatrains about her loss and religious consolation.[34] Another slightly less sombre sonnet may also date to this time.[35]

Widowed at the age of 34 Charlotte had, between the ages of 22 and 31, borne Jack Campbell nine children in as many years, and the eldest of the surviving eight was now only 11. Relatives and friends had tried to dissuade her from the proposed marriage on grounds of both rank and income, but the 21-year-old had been determined, as she termed it twenty years later—on a 'Marriage of Wilfulness and Love'.[36] Most women of Charlotte's rank and era were legally reliant on their menfolk for the arrangement and provision of their finances. Although her engagement to the handsome guards officer Jack Campbell had been of almost six months' standing, it transpired that her Argyll family and advisers had been less than assiduous in hastily drawing up the marriage settlement just a few days before the event, based on the aforementioned dowry of £15,000. Not only had no provision been made for a dower house in the event of widowhood, but she was immediately ill-advised to give up her rights to goods and chattels to her father-in-law.[37] Three days after his son's death, Walter Campbell and his heirs undertook to take over Jack Campbell's debts of £7,728 11*s*. 10*d*. (well over half a million pounds by now).[38]

Edinburgh and Scotland	2,716 8 1
Aylesbury	748 4 11
Stoke	830 17 1
London	3,433 1 9
Total	£7,728 11*s*. 10*d*.

Many of these bills, however, still remained unpaid at Walter Campbell's own death in October 1816. In 1817 Jack's sister, Elizabeth or Betsy Campbell married Stuart Moncrieff Thriepland, the third of five sons and a daughter of the third baronet of Fingask. Like many Scots as well as the Campbell family, he had been employed by the East India Company, from which he had just retired, and with his wife developed Middeton House and small estate near Uphall in Linlithgowshire. After the death of his grandfather in 1816 and to help pay off his father's bills, Walter Frederick Campbell borrowed from his new uncle-in-law, Stuart Moncrieff Thriepland.[39] (After Thriepland himself died in 1838 his heir, nephew and trustee was still dealing with Shawfield financial affairs into the mid-1850s.)

The education of Charlotte's two surviving sons, Walter Frederick and John George, was supposed to be taken care of by the Shawfields. Her annual income or liferent from her father's bond or dowry was only £750, supplemented by a voluntary contribution of £250, and an annual provision of £500 for the six girls.[40] Relative and absolute shortage of funds remained an unsolved problem for most of Charlotte's long life. The options for an aristocratic widow with so many young children were few, and the Shawfield Campbells were not only spending on their estates at Woodhall and Islay, but also comprised a very large family, many of whom were dowry-needing daughters. The new Duke of Argyll, now 40, was notoriously and utterly profligate. As well as the extravagances in building Rosneath Castle, his role as one of the Prince of Wales's bachelor bucks, his gambling and his sequence of courtesans and other liaisons continually ate massively into the resources of the Argyll Estate, parts of which had subsequently to be sold, as well as Argyll House in London.[41] He did, however, contribute £604 each year to Charlotte, paid quarterly, and her uncle Lord Frederick also helped not only with another £400 annually, but also with a legacy of £1,000 on his death on 8 June 1816.[42] Charlotte could perhaps have adopted her sister's strategy; having left her husband, Augusta often lived under the wing or roof of her younger brother John, at Ardencaple or nearby, and had also been bequeathed 11 Queen Street in Edinburgh. Lord John was an MP, FRS (1819) scientist, unhappily married and with indifferent health. Perhaps with Charlotte's household of a dozen or more, this was not really an option. Charlotte herself claimed that she had always tried to be independent.[43]

Her maid, Anne MacLean, was a constant throughout. Until old enough to have tutors or to be sent to public school, the two surviving boys and the six girls were all under the care of the formidable Swiss governess, Mlle de la Chaux, or 'Tiranna'. Eugenia Wynne on a visit to Inveraray in 1806 deemed the governess 'clever' but added that she talked 'a great deal';[44] the latter's surviving triple cross-written letters to the extended family in English and French corroborate this characteristic.[45] It is almost impossible, however, to feel anything but sorrow for her heavy work load, when reading in a letter from Susan Ferrier to Charlotte Clavering that not only was Mamselle 'in all the agonies of a sprained foot' in July 1809, but Lord John had led Lady Charlotte astray and given her the slip, for which 'if there is truth in transmigration, his soul will certainly be transfused into the body of a nursery-maid with the care of ten children, two of them teething'.[46] Mamselle was also entrusted with most of the children's travelling in Scotland and to and from the south, including arrangements for the boys' staying with tutors.

During her ten-month retirement until early April 1810, Charlotte was ensconced in Inveraray and Edinburgh. From the former she wrote at the start of 1810 to her lifelong friend, Mary Berry: 'I never knew before that I could live in Complete Retirement and like it. I am much fonder of myself in consequence than I ever was, and like most People that live alone, I believe I shall grow disagreeable to others—this Egotism is a specimen of it.'[47] She also admitted:

> As to my Bairns I interest myself in every possible way about them, but when People talk of Children being Companions they either talk nonsense, or they talk of what they know nothing about, except in Theory. Children speak and act very differently in reality, from what they do in Books of Education; and as what we seek for in a companion is sympathy and a capability of comprehending, neither of these things can be found in children, neither can we find them in Companions, but nobody makes use of appropriate words, and one thing that would make the world go on much smoother would be the perfect understanding of our thoughts.

The same encumbrance also made immediate remarriage for rank or financial security, let alone for love or companionship, equally problematic or even perhaps unlikely.

7

Reluctant Courtier

A possible solution had arrived out of the blue in a letter to Inveraray in November 1809, Lady Glenbervie offering her a permanent position with the Princess of Wales. Charlotte quickly determined to accept.[1] Leaving Inveraray on 2 April, after her 'retirement' Charlotte spent the next ten days staying with friends en route to London then went off to the country before the children joined her in London. On 24 April she was presented to the Princess of Wales at Kensington Palace by Lady Charlotte Lindsay. The princess enquired after her family, and told her she would have room for at least some of them, with the bait of a footman and use of one of the royal carriages, but she was strongly advised by one of the princess's other ladies, and sister of Lady Glenbervie, not to accept this offer. Charlotte was quickly presented at court by the Duchess of Buccleuch.

Charlotte was to record in her *Diary* 'Courts are strange, mysterious places', continuing:

> Intrigues, jealousies, heart burnings, lies, dissimulation, thrive in them as mushrooms in a hot-bed ... those who pretend most to despise them seek to gain admittance within their precincts; those who obtain an entrance there generally lament their fate, and yet, somehow or other, cannot break their chains.

She concluded: 'nevertheless they are necessary evils.[2]

The first sentence in Charlotte's published *Diary* encapsulated well over two centuries' experience of family courtiers from her grandparents to her grandchildren and into this century. For a widowed ducal daughter in the first decade of the nineteenth century, few were the possibilities of earning. Charlotte's mother had served in Queen Caroline's court for twenty years, but the legacy of her mother's dispute with the queen over her daughter, Lady Betty Derby, rendered a position in that court unlikely. However Lord Glenbervie, often included in the house parties at Inveraray, confirmed in his diary on 1 December 1809 that Lady Charlotte Campbell was to be a woman of the bedchamber to succeed his wife's sister, Lady Sheffield.[3] But the bedchamber on this occasion was that of Princess Caroline, the estranged and increasingly strange wife of the Prince of Wales. Entering court service, let alone becoming a member of a rival establishment, had probably never been envisaged by Charlotte and it became a situation which she neither much relished nor very much enjoyed, especially in the increasingly rackety court of the princess. Since only titled ladies could normally serve as courtiers, it was certainly one of the few directions Charlotte could take to improve her financial situation. Her faithful friend, 'Monk' Lewis, congratulated her, extolling the princess's 'many estimable qualities' which included 'reading a great deal, and buying all new books, while being fond of music, the play and the opera where she had boxes at both theatres', as well as having concerts at Kensington Palace.[4] In January 1810 Charlotte had received Mary Berry's account of her 'future Mistress and her agreeable dinners'.[5] The mini-court of the Princess of Wales was then centred in Kensington Palacc (and later at Connaught House), and at Montagu House on the southern edge of Greenwich Park bordering Blackheath. Lord Glenbervie detailed the rota of waiting: each of the four did stints of one month, three times a year.[6] The emolument was £300 guineas per annum, with perquisites for dressmakers, milliners, furriers, glovemakers, shoemakers and other expenses amounting to a further £200 guineas.[7] The 500 guineas, however, were 'taxed down by the property tax to 450 guineas'.[8] Given the use of a grace-and-favour apartment, use of a carriage and offered but declined space for her children (the eldest 13 and youngest 3), Charlotte's attendances were slated to start on 9 April, 9 August and 9 December, although the dates proved fairly flexible.

While the 'Delicate Investigation' had come and gone in 1806, by the time the regency was declared in 1811, Caroline's behaviour, understandably perhaps given the treatment meted out by her husband and his mother, became increasingly erratic, bizarre and often unseemly. Although critical, and despite constraints of various kinds, Charlotte did try to support her royal mistress, and this comes through in the *Diary.* George III, uncle of the princess, was a fond protector until his illness deprived her of his company. None of the treatment inflicted on her made the princess easy to work for and the scenario increasingly deteriorated, particularly in relation to Princess Charlotte, when the ladies had to act as go-betweens. They had to accompany Princess Caroline to the Court levees and drawing rooms, dinners and balls at St James's. Many evenings were spent at the opera and ballet then in Haymarket, and at the theatre in Drury Lane. Lord Glenbervie and others in 1810 made much of Charlotte's attraction to the Persian Ambassador, Abul Hassan, a recognised ladies' man (especially if they were short, which should perhaps have ruled out Charlotte).[9]

Concerning the early part of her royal service, Charlotte pointed out in a footnote in her *Diary*: 'It was said of the society at Kensington, that it was the lowest and most impure. At that period the accusation was *wholly* unfounded ... there was a galaxy of distinguished persons who sat at the princess's board.' She added: 'The nobles of the land flocked to her parties.'[10] Small dinner parties of the princess were 'peculiarly agreeable'[11] and after naming some who had been at one, Charlotte noted:

> This list of persons is but one of many such: equally high in rank, and more distinguished for talent and charm of manner, cannot well be conceived. There is no doubt that the Princess had the good sense to know, that the society of persons who are famous for talent or wisdom, casts a reflected light upon those with whom they associate.[12]

Charlotte's brother, the 6th Duke of Argyll, was one of the Prince of Wales's randy dandies, and some of the early dinner parties included some of the regent's coterie, whom the princess suspected of spying on her; as relations deteriorated many of these no longer accepted invitations. By early 1813 Charlotte was noting that the princess's circle was growing smaller 'every day', and company was becoming 'lower'.

Friends of Charlotte from Argyll and Edinburgh also numbered among the princess's guests, including the poets Thomas Campbell, Matt Lewis and Walter Scott. Courtiers or chamberlains participated, including the Glenbervies, Lady Charlotte Lindsay, the antiquarian Sir William Gell and his close compatriot Keppel Craven, contributing to enjoyable, if long evenings at Kensington Palace or Montagu House. Writing to Charles Kirkpatrick Sharpe in 1813, Craven noted that while dining twice a week at Kensington, he had formed 'a very strict alliance with Lady Charlotte Campbell, whom I cannot help having a very great regard for'.[13] Montagu House was described by Charlotte as an 'incongruous piece of patchwork. It may dazzle for a moment, when lighted up at night, but it is all glitter, and glare and trick; everything is tinsel and trumpery about it; it is altogether like a bad dream' (see plate 16).[14] Today there is only a tablet on the site of a bath, and the summer house in Pagoda gardens with its distinctive chinoiserie. Normally at both Kensington Palace and Montagu House amateur music 'was endured only for the sake of making a noise,'[15] 'as it is merely an affair of custom with the princess to have musicians, in order that it may be said She has had a concert; cats would do just as well'.[16] On one such occasion at Montagu House Charlotte had to endure the Sapios who made such a 'horrid din ... I think my ears never underwent such martyrdom'. She also wrote: 'The Princess sang or rather squalled.'[17] There, and at Kensington, she could become 'tired to death, yes, to the death of pleasure'.[18]

Many of the royal arrangements concerned displacement activity to fill time. However, forays to the Royal Academy and the British Institution, or to the new Dulwich Gallery, were much to Charlotte's liking, and on one such visit she greatly admired Cowper's version of Tam o' Shanter, 'the horse very good'. The launch of the *Queen Charlotte* at Woolwich was another memorable outing, summoned up later in her novel *Love*.[19] On a visit with the Princess of Wales to the British Museum and its gardens, statues and magnificent library, Charlotte was disconsolate at having to rush past the books.

> Whenever I view these collections my mind is depressed. I devoured with greedy eyes the outside of the volumes, and wished—oh! How vainly—that their contents were stored in my brain. A whole life of learned labour would not suffice for that; what chance have I, then, in the middle of my days, of accomplishing such a wish? ... I shall leave nothing to excite one emulative sigh when I am gone! I shall die, and nothing shall tell of my existence! But happier far are those who have never indulged a wish for fame. If a few who have loved us in life mourn us when dead, that is the only tribute to our memories which is, in fact worth seeking for. Down, then, proud thought, of living in after ages! Be that which you are destined to be—fulfil the course which is pointed out by providence, and be content.[20]

At times Princess Caroline would ask one of her ladies to accompany her on a walk in Blackheath or Kensington Gardens when 'all of a sudden she will bolt out at one of the smaller gates and walk all over Bayswater ... at the risk of being insulted, or, if known, mobbed—enjoying all the while the terror of the unfortunate attendant who may be destined to walk after her'. Other outings had to be thought up and planned. The Princess of Wales paid Mrs. Damer one of her visits to Strawberry Hill.[21] She arrived late, 'bringing with her only Lady Charlotte Campbell, Mrs. Damer's cousin'. After a cold dinner, at which the Princess was very lively and remained long at table, they walked and sat about the garden; she did not leave till twelve o'clock, although she had ordered her carriage for 9.30. On another occasion Charlotte addressed Mary Berry 'Samson, the Philistines be upon thee', having been commanded to tell her that the

Princess of Wales proposed visiting the Berries at Tunbridge on Tuesday 25 August 1812, along with 'Mrs. and Miss Rawdon—at least they are invited—and your humble servant'.

> There being a Dearth of Men throughout the Land at present, we have none, alas! to bring; but you are a good caterer in that way and have a certain pair of black eyes that are not bad Decoys for stray Birds. For Heaven's Sake use them vigorously in Our Service, for I think we shall be heavy in hand to you and ourselves without a little Male Aid.[22]

The arrangements were detailed from Montagu House on 21 August:

> I am commanded by Her Royal Highness to inform you, that about three o'clock She will be at your door on Tuesday. The Princess thinks that the Pantiles and the Ball will be very good fun *with* you; but rather wishes (unless you have some very Agreeable Brand) not to have any Company at Dinner.[23]

Lady Donegal described the visit when writing to Thomas Moore. The Pantiles had been 'put in an uproar last Tuesday'. The only men present were Sir Philip Francis and 'old Berry'.

> [The latter] liked the fun of gallanting her about, and enjoyed himself more than the fair daughters did, who were in a great fuss, and were forsaken in their utmost need by Beaux their former suppers fed, and had to amuse her, as well as they could, with the assistance of a few women that she did not care about.[24]

Private visits were also organised as when Charlotte accompanied the Princess of Wales on a visit in 1813 to the nonagenarian Emily, Duchess of Leinster, presenting her with a china cup which had belonged to the princess's mother.[25]

More pleasurable was the princess's espousal of Walter Scott (but he subsequently also became a favourite with the Prince of Wales and abandoned her table). Scott had sent both the princess and Charlotte a copy of his *Transcendent Poem* and, in May 1810, had also inscribed a copy of the *Lady of the Lake* to Charlotte on publication.[26] The princess often asked Charlotte to read aloud such recent works. In what he termed Charlotte's 'elephantine script an inch-and-a-half big',[27] she belatedly expressed her own 'Delight' for the gift of the *Poem* although it had taken her four months to concoct her gratifying communication.[28] She had been in bed with a 'severe sickness' but it had given her 'leisure ... to make wise reflections and good resolutions'. In the early summer of 1810, Scott gossiped to their mutual friend, Lady Abercorn, that he had seen Charlotte 'for an hour one evening as she passed through Edinburgh. She is still looking beautiful. We hear she is or was on the eve of marrying Lord Petersham.' He asked his correspondent: 'Don't you think that might be as well left alone?'[29] Lord Petersham, heir to the 3rd Earl of Harrington, was a tall and handsome eccentric and dandy in the Prince of Wales's circle.

In a bitchy letter from London on 13 November 1810 to her sister, Lady Frances Jerningham gossiped:

> You will perhaps have heard that Lady Paget is positively to be married to the Duke of Argyll. She was to set off yesterday with Lady Charlotte Campbell, and the Duke will receive them. It is a very odd affair and Lord Paget will not admire meeting his Quondam wife with the higher Rank of Duchess and an obsequious Husband, for he has always treated her with the most shameful Contempt. He must be a little more careful in his expressions. At the same time it is a most irregular proceeding.[30]

Having gone to ground in Perthshire, Lady Caroline Elizabeth Villiers had obtained a divorce from the then Lord Uxbridge.[31] While Scott subsequently noted it 'was a nine days' wonder, and is already forgotten',[32] others were less charitable. Lady Bessborough had written to Lord Granville Leweson Gower from Brighthelmstone in early September about 'the case that had just been decided in the Scotch courts, which will make a great noise'. She described the subterfuges necessary to produce adulterous evidence for a divorce, including an accomplice who retained a black veil over her face in bed in the appointed inn.[33] Lady Caroline had left Paget (with whom she had had eight children), while Paget himself immediately married Lady Charlotte Cadogan in what was widely regarded as collusion. Charlotte Campbell was indeed staying in Dumbrecks Hotel in Edinburgh on 18 November 1810 for her brother's Scottish marriage on 29 November. The Princess of Wales requested an account of the 'Duke of Argyll wedding and its antecedents and consequences'.

After the regency was promulgated on 5 December 1811, Charlotte was often caught in the crossfire between the Prince of Wales and his loathed and estranged wife, particularly over access to Princess Charlotte. At first the latter was allowed to dine once a fortnight with her mother, with specific instructions from the prince that they should never be left alone together. Governess Cornelia Knight recorded that on one such occasion in 1812 Charlotte played and sang to Princess Charlotte.[34] The affair escalated when Princess Caroline invoked the aid of the press after her letters to the Prince Regent had been returned unopened. As well as soliciting the advice of her chief Whig advisor, Henry Brougham, she had also asked Charlotte and her other ladies to turn her letters into 'good English'.[35] Normally they were dashed off just as she spoke.

Weeks turned into months when mother and daughter were kept apart; and after Princess Charlotte refused to marry the Prince of Orange, in order to spirit her away from England, she was isolated even further by her father and grandmother. Neither she nor her mother was allowed to participate in the great Hyde Park and other celebrations in June 1814 when much of the world came to London, to the disapproval and commiseration of Lady Charlotte.

Although she had expressed herself as uninterested in things political, during her time at court Charlotte noted various newsworthy events in her journal or correspondence. To Mary Berry she confided:

> I don't know what to say to the Victory [the battle of Salamanca on 22 July 1812 when Wellington defeated the French under Marmont]. Will it ultimately produce Peace? Carnage may be glorious, but I cannot say I enjoy it and I never hear the noisy thoughtless Mirth of the Populace upon such occasions without thinking of those Tears which no glory wipes away, and sighing for those to whom mirth is but Despair—but I know the World must be made *over again* for me. Won't—*Voila le malheur* you shall tell me all about it when we meet. I can only sign myself in violent Haste. CM.[36]

On 12 May 1812, writing to the same correspondent, from the Blue Chamber at Montagu House:

> You may think, my Dear Berrina, what a shock the tragical end of poor Mr Perceval has given to the Princess [the prime minister had been shot in lobby of the House of Commons on 11 May 1812 by John Bellingham, a bankrupt Lancashire broker with a grievance against his government]. I am commanded by Her Royal Highness to beg you will let us know all the particulars you may have heard concerning this awful event.[37]

The princess gave up going to the opera that night but 'she means to attend the Drawing Room on Thursday, as that cannot be attributed to any love of pleasure'. She asked Mary Berry for her 'opinion upon this business. Do you think that it is the action of a mad Individual, or the fulfillment of any settled plan?'

In 1813 the Prince of Wales discouraged Madame de Staël from visiting the Princess of Wales who had sat waiting for her, which even earned a black mark from Charlotte. But the latter also averred that her own life had then been far more interesting than 'when in the busy scenes of court life; for I have spent the hours with ———. She left town today, so I had nothing to do but to take to my books et je me suis fait raison'.[38] This probably referred to Madame de Staël, in whose company she had luxuriated: 'This meeting has given me fresh courage to bear my unhappy existence.'[39] While Charlotte felt very excited at meeting Madame de Staël on several occasions in London, the latter had claimed that 'there is no other woman I more desire to know than Lady Charlotte. I think the unique combination of rare beauty and a superior mind ought to influence the effect one should have on the other.'[40] Even more plangently she avowed, when first introduced to the lady herself, that she 'would gladly surrender all her genius, if in exchange, she could receive the face and form of Lady Charlotte Campbell', such 'was her espousal of the power of beauty to captivate, enthral (and too often, lead astray)'.[41] Charlotte's reading of de Staël included at least *Corinne*, *Essai sur les Fictions, Petits Romans* and *Essai sur les Passions*.[42] After an encomium of de Staël's womanly virtues, she asked herself rhetorically 'what do the other sex think of a female authoress?'[43] Her answer was that 'with one or two very sober, but very great exceptions ... there is not a man ... who does not think that those women are wisest and happiest who do not attempt that bold and dangerous adventure, authorship' and went on to opine that while men had 'the camp, the court, the senate and the field', women had nothing but thought and feeling left as they got older.

There were, thankfully, other reinvigorating moments. One day Charlotte walked by herself over the Heath to Lee. 'The day was fine, and I had not felt the fresh air blow on me so long, that it seemed redolent of life, and health, and peace, if not of joy and youth.'[44] When not in waiting, she sometimes returned to the Argyll family home in 13 Upper Brook Street. Writing on 2 April 1811 from 2 Lower Cadogan Place, at that time the home of Lord John, her niece Charlotte Clavering told Susan Ferrier that Lady Charlotte had no carriage, so that 'when we go out to walk it is for the good of our health, and we don't go into town at all, but walk for air and exercise in the park'.[45]

Charlotte recorded that she never left home for Court 'without regret; life is so short, so uncertain, that it seems to me as if all voluntary absence from what we love most, is folly'. Another time she asked Mary Berry 'why one ever consents to be absent from the Friends one loves most'.

> Is there anything that compensates for the absence of a beloved object? I know of none. Berrina, Dear Berrina, I shall never be wiser or better. My heart is still at fifteen, and not worn out—the more's the pity, say you—and sometimes I think so too. I took wing to-day to my own nest

> and nestlings—and am rather surprised why I ever leave either—but necessity teaches one to endure many things.[46]

She had earlier confessed to Charles Kirkpatrick Sharpe that she went about 'like other fools in quest of pleasure, and I generally find ennui', continuing:

> When by any accident I stay at home, I am sometimes agreeably surprised by a visit from pleasure. One assembly is so like another, everybody so dress'd out in their company face, so tired of themselves and of their pursuits, so dully gay and so gaily dull.[47]

Her correspondent had first met Matt Lewis at supper in Cadogan Place.[48] In the summer of 1810 the latter had also described her beautiful villa in Buckinghamshire as 'a long, low white house, all over verandahs and rustic colonnades and covered with fruit and flowers in profusion'.[49]

Financial worries continued to rumble on, and it was from Worthing that she penned a pained letter to the Shawfield agent in Edinburgh on 28 June 1811: 'I have now to acknowledge your having honor'd my draft of three hundred pounds which was no longer mine as I returned it to the Friend of whom I borrowed it.'[50] She also trusted that he had made a remittance to Coutts so that she could draw funds, explaining:

> I trust My Dear Sir you do not think I have any doubt of your wish to attend to My interests but the narrowness of my income and my determination not to incur any debt obliges me to require my remittance be punctually paid, therefore should Mr MacKinnes [Shawfield's agent] remain in arrear, I beg you will confirm me without loss of time, that I may myself apply to Shawfield, to have redress from that quarter.

She continued: 'Considering the last curious arrangement that was in a manner forced upon my Ignorance by Shawfield (giving up £2,000 for goods and chattels), I think I am at least entitled to punctual payment of my annuity'. She then reminded the agent of her 'oft repeated request, to have the Account of charge and discharge between you and I since April 1810 which I have been long particularly anxious about' and hoped that he would delay no further. Worthing was presumably cheaper for her family than London. In a letter to Mary Berry she signed herself off rather curiously—'Yours, writing and teaching at the same time'. She described herself as being 'in a sea of troubles', out of which she never expected to emerge, thanks to 'all my female train' for all of whom she was keeping 'School, without any interruption or temptation whatever.

We want nothing but a blue Board and Golden Letters ... with Young Ladies Genteely Educated—to complete the Establishment.'[51] To Charles Kirkpatrick Sharpe she admitted that she had been living at Worthing in the summer of 1811 'in perfect retirement, trying, for want of better amusement, to be romantic', continuing:

> But the unbounded ocean, and the trackless plains, and the glaring sun ... and the squalling of children, do not at all forward my endeavours that way. People talk of the sea's sublimity, but I declare it sublimely hideous here, rolling its monotonous waves upon a flat sand, and blighting with its salt breeze all the foliage.

She added: 'Summer without green robes and her garlands is not summer; for my part I am in a pet about it, and would as have it were winter ... What is it makes the hours and days so long?'[52]

The widowed Charlotte had not yet recovered her blitheness after the financial and health worries of the previous decade. 'I am only vulnerable through my affections; my weal and woe all lie in that quarter; what then can it have in common with a court?'[53] She continued in the same woeful vein: 'The vacuum in my existence, which one only circumstance can fill, still exists and a low languor enfeebles body and mind, But I hope—nay, I am not ungrateful for the blessings given.'[54] It may have been about this time that a 'near' relative came to her rescue with Westwood House, a large double bow-fronted house, gardens, pond and gardener's lodge, on Westwood Hill in Sydenham, Kent (see plate 17).[55] While it was certainly not in her beloved London, she could at least pursue another of her enthusiasms. On Christmas Day 1812, Susan Ferrier in Edinburgh had heard from her sister that Charlotte was laid up in bed with a severe cold which she had caught 'in her gardening operations', explaining:

> For she is grown a prefect hedger and ditcher, and works an hour every day in her garden with her own hands, which she thought did her a great deal of good, and in dry weather. I dare say it did, but the season is now too far advanced for outdoor work—at least for ladies.[56]

On another occasion she had returned 'after nine days absence to my little Home—I like it always—my garden is blushingly sweet in despight of wind and rain'.[57]

Living nearby in Sydenham was another of Charlotte's literary influences and friends of like age, the radical poet, later editor of the *New Monthly Magazine* and promoter in 1825 of a university of London, Thomas Campbell.[58] On 26 April 1812 he gave the first in his series of lectures on poetry at the Royal Institution where 'all friends struck me blind, except my Chieftain's lovely daughter, and now next door neighbour on the Common—Lady Charlotte Campbell. I thought she had the feudal right to have the lecturer's looks to herself.'[59] The Princess of Wales, to whom he was presented by Charlotte, 'has threatened to make an irruption into my house. Lady Charlotte Campbell has prevented her, but I am to be summoned to Blackheath to see her', when he had to repeat his lectures for the princess.[60] On 25 January 1813 he noted that he had been reading part of *Rokeby* to the Princess of Wales and Charlotte. The latter had written Walter Scott to express the princess's 'admiration and reception of Rokeby ... with transport', as well as her own 'humbler but not less sincere expressions, of delight—even at the very outside Sight of the Book'.

> Anticipate the delight I shall have in reading it this Night—this very Golden Hour with Her Royal Highness in whose service I am and with whom I have the Honor and pleasure of being en Tete a tete, a circumstance I doubly value as it affords the opportunity of immediately perusing Rokeby. I leave off writing to you to read you by which I have all to gain and you nothing to regret.[61]

In May of the same year Thomas Campbell recorded 'Lady Charlotte is a great accession to me. I spend evenings very often with her and her sensible Swiss governess.'[62] In turn, Charlotte composed some lines to Thomas Campbell:

> Bard of my country—clansman of my race!
> How proudly do I call thee one of mine!
> Perchance thou wilt not deem it a disgrace
> That with my verse thy name I should entwine.
> It is not write in borrowed wreath to shine
> Or catch reflected ray from light of fame;
> But a strong feeling, I may not define,
> Of honest pride, in friendship's sacred flame,
> Within my bosom glows while writing CAMPBELL's name![63]

In later life, however, she became somewhat dismayed by his having given up poetry for a busy life of socio-political activities.

Around this time too, Lady Charlotte, her niece, Charlotte Clavering, Lady Augusta's daughter, and Susan Ferrier, daughter of the Duke of Argyll's legal agent, became of mutual support to each other as aspiring authors. Lady Charlotte 'made a deep impression on Susan Ferrier's imagination, and they were on intimate terms', although her niece and Susan Ferrier were closer in age. Charlotte Clavering was writing on 10 December 1812 from Inveraray to Susan Ferrier:

> I must tell you of the success of your first born, I read it to Lady Charlotte in the carriage when she and I came together from Ardencaple ... If you believe I never yet in my existence saw Lady C. laugh so much as she did at that from beginning to end; seriously I was two or three times alarmed that she would fall into a fit. Her very words were. 'I assure you I think it without the least exception the cleverest thing of the kind that ever was written, far surpassing Fielding'; then she said, that as to our other books, that they would all sink to nothingness before yours; that they were not fit to mention in the same day; and that she felt quite discouraged from writing when she thought of yours ... I am sure you will be the first author of the age.[64]

Charlotte or her cousin Anne Damer (or both) were perhaps the inspiration behind Lady MacLaughlin in Susan Ferrier's manuscript of what was to become *Marriage*, while relations of the Argyll-Hamilton family, the Misses Edmonstone, probably evoked the archtypical maiden Scots aunts Grizzy, Jacky and Nicky. Two years later the manuscript was still being passed to and fro; Charlotte Clavering wrote from her uncle's in Northumberland to Susan Ferrier on 20 December 1812:

> I had an immense packet from Lady C[harlotte] the other day, which I confess rather disappointed me, for I expected volumes of new compositions, and on opening it what should it prove but your book returned, so I shall keep it safe till I see you. She was profuse in its praises, and so was Mamie [de la Chaux] who said she was particularly taken with Lady Juliana's brother, he was so like the Duke [George, 6th Duke of Argyll]. Lady C. said she had read it all deliberately and critically, and pronounced it capital, with a dash under it.[65]

She added:

> Lady C. begs that in your enumerations of Lady Olivia's peccadilloes you will omit waltzes. I back the request, and agree with her in thinking that people will immediately say she wrote it, and was Quixotising her own character. You may say she danced quadrilles in London if you choose. There were quadrilles, otherwise called cotillions formed entirely of married women of quality, in London when I was there.

In one letter from about 1810 to Charlotte Clavering, Susan Ferrier reported that she had 'sent off your production to your own care ... Whether it will be received or rejected the fates who preside over the Minerva Press alone can tell ... As I told you before, its extreme shortness is its chief crime and its excessive *personality* another.'[66] She continued: 'With regard to the others I am very desirous that you should get some person who is up to the art of bookmaking and bookmending to revise and correct it before you give it to the world.' Ferrier advised this 'because you may be well assured the authors will be no secret', adding: 'Robert Campbell [of Skipness] speaks of your writing not as a thing *suspected*, but quite ascertained. I affected to disbelieve it, but he said anybody that had ever seen it could not for a moment doubt its being the work of two people etc. etc.'[67] *Marriage* was not to be published, however, for another eight years when Blackwood gave Ferrier £150 for the copyright.

Charlotte contrived to create her own quiet times, whether in busy court life or her busy family life, for her new venture. Her first novel, the 110,000-word *Self Indulgence; a Tale of the Nineteenth Century*, was published in 1812. It was of this work that Sharpe wrote to Miss Bessie Mure of Caldwell: 'I have read your novel, or Miss Clavering's, or Lady Charlotte's, for to all these ladies it hath been attributed.'[68] She was in the right milieu to produce one of the earliest novels of 'ton'. Published anonymously, the title words appear in the fourth chapter when the reader is told that the hero's 'passions were impetuous, and a habit of self-indulgence had rendered them more so; but his mind was not devoid of brilliant endowments, nor was it deficient in culture. In order to be fashionable, he concealed these superfluous qualities.'[69] On 20 December that year Charlotte Clavering was telling Susan Ferrier that a few days after the previous package's arrival, she had received another parcel 'five times as big, and was all on the alert to open it, when, to my infinite mortification, what should present itself but "Self-Indulgence"!!' Lady Charlotte told her that Mrs. Damer had charged her 'with the fact of being its mother', adding that:

> [she] had begged and entreated that she would correct its inaccuracies to make it fit for a second edition, which she declared would soon be called for, and made her sit down and read it out in a slow audible voice, marking with a pencil where it should be corrected and amended.

Aside from the time this must have taken, it was this very copy that Charlotte put in the parcel requesting her niece to make a fair copy, incorporating the alterations. Susan Ferrier said she did not 'mind so much, as I am not obliged to look out for faults but those that are marked with a pencil'.[70]

Self Indulgence; a Tale of the Nineteenth Century was printed and published in two volumes in Edinburgh and London in 1812, followed by editions in Boston and Philadelphia. The novel was set in London where a wealthy city merchant in Bishopsgate was planning to climb up the social scale by moving from Islington to Mayfair. He was also plotting with the impecunious, but titled, Lord Donneraile to marry his only child, Sophy, to Donneraile's (reluctant) son with a dowry bribe of £30,000 and the promise of her entire inheritance. The different social standing of the two mothers was cleverly encapsulated: 'The easy assurance of ton got the upperhand of city tenacity ... Who thinks of high or low blood now-a-days? This is the age of gold, not the age of noblesse.'[71] The first of several icons were introduced which the author was to use frequently in her future writings—dogs, with the aphorism 'Love me, Love my Dog'. Books in libraries and feminine aspirations formed another theme. Sophy refused to marry at once since 'she would not marry any man whose character she did not know', and was left for many months, with her parents, at her fiancé's country estate. He had disappeared to the Continent and 'she sought for some object of pursuit to fill the vacuum of her mind of which she was conscious, and which her mind was not calculated to endure. Fortunately she found this object in books.' She cleaned and rearranged the library, then sat by the fire or at the reading desk 'deeply absorbed', even being referred to as a *bas bleu*. A year later Sophy and Mr Donneraile were married, only for him to set off immediately again for the continental mainland. A subplot, involving madness and suicide, was then introduced to develop 'The Tale' of bigamy and villainy in which Charlotte made use of her continental travels and observations in Paris, Pontarlier and the Swiss Jura. On return to England, Donneraile's bigamous wife Corissande was installed in an elegant villa at Richmond, then moved to Hampshire and the Isle of Wight. Meanwhile the anti-hero was ruined gambling, joined the English army in Portugal and fell during the battle of Talavera. Corissande then expired, while Sophy retrieved her exemplary life of virtue and piety. The sardonic Sharpe asked one correspondent whether he had yet 'met with a certain novel styled "Self indulgence"? It is written, O sympathetic Lysander! By the fair hand of my Sacharissa's aunt—by no less or lean a woman than Lady Charlotte Campbell herself. Certain civil people imputed it to me.'[72] To the Margravine of Ansbach he pronounced the 'romance a sad dog', with 'not much novelty in the work ... but what astonishes me greatly, some vulgarity ... all young men begin life by becoming drunkards'. Notwithstanding, one copy was owned by Major By of the Royal Engineers, then busily engaged during the American-Canadian War on the construction of the Rideau Canal in Ottawa. Another was acquired for the library of the eminent Maxwell family at Pollok House outside Glasgow.[73] A slightly altered version of the novel appeared under a different title in 1830, of which more later.

The end of each year sometimes found Charlotte in melancholy frame of mind. While she had confessed to Mary Berry in April 1812 that 'I now entertain sanguine expectations of bringing all my schemes to bear', Hogmanay or New Year's Eve in 1813 still found her reflecting in her *Diary* on the 'idleness of mind', and 'framing many good resolutions, which I hope I shall be able to fulfil'. She acknowledged that her private life had been calm; 'no very lively emotions have given a high zest to existence; and a constant pressure has lowered the tone of my intellect, and reigned in my imagination'. After wishing 'ardently ... individually, for peace', she confided that she wanted 'to be able to leave England, and visit foreign countries; I long for an opportunity to extend my observations and to acquire new matter for my mind to feed upon.' When hostilities ended between Britain and France with the Peace of Paris in April 1814, Charlotte swiftly put her plans into action. She had been with the princess for four and a half years. While she would finally serve for a short spell with the princess in Genoa and Milan during Napoleon's 'Hundred Days' in the spring of 1815 (and would keep in touch with her thereafter), she was giving up her salary, presumably assuming that it would be more economic to live abroad. Once Princess Caroline, contrary to all advice, had left England's shores, the Prince Regent not only deemed Montagu House beyond repair, but after a sale of its remaining contents, ordered its dismantling and demolition in September 1815.

For over four years, Charlotte had proved an increasingly reluctant, if loyal, courtier to the maltreated princess, having to be just short of a friend to her, thanks to developing a policy of never giving advice even when disagreeing with some proposal or action—'she has a bold and independent mind'.[74] At times such as the death of Percival in 1812 Charlotte had 'a higher opinion of the powers of her mind than I ever entertained before'. 'Had this princess been otherwise nurtured ... how different a person she might have been.'[75]

> She has excellent and strong natural feelings when they are stirred; but in general all her bad feelings are roused and her good ones smothered, by the unkindness and persecution she meets with. There is no knowing what a different person this poor Princess might be, had she the fair play of other human beings.[76]

8

Continental Escape

It was with a flourish on the first day of July 1814 that Charlotte recorded her satisfaction that 'At length I have been able to arrange my affairs, so as to be free to leave England and go where I like'.[1] She had given up her position with the Princess of Wales and provided for 'one or two old servants'; her 'dear old aunt' had died a fortnight previously, 'since which time she had been unable to write a word ... nothing except death can put an end to the natural affection which God has ordained between near relations'. Having fulfilled her aunt's last wishes 'to the minutest point, and I can now gratify my long-cherished wish of travelling in foreign countries'. When staying overnight in crowded Dover at its main hotel, 'The Ship', she felt happy to record in her journal: 'The only ardent wish I have formed for these last two years, is now fulfilled—I am on the ocean, on my way to the Continent.' The sun went behind a cloud momentarily on their way out of Dover harbour on 15 July 1814 and for that moment, 'a cloud of tender regret for what might have been, stole across my mind', but the sun gaily re-emerged and made her think positively about the 'new scenes which would occupy and change the current' of her thoughts. Over quarter of a century had passed since she had wintered in Naples as a 15-year-old with her parents and sister; and perhaps she also thought it would be advantageous to the physical and cultural well-being of her daughters, several of whom, Eliza, Eleonora and Beaujolois, appeared to have inherited some of the Gunning tubercular tendencies, as also did her son John. Although everything was recorded in the first person, the party consisted of Charlotte and her six daughters, Mlle de la Chaux, Annie MacLeod, a man servant and several others. Walter, 16, and John, about 14, had been left behind, Walter attending Eton, and John with tutor or away at school. Eliza was by now 17, Eleonora 15, Beaujolois 12, Adelaide 10, Emma 8, and Julia 7. It was perhaps with some mixed emotions, and motives, that Charlotte had determined to leave behind her sons, other family and friends in London and Scotland for a while. But as she was to note in Paris, while things were dear, she thought it would be possible to live more cheaply on the continent than in London.[2]

The fine crossing was of 'only two hours and fifty minutes', but as the tide was low on the French side they had to walk over wet sand for a couple of miles before climbing on to the long wooden pier jutting out into the Channel at Calais. They stayed at Quillac's Hotel and that evening went to three plays with music. Next day, just as she was stepping into her carriage to leave Calais, Charlotte received a message from Emma Hamilton—'the Lady Hamilton I had seen twenty-five years ago, at Naples'—who wanted to see her since she had 'known me long and well, and dearly loved those I loved (what a prostitution of the term!)'.[3] Feeling sorry for this 'poor soul ... a mixture of curiosity and sadness' made her decide to see Emma once more. 'Time had marred her beauty, but not effaced it', and when Charlotte complimented her as 'toujours belle ... although it was a little more than reality', Lady Hamilton's eyes became reanimated. Talk was of the past, and she was still denying that she was Horatia Nelson's mother. But it was Horatia who sadly arranged the funeral in mid-January the following year.

At 6.30 p.m. the family arrived in fortified but wet and gloomy Boulogne, having eaten some of 'the nicest bread I have ever tasted at Huitmille'. From the Hotel d'Angleterre ('it deserves the name, if dearness is one of the attributes of an English hotel', Charlotte noted), she walked round the ramparts of the upper town in the rain and imagined Bonaparte organising his threatened invasion of Britain. They set off again the next day through countryside described in detail, and it was again seven o'clock before they reached their next, comfortable inn at Samaces. The women's costumes seen on the following day were particularly noteworthy and colourful; and after reaching Montreuil the party visited the principal church where mass was being 'performed', with the authorities entering in a military procession (including drums) to sing the Te Deum. The inn at Bernay was 'the best of two bad inns; but what signifies for a night or two, when one is in health?' she asked herself rhetorically. Another long day, a miserable meal at Flicour, and yet another seven o'clock arrival on reaching Amiens, Charlotte immediately went out to see the great cathedral, where the guide regaled her with some of the horrors of the reign of terror.

Leaving Amiens on Tuesday 21 July, they arrived in Paris two days later, and immediately arranged to go in the evening to the Opera Comique, 'the prettiest salon imaginable': 'the drop curtain is the handsomest I ever saw: it is painted in imitation of blue velvet, covered with golden fleur-de-lis; the crown on a ball ... and the drapery very grand and simple in its folds.' There were again three plays with music, the latter being judged 'exceedingly good', if louder than her ears were accustomed to. Next day began at the Louvre, 'such a stupendous emporium of all that is fine in the arts ... Venus, Apollo, Bacchus, Diana', but 'time and circumstance' tore them away. They strolled through the Tuileries and their magnificent gardens, 'the profusion of chairs and benches in the sun and shade making a strong contrast to those in English public spaces ... which the English take such pains to destroy and disfigure'. She complained: 'There certainly never was such a country which had so little respect for public monuments or property, and so little love for the arts, as England.' With Lady Westmorland,[4] Charlotte then continued 'to every shop on the Boulevards', where the variety and relative cheapness of all the materials for ladies dresses tempted them. Only the height and immensity of the Parisian bonnets were displeasing. The two ladies proceeded to the Opera—Louis-Luc Loiseau de Persuis' 'spectacular' *La Jérusalem Délivrée* of 1812, whose last scene made Charlotte's 'very flesh creep'. And next day they planned to visit Versailles, noting along the way the 'magnificence of the city ... the superlative Pont de Jena ... St Cloud and its villas', but due to workmen doing repairs they couldn't get into Versailles, so retreated again to St Cloud to view Paris from the palace where they saw Bonaparte's 'voluptuous bed'; then on to the Trianon at Versailles, with its fascinating pictures. At last Charlotte admitted: 'I do not recollect ever to have been so fatigued as I was to-day in walking back to Versailles; and yet the warmth which kills others animates me.' Several invitations, however, awaited her on return, which she proceeded to fulfil, and even as she was eventually going to bed another English visitor called on her.

On Sunday 24 July she went with the same visitor to the Hôtel des Invalides, comparing it to Chelsea and Greenwich Hospitals which, in her opinion, were less vast but more beautiful. Then on to the Musée des Monuments Français before dining at Monsieur and Madame Giaridin's, where, over coffee in the garden she ventured to criticise the Parisian bonnets while all around defended them. The next day saw her at Ste Geneviève and the botanical gardens—the temperature was 83 degrees, and, like some others before and since, Charlotte found that 'as I do not understand botany, and saw no beautiful flowers, I was disappointed, and did not remain there long'. On Tuesday 26 July she visited François Gérard's studio, 'the person who is reckoned the finest artist in Paris'; he was busily engaged in two paintings of Bonaparte—'the one meagre and keen, a famished face, in pursuit of conquest; the other, bloated and surfeited by conquest and power—both handsome, and the eyes of both miraculous'. The final accolade for Lady Charlotte and Lady Westmorland was being presented to King Louis XVIII, by then re-established with his Court in the Tuileries. He had left Hartwell House, his exile home since Charlotte had given it up in 1809, and had arrived in Paris on 3 May 1814,[5] remarking that 'he should never forget what he owed to England'. Charlotte noted succinctly in her *Diary* that she had seen more and done more than she had ever before managed in the same time.[6]

Her diary resumed after a week, by which time Dijon had been reached. As she explained: 'I had been told I was to meet with all sorts of dangers and difficulties, and was advised to go by Voiturier, which has saved me no expense, and I have been nearly twice as long on the road as I should, had I posted.' The inns had again been poor, 'quite good enough for the purposes of animal existence, if not enjoyment'. She had learned 'to do everything in public' for there were no door bolts. By 6 August she and her party of almost a dozen were at last in a clean and comfortable Swiss hotel at Scheron, Geneva, with magnificent views of the lake and Mont Blanc. They then rented a house for a couple of months in Les Grottes district outside Porte Cornavain. 'Lady Charlotte took particular pains to decorate it', Madame de Staël observed, saying 'Ma Chère, vous avez trop de luxe!'[7] She renewed her acquaintance with Sir Humphry and Lady Davy,[8] and quickly met many others—Jean Charles Léonard de Sismundi, Auguste-Guillaume Schlegel, Ferdinand de Saussure, Benjamin Constant, Albert Jean Michel de Rocca and 'an Englishman, Mr Cumming, the flower of the flock', as well as Lady Westmorland 'who never rests herself, and never lets any one else rest in her presence', and was as charming as ever. After several weeks, although there is 'a picked society of intelligent and superior persons resident in or travelling thorough the country':

> After the great stage of life in London, Paris, or Vienna, it requires to let off gas of excitement before one can sober oneself down to the narrowed circle of 'L'imperceptible Genève' where the gates of 'this Lilliput republic' were locked at ten o'clock.

But she also admitted that there was much to love in the Genevoises even as one mocked them.

The talented, inveterate traveller and diarist, Lady Jane Griffin (who was later to marry Sir Benjamin Franklin), amusingly described the English church in Geneva about this time.[9] In front of a seasonal congregation of about fifty, the organist, M. Bertolini, played some airs that were so gay and rhythmical that smiles began to spread across the faces of the congregation. He continued quite happily, oblivious to the lay preacher's raising his arm and waving his prayer book around, until the latter was eventually able to start delivering his sermon. This 'happily related points of doctrine with moral precepts', the little church's preacher, Charles Sumner, later going on to become not only librarian to George IV, but eventually Bishop of Winchester, returning on 30 August 1853 to consecrate the present English Church in Geneva.[10]

Visiting outside Geneva, Charlotte was puzzled as to why the wonderful scenery of the lake and mountains 'more than any other, oppresses the heart with a sense of its own insufficiency to procure happiness'.

> Is it that, calculated as it is to excite the feelings to rapture, the contrast with the dull vacuity that reigns within, is more forcibly brought to view, and renders the burthen of lonely existence weightier? Perhaps it is—for since I came here my own cruel fate seems more vividly represented to my contemplation; the long years of 'fair occasion gone for ever by', which have blighted my youth, and will scathe my age'.

In part this may have been emphasised for Charlotte since she perceived that:

> The fine arts are at a low ebb here—here, where Nature puts forth all her Majesty ... the very magnitude and sublimity of this part of creation are opposed to the imitative power of the pencil. Landscape painting is scarcely practised ... each particular member of the landscape takes up too huge a portion of the canvas.

On a golden October day a sail across the lake to Coligny to visit Madame de Staël's cousin, Madame Necker, also made her feel more utterly lonely than ever. Although Madame Necker was, as customary thereabouts, 'without stays, slipshod, en papillottes and uncombed', she nevertheless managed to charm Charlotte.

The Princess of Wales had left England in August, with no clear plan of travel, and arrived in Geneva in October, spending only three nights, much to Charlotte's relief.[11] She had been dressed 'or rather undressed' most injudiciously at the ci-devant Empress Marie Louise's party in Berne. Charlotte 'was called upon to get up a ball for Her Royal Highness', and had to 'drive all over the town and country to beat up recruits, which was not an easy matter: so many wished to avoid ... her'. Poor Lady Charlotte had to take 'many rebuffs' but the ball did take place. One Englishman reported that the princess 'is gone this evening to a great ball, given by Lady Charlotte who is in Geneva'.[12] Definitely 'Poor Lady Charlotte'. The princess entered 'dressed' as 'Venus, or rather not dressed, further than the waist' which led her hostess to be 'all over shock'.[13] As she was 'really her friend',[14] Charlotte was vexed on the princess's behalf, particularly when the two large figures of the princess and Sismondi waltzed 'with pertinacious obstinacy'. The following day the princess returned the invitation, with dinner at Secheron where Charlotte was flabbergasted by some of the new retinue of Bartolomeo Bergami and his relations. It was as if the princess 'had cast off all common sense and conduct, and had gone suddenly mad'.[15]

After participating in a great fête of Madame de Staël's at Coppet on the other side of the lake, Charlotte and her family left Geneva on Tuesday 18 October 'with unfeigned regret', as she put it to Sismondi, to spend the winter in Nice. She hoped to see Geneva often again although, as she put it, 'with hope there is always a doubt—every thing in this life is so uncertain'.[16] Lyon was briefly explored, time being taken up with travel arrangements, but she considered the theatre not up to the mark and only used as a place of resort with no one listening or applauding the actors who 'acted as though they had been going to sleep'. Until, that is, Charlotte ventured to applaud once, which produced a 'remarkable effect from the stage'. The next day while visiting the cathedral and accompanying two women with whom she had dined, there were interesting discussions, ranging over catholic and protestant forms of worship, Kant's writings and Madame de Staël's views on religion. Charlotte pronounced the Roman Catholic church to be too bigoted, too cruel in its doctrines, to admit of sufficient tolerance for one universal gospel; the Episcopal she deemed to be too proud, and the Presbyterian too stern.[17] Embarking on the Rhône, in constantly wet autumnal weather, with overnight stops in inns at Vienne, Bieuf, St Vallière and Avignon, in each of which they doggedly trekked round Roman and later remains, the Campbell party finally reached Nice on Tuesday 1 November 1814 after a fortnight's journeying.[18] At first staying in a hotel they then rented the Maison Bavalis in the faubourg de la Croix de Marbre,[19] which she was to note in her novel *Love*, was peopled by English and other consumptives hoping to benefit from the 'perpetual spring, summer or autumn'.[20]

On previous occasions Charlotte had apologised for not writing to those such as Walter Scott when she had had 'a severe sickness', while her niece, Charlotte Clavering opined, 'I do not think Lady Charlotte is strong; her cold, however, is better. I wish she could stay here a little longer to recruit her health, but she will not hear of it.'[21] Her sister-in-law, Elizabeth Campbell of Ardpatrick, wrote to her niece Eliza in Nice in the autumn of 1815 hoping that 'your Mamma's health will soon be so much reestablished, as not to require to remain abroad. I am sorry to hear she still complains of the pain in her heart.'[22] Mary Macguire, family friend in Sydenham was looking after the monkey, perroquets, dogs and other pets left behind, and wrote to Eliza that she 'felt the strongest conviction that the end will be attained and that your invaluable and dear Mamma will return in vigorous health and that bloom of beauty which is given her so abundantly by the Almighty'. She added, perhaps percipiently: 'You know I am a desperate admirer of hers and if under these circumstances you sh^{d} discover anything bordering on romance pray attribute it to the real cause.'[23]

During her winter sojourn Charlotte read and corresponded widely, and kept in touch with the increasingly erratic Princess of Wales (referred to by correspondents as 'Mrs Thompson'). Sending new year greetings at the start of 1815 to her cousin, Anne Damer hoped that the excuse on the score of health would manage to keep Charlotte free of further commitment to the princess, although the latter's chief English staff of Keppel Craven and Sir William Gell were planning to leave her: 'You will, I think, hug yourself to think that you are out of this mess.'[24] One Sunday in February Charlotte admitted to allowing 'spleen to conquer [her] despite a good useful sermon on the value of time'; she fell out with her 'best friend' (presumably herself) and 'endeavoured to write and read at home, but the machine was out of order, and would not play', then spent a sleepless night followed by a listless day. To begin with the Sirocco and heavy rains enervated her but she also admitted to unsettled feelings at being so far from Britain. Perhaps such dispirits were dispelled on summer days by taking some of the many walks in the sheltered south-facing hills around the Bay of Nice, with its backdrop of snowy Alps. While on her way one day to collect some plants, 'the terraces of olives, vines, figs, and other fruit trees, intermingled with the cypress, the caroubier, and the almond' all in bloom in February, presented 'a magic scene', subsequently recalled in her novels *Conduct is Fate* and *Love*. She became part of the circle of overwintering English including Lord and Lady Glenbervie (the latter in precarious health), Lady Charlotte Lindsay, Lord and Lady Sandwich and others. One count brought her all sorts of books, and another acquaintance was Madame Davidoff, the Russian wife of General Davidoff, whose character Charlotte 'did not quite understand', but whom she found very good and agreeable company. One for whom she showed contempt was Madame de Villegarde, whose library of cabalistic books and interests focussed on the black arts and the occult. As well as very frequent dinners and balls among the English,[25] Charlotte was herself 'at home' twice a week.

She confessed to Sismondi that her daughters did not like Nice nearly so much as Geneva, where they 'were all too much spoiled'.[26] But Dr Gemelaro, the Aetnean philosopher, recorded that 'nothing in his life had made so great an impression on him', as the first of independent English ladies he had ever seen having been one of the daughters of Lady Charlotte Campbell, as he landed at Nice from one of H.M.'s men-of-war (in whose service he was). She was running about catching butterflies in a net, between that place and Villa Franca, 'when he had dared to think her mortal, he ventured to expostulate by saying "Ma Signora, sola in questa solitudine?" (alone in this solitude?) she tossed her head, and ran off here and there with her net, not deigning to answer his remark'.[27]

By the start of March 1815, Bonaparte, having evaded Sir Neil Campbell and escaping overnight from Elba, was near Grasse with several hundred men. No-one knew his next moves and Charlotte worried over her friends in England 'who will personally be anxious for us, not knowing how quiet poor little insignificant Nice is. They may imagine some scenes of bustle here, from which at present we are quite free.' On Friday 3 March Bonaparte had proclaimed that his eagles were flying from steeple to steeple and would soon perch on Notre-Dame in Paris, while Charlotte repeated her conviction that Nice was still a 'nook of safety'. The next day she ventured into the town making calls to discover anything newsworthy, but all 'conjectured till conjecture could go no further'. Visiting and having visitors continued busily; on Friday 10 March one such visitor was her abashed countryman, Sir Neil Campbell, who explained that he had been a commissioner, not a gaoler, appointed by the English government to 'provide Bonaparte with everything he could want' in Elba. Campbell had the *Partridge* but no men and 'no means whatever to prevent Bonaparte's doing whatever he chose'. As Napoleon had a small frigate, a bomb vessel, and several small boats with a thousand soldiers at his command, Sir Neil certainly considered 'that he could not be supposed to have any power to prevent his leaving the island whenever he might be so inclined'. While Campbell was away in Leghorn, allegedly with his mistress, Napoleon had indeed sailed off. As Campbell's enquiries on Elba had proved fruitless, he sailed for Antibes, and 'coloured violently' when confessing to Charlotte that he was 'in a pitiable state of uneasiness of mind, for I was aware how much the imprudence of the nations would be laid to my charge, and how much circumstances might make me seem guilty in the minds of thousands'. While she felt sorry for Sir Neil, Charlotte thought that he should never have accepted such a weak commission: 'Better, far better, to have been his appointed gaoler, and known by the prisoner himself to be such, than a spy in the disguise of a friend to provide for his wants.'

In February, the Princess of Wales had threatened to spend the following month in Nice, but this had not yet transpired.[28] By the middle of March, however, she had moved from Naples to Rome, intending to sail from the Civita di Veccia to Leghorn where she hoped Charlotte would take her offer of a frigate to join her 'avec toute sa famille et Mrs Damer' and thence go to Genoa. Charlotte's excuses on the grounds of poor health seem to have fallen on deaf ears.[29] The princess also suggested that Charlotte's eldest daughter, Eliza, might become one of the women of her bedchamber.[30] Only Lady Charlotte Lindsay and Mr Frederick North were still with the princess (and they too had decided to leave her soon 'for family reasons'), so it was never likely that Charlotte would agree to Eliza being exposed to the infamous Italian coterie assembling around the princess.[31] She replied offering to meet the princess in Leghorn but also advising her to return to England because of the increasingly troubled state of the continent. The princess did not reply. By the morning of Wednesday 15 March, Lady Glenbervie had heard via telegraph that Bonaparte was now at Lyon, with increased support. In town, Charlotte found that 'all the English, as if with one consent, were setting off in different ways, in order to get back to England. Most of them were flying to Genoa, where ... it was supposed we should find greater protection than here.' She accompanied Madame Davidoff to the *commandeur*, 'poor old Comte D'Osaque', to ask his advice on what best to do, to which he responded with a look of calm despair, that he would advise them, if they could, to leave Nice. Charlotte, however, 'determined to remain here until war is absolutely at the gate', in which event she planned to return to Geneva—perhaps easier said than achieved. One can only surmise at the strong reasons and feelings behind her rider 'for I dread returning to England, and many circumstances combine to make me doubtful whether or not I shall ever bring myself to go thither again'.[32] One Colonel Bourke offered to take her family along with Lady Glenbervie to Genoa, although the latter might itself have been a target for Murat's troops then in Florence.

The Princess of Wales had, however, written on 15 March to say that she now planned to stay with Charlotte in Nice, but since she was accompanied by her maid and her adopted son, William Austin, she realised that perhaps Charlotte would not have room, so she would take a house nearby, again desperately repeating her offer to Eliza. The last of the English, Archdeacon and Lady Waldegrave, had decided to go over the Col de Tende to Piedmont while the cleric, Mr Vivian, had preached his last sermon and taken leave of his congregation in Nice. Charlotte was beginning to feel melancholy at remaining behind, in a state of suspense. Nevertheless on Tuesday 21 March she and Madame Davidoff, with the latter's children and governess ('a poor quiet personage ... a governess's is always a miserable situation'), walked on a romantic path to Ville Franche, and were then rowed back across the bay. But her melancholy proved hard to shift and a week later Charlotte admitted: 'This last week, one of my overcoming periods of returning sadness stopped my pen. Suspense, astonishment, dismay, have all combined to make me feel that common daily notes were trivial and insufficient to express my state of mind'. What was 'as agitating' was news from Lady Glenbervie (now back in Genoa with her husband) written on Good Friday (24 March) that the princess had now arrived in Genoa and she, Lady Glenbervie, was acting as one of her ladies until Charlotte could get there. On the one hand this information made Charlotte tremble, but on the other, the resolution helped revive her spirits and once more she began to write up her diary almost daily.

9

'Transcendent Genoa'

The course of events seems to have been swift. The very next day after her last journal entry on Wednesday 19 March, Charlotte had spent the morning gazing at a large vessel that was on the horizon, 'without any presentiment that it was to convey me away so soon'. By Sunday 2 April 1815, she could write 'On board the *Clorinde*, Captain Pechell', posing the question: 'Who knows what a day may bring forth?'[1] The Consul had come to tell her that it was the princess's frigate, the *Clorinde*, which had arrived at Ville Franche to convey Lady Charlotte Campbell and her family to Genoa. Charlotte noted that a 'multitude of contradictory emotions rapidly chased each other through my heart! The secret wish I have long felt to go to Genoa was in some degree checked by the doubts and fears of the ultimate good of this wish being granted.' A note arrived from Captain Pechell recommending their going on board immediately, as Captain Campbell, commanding the *Tremendous*, the flag ship at Genoa, did not want the departure of the *Clorinde* delayed. It took until the Saturday, however, for all the arrangements and packing up to be effected. Captain Pechell had gone to Charlotte's to dine: he was a bachelor naval cousin of Augusta's husband.[2] Charlotte had 'expected to see a certain tall pata pouff son of Lady Pechell's, and to my astonishment I beheld a very well-looking young man, but a perfect stranger. I felt confused, from the nature of my own hopes and fears.' Living on her emotions, she wrote:

> My physical as well as mental nature is always much affected by any variety of events, particularly by the fulfillment of those which I have myself wished for, or endeavoured to bring about. I scarcely could persuade myself that my departure was so near at hand ... From

> the instant I heard the news, universal confusion succeeded in my occupations and hours, and I neither slept nor ate till yesterday, at four o'clock, when we embarked.

Her overcharged feelings also regretted 'leaving a place where I have passed some pleasant hours'. She continued:

> The general state of public affairs is so unsettled and awful, that to leave a quiet spot, one little likely to be disturbed by the general commotion, or any scene of horror, to go to one which, if war becomes general, cannot fail to be the scene of strife, made me feel nervous.

It was a beautiful evening when they went on board and, looking back to Nice, she felt 'a tender regret at the idea that I looked at it for the last time. The last time! There is a fund of sadness in those words.' Some compensation was, however, to hand. 'What a magnificent thing a forty-eight gun frigate is! How grand! How imposing. It is a command which must inspire a certain confidence in the commander.' She then recounted how well-looking Captain Pechell was, with his pleasing manners: 'The mastering of the elements is a noble prerogative; and when gentleness and suavity of manner accompanies strength, one feels respect for the being who unites these qualities. It would seem that Captain Pechell possesses them.' With the 'finest possible weather', they remained on deck till they got under weigh, gazing on the slowly receding shore. After tea they went again on deck:

> The stars appeared gradually in the heaven, till it was richly spangled with trembling light. A few sparks of fire ran upon the ripple of the wave, and we glided imperceptibly along the coast of the maritime Alps. The scene, the circumstances, and my own situation, together with reflections on the public history of the time, the wondrous convulsion in which the ambition of a single individual has thrown the whole of Europe,—filled my mind with thoughts too numerous, too vast, to be defined.

She noted that both the Captain and his brother 'draw prettily and have good taste for music, although no scientific or improved knowledge', and she elicited Captain Pechell's sad opinion of 'all the doings of the princess while at Naples'. Unlike Captain Briggs of the *Leviathan*, Captain Pechell had earlier that year refused to have the princess's newly promoted 'chamberlain', Bartolomeo Bergami, sit at his table.[3] The princess meanwhile had conferred on Bergami the title of 'Knight of Malta', and addressed him as her Chevalier. She ordered a separate table at which she was able to dine with 'the long stork', in Charlotte's moniker,[4] describing him as 6-feet tall with a 'magnificent head of black hair, pale complexion, mustachios which reach from *here to London*'.

They were still on board the *Clorinde* on Tuesday 4 April, by which time she confessed to liking 'my captain and his brother very much'; she felt more acquainted with them than if she had been 'years on shore, and had no particular subject of interest to have made us acquainted'. This was the outcome of a 'selfish feeling of being under his care for a time', which produced 'that sort of interest which long intimacy in other cases alone produces. Captain Pechell, in particular, has a respectable, good countenance, and a gentleness of demeanour, which is an excellent substitute for courtly manners'. They had danced on deck, and the 40-year-old Charlotte noted:

> I was surprised at my own security, and my ability to dance, as there was a considerable motion, and the wind constantly against us. But the scenery was so beautiful, and the weather so fine, that I found the time too short which I passed on board the *Clorinde*. The Captain, too, enjoyed the voyage.

A heavy rolling Mediterranean sea with contrary wind, however, prevented the vessel from reaching the harbour at Genoa on Wednesday 5 April when 'we came within seven or eight miles of the city, which was illuminated, and appeared like a magical crescent round the bay ... For the first time in my life, reality exceeded imagination'. She continued:

> The magnificence and beauty of this town, its situation, its gay and clean appearance, (so unlike all other Italian towns in that respect), exceed description, the city is built on terraces, which descend to the sea-shore. The form of the bay is that of a crescent, which is terminated on either side by rocks; on one of which the principal part of the town is built, the cathedral etc., on the other, the lighthouse. Orange, evergreen oaks, oleanders, and other trees and shrubs are mingled among the marble palaces, and the hills rise in grand amphitheatre at the back of this enchanted scene.

They anchored overnight in the harbour, and next morning Charlotte was first ashore with the Captain, in his gig.

Madame de Boigne colourfully recounted the Princess of Wales's arrival in Genoa on 26 March:

> The streets of Genoa had witnessed a sight which she would never forget. There was a kind of phaeton constructed like a sea-shell, covered with

> gilding and mother of pearl ... lined with blue velvet and decorated with silver fringes; this was drawn by two very small piebald horses driven by a child who was dressed like an operatic angel with spangles and flesh coloured tights!

The lounging princess was embodied in the following words:

> A fat woman of fifty years of age, short, plump and high coloured ... She wore a pink hat with seven or eight pink feathers floating in the wind, a pink bodice cut very low, and a short white skirt which hardly came below her knees, showing two stout legs with pink top boots.[5]

Bergami was in front, dressed like King Murat and on a similarly little horse, while the carriage was followed by two grooms in English livery, also on small horses. It was King Murat himself who had gifted this 'Neapolitan turn-out' to the princess and she used it for all her Genoese expeditions.

The princess had rented the 'beautiful Palazzo Durazzo di Scoglietti, without the inner walls on the west side of the town', as Lord Glenbervie described it.[6] Approaching the red and white marble palace (now Palazzo Rosazza in Piazza Negri) with its tiered gardens and parterres, Charlotte ventured to hope that 'this climate and its customs I should think ... must suit the Princess, if anything can suit her'. As for herself, breakfasting on a terrace at the palace next morning, Charlotte cogitated:

> There is a soothing power in this soft breeze, which in despite of every circumstance, lulls the mind for a time into forgetfulness. Certainly there is no place which, from its climate and its customs, combines so much to deaden mental suffering as Italy; but these contribute, even to a fearful extent, to an indolence of body and soul, which, though it gives temporary relief, is inimical to a healthful vigor of mind. And when we are aroused from that state of mental torpor into which it casts us, and are obliged to return to a ruder climate, or endure some new trial, or perform the active duties of common life, it is too often found that Italy and its opium have done harm in a moral sense, if not in a physical one.

Just as several years earlier, she again confided that she would prefer 'any occupation under the sun ... to that of waiting upon this royal lady; but, having none, I am glad of this one, unsuited as it is to my taste in every way'.[7]

In continuing the conceit of her diary when it was published anonymously over two decades later, she opined:

> Lady Charlotte Campbell is a sweet-mannered person; I should not say she was a happy one. Her children are a fine family; Miss Eleanor Campbell, I think, will be a beautiful girl, and they are all peculiarly agreeable for such young persons. Lady Charlotte's friend, Mademoiselle de la Chaux, is clever and must have been handsome.[8]

A fortnight after the family had left Nice, Captain Samuel John Pechell was writing wistfully to Mlle de la Chaux, au Poste Restante à Lausanne. He had been sent a 'document' in French signed by 'six very estimable personages', whom his brother had accompanied as far as Milan. Captain Pechell reminisced sadly about all their pleasant walks and evenings while he cast an eye of regret at what he termed the Red House 'from my Cabbin [sic] windows, suffering from the Blue Devils'. He hoped to meet them all again some day in England and asked mamselle to give Charlotte his 'best compliments and to tell her he had not forgotten the happy evenings they spent on board *Clorinde*'.[9] While one source recorded that the Princess of Wales had also rented a 'lodging' in Milan for the girls and Mlle de la Chaux,[10] the four youngest girls were more likely to have travelled on to Lausanne, while the two eldest may have remained with Charlotte or Annie McLeod, staying in their villa.

Like many today, Charlotte was enchanted when walking through Genoa, this 'most beautiful of all towns', sometimes deemed the discerning traveller's answer to Venice. On foot, she explored the streets which were almost a succession of palaces and gardens: through the Strada Nova (now Garibaldi) and Novissima, Bocca Negra and so on; past the Doria palace (now Palazzo del Principale), famous for its history, but reckoned the least splendid of the palaces. She viewed 'the grand remains of that magnificent man's magnificent ideas ... the gardens ... a superb fountain in marble ... eagles ... Neptune ... the Brignole palace, Il Palazzo Rosso and the Doge's Palace, now the Royal Palace [Palazzo Ducale]'. 'The great [mirrored] room of audience is the finest space I ever beheld a hundred and thirty feet long.' There were dinner parties at the princess's palazzo with many European royal and other grandees, as well as the Glenbervies, Devonshires, and Bentincks.[11] Sometimes the music at the opera was 'indifferent'. Maria Edgeworth told of one debate among Charlotte, Lady Glenbervie and others about her book *Modern Griselda* when a wager was laid with another lady that she would not read it aloud to her husband.[12] (The wager was won by astutely skipping bits.)

On 1 May the Princess of Wales gave a grand ball 'to the élite of Genoa. She quadrilled and waltzed with great zeal and alacrity, as did also the once lovely Lady Campbell, whose two beautiful daughters were also present' according to one military visitor.[13] Archibald Maxwell recalled first seeing her as a newly-wed in Edinburgh, 'the most lovely creature in "a bonnie Scotland"', along with her husband, who was just as great 'a paragon of manly beauty'. Although he admitted using an adverb much disliked by 40-year-olds, that Charlotte 'was still a very handsome woman, with one of the most lovely faces that can be conceived', Maxwell wished that she had followed 'the maxim ... of sliding gently down into the vale of years in a quiet unaffected manner'. Having danced a Scots reel with her a few nights before at a Bentinck party, at which the Devonshires were also present, he had decided that the once beautiful Charlotte had put on *beaucoup d'embonpoint*, continuing less than gallantly:

> It is an awkward thing, when mamma is closely followed, on going down a long country-dance, by two grown-up daughters, who are plainly telling her, whilst they are treading on her heels, that to grow old with dignity, is one of the most difficult of human lessons to learn.

Some years later, when giving evidence in 1820 to the Legislative Trial of Queen Caroline, one of the latter's entourage, Theodore Majocchi, also unflatteringly mentioned having met Lady Charlotte Campbell in Genoa. He observed 'I think she was a tall, rather fat lady, and had two daughters'.[14]

On Easter Sunday 9 April Charlotte went to the Cathedral (San Lorenzo), and the Pope mingling afterwards. Pope Pius VII sought refuge in Genoa from 22 March to 7 June 1815 during the Roman invasion of Joaquim Murat, King of Naples. 'Also went to our own service. It was not performed with that holy and reverent feeling which I have of late witnessed at Nice: still it is gratifying to meet with our own mode of worship in a foreign land.' The following Sunday was more to her liking when she 'heard a very fine sermon. The text was taken from the psalms. Missed the verse and could not find it, but the meaning was that evil company corrupts good manners. After what had passed the previous evening it came home to me in a most forcible manner.' Many other churches were also visited, whether for services or to see the interiors and the paintings, such as St Cyr (San Ciro), 'one of the most beautiful churches in Genoa, perhaps the most so, in respect to the richness of its decorations' and St Ambrosio (San Jesu), which contained 'the finest picture in Genoa, the Assumption of the Virgin, by Guido'. The Pope's 'truly magnificent present residence' and its 'truly sublime interior' (Brignole Palace, now Palazzo Rosso) and its paintings of Carracci, Giordano, Rembrandt, Tintoretto amongst others, were marvelled over. While the Pope sat with the princess, Lady Glenbervie and Charlotte 'had time to fall in love with the almoner and his fine countenance ... I felt quite a Catholic; or rather, I felt respect due to respectable age.' He also visited the princess in her palazzo, 'a circumstance so singular that it became quite interesting'. There were many other memorable outings including one to the renowned Institution for the Deaf and Dumb, under the direction and tuition of Arzarotti: 'I never was more delighted or instructed', so much so that she composed forty-six lines in his honour.[15] Quarter of a century later she was to refer to his healing powers in her novel *Love*, although by that time she had misremembered his name. Another 'glorious establishment' was the Alberghi dei Poveri, where '1319 poor are supported in peace and plenty'. April passed into May and 'this fortnight has been the most busy time. It is ever so. What is most worth remembering we are no longer calm enough to profit by.'

'And now I must end about pictures and palaces, and transcendent Genoa, to be engaged in all the hurry and bustle of an immediate departure'. The Princess of Wales had apparently determined on Milan, and although Charlotte thought the princess had bade her farewell in Genoa, she was once more summoned by her to Milan. Again Charlotte was sentimentally recording:

> How sad to look at scenes of wondrous beauty for the last time! To look at any object for the last time which has afforded us interest, is always painful, but at such transcendent loveliness, at such a scene, where fancy has once more floated in spheres of pleasure, it is doubly mournful.

Somewhat tantalisingly, she was then to confide:

> Above all, when the locale is associated with an individual—when a dear voice has echoed in that spot—a beloved footstep been listened to as it advanced to the place of rendezvous—there, where friendship and love have held sweet converse together, making a temporary paradise, into which the spite and malice and sin of the Evil one have entered not;—then it is indeed a bitter parting. I looked at this garden with infinite tenderness, I bade its soil be fruitful; I bade its flowers bloom in undiminished luxuriance; I bade the sun to shine on it, and the flowers to refresh it. All this looks very foolish on paper—what piece of sentiment does not? But so long as a third eye does not glance over the words, it matters not; and I would fain keep a record of these feelings.

This may have been a reference to Algernon Percy of the Northumberland family, then minister plenipotentiary to the Swiss cantons. The diarist had inserted in passing that 'Lady Charlotte Campbell is a little smitten with Algernon Percy ... his voice and looks are supremely interesting and she talked to him the whole night'.[16] Whatsoever, on Whit Sunday 14 May

Charlotte bade Genoa farewell, but 'not farewell the memory of thy enchantments'—writing forty-two lines on its transcendent glories, ending somewhat queruously: 'And then— farewell—ah! Since for ever/'Twere better I had seen thee never.'[17]

On the very next evening, at nine o'clock, she arrived in Milan to spend a 'winged' fortnight with the princess. The latter had left word for Charlotte to follow her to the opera at La Scala—she arrived only as the performance was ending but at least had the chance to have a *coup d'oeil* of the Gran Teatro in all its glory. She thought 'it was the finest building of the kind I ever saw'; and being lit up for the Archduke of Austria, it had 'an imposing effect'. The whole of Milan was *en fête* for the archduke's visit, and the next evening there was a great court ball in the vast and splendid apartments of the Duke of Milan. Another afternoon, chariot and other races for horses and men were held in the vast oval amphitheatre built by Bonaparte to hold 35,000 people. For once, the beleaguered princess was treated royally as an equal of the grand duke, and attended by Italian noblewomen.

In the short time that Charlotte spent in Milan, it was the Duomo that made the greatest impression: 'the dignity of its structure, and the rich, yet quiet beauty of its white marble walls and gothic pinnacles, are more in accordance with my feelings than the painted roofs and inlaid altars of the churches of Genoa'. She walked again and again around the great altar screen, and sat down to 'look and enjoy—to shut out the past and the future—and was satisfied—to be. A fortunate accident of light fell upon two statues in a once-to-be-seen-magic effect which never returns in the same way.' As one can to this day, she 'proceeded to the highest pinnacle of the cathedral and was well repaid for the trouble; for although these *mappe monde* views are not the most beautiful, it is gratifying to embrace a vast expanse of country at one view'. Walking around the roof, 'amid the most elaborate and beautifully-executed tracery of gothic ornament, spire, and foliage, and scroll innumerable, I looked over the rich plain of Lombardy, far as the eye can reach. It is bounded only towards the north by the vast chain of the Alps.' Later she was to add, 'I quitted the cathedral of Milan with regret. I have seen it since often, but it has never been the same cathedral to me.'[18]

By the end of May Charlotte finally left the Princess of Wales, having supported her longer than any other member of the English suite, the rest having quitted her.[19] She was then writing up the past hectic fortnight 'in the midst of clouds, and rain, and cold, on top of the Alps' at Simplon, with a good fire as her only consolation, on her way north 'out of sunshine and pleasure, transported once more to all the *morale* and all the *physique* of a cold climate, and the dull duties of common existence. Heavens! What a contrast!' Little did she perhaps realise: on 15 April that year, 1815, the volcano of Tambora in Indonesia had erupted massively (killing over 10,000 people directly). The earth was enveloped in a huge veil of dust that blocked out the sun's rays (the only positive comprised the subsequently glorious Turneresque sunsets). Temperatures were to plunge and the rest of the year or more was so cold that it became known as 'the year without a summer'. In the aftermath of the Napoleonic devastations, the cold, with incessant rains, hit continental Europe very hard, while in Britain, overcast skies and precipitation occurred almost every day with near famine, high grain prices, food riots and emigrations all ensuing.

The family did not head immediately for a cool, nay cold, English summer in 1815, but remained on the continent until November. In July Walter Frederick, staying 'for the holydays under Aunt Glen [Carter]'s hospitable roof' at Edgcott had been urged in a letter from Eleanor to 'go and pay Westwood a visit and see how it goes on'. He reported: 'Mamma has not been more unlucky than other people in not letting Westwood for there is a general complaint that nobody has let their houses this year.'[20] In June Lord John Campbell was writing from London to Eliza in Lausanne, thanking her for her letter of 24 May from Milan (which had reached London on 10 June), and reporting that her brother John had been in Town, looking 'perfectly well but delicate—I think he is however much better than he has been and quite free of any pain in his breast.' He mentioned an 'India appointment' being lost, but did not feel sorry since he suspected that his nephew John's constitution would not suit a warm climate.[21] Lord John even felt that there would be 'some difficulty in finding out a Trade for him, in consequence of his weak Health'. Charlotte apparently intended that John 'should follow the Diplomatic line'.[22] By July, John himself was reporting that he was at a new school which he liked, and which had the same 'holydays' as Walter at Eton.[23]

Charlotte's sister, Lady Augusta, had not followed in her mother's footsteps as a courtier, and by eloping then subsequently leaving her husband, had ruled herself out of court. But in turn the circumstances of the separated royals and the regency meant that Charlotte's daughters were also unlikely to become courtiers. Captain Samuel Pechell thought that Charlotte 'made no scruple of giving as her reason for leaving that she had daughters and would not allow them to stay where there was such an example'.[24] Despite renewed pleading by the Princess of Wales in Milan, a different outlook was beckoning for Eliza at the beginning of June 1815 when Charlotte finally left the princess and headed north over the Simplon pass to join her family in Lausanne. Charlotte's granddaughter recorded in her memoirs a 'curious detail' of fortune telling concerning Charlotte and her girls.

> It was foretold that within a few days complications would arise which would make their position [in Italy] very uncomfortable. But that, in their very hour of need, 'two fair haired Scotchmen would come to their rescue' and that her eldest daughter would marry the elder of the two. Strange to say, it all came about exactly as foretold.[25]

Sir William Gordon-Cumming of Altyre and Gordonstoun near Forres in north-east Scotland, and his brother, Charles, did arrive just when 'political complications had arisen, and hearing that some of their countrywomen were in difficulties, came to offer themselves as escort to Switzerland'. Thus, in the words of their descendant, they first met 'my beautiful grandmother Lady Charlotte Campbell of Islay, and her lovely daughters, of whom Eliza, the eldest, was my mother'.[26]

Like many of his generation of aristocratic or gentried sons, Sir William had held a military commission and had seen active service on the continent, to which his extant 'passports' bear witness. Surviving folded, unfolded and refolded documents entitling him to move around on the continental mainland are in the Gordon-Cumming family papers. One such 'passport', issued in 1814 to his brother, Charles Lennox Cumming-Bruce,[27] and allowing him to travel to Paris, comprised a large folio which described the '1m 80cm tall, fair-haired, blue eyed Chevalier, then 26, with dolore or ordue skin colouring'.[28] William and Charles had been much in demand socially in the autumn of 1814 when Charlotte and her girls were staying in Geneva. Charles, writing of Louis Albert Necker said he owed him at that time 'my introduction to the society of Coppet, and the kind and sustained friendship of Necker's mother, Madame de Staël'. He continued: 'There, with Schlegel, Sismondi, Dumont, Sir Humphry and Lady Davy, Lady Charlotte Campbell and her daughter [Eliza], Louis and I formed two of the dramatis personae in acting little plays adapted by our hostess from the lesser poems of Byron.'[29] Charlotte referred to a Cumming in Geneva at that time as 'the pick of the bunch' of young men, presumably Charles. Elizabeth Grant of Rothiemurchus subsequently described Sir William as 'the queerest creature, ugly, yet one liked his looks, tall and well made, and awkward more from oddity than ungracefulness'.[30]

As Charlotte's granddaughter subsequently put it, 'and so it came to pass that in the little Church at Zurich Eliza Maria Campbell became Lady Comyn Gordon', adding that the 'order of the double surname was then arranged and the old spelling was not finally given up till later'. Another version of the wedding between the 18-year-old bride and the groom, just short of his twenty-eighth birthday, is that it took place on 11 September 1815 in the house of His Excellency the British 'Envoi Extraordinaire et Ministre Plénipotentiaire de sa Majesté Britannique près la Confédération Suisse', Mr Stratford Canning.[31] Eliza was the first of Charlotte's children to marry—or to be married off—and her siblings were much taken up with the whole affair. Letters were addressed to the newly-weds at various Postes Restantes. Twelve-year-old Beaujolois was already a prolific correspondent (with better orthography than that of her brothers, thanks no doubt to Mlle de la Chaux). Charlotte often added long notes to Beaujolois' 'effusions'. Writing from Lausanne to Eliza ten days after the marriage, Beaujolois was glad to hear that the newlyweds were to return from a short honeymoon in Vevey on Lake Geneva before travelling to Italy, while her mother noted that Beaujolois felt a 'reflected Consequence in writing to a married sister'.[32] Mrs Damer and Mrs Sutton (of Dysart in Fife), were to be staying with Charlotte when the Gordon-Cummings were due back before setting off for Italy, so they had to be put up in the 'Lion D'Or' on Wednesday 27 September. In the meantime Charlotte was agog with the company of Madame de Staël, as can be seen from her line of thought:

> I have had some society however, in which I truly feel myself alive—you know who I mean—Madame de Staël—she goes alas! to Morrow—Existence is not stagnate in Her Company the Materialisms of Life, are concealed, and one feels disencumberd of the weight of daily cares—those petty Demons, that reduce the Mind, and sap the very Life of Life—I wonder I have a Spark of Soul left.[33]

The honeymoon travel document for Sir William and his new Lady described him as 'voyageant pour son plaisir dans l'Univers avec domestiques'. Dates are inserted thereafter for Lucerne on 20 September, Rome 12 October, Milan on 26 October, Como, then Pisa, Florence and Rome. Even before she saw them again, Charlotte was advising her daughter: 'don't have a Hundred and one children—trust me that is a great mistake—give my love to Sir William and believe that we shall be delighted to have you once more with us.'[34] Another letter seriously outlined the 'sacred duties of a married woman and a good wife, 'it ought to be your first wish to keep the Heart you have won' while admitting to envying her daughter 'in the Society of your Husband and in the Land of the Arts ... I only wish I could share it with you.'[35]

Even 15-year-old Johnny, having by now run away from his new school, sending the family into turmoil,[36] had been staying with a friend, William Oakeden, at Morges on Lake Geneva. As well as fishing in a licquet on the lake and shooting (though they 'never managed to kill anything'), he put pen to paper in a long, gawky but humorous scrawl to his new 'beau-frère' in Rome.[37] He hoped that 'you and I shall be friends' and that Sir William and Eliza would come via Geneva since he hadn't seen his sister for almost two years. There had been 'hels own Row' among Walter, Eleanor, Mlle de la Chaux and Charlotte, over a letter which Eleanor had written to the Gordon-Cummings in which she had called governess Tiranna 'the black cat'. Charlotte had used a 'false key' to get at Eleanor's letters; Eleanor was in bed but 'they turned her out neck or nothing and she was put in disgrace for a week. Walter settled them bot [*sic*] with a good blow up.' She added: 'Bye the bye if you write to Eleanor again you must write to Walter at Eton and he will send every thing privately to her.'

It was Eleanora who wrote to her elder sister in Milan on Saturday 21 October telling her that they were intending to leave Lausanne, adding she hated 'leaving this place'.

> We think we shall leave ... in two or three days ... We children are to go by voiturier and Mamma by Post so that we shall set off two days before Mamma and scarcely ever meet on the road—judge how delightful for me, I cannot tell you how I hate it and how melancholy it all makes me but I must submit.[38]

Charlotte was also writing from Bethusy near Lausanne to Eliza in Florence, yearning to follow her there instead of 'going to that bleak Sydenham of which the very thoughts give me the blue devils'. She admitted:

> Eleanor was rather sorry to go off with the young ones but it was arranged on account of Money and Room—they go all the way to Calais by Voiturier—I go only as far as Pontarlier and then Post the rest of the way—I expect to overtake your sisters on Wed, although we only set out on Monday morning the Children have got a Comfortable red Velvet Berline I sold the Basket for sixteen Louis (and conveyd as far Pontarlier free, into the bargain). All this is Mamie's management you may believe.[39]

She went on to say that 'Business and Money rule the Hours ... my Concerns, Plans, Hopes and fears ... It is my Earnest wish to come abroad again—you know the way in wh I am obligd to live in England is neither agreeable to myself or Advantageous to My Children.' They all met up at Sens, and in Paris Charlotte dined with the Castlereaghs while Madame de Staël also visited.[40] Eleonora, too, was already feeling melancholy at the prospect of being 'cooped up at Westwood'. The Swiss historian and genealogist Jacques Galiffe joined the family and escorted them back to Dover.

10

Sunless Sydenham

Charlotte's re-entry to Britain was signalled by Thomas Campbell in a letter of 3 November 1815:

> Lady Charlotte Bury is expected immediately at Sydenham. Her return will, no doubt make a change for the better in our society; but yet it makes me very sorry to see her change the genial air of the south at this period, and plunge into the temperature of world's end.[1]

By July the following year the lady herself was still complaining: 'Our weather is so very detestable that no Scotch rains I ever saw exceed the Gloom which covers these skies. I am constantly sighing for another Climate but have no chance at present.' One bright spot, however, was her Westwood garden, which was 'blushingly sweet in despight of wind and rain'.[2] Part of Sydenham Common had been enclosed to give Westwood House an impressive carriage drive. To the rear of the large mansion with its huge bay windows on either side of the front door, was the large garden, with a very long flask shaped pond.[3] From the front windows of the house Peak Hill could be seen, which encouraged Thomas Campbell to talk of Charlotte as being his next-door neighbour. Campbell and his wife had proved congenial friends and 'neighbours' during Charlotte's early widowhood when she was a courtier. He was also an intimate of the Mayow family, using their summer house as a quiet place for writing. There were five clever and attractive Mayow heiress daughters along with Thomas Campbell (since 1814 a somewhat disorganised editor of Henry Colburn's *New Monthly Magazine*, set up in opposition to Richard Phillips' *Monthly Magazine*). A coterie of successful men made their way to Sydenham, including Lord Byron, George Crabbe, Theodore Hook, Leigh Hunt, Washington Irving, Thomas Lawrence, Thomas Moore, Samuel Rogers, Tom Sheridan and George Ticknor. Perhaps, after all, Sydenham was not so far away. When out walking on the Common, St Paul's and Westminster Abbey could be seen (and the bells sometimes heard), as Charlotte championed in her thirteen-verse 'Stanzas Written at Sydenham'.[4]

That winter, the welcome Genevan friend who had accompanied them from Paris, was in London and paid frequent visits to the ménage at Westwood.[5] Jacques Galiffe, was being urged in December to come 'to eat at four o'clock and make music'.[6] The following February he was invited for an evening's dancing 'from 8 till one', at other times being urged 'to bring your Dog'. That same month Benjamin Constant's novel, *Adolphe*, was 'rehearsed in a private reading at their home'.[7] Writing to Jean Charles de Sismondi on St Valentine's Day 1816 from her 'little Book Room' and contrasting the snow outside with his then being in Tuscany she repined 'I think there is only one danger in going to Italy. It is never liking to live elsewhere.'[8] She told him she was reading 'an account of Iceland ... partly written by a friend of mine'. Another work which 'should be read by all Sovereigns', is written by a 'very Young Man—a very delightful one'. In March Charlotte ventured north, at least to Edinburgh and Ardencaple, spending ten days on the road during the return journey.

Walter had been persuaded to stay on at Eton, despite having been 'in great hopes to leave it, but the Meads and Persians have decreed it otherwise and here I am to stay till Easter', as he had complained to his sister, Eliza, in Rome in January 1816.[9] John had remained in Switzerland, staying in Morges, much in demand at the many winter balls, and building a new boat for the next summer.[10] In that summer of 1816, the girls' cousin, Douglas Clavering, on medical leave from the navy while daily receiving treatment with a doctor in town, renewed acquaintance with the family, staying for over a month at Westwood. He wrote to Eliza from Sydenham on 15 August:

> Commencing a correspondence which our intimacy in childhood might well have expected ... now that I am a second time returned and to remain ashore for sometime I cannot but be anxious to renew that acquaintance which I have already done in your mother and Sisters society and with whom I feel far more happy than with the cold and inhospitable people I have often met in my short career through life. I have already been here a week delightfully and charmingly amused for your Sisters all of them possess in an eminent degree the art of pleasing which added to the gracefulness, ease and vivacity the characteristics of

> the family render them to me who has seen nothing but a rough element ... going tomorrow to my Mother in Scotland where I shall remain for a month or two and then to return to England for the purpose of shutting myself up and dedicating my time to study and improvement for I am at present no more than a mere fish out of water.[11]

Beaujolois confessed to Eliza that she liked him 'uncommonly' and 'I believe I am rather his favourite', describing him as 'so very good and steady and so free from all the madness and wickedness of the generality of young men'.[12] He thought Eleanor too much like a butterfly, whilst considering Beaujolois erroneous in her views about wanting to return to the continent. Douglas gave them news of his sister, Charlotte and his brother, Rawdon, then with the army in Ireland 'without hopes of getting leave for two years to come'. But since the Irish ladies were so handsome and agreeable he didn't mind and 'was frequently in Love and even violently so ... but he has taken care not quite to loose [*sic*] his senses or his heart'.

Eliza, meanwhile, had arrived in Edinburgh en route for Altyre. Elizabeth Grant described the household in Charlotte Square: 'the Cumming Gordons, the old Lady and her four unmarried daughters, [son] Charles, and Sir William and his Bride on a visit to them'.[13] She reported:

> Young Lady Gordon-Cumming, as she called herself for distinction, was not handsome, very tall—five feet ten and a half—thin, not well made, neither were her features good, yet altogether, when well dressed, I have seen her look magnificent ... She carries her heart in her countenance, and it is so good a one that it makes one happy to look at it.

The whole family was 'in a dream of joy at Sir Willie's wife being the daughter of Lady Charlotte Campbell, neice [*sic*] to the Duke of Argylle'.

> It was Eliza here, Eliza there, and Eliza only; they were awakened by [*sic*] and bye, and rather rudely, but this winter it was all an intoxication of happiness ... every evening ... young Lady Cumming sang ballads neatly ... All the Cummings were queer, queerer than one ever sees people now.

To the rest of her family, Altyre perhaps seemed a long way away. Charlotte wrote to Eliza:

> There is something awful in every Change of Life and it is not till we are settled in our new habitations that we feel the change. I trust however that the beauty of the Country you inhabit and the interest which you

> will feel in it and which habit and use will daily render more dear to you, will quite take off any little melancholy you at first experienced in being so far from me and your Sisters. Sir William will I am sure as Circumstances allow and your own Children and connections will give you so much to do that you will not feel the intermediate time irksome or heavy.[14]

More polemically, she hoped that 'whatever you feel My dear about the Coarseness of Scotch Society—and the vulgarity of the language, you will have the good Sense not to hurt the feelings of those around you by betraying your disgust'. She went on:

> God knows how much for years I labourd to conceal my distaste for the Manners and Habits and Sounds in which I lived—I could not do it again—but you have a Husband who is devoted to you, and while that is the case one can do any thing, and do it cheerfully.

However, while Charlotte claimed that she 'should like to be transported to Altyre to see you and yours', she also confessed that 'I dread going to Scotland or even seeing it—it always brings to Mind such a long state of trials and sufferings that I do not think it very likely I should ever go there'. On 30 August 1816 she was perhaps only exaggerating slightly when she told Eliza 'since June last twelvemonth when I left my beloved Milan I have never known what a summer day meant'.[15] The English weather that 'year without summer' produced great storms, massive rains and appalling cold.[16] While she professed to her daughter her 'belle passion for London', averring that it was the only place in Britain worth living in, she confessed:

> My greatest Interest is the idea of wandering about on the Continent—in the first place my health requires a warm Climate—and my sickly disappointed spirits require scenes wholly unconnected with my past Life. I see no prospect at present of my getting abroad, but as soon as I can I will go there.[17]

Apart from volcanic dust causing gloomy skies, there had been another unusual event that summer—an earthquake of 5.1 on today's scale had shaken the north-east of Scotland on 13 August at about 11pm. From 29 Upper Brook Street on 22 August 1816 Charlotte enquired of her daughter:

> Well dearest Eliza, what have you done with the Earthquake, and has the Earthquake done with you? If your first born comes forth in the way of

> these prodigies of nature, what a prodigy it must be. I shall long seriously to know that you have not been frightend ... and have got over the Evil hour.[18]

An heir for the Gordon-Cummings, Alexander Penrose, had indeed been born at Altyre on 17 August 1816. Mlle de la Chaux congratulated Eliza on her newborn 'héros—car c'est sans doute à son honneur et gloire que le Tremblement de terre a eu lieu'.[19] In writing to congratulate Sir William, Charlotte thought 'being a Grand mother certainly alarming ... yet in good truth I have only to wish that all my Daughters may follow Eliza's example as fast as possible'.[20] Husbands would have to be found for five further Campbell daughters, the youngest only 9. While congratulating Eliza for 'not having followed my bad example in being a Girl Maker', she asked Sir William to remember 'there may be too much of a good thing. It is all Nonsense to talk of the blessings of a large Family. I wish you enough but not too many ... a few and good that is my Wishes for you and yours.' Days later she was also giving the new 19-year-old mother some dubious advice and warnings:

> I hope dearest Eliza you will take the greatest care of yourself all depends upon that; remember you will have to repeat the Job, every year, and nothing but the greatest attention will preserve your beauty lace yourself up at all hours of the day and do not walk too soon. Without health there is no happiness and your health as well as your Beauty depends entirely upon care. Do not drink any liquid hardly and live entirely upon Chicken—for the first three weeks I lived upon nothing else—a dry Chicken Sandwich. I was far smaller than ever you were, and yet alas! What an enormous size I became with the trade. So take care of yourself. Keep this Note a secret.

She continued in non-maternal refrain:

> The good people will think I am not a good Grandmama—but I own I care very much for you only and the babe because it is yours ... only I mean I do not know myself in babes—like 'the Man who did not Know himself in a tree'—when it is fifteen if I live so long I shall be very fond of it.[21]

After further advice on nursing she expressed the hope that Eliza would 'avoid growing into a Squashy Milk Cow—or Brood Mare' and averred that 'nothing but mental Cultivation—nothing but striving that Matter should not get the better of Manner is the path to follow'. Since her daughter would 'probably have a Child every year—do not because you feel happy (as I call it) allow yourself not to be occupied—read—one may always read—it is the light of Life. I know nothing else in this World that completely answers to one.' This homily was accompanied by a heartfelt warning not 'to let Women prose to you all Day long about Cake and Cawdle and Clothes. Most Women lose their place in the Scale of Intellectual beings—by sinking under the weight of their Phisical [*sic*] Natures.' The letter ends 'so much for my way of thinking and my advice but you know it all pretty well already'. At the end of the month Charlotte was replying to Eliza's news in somewhat more emollient vein.[22]

> It is most fortunate that you have all those maternal yearnings towards your nouveau né, and that the pain is compensated to you may it ever continue to be so. As to your nursing you are quite right to do whatever Sir William and yourself like best. Nobody has a greater idea of the Duty owed by Wives to Husbands than myself. There is no happiness and no virtue without it. I think you seem to be perfectly happy, and happy in the way most calculated for your happiness. What can one wish more for oneself—what more can I wish for you.

This epistle ended with the admonition 'Good bye my love don't grow large and lubberly like your Mama if you can possibly help it—continue as happy as you are'.

The birth of their first nephew occasioned a rush of letter-writing from the Campbell sisters to Eliza, a correspondence that was to continue for over a quarter of a century, through a dozen further births at Altyre. Next down the line, 17-year-old Eleanora wished that as 'an old maiden aunt, I hope people will begin to respect me'.[23] None of the family at Westwood appears to have been at Penrose's christening, though Annie MacLeod attended, having been spared by Charlotte to help Eliza.[24] Charlotte had already requested that MacLeod return immediately to Westwood:

> I must be despotic and request you to send Macleod off immediately as we really cannot do any longer without her. She may spend a few Days with her Friends—but she must not stay longer at Altyre. I know by experience she is of no use whatever in The Crying—except to cry herself.[25]

This was followed by another letter in which Charlotte rather callously hoped that 'MacLeod is on her way': 'She can be of no use to you and My Household cannot go on without her any longer.'[26] Eventually, after six days of rough sailing from Leith to London, and frequently suffering from seasickness, MacLeod returned, bringing christening ribbons along with details of the extended Gordon-Cumming family, all much devoured by the Campbell sisters and their mother, who had 'tears in her Eyes'.[27] Charlotte admitted to Eliza that as a grandmother she had looked 'in the glass I was comforted there's vanity for you',[28] while in October Alexander Baillie (Harley Street and of the Dochfour family in Inverness), one of Charlotte's escorts about London that summer, related to Eliza that not only was Charlotte looking very well, but she was 'much devoted with the idea of being a grandmother. She is certainly the most delightful of all grandmothers; I might say, of all mothers, for no person is like her.'[29] Charlotte was also beseeching them to 'watch the first Northern Lights you have'.[30]

When Henry Raeburn's painting of Eliza was exhibited at the Royal Academy the following spring of 1817 he himself deemed it 'much the best and handsomest female picture I have yet painted' (see plate 18).[31] With its highly elaborate head gear and dress it is hard to believe it to be of a young married woman of about 20. The likeness appeared much more Shawfield than Argyll and Gunning, a feature echoed in later portraits. In her right hand she was depicted holding a stylus or pen which was much more her icon than some fashionable item, or even perhaps a favourite pet. In telling Eliza that 'in general I think Raeburns women are harsh and coarse' her mother hoped that 'he has made an exception in painting you', and she had heard that it was 'very handsome'.[32] Eleanor reported, 'Your picture has been more admired than I can tell you', but was highly critical of a 'copy' of it made by Bessie Mure. As Eleanor put it', if the original is no better it really might do for you fifteen year hence, such an old hard looking thing'.[33]

On occasion Charlotte ventured from Sydenham to town, once to see brothers in law 'Walter and Collin [*sic*] before they left England', leaving Eleanora and Beaujolois with the Carters at Edgcott, while she herself visited Anne Damer. Serving in the East India Company from the time he was 19 in 1797, Walter had progressed up from 3rd, through 2nd and 1st officer to his first command of an Indiaman by 1803, and his many voyages to the Far East come to life in his detailed logs now in the British Library. His younger brother, Colin, had been a 20-year-old midshipman in the Royal Navy at the battle of Trafalgar in 1805, sending a vivid account of the battle to his father at Woodhall.[34] Ten years later, with Walter contemplating leaving the Company (perhaps due to faltering health), and himself taking a break after the end of the Napoleonic wars, Captain Colin and his servant joined Walter at Portsmouth on the Company ship, the 1,332-ton *General Hewitt*, as a passenger on a round voyage to China. He kept a colourful journal, the homebound part of which included visiting Napoleon on St Helena.[35]

Charlotte wrote:

> I continue in favour with P/s C: [Princess Charlotte] whom I have seen frequently. It is reported about Town that the Regent is to try for a Divorce and of course for a Mariage [*sic*]. What follows is also of Course—an heir—I confess I am too much interested for P/s C not to hope all this may not be. But there is no saying. There is to be a great Fete at Carlton House ... every Body is asked—tag and bobtail but not me—this is very mark'd. Mrs Damer was invited, but has been so unwell all year she will not venture into so great a Crowd, which I am half sorry for, but perhaps she judges wisely.[36]

During the winter months, other old friendships were renewed in person, Mary Berry writing from Paris to her sister in London commiserating on a migraine: 'Dear Charlotte's visit would do for it completely. But there are people whom in sickness, or in health, one would always rather see than not see, and she is in distress too: good cheerful soul! Is certainly one of them.'[37]

Lord John's unhappy marriage did nothing to improve his poor health, and Charlotte was often called on to nurse him through quite serious bouts of illness at the Argyll home at 29 Upper Brook Street in Mayfair. At the end of June 1816 she described him as having had severe inflammation on his chest and 'Oppression at his Heart', for which he had been repeatedly bled and blistered.[38] After another relapse, his life being once again in extreme danger, she worried that 'it is a vile Species of Malady against which there is no security', with only laudanum able to give some relief. She and Eleanora stayed in town for weeks at a time, while Mlle de la Chaux was left in charge at Westwood. When Lord John could be left for a little while, Charlotte and Eleonora would go out into the park for the fashionable hour of five o'clock. By the end of August, Eleanora gave her version of their daily routine to Eliza:

> Breakfast at 1/2 past ten and letter writing for Lord John and ourselves till two, we then proceed to take an airing in the Dukes carriage round the ring and latterly Lord J gets out and walks with me a little ... he hopes to return to Scotland in ten days. At 1/2 past 4 we dine and after that we, that is Mamma and I drive up and down in the park til it is quite dark and there are still a good many dandies in town. Alas! Mamma fixes all the beaux eyes and I none amn't I to be ?pitied; but no wonder when you have made me an old maiden aunt. After that we read to Lord J. till 1/2 11.[39]

Charlotte hoped that her brother's doctors would advise him to spend the forthcoming winter abroad, when she would have jumped at the opportunity of accompanying him, but it was not to be and instead he set off for Ardencaple in September with Eleanora and Mlle de la Chaux.[40] Lord John's brother, George, Duke of Argyll, had been 'most amiable' and assiduous in visiting, and when he came to town from Bognor with his duchess and step-daughters for a ball at the Queen's house, 'there not being room … for so many persons', Charlotte was able to return to the rest of her family at Westwood, or take Eleanora to visit friends or relatives such as the Hooks now at Winchester, or the Carters at Edgcott. But they also managed to get a box to see Mrs Siddons, and were 'all Summer and Autumn … backwards and forwards at the Priory' in Stanmore, Middlesex.[41]

Charlotte had confessed to her eldest daughter: 'You will be surprised to hear that in the midst of my anxiety I have pass'd three days at the Priory with Eleanor in a great and brilliant party of Royalties etc.'[42] The grandee Lord Abercorn and his new Lady and third wife resumed invitations to Charlotte, making a great fuss over 16-year-old 'Miss Campbell'; it was now Eleanora's turn to be launched into society. They were frequently invited to stay for several days at a time in the Abercorns' sumptuous Priory home. 'It is impossible for anything to be more kind than Lord A. is to me and to everything that belongs to me—and to every Body that I call a Friend—I feel his House really like my own' was how Charlotte expressed her feelings about Lord Abercorn and the Priory.

> I can not say as much of My Own Brothers but there is 'a friend that Sticketts closer than a Brother'. I only wish he may not turn Eleanors Head for he admires her so much—and says there is nothing He will not do to render His house pleasant and useful to Her.

Known as 'Don Magnifico', immensely rich and vain, as well as being a considerable womaniser, the 60-year-old Lord Abercorn was about to buy 8 acres in Regents Park to build a magnificent town residence, to be completed in two years, but meanwhile he also rented a house in London for the winter. Charlotte wrote:

> The Splendour in which he lives is a little dangerous to behold, for one forgets there are a few persons who can so live, and it is necessary in the melancholy world to be always building up fences against unruly wishes, and impracticable schemes of happiness. In My early days when an unbounded prospect lay before me Lord Abercorns House was my first Sphere of Motion, I never then expected to move in any other. One is never sufficiently taught the reality of Life—or to consider how much everything depends upon ones own Actions. If all such splendour now became mine, it would only appear to me to be my due, and although

> I struggle hard against my present Fortunes [I] endeavour not to shew how much they oppress me.[43]

At this point the extant letter runs out, but not before she had expressed her opinion that:

> The Priory had all of Magnificence which can be display'd but there is nevertheless in some places and with Some Persons a Gloom which no Magnificence brightens—and that is the case there—Eleanor did not feel this it is not her time for feeling these things.

Eleanora's gossipy letter to her elder sister elaborated all of this social activity.[44]

> Last Thursday William [?her cousin] came here for me and took me to join Mamma in town who was staying for two or three days at the Duke's and he went on with us to the Priory. Lord and Lady Abercorn received him very kindly and he seemed to like his visit there very much.

She went on to describe how in the evening they had danced 'a little':

> But not much as besides Lady Julia Gore, William, a Mr Ellis a douce kind of laddie and myself the rest of the company were neither dancingly disposed, or constructed, they consisted of Lord and Lady St Germains, nothing particularly ornamental, or agreeable, and Sir George and Lady Hill, whom I had seen there before.

Eleanora cattily observed that 'Lady Aberdeen played for us very good naturedly but she does not much excel in that art. I think her very beautiful, that is to say her head and bust for her legs and arms are rather heavily made.' Another house guest was 'a Captain Gaven Hamilton, a very handsome man, a sort of relation of the A's I believe, and who has distinguished himself in the navy, who saw a good deal of Mr Cumming abroad' as well as Alexander Baillie. 'Lady A. thought Mr B the handsomest ... man she had ever seen'. Eleanora ventured her opinion that 'upon the whole nothing can be more kind than Lord A. is to Mama and all that belongs to her and he is so handsome and has so perfectly the manners of a grand seigneur with all the kindness and attention possible that I think him very agreeable'. Name dropping continued after another sojourn at the Priory; Eleanora and her mother had dined with the dukes of Cumberland and Fife; the latter's son, Lord Fife, 'talked heaps to me of the magnificence of your beauty and of the wonderful improvements you had wrought upon your worthy husband'.[45] She continued: 'I wish L. F was a little more elegant for he is immensely rich and might do very well for me. I trust you like Frederick North for a brother-in-law, be prepared. There was a great dinner at his house the other evening.'

Eleanora herself had come in for some criticism in 1816, when in Edinburgh Susan Ferrier observed: 'I think Miss Campbell critically beautiful, and *nothing more*. She has all the Argyll elegance, but she wants their look of *esprit*; and in short, she is a person I don't think I could ever feel much interest in.'[46] Elizabeth Grant, for her part, wrote that Eleanora was 'a pretty creature, the image of me! It was really curious the extraordinary likeness to us that ran through this whole Campbell connexion, and no relationship between us.' She rambled on:

> Even Charlotte Clavering, Lady Augusta's daughter, had a look of me ... Emma Campbell could hardly be known from my sister Mary, and Mary and I were both so like the Miss Gunning, Duchess of Hamilton and Argylle [*sic*], that they used at Altyre to dress us up and set us underneath her picture as a show.[47]

Charlotte Clavering had written to Eliza,[48] saying that she was delighted to see her cousin Eleanora 'so like Lady Charlotte she reminded me of her in every gesture and movement so much grace and elegance and such a lovely figure', continuing 'though indisputedly not so handsome as Lady Charlotte nor like in expressions yet there were constant looks in her countenance, or rather the notion of her features which so fondly recalled Lady Charlotte to my mind'. She added: 'Pardon me but I think she has learnt from Lady Charlotte to be a little what I call fine and fastidious ... you have none of it about you, I am sure Eleanor will be prodigiously admired which she will like not a little'.

Charlotte spent some time in Edinburgh in the spring of 1817. As Susan Ferrier put it to Charlotte Clavering:

> You would hear how Lady Charlotte had tarried in this place ten days, but I got very little good of her. She was so *cherché* and *recherché* ... Lady Charlotte seems more eat up with sentiment than ever; all *her* sayings and doings are delightful, to be sure, but how odd they would seem in the ugly part of the creation! ... I thought Lady Charlotte looking more like herself, for she would dance and sing and go about and *talk blue*, and that is hard work in this town.[49]

On their way south from Scotland, Eleanora and her mother had been visiting Lady Exeter, for Charlotte Clavering passed on the news that:

> She liked Burghley very much, and I wish heartily she could captivate the young owner thereof, for she professes now to be very particular about beauty and seems not the least tinctured with romance respecting Love etc. What think you of her opinions on these subjects?

The said prospect was 'eye-watering'.

Back in London, Eleanora reported to Eliza that her mother had 'not yet begun to sit to Geddes,[50] but intends to do so, as soon as she can find courage to get up in the morning: he wanted her always to come to his house, but really that was a little too much'[51]. At the same time Walter wanted Eleanora 'to sit for Allan',[52] whose whereabouts she asked Eliza to discover. Eleanora had told her sister that people who had never seen Eliza thought Raeburn's portrait 'was my sister and some thought it was me. Only conceive how flattered I was.'[53] Eleanora's letters during the spring detail many of the giddy concerns of a 17-year-old participating to the full in her first London season. Writing on 25 April 1817 she admitted to feeling 'angry and enraged with myself for being schockingly [*sic*] capricious'.

> Somebody pleases me for a short time, a week at most, and then some other person comes and quizzes [ridicules] them to me and I feel quite schocked [*sic*] at my own bad taste in ever thinking them agreeable. This is horridly unamiable but I can't help it.[54]

She went on:

> There are one or two luckily whom I still continue to like notwithstanding all the evil I hear of them. Charles Percy [of the Northumberland family] is a very great favourite and Lord Uxbridge though quite a boy, might be rather dangerous, but he returns to France in a few days, and I am half sorry and half glad of it; why, I have not had time to ask myself yet.

Other 'dangerous' beaus included Lord Strathmore, one of Eliza's former admirers, having come up to her one night at Almack's 'in the midst of a quadrille … and besought me to allow him to come to us in the mornings that I may teach him' to dance waltzes and quadrilles properly. 'Don't you think it will be too dangerous for me. Luckily I have got a very comfortable égide [thick skin] which will repel the shafts even of this beauty who is reckoned so irresistible.' Lord Roseberry was another. He had interrupted the writing of a letter at four o'clock one afternoon when she had to entertain him alone at 77 Gloucester Place, which they were renting. 'I hate it, it makes me so nervous, and I suppose he saw it for he went off saying that he hoped there was no impropriety in cousins being left alone together, ha ha.'

The reason for her having to serve him tea on her own was that 'Mama continues like myself to be weak and side painy' and was still in bed. Eleanora confided to Eliza that 'there is nothing that will do her good but going abroad, half from the strength of imagination half from reality'. Ten days later Charlotte confirmed this to Eliza: 'I am not without pain in my side and ever since my Journey to Scotland I have never been quite well.' After commiserating with Eliza's being 'so unwell' that she advised going to a warm climate again in the autumn and winter if she were not better, she disclosed that 'on My Side of the House' there was a 'Breast Complaint—I am not free of it Myself.' While she was happy to hear that 'Mr Penrose' was thriving, she added her familiar refrain: 'When he is Eight years old I shall deign to look at Him—by that time you will have seven more seedlings. Count the grandchildren I may have—if you have eight a piece.' She regretted that she would not be able to see Eliza 'before we go to the Continent but besides that I dread a Northern Journey upon a thousand accounts, I really have not the Money to go out of my way'.[55]

Bessie Mure had divulged to Eliza that Eleanora had spent 'a dreadful deal of money this year,' that Charlotte 'from indolence has let her spend much more than she ought', and that she 'drest much beyond most Girls'.[56] In one of many long letters to her sister at this time, Eleanora mentioned Eliza's 'present for which I thank you a thousand times, it will plentifully supply all my deficiencies', in four pages of riposte to 'Bessie Mure's intelligence'.[57] In what was probably just a main concern of such a young girl or woman during her first London season, her wardrobe, Eleanora did admit:

> Comparatively speaking I have been extravagant for there has been a good deal of money spent upon my dress, but as I began without having any of those sort of clothes which one cannot appear in the world without, of course I cost more than I should do any following year if I were to be in London; I believe that in the space of 10 months what with mourning my court dress, and the milliners bill I have cost Mama £150. You are much shocked I am sure, and it sounds very horrible, but included in this there are my subscriptions for Almacks, the French Play, and occasionally the Opera and the £15 they allow me for gloves, shoes, ribbons and bonnets.

She then went on to give Eliza an account of her clothes, 'at least as well as I can remember', beginning 'from the end of mourning' (for her grandfather, Walter Campbell):

> A black poplin for the morning and a grey d[itt]o trimmed with two deep full flounces of black and grey Bowmans gauze, for the evening a black flowered gauze I used to wear over a white satin slip trimmed with mock white blonde at bottom and at top your real white blonde, besides this one white crape gown; these two I wore alternately all the time I was in mourning: this with a black satin spencer made up that business. After that I wore the satin slip that had been under the black, for some time under colours (which by the bye was the same one Lord Abercorn had given me with a white gauze gown last year at the Priory before I came out, which you may remember I told you of) but at last it was so dirty I was obliged to have another and these two slips have served me all the time. For coloured evening gowns I have had your pink one made up in the way I told you, a light blue spotted gauze, a white one d[itt]o Walter gave me and a lilac d[itt]o.

While admitting that these might be considered 'a great many', she explained that they had gone out 'a good deal', while 'in walking with the men their dirty coats and hot hands destroy one's gown behind dreadfully, and crush and shabby them directly. I always give a lecture to each in beginning about holding me properly but to very little purpose.' She then said that they all cost so much because:

> They have all been made out, and that whatever trimming they had the milliners furnished. They were generally made so as only to reach to the top of the trimming of the white satin slip under, and the gown itself had mock blonde on it headed by a double quilling of net, or else net wreathed round a rouleau of satin. With a pink silk spencer Mama gave me and a white satin one I gave myself this is all at present that I can remember of my cloathes [*sic*] and I am sure you must be heartily bored with the list. Out of the £15 Mama gives me I was always obliged to buy myself whatever artificial flowers I might want, as she never gave me any and you have really no conception of the quantity of white shoes and gloves one dirtys [*sic*] in dancing what with the chalk upon the floors, and the dirt of the men's coats.

Only one of these gowns was by this time 'tolerably clean ... but as I am only going to two more balls it will do perfectly, one of these is to be I believe a fancy ball at Almacks in which case I shall go in a Swiss peasants dress I had made for a masquerade'. Eliza's money she intended to use to pay off a shoemakers bill and 'in fitting my self out with a few pairs for the continent'.

> I have too bought today a russian leather case which cost two pounds 15. And I mean too to get some bottles for an old dressing box I have, and send the person some sort of a gold ring; I wish you would draw me a pattern dear and send it to me as soon as you can that I may have it made before we go abroad. This is all I can remember and now you may pass your judgment upon me.

Eleanora thought that her sister would probably have seen in the papers 'that we, that is to say Mama was turned out of Almacks for coming without Tickets, and it is a literal fact'. She continued:

> We applied too late to the Lady patronesses, and they had no tickets left for us, but Mama thinking that from her rank etc etc she had a right to go, and that the people would certainly not turn us back at the door, proceeded there with me. At the door we were admitted but no sooner had we entered the ball room, than the whole possy of patronesses marched up to us, begging to know by what right we were there, and though in civil terms requested Mama to march off, for examples sake, as they had that moment turned Lady Worcester from the door, who had like us come without a ticket. She out of courtesy they allowed to remain as being a dancing dog, but Mama retreated, and upon the whole I think I never heard of such a piece of impertinence; Lady Jane [Paget], one of Lord Uxbridge's sisters, my great croney [*sic*] was in such a rage with all the ladies about it that she wished to persuade us never to speak to them again, but that would be quarrelling with ones bread and butter.

While Charlotte's mother had been one of the founding patronesses of Almacks, set up in 1765 by the Duke of Argyll's valet, Charlotte got her own back in her novel, *The Exclusives*, published in 1830, with a subsequent key published suggesting the principals.

Justifying her decision in the summer of 1817 to leave Britain again for the Continent, Charlotte claimed to her eldest daughter: 'I am too poor to live in London—that is quite out of the question. I am convinced of the impossibility of doing so—under four thousand a year with my family and as I ought—without any extravagance even ... but in my two thousand it will never do.' She added that to remain at Westwood 'in total seclusion would not do either'. When walking in the park in London, she and Alexander Baillie often talked of London being the only place to live in Britain, finding it 'still quite full and agreeable' even in its August heat.[58]

> But as I cannot live in London as I should like to live, I think my Life will be sweeter to me on the Continent—where my means will certainly

> go further and where a change of Scene and persons will not constantly remind me of what I might have been, of what I might enjoy—there are many reasons to make me love a Wandering Life.[59]

Her rationalisation continued: 'Then my health—your Brothers being on the Continent etc etc, last not least, my own inclination all combines to make me go to Italy and to Italy please God I go at the end of the month.' The plan was to go to Marseille, thence by ship to Leghorn or Civita Vecchia, aiming for Rome. 'Oh! How I shall enjoy it. Going away is always heart breaking and heart breaking it will be. But yet I shall be happier there than I could be here. A change of scene and climate is necessary to me.'

Further explanation followed with her belief that Eleanora had 'not yet got a Husband but time enough. Only the great World of London and vapid admiration is not so likely to procure that Solid good as the wilds of Switzerland or the romance of Italy.'[60] A few months later this was reinforced: 'At all events she is young enough to wait for a couple of years.'[61] While Charlotte liked the thought of 'dear amiable Lord Rocksavage' as a son-in-law, she percipiently feared that he was 'too grave for Eleanor'. 'My own cousin Lord Roseberry I should like also. But still he is too grave I fear. She would like Lord Uxbridge a mere boy. But he is gone to France.' His father, Lord Anglesey, moreover, had 'look't at us both as if he would have breathed out flames upon us'. Eleanora herself elaborated: 'His father used to examine us with eyes that terrified me to such a degree that I was glad to shrink behind anybody who could hide me from him. I am convinced he hates me.'[62] The 18-year-old however expressed her unhappiness at leaving England for two years, during which time she and Lord Uxbridge would probably not meet: 'I am really wretched at the thought of it, for though I know that upon the whole it is better that we should go, as Mamma cannot live here as she would like … it is really heart breaking. And then too such a caravan of people as we are.' Mlle de la Chaux was going ahead to have some time with her family in the Swiss Jura before meeting up with the Campbells at Marseille and Eleanora bewailed her absence:

> Only conceive what poor Mama will do without somebody to scold for her at the inns. I think I see already some of the ludicrous scenes that will infallibly take place … When I hear Mama talking over all her plans every morning with a sort or enthusiasm of joy, to me quite incomprehensible, I feel so melancholy that I sometimes cannot bear to sit in the room.

Eleanora continued to pen long letters to her elder sister—four of the eight pages dated 5 July were taken up with the problems of communicating secretly with Lord Uxbridge.[63] The latter's dandy cousin, Francis Russell of the Bedford family, often came into their box at the opera, acting as a courier and go-between to avoid Lord Anglesey or Lady Charlotte finding out. Eleanora felt that her mother thought it was 'merely a folie de Jeunesse' and she herself owned that that Lord Uxbridge had 'never really popped the question as Sir William calls it'. Despite not having known him for long, Eleanora was of the following opinion:

> As to the amiableness of his character I am thoroughly convinced of it, from all I saw of his behaviour to his Mother and Sisters, and the way they all adore him. He is not handsome, but elegant and high blood looking, and most excessively gentlemanlike in his manners.

With all the assurance of an 18-year-old, she was altogether 'sure I shall never like anybody better, or half so well'. Eliza had scolded her younger sister for not locking up this secret correspondence from 'the person who was in despair at not having heard from me … he wanted to meet up at Calais or somewhere thereabouts as Cassell his quarters is in that direction'. But Eleanora pointed out that she did not have 'a single place to do so either in my own room or elsewhere and whoever has done me the kindness of reading them must have routed in a press in my room where not a soul has business to enter <u>nasty prying beast or beasties</u>'. This was later to be a reprise for her next youngest sister, and in the end Eleanora had had to confess the whole thing to her mother 'en long et en détail'.

Bessie Mure had relayed to Eliza that the 'Thermometer in the shade is at 80' that hot June of 1817, which was said to be the hottest for nine years, but also gossiped that she had heard from both Charlotte and Mlle de la Chaux the sum expended on Eleanora. Some had remarked that she was thought 'drest much beyond most Girls and that Even the greatest liberality of Walter to whom charges impute it would hardly justify it of course the blame has fallen on Lady Charlotte'.[64] Bessie Mure obviously thought Eleanor somewhat spoilt, as she had been very disappointed and upset at not being allowed to go to a ball at Almacks one Wednesday evening when everyone had to wear national costume. She averred that Charlotte 'had not a sixpence of Money to buy a dress for her to dance in the Quadrilles'. She also let slip that Charlotte was not keen to encourage Lord Worcester's attentions to Eleanora as 'his character is so notoriously and glaringly vicious'. Writing of the other girls on the eve of their departure for the continent, Bessie Mure opined that 'Beaueujolae [*sic*] does not look well now and I don't think she can ever continue to be as pretty as Eleanora [*sic*] tho some people say she will be much more so.

I think Adelaide Emma and Julia will all be very handsome.' Her stream of consciousness continued:

> Emma would be perfect if her mouth was not a nuance too little especially when she laughs for perfect beauty and a little squareness about her cheeks but her nose and eyes are perfect and the Expression of her face and I think her figure and démarche very Magister and Elegant.

Adelaide and Julia were spared her pen.

Even though she had given up her horses on 1 July,[65] Charlotte enjoyed London's summer heat. For five 'Delicious Days we have had the thermometer at 83 in the shade', she told Eliza in cooler Scotland at the start of July, adding that it was, however, 'too delightful to last'.[66] She was frequently given the use of a box at the Opera, the only social activity 'that I like' of all the balls, parties, visits to the Priory and so on during the season. While yearning for 'the certitude of a box' of her own at the opera she explained ''tis the doubt and turmoil of Love rather than the quiet enjoyment of married felicity. I do like to be married to the Opera.'[67] Nineteen-year-old Walter arrived at the start of July and had to be introduced to society amidst a whirl of engagements,[68] being 'admired and liked and he certainly has very pleasing and gentleman like manners'. According to Eleanora, they had gone to the Opera to Sontini's *Agnese*, 'which was acted here for the second time and the music is really heavenly, but upon the whole I don't like it, for the subject is too horrid and one does not go to the Opera to weep and wail'. She continued:

> We went too after it to sup at Mrs ?Standish's, otherwise surnamed the Zephyr de Plomb where there was a little chosen collection of dandys, [*sic*] Montagne Bradshaw etc etc and everything was the most perfect Style. Upon the whole it was very agreeable, and I liked it because it was out of the common order of things. Next week we have heaps to do, but I like nothing but Almacks and the French Play, for there at least one has all the best people, stupid and disagreeable as most of them are.

The family's paternal grandfather, Walter Campbell of Shawfield and Islay, had died in Islay House on 19 October 1816.[69] Instead of his son Jack (and Charlotte), it was his grandson, Walter Frederick Campbell (see plate 19), then only 18 years old, who succeeded to the estates of Woodhall and Islay. Walter had spent time with various of his Shawfield and Argyll relations a couple of autumns before and became a great favourite with his grandparents when in Islay.[70] Despite a big storm in the Kyles of Bute when Walter had had to go ashore to shelter and dry out in a cottage, his aunt reported that she was very glad 'to see him like Islay so much, where he will one day have the power of influencing the comforts and happiness of 12,000 people, and who, if he does not, will be left to the care of rapacious agents, to his own loss, and their discomfort'. He had also spent a week fishing, stalking deer and staying in one of the caves on Jura. After leaving Eton in 1816 his guardians had looked for a bearleader or tutor to accompany him on a proposed Grand Tour. Eleanora informed Eliza on that Walter had seen 'Bury, the person designed for his tutor, and luckily does not dislike him, though in my opinion, he might at first strike one as being rather ?Simon Parish'. She added:

> Mama wishes to make him set off directly and I believe upon all accounts the sooner the better but my friend is not quite of the same mind and as he has a carriage preparing for him and various other things to procure, I think it will be three weeks before he is fairly off.

Charlotte intended setting off on 21 July 1817; 'the idea of all the fuss that must infallibly take place, and which is indeed already commencing, gives me the horrors' as Eleanora put it to Eliza. 'Perhaps I may like it well enough when I am once at Rome, but being two years away from England is a perfect Exile.'[71] According to her mother, they were 'awaiting the little rebel John and scarcely knowing whether he will be caught or not'. As Charlotte told her eldest daughter on 2 July: 'It is really a most mad and disgraceful Boy—only one hopes Age may improve Him.' Seventeen-year-old John's escapades of the previous winter were hinted at by Beaujolois.[72] She mentioned that she had already told the story of John in 'her red book' which 'throws a shade over us and all our countrymen ... quite sufficient to give the English a bad character'.[73] Nothing else had seemingly been talked of during the previous winter and Beaujolois claimed that every person she met thereafter on the Continent asked 'et qu'est donc devenu votre pauvre frère?' to which was added some excuse and condolence. De Saussure quizzed her when visiting in Lausanne, letting out 'fresh accounts of his cunning and deceit'. She worried that the whole affair might throw 'a veil in the eyes of the world over every future merit that John may have'. Eliza received another titbit from Bessie Mure that Charlotte would like to have secured 'an elligible [*sic*] situation for Him ... several have already failed which were the most desirable'. Gratuitously she hoped that Eliza's first son, Penrose (then less than 1 year old) 'will not be such a troublesome concern as this Brother of yours'. John finally made his appearance in London on Saturday 12 July, having first sent his uncle, the Duke of Argyll, 'as his Ambassador to acquaint Mama with his arrival, and his Grace desired particularly not to lecture John too much, as it might have the worst possible effects upon him saying that he thought gentle means would prove more effectual', as Eleanora reported to her elder sister.[74] She then explained that John 'seems sorry to have contracted the debt he did and to have displeased Mama', but he also thought that a 'prodigious blackguard' of a friend was wrong to have had him arrested'. John explained to his mother that he thought he had done 'nothing dishonourable in getting into debt which he meant to pay off little by little', and since his mother only gave him half a crown a week 'and never sent him any present of money' he could hardly be expected to stay out of debt. Eleanora had tried to make him understand the stain on his character, but admitted to Eliza: 'You know he is very warm hearted and affectionate and it is impossible from his agreeable manners not to be kind to him and fond of him.' A clergyman near St Neots with several other boys of the same age (16 or 17) had been engaged to keep him for six months, after which he 'seems strongly inclined to go into the army', in which the duke had advised his mother to secure for him a commission. He had arrived back, as tall as, 'but much better made' than Walter, and 'though God knows he came dressed very much like a half starved apprentice looked gentlemanly. He literally had not a stick with him, but what he had on his back the rest he had sold at different times for actual food.' Before leaving, however, they had already received several melancholy letters from John, 'safe at St Neots', on receipt of which Beaujolois had written to him 'begging him to keep up his spirits'.

A further problem Charlotte had to solve was that of her maid 'poor Fanny' who was being left behind. She did not want to go to Lady Augusta 'because she has no home of her own and ... she is sure that she would be miserable there'. So Eliza was prevailed upon to have her at Altyre where, for £50 a year and her keep, she could be relied upon to help with 'any sitting still business she is up to', in Charlotte's words. Before they finally left London on 25 July 1817 the travel plans had changed, as Charlotte explained to Eliza on the eve of departure.[75] They were to go by land instead of sea:

> For I find that a vessel coming to Marseilles was a very doubtful affair and then comes the Equinox and then comes my sea fears. So after all we go to old Lausanne—and through dearest Milan—over the grand and melancholy Simplon—then Bologna etc. etc. Who will be delighted—the wandering Romantic Mama—yes—will be.

She was to pay 140 guineas to travel from Lausanne to Florence, 'and further than Florence I do not think I can go this year unless I take a little flight with my Son and Eleanor and leave the heavy baggage [the rest of the family] settled at Florence. This I think possible.' But she confessed, like many prospective travellers, that at that moment she was 'very melancholy—melancholy for a thousand reasons past, present and to come'.

> It is a different thing to leave ones Country for a short time for mere pleasure with a power of Money to command going or coming. But to go from a necessity from painful reasons—from a sort of restlessness of never having been happy—this is not Happiness—or pleasure.

A few weeks earlier she had expressed similar sentiments when telling Eliza of their forthcoming travel plans, at the same time apologising for not writing more often because her frequent 'despondency of Spirits of which I am not the mistress would only breathe a desultory sadness over my letters'. She continued: 'There are past Glooms which never wholly pass but which colour Life with their murkiness—and tint the whole of existence with a dark and Cheerless hue.' However, she had emphasised her 'love for the Continent ... when I am ruminating in My Carriage going slowly on and allowing my Imagination to fly—then I live in a World of my own, the only world I delight in'. Even this she had tempered with the uneasy thought that, when reunited at Lausanne/Bethusy with former acquaintances and friends, as well as Walter and Mr Bury, 'one always regrets the past if it is merely because it is past. Such strange Beings we are.'

Fourteen-year-old Beaujolois had added a note to her mother's letter, in which she asked her oldest sister to 'entreat of mamma' to allow her to 'keep upon a sheet of paper an accu^t^ Journal written every night of what we do and send it to you every fortnight as a letter'. She felt like crying every time she saw Eleanora writing and receiving letters from and to Eliza, while she was not allowed to do so by her mother. 'After all I am old enough to be trusted in what I write.' There had apparently been another 'fatal' episode of letters unbeknown to Charlotte, and Beaujolois had had to 'swear to desist'. She charged Eliza with having hidden her 'affair snug enough from us but I am determined none of my other sisters shall do so' suggesting she knew what Eleanor was up to, although the latter denied it. 'Oh, dearest Eliza, how happy I am to go abroad and how I hope you will come. This is a selfish wish but you will forgive it. Do pray.' In the end, not only was Beaujolois apparently allowed to go ahead with the journal, but she also then composed long and detailed letters to Eliza about the journey and their sojourn in Florence.[76] Eliza was again pregnant, and about to spend two winters in Naples for her health (although after a dozen further children she lived until she was 45). Eleanora was to have more 'lovers' and beaux, before Lord Uxbridge's father, by then Marquis of Anglesey, relented to allow them to marry in 1819. While both of these girls' marriages were probably deemed more suitable by the outside world than had Charlotte's for love, the marriage possibilities for the remaining girls as the years passed were probably at least as interesting amongst the English on the continent as at Sydenham. And, according to Mlle de la Chaux, she could not 'bring them to give one regret to Westwood or fear of being killed by the heat of Italy'.[77]

11

Florentine Intrigue

The neatly written journal which Beaujolois was delighted to start was found on the floor of a secondhand bookshop in Charing Cross Road in London in the middle of the following century. Sir Gavin Rylands de Beer, an eminent scientist, was intrigued not only by the manuscript journal itself, but also the maturity with which it was composed by what turned out to be a 14-year-old. He arranged for a 'portion of it' to be published in 1951,[1] and in his introduction drew up a 'dramatis personae' which included many of the names of people met in the foregoing chapters of this book. He chose to finish the transcription at Easter Sunday of 1818, although, after an understandable lapse, the journal apparently continued for some time. The survival or whereabouts of this later part is not known.

Friday 25 July 1817 was the start of what 14-year-old Beaujolois refers to as 'being on the wing', her 'third' single journey through Europe. It is hard to imagine the bustle that had to be orchestrated by Mlle de la Chaux, the butler, Annie MacLeod and the maid, Mary, to organise Charlotte and her five girls to set off for a lengthy continental residence of perhaps a couple of years. Westwood had been readied for letting, and it was from 77 Gloucester Place that the party left in a carriage and a berline at 2 p.m. instead of the planned 7 a.m.[2] They thus only reached Sittingbourne by about eleven o'clock at night.

> And although mamma's first intention had been to go as far as Canterberry, we were all glad to stop at Sittingbourne for the night. The first day's journey is always the most fatiguing. At least so I think as afterwards one gets used to rumbling of the carriage and all the other agrements of travelling.

At 'Canterberry' they were to have visited the cathedral but one coach went on to Dover with Adelaide and Emma, Annie MacLeod, a Mlle Perillow and Miss de la Chaux who was apparently travelling with them after all. Charlotte's carriage, with herself, Eleanor and Julia in the inside and Beaujolois and Mary in the dicky at the rear went on a long detour to visit a M[rs] Sandys at Upper Hardes. During the whole journey, in typical July weather, it poured incessantly, a high wind making it impossible to shelter under an umbrella, while the carriage nearly shook to pieces on the very bad side road. The rain continued the whole afternoon 'most provokingly and we could not walk at all to enjoy the beauties of the place'. After dinner they set off again and reached Dover at about ten o'clock, by which time the rain had just ceased; Beaujolois was glad 'to have the pretence of its being late not to sail'. The captain with whom they had crossed the Channel both times before in 1814 and 1815, Captain Frasier, had his ship laid up so a Captain Meire was engaged by Charlotte for the following morning.

In Dover Charlotte was also penning her thoughts on leaving Britain (deliberately Britain, not just England) and its liberty. Passing through the 'happy landscape of English scenery, its plenty, its peace, awoke the note of poesy, which has never yet been quite silenced in my heart ... It is possible to write poesy with a broken heart.' Six nine-line stanzas elaborated her own restlessness which she hoped would once again be alleviated by 'change of place'.[3] On Sunday 27 July the two carriages, Charlotte, 18-year-old Eleonora, Beaujolois 14, Adelaide 13, Emma 11 and Julia 10, their governess Mlle de la Chaux, Mlle Perrilow, Annie MacLeod, maid Mary, the butler and man servant, all embarked on the *King George*. They were on board by eight o'clock just in time to catch the tide on the turn.[4] The Custom house officers behaved 'very civilly to us and nothing was touched'. Beaujolois noted the beautiful morning, the sun shining and a fair breeze, continuing:

> Having resolved to put a bold face upon the matter and to drive away sickness accordingly I placed myself in the carriage on deck and tried to write. Miss de la Chaux soon joined me and laid groaning for some time. I was quickly obliged to put away all writing implements and mamma likewise. The sea grew higher and higher the farther we got. And the wind more strong. You may judge of the happy effects of these delights on Squeamish travellers. The ship was pitching the whole time and one side of it within a foot of the sea. We had several cold baths during the journey as the waves poured all over the Deck. Some of the company were wet to the skin. We had never seen the sea so high: the sailors even owned it was pretty freshish.

After three hours of 'this happiness (which mamma declared she likes)' they came safe into port, and as the tide was up it was easy to land on the quay. Mlle de la Chaux was still groggy and was at first unable to find the collective 'passport' for the Custom house officer. Beaujolois was aware that 'the rogue had seen it but sat quietly waiting without saying so'. Fortunately the document turned up, and since MacLeod had percipiently removed from the trunks certain petticoats which might not have been approved of, and made all the women and girls wear one, all was well. Duty had to be paid on all the packed books, while Charlotte had to deposit about one-third of the estimated value of the two carriages, two-thirds to be refunded on return through Calais.

Waiting on the pier for the bedraggled arrivées were two officers of the 7th Queen's Own Light Dragoons. Eighteen-year-old Lord Uxbridge and his friend, George Molyneux, were at the time quartered near St Omer some 25 miles south-east of Calais, and walked with the party to their hotel. They forswore the best hotel, Quillac's, of which they'd last had a poor experience, and stayed instead at Meurices Hotel. The Campbell female party of seven sat down to dine *table d'hôte* at one o'clock with a 'great variety of dishes'. The two officers 'came in and out all day', and finally went off to the theatre with Charlotte and Eleanora. Then the family set off the next day, Monday 28 July, which was windy and cold, particularly for those sitting on the outside of the carriages, and after delays for horses at Montreuil, they slept at Bernet. Reaching Amiens by four o'clock the following afternoon in time for dinner, they visited the cathedral before going on to spend the night at Breteuil. After dining next day at Chantilly and passing Paris on the outskirts only, they stayed at Mangeron where 'we have already been twice'. On the last day of the month they went on without stopping to Sens ('Le Grand Cerf') via 'Ancy le Franc' and Besançon. They reached the border town of Pontarlier and were delayed at Jougne in the Jura mountains, then stopped at Vallorbe, arriving eventually in Lausanne on 6 August, after twelve days on the road. There they stayed for five days in the Hôtel du Lion before moving into the less expensive 'Campagne Ribe', near Ouchy on Lake Geneva. Bathing in the lake and socialising with various other English visitors such as the Earl and Countess of Sandwich, they were joined by Walter and his tutor, 'the long-nosed companion *de voyage*' Rev. Edward J. Bury, whom Beaujolois reckoned felt 'the charm of what he sees more than Walter'.[5]

Charlotte and Eleanora renewed acquaintances in Geneva during the last week of August, then, by the afternoon of 2 September the party was on its way again. Stopping in Vevey, passing Château de Chillon and 'baiting' at Aigle, they arrived in Bex, then next day drove through St Maurice, stayed with the same innkeeper at Martigny as they had done in 1815, and later slept in Sion at the 'Lion d'Or'. On 4 September they dined at Tourtemagne and slept in the new large 'Hôtel d'Angleterre' at Brig. Next day they were called at three in the morning and were on the way by five, to mount the Simplon with 'five horses to the berline and four to the carriage'. The ascent took eight hours, parts of which they chose, or had, to walk. The southern descent was easier—a good road, thanks to 'the great Napoleon', and a bribe to customs' officers at the foot, at Yselle, to save all their luggage being searched, before sleeping at Domodossola. On they rumbled along the shores of Lake Maggiore which Beaujolois 'viewed again with the greatest pleasure'[6], past the Isola Bella. When there was no bridge, carriages and people had to be ferried across rivers. After having their document stamped, they tried to sleep in a flea-ridden inn at Sesto Calendo. Continuing down the Lombardy Plain they endured an eleven-hour journey before reaching Milan on Sunday 7 September, where they stayed at the 'Albergo d'Italia' on the Corsa della Palla. On their way into Milan, they passed the Piazza Borromeo where Charlotte had been with the Princess of Wales in 1815, and also saw Bonaparte's unfinished triumphal arch 'which was to have terminated the beautiful road he has made to enter Milan'. Beaujolois was impressed by the 'well dressed women and ... their beautifully arranged hair' especially as the next day, Monday 8 September, was a feast day with everyone parading in their 'gala dresses' on the Corso on the way to and from church. They revisited the Duomo and once again admired the aerial spires and finely wrought statues. Beaujolois deemed the organ and choristers much 'like an opera and scarcely appropriate to a Cathedral but as musick it was fine', the whole service lasting two and a half hours. After dining, they went to the Palazzo Brera ('with statues not proper for us to see') and on to the overwhelming Ambrosian Library, returning 'dead tired' to the albergo.

In the carriage on the following day Beaujolois averred 'Milan is a delightful town and I should very well enjoy living here for some weeks', but they were already on the wing. She described how they were always up between three and four, would breakfast then stop for several hours at about eleven, dine, sightsee or rest, then leave again at two or three o'clock. They tried to be at an inn no later than six o'clock and certainly before dark. After visiting Lodi they slept at Casello about 9 miles from Piacenza, with guards at their doors. It was the turn of the cathedral at Piacenza to be admired the next day after which they slept at Borgo St Donnino. The Princess of Wales was then also travelling in Lombardy, but they did not meet. Parma was the next stop—at each of the duchies of Milan, Piacenza and Parma, the 'passport' had to be stamped, luggage being cursorily searched after paying a bribe—and the night was spent at a very full inn in Reggio. They lumbered on for another whole day through the Lombardy plain before continuing their ladies' grand tour in Bologna, much admiring the Virgin Mary church and convent, porticos, the wide arcades, St Pretronius church with its Cassini meridian, and the notable bronze statue of Neptune by John de Bologne in the nearby main piazza.

It took six hours to ascend the Apennines on Saturday 13 September, stopping at Loyano to dine and sleeping at Covilayo, before reaching Florence on Sunday 14 September, having left London on 25 July. For a week it was a treat to stay in the renowned Schneiderf's Hotel by the Ponte della Trinita over the Arno. As Beaujolois noted, 'it is considered the best in Florence and certainly is very good but the expence is enormous. However all the world come here and half by prejudice and half by advice and the recommendations of others, so we do so too.' She then went on to point out that a suite of very good apartments comprising five rooms was charged 32 franks a day per head (a frank was then about 18 British pence), and 16 paoli for dinner (about 3 British florins). Henry Matthews, a Fellow of King's College, Cambridge, corroborated Beaujolois's comments, deeming Schneiderf's 'a magnificent establishment', claiming that dinner alone would cost more than the whole daily expenditure.[7] Beaujolois' verdict confirmed that Schneiderfs was 'ruinous though excellent as an Inn'.

Before they had left London, on 16 June Charlotte had the sad task of informing the author, poet, dramatist, critic and fervent patriot, Ugo Foscolo, of the death of his mother.[8] The girls all wrote to him from Calais, in English or French.[9] Beforehand he had advised his 'Donna Gentile', Signora Quirina Ocenni Maggiotti, that 'Milady Carlotta Campbell' was going to Florence for reasons of economy, with all her family consisting of 'a large number of girls'.[10] Since Charlotte would have to take a house and incur considerable expenditure, particularly at first, he beseeched the signora 'by the entrails of our love to do your utmost to see that Milady does not fall into the hands of some Florentine shark who preys upon foreigners and especially upon every poor English person'. Affirming that Charlotte was 'coming to the Continent because she is unable to afford the enormously high cost of living here; indeed it is so high that it would appall [*sic*] you', he asked her to guide on how to take a house, a box at the opera, hire a carriage and engage a cook, so that Charlotte did not spend more than 'what the people of the country would pay'.

Whether or not Signora Maggiotti or Charlotte followed Foscolo's advice and behest, Beaujolois described the week as being 'dedicated' to looking for a suitable house. After seeing many 'in what is considered the fashionable situation', Charlotte finally settled on the Casa Torregiana verso della Porta Romana, within easy reach of the Bobolo Gardens and the Pitti Palace. Though 'rather out of the way … dirty and ill-furnished,' it had the advantages of being large and commodious, was situated in the middle of a 'large and really beautiful' garden and the rent was affordable at about £200 a year. The Berries had just arrived from Genoa and were renting 'a fine house in the Piazza Santa Maria Novella'; with them they shared a box at the opera three times a week for three months at 14 guineas. A male cook could be hired every day for 16 franks to cater for the whole family—'nothing could be cheaper', while the 'lacquaid de place' was an extra 4 paoli a day. So 'living moderately and with some care the expence is less here than in England considering all the extra luxuries which may be had at a very low rate'.

Foscolo's report of Charlotte's deciding to live on the Continent for reasons of economy was well borne out in various of Beaujolois' comments. More telling was Beaujolois' view at the time that, for her, unlike Eleanora perhaps, living on the Continent was infinitely preferable to Sydenham in Kent. 'I prefer remaining abroad as here is more chance of variety and entertainment than there would be in living at Sydenham or indeed in any part of England.' But it is worth recalling that Charlotte had also wintered abroad, particularly in the 1780s. Charlotte intended to remain away for two years, and in the first instance took a year-long lease of the house in Florence in September 1817. But it was to prove longer than that before she was perhaps to reclaim the coach deposit at Calais. More than eight years on from her first husband's death, her father-in-law had died in October 1816; she was now dependent on her 19-year-old son and his agents for her yearly income of £750, sometimes augmented to £1,000, based on her dowry, a contribution of over £600 from her brother, the Duke of Argyll, and £1,000 for the five girls. She no longer had the salary and expenses from the princess of Wales, erratic though it had sometimes been, nor was their any further contribution after her uncle Frederick died.

The Campbell daughters were growing up under the tutelage of their Swiss governess and, like their mother, were to become proficient in speaking and writing in several languages, reading widely amongst themselves and with others, and often taking part in various family musical and dramatic activities. Beaujolois made frequent reference to sketching and its difficulties, including an interesting altercation with Mlle de la Chaux over art criticism. She explored this further with her mother, who agreed with her argument that 'for the gratification of the eye any foreign town was certainly far superior to the view outside the window at Gloucester Place'.[11] She also mentioned that her mother had then 'talked and conversed with me most kindly and amiably, chiefly about the continent'. Eleanora as 'Miss Campbell', accompanied her mother socially and with the Berries was presented to the Duke of Tuscany in the Palazzo Pitti on Sunday 28 September, prior to the celebrations given in honour of the marriage of his 16-year-old daughter. Only the Campbells and the Berries were given the honour of being spoken to by the grand duke, according to Mary Berry.[12] Two days later Charlotte and Eleanora were invited to the marriage itself and were ensconced in the Duomo 'in full dress'.[13] The four other girls went to spectate with Mlle de la Chaux and witnessed the whole event, remarking that the Italian ladies were 'particularly well dressed with great profusion of jewels and very good taste. They disgrace the English', apart from Charlotte and Lady Octavia Law.[14] That same evening Charlotte went to the Court held in the Appartamenti of the Pitti Palazzo, followed by a masked ball; another grand ball was to take place later in the week.

More prosaically, Charlotte normally breakfasted at nine o'clock, went out in her carriage half an hour later, sometimes taking some of the girls with her, dined at three, had a rest, then either went out to the Cascine, the public drive, to the Miss Berries, to the Opera or for a wide miscellany of other social occasions and activities among the English 'colony'. Henry Matthews declared:

> The English abound so much in Florence, that a traveller has little occasion for any other language ... English shops abound with all sorts of knick-knacks—from Reading sauce to Woodstock gloves; and the last new novels stare you in the face at the libraries.[15]

Meanwhile the girls were up at six o'clock, walked till breakfast on the shady Cascine along the Arno, or in the nearby Boboli Gardens. Their breakfast was at eight, and they dined at one and five. Overwhelmed, and often fatigued by paintings and sculptures in the Uffizi or the Academia, Beaujolois was also taken on outings with the Berries, but she and her younger sisters missed out on many of the grander events. Charlotte, however, sometimes took them out walking from the Porta Romana of an evening, and she also frequently entertained in the Casa Torregiana, names reappearing that included the Fabrinis, Tonellis, Fremantles and the Laws. Despite her professed ideas and hopes of economy, in early November 1817 Charlotte held a 'crowded party for the whole world of Marquisses Princes Princesses Marchionesses etc etc', including Prince Borghese and his mistress, the Duchess of Lanti (his princess, modelled naked by Canova, meanwhile being at the Baths of Lucca). England was mourning the death on 6 November of Princess Charlotte; however, on Saturday 14 November a ball was given by Charlotte for Walter, who had come of age on 9 April. This 'everybody thought was splendid ... it began near ten, and from that moment till three I never stopped dancing' as Beaujolois was to record—she had enjoyed herself 'exceedingly', but was stiff and sore the next day.[16] The Gordon-Cummings arrived in Florence at the end of November with their son, Penrose, and after spending three weeks, moved on to winter in Naples for Eliza's health.

With all of this social activity it is also questionable how much further Charlotte's next novel was able to progress. Beaujolois had mentioned her working on it as they were admiring the scenery near Besançon, and Charlotte did incorporate the scenery of the 1815 and 1817 journeys and that of Scotland, almost step by step. But it was to be another five years before Blackwood published *Conduct is Fate*. Her motive for writing this novel may even have been as much financial as literary, despite the economies of leaving London for the continent. If, like most diarists, it was often written up in arrears, more especially while travelling, Beaujolois had caught up with her journal in Lausanne/Ouchy: 'Another long interruption in my journal. But alas I have so often had to regret the same thing that my only resource now is to do better in future.' Later, in Florence, Beaujolois confided to her journal that she was often alone by the fireside, being too young to accompany her mother and elder sister socially. Beaujolois' published journal, however, stops abruptly before detailing the momentous event that now shook the household, and eventually friends and others, to the core.

Had he lived for another seven years, Charlotte's husband, Jack Campbell of Shawfield, would have succeeded to his father's estates of Woodhall in Lanarkshire and the island of Islay when his father died on 19 October 1816. How differently might Charlotte's life have turned out. Instead, it was Charlotte's elder surviving son, 18-year-old Walter Frederick, who succeeded, his father having died aged about 37 in 1809. Grandfather Walter Campbell had himself inherited unexpectedly in 1777 when his elder brother, Daniel, died unmarried, aged about 40. The entail of the estate had at that time been rearranged and, although Walter then acquired other estates through his second marriage to Mary Nisbet of Dirleton; by 1816 the Campbell of Shawfield estate comprised Woodhall in Lanarkshire and the greater part of the island of Islay. Walter had bought the estate of Sunderland in Islay for his second son, Walter, while the Skipness estate in Argyll had been given to the next son, Robert, and Ardpatrick acquired for Colin.

After leaving Eton the 18-year-old Walter Frederick came into a substantial rental income from the Islay and Woodhall estates. However, not only were the encumbrances on the estates still very draining, but his grandfather, Walter Campbell, had not completed his arrangements on the entail. Amongst others, creditors of his father, Jack Campbell, were still clamouring for payment. An unexpected rescuer for about half of the latter debts of over £7,700 had appeared, Stuart Moncrieff Thriepland of

Middleton in Linlithgowshire. After a career in the East India Company, on 2 July 1817 at the age of 46, he had married 'Aunt Betsy', Elizabeth Campbell of Ardpatrick. A letter to his new uncle-in-law from Walter Frederick thanked him for a loan, and arrangements were put in place to access the money in thirds payable on 1 August 1817, 1818 and 1819. But no provisions appear to have been made for repayment. Thriepland died in 1838, and his nephew, heir and executor, was still trying in the 1850s to recover the moneys with some interest from trustees set up after Walter Frederick's bankruptcy.

In 1817 the Campbell guardians had appointed a young man some eight years Walter Frederick's senior, Edward John Bury, as tutor or bearleader and travelling companion for him. Bury had graduated from University College, Oxford, and after being ordained at Newton St Looe in the diocese of Wells, had become rector of Litchfield in Hampshire in 1814, although it was perhaps rather titular and as customary he probably spent little time there. Beaujolois considered that the 27-year-old Rev. Bury was probably more aesthetically interested in, and enjoyed their travel more than, her brother.[17] When the two came from Bologna to Florence in November 1817, they accompanied Charlotte to the Boboli gardens one day and were joined by Agnes Berry and Beaujolois, but 'there was no drawing ... as Miss Berry was afraid of Bury' who was a talented amateur artist, his paintings subsequently being described as 'in the style of Turner ... some of them comparing most favourably with those of the great master'.[18] Even as a student, Bury had called on Thomas Lawrence, with an introduction from a Mr Jennings of Bath.[19] According to Lawrence, his mind was then already 'much devoted to painting as an amusement, and He said, He makes it a principal study, and, after taking his degree at Oxford, he shall apply still more closely'. Bury had spent two summer months drawing landscape studies in Wales at Dolgelly in Caernarvon. He had also mentioned to Lawrence 'a process for making studies which he had hit upon', and had also expressed 'a wish that there should be a College established at the Nation's expence for the instruction and support of young men whose talents should appear to promise their being able artists'. By the time he was accompanying young Walter Campbell, Mr Bury had visited the Princess Borghese, Napoleon's sister, Pauline Bonaparte, and had even, much to the displeasure and wrath of Mlle de la Chaux, viewed Canova's renowned, if infamous, statue of the princess as a nude Venus (1808), which her husband had normally kept out of sight in the Villa Borghese in Rome.[20] Charlotte was perhaps writing to keep in touch with Walter and his tutor on their travels; one later author went as far as suggesting that 'without a shadow of doubt', several of her letters from about this time were specifically written to Edward Bury.[21]

Mr Bury was to incur Mlle de la Chaux's further displeasure. Her sister died on 5 December 1817 (Beaujolois and her sisters had to pay respects to the corpse) and the protestant funeral and burial were held at Leghorn, where Charlotte 'apparently paid more attention to Mr Bury than to her', as Beaujolois wryly noted.[22] She added that Mlle de la Chaux frequently complained of this, which made Beaujolois remark to her sister, Eliza, that with hindsight she began to 'observe what was going on'.[23] 'Mr Bury was in love with mamma or rather mamma sought to make him so by her endearing conduct to him', she confided to her eldest sister 'even before I imagined things were as far advanced as I afterwards found them to be'. Charlotte apparently soon 'confessed the whole' to Eleanora, who in turn told Walter, to whom Charlotte 'did not venture to speak about the affair foreseeing what would naturally ensue'. Walter and Bury had planned to set out for Rome on 11 February and Charlotte wished 'to heaven' that she could have accompanied them, 'but indeed my Duty, my fear of being an expense to Walter, an expense unnecessary, which his Guardians might condemn as such, prevented the possibility of what would have been to me in every way—happiness'. Instead, Edward Bury abruptly resigned his tutorship—as Charlotte disingenuously put it to Eliza: 'Some Domestic circumstance obliged him to do thus'. Charlotte urged Walter's guardians to find a replacement tutor as soon as possible, adding to Eliza, more percipiently than she could possibly have predicted for the long term, that what she dreaded for Walter 'if left entirely to his own devices, is his becoming the prey of artful designing Men, or of poor beggarly toad Eaters who will flatter his passions to live upon his purse'.

A furious Walter agonised for ten days before approaching his mother and imploring her at least not to marry Bury without more time for reflection. Even the 19-year-old's tears and 'violent hysterics' did not, however, deflect her; so Walter left the Casa Torregiana, vowing never to enter it again, never again to see Bury, removing his carriage and belongings to the residence of the English minister, Lord Burghersh. It was little wonder that Charlotte was not in spirits to enjoy the pre-Lenten festivities at the beginning of February. 'The Carnaval [*sic*] here disappointed me', she told Eliza.

> The Masks were few and stupid, and the dresses not the least magnificent. What they call the religiones are the Theatres, and late Masquerades—Where the English find amusement in abusing and scandalising their own Countrymen—and treating with contempt the people of every other nation.

She told of the balls and parties given by the continentals, of whom she liked Madame Appary best: 'she has quelque chose de la séduction d'un homme'. This was all breathlessly relayed to Eliza in Naples on 5 February in the midst of a desperate letter, the first part of which has already been divulged.[24] Now she was trying to justify her chosen direction. She had felt 'constantly oppressed by difficulties of Money—in my Married Life, wretched—in my widowhood suffering all but Penury'. Her faithful servant, MacLeod, was 'the only stay and support I have got to help with all your younger sisters ... their cloathes ... household affairs etc.' While all this was going on, and to the delight of Florentine gossip, Edward Bury left Florence on 8 February to stay in Pisa for a month. In the end, Walter set off on 12 February for Rome and Naples, with 'Strickland a good natured fatty', and 'still at war' with his mother, as Beaujolois put it. His mother had intended delaying her marriage until Eleanora's 'was accomplished lest hers should injure Eleanor's',[25] but now it was fixed for the following month. Walter instructed his agents in Edinburgh to cut off Charlotte's allowance on the day of the proposed marriage, which Beaujolois felt 'ashamed to say that this alone has affected her'.

While she perhaps underestimated the extent of the furore that her second marriage would create, Charlotte had filled twelve pages in six folded sheets in, for her, unusually small, neat and tidy handwriting in her letter to Eliza: perhaps she had made so many changes and scorings out that this is a fair copy.[26] Addressing Eliza as much as a friend as a daughter, the first part of her mother's letter made very distressing reading, as Charlotte admitted to the realised folly of her first romantic marriage twenty years before. When what she termed the storm ceased with Jack Campbell's death in 1809, and recognising that children alone would not give her the happiness she aspired to, after a year, and thinking that 'fate owed me a white Hour before I died', she had hoped to attach 'Myself to Another Husband—hitherto I have been disappointed but now comes the event for which I have tried thus to prepare you'. She continued: 'I think I have found a Person calculated in every way to make <u>my individual</u> happiness—but one, whom in every possible worldly light—it is imprudent and almost ridiculous to have chosen. But <u>I have chosen Dearest</u> Eliza <u>He will be my Husband</u>.' She admitted that she was to marry a man her inferior in 'rank and circumstances', a man almost young enough to be her son, a man 'whose very situation in my Family will add an additional Stigma in the Worlds Eye to his Character as well as my own', but she repeated: 'I shall marry Mr. Bury.' She foresaw that the world would say:

> Well! Is it come to this Lady Charlotte Campbell married to a young Parson Bury, her son's Tutor—a Grand Mother—a woman of her rank—of her age—of her character thus to have let herself down—thus to have forgotten what she owes herself and her Children.

But she asked her daughter to look at the action philosophically and morally, optimistically predicting that the wonder and abusive gossip would shortly disappear, 'particularly if my children excuse and protect me', while avowing that the consequent happiness will, 'I firmly believe—be to me great and lasting'. She was realistic enough to aver that 'the passion of Love always subsides sooner or later—at my time of Life I cannot expect it to last long'. But she pointed out instead 'the sweets of grateful affection' and of 'a similarity in tastes and pursuits (the greatest and most lasting of all happiness's)', betokening Mr Bury's 'high consideration for my Intellectual endowments and a pride in me as a Being of no common order' which she firmly believed would 'protract the Hour as late as it can be protracted—and gild the latter part of my days with sunshine—I shall not die—and feel that I have never lived—once at least I shall taste of happiness'.

Her long letter then went on to foretell, if not forestall, all the gossip that would come to the ears of Eliza and the others—of how she was supposed to have seduced Mr Bury and that she had 'merely a sensual passion for Him—that He has none of any kind in return', and so on. She realised that he could not be marrying her for avarice, for 'thank God I have no money to give Him'. She emphasised that none of such allegations was true:

> Mr. Burys talents—his Manner—his Mind pleased and attracted me. His situation gave me his constant company. I yielded to the attraction with all the ignorance of an inexperienced person—although an old one—and with the more security, because I never dreamt so young a man could feel a passion for me. And from his no rank—his being my Son's tutor—his being Melancholy—and serious—Love between us appear'd to myself as to all the World out of the question.

She declared to Eliza that they themselves were unaware of the truth ('it was made known to us by the scandal of Florence') saying that she 'was more surprised than the World when I found that we loved each other'. She pointed out that she had never intended to have married Bury so quickly, wanting time to 'give a decent sanction at least to the deed', with the additional dread of its being detrimental to Eleanora's marriage, but had been driven to it 'by the publicity which is now attached to the business'. She had not felt able to agree to Walter's threat that if she did not swear that her marriage would be put off for a year, he would never see her again. She then described her son leaving in a violent rage for Rome and Naples, all Florence knowing why, and Mamie de la Chaux being 'furious'. In defence of her future she wrote that 'Mr. Bury has behaved throughout like an Angel'. He had offered to withdraw her promise to marry him but 'I could not repent—I feel that my own happiness depends on the fulfilment of that promise—and if I did not, I were a wretch again … I do not for an instant wish it—on the contrary I am irrevocably determined'. Sadly for all concerned, Mamie de la Chaux became a casualty of the whole affair, and determined to leave the family by the wedding day. She had been governess to all of Charlotte's children, and had been with the Argyll family for over twenty years.[27]

Mlle de la Chaux's cross-written letter to Eliza on 12 February 1818 was unstinting:

> From what has passed between B[ury] and I my staying is quite out of the question—he knows what I think of him, and consequently must hate the sight of me. But previous to this, my resolution had been made. I told Lady C I could not bear to see her in such a situation and her children crushed by it … I feel a sincere pity for her future sufferings for I cannot expect that such a man can make her happy.[28]

She went on to explain that Charlotte had told her:

> 6 or 7 weeks ago, that she thought he was ill tempered and very tyrannical, full of prejudice, and that he held almost every body cheap, that his manners were so unpopular that his presence was enough to prevent people from coming where he was etc. However he persevered in his constant attentions and assiduities and it was not in vain unfortunately. I wrote to tell him I had seen it all and what I and every well thinking person would think of his conduct etc.

While a first letter had been, in her terms presumably, 'very moderate' she had subsequently been less scrupulous in letting him know what she felt. A further effusion to Eliza in a mixture of French and English ten days later went even further: 'Il est vrai que je suis coupable encore d'avoir très mauvaise opinion de Mr. B dont les moeurs, comme Ministre surtout, sont tachées d'un crime, qu'il ne nie pas lui même, et qui est bien connu de plusieurs personnes.'[29] Backed by many inferences, she vowed she could never serve in a household of which he was the master, in whom she had no confidence either as a husband or stepfather.

Eliza's response to her mother appears to have been somewhat more conciliatory, as her mother's letter of 24 February puts it, at the same time asking Eliza not to be influenced by Walter's opposition: 'The way in which you have taken my communication does equal credit to your Head and heart dearest Eliza.' She admitted that it was impossible that Eliza should 'like my Marriage' but hoped that when they met her daughter would see her happiness, 'the only thing which can ultimately reconcile you to it'. She also expressed the hope that Eliza had reasoned that her mother 'is not happy—has never been happy—if she is so now, Let us, her Children forgive what may hurt our Pride in the connection she has formed and since there is neither imorality [*sic*] or vice in her conduct let us support her before the whole World'. Charlotte went further, apparently ignoring Eliza's imminent confinement, imploring that it would be of 'unspeakable Comfort' to have Eliza and Sir William present at her marriage. She announced her intention of travelling immediately to Naples, setting out on 10 March without stopping a day in Rome, asking Eliza to tell her by return of post whether she 'would receive her with open Arms and if her husband, Sir William, will'. Whether or not the proposed journey took place, the Gordon-Cummings had other things on their minds for Eliza's second child, a daughter, was born in Naples on 5 March. In the same letter Charlotte had once again tried to exonerate Bury from the blame of the gossips in the whole affair: 'I am more than anxious to do justice to Mr Bury's conduct towards Myself ... as to doubting his having a real passion for me—you will not when you see and know Him better.' She described his attributes as:

> Grave and melancholy—his mind is not young—his tastes and pursuits are exactly what suit mine. If I had drawn a character, that could be companionable to me it is his own—Romantic—highly cultivated—full of Talent. It is impossible not to feel proud of having attach'd such a Mind.

Charlotte was also well aware of the faults that obscured his finer qualities: shyness, fear of not pleasing, a 'kind of gloom of Soul', but averred that this dissipated on getting to know him and 'unlocking the key'. She ended with the somewhat staccato thought that 'you know his Love of Penrose [the Gordon-Cumming heir and her first grandchild] must win your heart—was it that it was My grandchild—how comical!!!'

In her monumental volumes on Italy, Sydney, Lady Morgan described the society at the British Embassy in Florence as 'pre-eminently brilliant and numerous; and in the splendid salons of Lord and Lady Burghersh, British hospitality found its best representation'. Lord Burghersh was the son of Charlotte's friend, Lady Westmorland, while his wife, Priscilla was a niece of the Duke of Wellington. In their palazzo 'Tory met Whig in amicable discussion on the merits of Niobe' and other Greek myths, while French Ultras and Jacobins, Romanticists and Classicists 'affected to forget their feuds, all participating in dinners, fine food, good music and quadrilles'.[30] It was in the chapel of this ambassador's palazzo in Florence on Easter Monday, 23 March 1818 that Admiral Sir Thomas Fremantle gave Charlotte away. His wife Elizabeth was Eugenie's sister, and in his present role as Commander-in-Chief of the Mediterranean, they were renting a magnificent palazzo for a yearly sum of £150. Supporting the 43-year-old grandmother when she married 27-year-old Edward John Bury, were her longstanding and loyal friends, the Misses Mary and Agnes Berry who recorded that 'Nine o'clock this morning was the hour fixed for the celebration of Lady Charlotte Campbell's marriage. We had been friends for thirty years, and we offered to be present ... Lord John Russell was invited.'[31] The chargé d'affaires was one G. Dawkins, and the chaplain who solemnised the marriage was Samuel Oliver, who was on half pay to the 22nd regiment of Dragoons.[32] It took Beaujolois several weeks to record the marriage in her journal, along with the departure of Mlle de la Chaux to her family home at Yverdon and of Eleonora to stay with Eliza in Naples. Beaujolois confided:

> I could write much but I am unable. Perhaps at some future period I may endeavour to relate all that has happened. The last weeks have been a painful trial for me. I am far from happy, every thing I see vexes me and in such a condition I could not put myself to write.

According to Gavin de Beer, her diary then became more spasmodic with pages torn out.

Thereafter the tongues and pens of all and sundry expressed their disapproval at this, the second 'unwise' marriage made for love by Charlotte. Snobbery was an important factor. Although of a 'respectable Somersetshire family'[33] allegedly descended through the maternal line from an earl of Morton and only son of Edward Bury of Taunton (and later of Ivor Lodge, Buckinghamshire), Edward Bury was apparently without many material means but, like Charlotte, of expensive tastes. Even on Good Friday, Lady Frances Jerningham had relayed the gossip to her sister, Lady Bedinfield that 'Lady Charlotte Campbell who has a very Large Family has married her son's Tutor'.[34] Charlotte's younger brother, Lord John Campbell, writing to Mrs Damer on 26 June averred that he could 'learn nothing favourable of Mr Bury, all correspondents seem to unite in Disliking him'.[35] But he did add that 'Walter had consented to come home by Florence, in order to visit his mother'. Professor John Playfair, the eminent mathematician and professor of natural philosophy at the University of Edinburgh, took a somewhat more conciliatory view when he wrote on 5 August to his equally longstanding friends, the Misses Berry. Commiserating that their enjoyment of Florence must have been somewhat diminished by the circumstances of Charlotte's marriage, he added more kindly:

> After all, it is an action on her part more unwise than wrong, and I think ought not to be visited with the continuance of indignation and reproach. It brings her down a step below the *heroic* level to which her conduct and her beauty (for this last had its full share in fixing our opinions) had raised her in the estimation of the world, but she stills remains at a height much above the common run of Men and Women even of her own rank.[36]

Beaujolois referred to her new stepfather as 'long-nosed Mr Bury', who could be 'furious in his sleepy quiet way'. Walter Scott meanwhile had written to Lady Abercorn of his 'old friend, Lady Charlotte, who has made a sad mess of it. Our Scottish proverb says there is no fool like an old fool'.[37]

Since her teens and her subsequent widowhood Charlotte herself and others had linked her name romantically with men. But it was for the Reverend Bury that she chose to end her widowhood, once more despite opposition and probably without much advice. It was probably their shared love of art and fine art that was part of the attraction between Charlotte and her second husband. But a contributing factor may also have been that he was a cleric and she a staunch believer. Walter and Johnny apart, the family into which Mr Bury married then consisted of Eleanora (about to become 18), Beaujolois (15), Adelaide (14), Emma (12) and Julia (11). Replacing Mlle de la Chaux in the family was not to prove easy, and various Swiss governesses for the younger girls were in turn attached to the family.[38] Charlotte's faithful maid, Annie MacLeod, continued to be her mainstay. In the meantime Eliza's first daughter had been christened, according to the rites of the Book of Common Prayer in the Anglican church, by James Walker, the minister of St Peter's Episcopal Chapel in Edinburgh. This event took place in the Albergo della villa di Londra in Naples on 5 April.[39] The baby girl was given the names of her mother's cousin, the sculptress Anne Damer—Anna Seymour Conway, and was always known as Seymour. Proxy for Mrs Damer was Seymour's paternal aunt, Miss Emilia Ann Cumming. Other relations who were sponsors included William Hamilton-Campbell of Winton and Pencaitland, a Shawfield granduncle, and a Shawfield grandaunt, Lady Ruthven, while other witnesses present were her uncle, Walter Frederick Campbell of Shawfield and Islay, Lord Ruthven, George Forbes, banker in Edinburgh and John Hay, an Edinburgh advocate. Civic registration followed on 8 May.[40]

12

Lady Charlotte Maria Bury

Early in July 1818 Charlotte's nephew, Rawdon Clavering, arrived in Florence, and some weeks later he accompanied Charlotte, Mr Bury, Beaujolois and Adelaide on an excursion to Poppi, Camaldoli, Vallombrosa and Laverna in the Casentino in Tuscany.[1] Charlotte's journal and perhaps a commonplace book and Edward Bury's sketching pads were to be mined for a joint ambitious and expensive folio volume of prose, poetry and drawings, *The Three Great Sanctuaries of Tuscany*. With her husband's selected illustrations, part of Charlotte's journal was transcribed for the volume, and described the road up the fertile and cultivated Arno valley out of Florence before it changed abruptly to wilder scenes at Monte Somma. The little town of Poppi stood 'on the very pinnacle of a steep conical hill ... crowned by a building of the middle ages, very much resembling the Palazzo Vecchio of Florence, and said to be of an even earlier date'. Although there was no regular inn at Poppi, the hospitality of the inhabitants, like that of the Scottish Highlanders, was such as to detain the party 'from their researches', though they did not like to complain. They continued on horseback and foot up the rugged path into the Apennines and Charlotte remarked that the appearance of the Casentino and the convent of Camaldoli 'if first viewed by a bright moonlight, is peculiarly impressive and sublime—to a degree, indeed, that no beam of day can equal'. Amongst the pines and firs, the stone cells of the ruined hermitage of Sagro Eremo had 'nothing to recommend them to attention except the recollection of the enthusiasm which induced men to undergo the rigours of the order'. After shuddering at the thought of the severity of winters endured in these stone cells, Charlotte gave the names of the priests recorded in the shrine of the larger Camaldoli itself, with one of whom, Padre Don Michele, 'we had more opportunity of becoming intimate'. It was his 'polite benevolence and cheerful good-will which marks his general character', as well as his name, that Charlotte was to depict in the novel on which she was still engaged, *Conduct is Fate.* She so admired 'the highly industrious and beneficial community' of the Camaldolesi that whenever she heard the name of Camaldoli 'a thrill of pure delight courses through my veins; and so long as memory retains its power, the time I passed there will be beloved—revered—mourned'.

The Bella Acqua or Val' Ombrosa of Milton comprised an extensive building established by the Benedictines in the eleventh century, once renowned for its library and other treasures. Charlotte was excursive about Napoleon's plundering of such places, and although 'the more noted works of art have been restored in part ... to their parent land, many of them have never returned to their original destination, but have gone on to enrich the public galleries and libraries of the various capitals'. She was ambivalent over the whole question of provenance and collection, but in the end:

> As I mused in the certosa of Valombrosa, its bare walls and half-ruined refectory, I was not at all consoled for its spoliation by the reflection that many of the beauties by which they had been formerly decorated, were to be searched for, and perhaps found, in the different public museums, even of Florence ... there is a more intense and effective benefit to be derived, from holding a single work of art in the very place for which it was designed.

St Francis of Assisi in the early thirteenth century was the founder of the eponymous Franciscan order, and of the Lavernian sanctuary, comprising two churches by the time of the Burys' visit. While many of the original statues and friezes were still intact, and the vaulted roofs 'deep azure and spangled with golden stars ... many of the pictures had been carried off by the French'. While also admiring the whole mountain of Laverna and the neighbouring countryside for the abundance of objects of interest, not only to the contemplative and imaginative traveller, but to the botanist, geologist, and naturalist', Charlotte thought it appealed above all 'to the poet's eye'—visionary inspiration which spurred her then or later to compose her poetry for the lavish folio volume discussed later.

As the lease on their house in Florence was soon due to expire, Charlotte, Mr Bury and Beaujolois ventured to Sienna on 21 August to look for their next residence but without success. In October there was another excursion for Charlotte, Mr Bury, his friend, Mr Lister, and Beaujolois to Volterra.[2] By the end of November 1818, however, they had arrived in Rome where they were now going to spend the winter, living at the Porte Pia. There is one section in the second volume of Charlotte's published *Diary* in which the named days and dates for a short spell of twelve days in Rome appear to relate to December 1818.[3] Within a few days of arriving in Rome and leaving visiting cards, Charlotte, despite being pregnant in her mid-forties, was indulging in and enjoying a hectic round of activities. As ever, it made no reference to her husband or family but did give the names of various friends and acquaintances whom she accompanied to see some of Rome's outstanding churches, palazzi, villas and paintings. The views from St Onofrio on the summit of the Janiculum on a clear December day were 'transcendent'. Sir Thomas Lawrence was in Rome and Charlotte went to see his portrait of Lady Burghersh and her son. On another occasion the Duchess of Devonshire accompanied her to marvel over Lawrence's 'magnificent' portraits of the pope and Cardinal Gonsalvi. Charlotte also dined on occasion with the latter, as well as with other English such as Lady Saltoun, Sir Humphry and Lady Davy among others. In the sacristy of St Peter's 'miraculous building', she was not only once again presented to the Pope, but along with 'several other English persons prostrated ourselves at his feet, and felt no degradation by the homage'. The Scots sculptor, Thomas Campbell, spent ten years in Rome from 1819, his studio being in the Piazza Mignanelli; he exhibited almost annually after returning to London and was then in contact with Charlotte.

Lady Morgan described the Piazza di Spagna and the Via del Babuino and one or two other streets nearby as 'literally British colonies, and the bustle, noise and life which their foreign inhabitants lend to them, are almost unknown in every other part of this 'city of the dead' (Città Morta).[4] Henry Matthews, a Fellow of King's College in Cambridge, described the haunts of the estimated 2,000 English visitors and residents in Rome, who 'swarm everywhere', thanks to the 'partiality of the Pope to the English'.[5] The Piazza di Spagna was 'the focus of fashion, and the general resort of the English. Some travellers have compared it to Grosvenor Square'. Similarly he characterised the Corso as 'the Bond-street of Rome (also the Billingsgate)'. On Sunday mornings the English ladies (what about the men?) attended the English church in the Via del Babuino, 'which is now established with an éclat that scandalises all orthodox Catholics' and 'boasts a very numerous congregation. The door is thronged with as many carriages, as a new fancy chapel in London.' On Sunday evenings Vespers at St Peters was 'the favourite lounge of the English ladies': they 'parade up and down in St Peters ... which then becomes the fashionable promenade. After Vespers ... all the equipages in Rome are to be found in the Corso which then answers to our own Hyde Park.' He thought that the same English ladies had 'metamorphosed Rome into a watering place.

One or other of them is "at home" every evening, and there are balls twice a week.'

A welcome guest in the following spring was a talented young woman and heiress, Joan Glassel of Londniddry in East Lothian, who subsequently became the second wife of a widowed Lord John Campbell.[6] She had been brought up when orphaned under the wing of Anne Grant of Laggan, and was visiting Rome with the Smiths of Jordanhill, mentors and friends who were also Argyll tenants at Rosneath.[7] Her closely-written journal with its cramped script details many of the activities in which she participated with the Smiths and the family at the Porte Pia between 15 March and 20 April 1819. There she enjoyed meeting the sculptor, Antonio Canova, going with him to hear Signora Pellegrini sing, also visiting his studio to discuss the then fashionable craniology. Lady Morgan deemed Canova's studio 'by far the most extensive in Rome', with various workrooms and galleries, 'masses of marble, almost mountains, fresh hewn from their native quarries in the lower stories, and many others in various stages of execution—living groups of beauties, wits, kings and pontiffs'.[8] After dinner, in the relative cool of an evening, Joan Glassel, Beaujolois and Rawdon Clavering often went walking or took the carriage to the nearby Pincian hill to marvel at the domes of Rome. While admitting that the view was delightful, Joan Glassel found the air of Rome 'very unpleasant to me and on most days here I have more than my usual headache'. One day they all went out to a 'vineyard at Porte Salaria which leads into the Borghese woods. While the children hunted stones I made a couch of reeds in a shady summerhouse for Lady Charlotte.' At other times they attended concerts in the Sistine Chapel and elsewhere, though she thought 'most provoking this system of giving such short notice for everything'. For the first anniversary of the Bury marriage on 23 March, after buying presents for Charlotte, Joan Glassel herself was given a 'glorious antique ring' by Mr Bury. After the dinner party that evening Charlotte sang Lady Augusta's 'most recent song'. Letters from Scotland and England were eagerly mulled over and boxes of books also arrived; Susan Ferrier's *Marriage* which had finally been published in 1818 was read aloud. The womenfolk often went into town to shop, stroll or saunter and sit around for several hours on a 'glorious day' such as that of Thursday 25 March. Although Lent was more strictly observed in Rome than for instance in Naples, at the start of April the city was en fête for the arrival of the Emperor and Empress. All the windows of the main Corso were bedecked with 'Tapestry and Damask', and Charlotte and the children wondered at the state coaches, while Lord Guildford was accompanied by Mr Bury to dinner with the Queen of the Etrurias.

For the court at the end of Lent on the evening of Palm Sunday, 4 April, 'a dress for Ly Charlotte was bought and made from ½ past 2 to seven' and she appeared 'splendidly lovely in her court dress'. With Holy Week approaching, 'black things for the Chapel' had also to be conjured up. Earlier that day they had made an unavailing attempt to get into the Quirinale, but on the following Wednesday and Thursday they entered the Sistine Chapel 'with unexpected ease', saw the Emperor and Empress and enjoyed 'the fine music'. The 'splendid spectacle' occupied three pages of Joan Glassel's closely written journal. On Easter Day of 1819 itself Charlotte (and presumably her husband) went early to St Peters with Beaujolois, Joan Glassel and the Smiths, the spectacle being 'the most splendid imaginable', and after dinner they ventured out to admire the illuminations and fireworks, 'the most indescribable spectacle ... rockets, Roman candles, Catherine wheels etc.' according to Lady Morgan.[9] Understandably, by the following day, Easter Monday, the six months' pregnant Charlotte was 'not at all well as she was fatigued sitting long in Church yesterday and was obliged to put off some people who were coming to dinner'. Instead, Beau and Joan walked in the grounds of 'Paulines Villa, quite a little Paradise ... close by their house'. Joan Glassel spent her last day in Rome, Wednesday 14 April, at Charlotte's, going into town and 'walking with the girls and Lady Charlotte', then to the Villa Borghese which was 'quite delicious only too many people'. Charlotte had enjoyed the company of Joan Glassel who had been 'a most indefatigably obliging person. But I always comfort myself with the idea that we shall enjoy one another's company.'[10]

Charlotte gave birth on Friday 9 July 1819 to another daughter, Bianca Augusta Romana. The first name was perhaps optimistic, after the patroness of heavenly harmony, and she was usually known as Blanche. The other names were after her maternal aunt, Lady Augusta Clavering, and to the city of her birth, a circumstance to which Charlotte was often later to refer. Johnny Campbell had apparently been in Rome at this time.[11] By 16 September Charlotte was writing to her brother that she was quite recovered,[12] though, as he remarked to Joan Glassel, 'I am easy as to her life upon this occasion, but alas! What has she left herself to desire in Life?' The eventful year had seemingly done little to assuage the family antagonism to the Bury marriage. In writing to Joan Glassel in October 1819 Lord John reported a letter from Eleanora[13] confirming her mother was quite well again and had written to her in high spirits. But that she was also full of abuse of 'Wood Hall and all its former inhabitants'. He continued:

> It is curious that Death, which usually calls forth any lingering affection for its victim should have awakened all Charlotte's hatred against her

husband and all his family to a curiously inveterate degree ... upon my conscience, I think she is gone distracted altogether.[14]

In November she and Mr Bury embarked on a journey to Assisi. In the middle of that month an old acquaintance, the Irish poet and song writer, Tommy Moore, was taken to visit the Burys. Earlier in the summer, Charlotte had once again been captivated by his singing: 'the distinct enunciation, the expression, the nationality of his genius—when heard, delighted in, and never to be forgotten'.[15] But Moore himself sadly recorded of Charlotte in his memoirs that she was 'much changed from the creature I first knew ... about 17 or 18 years ago'.[16]

In a letter to Eliza a few months later Mlle de la Chaux also described Charlotte as well, although apparently 'thin and much altered'.[17] Eliza had been outraged by her mother's pregnancy (while herself again pregnant). Eleonora had been under Eliza's wing since the events of spring 1818, and Lord Uxbridge must also have reappeared on the scene, for, on 5 August, in the drawing room or the dining room[18] of Eliza's home at Altyre, Eleanora and 'young Paget' were married. On 7 December the new countess was taken to Beaudesert in Staffordshire, a grand home of the formidable Anglesey family.[19] She related to Eliza 'You may believe I was in a fright', and apart from the music-making of the many womenfolk, there reigned 'a sort of whispering silence which one hardly ventures to break', all and sundry being terrified of Lord Anglesey and his punctiliousness. The house itself she considered, with some understatement, 'very large and handsome ... and the place quite beautiful but it appears ... with the ground covered with snow, rather melancholy'. Lord Anglesey and his legal advisers thought that his son's marriage at Altyre required ratification in England, so, 'to prevent the possibility of any shadow of doubt hereafter', Eleanora and Lord Uxbridge were remarried on 'the very cold morning of 8 February between 10 and 11 in St George's Church' in Hanover Square.[20] But as Eleanora put it: 'Our remarriage was so soon got over and occasioned so little sensation in our part of the world that I really never thought of mentioning it to you.' Not only for Eleanora but for her husband and the rest of the family, excursions to Wales for his electioneering seemed utterly distasteful; Eleanora even described Anglesey's Plas Newydd as melancholy and it did not compensate for either the long journey nor for their having to meet and mix with the Welsh.

Persistent problems, particularly over finance, continued with Walter. He had come of age in April 1819, and on 14 January 1820 married Lady Eleanor Charteris, daughter of the 8th Earl of Wemyss,[21] although his sister Beaujolois thought him 'too young', as well as disapproving of marriage between cousins. The family in Rome only heard of this marriage in a subsequent letter to Charlotte from the bride's mother, Lady Wemyss.[22] Beaujolois spent hours of her time writing to Eliza at Altyre. Charlotte had perhaps become somewhat paranoid and had resorted to opening her daughter's outgoing and incoming letters. By the end of February 1820, Beaujolois reported to her sister that their life during Lent had been so tranquil that she had not had much news to write:

> It was rather a good thing for me that the dancing stopped for although we had only one ball a week I contrived to make myself ill with it. I was only able to go out twice during the whole week of carnival. The French ambassador had a very fine masked ball which entertained me ever so much.[23]

Like Beaujolois, Mlle de la Chaux passed on news to Eliza that Charlotte had wanted 'to avoid the trial of meeting or not meeting the princess of Wales' (now Queen) and had considered fleeing to Naples 'and got the child weaned all at once, which circumstance Julia thought very hard. But on further consideration, she thought she would do like the other English people and wait quietly the event—do the best—or worst.'[24] In the event, the queen arrived in Rome on 22 February, however, since the papal government had not received instructions from the British Minister, she was refused the panoply she considered her due as queen, and saw only a few English people,[25] before moving on. But it also led immediately to another pregnancy for Charlotte.

Most of Beau's letter of 28 February 1820 to her eldest sister was taken up with a long discussion on the whole family situation as seen through the surprisingly mature eyes of this 17-year-old. Although she had promised to do so, Charlotte had never forgiven Beau for writing to Eleanora 'about twenty months ago'.[26] Beau reiterated that it would be easier to meet than to write under such conditions of censorship, as well as apologising for having to write such a difficult letter on such unpleasant matters. Beau's allegiances were divided. She was also aware of her continuing separation from other members of the family: 'Nobody can wish more sincerely than I do that all uncomfortable things were at an end ... and the time will come when we shall be happy together.' She hinted sadly at an abortive plan for her to accompany Walter back to Britain. 'The time of our return to England is always put off and now mamma speaks of another year and a half.' Charlotte apparently complained that Beau's 'living peaceably and amicably with Mr Bury' was hypocritical, as was her attitude to baby Blanche. But Beau defended herself, pointing out:

> Mr Bury acts towards me exactly in the same way as I do to him. He is attentive and kind towards any of us who are ill and having no course

> of complaint against him why should I not behave in the same way. I suppose even [if] things did not go on so peaceably as might be wished I could meet with no redress especially living away from every body belonging to me without the possibility of applying to them and I should always think it my duty to be the same to mamma and purely for peace sake try to be as well as I could with M[r] Bury.

With regard to Blanche, she averred:

> I really think it would require to be more unnatural to be any thing but kind and fond of a remarkably pretty wee harmless little baby which one sees two or three times a day—laying aside that she is mamma's child. Were she old enough to affect us in any way then indeed there might be reason for liking or disliking her yet mamma hints that this is hypocrisy.

Beau mentioned the subject of an additional complaint of her mother's:

> It is mean in me not to mention any thing of the sort to you or Eleanora—not to speak of how comfortably we live and of what a good domestic husband M[r] Bury is. It would on the contrary be mean in me as mamma reads my letters to say any thing in praise of M[r] Bury—as that would certainly look like hypocrisy.

She then added:

> As for M[r] Bury, making mamma a good husband I really think she is the best judge of that and that it belongs more to her than to me to tell you so. During the time of mamma's terrible illness [childbirth at the age of 44] M[r] Bury was every thing one could desire and, at such a moment it would have been wrong in me not to have said. I did so either to you or Eleanora I forget which and I remember even speaking so warmly about it that John [her brother] called me a great hypocrite for ones pains.

It is hard to realise that these are all the thoughts of the young Beau; she found it very difficult 'to regulate the expressions which one may ... in a moment of emotion so that they may not appear exaggerated to others and even to oneself when read coolly sometime afterwards', adding: 'For this reason I always study to avoid all that might be misinterpreted and all that might lead to long and disagreeable arguments.' She went on to say that after her mother's 'illness' she or Johnny had sent daily letters to either Eliza or Eleanora, and 'the same to Ld John and Mrs Damer'. All this effort, however, had probably been undermined or actually nullified by an unscrupulous and dishonest servant because all the letters 'missed as well as many other letters at that time, even one containing money was never received'. She vowed to continue sending letters in the hope that some would get through. This particular one she sent to Sir William 'in order that he may judge whether you are capable of receiving letters or not'. Since letters took about a month they would 'still have some weeks of anxiety before we can hear of your safety (a second son, Roualeyn George was born to Eliza on 15 March). I hope Sir William will remember to write to us.' She ended on a lighter, though slightly admonishing note: 'I was very glad to hear some thing about your children ... Do not let them talk Scotch if you can help it.'[27]

Another of Eliza's correspondents at the time was her cousin, Charlotte Clavering, who had in December 1817 been married at Ardencaple to Miles Fletcher. She wrote from Edinburgh on the last day of March 1820 that Mlle de La Chaux and Susan Ferrier had gone that day 'to our aunt elect' at Longniddry, asking if she didn't think it strange to fancy Miss G[lassell] in the character of the Duchess of Argyll sailing about at Inveraray with all that majesty of demeanour which characterises her?'[28] Charlotte Clavering's nickname was 'Chatty' and her letter goes breathlessly on talking about her mother, Lady Augusta, having taken 'a nasty little house in the skirts of Helensburgh which I am horridly vexed at'; about her surviving brothers, Douglas and Rawdon, as well as her cousin, Walter, and his already pregnant wife (Margaret Susan was born on 15 October 1820). To Eliza, Mrs Damer rejoiced at Lord John's marriage 'with a woman whose tastes and habits ... are suitable to his own ... and then Miss Glassell's Fortune is such as to enable him to live comfortably at Ardencapel [*sic*] Castle, the place of all others that he prefers'.[29] She was not to let up on the Bury marriage, however.

> From Rome I have received several letters, all, as you says of yours from the same quarter, filled with expressions of delight and details of enjoyment etc and not one word of what one really wants to know, nor of things that must, at times at least, seriously occupy her mind! One passage in a letter I must give you. She says ending her letter 'farewell Dear Cousin—I entertain a hope that you will one day be reconciled to Mr B. for he is really a person to be honoured and liked for himself and one whose tastes and habits and very ways I dare venture to predict would please you'! and this to me is lamentable! Could I even believe in the dream of perfect happiness Charlotte affects to boast of, it would at least be something for the present I should say 'may it continue' but I cannot ... What is to become of her, with this most vain and extravagant

> Husband and her own too well known carelessness about her own affairs and I am sorry to add, about all serious concerns.

Fortunately for today's reader, Eliza disobeyed Anne Damer's request to burn this letter written from the 'openness and grief of my heart'.

'Roman fever' was virulent in 1820, and like many other visitors, Alexander Baillie had fallen victim, as had Lady Ruthven.[30] At the start of the year, the family maid, Mary Mcintyre, had also been very ill for three weeks, and was nursed by Annie MacLeod, who then herself fell ill. Both eventually recovered 'thanks to the ministrations of a very good "Scotch doctor"'.[31] In early March of 1820 Beaujolois told her sister, Eliza, that the family was moving to Naples at the end of the month.[32] By June she was writing to say that she would rather be with Eliza in Scotland during the summer than being 'with Walter entre nous soit il dit'.[33] By then they were established quietly in their villa and 'as there is a good hill to walk up besides driving all through the town to get to our house we have not many visitors'. She talked of the English in Naples giving parties but 'we go to none of them as it would have been very disagreeable for different reasons to have lived more in public'. Not only was Charlotte pregnant once more, but Beau had her own reasons for wanting to keep out of the limelight. The girls had only been out twice since they had arrived, once to go to Pompeii with their aunt, Lady Ruthven, and the second time with her to the theatre.

Although it was very hot in Naples it was infinitely preferable to Rome, but the family only went out after dinner about seven to walk about the villa's grounds which were large enough 'to take the little exercise one feels inclined for here', as Beau told her eldest sister.[34] Unfashionable German was added to the girls' French and Italian; Beau thought that despite the German master spending more than an hour with her three times a week, 'I think him rather a bore by the time it is done'. She informed Eliza that she sang 'tant bien que mal', although she thought her voice weak in itself and 'the heat did not much improve it. My sisters are getting on in "musick" and there is always the most invariable succession of the best musick in some part of the house during the whole day.' Adelaide was apparently very skilled in drawing and had delighted Mlle de la Chaux by despatching some family portraits to her. Beau herself would also have liked to draw but felt that she had 'no fancy for figures and it is impossible to get a good landscape master'.

She mentioned the plan—if it did not change: 'I do not know exactly what will happen in the intermediate time but Paris is to be the winter resting place of the Caravan. Time will make this out more distinctly.'

Charlotte and her husband visited the 'green' island of Ischia (presumably also 'Blue Capri') and intended exploring Paestum, south of Naples. Beau, however, did not want to accompany them as 'it would be a great additional expense upon ones account and a very hot journey of five or six days as mamma intends also to see other places on the road and I do not want to be out of Naples for so many days', and she 'may just as well remain quiet in the Convent', another of her epithets for the household. Adelaide's letter in French to Mlle de la Chaux on 9 July 1820 described the past few days' movements of soldiers in Naples and the new constitution, agitation also in Rome, as well as imparting news of the family (Lady Ruthven still poorly after the fever) and the Duchess of Devonshire.[35] Letters were tampered with and post was highly irregular. A letter to Eliza from Anne Damer on 12 July quizzed her about Beau's marriage plans, as well as offering her usual slander of her cousin, Charlotte: 'she and her deary are I hear going on in the same state of extravagant living at Naples that they did at Rome'.[36] About the same time, Eleanora was writing to her elder sister, 'I hear Mama is to lay in again in November. Is it not too shocking.'[37] Towards the end of July 1820 when her husband had been ill, Charlotte was beseeching one Captain Bosville to take them from Naples to Leghorn by sea in one of the only two vessels available 'in the present state of this Country'.[38] Another plan had been to try to go in Douglas Clavering's ship to Leghorn, and then to Florence where they might winter, but neither plan transpired.

The family left Naples in mid-August and by the end of September they were settled for the winter, not in Paris, but in Pisa, with 'a very nice house ... and half as cheap as those in Florence'. Charlotte was by then over six months pregnant and 'it would of course be quite impossible for us to appear any where now until after mamma's confinement'. Beau was 'glad we are to be in a quiet place free from the observations of all ones kind friends. They have not spared them already.'[39] However, sailing from Greenock, an Edinburgh friend, Eliza Wilson, overwintered in Pisa that year and with her sister, Jane and brother, James, frequented the household.[40] Arriving in October in Pisa, 'the quietest of all quiet places', she continued her travelling journal with detailed, if ultimately cloying, descriptions of all the social comings and goings with the 'beautiful Campbell daughters, including Lady Tullymore to be'.[41] Characterising Charlotte as 'the same as ever' and 'looking extremely well, with a lilac crepe turban and kid boots of the same colour', she added: 'I never saw such beautiful feet as she has.' On another occasion, Charlotte was elegantly dressed in 'ermine, with a black velvet hat and feathers'. Eliza delighted in her being 'very blue', enjoying 'some interesting conversation ... on the power of love and the beauty of Italy, two subjects she is well qualified to talk upon'. While it was not so surprising that she confessed 'I admire her so much, her manners are so sweet and unaffected', it was for once a pleasant change to find that someone deemed Mr Bury 'very young looking, modest and agreable ... pleasing and like a gentleman—very attentive to, and fond of Lady Charlotte'. Argyll family miniatures were pored over and Charlotte gave lessons in harp and singing. To Eliza and the older girls Charlotte also gave 'the novel she is writing to read'. Eliza recounted that she spent three days between 22 and 24 November reading *Conduct is Fate*, thinking it 'very interesting' and expressing the view that it 'has much merit. Few women with her personal beauty, could take so much pains to cultivate the mind.' In weather 'cold and Edinburghish', excursions were made to Leghorn 'for trifles'.

Beatrice was born to Charlotte, almost 46, on 17 December 1820. By the 30th Eliza Wilson noted that Charlotte was already 'making a charming recovery', and by 10 January she and Mr Bury had called in their carriage on the Wilsons. A week later Beaujolois and her mother were out sketching the 'old tower' at the end of the bridge over the Arno, and despite the weather being 'too Scotch', there were other sketching trips for mother and daughters. The babe's christening day was to take place in February. Eliza Wilson and her brother arrived at twelve o'clock to watch Mr Ellis christen Beatrice Emma Margaret Bury who was 'rolled in pink satin'; her half-sisters were all in white gowns and ribbons, and Lords Montagu, Blantyre and Tullamore were also there to participate in the 'elegant collation' afterwards, with 'good music. In short the whole thing went off quite beautifully and Lady Charlotte looked uncommonly well.' The Burys' third anniversary on 23 March 'occasioned a delightful evening ... after tea wine and a beautiful sugar'd cake there was singing and harping by Lady Charlotte and the girls'.

On settling in Pisa, Beau had poured out her heart in a long letter to her sister, Eliza, covering eight pages of the saga behind her and asking Eliza 'to share with me in my happiness in knowing that all the difficulties attending my marriage are at an end'.[42] Beau had first met 19-year-old Lord Tullamore, son of the 1st Earl of Charleville, and his redoubtable countess, Catherine, in Rome in the middle of November 1819, when she 'used to talk and dance with him. But he was never even presented to mamma till after we went to Naples. We also knew his brother [his half-brother, Charles Tisdall] very well and he and I used to be great friends.' After some escapade in Ireland or London, Lord Tullamore had been sent abroad by his parents. The brothers left Rome for Naples about the end of February 1820, and according to Beau, although she was 'perfectly ignorant of every thing of the kind', apparently Lord Tullamore 'was then much in love with me'. On an excursion to Vesuvius he however had a bad fall,[43] and was initially attended by the medical husband of Sydney, Lady Morgan. As the latter wrote to Tullamore's mother, the Morgans were both 'greatly delighted with Lord Tullamore ... We have ... rarely, if ever, found so much unbiassed judgment in so young a person ... he speaks Italian wonderfully.'[44] Be that as it may, Lord Tullamore subsequently spent months becoming more and more ill in Lausanne, recommended for convalescence as being cooler than the Italian south. In his delirium he had constantly called out Beau's name, she averred in her letter to Eliza. His parents did not want him to marry young, or someone so young, but five successive doctors advised them that if he wasn't allowed to marry, it would probably be fatal for someone of such a nervous disposition: 'his illness came totally from the mind ... and he could never recover till the cause of his unhappiness was removed'. So in September 1820 the earl and countess had eventually relented and agreed that the marriage could take place after Christmas.[45] To Eliza, Beau pondered whether, by delaying, they perhaps hoped that the marriage would not take place at all; indeed his parents took him off to Paris. Friends interceded on her behalf, however, and Beau herself argued her suitability to her sister: 'I am eighteen in two months and if they choose they may call me nineteen or twenty for certainly I may safely in appearance pass for any age under thirty.'

As she was writing, Lord Tullamore was garbed totally in black, and scarcely ever moved out of his room in Lausanne or had any company except that of the elderly Sir John Dalrymple. But the young lovers wrote daily to each other, his letters being sealed with black wax, and Beau sent him a 'shell' made of herself from her Roman bust. She brushed aside people's views that Lord Tullamore was poor, like herself, one of the 'penniless ladies'. Her naive rationalisation was that 'his father though laden with debts is exceedingly rich and therefore although he has not thought it necessary to make a bargain with me about such matters I suppose he is not quite a beggar'. One wonders whether Charlotte pondered the whole medical and financial situation before replying in the affirmative to the formal letters from Lord Tullamore and the Charlevilles.

In the disturbances around the Mediterranean letters apparently continued to go astray, for Beau told Eliza in January 1821 that she and Charlotte had only received one letter from Eliza since arriving in Pisa six months before.[46] Charlotte had recovered from Beatrice's birth 'as well as possible' by her 46th birthday in January 1821, when Beau asserted to Eliza that there would be no reason for delaying her own marriage beyond the middle of February. By this time the Earl of Charleville had agreed an allowance of £1,600 a year, which Beau recognised would not 'allow of our living ... in England ... certainly not in London'. The plan was for them to live on the Charleville estate at Tullamore in Ireland and for

Lord Tullamore to go into Parliament and rent a London home. Eliza had been pressing Beau to come and visit Altyre, but this was not apparently to Lord Tullamore's liking, and Beau pled that she was worried about his still being delicate: 'Three times he escaped death … and I dread anything which might agitate or vex him.' While she had been 'practicing [*sic*] economy ever since arriving in Pisa', Beau admitted to having been 'very awkwardly situated with regard to money'.

> I have drawn for 200£ which I could not avoid and I shall think as you advise accept of 1,600£. This is not for myself as much less will serve me. I have not the slightest intention of getting any thing in the least fine. I am totally without clothes therefore I must buy some but I shall do that as sparingly as possible [unlike her sister Eleanora]. I am quite aware that a good trousseau is very useful but beggars must not be choosers and in the present case we are very poor.

By the time Eliza received this, and almost three years after her mother, Harriet Charlotte Beaujolois Campbell was married, also in the chapel of Lord Burghersh's Florentine palazzo on a very cold Monday, 26 February 1821 to Charles William Bury, Lord Tullamore. Eliza Wilson had talked of new dresses that Charlotte had commissioned for the occasion, and her husband Edward Bury remained in Florence after the marriage to sketch. The earl recounted to his agent at Charleville:

> You have heard before this, I make no doubt, of a very important event to us, that is, Tullamore's marriage. It took place on 26th February last, and was solmenised in the ambassador's chapel. As you may reasonably suppose, I was little inclined that he should marry so young; but I am more reconciled to it now, as I like the young lady, who appears to me amiable and sensible. In consequence of his marriage, I allow him at present £1,600 a year, which I intend you should pay him out of Charleville estate [twice a year], at least till my return, when perhaps I may be able to settle it otherwise.[47]

From Leghorn Beaujolois wrote to Mlle de la Chaux on 12 March saying that they were to be remarried by the English chaplain there and that they had stayed at an inn in Pisa to see her mother.[48]

Beaujolois' long letter to Eliza from Pisa in the autumn of 1820 had described the three younger sisters that Eliza may not have seen for some time. They all looked perfectly well, the winter 'having quite removed the pallid skins which the delights of an Italian summer gave'. Adelaide was as tall as Charlotte 'but very slim. She is letting her hair grow and it is a very pretty colour and she does it very nicely. She has a pretty complection [*sic*] and looks very young for her age' (16), and 'will be remarkably handsome.' Her mother deemed Adelaide 'the most handsome of all'. Emma, 15, was thought by Beau to have been very thin, but 'she looks now much better. Her face is pretty although her figure does not shine much as yet.' She was no taller than Julia and 'I daresay she will be the least of the family'. Beau described the 14-year-old Julia as 'not at an advantageous moment although she will do very well en temps'. Another comment is added which clarifies a later view that 'all but one of Lady Charlotte's children takes after her good looks'.[49] Poor Julia 'still squints and it makes her very angry to tell her so. She tucks her hair tight up which is not too becoming but that is to make it grow. She is as clever as ever and entertains us often by her pictures of talent and presumption.'

In the same letter Beau promised that she would 'certainly execute your commission to Bartolini and send you the answer'. Tuscan Lorenzo Bartolini had studied in Paris with Jacques-Louis David and was a friend of Jean-Auguste Ingrès. He opened his Florence studio in 1815 and on several occasions referred to this particular commission as 'The Dancers' or 'The Ballerinas'; it has also been called 'The Campbell Sisters' (see plate 20). Lady Morgan felt that Bartolini's studio was particularly delightful for English travellers. 'There is scarcely a living bust in Great Britain, on which fashion has set her mark, or notoriety stamped her signature, that may not be found in the studios and galleries of Signore Bartolini.'[50] She averred:

> The lovely children of Prince Esterhazy, and the beautiful daughters of Lady Charlotte Campbell are historical works; and independent of the extraordinary fidelity of likenesses ... they are eminently precious as specimens of the perfection to which modern sculpture has arrived.

It has also been suggested that it was 'Mr Campbell', i.e. Walter, who commissioned the statue. Someone must have decided that it was to be of the two younger sisters in 1821. Emma and Julia were then aged about 16 and 15, but one might wonder why all three of the youngest girls were not represented—the tall Adelaide in the centre, perhaps, and her two younger sisters of more equal but lesser height on either side. A full-size plaster model is in the Gipsoteca Bartolinia in Florence. The dancers are skilfully executed on tiptoe with gently wafting draperies delicately carved in the final marble version. The inscription of the plinth is dedicated to the English sculptor, John Flaxman, whose engravings of Homeric subjects Bartolini greatly admired. It was shipped from Leghorn to Leith, its immediate destination not known; although the Campbells were no longer in Islay by 1886, the statue may then have been in Islay House.[51] It subsequently graced the dining room at Inveraray Castle before being placed in the gardens there, then loaned in 1991 by the trustees of the Duke of Argyll to the then National Gallery of Scotland, where it enchants all.

While the arrangements and execution of this statue were being effected, the much less kindly pen of another sculptor gave news of Charlotte to Eliza. In February 1821 Anne Damer wrote to the latter congratulating her on her recovery from another birth.[52] The scrawl has almost to be read twice to realise the full effect of her continuing venom against the Bury marriage.

> From Charlotte herself I have not yet heard since her laying in. But Beaujolois has been very attentive in writing to me ... All there goes on as ill as possible, as you well know and Mr B has turned out just what we expected and the suspicions so often repeated over—of 'perfect content and perfect happiness' do, I confess, quite disgust me and such letters only make me melancholy. I shall be most glad to hear Beaujolois is actually married and like you, I can not see (if all is as it is represented) why the marriage did not take place at Ld Tull:'s return.

Sadly, according to the uncharitable Mlle de la Chaux another casualty of the Bury marriage appears to have been the long-standing family friend, Alexander Baillie, who was 'not the least reconciled to the change he found in Lady Charlotte's manner towards him'.

After George III died and his son was proclaimed king on 26 June 1820, his queen returned to England following failed financial negotiations to persuade her to stay on the Continent; events moved very rapidly and the trial of Queen Caroline was initiated. Before it had begun, Anne Damer—who had never met the princess before—had intended leaving her card a few days after the queen's arrival when the latter was staying with Lady Anne Hamilton in Portman Square/Street before moving west to Brandenburg House at Hammersmith. Anne Damer wrote sympathetically of her queen to Eliza, describing a morning only two or three days subsequently when the Queen had returned the visit 'quite without notice or form'. Her arrival at Twickenham was no sooner known than 'Bells began ringing Cannons firing and every testimony of joy ... was shown ... people crowded round my door as she went out crying "God bless the Queen and Long live the Queen" etc. etc.'[53]

It has been suggested that Charlotte was called as one of the defence witnesses at the trial of Queen Caroline in the summer of 1820. 'Among the names of witnesses moved for in 1820 to be summoned on behalf of the Queen is that of "The Lady Charlotte Bury".' Ignoring the verb, Rosa's superficial view was that 'the happy couple stayed abroad until they were forced to return to England because she was needed in the trial of Queen Caroline in 1820'.[54] In October 1820 Lady John Campbell thought that Charlotte was 'on her way home summoned by her Majesty'.[55] But another correspondent opined on 4 November 1820 that 'it must have been a relief to you all that Lady Charlotte was not plagued about that troublesome Queen—for however little she had to say it was very agitating to appear before all the Lords'. It was also face-saving for Charlotte to avoid hearing the scurrilous references to her by the princess's bribed servants. In any event, it seems unlikely, since Charlotte not only wrote to Eleanora from Leghorn on 31 August, but she was to give birth in Pisa to her last child on 17 December 1820. By then Charlotte had written to Queen Caroline who responded with a friendly letter saying:

> No-one's congratulations have been more welcome to me than yours ... That I should have been saved out of the Philistines' hands is truly a miracle, considering the power of my enemies and their chiefs, for nothing was left undone that could be done to destroy my character for evermore ... I was sure you would rejoice at my glory, dear Lady Charlotte; no one has been more true to me than yourself at all times.[56]

Although those such as Lady Anne Hamilton and Anne Damer had been brave enough and loyal enough to visit and support Queen Caroline, Charlotte was saved from any decisions as to attending the Queen's thanksgiving service in St Paul's Cathedral on 29 November and was still in Paris when Caroline became ill and succumbed on 7 August 1821, shortly after being prevented from attending her husband's coronation. Two days after the latter, George IV descended on the Anglesey family at Plas Newydd en route for Holyhead and Dublin. In a letter to her sister Eliza, Eleanora described how they had been given three-quarters of an hour's notice: 'dinner and beds had to be summoned up'. But Eleanora must have been overjoyed, even if her daughter 'little Ellen' was perhaps less so, when the King remarked that her daughter was 'the beautifullest little Angel he ever beheld and kissed her with great delight'.[57]

Perhaps it was as well Beau had gone from the Bury household; one wonders how her heart and pen could have coped with the subsequent death of Beatrice, 'after much and long suffering'. Lady John Campbell was Beatrice's godmother to whom Charlotte later sent the searing verses which she wrote 'without taking My pen off the paper three days after Beatrices death'.[58] They are dated Paris, 10 October 1821. Charlotte asked Lady John (in February 1822) not to give the lines away, acknowledging that Beatrice's father 'never could read them'. She added that 'sometimes I look at Blanch [*sic*] and tremble for She is his only One now—and what would he be if He lost her—but we are not ought to anticipate Evil'. The loss of little Beatrice Charlotte herself could 'by no means get the better of'.

> For in times of youth, Children seem the natural consequence of marriage and appear to spring from the parsley Bed every day and Hour; but in after life we feel them more especially the 'Gift and heritage of the Lord' and the doubt of having such a loss supplied, renders it ten thousand times more deeply felt, thus are poor Mortals, ever repining against what is it is—ever thankless and erring—I hope not quite so.

Perhaps it was the loss of her last child, when she was 46; she had after all lost at least one son, Henry, two decades earlier. Or maybe it was because this was only her second child with Edward Bury, himself often apparently ill, although only 31 years old. She had not conceived how lasting and how bitter such an affliction would prove and bemoaned that 'the triumph of bringing our two beautiful babes Home was not to be mine'.[59]

A few days later, from Paris on 15 October Anne Damer was unsympathetically describing to Eliza how 'your mother is sadly altered I am grived to say. Her face once lighted up by cheerfulness and content, is now thin and careworn.'[60] She would have felt pity for Charlotte if she did not 'still persist in distrust of her professions of happiness with the unprincipled and tyrannical Coxcomb, Mr B'. She continued:

> He returned here on Friday night last and since that I have not seen either your mother or your Sisters, they have not been near me and I begin to think that Mr B has forbid their coming. Then as in England now he did not call upon me, which I was glad of it is true to say.

She piled on her complaints:

> In short I find all you have seen and heard of this lamentable marriage so far from being exaggerated falls shorts of the reality. Your sisters are sadly dressed have no Education given them of any sort here, they never go out, scarcely to walk. Surely this ought not to continue?

Suggesting additional reasons for Charlotte's wan appearance—if indeed any were required—Damer thought that Mr Bury's business in England had been 'about Westwood and money matters but what has been done I know not'. She went on:

> Yours sisters I doubt not will have informed before that little brother [Damer's error] after much and long suffering, is dead this may therefore

> be a moment of distress I think and to her anxiety about Mr B's coming or not coming, made dear Charlotte appear somewhat worse than otherwise she might. But that could only be a shade of difference!

Beatrice had died on 7 October when her father was presumably in England. Damer's last arrow was even directed at Bury's supposed treatment of the hapless MacLeod 'Poor MacCloud is a victim to Mr B's insolent Folly ... not treated as her faithful service deserves'. Her invective was only bettered by that of the diarist, John Wilson Croker, who cruelly depicted the difference between the Lady Charlotte of Lawrence's day and that of twenty years on when he met her again: 'she had grown coarse, and one of the most mortifying spectacles of dilapidated, but still pretentious beauty I could imagine'.[61]

This is published later in *Journal of the Heart,* 1830, p. 72.

> Tis past, the fitful fever of Lifes dream
> For Thee, my Infant Beatrice is oe'r
> For Thee, how vain to swell the mournful theme
> For Thee, how idle all that I deplore;
> Thee blessed one in Christ regenerate;
> Translated now to beatific state
>
> Oh! Infant mine, I did not think such pain
> For one so lately lent could thus be felt
> Although the blessing were recall'd again
> I did not deem such anguish would be dealt...
> I did not deem how hard it was to say,
> The Lord hath given, the Lord Hath taken away
>
> Perhaps, it was thy Suffering in that hour,
> Which leaves so piercing, and so bruised a Woe,
> Perhaps, it was the Crushing of that flower,
> Which to my heart hath given this deadly blow:
> Perhaps—ah! Cease: enough vain reasoner
> To know that He who wounds Thee cannot err.
>
> Nor for myself alone this bitterness
> Overwhelms a heart that would not be ingrate:
> But when a Fathers Husbands deep distress
> Swells the dread tide of sorrows aggregate
> I sicken at those floodgates of Despair
> Which tis my task to open and bid him share.

For I must tell him of the dreadful scene,
The awful ?Issue of that withering strife,
Which hung in dread suspense, so long between
The gleaming hope, and dark despair of Life:
"Till the torn heart was wearied stricken sore
And when the blow was struck, could feel no more

That bitter strife, that suffering feeble shriek,
The rolling Eye, the restless grasping hand,
The look of innocence so angel meek
Like heavenly beam on tempest stricken Land
With busy busy bustling of the attendants round
And all the madness of that mingling sound

Alike are still'd—and of the awful Hour,
Nought now remains save the hushd sigh of sorrow
That dares not breathe upon that fallen flower
One wish that it should have outlived the morrow
Since it is freed from all this Earthly evil
To thrive unblighted in mortal soil.

I could have thought she Slept—so beautiful
The smile of death sat on her innocent face
But that the lustre of those Eyes were dull
And lay night closed in melancholy grace
Beneath their silken fringe of golden brown
Which stood immoveable half bended down

Still on the Life the hue of Health was spread
As if the vital spirit linger'd there
And loved the Roses of its native bed
Too well to leave those flowers of beauty rare
But on the marble cheek no colouring told
Deceitfully of Life—I saw 'twas cold.

This was at first—but when I gazed again
An awful change in little space had pass'd
The marble brow with yellow did distain
The violent Eye contracted, paled* and Glass'd
The tightened Lip resigned its brilliant glow
And Death stood manifest—array'd in Woe

The ran that creeping Horror through the veins
The tribute Nature pays to kindred clay
When bending oe'r the mass we call remains
What made it dear; the Soul—has pass'd away
And gazing thus—the dearest youngest thing
Gives but involuntary shuddering.

Then on our knees oh Lord in agony,
We life our heart and pour unfeigned prayer
Then do we feel our insufficiency
Confess our weakness and our wants declare
Bend to the chastening Rod that lays us low
And own the nothingness of all below.

Not in the Grave oh! God of wonder
Direct the mourners dark despairing
Not in that loathsome, that terrific place
Whence shrinking Nature turns instinctively:
But bright in faith of a redeemers Love,
See Heavens own Portals opening from above

See the glad day spring shining from on high
Lighten the dreary darkness of the Tomb
When death shall swallowed be in victory
And all come forth to meet th'appointed doom
Then 'mid the Angel Choir that Angel see
Rise with Heavenly Host exultingly

*Paled its ineffectual fires—Milton, I think

13

Crises

Correspondence amongst her daughters in the autumn of 1820 had reiterated that it was Charlotte's intention to return to England in the spring of the following year. Perhaps the condition and demise of the little infant delayed the return. Instead of going back with the four elder children married, her younger Campbell son in the army, the three younger girls, and two new daughters, the sorrowing Charlotte and Mr Bury were leaving Paris for Westwood House in Sydenham in another November, that of 1821; it was to be another two decades before Charlotte was again to experience Italian warmth. Mr Bury's father was enduring a long and painful illness,[1] while ongoing—and increasing—financial and legal problems had been hinted at in Anne Damer's October letter from Paris.[2] The year that followed was often referred to as the year of crisis, both in familial and financial terms. Family correspondence over the next decade charts many of the ensuing turning points as well as some happier events and doings in the lives of Charlotte, her husband, Blanche and the rest of the family.

The first immediate crisis was bitterly described by Charlotte soon after her return, when writing from Westwood on 13 November to her brother, Lord John.[3]

> Mr Bury has contrived to do what no one else would for me, and has actually brought me once more here. Had it pleased God to have spared us our Infant, I should be quite happy though the pleasure of my return to this Place has been overthrown by the unjust and cruel hatred of the Friend I once loved most.

Although he had promised to pay her £1,000 in six months' time, Mlle de La Chaux had taken out a writ against Mr Bury, while at the same time she had sent a congratulatory letter to Charlotte upon her return to England. Charlotte bitterly charged Lord John with Mlle de la Chaux's assertion that 'she was sanctioned in this violent proceeding by your advice and [her son] Walter's' adding, however, that 'in so far as regards you, I cannot believe to be true: it is so unlike all your usual gentleness and kindness'. She continued:

> This unjust persecution and bitterness towards Mr Bury for a debt which his most prejudiced Enemies must know to have been incurrd by me when a widow for the maintenance of My Children and myself appears to me so decided a shame upon Walter, that I think every unbiass'd mind would cry out against him for allowing My Husband to pay <u>such</u> a debt—much more for backing Mlle de La Chaux in this unseemly violence.

Among all the 'injustice and unfair abuse lavish'd upon Mr Bury on the score of expense ... that He married me to pay his debts and run away with my Substance and my Childrens', she pointed out that the purpose of the writ was to prove 'that He on the Contrary is to pay theirs, and mine—and that My Son is well pleased to be under this obligation to Him'. She herself could not 'remedy the trouble I have brought upon Mr Bury' and asked her brother to intervene with his nephew, Walter. She ended by saying that she was 'dead sick of the strife I live in—and those who pretend to be my Friends must not be My Husband's Enemies for how can Man and Wife who love each other have any separate interest'. The views of some others in the family appeared at variance with Charlotte, her cousin Anne Damer dissembling to Eliza: 'Walter's generosity has enabled her to live at ease where she may chuse.'[4]

It was Mamie de la Chaux's turn to complain in a cross-written letter to Lady John from Geneva dated 14 January 1822 that Charlotte had reported to Beaujolois in Geneva 'that I had caused Mr Bury to be arrested, tho' he had offered to give me security for the payment of the debt in 6 months etc. etc.'[5] Mamie had ended by saying that her own solicitor 'had refused to act a violent part', continuing:

> And I had been obliged to withdraw the writ. Can you conceive how Lady C. could be brought to write with her own hand facts so entirely false? Merely to please her husband and try to prevent her Daughter to continue to be on good terms with me for she abuses me for my ingratitude, unchristianlike disposition, and particularly says I must be for ever wretched from <u>remorse of conscience</u>.

While thinking it all 'so *outré* that it does not offend me', Mamselle averred that is was perhaps all part of 'the Burrian system'. The acidulous Bessie Mure of Caldwell was soon writing equally vituperatively to Lady John, wondering whether Mamie might get 'the money' but also attacking the Burys:

> I could forgive Mr Bury being a puppy and rude to Ly Uxbridge if he did not lie and make poor Lady Charlotte believe Mamie intended to arrest him and that her own Solicitor withdrew the writ. It is very unfortunate Lady Charlotte having fallen into the hands of a man of so little truth sense or good temper because her mind is so completely biased by him, the sunshine of its own radiant good tempered obscured for ever by his folly and absurd self consequence.[6]

No more is heard of this affair after Mlle de la Chaux withdrew, but while she visited and for long corresponded with many in the extended Campbell and Argyll families, helping out at the times of their various confinements and so on, the rupture with Charlotte was never to be repaired.

In the meantime the vexatious relations with her elder children had caused Charlotte to plead with Eliza's husband, Sir William Gordon-Cumming, on 26 November 1821:

> You are all kindness and affection. I am too when I can be so—but I think Myself so ill treated by My Children that I have once for all written a decided Letter to Eliza as I mean to do to each of the others. The thing must be settled one way or other—but well knowing that Husband and Wife cannot—or at least ought not—to act in any point with a separate feeling, I submit the History of My Wounded Heart to you as well as to Eliza ... if as a Husband yourself you do enter into My Sentiments it would be most gratifying indeed to have you as a Mediator of peace.[7]

The letter to Eliza on the same day starts off with a complaint that her mother had only a few days earlier received the first and only letter from her daughter since before her confinement at Pisa 'now Eleven Months ago!!!'[8] Ignoring the possibility that letters to and from the Continent might have gone astray, she went on to say that she was sorry to have to 'enter into long and painful details which hurt me much more than they do you', declaring that 'it was the last time I shall ever make known my sentiments to you in regard to your Conduct towards me and on your Answer in writing will depend, whether we can ever meet as Mother and Daughter ought to do or not'. While Eliza had apparently sympathised over Beatrice's loss, 'the silence of all mention of Mr. Bury, forms a part of a system adopted by My three elder Children to make known their dislike to My Husband'.

> [This had] shown itself uninterruptedly during three years in some shape or other—either by round about and artful Insinuations—or as in the present case by Contemptuous Silence, or else by open impertinence, as in that when I was first with Child of Blanch and that you cruelly wrote me word 'You had hoped that humiliation might have been spared you'!!!

She did not expect 'long professions of regard to Him' which would be:

> From you as unnatural as they are unsought for but not a word—not an allusion—no more than if I had had a Child without a legitimate Father to it—can this please me? No ... Mention of Him to me would have been the only cordial to my Spirits at such a time. Had you witness'd the suffering Death of the dear Infant I don't think such Stony hardness could exist in Human breast—but I do not attempt to touch you—tears shed at one Moment and Daggers drawn at others—is only the scene of Florence and what has pass'd since acted over again.

She described how for long she had been made unhappy by the conduct of her elder children and, 'except when roused by extraneous torments I have long thank God ceased to feel the Stings of mortified Vanity and frivolous mischief with which they beset me as I once did; but certainly to be at Enmity with ones Children must always leave a Pang'. But she vowed that she would 'never cordially meet those who do not verbally and personally pay these outward decencies of Life (politeness and humanity) and respect to me through my Husband'. Unless Eliza, as also Walter and Eleanora were to:

> Write me a full and explicit apology and confess yourself to have been in the wrong and acting under the instigations of pride and prejudice I beg leave in future to avoid all the cold unnatural pretenses of correspondence with a Child who only seems to try to wound and make me miserable—as far as is in her power.

Beaujolois was not included in the ultimatum. She and Lord Tullamore were being cherished in Geneva by Mlle de la Chaux. The latter had been cordially received by Lord Tullamore of whom she expressed 'great hopes that he will make an excellent husband', being 'a very gentlemanlike person and ... much more formed, in his ideas and principles than any young man of his age I ever saw. Above all he is orderly in the management of pecuniary concerns.'[9] She averred that 'nothing can be more affectionate than dear Beaujolois is towards me. The change of her situation has not made her the least less natural and agreeable, thank God.' She noted that the Genevese were snobbier than the English, citing their refusal to receive the (erstwhile divorced) Duchess of Argyll while accepting her husband, also claiming that the Tullamores are 'the only people of distinction here at present amongst the English,'[10] but:

> Their living so much at Home astonishes the Genevese very much, who like the French don't understand how it is possible to prefer quietness to constant visiting, unless you are absolutely at death's door. Tell Lord John that he will find in his nephew Lord Tullamore a similarity of taste, for he is very fond of turning to domestic enjoyments.

Beaujolois was pregnant, and 'ready to face this awful trial cheerfully—but I confess I dread the idea of seeing this young creature in agonising pain'. Following the new infants of Lady John, Eliza and Eleanora, Beaujolois produced the Tullamore heir on 8 March 1822. In the summer, while the Tullamores went to Lausanne, they left their son at Yverdon with Mlle de La Chaux, along with his Swiss nurse and English maid.[11] At 5 months, in Mamselle's eyes, 'the dear Child is prosperity itself and full of intelligence'.

Just after Easter in early April 1822, Charlotte was apologising from Sydenham to Lady John for her pen having been silent since she had sent her sad tribute to Beatrice's godmother a couple of months previously. Silent her pen may have been, but she now composed a long and repetitive cross-written letter.[12] She explained her reluctance to write being partly on account of the troubles with her three elder children, but also because for three weeks she had been in 'great wretchedness' about her husband who 'was between Life and Death' (she talked of 'Germs'). Thanks to one 'unpardonably careless' Dr Scott of Bromley, Mr Bury had seemingly been 'within an ace of losing His life'. He had subsequently gone to London for ten days to take the 'warm Baths'. Charlotte was unhappy at not being with him, but felt obliged to stay 'at my Post here with my big Girls'. She continued somewhat plaintively: 'I live here just as I used to do—never going to Town when I can possibly help it for without Money London is as detestable as it is agreeable with it. But one must have all appliances and means to boot otherwise it is melancholy and profitless.' Some 'real Friends' were prepared to drive 'seven Miles into the Country', some only able to do so 'but rarely'. Adelaide, Emma and Julia, as well as 'my little Blanch [*sic*], not quite three, who is grown quite captivating as well as beautiful' formed 'our only Society'. She continued:

> Yet now I am married I never tire of this little retreat and my Garden is as constant a resource of amusement to me as usual ... In my own pursuits and in my Husbands talents and society I feel real pride and pleasure independant of the World and in my own breast a peace which the World can neither give or take away. But I never hope to live again with My Relations they behave in such a way to My Husband that I never can.

One such was her brother, George, Duke of Argyll, who had been 'long in Town' but had taken no notice of her. So she had written saying she would be happy to see him, to which he responded with a 'kind enough note as a Single woman and offerd even to come here?!!' She had answered that she did not want to put him to so much trouble, also reminding him that she could have no real pleasure 'in constant intercourse' with anyone who did not receive her husband. Nevertheless she ventured to town the very next day, accompanied by Adelaide, Emma and Julia. She found the 59-year-old duke, 'as always, delightful, suave, gentle and kind, but much alterd in person. How different a descent of the Hill he has chosen from bad habits to that my Father made. What a different old Age will it necessarily be.' His duchess was another matter:

> I am not apt to be chil[l]ed. But such repulsive coldness I never met with. She literally never spoke to me and and hardly even answerd me when I addressed a speech to her—and what an expression of countenance and what a change five years have made. She literally behaved in such a way that I never could ... return within her Doors.

Moreover, since her brother had never even mentioned the name of her husband or Blanche, nor alluded to the loss of Beatrice, Charlotte thought it a 'melancholy certainty but never will I voluntarily return to persons who behave thus to me', continuing: 'And except that instinctive tie of Blood which one cannot get rid of—I look upon all my relations as parted from me for ever, for never will I (and I am pretty determined) go twice into anybody's House that does not receive my Husband.'

Lady John was one of the few (when Joan Glassel) who appear to have got to know Mr Bury in Rome in 1819, rather than just having opinions about him from hearsay or snobbery. But as Bessie Mure opined to Lord John, 'Lady C. said she would like to go to Scotland this autumn but that tho she is sure Lady John would be glad to see her you wont have Mr Bury'.[13] Several months later while thanking God for 'plenty of Friends ... who act a very different part', Charlotte gratefully acknowledged that the Shawfield relations who had shown most 'civility to my Husband' included her dear sister-in law Glen(cairn) Carter and her husband, with whom they often stayed at Edgcott in Northamptonshire.

Matters were, however, coming to a head. There seems to have been some incident in which Mr Bury gave offence to Eliza. According to Bessie Mure, he had not 'budged from his chair when she had entered the room' but had 'sat with his back to her the whole time, Lady Charlotte as cold as an Icicle and the tears trickling down Adelaide's cheaks [*sic*]. When in turn Lady Uxbridge went to Westwood, he went out of the house.' Charlotte had also only spent ten minutes visiting Eleanora after the birth of her son and heir in December and had discouraged any of the girls from accompanying her. The Gordon-Cummings came as planned to London for the season in June 1822, despite no apology ever having been received, which might have 'placed us on a better footing'.[14] They also even reached as far as Sydenham, as Charlotte explained in a letter to her son-in-law:

> Mr Bury was still prepared to meet Eliza with every politeness whenever chance brought us together for my sake. After the unprovoked outrage of Eliza at the period of our Childs Birth I cannot wonder at Mr Burys feeling as he does and I think that in permitting me to see Eliza in his own house. He did as much as I could expect from Him under existing circumstances.

She went on to elaborate to Sir William why she had not called on Eliza and himself when they first arrived in London, which had apparently caused offence:

> I do not think He would wish to prevent my calling on her, but as she has shewn in her manner to Mr Bury since we have met in Town so much evident dislike not to say rudeness; and wishing always my own and my Husbands visits to go hand in hand I own I have felt no desire to call on Her alone. Mr Bury begs me to express to you his sense of the kindness and politeness he has always received from you and his regret that he is prohibited from cultivating your acquaintance as much as He is desirous of doing so.

The Burys did go to stay in town, also at Kirkhams Hotel. But something appears to have gone even more seriously wrong between the two families. The sequence of the correspondence is not always dated nor clear. In ponderous prose and long sentences, written from Westwood in the middle of June in his small precise script (one of only two extant letters in his hand), Mr Bury felt compelled to write to Eliza, addressing her as 'Madam':

> As I understand from Lady Charlotte that you state me to have rejected your hand, when you did not the Honor to offer it, I am at a loss to comprehend when and where that circumstance could take place. I remember that your Ladyship on entering the room, during Mr Lambert's dinner, was pleased to give me your hand, which I unquestionably had the honor of taking.[15]

The effect was somewhat spoiled when he continued 'candidly' that considering her conduct to him and his child and 'our mutual opinions, such a formality might have been waived, without the sacrifice of any of that outward politeness which I was most anxious should exist between us from considerations to my wife'. He suggested that, despite the 'length of time and your Ladyships avowed dislike of me', for 'Lady Charlotte's comfort' Eliza might 'make the sacrifice of bowing to me when we meet and replying to me when I have the honor of addressing you'.

Charlotte subsequently tried to explain to her son-in-law:

> I had hoped that all discussion was past between us yesterday morning and My Husband and Myself were going to you and Eliza this morning but your manner to Mr Bury last night makes me conceive that <u>now you</u> are quarrelling with us—a thing I could not have supposed from your hitherto unfailing kindness and your known good nature. I trust you will not continue to put any bar on our perfect reconciliation for really it is a melancholy thing to be always at War and either this discomfort must end <u>now</u> entirely—or entirely part from us for I have not nerves to go on quarrelling and we had better meet no more than meet unpleasantly.

She felt that her daughter's mind had been poisoned 'by those who ought to have acted a very different part—and that they said to Her shew every kindness to your Mother but marked dislike to Her Husband', adding: 'I fear imagined that whatever I wrote or said was written under Mr Burys influence and was not the spontaneous dictates of my own heart'. Affairs escalated further when Eliza was accused by her mother of 'indulging her pride and capricious hatred of My Husband' in having 'framed an excuse that has no foundation in fact for affronting Him twice publicly when Accident brought her near Him.[16]

Next Charlotte abruptly fired off an unusually fulminating letter to her son-in-law in her large hand, to which she did not expect a written response while regretting that their intercourse 'must cease now entirely'.[17]

> Now mark me Sir William I have no intercourse with those who do not speak to My Husband and who make <u>me</u> the means of passing an affront

> on Him. Therefore when we meet pray do not address me and bid Eliza follow the same rule. Our intercourse is for ever at an End.

She ended the letter hoping for 'more peace in its loss than I have found in latter years in Endeavouring to maintain it'. Sir William did send a brief riposte to his 'dear Lady Charlotte':

> You shall ever find me what I ever have been to You—all affection. Having ceased to esteem Mr Bury I must decline ever entering on any subject connected with him. 'My right hand is my own' and mine shall never go where my heart does not. If on this account you make any difference in your conduct to Eliza I must indeed regret it after the very humiliating scene she subjected herself to yesterday and which I am sure no other Daughter in England would have. She has indeed shown her love to you whether you are willing or no believe me I shall ever love you both on your own account and Elizas.[18]

Bessie Mure was the one to pass on the gossip to Lady John.[19] Her 'circumstantial account of the Campbell blow up exactly as I received it' she relayed to Lady John a month later.[20] After alleging that Bury had turned his back on Eliza when they met, Eliza had indicated that she would never bear such conduct from any man. At which juncture 'Lady Charlotte was in a dreadful rage and suffered her violence to get too much the better of her—altogether it was a very disagreeable business'.

> Lady Charlotte flew into a violent passion started up seized Lady Cumming by both shoulders and shook her as one does a naughty child and she was exceptionally frightened and dropped almost fainting in a chair and was only relieved by a violent fit of tears. Before she had recovered Lady Charlotte began abusing her again and ended by saying it was the last time they should ever meet except in public where she commanded her never to presume to approach or speak to her.

As soon as she got back to the hotel Eliza had sent for Walter, also staying in town for the parliamentary season, and related what had transpired to him. Walter was so indignant that he vowed his three younger sisters should no longer be left to the mercy of their mother and Mr Bury.

This possibility had been in the air since the family's return to England. After succeeding to the estate in 1816, followed by his European travels, Walter spent most of his life and fortune in the amelioration of his estates in Islay and at Woodhall in Lanarkshire, and as an MP. Although his sister, Eleonora, was concerned at his being too young at just 21 to marry, and also had reservations about first cousins marrying, his marriage to Lady Ellinor or Eleanor Charteris, daughter of the 8th Earl of Wemyss, had taken place in January 1820.[21] His wife gave birth to a daughter, Margaret Susan, in October 1820, but she was 'a sickly child' who died before she was 2 years old and is commemorated by a plaque in Bowmore Church in Islay. Their son, John Francis, arrived on 29 December 1821, and while he was never to succeed to Islay and Woodhall, he was to succeed in many other avenues of his life. Despite all his commitments of estate, family and parliament, the 24-year-old Walter had determined to remove his three younger sisters from the influence of Edward Bury, for reasons probably more imagined than real, if legal. Eleanora was at odds with Eliza and Walter over the measures proposed for the younger girls. She did not think them 'at all practicable', continuing:

> Nor indeed do I think they would be for their advantage, in the first place any thing violent or at all like an éclat goes against my grain if there is possibility of avoiding it, and as my sisters are now thank God more under ones own eye and certainly not likely to leave England for some time to come, I think if Walter only setts [*sic*] about it properly he may in great measure sett things to right.[22]

Eleanora also thought her mother would never consent voluntarily to her younger daughters leaving, and mistakenly considered the law would never allow it to happen without Charlotte's agreement. Trying to make peace, she suggested that 'some trustworthy person in the shape of a governess' should perhaps be appointed to help Adelaide superintend the financial and other affairs of the girls.

Nothing had been effected by the late spring of 1822, but when in June 18-year-old Adelaide (staying in London with Eleanora at the time) and 15-year-old Julia (in London with Eliza) were asked by their 24-year-old brother, Walter, if they would constitute him as their guardian, they consented. A lawyer was sent for who drew up the appropriate document, after which Walter wrote to inform Charlotte that in consequence of the ill treatment his elder sister had received at her hands Adelaide and Julia had constituted him as their guardian. In indicating that he would call on his mother very soon with the signed paper, he also requested that his remaining sister, 16-year-old Emma, might be at home when he called. Not for nothing perhaps had Bessie Mure referred to Walter as 'an abusive spirit'. In February she had hoped that the 'unruly' older children would be reconciled to Charlotte but 'that is a Shawfield feature they have in great perfection'. Bessie Mure was fearful for Charlotte, as she piously wrote to Lord John:

> Lady Charlotte who passed for forty years of her Life for being of the utmost heavenly disposition should allow those heartburnings jealousies suspicions and injustices to get possession of her old age [47] when all turbulent passions should be laid aside and nothing practiced [*sic*] but forgiveness and forbearance to prepare us for that world where nothing enters but peace and Love.[23]

On receiving her son's letter the response of Charlotte and her husband was immediately to seek advice from several lawyers. But the latter all declared that, as a woman, she did not have the legal right to keep the girls. According to Bessie Mure, when Walter arrived the meeting that took place was 'most unpleasant'. Walter told a tearful Emma that he had brought her the paper to sign. While she felt 'miserable at home' Emma, however, opined that if they all left, her mother 'would be completely at Mr Burys mercy who from being deprived of the large sum [£200 each annually] allowed by Walter for their education would become more ill tempered than ever and end by using their Mother ill'. Emma said she would consider everything for a week before giving her answer, while a few days later Adelaide and Julia had second thoughts and attempted a reconciliation. At the same time they asked their brother to formalise various conditions, including unrestricted intercourse with all the family, as well as the money Walter allowed for their education to be disposed of as Adelaide, being the eldest, thought best. A tear-blotched letter to Lady John from 16-year-old Emma in the London Hotel where the Gordon-Cummings were staying echoed the earlier emotional dilemmas faced by Beaujolois in Florence.

> Were Mr B thinking of taking us abroad again or did Mamma forbid us seeing you all, I would not hesitate in leaving them directly, but as Mamma promised me yesterday that we should meet as often as possible, I cannot resolve upon leaving her unless I hear something to the contrary, or she herself consents to it.[24]

Emma would have liked Julia to have stayed at home as well; 'Julia and I could easily go on as we have hitherto done and as long as we are in England it would be easy to leave them were things to become worse.' Poor Emma felt 'so confused, with fright and the misery of these last three days that I do not know what I say'. She continued:

> All that I wish is to prevent anything violent towards Mamma and she will never forgive us if we all leave her. However as things have broken out again just as I thought peace made I am afraid they can never be

made up again and if there is no better way, I think Mamma will not prevent us from living where we are in peace. I wish some of you would represent this to her.

Kindly Emma did not want to make her 'Mamma' unhappy and probably stayed on at Westwood until 1823. It appears that Charlotte had also had to promise Walter that one of the girls at least should always be in Scotland.

After noting that 'Emma was always my pet and she behaved best of any', Bessie Mure had mentioned to Lady John that the girls' brother, Johnny Campbell, had been in Edinburgh. She would have liked to have seen him as he was 'so agreeable they say'. He had told his cousin, Chatty Fletcher, that the girls were 'to change about between Lady Charlotte and their friends in Scotland'. This seems to have taken immediate effect for Adelaide and Julia were to sail from London to Leith with the Uxbridges and the Gordon-Cummings respectively, Bessie Mure adding that 'none of them are to live with Ly Uxbridge as they could not be kept from the pollution of Lady Anglesea' [*sic*], while 'Altyre would be 'a bad abode for Julia'. In less acerbic vein she pondered to Lady John:

Now is it not a melancholy thing that Lady C who seemed to be made up without one jarring atom full of peace and gentleness should since this most unfortunate union have lived in a constant state of jealousy and quarrel utterly alienated now from her sisters and all her own family. Who if this Man could have behaved like a gentleman or rational creature would have overlooked everything else. Ly Charlotte being quarrelled with Mamie her children and Brother is the most inconceivable moral change that has taken place in the course of my experience. It is said she and Mr Bury are going abroad again never to return to England.[25]

Much as Charlotte might eagerly have embraced such a move, it was not to be. Eleanora had confided to Eliza in November 1821 that 'Mama cannot leave England even if she wished it ever so much, as I do not believe they have a single farthing to pay for post horses'.[26] Charlotte confirmed the current family arrangements to Lady John when writing in her large scrawl while 'lieing down on a sopha' at Westwood.[27] Julia sailed to Scotland with Eliza and went on to stay with Walter, his wife and son in Islay, while Adelaide travelled with Eleanora. Johnny had also been in Edinburgh for the first time in five years (from Switzerland), and had gone to Pencaitland with his uncle Colin, while Emma had remained with her mother. In her earlier letter of 13 April to Lady John, Charlotte had remarked on Walter having replaced Lord John as Member of Parliament for Argyllshire, the latter having applied for the Chiltern Hundreds.[28] She was glad for his sake that Walter had acquitted himself so well but claimed not to understand 'the Politics of the present Day where each man brought in to parliament gives his Vote as his employer chuses though He often professes himself (as in my Brother Johns case) that His Judgment and His tastes would lead Him to vote on the other side of the question'.

> I don't wonder with his way of thinking that He got rid of the thing as soon as He could and gave it into the hands of a more Suple [*sic*] and younger stager—but ... I cannot help laughing at the idea of Walters taking the ? so easily for two years ago I heard Him violently declaiming against The Dukes Politics—all this does not raise much patriotic enthusiasm in My breast.

Now in mid-July she talked of Walter and Lady Eleanor also having returned to Scotland and ventured her opinion of Walter's wife as a 'thoroughly amiable Person and I like her very much'.[29] Much must have been resolved, forgotten or even forgiven, for Walter had seemingly asked the Burys to visit in Scotland: 'Next year I hope we may be able to make it out and then I trust I may have a chance of seeing you.'

When Charlotte had sent Lady John her elegiac Beatrice tribute in February, she had added at the foot of the letter, 'My Husband returns your remembrance with all of courtesy and good will', and expressed the wish 'if only we could meet once more the remembrance of the Dear Palatine and of Porta Pia would set exactly on the same ground of talking again'. But she wondered also 'shall we ever meet again as we then met', as 'so many things have happened since that time ... such bitterness's and heartburnings and prejudice'. She hoped fervently that they would meet again at Ardencaple which she eulogised:

> The Place in its own local self had always the greatest charm for me—it has a smilingness about it that none other has—Roseneath [*sic*] is more beautiful Inveraray more sublime—but there is a laughing sweetness about Ardencaple that I would rather Enjoy than any of the qualities or consequences attendant on the other two.

She then continued, going from 'Place to People':

> You know pretty well what I think of you—because people always feel those feelings tolerably mutually and as to My brother you know what I think of Him. And what pleasure it would be to me to see Him for the first time in his stormy Life really happy and happy in a Wife and child—the only real happiness after all.

But by the end of the year she was still trying to get Lady John to use her influence with her husband on Walter, now giving her only £750 a year, with no allowances for any of the girls, while he had a nominal income of £20,000 a year. Neither Walter's grandfather nor he, on coming of age, had acted decently by the mother who 'under very trying circumstances' had been a good and faithful wife but who had been left 'in the bounty of strangers and distant relations, Mrs Damer and Lord Frederick'.[30] She wanted her son legally to settle her home and £1,500 a year for 'My Life' only, a recurrent refrain, never to be achieved.

The June crisis of 1822 appears to have been put behind her (at least for the time being), and Charlotte and her husband had been visiting her friend 'Lady Berkeley—Lady Sutton's Daughter. She is a clever agreable person with a very good natured husband who allows her to do pretty much what she likes.'[31] They had intended going on to Mr Lambert's in Wiltshire and afterwards to the Isle of Wight to the Hooks', but Mr Bury had been recalled for business that remained unsettled. She thought it unlikely they would move from Sydenham again—'we have been such constant wanderers lately that six months of a stationary Life will be perfectly to my taste', and 'my Rosebushes and my Duck pond with all my indoors occupations fill up all my time'. One friend who made his way to Sydenham was the recently widowed Lord Glenbervie. In June Charlotte wrote to congratulate him on his gifted translations of Ricciardetto, while asking if he would allow Mr Bury's carriage to follow his from Argyle Street in town so that he could be presented by Lord Rocksavage at a Levee.[32] When Lord Glenbervie in turn accepted Charlotte's invitation to dine and stay overnight in Sydenham, he hoped to have 'the pleasure of talking over certain recent publications, one of which, in three volumes, I have read over, I will tell you with what pleasure. I am sure I need not say to you, with what interest?' While trying to fix on a date for the visit, Charlotte was looking forward to receiving his 'commendations and very instructive to profit by your corrections on the little novel you so kindly mention'. Bury again 'having been ill', then 79-year-old Lord Glenbervie himself being indisposed, it was Friday 23 August before he finally reached Sydenham to enjoy 'the quiet country air' when their 'only room ... Books, Leisure, Liberty, and Welcome await you'. His regimen was 'very plain', his only beverage being 'a little sherry with warm water and sugar'.[33]

After a long period of gestation and negotiating with the publisher, Charlotte's second novel had been published earlier in the year, again 'anonymously'. In August 1817 Beaujolois had referred to her using the scene when leaving Besançon 'in the novel she is now writing'.[34] While Charlotte was in Italy, *Conduct is Fate* was handled for publication by Susan Ferrier, Blackwood having published Ferrier's novel, *Marriage* in

1818.[35] While he had a high opinion of parts of Charlotte's manuscript that he had read, and 'commercially speaking', was very happy to publish the work, William Blackwood was shocked by Charlotte's count and countess, as he had written to Susan Ferrier on 18 January 1820:

> I hope the author will pardon me for the liberty I take in hinting that I feel confident that she could very greatly improve the first volume so as, in my humble opinion, to make it more acceptable to British readers, who are not accustomed to a husband knocking down his wife, nor yet to some other traits of Continental manners. Of all this, however, an author, and not a bookseller, is the best judge. If she is determined to publish I shall be happy to take charge of the book, and when I see the conclusion of the work I will let you know what sum I could afford to offer for it.[36]

The third volume was finished before midsummer 1821. Susan Ferrier recounted an occasion on which Charlotte was dining with her in Edinburgh, and had John Wilson ('Christopher North')[37] 'to show off with'; the question arose whether a woman of a right way of thinking would not rather be stabbed as kicked by her husband. 'I am for a stabber ... it was talking of Lord Byron that brought on the question. I maintain there is but one crime a woman would never forgive in her husband, and that is a *kicking*.'

On 5 March 1822 Blackwood reported to Thomas Cadell Jr in London, with whom it was being jointly published, that the novel would be ready in a fortnight, and advised him to get advertisements out for it.[38] These appeared in the *Morning Chronicle*, *The Star*, *and The Edinburgh Evening Courant*. A month later, Blackwood was urging Cadell not to spare the advertising for the novel, as well as wondering how the sale of it 'was coming on'. Readers found copies in the circulating libraries—in Bristol, Cheltenham, Bath and Belfast, as well as in London, Edinburgh and Newcastle-upon-Tyne and elsewhere. The triple-decker was priced at one guinea for each volume which ran to over 300 pages. Altogether just under 200,000 words had been composed, copied and recopied. The heroine lived near Lausanne and the first volume ranged over the parts of the Continent familiar to Charlotte including Switzerland, the Rhône, Avignon, Fréjus and Genoa; the heroine crossed the Channel to serve as a lowly London governess, with family travels in southern England, and Scotland—Edinburgh, the Highlands, the Clyde, Ardkinglas and Inveraray, Oban, Mull, the canals and Kyles of Bute comprising foreground more than background in the evolving plots. The soulmate that she met, Miss Oswald, then returned with her to London and the Continent and the third volume encompassed Calais, Paris, Nice, Genoa, Milan, Bologna and Florence before a gothic climax centring on Camadoli and Laverna; the heroine finally returned to Lausanne. This was not a novel of *ton*, but the strictures of a reviewer of her next novel could similarly have been applied—the material might have been spread over several novels.

After discussing various books she had been reading, Charlotte sent a copy of *Conduct is Fate* to Lady John, asking if she had 'made acquaintance with a certain *Miss Oswald* ... What do you think of her Character? and what thinks my brother John?' She neither denied nor admitted authorship: 'It may or may not be that is the best way to take it. 'Tis an amusing thing at all events—and I shall proceed now swiftly in that career. Tell me if you hear anything of the said Book.'[39] Bessie Mure had just got her copy on 2 May 1822 and 'had read only a little bit and I think it has a charm'. A fortnight later she had read it all: 'I like the first two volumes pretty well the third is intolerable have you read it.' She had, however, read it all before in manuscript, but added that 'people don't trouble themselves about it—nobody reads novels but Walter Scotts now, and I think they are very right'.[40] To her sister, Mrs Connell, Susan Ferrier also sent a copy:

> I believe it is scarce published yet, so I have no idea how it is to take or what is to be said of it in the world; but for my own part I think there is a great deal of talent in it, though not very well directed. Some of the descriptions are beautiful, but there is too much of them to please the generality of readers. Altogether I am not sanguine about it, but I shall be happy if it succeeds.[41]

In thanking Blackwood on 27 March for his copy, Theodore Hook, son of her family friends, referred to the anonymity of the author: 'She makes no great secret of it here but stops till its fame is complete to announce herself.' Less than a week later he had read it and was telling the publisher that 'it is a very sweet novel and contains much good writing and a great deal of good feeling. I have no doubt it will be a hit.'[42] John Galt was going to read it when the Easter holidays started on Friday 19 April when he would have more leisure.[43]

The reviewer in Blackwood's *Edinburgh Magazine* or 'Maga' of April 1822 considered that *Conduct is Fate* ranked between 'the blood-and-thunder romances of the Ratcliffe School, and the sober plebeianism of the natural and matter-of fact genius of Novelists ... Powers of invention and fancy' were sprinkled with 'adultery here and there—a good deal of murder—robbery *ad libitum*—queerish doings', all cited as straining the reader's credulity, as well as the fortunes of the characters moving across

Europe to Scotland and back.[44] The presumed male reviewer confessed that he was not sure that the assumed female author herself 'saw the end from the beginning' and wondered whether the denouement was planned or not. He then proceeded to 'confine' his remarks 'to what may be of more service to the author'—some columns of criticism on the style, focusing in on the ungrammatical 'who' for 'whom', abundant tautology, the 'precious fanfaronade and jumble of metaphors' and other infelicities. Somewhat pompously he could not decide whether to lay the blame on the author or the printer for the 'barbarously mutilated' French of the chapter 'mottoes'—amounting essentially to the missing accent over *où*. Since the novel was 'the infant lisp' of the author's 'pencil, as she somewhat ludicrously calls it', the reviewer felt that she was entitled to 'considerable indulgence'. But his pièce de résistance was the suggestion that the author had plagiarised a passage *in toto* from "The Earthquake" whose author had been 'deeply read' by the reviewer. In view of the timing, it is not clear whether this reviewer was Galt himself—who was at the time writing for the 'Maga'. Was the accusation entirely valid? Having dropped this bombshell, however, the reviewer finished by thanking the author 'for the pleasure (not unalloyed)' of her work, and looked forward to her next work, 'the better for our good-natured strictures'. It was probably not difficult in the close society of Edinburgh for Charlotte quickly to discover the identity of the reviewer.

The late summer calm in Charlotte's life after June 1822 had not, perhaps unsurprisingly, lasted. She often tended to be melancholic and contemplative at the year's end. This time she began on a more cheerful note to Lady John concerning the latter's second pregnancy, telling her:

> It must surely be a pleasant thought to you that you are propping up the tumbling down Old Castle of Argyll—no one rejoices in this more sincerely than I do—May it please God to grant you His Blessing to your Lifes End here and to a better Life here after and to make your Childrens Children for ever more Heirs to a Family that is yet to arise on Earth and Do honor to its progenitors—this is a Prayer in which we ought all to join for without Prayer we can have no manner of thing that is good.[45]

Such pious thoughts, however, were quickly dispelled in the following six pages of diatribe against her son, Walter and about finance. In addition, Edward Bury's attack of fever had recurred and she had once again 'only just recovered from the painful anxiety of watching Him'. She expanded:

> He is removed to London for Baths and Doctors but I alas! Am doomed to be separated from Him owing to want of Money—a most wretched

> tryal to me—to be parted from Him at such a time—Thank God He is Alive—what a Desolate Creature I should be without Him.

Much of the letter may have covered old ground, but the financial problems had not been resolved, and in spelling them out again in detail, Charlotte besought her sister-in-law once more to use her influence to get her brothers, the Duke of Argyll and Lord John, to intercede with her son, as she thought they should have done with his eponymous grandfather when Jack Campbell died in 1809.

Through his wife, Charlotte appealed to her brother Lord John 'to try and persuade Walter to settle legally upon me for My Life only this little Home', continuing:

> I have a letter from My brother John at the time of Shawfields Death which says a thousand a year additional is all that I would hear of for you settled on Yrself. This to me His Mother who had a cruel and trying past to act by His Father which thank God I was enabled to go through to the last—and who was left in a manner destitute without a Home of any sort provided for me to fight through the world with My Eight Children as I might. I cannot help adverting to that period of my Widowhood when I have ever thought My brothers might have shamed Shawfield [her father-in-law] into doing something for me—however they went on to trust to my son—and alas!

She argued:

> £750 is really incompetent to the Common Comforts of Existence—and ought to make Him Ashamed—if My expectations of having it raised to 1200—and a Home are unreasonable—say at least what you think reasonable—and above all see that it be settled on me by Law ... it is painful enough to be a beggar to my own Son.

Had it not been for help from her uncle, Lord Frederick, her cousin, Mrs Damer, and her brother, George, together with the monies she received from the Princess of Wales she 'could not have lived'.

> Whatever boastings and appearances may be—certainly it ends in this. He supports His three unmarried Sisters—but He gives His Mother only £750 pound a year—Now I trust I am not greedy—and I know that I have learnt it in the School of Adversity—I am not extravagant—but such treatment as this from a Son who has a nominal Estate of £20,000 a year and a real one of £10—His shabbiness and cruelty which I cannot

> but feel most painfully—that he should not at least give me a House over my Head—that He never should have provided a Home for me when He came of Age is I believe an unheard of thing at all events a most cruel one.

She continued:

> How can you think that I can go cordially to a Son, who does not give me a House over my head and who has positively refused to settle more on me than the £750—which at Mrs Campbells Death He must give me by law—and in the mean time boasts Himself of the £500 he is not obliged to give. Let Him provide me a Home—a humble Home I do not expect any thing like what I once might have thought myself entitled to—this poor miserable little place would satisfy me to lay my bones in and give me £1500 a year settled upon me for My Life ... nay even £1200 a year and a House over my head would satisfy me. We are preparing to leave this little Home—which I in a manner made for myself and which would have been mine had My Brother not refused to give me the five Thousand of My Fortune which might have been vested in it seeing I had no Shelter for My Head—well we are preparing to leave it to be turned out Houseless and Shelterless—and this through My Son. Should things remain as they are how can I ever revisit Scotland? I must think all My Relations have treated me with Cruelty and neglect and I cannot wish to give myself pain by being in a place where all things recall such treatment most forcibly to my remembrance—nay more I must wish to see as little as possible of a Son who has treated me thus.

It is difficult to know how much real income there was to help finance Westwood, Charlotte, and her husband, Emma, Blanche, MacLeod and the other servants. Bury was still titular rector at Lichfield or Ludshelfe, a parish of 'only thirty souls'. A revealing and formal letter had been written by his wife on 22 July 1822, addressed 'Dear Duke Devonshire'.[46] Not beating about the bush, she boldly asked whether the duke could provide a living for her husband, should 'his Grace ever have one vacant'. After the duke had replied a month later, presumably unable to comply, she thanked him in 'my anxiety, in the midst of turmoil' for his kindness and remembrance. To use her own term, she herself had, however, embarked on her new career, although she was perhaps only paid a few hundred pounds for her novel. Finances indeed reached such a parlous state that Westwood House, which had been left to Charlotte by 'a relative' (during her first widowhood) had to be relinquished.[47] Even a decade later, Edward Bury was still engaged in trying to put Charlotte's finances on a more stable and, he thought, equitable footing, explaining the circumstances yet again to her son, brothers and their various agents. The root cause of Charlotte's financial difficulties since her widowhood in March 1809 was the hastily drawn up marriage contract of May 1796. As her second husband put it:

> No anticipation of her early widowhood had been entertained ... and much had been left to contingencies ... To the absence of foresight and precaution as well as to blind reliance upon the honour and affection of the family with whom she intermarried, is alone to be attributed the inadequate provision secured to Lady Charlotte from the Shawfield Estate.[48]

No dower house or any provision in lieu of such had been arranged. Her jointure, 'so disproportionate to the alliance and unequal to the rank of the part', yielded only £750 per year. Charlotte had sought to augment this with her income from the Princess of Wales, of about £200 plus expenses of £300. When this contribution was given up and Walter had succeeded to the Islay estate, an additional voluntary sum of £250 was decided upon in February 1817, but the monies were not always paid during the difficulties incurred by her remarriage. In addition she had been ill-advised at the time of her widowhood to give up a claim of £2,000 for goods and chattels in Walter Shawfield's favour. The costs of education of the heir, Walter, were not wholly paid for as promised. Inevitably the allowance of £200 per annum given for each of her unmarried daughters fell short of their requirements as they were successively launched into society. So from the start of her widowhood, with eight surviving children, debts and the interest thereon had never been absent. Since she could never really afford to live in London in the style which she had expected, living at Sydenham or on the continent had been other attempts at saving money, if not making ends meet. The unforeseen loss of £600 income from August 1822 when Adelaide and Julia left home, followed in May of the following year by Emma, cannot have helped. Her husband spent much of his time trying to sort out the financial situation with her son, while her elder brother, the 6th Duke, also tried to intervene legally (he could not afford to, financially). To pay off the debts accumulated, the irreparable loss of Westwood had to be decided upon, that in itself incurring costs and 'without a single prospect, or the possession of a single shilling, by which another roof could become hers', as her husband emoted.[49]

How upset and rankled Charlotte felt at the prospect of relinquishing Westwood House is revealed in a letter of 3 February 1823.[50] Six months after leaving home in August the previous year, her youngest Campbell daughter, 16-year-old Julia, was staying at Woodhall with her brother, Walter, and his wife, Lady Ellinor. Charlotte's letter expressed little sentiment or concern at her daughter's continued absence from her mother, apart from the signing off which ends 'Mr Bury desires to be kindly remembered to you. And I am your affectionate Mother, Charlotte Maria Bury'. It was mostly concerned with the financial difficulties allegedly created by Walter. Deeming a recent letter from Julia intending a change in her 'residence' after six months to be 'rather in a Cavalier Style' her mother explained the circumstances from her viewpoint. She alleged that no period had been fixed for Julia's 'Visit' with Walter which Charlotte had 'certainly at the time was consider'd one of temporary amusement to you'. Walter had then apparently withdrawn Julia's allowance and when Julia had then gone to stay at Altyre, had given the annual £200 to Sir William 'as board Wages (I suppose) for you'. Charlotte continued:

> And on my appealing against a change which made your Visit, from a temporary, become a permanent one, he answered me (which Letter I now have) that it was never consider'd temporary and thus the matter ended. Both parties knew at the time of your departure that it was understood to be temporary; and optional with me whether you went or not at all. But your brother croit qu'il trompe parce qu'il ment.

She emphasised Walter's determination to make Julia's leaving permanent, 'either to put two hundred pounds in Sir Williams pocket or save it for his own—which ever it is—no matter'. She also wanted 'some written Engagement and Understanding respecting your stay with or your absence from me'. Her concluding chilly sentence verged towards emotional blackmail, for, 'according as he decided, I shall know whether I have a Home or not over my head'. What a very sad sentence this last was for the beauty and daughter of Argyll, even if only part of the situation was to have to depend on her son's decision over the allowances for her daughters. She stressed:

> This Mischief has been caused by your selves and that if you had not shewn the total want of affection and the very improper want of duty in your mode of leaving me—the now necessary change in Mr Bury's, and my residence, would not have taken place. We should in that case have had this Elligible [*sic*] House for you and your sisters; to have come and gone to, as you chose where as in the present instance we shall shortly have no Home whatever.

14

Aftermath

Westwood House was finally given up in 1823. By March 1824 the Burys were appearing in court at Bristol to arrange a loan of £300 from Lord John Campbell,[1] Edward Bury still being described as rector of Litchfield in Hampshire, and the loan having to be repaid at £100 for the following three years. They appear to have been staying for some time at Clifton on the outskirts of Bristol.[2] It is good, if surprising, to read Eleanora informing Eliza in July 1824 that Charlotte was by then 'on very good terms with us all'.[3] However, Beaujolois, writing to Eliza from Ireland that autumn, wickedly recounted some 'wonderful accounts of Mamma' that she had heard 'from a gentleman who saw her lately. It seems she and Edward are the amusement of all children and that a short time ago when they went to the fair at Bristol they were so mobbed that they escaped after having had a tremendous fright.'[4] She explained:

> Mamma is rather worse instead of better in her dress and ... Edward now wears a light grey coat cut like a shooting jacket with black velvet collar and cuffs, he has let his hair grow long like a womans and wears it in large curls on his back and shoulders. When it is cold he walks about in a sky blue cloak lined all through with fur. I assure you the gentleman who told us was in fits of laughter at the mere recollection of the sport he had had.

Perhaps it is not then surprising that she went on to say:

> Mamma is in a great state of fury with my sisters God knows what for. I begin to think she must be affronted with me for nothing will make her

answer my letters which are always most courteous. Poor woman. Does she always continue in the same terms with you.

Bessie Mure was equally spiteful when referring to Charlotte having gone 'without stays in that neglected state she did at Clifton'.[5] Her comment on visiting the Burys had been that 'he was as sickly and lanky as usual' but she admitted that he had also been 'by way of being decently civil'.

Some of the circles in which the Burys were moving were clerical. Writing from Winchester on 16 April 1825, Charlotte resuscitated her connection with the by then, Sir, Walter Scott, in asking him to further the poetic ambitions of the Rev. Walter Hook, the 'Son of my oldest and best Friends' and who had 'some of his lines in a Collection of Miss Baillies'.[6] In a postscript, she reminded Sir Walter of 'Doctor Hook now Archdeacon Hook and all our gay parties—at Woodburn—Queen Street etc'. At this time the Burys were probably living in Winchester, courtesy of these, her closest friends, the Hooks. Lady Louisa Stuart had earlier described Mrs Hooks' having 'fair locks, dressed after Lady Charlotte Campbell'.[7] James Hook was a polymathic cleric who in 1792 married Anne, the daughter of Sir Walter Farquhar, physician to the royal household. By the 1820s he was rector at Whippingham in the Isle of Wight, and archdeacon in Winchester before being appointed dean of Worcester in 1825, at which point Bessie Mure noted that the Burys then had to pay for their lease in Winchester. This smuggling part of the world was characterised by Charlotte in her novel.

Other friends she mentioned particularly were Lady Exeter, the Lamberts and the Scropes. The first was the widow of Charlotte's Hamilton half-brother, the 8th Duke of Hamilton, when she married the 1st Marquis of Exeter in 1800, thus becoming chatelaine of Burghley House near Stamford. Aylmer Burke Lambert, cousin of Charlotte's mother, was a wealthy and somewhat eccentric man of many interests who had inherited from his father in 1802.[8] With estates in England and Ireland, and Jamaican plantations, he also spent time in his homes in Salisbury and London, and Boyton House near Heytesbury in Wiltshire. An avid naturalist and collector, he had been one of three founders of the Linnaean Society in 1788, along with Samuel Goodenough, James E. Smith and T. Marshan, and counted Sir Joseph Banks and the Hookers amongst his close associates. With his wife Catherine, their hospitality was gracious and charming, and they were especially kind to the Burys at this time. Widowed in 1828, Lambert dined with Charlotte until his death in 1842. The classicist and sportsman, William Scrope, inherited his family property of Castle Coombe in Wiltshire in 1787, as well as other lands in Lincolnshire. As an amateur artist, he exhibited at the Royal Academy but it was as a passionate sportsman that he rented property near Melrose, becoming a friend of Sir Walter Scott and writing and illustrating books on deerstalking and salmon fishing.[9]

Charlotte's elder daughters had married men in uniform, or with titles and likely to inherit grand houses or estates; Eliza, Sir William Gordon-Cumming, Baronet of Altyre and Gordonstoun; Eleanora, Lord Uxbridge, son of the Marquis of Anglesey, with various large estates and houses, in Staffordshire, Sussex and Anglesey; and Beaujolois, Lord Tullamore, heir to the Earl of Charleville, with houses in London and estates and castles in Ireland. Houses were owned or rented in London for the 'season' or longer. Walter had married Lady Ellinor Charteris of Wemyss, and at last there was better news of the black sheep of the family. Johnny had been back in Britain in 1822 after five years' absence, and had seen some of his sisters and relatives. After some other unsuccessful episode in London, he was next posted to his regiment's depot on the Isle of Wight. There he met, and on 16 May 1824, married Ellen, daughter and co-heir of Sir Fitzwilliam Barrington. Walter was the only family member to attend the wedding, although Beau would have liked to accept his invitation, if finances had allowed; Walter had not asked any of his younger sisters to accompany him.[10] Eleanora thought it odd that John should have married at all—he did not seem to be 'the least in love'.[11] Since Charlotte's friends, the Hooks, were also in the island, the Burys could have attended, but this seems unlikely. Indeed, this must have been another fractious relationship, for when Charlotte was in Winchester she had bowed slightly and passed John by in the street. Johnny and his wife occasionally joined the extended family in London, Edinburgh, Woodhall and, sailing in the Campbell of Skipness yacht, in Islay. They had a son, Walter Odenal, and two daughters, Edith, and one who died in infancy.

From letters to Eliza and between and among the sisters the somewhat peripatetic life of the younger girls after leaving the Burys can be glimpsed, illustrating the rather different social interactions and possibilities from those of their elder siblings. In the immediate aftermath of the family disruption when the Burys were staying in the West Country there were only a few references in the sisters' letters to them or about meeting them. Adelaide, Emma and Julia remained peripatetic until their own marriages, staying with and helping with their siblings' young families, especially the Islay Campbells at Woodhall, Islay and Gosford, as well as with Lord and Lady John Campbell and their growing family at Ardencaple. Only occasionally did they get as far as the somewhat distant Altyre, though they at times saw Eliza in Edinburgh or London. Steamboat travel was in its infancy and required varying degrees of fortitude. The voyage up and down the east coast between Leith and London could take anything from two and a half days to a week or more.

Walter, however, still only in his early twenties, saw it as his responsibility to look after his younger sisters' interests, albeit in a somewhat authoritarian manner. Twenty-year-old Adelaide's affair of the heart with one 'BM' in 1825 was apparently an early casualty. At Almacks in April, B.M. had been there, talking to and dancing with Adelaide; as Emma reported to Lady John:

> He touched upon nothing gone by, but never left his eyes off her all night and talked to no one but some of our family. In short it seems that he does really still care for her, though the obstacles are of course still the same. Adelaide however is in a third heaven of delight and Walter does not seem to dream of things coming round again. I do not know how it will all end.[12]

It was, however, to be not only another ten years before Adelaide was to marry (but not BM), and she was not back in London for the first six of these.

What were the marriage prospects for the younger Campbells, successively Miss Campbell until they wed? Although Charlotte had returned to live in London by 1825 and was often in the company of her older daughters, there is little evidence that she saw much of the younger ones, only sparse correspondence surviving. Despite her own experience of youthful marriage, and contrary to her reservations about her brother's marrying at a young age, Eleanora was at pains to see her sisters wed, while Beau organised parties at her home in St George's Place for them to meet whichever suitable beaus were around. Each year for the London parliamentary season in early summer Walter and Lady Ellinor took a house in Montagu Square for three months. The girls took turns to go in pairs to 'All Macks', Emma reporting that Julia 'is very much admired by everybody who sees her and is in high good looks and spirits'.[13] There were many balls such as that of Prince Esterhazy, where Emma was 'thoroughly ennuiée' [*sic*], or of Lady Wemyss and Aunt Glen Carter, or the Caledonian Ball at the end of May for which Lady Ellinor was one of the patronesses. For the quadrilles, 'all the young ladies are dressd alike, like a corps de ballet', but the Campbell girls decided not to take part in the quadrilles and go their own way. Emma borrowed a Mary Queen of Scots costume from Eleanora, while Adelaide put together a Milanese costume and Julia got togged out in a pink and silver 'Spanish full dress'. Although she thought it an agreeable ball personally, Adelaide did not think it had been an especially good one. She thought Emma's costume not particularly becoming but 'Col d'Este and many others thought her and her dress divine'. Mrs Coutts's breakfast was 'a very gay thing' written up in the *Morning Post*. Julia spent a week in Windsor at the Ascot races with the Tullamores. There were also theatre and opera trips. Many young beaus, presumably vetted and approved of by the Islay Campbells, dropped in at Montagu Square, or walked the girls in the square or park. But even when Adelaide and Julia were out one day in the carriage and saw Angus Fletcher, their cousin Charlotte Fletcher's brother-in-law and sculptor, and stopped to speak to him, Emma knew that 'as he does not know Walter and Ellinor they could not ask him to come and see us ... it is very difficult to do any thing one likes', even such as going to meet their former Sydenham acquaintance, Thomas Campbell. Hours were assiduously taken up in singing lessons with Mr Hawes, learning the latest glees and catches, preferably with Campbell of Saddell singing the bass parts instead of Adelaide and Emma.[14] Chess became another enthusiasm, taught by 'little Mr Cochrane' whom Emma quickly learned to beat. She had gone to dine with Eleanor and Uxbridge one evening but did not 'certainly wish to spend another such again'. Like her mother, Adelaide was devoted to her dog, and was quite content to miss Almacks one evening when the poor dog was ill. London's spring viral colds, smoke and fatigue affected them all at some stage. On 14 June 1824 their brother, Johnny, brought his new 'amiable and very sensible' wife to meet them for the first time.

On one occasion at the end of June 1824, Lord John hired a steamboat at Greenock to proceed via Ardlamont, an embarking place for Islay, and round the Mull of Kintyre. But he found that the captain 'had played false and crammed the boat', so alternate arrangements had to be made. Luckily for the girls, the boat had made two attempts to get round the Mull but was driven back and had to land at East Tarbert on Loch Fyne, from which they crossed to West Loch Tarbert and eventually sailed for Islay.[15] The following summer Emma admitted to Lady John that she was 'alive' after another passage to Islay.[16] She had stayed in the cabin:

> But after a good deal of interesting and profitable conversation with the female tourists, and an old Glasgow wife who was anxious to give me an idea of her importance, I turned into bed, and had the amusement of watching through a chink of my curtain, the proceedings of the English party, they were extremely surprised at my not undressing but I had no mind to pass the night there.

The 'Pollock Shaws lady' had also given her uninvited accounts of the splendiferous 'King's visit to Edinboro'. At the mouth of the Sound of Islay, 'they were obliged to lay more than an hour ... as it was so dark and misty they were afraid of going on'. It was four in the morning when they landed at Port Askaig where carriages met them and took them off to Islay

House. Enclosed with the letter was one of Julia's sketches, an interesting view of Lady Ellinor with Campbell of Jura, their backs to the sketcher while looking at the stunning Paps of Jura.

The ennui felt by these energetic young women cooped up in others' homes, reading, sketching, needleworking and netting (knitting) is palpably conveyed by poem and ink in frequent and lengthy letters to each other, and to their older sisters. A pretty cottage ornée had been built on the south-east coast of Islay at Ardimersay as a base for Walter's sundry sporting interests, and the girls were writing, sketching and sewing there even in the short days of dim wintry light.[17] In return for presents of hens, eggs, butter and so on given by the islanders to Lady Ellinor, and also to give away to the poor, the girls had to 'work away at old wives' bedgowns, Flannel dickies and such like'.[18] At other times the young women's energies were taken up with preparing for balls in these homes, or in those of their neighbours. In August 1825 Adelaide was in charge of the decorations for the Islay House ball. As Emma told Eliza:

> We were all very busy dressing up the staircases with pink and white festoons and lamps of Adelaide's invention, I assure you she was very proud of her contrivances for lighting the dancing room, branches of wood dressed up with heather and ferns and small lamps amongst it all ... very gay and pretty.[19]

But sadly she thought it all 'lost on the sort of people who saw it'.

> You would not have believed it but we got in the Island about a hundred people who call themselves ladies and gentlemen which with our own party made a very respectable assemblage ... John, Ellen, Colin, Elcho, Mr MacAllister, the whole Colonsa party and the Skipness boys.

There had been frantic preparations on the island all day. Despite the constant rain which might have ruined his efforts:

> Urquhart the Glasgow hairdresser having had a report that the said ball was to take place, repaired here from Glasgow with silk stockings, gloves etc., and he afterwards told us he had been from eight that morning dressing heads ... short and almost frenchified.

Some had to come over twenty miles in carts and 'adorned themselves at the Inn or rather the ale house' at Bridgend in time for the start of dancing at eight o'clock. Ten Islay fiddlers made up the band, 'some of whom played well enough, but not being accustomed to play together, the crash was occasionally rather discordant'. There were also quadrilles with the help of piano and cello, and members of the house party contributed to the music which went on till five in the morning.

The later summer season in Islay found the girls busily engaged in many of Lady Elinor's charitable projects—sewing schools, prize-givings, making bunting and decorating Islay House for the seasonal ball, races, annual boat race and so on. Adelaide and Julia were busy drawing portraits and modelling in wax any relatives and guests who could remain still for long enough. Just as with previous generations at Inveraray, Islay House was often 'full of company' during the shooting season; it was perhaps not quite so high flown as twenty or more years before in Inveraray, but consisted of a wide circle of kin from Argyll, others such as Charles Tisdall, Lord Tullamore's half brother, and 'last but no means least, Mr Hawes, the person who gave us lessons of singing in London and who in the country proves daily more agreeable', as Adelaide averred in a letter to Lady John.[20] Noting that he was very handsome she intended 'trying to take his portrait one of these days'. They made him 'sit at the Piano forte all night' accompanying their songs, after he had been out fishing and shooting 'all and every day whatever the weather'. Another tradition had been handed down—the production of 'a Sunday evening newspaper' which included prose by Hawes and verses by Emma to Charles Tisdall, though supposed to be from Miss Campbell of Carradale. Many of the young men fell in love with the lovely Emma, but as Adelaide confessed to her aunt Lady John:

> Your Angel Emma is again at her old tricks ... adding many moths to her list of victims of her charms, who, singed as they may be, still hover round the light and court their own destruction. Were you but to see the bewitching smile that plays around her lips and the glance that flashes from her dark blue eye [*sic*] when he is near you would feel for his mishap and pity him.

The partying continued well into the autumn, with the Inveraray 'meeting' and three nights of dinners, balls and suppers there, so that with all the singing and dancing Emma felt so 'completely knocked up that I can hardly speak'.[21] Adelaide had produced not only a 'capital collection of portraits' of the principal figures, including those in fancy dress on the last night; she had also been asked by Walter to do a water colour of the three sisters, 'all extremely like', Emma not being able to resist the additional comment 'I think everybody agrees in saying that the one of me could not be better', although the composition was as yet not finished. There was also electioneering; they returned to Islay before proceeding to Woodhall and then Edinburgh for its New Year season.[22] In 1824 Adelaide and Julia had been painting frescoes at Woodhall, when Julia found herself on her own there for several weeks, her imagination fearing 'Evil Spirits' and giving her the 'Blue Devils'.[23] While she regretted that there would be no more of Lord Byron's poems over which to shed tears, she managed to get through Elizabeth Benger's *Memoirs of Queen Mary*, Lucy Aikin's *Memoirs of the Court of Queen Elizabeth*, Lady Morgan's *Salvator Rosa* and Theodore Hook's *Sayings and Doings*.

In the background there was a litany of the strange medical history concerning Lady Ellinor. She suffered severe facial rashes and regularly ordered medicine from a doctor in Glasgow, often taking more than the recommended dose of what appeared to be a strong suppressant. Subsequent fevers and delirium were attributed to these Steele medicines. The local Islay physician Dr MacTavish treated her for these various complaints, but other medicals were also required to make their way to Islay from Glasgow.

Many of the letters amongst the female correspondents in the extended family included references to the ongoing childbearing of the older sisters and their sisters-in law. Charlotte had advised Eliza's husband in her first letter after the birth of their first child and heir in 1816 not to have as many children as she herself had had, particularly 'of the female variety'. She also strongly advised against nursing one's children, to save the ruin of the mother's figure, although she nursed Blanche herself in Italy in 1819.[24] Eliza certainly did not act on the first piece of advice, although ignoring the second may have contributed to her having her children at almost biennial intervals, instead of her mother's having had nine children in under ten years. Eliza gave birth to at least thirteen children who survived (although two of her younger ones died of scarlet fever in 1837), and she was child-bearing for over quarter of a century. All her children were born at Altyre except her first daughter (in Naples, 1818) and her last daughter (in London, 1837). At the same time many of her energies were expended on the Altyre estate and its dependent families. The estate was being 'improved' in the manner of the times and, together with various projects for female employment, Lady Gordon-Cumming's special interests were in the layout of the policies surrounding the house. Mlle de la Chaux hoped to see all the gardens, shrubberies, walks and the greenhouse, and also aspired to tread on the iron verandah that had been despatched from Carron iron works.[25] One visitor to the garden later eulogised:

> As a perfect cluster of arbours and greenhouses apparently meant for the muses and graces, for pleasure, gayety and romance, but never intended for the mere vulgar, ordinary purposes of life. Within, without,

> and round, you see nothing but flowers rushing in at every window and besetting all the doors ... the green lawn is like Genoa velvet studded with fuchsias, geraniums, carnations, every flower, in short, that has a name ... the hall had the fragrance of a conservatory.[26]

Even in this apparently exemplary household however, a crisis had erupted in 1823. It was Bessie Mure, as ever, who gave the first hint, gossiping from Edinburgh to Lady John Campbell at Ardencaple: 'At a large dinner at which I met Dundas of Dundas he came and sat by me laid his shoulder to mine and brandishing his legs and arms asked me if I had heard the story of the French widow and Sir W C. I can tell you all the particulars he added.'[27] Not only does Sir William seem to have been disloyal to Eliza with the governess whom she sacked, but he had apparently encouraged her to have beaux to stay so that she could also be blamed for being an unfaithful wife. Characteristically Bessie Mure had

> a great mind to write him an anonymous letter and ask him where he thinks he will go when he dies having the well being of a Girl ... intrusted to him whom he vowed to love cherish and protect and he fulfilled them by violating the delicacy of her mind by every impure discourse and then encouraged and surrounded her by every idle youth who admired her and insulted her by such dissolute conduct even under his own roof.

Bessie Mure considered that Beaujolois would have coped better with the whole affair than Eliza but although she deemed Sir William to be 'really half a fool half a madman, I think she will remain with him tho she is a person more swayed by the passion of the moment than by deliberate resolve'. Eliza's grandmother, 'old Mrs Campbell' (of Islay) had apparently tried to persuade Eliza that 'wanderings were very usual in men' and that she knew of 'so many instances of women who are now in their Graves who had dissolute husbands and who grinned and bore it and were generally rewarded for patience even in this world'. She contrasted this with 'the women who separated were happy no time', adding percipiently: 'I sometimes think Eliza destined to be tyrannised over by her husband as her mother was by all of hers. She resembles her in many points of her character. Mercifully she has more maternal love.' Bessie Mure's next effusion gossiped further. In another long letter, she detailed all the comings and goings of the Cummings and the governess in what was for a while the talk of the town (in Edinburgh)—the lawyers, the recriminations, the reconciliations and so on.[28]

It is presumably to the same affair that Mlle de la Chaux referred in her cross-written lengthy letter to Lady John relating:

> It was a sad confirmation of what I had lately heard, and expected, ever since the last visit I paid to my unfortunate friend. Things were going on in a way which could not but overthrow all family happiness. It made me miserable. Seeing I could not mend matters, I went away as soon as I could with a heavy heart![29]

She hoped that Eliza's 'own dearly bought experience and her future prudent conduct may bring back some peace of mind for herself, and better behaviour on his part occasionally but not permanently I fear'. She added: 'He has no control over his passions safe what is suggested by self interest now and then and by a sort of good nature.' Mamie de la Chaux went further, observing:

> I had an opportunity to make respecting the leading point of his temper and peculiarities, before he married were such, that I certainly should have broken off the engagement had she been my Daughter, at least I should have required a few months for deliberation, but such things were not to be thought off [*sic*], according to her Mother's notion, who was the only person who witnessed the Ceremony with my eyes and without anxiety for the results of that married union.

She thought his Cumming sisters had too much influence over him, and were all 'prejudiced ... in their blind approbation' of all that he did, and she expressed the hope that 'as many as can should be silent upon it—Try dear Lady John to make her own relations, at least adopt this plan', continuing: 'Especially if possible, her Mother. In answer to your ever kind manner of inviting me to return to dear Scotland, I shall say candidly that I feel at present less inclination to take advantage of it, owing to the circumstance of our mutual regret.'[30]

Mlle de la Chaux was often helping the sisters at parturition, her accounts being on the graphic and dramatic side. When Beaujolois was pregnant in Switzerland in the winter of 1821/2, she looked 'very well indeed considering her present burden and her health having improved of late I hope she will get rid of it safely. She is ready to face this awful trial cheerfully. But I confess I dread the idea of seeing this young creature in agonizing pain.'[31] She added: 'I think if there was nothing but that, to make a man feel tenderness for his Wife, it ought to be enough.' Beaujolois' son and heir, Charles, was born in Geneva on 8 March 1822, as the Earl of Charleville informed his agent back in Ireland:

> I have great pleasure in announcing to you a family event which I am sure you will rejoice with me in. I mean the birth of a grandson. Early

> this month Lady Tullamore was safely delivered of a fine boy, and both mother and Child were going on as well as possible when we heard last from Geneva.[32]

Another son, Henry Walter, arrived in March 1823, but writing from Charleville Forest Castle and its 'penetrating damp' in October 1824 Beaujolois expressed her conviction that her next child would be a girl, since she felt 'different' this time.[33] The doctors had told her she was to lie in on 15 November but 'I do not myself count before the last days of the month'. The longed-for daughter appeared on 4 December, and was named after her mother and always referred to as 'Little Beau'. Eliza was also pregnant again, and Beaujolois advised her 'to wear Dr Hamilton's straps immediately for certainly they preserve the figure amazingly'. In advance, Beaujolois said that she wanted to attempt nursing this time. 'But I should think it will only be an attempt for Lord Tullamore already seems rather to disapprove of the plan.' She also hoped to see Eliza in London, with her daughter, Seymour: 'I only wish all the children were to be of the party.'[34] She had two further living children, John James in 1827 and Alfred in 1829, while a second daughter, Julia, was born on 15 January 1832 but died the same day.

On their return from their continental sojourn in 1821 and 1822, Lord Tullamore had become an assiduous MP, representing Carlow and then, after 1832, Penryn and Falmouth until his father's death in 1835. He and Beaujolois were in London for parliament and the season, and set up home at St George's Place on Hyde Park Corner. The senior Charlevilles rented the Duke of Queensberry's house in which the redoubtable countess, though severely disabled by rheumatism, held sway over one of London's most lively salons at this time. The Tullamores sometimes travelled to Scotland in late summer,[35] and most autumns saw them at home in Charleville, whose gates and driveway were on the edge of the town of Tullamore.[36] The earl had brought the Grand Canal to the town and had also instigated many civic improvements including the church and court house. The Castle must have held strange echoes for Beaujolois. Built by Johnston in the decade after 1806, its central tower was modelled on that at Inveraray, although the latter's four corner towers were surpassed in height and variety by different designs at Charleville. The interior was not French but almost outdid Strawberry Hill in the extent of its Gothic decoration and remains one of Ireland's most renowned and complete Gothic interior. Estate buildings and glass houses complemented the house. In the immediate aftermath of the Union, Charleville was built to impress and to entertain envoys, luminaries and society at large. The Castle and grounds with plantations and walks have now seen better days but it is easy to conjure up images of the Tullamore balls in the cream and gold salon with its ornate Gothic ceiling; the soirées in the music room and table conviviality in the darkly panelled dining room. A grand staircase led to galleries off which were the bedrooms and boudoirs, some in the turrets and a small octagonal library. Although the main rooms were south-facing it is no surprise to find Beaujolois bemoaning the Irish mist. Perhaps it was no wonder either that Charleville's atmospheric Gothic setting and rumoured paranormal instances were used in 2007 for two Jane Austen films—*Northanger Abbey* and *Becoming Jane*.

Almost from the start, there had been rumours on the Continent and in London about the fortune of Eleanora's marriage. The young socialite often recognised that while not ill, she did not feel well enough 'to enjoy anything'.[37] She suffered headaches and, as with many in her family, an ordinary cold led to complications and frequently laid her low. Moving with her husband's regiment, and enduring long journeys between London, Beau Desert in Staffordshire and Plas Newydd in Anglesey, fatigued her, as did sharing homes with the fractious Anglesey family. Longing for a small house of her own, she and her husband rented a house in London's Lower Grosvenor Street for six months in early 1820 then moved into a larger one.[38] The Duke of Argyll was very partial to Lord Uxbridge (his stepson), and his duchess was also very supportive of Eleanora.[39] But pregnancy meant that she had to forego London's social life and she was often left alone at home, only going out three times in one season. Perhaps the frailest physically and psychologically of the Campbell girls, she was just 22 when her first child was born in May 1820—not a son and heir, but a daughter, Eleanora Caroline. Her searing letter to Eliza described what many women through time, and a near conspiracy of silence, are surprised to discover about their first accouchement, the almost unbearable pain:

> I think the whole concern so superlatively horrible that I only wonder how people ever have <u>second</u> children. On the Thursday I suffered all day a good deal of pain and had reasons to expect it might come on in the night, however I slept pretty well till four o'clock on the Friday morning and then the pain came on so bad I could not stay in bed, but got up and walked about the room till eight when I rang for Mrs Norton and desired her to send for Mrs Whitehouse and the woman who was to attend me.[40]

All this time her husband 'Ux' was asleep as he had been unwell for ten days after a riding blow which became so inflamed that the pain 'kept him entirely confined to his sofa'. She related to Eliza, who had been through childbirth several times already:

> I was in constant pains till six oclock the next morning, without a minute's sleep, etc I kept hopping in and out of bed for I could not lay, like a mad creature I did not conceive human nature could have borne what I went through at the last. I as firmly expected to die as possible, and the old lady said she had not known such a hard labour for many a day. I suffered horribly too from the after concerns when I hoped all was over.

Like many others before and since, she continued: 'My joy and gratitude when I heard my darlings voice I cannot describe, but if I were to live a 100 years I never can forget what I suffered.' Her spouse was 'a very indifferent papa at present but I trust will improve'. In time, Uxbridge did play with his little red-haired daughter, but it was no doubt with some relief all round that Eleanora bore him an heir, Henry Paget, in December of the following year. Another daughter, Constance followed later.

The difficulties in the Uxbridge marriage were given by Beaujolois as a reason for her delay in writing to Eliza from Windsor in 1824, since she had 'had nothing pleasant to tell you about Eleonora and Uxbridge and she wrote to you herself'.[41] She expanded: 'I think theirs is now a hopeless case. He has so completely lost her affections and treats her so as to harden her every day more and more against him.' Julia considered that no 'mortal could continue to live with him in his present ferocious state' and added: 'all agree that none but such a perfect disposition as hers could have gone on so long with him. She constantly says that were it not for the children she would leave him immediately.' Eleanora was writing to Eliza in June that there had seemingly been some 'vile woman who effectively succeeded in filling his mind with jealousy mistrust and suspicion. He broke entirely with her in the autumn just after we left Worthing', but his temper had been dreadful in the long winter of 1823 at Beau Desert, and even worse when back in town.[42] Beau blamed the 'dreadfully bad set altogether men and women and it was a great misfortune ever to have had any thing to do with them', adding: 'Uxbridge and I are no longer on speaking terms. We only bow most respectfully. I believe he looks on me as little better than the Devil and cannot endure that Eleanor should associate with me.' This sits uneasily with some of the gossip parlayed to Bessie Mure who blamed Beau for being the cause of the Uxbridge problems: 'What an unfortunate friend Lady Tullamore is for her.'[43]

The world, including all of Eleanora's relatives, certainly agreed that it was very difficult for a separated woman to thrive. Beaujolois had opined 'in cases of separation ... a woman always comes off badly and all the blame falls on her'.[44] Even Bessie Mure queried 'what she will do and where she will live. She will get head and ears in debt.'[45] According to Beaujolois, Eleanora had stuck it out with 'Uxbridge at Beau desert and all its odious inhabitants', and considered that she should perhaps spend the winter months in London with the Tullamores. Charlotte thought that Eleanora should go to Eliza's at Altyre 'to fish in less troubled waters'. When she was indeed at Altyre she can hardly have been very happy to receive the advice of her 21-year-old sister, Adelaide.[46] After cogitating for a while, she wrote from Ardimersay Cottage in Islay on 1 December 1825:

> I wish though, most ardently wish dearest Elinora I had any ground to hope that you would bring yourself to return to Uxbridge ... our duty to God is the first thing in Life certainly then according to the laws of the bible your duty is '... unto your husband'—for did you not say for better and for worse ... if you make the virtuous exertion to return to your duty, God will give you strength to go through your trials. May I beg of you ... to read the Bible more regularly. Know dear you have rather neglected it for many years ... (also Uxbridge). You would both have been happier ... Reflect on the melancholy consequences of being a single woman.

A few days later Beaujolois, bemoaning 'the terrible abuse that is lavished upon Eleanora', was also censoring Eliza.[47] She was sorry to hear that 'even in Scotland you are both dreadfully abused', continuing:

> It is said that Eleanora was not content till she had bought up all the finery Edinburgh could produce and that she was going about looking the gayest of the gay and in high spirits. This was said in the Clubs. They say she does not care about her children since she could leave them with so little difficulty.

Above all many people had seen Eliza and Eleanora dining out,

> dressed with extraordinary magnificence to the great envy and malice of all beholders. In short the county rings with Eleanora's indifference and gaiety and readiness to amuse herself when only a few years ago they saw all she did to marry the man she has now discarded.

The admonishment continued, hoping that they would not go out 'amongst all those chattering people who from envy alone will abuse you and your finery'. She finished by repeating some Edinburgh gossip passed round at London's Crockfords where it had been said that Lady Uxbridge had gone to Altyre with Lady Cumming. 'I hope' said the wit of the party 'she is going to Alter'.

Just before Christmas 1825 Beaujolois wrote to Eleanora, having in the circumstances felt 'afraid of every word I say ... At least I feel very differently from what I did formerly. I hear more and more every day how shamefully Uxs family have abused me Ld A[nglesea] at their head ... but to this make no answer.'[48] She reported that Uxbridge had joined his regiment at Windsor and the children were still in town but, sadly, 'are always made to cut mine whenever they meet'. This, despite Julia's observation that Uxbridge 'is quite broken hearted and literally has not a moments rest except when he is with his children'. As through time, the approach of Christmas occasioned a flurry of emotional letters among various members of the family. From Altyre on Sunday 18 December 1825 Eleanora wrote a short letter to her husband attesting her 'firm belief that we cannot be happy, living together', continuing:

> No real harmony could exist between us ... you ask me how I can hope for anything like happiness constantly separated from my dear Children. You promised to me to allow them to be with me frequently ... God bless you my dear Uxbridge and make you happier than your Ever affectionate Eleanora Uxbridge.[49]

Eliza, seemingly *in loco parentis* for many of her sisters, was the recipient of several anguished letters from Uxbridge at this time. Even Bessie Mure had reported breathlessly that 'Lord Uxbridge felt the separation most keenly that it almost killed him that he was going about London the Ghost of what he was'.[50] His children were either with him in town or with his sister, Caroline, Duchess of Richmond, at Goodwood. 'They say he is a picture of misery', wrote Bessie Mure,[51] the day before he wrote from London to Eliza, answering some of her questions. 'I own myself guilty of ferocious looks, and severe and unkind speeches ... horrid reports about Eleanora, she acting contrary to my wishes ... mutual acknowledgment of error surely ought to take place.'[52] On 19 December he sent a much more emotional letter to Eliza, perhaps in response to hers of the previous day, about Eleanora's leaving her home and her children, and on Christmas Eve he enclosed that same letter from Eleanora to Eliza.

Eliza and others had been communicating that Eleanora was also ill. There had been previous references to her use and abuse of laudanum. In October Bessie Mure had hoped that she would 'break the dreadful habit of taking Laudanum and allow her judgement to act unbiased by that horrid potation', though she conceded that she had no hope of this happening.[53] On 5 December 1825 Uxbridge had written from Goodwood, hoping that Eliza had 'persuaded her to give up the Laudanum or she cannot live to see the dear chicks again'.[54] The London financial agent to the upper classes, Moses Hoper, advised Sir William on 29 December 1825 that Lady Uxbridge was to be invited home again to her children and Lord

Uxbridge.[55] But by 4 January 1826 his associate, Tupper, was pleading with Sir William[56] about Lady Uxbridge and laudanum.

> Let her be implored therefore not only for her sake, but for the sake of all she values and holds dear on earth to forbear to the utmost her power from the use of this medecine [*sic*], I am aware this cannot be done at once but in her case she ought to summon resolution to Do so by degrees, but let this be done quickly for Gods sake.

Even writing from the George Hotel in York on 2 January 1826 Uxbridge responded to Eliza's worry of Eleanora's getting Laudanum 'in a way you never dreamt of—What do you mean? Who does she employ, and how does she get it?'[57] While Bessie Mure had referred to the strong Campbell and Shawfield stock the Gunning heredity probably contributed to Eleanor's ill health for which laudanum was prescribed. Lord Uxbridge had been on the quay in Calais in 1815 waiting for her when he was a young officer only 18 years old, she 16. They had married in 1819 in the face of his family's opposition and life in London and at Beau Desert had probably produced their own stresses. Childbearing may also have contributed, but in her own words that Christmas Eleanora had written to her husband 'I often think that I do not have long to live'—and she was only 20 years old.

A further complication had arisen for Uxbridge just at this time. His brother, Lord Arthur Paget, was injured in a hunting accident in Yorkshire, and died on 28 December 1825 before Uxbridge could reach him.[58] After taking part in the military cortège through York and the funeral service at Lichfield, Ux himself became ill when he returned to London. The emotional see-saw continued with letters to and fro. About this time Eleanor had written Uxbridge and he in turn wrote to Eliza on 19 January 1826 'to express the pleasure I felt at her beginning to shew some wish to return to her home; though at so distant a day'.[59] While rueing that his future life was to be settled by a letter from his wife, he anguished: 'Oh Eliza, if Eleanora could only see the Chicks she would never leave them again.' By early May Hoper reported from London to Sir William that 'Lady Uxbridge on the whole was looking better than I expected ... I am told she has left off the use of laudanum.'[60] But a month later Uxbridge was telling Sir William that his wife was again 'looking very ill indeed. She is much reduced and is shockingly weak and takes scarcely any nourishment.'[61]

By the start of 1827 Eleanora was wintering at the Sea House Hotel in Worthing and had again become so ill that Beaujolois and her husband, Lord Tullamore, were sending reports at least daily to Eliza. Local doctors and a Dr Burnett from London were in constant attendance. Charlotte engaged in correspondence over Eleonora's condition with the doctors, asking them not to conceal how dangerous her condition was, and hoping to talk to Dr Burnett personally.[62] Perhaps surprisingly, she made a rather formal request:

> Should it be ... your opinion that my presence will not tend to agitate Lady Uxbridge or that there is any danger to be immediately apprehended, I shall immediately proceed to Worthing. Indeed I beg the favour of your alluding to my intention to my Daughter and endeavoring to ascertain from her if my presence would contribute to her comfort and tranquility [*sic*].

The reply is not known, but Eleanora's fevers caused her pulse to rise. Night times were particularly bad with persistent coughing and she rarely managed to get out of bed by day; if she did, she had to be carried downstairs. Laudanum was still in the picture, but as Beaujolois noted, 'while we are here and she cannot move she does not get much contra bande'. Beau calculated:

> She must have taken two gallons of laudanum since last January—at one chemists in London the bill sent in to Ux for her contained 23 half pints—besides we know two other chemists in London who furnished her with it. She firmly believes that she is given no Laudanum although they are still obliged to give her a good deal—and she says she is delighted to think that she is cured of taking it. It is the first time she has spoken on the subject or that I have mentioned it to her and decidedly that is the best plan.

Beau's view, however, was that 'all the expense and kindness by Uxbridge would in all probability be repaid by her leaving him if she recovers'.

Walter had set off from Woodhall on 12 January 1827 to see his ailing sister.[63] Although Eleanora was apparently not keen, Charlotte also came to visit, and Beaujolois informed Eliza that 'Mamma went away this morning quite enchanted with Uxbridge and herself'. Beau acknowledged that 'Uxbridge has been very kind to all of us'. But in the middle of January he had to leave Worthing to be on duty in London for the Duke of York's funeral. On his return he arranged for Eleanora to be taken to London for further medical treatment. Dr Burnett was to 'set her asleep with laudanum and bring her up in a quiescent state in the spring carriage'.[64] When they awoke on 22 January, the ground was covered thickly with snow, 'altogether the weather in a most unfavourable [*sic*] state for an invalid'.

Notwithstanding, Eleanora was put on a bed 'like a bier ... shoved in like a coffin to a hearse ... her maid with her'. The Tullamores accompanied the invalid in a separate carriage. They left Worthing at midday, but as the snow continued to fall steadily it took seven and a half hours to reach Berkeley Square. Beau sent 'Betty' a 'bad account of Eleanora's fever and cough, her pulse above 140 by evening'.

> Dr Barnett on his second visit ordered her bled instantly—a large breakfast cupful from a blister put on her chest. She passed very sleepless nights talking incessantly, vomited and defecated until almost fainting. Poor Eleanora repeatedly said 'surely this must be just like dying.'

Three days later Charlotte descended again, as Beaujolois graphically relayed to Eliza: 'I am horrified to tell you that Mamma has really conducted herself in such a manner as quite to incense us all, by her disgusting want of feeling.'[65] Eleanora had written her mother to say that the Duchess of Argyll, who daily appeared at the same time, wanted to avoid meeting Charlotte. The latter sent back an open note saying she had no kind of objection to meeting the duchess and would certainly come. This she did, and in spite of the footman begging her to walk into the drawing room to avoid the duchess at Eleonara's sickbed, she rushed past him, 'dragging Blanch after her and before any soul could announce her darted into Es bed room and was by her side in an instant. She turned to the D/s—held out her hand saying how do you do D/s. The D/s could not refuse it but instantly left the room'. As Beaujolois put it: 'Mama talked chalk and cheese ... she looked perfectly well and then went away quite proud of her performance'. Poor Eleanor said the agitation of this scene was so much that she felt as if something 'had burst at her heart'. Dr Burnett then bled her again and insisted that no one should be admitted but Beaujolois. Charlotte was put in an even poorer light:

> Mamma has written since one unfeeling unnatural enquiry after another. In short Dr Barnett and every body are quite scandalised ... She told my nurse yesterday when I sent her maid to tell all the particulars of Eleanor's state that she did not believe she was by any means as ill as I imagined that she must know our constitutions mental and physical better than any body.

Beaujolois also sent a following letter to Sir William reinforcing her horror at Eleanor's agitation, saying that she herself had taken her mother by the hand and had led her from the bedside:

> After which she stayed for three-quarters of an hour under the pretext that she wanted to hear Dr Burnetts opinion ... she felt no anxiety etc she talked of every indifferent consequence you can well imagine ... Dr B told her very seriously that Es life now depended on her being kept perfectly tranquil.[66]

On 12 February a Welbeck Street consultant, after calling in other specialists, sent a report on Eleanor to Eliza: 'Both Lungs and heart are implicated ... and the continuance of these complaints have [*sic*] produced both weakness and emaciation.' They had also told Charlotte that there remained some other hidden malady which they could not understand but which they thought was destroying her. They had warned Beaujolois that unless some decided improvement were to take place within the next two or three weeks 'no human power could save her and that she must then sink rapidly'. Beaujolois herself thought that 'others may be deceived but I cannot and have everything to fear'. Eleanora had asked whether Eliza could come, but there was illness at Altyre, and on 21 February Beau was feeling very 'distressed you are not likely to come to town for a whole month ... I do hope Sir William will let you come without loss of time even if you have to do so without him.' Uxbridge had seen his wife's emaciated body and 'turned away quite sick and cried like a child. I wish I could have any such relief but I have never yet cried once.' She continued:

> I have loved her like a sister ... I do not regret the course I have always pursued towards her much as I have been blamed. I acted disinterestedly and (however mistakenly) as I hoped for the best ... Nothing can have been kinder more friendly and obliging than poor Ux.

The surviving correspondence comes to a stop, and Eleanora survived into 1828.

Charlotte was at Lord Uxbridge's villa at Twickenham in February that year and Eleanora died there on 3 July 1828, aged 29, after what *The Times* described as 'a severe and lingering illness, which she bore with the greatest patience and resignation'. The eldest of her three children was only 7 or 8. Despite the turbulent history of her marriage, she was reported as having been buried in the Anglesey vault in Lichfield Cathedral. In death the family, as in many others, was not immune from squabbling. Before Lord Uxbridge had even returned from the funeral, Beaujolois had exchanged a chair he had given her for another which he claimed was the one in which he had often watched his 'blessed' Eleanora sit. Eliza implored her sister to return it immediately and when harmonious relations had been restored, a year later he was distributing some of Eleanora's jewellery to her five remaining sisters. Four years later he remarried. Like Tullamore, and echoing the Argyll tradition, he spent much of the rest of his life at successive courts.

The year 1828 also witnessed other sad family events. On 21 January Joan Glassell, Lady John, died and was shortly followed by her new-born daughter. Adelaide had helped to nurse them and then stayed for several years to look after the bereft Lord John, his two young sons, John and George, and remaining daughter, Emma, until he remarried four years later.[67] On 13 February 1828 Lady Augusta was advised that her son, Douglas Clavering, by then in his mid-thirties, must be presumed to have been lost at sea, since nothing had been heard of his vessel, the *Ardwing/ Redwing* after sailing from Sierra Leone on the 16 June the previous year.[68] By then a Commander and a Fellow of the Royal Society, Douglas had been gazetted for his coolness and gallantry in Chesapeake, and had been involved over the previous decade in much oceanic research in the Caribbean and Atlantic before surveying Spitsbergen and the east coast of Greenland. His journal of the latter was posthumously published as promised by James Smith of Jordanhill, his premature demise having cut off 'the promise of future eminence'.[69]

Charlotte's cousin, the sculptress Anne Seymour Damer, died on 28 May 1828, aged 79, at her house in Upper Brook Street, her favourite cousin, the Duke of Argyll, being present. Mourners at her funeral and burial at Sundridge[70] in Kent included the Rev. Edward Bury and Sir Alexander Johnston, cousin Louisa's husband. The year before, Charlotte had composed a preface to a proposed second edition for Henry Colburn of Anne Damer's romance *Belmour*[71] which had been 'published many years ago, but, owing to various unfavourable circumstances, was never so generally known as it deserved to be'. Friends had hoped that Anne Damer would consent to a new edition of *Belmour*. But her cousin's reply had been that the time would come when, 'you may (and I am pleased with the thought), affix your preface to Belmore [*sic*], and I feel that you will do so with a sense of melancholy pleasure'. Seven years later, Charlotte was moved to write a corrective to a recently published biography of Mrs Damer in which there was 'a sneering depreciation of her character and talents'.[72] Charlotte voiced the following opinion:

> All women who aspire to fame are subject to severe criticism. Happiest and wisest are those who, not being compelled by circumstances of a pecuniary nature, rest in the tranquil shade of domestic life, and whose duties and cares are repaid by the love of a husband, of children, and of kindred ... During the short time that she was a wife she behaved excellently well to a singularly depraved husband; and at his death she

> despoiled herself of every thing to pay his debts, as far as her means allowed, even to the very diamond buckles of her shoes. To her husband's brother, for many years, she gave a fifth part of her jointure.

She went on to pay tribute to many of her exemplary characteristics as a daughter and friend, and especially as far as Charlotte herself was concerned,

> as a benefactress (and who can speak to this better than myself?), noble and munificent. To her dependants, the best and most generous of mistresses ... No one more implicitly obeyed the golden rule of doing as she would be done by. Her conscientious use of affluence was at once noble and judicious.

Her education and intellectual talents had been impressive as well as highly valued; less so perhaps were her many sculptures in terracotta and marble. The most notable of the latter are probably those in the British Museum, Register House in Edinburgh, Goodwood House, Marlow Bridge over the Thames and elsewhere, as well as a self-bust in the Uffizi in Florence.

From the age of 18 or so, Emma's hopes for William Russell, a grandson of the 4th Duke of Bedford, had also been opposed by her brother Walter. The girls had been out to visit their Mayow friends at Sydenham one day, and William Russell had ridden there. However, as Emma told her aunt, 'this so enraged Walter, although I did not even see him, that he cuts him now whenever he meets him'. Worse was to follow. The girls all went to a party (at Lady Matthews), where Emma had shaken hands with Russell who 'had placed himself in our way' when leaving. 'Walter told me that if I did so again he would take the liberty of knocking him down on the first occasion and that as it was he felt much tempted to do so for haunting us so, as if a man has not the right to go to a public place. This is an agreeable way of going on.' Poor lovers—Lady Ellinor was all for packing Emma off at once to Ardencaple. William Russell continued to appear at any event which he thought likely to be attended by the Campbell girls; at the Caledonian ball he was rigged out in highland dress—Campbell tartan, no less, 'in which he certainly looked very well'. In glorious weather in the middle of June Emma made a five-day visit to Fanny Mayow in Sydenham.[73] The fine weather recalled an excursion with Lady John the previous year to Loch Long and Loch Lomond—'certainly more enjoyable than any I have ever made'. The Mayows had asked one of that party, the same Angus Fletcher, to come to meet Emma again, but he was not able to do so, and Emma repeated the plaint that Walter's not knowing him put it out of the question to meet in town. Fanny Mayow included a note in Emma's letter to Lady John explaining that 'Mr Campbell is so very violent that I am afraid of any word escaping which he "can spell backwards"'. She was trying to 'preserve her faith with him and her truth with Emma and Mr Russell', but thought Walter 'not cool enough to be reasonable'. She considered William Russell to be conducting himself as handsomely as possible, even as far as not sending letters to Emma, but felt that when they were to go north at the start of July, Emma would be 'deeply sorry to quit her chances of meeting with Mr R'.

Members of the Russell family had similarly disapproved of William's relationship with the fortuneless Emma Campbell. Bessie Mure had once worried to Lady John Campbell that the scandal of the Uxbridge affair, Eleanora and Beau having been 'so unpleasantly in the mouths of the world will be a great loss to the other girls'. She continued: 'That any of them will ever marry and subside into a domestic wife I see no chance of and least of all it is said your friend Emma as she had supposed to have a double thirst of admiration of any one of them and they are all pretty well in that way.' However, they managed to overcome such obstacles over the next few years, the constancy and determination of the young couple were such that by January of 1828 his mother had been able to write to his grandfather that she was 'glad of his young and innocent marriage—may it be happy! Or at least may they think themselves so. I always protected it when the sager members of the family thought it a folly.'[74] Finally *The Times* reported that on Saturday 17 May 1828 in the rococo St James's parish church in Piccadilly, 'by licence', the Rev. Gerard Thomas Andrews had married 'the Hon. William Russell, eldest son of Lord William Russell, and nephew to the Duke of Bedford' to 'Miss Emma Campbell, daughter of Lady Charlotte Bury and niece to the Duke of Argyll'.[75] This was a society wedding, in London, such as none of the elder Campbells had had. Attending the 23-year-old Emma as bridesmaids were her sister Julia, and William's elder sister. The Duke of Bedford had been 'severely' indisposed and was therefore unable to attend, but, before the church ceremony his son, the Marquis of Tavistock, gave a 'public breakfast' for his cousin and his bride. This was the first of her children's marriages in Britain which Charlotte had attended; happily restored to her London life, she must have been in her element on the evening before the marriage providing 'a sumptuous celebration' for the many relations and friends. The bridegroom's father had given the couple a pair of saltcellars[76] to grace their table on which the Duke of Bedford's 'magnificent service of gold plate' would be arrayed.[77] After the ceremony, the newly-weds went to Chiswick for some time. They were to live in Lincoln's Inn as he was in the Chancery, and sisters Adelaide and Julia came to visit or stay. It is heartwarming to read Julia's account to Eliza in May the following year: 'dear Emma is going on delightfully and William and she are as happy as possible with their wee Lassie', although Julia herself had still not found any 'sentimental alliance of heart in London'.[78]

15

Prayers and Projects

When they had returned to London from the West Country in 1825, the Burys were house hunting.[1] At first they stayed in 'a house of Mr Lamberts [*sic*]' in Grosvenor Street.[2] Bessie Mure subsequently visited Charlotte and related to Lady John that the Burys 'have got a house', not in Mayfair, but 'in New Cavendish Street which is very near the Regents Park of which she is distractedly fond. I told her I wondered she could endure it after the lovely downs of Clifton. She walks there every day.'[3] Blanche was now 6 years old, delicate and 'a sweet child', with a governess and a footman 'who if not quite such a Skeleton as ?Hypolito is certainly not a ?Here awa Crater'. Charlotte's brother, George, the duke, did visit Charlotte but his duchess refused to have any interaction, at that time also 'cutting' Eleanora and Beaujolois. The duke, however, had 'taken the trouble to wade through' all Charlotte's papers and had 'declared in her favour in her claims on her son'. As ever, the inquisitive Bessie Mure wanted to know from Lady John whether she knew 'what these claims are and if she is likely to be successful in them'. Bessie Mure was informed by Lady Exeter that Charlotte and Mr Bury got asked to 'all the first parties in London of course she is quite happy tho she has no notion how that will agree with their finances'.[4] That season, Charlotte was apparently accompanied everywhere by her daughters Eleanora, Lady Uxbridge and Beaujolois, Lady Tullamore. Lady Exeter had also gossiped that a slimmer Charlotte astonished 'all the world with the great extraordinariness of her dress and appearance'. On 7 September 1825 Tommy Moore met up again with Charlotte and Lady Davy when invited to dine and sing at 'Miss White's party'.[5] Of Edward Bury, Bessie Mure related that her sister-in-law, Mrs James Mure, had been 'very shocked' by Mr Bury's caricatures 'if caricatures they could be' which he showed 'to everyone he saw'.[6] But she was occasionally more fair to Charlotte's husband. In December 1825 she thought Charlotte 'was looking very handsome indeed and in better spirits and better dressed than usual'.[7] This she attributed to Bury seeming to be 'in better humour and less savage than formerly', while admitting that she had 'never seen him yet'.

While her husband was drawing, and in amongst her social activities, Charlotte was writing. Given that she herself had used the word 'career', it is against the continuing litany of financial, familial and health scenarios and crises, however, that Charlotte's future writings had somehow to be fitted in. Her diaries and writings show her to have been conventionally religious; and she had married a clergyman. So perhaps it is not surprising that at this juncture her writing followed a different direction. A commonplace book of 1823 mostly comprised religious themes copied from a collection compiled by her mother-in-law. *Suspirium Sanctorum or Holy Breathings: A Series of Prayers for Every Day in the Month* was sent off to publisher Saunders and Otley on 10 November 1825.[8] Although still anonymous and 'by a Lady', it was, with his permission, dedicated to the Right Rev. Dr Samuel Goodenough, the Lord Bishop of Carlisle:

> To whom, indeed, can an attempt to render homage to our holy faith be more appropriately dedicated, than to one who is so eminently distinguished by his piety and learning; and to whom (under Providence) I am indebted for the preservation of my life, at the peril of his own?

It was the all-knowing Bessie Mure who provided the explanation for this dedication when writing to Lady John Campbell on 20 October 1825, asking whether she should send her 'a copy of Lady Charlottes Prayers when they come out', at the same time wondering whether the prayers were being published 'at her own Expence or her Bookseller gives her 5£ for them'.[9] Talking of the dedication she imparted the news that it was Dr Samuel Goodenough, who 'once saved her life when he was a Domine and she a child of five years old. Some carriage was about to drive over her but he gallantly seized the horses by the heads.' The reference is probably to the time of the Argyll family's residence in Ealing when Goodenough, himself the son of a clergyman, having attended Westminster School and Christ Church Oxford, had in 1772 established a school at Ealing with a high classical reputation, for the sons of the many 'noblemen and gentlemen of position'.[10] The school was to last almost to the end of the century, and presumably Charlotte's Argyll brothers had attended. He only gave up the school when appointed canon at St George's, Windsor in 1798; he was subsequently dean at Rochester (1802) and then consecrated Bishop of Carlisle in 1808, one of the last to wear a wig. Although spending most of his time in London, at his residence outside Carlisle he cultivated his interest in cookery and gardening. Not only did he create a recipe book which survives in manuscript today, but this polymath also had strong interests in botany, and along with one of Charlotte's Gunning relatives, Aylmer Bourke Lambert, had been one of the founders of the Linnean Society in 1787.

The book of prayers of which Charlotte sent a copy to the bishop, and which is now in New York Public Library, was published in London in 1826 by Saunders and Otley and printed by J. F. Dove in St John's Square. In a preface of one 166-word sentence, the author explained her rationale:

> Forasmuch as I have heard many persons express a wish to have their private devotions varied in form of words (the Lord's Prayer excepted, which, coming directly from God, carries with it a divine blessing, and cannot be subject to any objection or imperfection), and that I have myself, in the weakness and waywardness of my spirit, found attention lagging when it ought most intensely to have been engaged, frequently owing to a repetition of words, which, however well chosen, the tongue pronounced mechanically, I have in consequence, for mine own especial benefit and satisfaction through the grace of God, composed, on one or more verses of the Psalms, a different prayer for very Morning and Evening throughout the month; and having, by God's favour, completed this work, I am induced to send it forth into the world, in the humble but earnest hope that it may call some souls to partake in the holy satisfaction, and divine peace, which it has afforded to my own.

Susan Ferrier thought the prayers 'far superior to her novels, and highly creditable both as compositions and as showing so much Biblical research'.[11] But they were parodied by W. M. Thackeray. Although the prayers were 'serious enough' Thackeray, whose instinctive dislike of snobbery was aroused by titled authors, thought they were rubbish. In his paper, 'The Fashionable Authoress', he reviewed *Heavenly Chords, a Collection of Sacred Strains, selected, composed, and edited by the Lady Frances Juliana Flummery*'.[12]

While she had been 'longing to see the whole production', Bessie Mure seemed to have the last word for the time being.[13] Since Charlotte had come back to town in 1825, she had been 'very magnificent in dress'.

> She always wears what I call a pink Satin Drum on her head. Lady Tullamore calls it a pot but it is an erection of near twelve inches heighth

> [*sic*] with a puffing of White net round it and with the addition of ringlets is enough to make any one stare their eyes out.

Fifty-year-old Charlotte had been in great good humour when Bessie Mure saw her in London in the autumn of 1825, but had talked of Lady Uxbridge and her concerns in a way that made Bessie Mure's hair stand on end. The latter relayed Charlotte's words to Lady John: 'I always prophecied none of the three eldest would come to good and we cannot but triumph that my words have been verified.'[14] Charlotte had also said she had done everything she could to persuade Eleanor 'to bear and forbear':

> Asked if he ever beat her to which she replied if he had she would have left his house that moment and Lady Charlotte said she had suffered that often and had never complained ... She told her the only thing she had for it was to run away with the first man she could get be divorced and marry her lover.

Perhaps taking this more seriously than had been intended, the humourless Bessie Mure rhetorically asked, 'Was there ever such advice from a Mother to a daughter', then added her pièce de résistance:

> Especially a mother who is publishing prayers for every day of the year. I told her nobody would buy or read them. If she wrote another novel all the world would read it but as for prayers they would chuse some other diversion than one with a Pink Satin Mitre.

Nevertheless, a second edition of the prayers followed in 1830, expanded into two volumes and still being advertised by the publishers a decade later.[15]

Saunders and Otley were also responsible for her next 'anonymous' publication, printed in 1826 by S. and R. Bentley in nearby Dorset Street. In this very different mindset, Charlotte again incorporated her travels and research whilst in Italy—Volterra, Pisa and the Coast—to produce a three-decker romance of a crusade.[16] Two sets of the three volumes, in which he inscribed his name, still sit in her son's library collection in Islay. John Murray, the publisher, received a request from Fanny Richardson asking for *Alla Giornata* saying that she thought there was 'a great deal of merit in it'.[17] Lady Holland wrote more vituperatively to her son, '*Alla Giornata* is written by Lady Charlotte Bury. I have not read it, tho' it is said to be better than her former publication. It had to be so, to be worth anything'.[18]

As she explained in the frontispiece:

> Above the door-way of a marble palace which stands on the banks of Arno, in Pisa, the inscription that gives the following story its title, is to this day read. The words, "ALLA GIORNATA", or To the Day, allude to a fact which has often been a subject of inquiry, and which the following romantic legend will tend to explain. May its perusal afford a degree of interest to those, who, like myself, have wandered by Arno's side, and have perhaps asked in vain for the meaning of these mysterious words.

On the title page of each volume she chose as epigraph a verse from Burton's *Anatomy of Melancholy* which read:

> When I go musing all alone
> Thinking of divers things foreknown;
> When I build castles in the air,
> Void of sorrow, and void of fear,
> Pleasing myself with phantasms sweet,
> Methinks the time runs very fleet.

The triple decker appeared to warrant eleven pages in *The Monthly Review*.[19] Acknowledging the 'apparently well-founded' rumour of its author as 'Lady Charlotte Berry [*sic*], better known, perhaps, as the beautiful and accomplished Lady Charlotte Campbell', the reviewer deemed it a 'complete god-send' for the patrons and patronesses of the circulating libraries. There followed a list 'precisely of those materials which fill their thirsty souls with never-ending wonder and delight: Italian banditti, monks, nuns, pilgrims, condottieri, witches, minstrels, muses, Love and slaughter, caverns, castles, sieges, battles, tempests, shipwrecks'. While again scolding the 'fair and noble author' for squandering 'as much of imagination in these three volumes, as would in more economical hands have easily given rise to a hundred', he suggested that each chapter, usually a surprising story, could have been 'spun out into a separate work'.

The doughty late-fourteenth-century heroine of Pisa is fighting the Florentine enemy on several fronts—for freedom of liberty, and freedom for church, State and marriage, the latter 'a message to her own sex', until she meets her hero. Their trials and tribulations occupy the three volumes until 'Alla Giornata'—the day on which they finally come together at the end of the romantic legend. Charlotte employed 'a prodigious congregation of machinery, and of dramatis personae drawn from every class of life'. The reviewer thought the third volume 'almost unreadable', but that apart, many passages had been composed 'replete with good sense, and full of instruction for the sex to whom they are advanced'. Notably, he also considered it 'impossible that the strenuous idleness of fashionable life can have any real attractions for a Lady who thus lingers over one of the happiest periods in the career of her heroine ... dreaming of empire ... superintending her affairs at the centre of her Volterra seat', before love was to complicate her life. It was also presumed that 'Lady Charlotte often spoke her own sentiments under the masque of her heroine using the natural powers of description, expression and use of appropriate poetical similes', or aphorisms such as: 'When parent-offspring relations break down, anarchy ensues, God never forgets.'[20]

Again, however, the reviewer (perhaps the same one) castigated Charlotte's grammar, the absent article 'a' or 'an' perhaps due to 'her having lived abroad where in French and Italian the articles are seldom used'; worse were the mismatches between single nouns and plural verbs, as well as using 'who' where it should have been 'whom'. Notwithstanding, the lengthy review justified itself finally: 'Our principal purpose ... has been to select ... some passages which struck us as containing unquestionable indicators of a fine imagination, and of an observant and highly accomplished mind.' One of the many quotations illustrating the review was the 'magnificent description of the appearance of Pisa':

> The deep roseate hue of the setting sun illumined the Arno like a glowing gem, and turned the meanest things it touched to beauty; the very roofs of the houses and palaces seemed broidered velvet, and the innumerable colours which tinted the walls, resembled the precious inlaid work of a rich cabinet, rather than the stains and depredations of time and weather,—such a magician is the sun of southern climes. Yet the minute detail of objects did not lessen their general effect; over this glittering brilliancy a veil of middle tone was spread, shrouding its effulgence, and uniting it by a thousand delicate reflexes with the deeper shadows. The clearness of these very shadows was a thing to wonder at apart, while the whole picture absorbed attention, as being entire and harmonious, although in its several markings distinct, detailed and defined.

The ancient tower which flanked the Ponte Vecchio, rose darkly against the panoply of the golden sky; yet the small Moresque arches which so gracefully support its widening brow, together with every projecting moulding and prominence in the deep-toned mass were traced in clear and sharp outline. Beyond the tower, the eye stretched to the distant reach of the river, studded with boats, which gave a heightened value to the landscape, opposing their dark brown and orange hues to the flood of light that beamed around them, while the parting orb of day again returning, streamed over the beautiful building of St Paolo, situate on the southern bank, and which cast its softened image in the stream. Lower down rose the fair Spina, a mixture of Saracenic and Moreque taste, which, rich in foliage, figures and fretwork, delights the eye in despite of all the rules of architecture. Opposite to this, marble palaces shone in bright array, backed by the square towers, which reared their massive forms, the lofty and permanent monuments of family greatness. Such was the fashion of the times,—and every noble house boasted one or more of these fabrics as marks of proud distinction. Beyond them, the eye passed over the receding buildings of the town, till it reached the forked Apennines, which framed as it were this most beauteous picture.[21]

Flirtation was Charlotte's triple-decker for 1827.[22] Saunders' rival, Henry Colburn, became one of the most notorious publishers of nineteenth-century fiction. Progenitor of the so-called 'silver-fork' genre of novels[23], often by aristocratic authors, depicting the life of aristocrats for the aspiring middle classes, he ensured, with advertising puffs in his journals, the *New Monthly Magazine*, the *Literary Gazette* and the *Athenaeum*, that *Flirtation* was very well received in the circulating libraries and by the public. It ran to three editions by the following year, even at the price of one and a half guineas or 31*s.* 6*d.* The puff in his *Literary Gazette* claimed that the novel possessed:

> Three popular recommendations: the name of the author, Lady Charlotte Bury (so much for anonymity!); its own name, 'Flirtation'; and the excellence of its purpose. The whole tendency of the work is to discountenance a reigning vice, and implant a worthy virtue in its stead. It may teach some women (and even fashionable ones) to set a proper value upon themselves.

By the time of the third edition the following year, the puff in Colburn's *New Monthly Magazine* had become even more extravagant:

> 'Flirtation' is not merely the title, but the prevailing genius of this novel; as indeed it ought to be. The noble authoress follows her subject, and never wanders from it; every incident is metamorphosed into it. How redolent of flirtation is every chapter! What an entireness of subject pervades every line! Flirtation on the part of men; flirtation on the part of women; flirtation abroad; flirtation at home; flirtation in low life, and in high life; flirtation among the single, and among the married; private flirtation, and public flirtation; and many phases more than we have room to enumerate of the same vice. If this picture should fail in

> reforming the male coquets who indulge in it, we entertain confidant hopes that the fair will listen to her Ladyship's exhortations, and be taught to renounce so dangerous a pastime.

Further editions were produced in London (1834 and 1836), Paris (1836) and America (1828).

Flirtation was the story of two nieces of a General Montgomery, Lady Frances and Lady Emily Lorimer. Lady Frances was haughty, highly strung, stylish and very worldly. Her life was selfish and unhappy, her flirtations after marriage causing her husband to leave her to a solitary death. On the other hand, Lady Emily was gentle, kind, and self-effacing; her marriage towards the end of the third volume was complemented by a life spent in doing good for others. Quite specifically linking the immoralities of *ton*, other flirts, male and female and of several generations, were woven in; when flirtation developed into unrequited love, male suicide resulted while females withered away. Again the three volumes ranged breathlessly from London to Dorset, Hampshire and Somerset as well as the Bay of Naples, where Lord Mowbray became embroiled in a flirtation with an opera singer on locations around Naples, well known to Charlotte—Castellammare, Sorrento, Amalfi and Ischia—before following him to London and expiring with a broken heart. As well as incorporating true-to-life smugglers on the Dorset coast, authorial views were aired on topics such as landscaping and legal skullduggery. Many of her poems were used in illustration but one notable feature which one perhaps wishes Charlotte had developed further in these and other novels was direct speech. This was the preserve of one strong character, a family retainer named Marian Macalpine or Alpina. She thought, spoke, quoted and wrote in Lallans; appropriate epigraphs, extracts of poems, ballads and songs all enhanced her characterisation. While the author could not be criticised for orthography it was perhaps as baffling to the readers of the circulation libraries as if it had been Gaelic which Charlotte also heard during her Argyll childhood. In the last two paragraphs at the end of the third volume the narrator spelled out the dangers of flirtation:

> Not so is it in the illusory bliss of illicit passion; there every added hour of guilty communion destroys the illusion, and blasts the short-lived happiness of such unholy love, and in the ending, for the end comes quickly, what an arid desert and hideous devastation are left behind! In the foregoing narrative, the picture of virtue and of vice, under these forms, has been attempted; and it is believed, that in the different fate of the two sisters, may be traced the fate of all who like them shall choose either the pure path which leads to lasting happiness, or follow the

downward road to misery and shame, through the PERILOUS MAZES OF FLIRTATION.

She had produced a novel of 'ton' with *Self Indulgence* (1812) but by the time of *Flirtation* in 1827 the author was already in her early fifties writing fashionable novels that may have appeared old-fashioned to some. 'Owing far more to Plumer Ward and Maria Edgeworth than to Hook and Disraeli, *Flirtation* was hardly contemporary in tone', in Rosa's view.[24] Be that as it may, Nathaniel Parker Willis, an American journalist visiting London, observed that Charlotte's books 'sold well and she obtained as much as £200 for each of these sentimental tales'.[25] Colburn hinted that *Flirtation* was a *roman-à-clef*, thus achieving a mention of it in the 'High Life and Fashionable Chit Chat' column of *World of Fashion*. 'Lady Charlotte Bury ... has quite put some of her high-life acquaintance into a flutter by writing on "Flirtation", so uneasy has the cap fitted some she has placed it on.'

The novel was indeed sentimental; but *Flirtation* had a vein of thoughtfulness and strong moral principles, as well as its knowledge of fashionable life. 'While flirting was sometimes depicted as fun and light-hearted' in the Romantic era, as one more recent critic put it, Charlotte's novel demonstrated that 'for a woman, flirtation was much more dangerous ... precisely because of its uncertainty, and its undermining of accepted forms of sexual and marital conduct'.[26] But the novel also clearly indicated 'an increasingly prevalent association between flirtation and reading, with deleterious effects on the imagination and inner mind' of the 'bad' flirt, Frances, as opposed to the old fashioned values of the her sister, Emily, and Miss Macalpine. Frances was a voracious reader of poetry such as Byron's, of which Alpina disapproved. Throsby explained this attitude further, emphasising that 'the anxiety surrounding flirtation went beyond a fear of sexual deviancy: it was closely linked to a woman's intellectual development as well. Bury's novel indicates an increasingly prevalent association between flirtation and reading.'

The third edition contained an advertisement for the forthcoming *A Marriage in High Life*, 'by the author of *Flirtation*'. Colburn probably persuaded Charlotte to edit this novel for Lady Caroline Lucy Scott (née Douglas), to whom she was distantly related through her mother's Hamilton marriage, so that he could promote it as another novel of *ton*.[27] While it therefore did not employ Charlotte's own continental experiences and background, the story of an aristocrat who neglected his pious, middle-class wife to devote himself to his mistress, was again supposed to be based on fact. In her preface to the first of the two volumes Charlotte expressed the hope that since it contained 'a few passages in the history of the heart and feelings of an individual placed in singular and trying circumstance', continuing:

> Those who should recognize beneath the feigned name of Lady Fitzheury, one whom they remember to have seen in the gay scenes of fashionable life, will probably feel some interest in the events which occasioned her first introduction into the world, and her sudden disappearance from it.[28]

The parents of Lord Fitzheury and Emmeline Benson had arranged their marriage when they were children. On the eventual wedding day, Lord Fitzheury told his bride that he did not intend 'to live with her intimately', as he 'was allied in consummated love' to Lady Florence Mostyn. Lady Fitzheury becomes devoted for a while to Almacks, 'even if only as a Wednesday night anodyne for despair',[29] and only towards the end of the third volume does her husband, dying of consumption or tuberculosis, awake to the sterling character of his wife and the falseness of his mistress. As in most of Charlotte's novels, wrong usually comes to a bad and sad end; she herself had enough experience of the world, even in her own family, to know that virtue was not always rewarded, or, as in her virtuous heroine, could often be rewarded too late. Colburn's puff in *Flirtation* suggested to Charlotte's readers:

> 'Marriage in High Life' is a novel likely to become a permanent favourite with the public. The narrative is constructed upon an event of deep interest: it reaches the feelings in the simplest language of conversation. It is perhaps one of the most unpretending tales of the day. It impresses itself upon the mind, and we close it with high respect of the amiable feelings of the authoress; she possesses the merit of suggesting events of no common power over the feelings of the heart.

This novel was translated into French (1832) and German (Vienna, 1837), and another edition was published in 1857, when Charlotte was 82 years old. One 'Scotch' gentleman is reported to have remarked shortly after publication of both of these novels that Lady Charlotte Bury 'was certainly a very sensible woman for she had proved to the world that Marriage was the only remedy for the sin of Flirtation'.[30] Colburn's hand in the fashionable titles of such novels probably ensured good sales, while the author might reflect that her tales were morals that might do good.

Sundry other projects were discussed with a variety of correspondents although, as one would expect, not all of these came to fruition. In April 1828, her friend and former court colleague, Lady Charlotte Lindsay, described Charlotte to Mary Berry as seemingly 'over head and ears in

Belles Lettres, and Royalty, Cookery, Bazaars and Dress', her visit having been curtailed by Colburn's waiting to see Charlotte.[31] The publisher had involved his aristocratic author and editor in a rather large venture, although details are scarce. Lady Charlotte Lindsay's is one of only three references to the 1,600 receipts or recipes which Colburn produced from 'a Lady of Rank' in *The Lady's Own Cookery Book and New Dinner-Table Directory*; the subtitle continued '*in which will be found a large collection of original receipts including not only the result of the authoress's many years observation, experience and research, but also the Contributions of an extensive circle of acquaintance; adapted to the use of persons living in the highest style, as well as those of moderate fortune*'. Colburn further enthused in the Preface:

> The Receipts composing the Volume here have been collected under peculiarly favourable circumstances by a lady of distinction, whose productions in the lighter department of literature entitle her to a place among the most successful writers of the present day. Moving in the first circles of rank and fashion ... mass of materials thus accumulated ... Editor [he] task of arranging them.

Maria Edgeworth told her sister, Honora, on 4 March 1831 that at a dinner hosted by Sir Walter Scott's son-in-law, John Lockhart, Lady Lyndhurst had quoted 'a cookery-book lately published by Lady Charlotte Bury (it is said) for quiet people'.[32] Although the cookery book has always been attributed to Charlotte, of the letters sent and the recipes received from such a circle there is little sign. But Colburn's hints, if not claims, seem robust. There were three editions, the first about 1831, a second in 1835 and a third in 1844. It is not known how many were published, purchased or used, but it was one of the scarcest of her publications until available online or by print on demand.[33] Only a few library copies exist and rarely appear at auction. It has to be presumed that it was Colburn's minions for assembling all the table setting diagrams and essays as well as the 1,600 recipes. If Charlotte's cook had in fact produced—or tested—the quantities of food either at home or for guests, it is perhaps unsurprising that the household was in perpetual financial difficulties.

Prince Hermann von Pückler-Muskau was in England and Scotland from 1826 to 1828; this colourful, dandiacal figure was a soldier and author, and introduced landscape gardening to Germany. He was interested in meeting literary figures such as Charlotte, who had 'exchanged the celebrity of a beauty for that of a fashionable author', as Paston later put it.[34] Calling on Charlotte the morning after meeting her, the prince 'found everything in her house brown, in every possible shade; furniture, curtains, carpets, her own and her children's dresses, presented no other colour'. This is perhaps surprising enough, but he added: 'The room was without any looking-glasses or pictures, and its only ornaments were casts from the antique.' While he was there, Scots publisher Archibald Constable was announced—he who had at first refused Scott's *Waverley*. The prince hoped that 'the charming Lady Charlotte had better cause to be satisfied with him'. Constable was just one of many publishers who made their way to the drab brown drawing room, although he was never to publish any of her *oeuvre*. Sir Walter Scott was also in London in the autumn of 1826 and his journal for 18 October recorded that he 'sallied forth again after breakfast and visited the Piccadilly ladies [the Dumergues]. Saw Rogers and Richard Sharp, also good Dr. and Mrs. Hughes, also the Duchess of Buckingham, and Lady Charlotte Bury, with a most beautiful little girl' (by now 12 years old).[35] For this little girl, Blanche, Charlotte at this time had composed twelve alternately rhyming quatrains in a 'Christmas Hymn, for a child, addressed to "Bianca", by her affectionate mother'.[36]

Surviving scattered correspondence reveals that Charlotte's advice was sought out by aspiring writers and poets. From Lambert's house in 26 Lower Grosvenor Street on 14 September 1825 she responded to one Mr Sotheby:

> For the delight he has procured her, in the perusal of His Poems ... The lines to Mrs Sotheby must create a loving envy in the breast of every happy Wife; and the high religious feeling which pervades the whole work renders the beauty of the Language its least merit.[37]

She continued, 'The Pictures of Italy breathe of the clime, and Mr Bury will gladly endeavor [*sic*] by his Pencil to prove how beautifully true to Nature they are', while mentioning:

> At the present moment Mr Burys Portfolios are pack'd up and He cannot have access to them, as He is on the point of moving from one House to Another, but the moment he is settled, He will have great pleasure in being allowed to illustrate one or two of the subjects.

The letter ended hoping to make the personal acquaintance of Mr Sotheby and his wife when they returned to town.

16

Public and Private Lives

From Edinburgh in August 1828, the essayist, poetess and a leading authority on Scots folklore, Anne Grant of Laggan, wrote to their recently widowed mutual friend, Mrs Anne Hook, characterising Charlotte as 'certainly much changed in appearance, though her charming manners, all ease and simplicity, are unchanged'.[1] She mentioned Bury's ill health and Blanche's apparent fragility, but added that he was 'much engaged in preparing some publication, the subject of which, I believe, is connected with the fine arts'. She had gone to a select party 'the ornament of which was Sir Walter Scott', where many of Mr Bury's drawings were displayed'. Charlotte's Shawfield brother-in-law, Lord Ruthven, 'the first of judges and himself an artist', had deemed them 'very fine'. While little is known of Bury's artistic activities, he was apparently in touch with the leading artists of the day, including Sir Thomas Lawrence, who had had to postpone a proposed meeting of professional friends in March that year until he was 'less harried and harrass'd' by the approaching Royal Academy annual exhibition'.

As Edward Bury explained in his rather formal style in a letter dated 3 October to Sir William Gordon-Cumming, the Burys' original plans had had to be altered.[2] Writing from Islay House, he also reported that he had been ill, while:

> The storms have declared against the possibility of any communication, or I had earlier thanked you for the letter in wh: you so kindly press us to Altyre, and have endeavoured to assure you of the <u>very great</u> dissapointment [*sic*] we experienced, when our visit to you, this autumn, became impossible.

On leaving London, they had intended to visit Walter at Woodhall, then proceed to Altyre, and on the way back to have stopped at Inveraray and Ardencaple. But on reaching the Wemyss' Gosford House on the East Lothian coast, letters were waiting from Walter in Islay, telling his mother that he would not be at Woodhall, and that such preparation had been made to receive Charlotte in Islay, that it would be 'the severest mortification and dissapointment [*sic*] to all', if she did not appear in the island. Edward Bury had left it to Charlotte to write to Altyre saying they had reluctantly had to abandon thoughts of going north so late in the season. It seems that she had not done so, however, since:

> From the expression of your having expected us for the last two months, I am led to doubt her punctuality in this respect—and if she has been so negligent, I am doubly sorry, and would, were the thing possible, repair the oversight by coming to Altyre directly.

He did hope the visit would only be deferred until the following year, and that in the meantime they might all meet at Inveraray or Woodhall.

Charlotte often confessed to being a poor sailor, especially under sail, however she might even have ventured on the new steamer *Maid of Islay* which her son had just introduced to the island. The bill for the 'aqua' or whisky given to the 'Highlanders assembled to receive Lady Charlotte', in the curving driveway sweeping up to the lovely Georgian Islay House, was for five guineas.[3] There was much to see on the island, especially for Edward Bury—the house itself much expanded at different periods during the Georgian era, the incipient 'policies' of plantations, drives and pleasure gardens, including aviaries, all materialising from plans recently drawn up by William Gemmill.[4] The farming landscape was being remodelled and villages and various industries were being introduced and developed, along with roads, bridges and piers. Some of the English street names had royal connections, such as King Street and Queen Street in Portnahaven. But that year Walter Frederick was to name one of the new villages after his mother, and one after his wife. Sixteen slated houses had been built in Port Charlotte by the following year, with another eleven built, but not roofed.[5] Both Port Charlotte and Port Eleanor or Port Ellen housed day-labourers, fishermen and craftsmen, as well as shopkeepers, innkeepers custom officers and the like. As with many of the other villages on the island, they also supported whisky distilleries.

Dr Samuel Crawfurd, the surgeon and agent for Walter Campbell, lived nearby in another lovely, if relatively smaller, Georgian house in the centre of the estate at Eallabus. His son, John Crawfurd, had been 'late Envoy to the Court of Ava etc etc', during a colourful career in the East Indies.[6]

Two daughters had been born to his wife, Horatia Ann, while he was in the service of the East India Company. On 4 September 1828 an unusual entry was copied into the parish register of the Church of Scotland for the parish of Kilarrow. The Reverend Edward John Bury, using the Anglican form of service, and signing himself as Rector of Ludshelfe in the County of Southampton, baptised 5-year-old Horatia Charlotte Campbell and her little 9-month-old sister, Eleanor Charteris Julia Campbell.[7] The sponsors for Charlotte, born in Calcutta on 9 May 1823, were Charlotte, Charles Carter Esq. of the East India Company's Service, for whom Walter Campbell stood proxy, and Mrs Monro, for whom Lady Eleanor Campbell stood proxy. Little Eleanor had been born at sea on 26 November 1827 and her sponsors were Walter Frederick Campbell himself, his wife, Lady Eleanor, and Miss Julia Campbell.

In Islay House Charlotte would often pass Bartolini's delightful likeness of her two youngest Campbell daughters. As the Burys apparently stayed on in the island for at least another month, it has to be assumed that relations were easier between the laird of Islay and his mother, despite the obvious expenditure being lavished by her son on his island. But, unfortunately, there are no other letters or records of their stay. Visits are likely to have been made to the newly-finished *cottage ornée* at Ardimersay on the south-east coast of the island, as well as to the eponymous village of Port Charlotte described as 'showy' a decade later by Lord Teignmouth on his tour of the Scottish coasts.[8] The stormy weather may have allowed Charlotte the opportunity to work at her desk overlooking the sea loch of Indaal and she may have been revising and expanding her first novel for Colburn to re-launch, an advertisement that year claiming that it was 'nearly ready for publication', although it was not actually published until two years later, in 1830, as *The Separation*.[9]

Another of her projects was a proposed Argyll family history. Much correspondence was generated by this project, and Julia was involved as a research assistant, although she admitted, after sending her mother some notes: 'I do not think this very interesting, even should you not know it.'[10] From her new address at 6 New Cavendish Street on 30 December 1826 Charlotte confessed that writing in the third person 'puzzles me'. She was apparently still working on this project several years later, when Charles Kirkpatrick Sharpe referred to a paper which she might 'care to have for her Argyle history'.[11] One London correspondent was at pains to prove that a 'most curious and costly illuminated' manuscript in the British Museum could throw 'some Light on the Hypothesis of a direct connexion between the male Stems of the English Beauchamp family and the Scotch Campbell'.[12] The same writer hoped that Charlotte was 'in possession of Edmonson's *Genealogical History of the Earls of Warwick*, a small octavo publish'd about 60 or 70 years ago, which may be pick'd up any where second Hand in London for 6 or 7 Shillings'. She was then advised to read Collins' *Peerage* of 1756 and was to bear in mind:

> Biographical Sketches of the brother Dukes John and Archibald [of Argyll], who may be emphatically styled the Wellington, and the Pitt of Scotland of their Day will require a Course of minute research through every historical work or collection of papers of distinguished families published in Great Britain in the past century.

An extract from a 'grand dictionnaire' was enclosed. Poor Charlotte: 'Even the Notes annex'd to every Edition of Pope's *Works* ought to be look'd through.'

The Duke of Argyll's Inveraray agent, Robert MacGibbon, had been enrolled by Charlotte to inquire whether she could have a look at 'a manuscript account of the Argyll family' in the possession of John Campbell at Auchinleck. This was based on 'a vast number of valuable documents at Dunstaffnage',[13] and although MacGibbon judiciously regarded its authenticity as 'not favourable', it was forwarded on to Charlotte at Ardencaple Castle on 8 November 1828.[14] MacGibbon recommended that she should get in touch with 'a literary man', Mr John McArthur of Henton House in Hampshire, who had a 'very valuable history of the Clan Campbell' in his possession. Further time-consuming probing was also suggested: 'Connected as the Family of Argyll has been for a very long period with the public transactions of Scotland, as well as involved in many of its most vital interests, much valuable information may be obtained by research in the Advocates Library' whose then curator was Sir William Hamilton. Charlotte corresponded with Mary Stewart Mackenzie of Kinmount, near Annan in Dumfriesshire, asking her for 'any unpublished documents', particularly hoping to find the diary of Lady Sophia or Harriet Lindsay, 'who assisted Archibald, 9th Earl of Argyll, her stepfather, to escape from custody in Edinburgh Castle in 1681'.[15]

A different project comprised collecting folk tales, some of which Charlotte was to use in her novels and in the miscellanies of 1830 and 1835. In a letter of 16 December 1828 from Inveraray to Charlotte, then at Woodhall, Robert MacGibbon said he would send some of the stories he had been gathering for her, care of 'Miss Campbell' (Adelaide) at Ardencaple.[16] This would not, however, be easy, 'as there is not now a carrier from Inveraray to Glasgow, and my packets would not be worth postage'. He advised her that as long as they or 'Islay' (i.e. Walter) remained in Scotland, he would continue to enclose such oral tales to Walter to be forwarded; otherwise they would go to Ardencaple. One of the stories sent on Boxing Day, 1828, probably in his wife's hand,[17] was 'A Story of Fairies', set on a bright moonlit Christmas Eve in Invernesshire, when Mr Grant of Drumcork felt sure that on such a beautiful night the fairies would be out and about. He proposed that his house party should venture forth on the moor to find them, or at least hear them, even though he admitted 'never yet knowing of anyone having heard them that a death did not follow'. When they reached the moor, the stillness of the night was broken by a far-off cry, repeating 'Have you got?' to which the close-up answer was 'No'. This continued for a couple of hours, until all except Mr Grant returned to the house. After hearing many further repetitions, the answers became voices from all around the moor, shrilly screaming 'Yes, Yes, Yes'. Mr Grant then heard the single voice call out "Who have you got? To which the shrieking voices replied at once 'Donald Mor in the Dell'. Confirmation came next day with news of this very death having taken place at that very time. Another well-known tale of the supernatural which Charlotte employed several times, concerned the apparition of an army marching along the Inveraray road, marked by a thorn tree (which stood until it and the breast wall on Loch Fyne were washed away in the 1920s).[18]

At the beginning of February 1829 Anne Grant of Laggan was writing from Edinburgh to Charlotte's longstanding friend, Anne Hook:

> I very much wonder that I do not hear more of Lady Charlotte Bury: she was expected to pass the winter in Edinburgh; and her staying so long in the west country [presumably Islay and Woodhall] seems proof that her most amiable daughter-in-law has made their residence agreeable to her and to Mr Bury.[19]

Anne Hook may have been somewhat surprised, if perhaps, relieved, when she read such news. Anne Grant continued:

> Lady Charlotte is particularly happy in her family; Adelaide is the object of admiration and the highest esteem to everyone in that country: her attendance on Lady Ellinor in the last period of her disorder was more like that of one of the Sisters of mercy of whom we hear on the Continent, than what one would expect of a delicate young lady. Since that time she has been an unspeakable comfort to Lord John in the direction of his family and the management of his ... very promising ... children [after the death of their mother].

Charlotte and Bury may have at last managed to include Altyre in their travels in 1829. In a letter of 12 May from Julia to her sister, Eliza, she hoped that her sister would be gathering strength for another confinement and 'to be well to receive Mamma with joy and comfort, and that you will not allow any past recollections or future circumstances to agitate you'.[20] Sir Walter Scott and his wife dined with Charlotte and her husband in Edinburgh on 27 May, after which Scott confided in his journal that Bury was 'an egregious fop but a fine draughtsman'.[21] The visit was reciprocated at a lunch on 8 June when his wife 'had a little party, where Lady Charlotte Bury, Lady Hopetoun, and others met the Caradori, who sung to us very kindly'. He went on: 'She sung Jock of Hazeldean very well, and with a peculiar expression of humour. Sandie Ballantyne kindly came and helped us with fiddle and flageolet. Willie Clerk was also here.' Scott claimed that 'they had all been very gay, and not the less so for the want of Mr Bury, who is a thorough-paced coxcomb, with some accomplishments, however'.[22] Anne Grant reported to Anne Hook in late August 1829 that she had seen Charlotte several times while she was in Edinburgh.

Perhaps, in the end, all Charlotte's work on the history of the family was only to serve as background for several 'illustrative memoirs' which were not only to appear in the fashionable press but may also have been intended to boost Charlotte's profile in the public eye as an author. Charlotte appears to have been acknowledged in society once again. In spring 1828, she was the first in 'a series of characteristic sketches of … celebrated contemporary Personages' to be profiled in *The London Weekly Review*.[23] The history of the Argyll family also took up most of the space in the biographical memoirs of Charlotte, Eliza (Lady Gordon-Cumming) and Beaujolois (Viscountess Tullamore) which appeared in various numbers of *La Belle Assemblée*. 'The Lady Charlotte Bury' who was introduced as 'a woman distinguished as much by her literary attainments, and the superiority of her intellectual powers, as by every charm of person, very elegant and graceful accomplishment'[24], was illustrated by Thomas Wright's engraving of Lawrence's portrait of Charlotte from 1803.

A rather different portrait was promulgated, however, by Maria Edgeworth when writing to her mother later that year.[25] Possibly meeting Charlotte for the first time at the Lockharts (Sir Walter Scott's daughter and her husband) the all-seeing author opined that she 'must have been a very fine perhaps beautiful woman with a fair complexion and bright colour but on a very bold scale and now the remains are melancholy not interesting'. She scathingly amplified:

> She dresses too young and presented an unappealing picture and is not well made-up—her own gray hair coming here and there into view between the false—too evidently false masses of brown her own hair is dragged up some way so that it gave me a pain in my temple to look at her!

Her sarcasm became more biting: 'her mouth once beautiful is now all fallen in and she is like a much-worn antique bust—Strong marks of the passions having passed over the countenance' but '*L'amour a passé par là* [*sic*] is not the first thing that occurs to me'. However, Edgeworth did admit that she had 'not done justice to Lady Charlotte Bury's manner which is high-bred and quite easy. Her voice and conversation are both agreeable—unaffected—free from authorship pretension of any sort!' Perhaps this was just as well—the 'ugly' and 'vulgar' John Murray was 'rather awkwardly puzzled tho' how to be paying his devoir to two lionesses at a time—Lady Bury and Miss E'.

Formal and recent accompanying illustrative portraits of Eliza and Beaujolois had also been specially engraved for *La Belle Assemblée*. Many of Charlotte's daughters appear to have inherited more of the Argyll and Gunning looks than the Shawfield ones. However, in both Raeburn's oil of 1817[26] and Thomson's 1830 engraving of Ross's miniature of Eliza[27], the Shawfield resemblance is very pronounced. During the spring and summer of 1831, Charlotte presented both Eliza, Lady Gordon-Cumming, and Walter's wife, Lady Eleanor, at the new court of William and Adelaide.[28] A miniature of Beaujolois by F. W. Wilkin had been engraved by J. Cochran for *La Belle Assemblée* in 1826, but was much less flattering than an earlier one—later published by Finden based on an earlier drawing—and she too shared some Shawfield features (see plate 21).[29] Perhaps the rather haughty and supercilious air fitted with the Countess of Charleville's views of her daughter-in-law about this time. Tullamore's mother, Lady Charleville was greatly troubled by the restless extravagance and rumoured insecurity of her son's establishment. While Creevey was to describe Tullamore himself as 'the greatest bore the world can produce', he considered Beaujolois, 'a very handsome woman and somewhat loose, but as she is dying of consumption, we will spare her'.[30] Sadleir deemed her 'of consumptive tendency and made free of society during the hectic eighteen-twenties', who had developed into 'a pleasure-mad neurasthenic, typical of a time of post-war carnival'.[31] She belonged to a raffish and dissipated set, which included her brother-in-law, the widowed Lord Uxbridge, Lord Sefton and various of the younger Campbells. Tullamoore himself seems to have been easily led but temperamentally a conscientious young man, who consoled himself for his inability to curb his wife's extravagance and wildness by spending hours at the House of Commons, only then joining in her revels. Lady Charleville strongly disapproved of her daughter-in-law and her friends, and in letters to her own daughter, Mrs. Marlay, was much concerned with the seemingly blatant indiscretions of her son and his wife. By July 1831 gossip was again linking Lady Tullamoore's name with that of Lord Uxbridge, and, 'as if this were not enough, Tullamoore, already friendly with count d'Orsay, was becoming (or so the world said) more than friendly with d'Orsay's wife Harriet'. These affairs formed the basis of a *roman à clef* by the Countess of Blessington, *The Repealers*, which included an appendix to the characters, not least the formidable Countess of Charleville.[32]

One project on which both Charlotte and her husband spent much energy was first referred to in the middle of 1826. From 6 New Cavendish Street, Portland Place on Thursday 1 June Charlotte presented her compliments to the publisher, John Murray II, and 'being anxious to speak to him on the subject of a little work she contemplates publishing, will attend to any appointment it may suit Mr. Murray to make for that purpose'.[33] This meeting is likely to have taken place, but by 20 June she was already requesting 'the favor of an answer respecting her Poem, as soon as he can conveniently come to any decision', adding 'Lady Charlotte would not trouble Mr. Murray with this Note, but for some circumstances which have arisen, that render it necessary for her to entreat Mr. Murray's answer speedily'. Six days later she expressed her regret at having to send him a reminder but:

> Owing to arrangements which Mr. Bury is making with his Engraver, in order that the plates which are to illustrate the work, may be executed before Christmas—Lady Charlotte finds it necessary to request Mr. Murray will have the goodness to give her his decision without further delay.

This was a period of general depression for publishers, and even those like John Murray were in difficulties, so perhaps he played for time. On the last day of the month he sent a peace offering to Charlotte noting that the copy of *The Representative* with 'the very flattering notice it contains of Alla Giornata, cannot but be grateful to her'.[34]

When they returned to London from Scotland in late 1829, the Burys resumed their pursuit for a publisher of the magnum opus. One of the 'able heads' whom Charlotte had asked to read her manuscript was her former neighbour, Thomas Campbell.[35] She asked him 'without fear of offending my vanity or my cupidity, tell me as a friend what you think (under all the circumstances of my necessities which I have confided in you) I may ask for it … remembering that my name at full length is to be attached to the work'. On the strength of 'the Laurel' he bestowed on reading her work, 'worth a Crown of Gold', she had shown his letter to Henry Colburn, but the latter had declined to make her any offer.[36] Any bargain with Colburn was to be 'for the copyright and not an Edition'.

Dear Duke of Devonshire

Your goodness encourages me to the painful task of asking a favor of You – a liberty for which I have no Apology to offer, except the heartfelt interest I take in succeeding in my Object, and the serious consequences to us of my being enabled to do so.

This favor is the presentation of a living to my Husband Mr. Bury should Your Grace ever have one vacant which You may not otherwise dispose of. –

reiterating my Apologies for this liberty & earnestly entreating You to consider how deeply I am interested in obtaining my request –

I remain Dear Duke
With great Esteem
Yours most Sincerely
Charlotte Maria Bury

Letter from Lady Charlotte to the Duke of Devonshire, 22 July 1822. (*Devonshire Collection, Chatsworth*)

The front of Argyll House in Argyll Street by Thomas H. Shepherd, 1854. (*British Museum / The Trustees of the British Museum*)

Above left: John Campbell, 5th Duke of Argyll by Thomas Gainsborough. First exhibited at the Royal Academy, London, in 1779. (*Inveraray Castle / Argyll Estates, by kind permission of the Duke of Argyll*)

Above right: Elizabeth Gunning, Duchess of Hamilton and Brandon, and Duchess of Argyll by Katherine Read, engraved by R. Lowry and J. Finlayson in 1770. (*Inveraray Castle / Argyll Estates, by kind permission of the Duke of Argyll*)

Left: Elizabeth, Duchess of Argyll with Lady Augusta and Lady Charlotte Campbell as a baby by Angelica Kauffman, *c.* 1775-6, in Lady Russell Constance, *Three Generations of Fascinating Women and other Sketches from Family History*, 2nd edn (London, New York, Bombay: Longmans, Green, 1905).

Lady Charlotte Campbell, 1775-1861. Writer and famous beauty by Johann Wilhelm Tischbein, *c.* 1789. (*National Galleries of Scotland. Purchased 1975*)

Lady Charlotte Campbell by Anna Tonelli, mid-1790s, in Lady Russell Constance, *Three Generations of Fascinating Women and other Sketches from Family History*, 2nd edn (London, New York, Bombay: Longmans, Green, 1905).

Modern Elegance by James Gillray, published on 22 May 1795. (*Photograph by Mark Unsworth*)

Lady Charlotte Campbell as 'Flora' by John Hoppner, first exhibited at the Royal Academy, London, in 1796. (*Inveraray Castle / Argyll Estates, by kind permission of the Duke of Argyll*)

Lady Charlotte Campbell's Medley and Reel in *Skye collection of best reels and strathspeys extant; Embracing over four hundred tunes collected from all the best sources, compiled & arranged for violin & piano* by Keith Norman MacDonald (Edinburgh: Paterson & Sons, 1887), Glen Collection of printed music, National Library of Scotland. (*Creative Commons Attribution 4.0 International Licence*)

Lady Charlotte Campbell (with turban) by Archibald Skirving, 1802. (*Private collection / Public Domain, Wikimedia Commons*)

COLONEL AND LADY CHARLOTTE CAMPBELL.
From a Drawing by Edridge, at Swallowfield

Colonel John Campbell and Lady Charlotte Campbell by Henry Edridge, late 1790s/early 1800s, in Lady Russell Constance, *Three Generations of Fascinating Women and other Sketches from Family History*, 2nd edn (London, New York, Bombay: Longmans, Green, 1905).

Colonel John Campbell, of Shawfield and Islay, unknown date and artist, but possibly George Sanders (Saunders). (*Eallabus House / Islay Estates, by kind permission of Alastair Morrison, Baron Margadale*)

Above: Cartoon of Walter Campbell of Shawfield's family, unknown date and artist. (*Eallabus House / Islay Estates, by kind permission of Alastair Morrison, Baron Margadale*)

Left: Lady Charlotte Campbell by Thomas Lawrence, 1803. (*Abercorn Collection / Abercorn Heirlooms Settlement Trustees*)

View of Montagu House on Blackheath, London; possibly after a drawing by Paul Sandby, *c.* 1779. (*National Galleries of Scotland. David Laing Bequest to the Royal Scottish Academy on loan 1974*)

Westwood House as Passmore Edwards Teachers' Orphanage, Sydenham; unattributed photograph on a postcard, *c.* 1904. (*Mary Evans / Peter Higginbotham Collection*)

Eliza Mary Campbell, Lady Gordon-Cumming by Henry Raeburn, between 1815 and 1823. Current location unknown. (*Public domain, Wikipedia*)

Walter Frederick Campbell of Islay, 1798-1855. Member of Parliament for Argyllshire by Thomas Dick, after Kenneth McLeay, unknown date. (*National Galleries of Scotland. Purchased 1937*)

The Campbell Sisters dancing a Waltz by Lorenzo Bartolini, 1821-22. (*National Galleries of Scotland. Purchased jointly by the National Galleries of Scotland and the Victoria and Albert Museum, with the aid of the National Heritage Memorial Fund, Art Fund, with a contribution from the Wolfson Foundation, and a donation in memory of A. V. B. Norman, 2015*)

Above left: Harriet Charlotte Beaujolois (née Campbell), Countess of Charleville by Edward Francis Finden after John Hayter. Stipple engraving, published 1841. (*National Portrait Gallery, London*)

Above right: Miss Blanche Bury, daughter of Rev. Edward and Lady Charlotte Bury, engraved by William Henry Mote after Sir Charles Lock Eastlake, unknown date. (*Royal Collection Enterprises Limited 2024 / Royal Collection Trust*)

LIST OF ROYAL SUBSCRIBERS.

HIS MAJESTY THE KING.
HER MAJESTY THE QUEEN.

HIS ROYAL HIGHNESS THE DUKE OF CUMBERLAND.
HIS ROYAL HIGHNESS THE DUKE OF SUSSEX.
HIS ROYAL HIGHNESS THE DUKE OF CAMBRIDGE.
HIS ROYAL HIGHNESS THE DUKE OF GLOUCESTER.
(*Two Copies.*)
HER ROYAL HIGHNESS THE LANDGRAVINE OF HESSE.
HER ROYAL HIGHNESS THE PRINCESS AUGUSTA.
HER ROYAL HIGHNESS THE PRINCESS SOPHIA.
HER ROYAL HIGHNESS THE DUCHESS OF GLOUCESTER.
(*Two Copies.*)

HER ROYAL HIGHNESS THE PRINCESS SOPHIA MATILDA.
HER ROYAL HIGHNESS THE DUCHESS OF KENT.
HER ROYAL HIGHNESS THE DUCHESS OF CUMBERLAND.
HER ROYAL HIGHNESS THE DUCHESS OF CAMBRIDGE.
HIS IMPERIAL MAJESTY THE EMPEROR OF AUSTRIA.
HER IMPERIAL MAJESTY THE EMPRESS OF AUSTRIA.
HIS MAJESTY THE KING OF THE FRENCH.
HER MAJESTY THE QUEEN OF THE FRENCH.
MADEMOISELLE ADELAIDE D'ORLEANS.
HIS MAJESTY LEOPOLD KING OF THE BELGIANS.

The remaining Portion of the List of Subscribers' Names will be published when the Subscription is closed.

'List of Royal Subscribers' to *The Three Great Sanctuaries of Tuscany* by Lady Charlotte Bury, 1833. (*Photograph by Mark Unsworth*)

Above left: Adelaide Constance Lennox (née Campbell) by W. Joseph Edwards after Sir Francis Grant, published mid-nineteenth century. (*National Portrait Gallery, London*)

Above right: Lady Charlotte Bury by James Posselwhite after Sir George Hayter, unknown date. Used as frontispiece to *The Three Sanctuaries of Tuscany*. (*National Galleries of Scotland. Given by J.S. Duncan, 1937*)

NOTE FROM THE AUTHORESS.

In apology for the long delay of the publication of this Poem, it may be allowable to state, that its postponement has been occasioned by the deepest affliction which could befall its authoress, namely, the loss of him to whom the Work is indebted for its brightest ornament in the graphic illustration of its subject—of him whose unrivalled talent and judgment would have guided and directed its progress, and who would have shared in the satisfaction of its completion.

The desolating reverse of such a happy prospect will plead in excuse for this testimony of love and respect to the memory of the best of husbands, from his fond and mourning widow,

CHARLOTTE MARIA BURY.

Mount Street, London,
October 1833.

'Note from the Authoress' prefacing *The Three Great Sanctuaries of Tuscany* by Lady Charlotte Bury, 1833. (*Photograph by Mark Unsworth*)

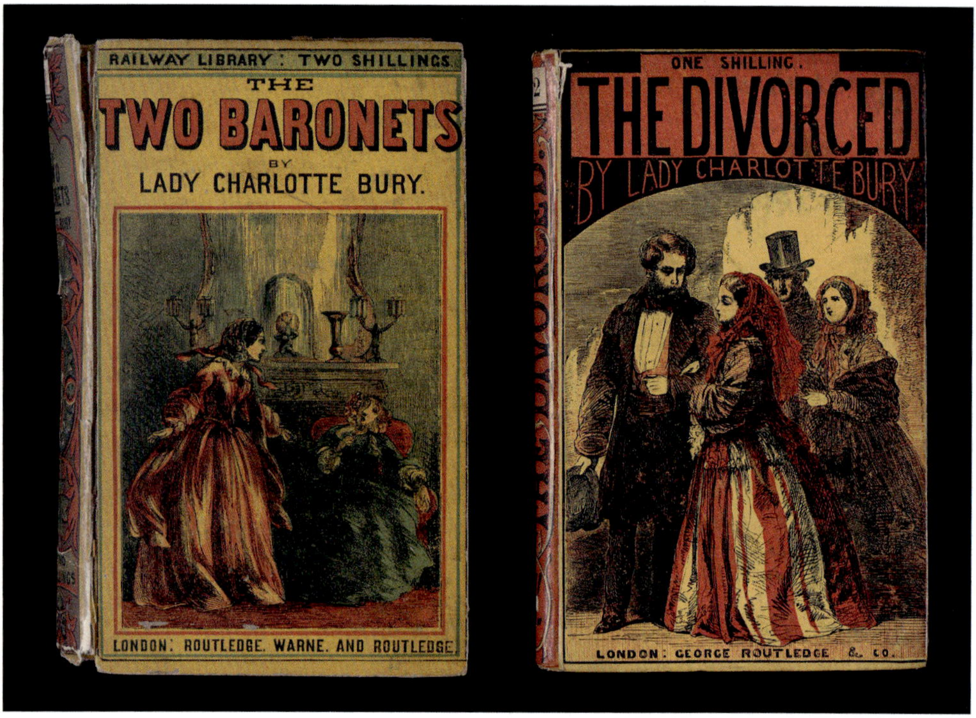

The Two Baronets (London, New York: Routledge, Warne, & Routledge, 1864) and *The Divorced* (new edn ; London, New York: G. Routledge & Co., 1858) by Lady Charlotte Bury (*Photograph by Amélie Deblauwe / Cambridge University Library, reproduced by kind permission of the Syndics of Cambridge University Library*)

Panoramic View of the Bay of Naples seen from the Hotel Della Vittoria by John Francis Campbell, 1842. (*National Galleries of Scotland. Purchased 1942*)

A selection of Lady Charlotte Bury's publications held by the Cambridge University Library (*Photograph by Amélie Deblauwe / Cambridge University Library, reproduced by kind permission of the Syndics of Cambridge University Library*)

Lady Charlotte Susan Maria (Campbell) Bury (1775-1861) by James Rannie Swinton. (*Private collection; photographed by Mark Unsworth; print reproduced by kind permission of National Galleries of Scotland*)

Asking Campbell to return the long poem, she added that she did not have 'another correct copy'.

Perhaps it was as well the Burys had probably been unaware of Scott's sentiments about Edward Bury, for at this time Charlotte was writing to Scott soliciting his help. She requested her letter of 12 March 1830 to Sir Walter to be 'altogether a Secret'.

> No one knows I write it—It is to ask a service at your hands ... Now for it—I am going to publish Some True account of the Three Great Sanctuaries of Tuscany, Laverna, Camaldoli, Valembrosa—short verse—and long Notes—some able heads have looked it over to see that there is neither bad grammar or nonsense in it.

She then humbly explained that she was 'in distress for Money ... not expecting much from any other source'. She intended this work to be the first to which her name was attached. But she required 'some Panygerick some recommendatory opinion in sentence from you, that I want d'avance, in order to make Colburn pay me well. Your word of praise is literally a Bag of Gold'. She ended 'This is My Secret This is My petition' and asked him to burn the letter when read, signing off as his 'affectionate and admiring Friend from the first to the last'.[37] It must have been a very disappointed household when the reply was received. Scott's endorsement on the original petitioning letter, which he did not consign to the flames, read 'Answer'd I could not do as required, but would review the performance'.

Towards the end of April 1830 Charlotte asked Susan Ferrier's sister, Mrs Kinloch 'to send her a person (I had once inquired about for her) to copy for the press, as she wished 200 pages copied in two or three days. I sent her a dirty body Duncan "Lady's Chamber".' Mrs Kinloch thought it was another 'Journal of the Heart', but it was more likely to have been the grand oeuvre.[38] Sir Walter Scott had apparently had a change of heart and Charlotte must have been most gratified and spurred on by some better news which had arrived in Park Square in the middle of June. Addressing Sir Walter Scott as her 'very Dear ... and honoured Friend', she replied on 15 June: 'It was Your Name and good will I sought far above your Generous Subscription—for both however I deeply thank you—and for your precious note. I hope I shall not disgrace your kindness, or commit such a Name as Yours to anything very indifferent.' She added that for 'fear of any Sin against Gramar [ch] or common sense, I shall have my work carefully looked over, by competent Judges. The moment I have a Prospectus printed, I will send you one.'[39] Her husband was personally going to bear the cost of making the copper plates of his drawings.

The kind of volume envisaged was perhaps not quite right for the Colburn stable in any case. Charlotte and Mr Bury next invited John Murray to 'a family dinner with them ... at Seven OClock' on Saturday the 10th of July 1830. This perhaps did the trick; an undated letter written by Mr Bury thanked Murray for becoming 'the Publisher of her little work, on the Terms you proposed'. He continued: 'Her Ladyship is anxious to render it as correct as possible before it is placed in yr hands, and the MS will therefore be delayed for a few days, but as soon as it is revised I will have the pleasure of forwarding it to you.[40] The 'little work' turned into a much bigger operation and it was to be several more years before it finally came out under the Murray imprint.

During the winter of 1830-31 Charlotte and her husband were invited about once a fortnight to dine with Beaujolois at 8 St George's Place.[41] At other times Charlotte and Beaujolois dined alone, or accompanied by Julia who was probably staying with her sister at that time, appearing frequently on the lists of diners. On occasion dinner was hosted by both Lord and Lady Tullamore. For instance, the Duke of Argyll, accompanied by his duchess, were joined on Sunday 21 November 1830 by the Dukes of Sussex and Portland, Lord Uxbridge, Lord Deerhurst (Charlotte's cousin). The last dinner entry, which included Charlotte that winter season, was on Wednesday 13 March when she and Blanche dined alone with Beau. Other members of the family also dined with Beau, including her aunt, Lady Augusta, on Saturday 22 January 1831, along with her paternal aunt and uncle, Lord and Lady Belhaven, and her sister, Emma with her husband, William Russell. Eliza and Sir William Gordon-Cumming, Walter Frederick with his wife, Lady Eleanor, and John's brother-in-law, Captain Vandeleur, were guests that summer. Julia was frequently present, either alone, or with others, presumably still staying with the Tullamores. But rarely were the Burys at the same table.

Perhaps that is not so surprising when letters sent to Walter Frederick by an increasingly desperate and often indisposed Edward Bury, are read.[42] On 11 February 1831 he had felt obliged to re-open the ongoing financial problems with his stepson. 'It is a painful task to me to write this letter, and a still more distressing alternative which urges me to do so.' He felt grieved to have to tell Walter that once again 'your dear mother cannot retain the house she lives in without your assistance'. The loss of Westwood was being loomingly repeated for 3 Park Square. Explaining that 'although its cost has long been paid, still, debts which it would have been extremely painful and difficult for me to prevent, and some which it was impossible, have accumulated to a great extent; and I have at last no means of covering them, but by a sale'. Sadly he continued:

> I have no other property now or I would not make this appeal to you. To spare your mother, however, the misery of leaving her present home, I take this only alternative that remains in my power to solicit you, dear Mr Campbell, to take it for her benefit and (with the exception of my books and prints) everything I possess in the world, if such a step, by your kindness, can be the means of preserving to her the future permanent comfort of it.

He admitted that its value would probably not, 'some years hence, bring you the sum we require of £6000'. He expressed the hope that by offering the sale of the property to Walter:

> It may be secured, or in some way granted to your mother for her life by you, apart from any interest which I might retain in any thing that was hers—the payment of every thing affecting it being discharged from the proceeds of the sale, for the rest in all connected with your mother's future happiness and security, and which she and yourself might decide upon, under the present circumstances, you will find me a perfectly willing and cheerful co-adjutor.

A second letter of 25 February from Bury, apparently in answer to a reply from Walter, was delivered to the latter by his uncle, the Duke of Argyll. It reiterated that Bury himself had already surrendered everything he possessed, and once more asked Walter's

> indulgence to listen to the proposals which may ultimately be laid before you, and if any method to lighten future responsibility to yourself can be devised, or any means of reimbursement which may hereafter be in my power, can be rendered available to the object we both have, I am convinced ... that I will cheerfully and thankfully subscribe to any conditions to this effect.[43]

A month later Edward Bury asked Sir Alexander Johnston, the husband of Charlotte's cousin, Louisa, to deliver a third plea, but this was returned unopened.[44] In this he discussed the interviews that had taken place between James Macinnes, Walter's elderly agent in Edinburgh and Mr Monypenny in London acting for Charlotte. The outcome must have seriously upset the Burys. Macinnes had declined assistance on the ground 'that he believes the embarrassments to arise not from Lady Charlotte's but Mr Bury's extravagance, to which he is not at all disposed to administer'. Macinnes had given no authority for his claim and Bury thought:

> The justice of the term 'extravagance', however, applied to some excess of expenditure, over and above the annual sum of £1290, the gross amount of your mother's diminished income, since 1822, is rendered somewhat questionable, unless rank and situation are lost sight of by the knowledge of the fact, that such was its amount, that out of it your mother had to provide for herself a residence, furniture, and every portion of household establishment, and that, from the period named the only gratuitous advance made to her, independent of income, were limited to £1000.

He explained that he had used the term 'diminished income,' from the circumstance which led to the diminution 'very well known to us all', adding they proceeded

> neither from extravagance nor inclination, but positive necessity of events forced upon us in the year 1822, some of which had their origin so far back as your mother's widowhood, and in the very straightened means she possessed of maintaining her family. Upon a general view, then, the term 'extravagance' would appear somewhat ill-founded.

To refute Macinnes' claims, Bury produced lengthy and detailed arguments and details of 'the embarrassments gradually on the increase for sometime owing to inadequacy of income'. He stated these at £6,000, but including a previous advance of £1,000, they actually amounted to £7,000, which 'added to your mother's income of £1,290 from that period, renders its amount within a trifle of £2,000 per annum'. He asked: 'Would such an expenditure have been considered as "extravagant" even had she possessed it, instead of having to provide residence, furniture and household requisites?' Confining himself only to Charlotte's expenditure, he continued:

> At the same time, I appeal to yourself, has she lacked any of these requisites, or any of the moderate appendages of her rank, carriage, dress or society, such as an imaginary income of £2000 per annum, would annually have given her? and if she has possessed these, would a less sum have afforded them? if not, where is the plea of 'extravagance?' Again, and still more particularly, if having possessed them to a given period, there should remain, from the source of such an income, a portion of the annual outlay accumulated in the shape of a residence, furniture and household requisites, to the amount of £5000, serviceable and sufficient for many years to come, would not the yearly expenditure, during which this accumulation had imaginary income expended fall from £2000 to something like £1700 or £1800? and yet this is the state

> of the case and of the present question. Let your mother's income have been £2000 per annum for these last 10 years, and there would have been no embarrassment. Let it be made up so from that period, and there is residence, furniture and all other household requisites, and no embarrassment remaining.

Bury explained to Walter that he had argued hypothetically, to illustrate that 'as far as the plea of Mr Macinnes's excuse goes, and as far as he has a right to extend it, *no* "extravagance" in your mother's expenditure'. He summed up by emphasising that £6,000 could only be raised by 'the sale of our house, furniture and household requisites', adding: 'To avert the distress such a measure would entail on your mother, I have offered to divest myself, and make sale of them to you, in order that the embarrassments being removed, the whole may be secured to her.' Bury was also ready, 'if you desire or think it expedient to resign, with her consent, whatever right I may hold over her jointure, leaving to yourself the disposition of every thing connected with her mode of life, establishment and domestic expenditure'. The heartfelt petition ended in ever more serious vein with a florid testimony of his devotion and affection for Charlotte and deep concern for placing her future on a firmer basis of 'tranquillity and happiness'.

Although Lady Augusta had been described as far back as 1806 by Eugenia Wynne as 'once lovely' but 'now crooked', 'deformed', with 'no remains of beauty' and with 'a bad Husband and bad health',[45] Adelaide wrote to her eldest sister from Ardencaple on 16 April 1830 that their aunt, Lady Augusta, was 'remarkably well in bodily health—but I daresay you will find her grown very old in appearance'.[46] Nevertheless it comes as something of a shock to read of her burial in Rosneath churchyard.[47] She had been born at Rosneath on the last day of March in 1760, and died there on 22 June 1831. The younger Lady Augusta was usually depicted by family and friends in portrait, memoir or when acting as chatelaine for her widowed father, as disappointed in and by life. Elopement in February 1788 to a man six years younger, had turned into estrangement; her surviving three children, Rawdon, Charlotte and Douglas, however, participated at various times in the lives and activities of their aunt Charlotte and their Campbell cousins.[48] Lady Augusta only rarely appears to have followed her relations south for the London season or continental travel, and divided her time between 11 Queen Street in Edinburgh, and Ardencaple or Rosneath near her younger brother, Lord John, up till the time of his second marriage in 1820. It was at Ardencaple, then described as the home of Lady Augusta and her daughter, that the latter had been married on 27 December 1817 to an Edinburgh advocate, Miles Angus

Fletcher.[49] Adelaide had also mentioned her brother John's illness in her letter of 16 April 1830, and his death a few days before his thirtieth birthday was recorded in Madeira on 6 August; it is conjecture whether he was there for his health or with the military. Less than two years later John's widow, Ellen, and her youngest daughter died in Brighton on 7 and 11 May 1832.[50] Guardians for their remaining orphaned young children, Walter Odenal and Charlotte Edith Eleonora (known as Edith), were Captain Vandeleur and their by then widowed uncle, Walter Frederick, who looked after them with his sisters' help.

By November 1831 Charlotte was writing from Park Square to her long standing friend, the Countess of Charleville, that she was 'still on the verge of a precipice—and nothing is decided'.[51] Under this shadow, she was unable to escape into a 'world' of her 'own', but expressed gratitude at having a loving husband and child, and good relations and friends, including the 'most amiable Lady Kirkwall'.[52] The Duchess of Richmond had come to tea but must have been 'terribly bored, for she had lighted on a knot of reformers ... and the talk of works of Art and matters of general Science was not much in her way, but she had no where to go and she got a cup of tea and my good will'.[53] The day before, the town had been 'paraded by Reg^{ts} in all directions', but she had not heard of any riots and was not alarmed.

Alarm of an altogether different dimension was, however, to be Charlotte's lot during the following spring of 1832. On the Saturday night of 13 April Adelaide penned a letter in Rosneath Castle to her sister Eliza, in Altyre, saying that while she knew her mother wanted to return to London and 'seems to look forward to the possibility of Mr Bury's recovery ... the Drs say the only thing is for him to go abroad'.[54] But Adelaide did not think 'there was much probability of his ever getting better. In the mean time however there is no great change in his health either one way or the other.' In an even larger than usual script, Charlotte wrote to a family friend, the Rev. J. Lillie, thanking him for the loan of books, however she hadn't had 'leisure and freedom of mind to read again, but though Mr Bury I thank God is better, He is in a very feeble state, and I seldom read or do any thing but attend to Him'.[55]

Adelaide was alarmed by Beau's also having been ill, expressing the hope that 'the Lord [may] not see it needful to send us further calamities for already we are certainly much chastened'. Beaujolois was much thinner, weakened by 'five week long periods', when on 10 May Charlotte dashed off a rushed note from Rosneath Castle to Lord Tullamore saying she was heartened to hear that Beau was on the mend. She talked of being 'in the midst of my own heavy tryal ... My heart is very heavy and I will add no more.'[56] Writing to her sister Eliza about the deaths of John's widow, Ellen and her youngest daughter,[57] Beau complained about her mother's writing to Lord Tullamore instead of to herself. Beau considered that 'the style of her composition is totally different this last time she wrote and found she could not do us out of any money'. Even more unkindly she opined: 'Mr Bury is I fancy gradually sinking and I must think that once he is gone she will be quite happy.' Worse, Beau had pencilled on her mother's letter to her husband:

> The undersigned are of the opinion from the warm expression contained in the above note—that Mr Bury has been ill much too long ... Lord T says he is very glad he happens to be so far separated from her—as he thinks otherwise he might be called upon inconveniently. How very refreshing the idea.

It was signed Bittie—BT (Beaujolois Tullamore). This would appear to be a very different sentiment and woman from the younger, more reasonable and kindly disposed Beaujolois.

To Eliza, Adelaide also made 'one more allusion to the painful subject of Mama's affairs, which are still as unsettled as ever'. She had hoped that:

> More union was likely to be promoted by all Mama's children acknowledging (that is if they can conscientiously do so) what Mama requests is that she has said to me more than once that upon this depends much her feeling towards her children as their doing so would prove their desire to please her and do her justice and that if they do not do so she never can feel that pleasure in them or the same degree of affection towards them she would otherwise. Of the reasonableness or rationality of this declaration, as Mama's child I will not presume to judge, but merely state this much to you that you may not mistake the cause of her coldness from which I myself suffered for a time but upon my remarking the difficulties under which she had laboured and the unfairness of the account given in by Mcinnes—which any body might see who chose to examine it—Mama became and has remained ever since quite kind to me.

Walter's wife was also very ill in Islay, and in April 1832 Adelaide considered that 'Julia was beginning to be quite worn out with attendance on Ellinor and anxiety on her account'[58], although early in May she still thought her sister-in-law would 'fully recover'.[59]

> [Adelaide felt] a great longing to go to her and endeavour to be of use there for at present I do not feel that I am of any here excepting just that I am somebody for Mama to speak to when she is not in the sick room,

> but the dread of Mr Bury's becoming suddenly worse and of his dieing when Mama would be almost quite alone makes me fear to leave her. However I shall be guided partly by what the Doctors say of Mr Bury in a day or two and partly of course by what I hear from Islay. Perhaps I may hear again tomorrow but you know the posts from thence are terribly uncertain. Now good night dearest for I am wearied in body and sore at heart and I desire to seek His face who alone can impart peace in the time of tribulation.

Adelaide did indeed leave the Burys and go to Islay to help. The Islay physician Dr MacTavish had been treating her, but called in Dr Balmanno by special boat to Islay from Glasgow in 1832. However, Lady Ellinor succumbed to what has often been described as insanity at Woodhall on 16 September 1832. Her body was brought to Islay for the funeral, Islay House and the servants shrouded in black, as was the pulpit in Bowmore Church.[60] Several years later, Lady Ellinor's remains were placed in one half of a heavy black marble sarcophagus inside the church.[61] Walter Frederick Campbell commemorated her with the lighthouse guarding the bay at Port Ellen, with its sentimental inscription of five quatrains entrusting her light as a guiding star to mariners.

Writing from the island on 7 May, this time to her sister Beau, Adelaide had heard the day before 'that poor Mr Bury is still continuing worse and should I again hear tomorrow that he is near his end I think I ought to go to poor dear Mama on Thursday but my movements will depend entirely on what news I get tomorrow'. She added: 'If I do not go next Thursday I must wait for another week' (for the steamer). The Rev. Edward John Bury died aged 42 at Ardencaple Castle, home of his brother-in-law, Lord John Campbell, soon after the middle of May 1832. Less than a year earlier, Lady Augusta had been buried in the churchyard at Rosneath, which was said, at the end of the nineteenth century, to contain a grave, 'much overgrown with ivy and moss, which is understood to be the resting place of the Reverend E. J. Bury, a clergyman of the Church of England, who was the second husband of Lady Charlotte Campbell'.[62] In 1893 one of the older inhabitants of the Rosneath peninsula remembered the funeral, which was attended by several of the women members and friends of the Argyll family, 'the first time she had ever seen ladies at a funeral'. She had been told the day before by the gravedigger, 'ye'll see a strange sicht on the morn, a minister walking through the kirk-yard readin' oot o' a book, wi' his sark on the tap o' his claes'. Even in his last weeks, Edward Bury had still been trying, with Lord John, to put Charlotte's future on a more secure footing, and on 24 May Charlotte, widowed for the second time and now aged 57, was already taking up her pen to send the corrections on a printed memorandum of explanation and appendix of financial transactions between the Burys and the Shawfield estate from 1819 (perhaps it should have been 1818) to 1832, prepared by her husband in his last dying days. Various bonds were subsequently taken out on Charlotte's life by Lord John, the interest to be paid amounting to over one-third of any future income she might expect or receive.

Lady Charlotte had always hoped that her relatives and children would be 'reconciled to Mr B. for he is really a person to be honoured and liked for himself and one whose tastes and habits and very ways I venture to predict would please you', she had written to her cousin Anne Damer in 1820.[63] The latter's response, writing to her niece Eliza was 'what is to become of her, with this most vain and extravagant Husband and her own too well known carelessness about her own affairs?' When Charlotte had sent her threnody to Beatrice's godmother, she had added at the foot of the letter to Lady John: 'My Husband returns your remembrance with all of courtesy and good will expressed.' She hoped fervently that they would meet again at Ardencaple, which she eulogised: 'the Place in its own local self had always the greatest charm for me. It has smilingness about it that none other has, Rosneath is more beautiful Inveraray more sublime ... there is a laughing sweetness about Ardencaple.'[64] Rosneath's association was to be saddened for Charlotte by the last illness and death of her younger husband. She herself had always protested the happiness of her choice. Her granddaughter, Lady Constance Russell, wrote of her 'apparently having led a happy life with her husband'.[65] She quoted Charlotte as saying:

> He has his faults, like all of us ... but as a husband has as few as possible—inexpressibly careful and tender to me—quite lover-like, never leaving me, and all his tastes and pursuits those which are most refined and most of a nature to keep him constantly at my side; indeed he has no wish ever to leave me and his child for a moment.

In the November before he died, Charlotte had written to the Countess of Charleville:

> I love My Husband and in that alone and the mutual possession of our Child there is much blessing; So long as I have Him and her I have nothing to repine at. Trouble is trouble it is true, but it is very differently modified when it is only of outward circumstances and not of the heart.[66]

When younger, Beaujolois had defended her stepfather against her older siblings, and her younger ones, Adelaide, Emma and Julia never resorted to the snobbish hatreds of their elders, including Anne Damer and Bessie Mure. Recurrent illness may have made Edward Bury tetchy at times, but perhaps the obituary notice in the *Quarterly Review* got nearer to the essence of the man when in 1834 it reckoned that 'the world has lost a truly great artist by the death of Mr. John [*sic*] Bury, though the modesty of his character prevented him from making any public display of his extraordinary accomplishments during his too short life'.[67]

17

The Three Great Sanctuaries

Reference had first been made on 1 June 1826 to the magnum opus on which Charlotte and Edward Bury devoted much time and energy composing, illustrating and financing. Finding it difficult to procure a publisher, especially after Colburn's rejection, the Burys must have decided to finance its production by subscription, John Murray having agreed to publish from Albemarle Street. Prospectuses were concocted which Charlotte began from 1830 to send out to her wide social range. A printed list of grandee subscribers was headed by King George IV and the fliers were intended to encourage others to send two guinea subscriptions to various bankers in London (Coutts and Co, Herries Farquhar, Masterman and Peters), and Sir W. Forbes and Co. in Edinburgh. Many letters in Charlotte's hand were penned from this time on, with the promise of a subsequent list of subscribers being published. Mr Wilson Craig of Riccarton rather grudgingly replied, adding his name to the list but also gratuitously writing to a colleague: 'Lady C. Bury is a selfish and most extravagant Woman, a most worthless Scion of a noble stock, and from what I know of her circumstances, that although she may possibly raise some thousands by this manoeuvre, yet her ruin is certain.'[1]

After the king died on 26 June 1830, altered fliers had to be produced, with the new king and queen now heading the list of subscribers. Considering that her siblings, eldest children and many of her friends thought that, at least for some time, she had lost status by her second marriage, her stock seems to have returned in court circles, for she had managed to enlist as subscribers not only George IV, but then King William IV and Queen Adelaide, a prince and three princesses, the Austrian emperor and empress, the French king and queen, and Prince Leopold of the Belgians. There were also changes between the earliest fliers and the final published list (see plate 22); the Duke and Duchess of Gloucester had ordered two copies each but the names of all the Scottish dukes and their duchesses, though presumably not their subscriptions, had disappeared: the premier Duke of Hamilton followed by Argyll, Atholl, Buccleuch, Gordon, Montrose, and the Dowager Duchess of Roxburgh.

Thomas Thomson of 127 George Street Edinburgh received one of the fliers on 6 July 1831:

> My worldly fortune and comfort, depends upon the enormous success of the work of which the accompanying Prospectus will give you all the particulars. I entreat you to interest yourself for me. It is your Influence in the wide extended circle of y[r] Acquaintance for which I solicit not for your own cash—the Artist and the Author must Sup for their bread by the Sweat of their Brows, and it is the idle part of the Community who ought to administer to us—don't you think so?[2]

She exhorted him, 'If any Scotch enthusiasm remains rouse it for the Daughter of the House of Argyll', also requesting him to pass it on to his brother, the Rev. Mr Thomson of Duddingston 'to whom it is equally addressed'. Her father's aged agent, John Ferrier, also received one of the new prospectuses, telling his daughter Susan that he would try to get two or three subscriptions although he despaired 'of being able to do more, as it is only in very peculiar circumstances that such can be asked or expected'.[3] He had noticed one flier 'figureing [*sic*] away on the mantelpieces of the [Edinburgh] Club houses, but no subscriptions yet'. To Sir Duncan Campbell of Barcaldine Charlotte laid it on thickly in her appeal for his subscription as 'one of my trusty Highland Knights … in the ancient spirits of Clanship, to uphold and befriend a Daughter of the House of Argyll'.[4] His scrolled response promised to take six copies. Other known addressees included Sir William Clayton, Lady George Murray, Mrs Harriet Scott and Mr Archibald Smith, while Lord and Lady Winterton were also approached as being among the most 'Illustrious and talented people of the Land'.[5] Unfortunately the results of all her endeavours are unknown, but enough must have been secured for the project to proceed, although the promised secondary list may not have materialised in print.

In April 1832 *The Lady's Magazine* regretted 'to hear that Lady Charlotte Bury's work on the *Three Great Sanctuaries* is delayed, for a melancholy cause—the serious and alarming illness of Mr Berry [*sic*], who was to have etched the plates'.[6] All too soon, correcting the printed financial statements prepared by her late husband in his last days in May 1832, with what must have been a very heavy heart, she then focused on publishing the ambitious volume on which they had together laboured for years, *The Three Great Sanctuaries of Tuscany, Valombrosa, Camaldoli and Laverna*. Writing on black-edged notepaper and addressing an undated letter from 'Messrs Clares Decorators, Mount Street' to James Moyse, printer in Castle Street off Leicester Square, after 'placing her M. S. of the Sanctuaries of Tuscany' in his hands, she told him that the number of pages would not exceed 180.[7] She was hoping that he would be able 'to make some difference in the price ... bearing in mind that Lady Charlotte is for her Rank and Situation in Poverty'. The actual printed number of pages turned out to be 138 with a dozen preliminary pages and half a dozen plates. By reducing the number of pages and costs, the monies raised would stretch further. During May she was in touch with the Rev. Edward Scobell of 14 Blandford Street concerning the proofs[8] and Moyse was urged to insert advertisements in the 'various papers and Magazines of the Day' and was invited to discuss these and other points 'any day between 1 and 3 o'clock'. She pressed him for an answer as soon as possible, as well as asking for the volume's exact size 'to give it to an artist for a particular Plate which is to form the Frontispiece'.

It was eventually in October 1833 that she sat down to pen her prefatory apology for the long delay in its publication (see plate 23), occasioned by

> the deepest affliction which could befall its authoress, namely, the loss of him to whom the Work is indebted for its brightest ornament in the graphic illustration of its subject—of him whose unrivalled talent and judgement would have guided and directed its progress, and who would have shared in the satisfaction of its completion. The desolating reverse of such a happy prospect will plead in excuse for this testimony of love and respect to the memory of the best of husbands, from his fond and mourning widow, Charlotte Maria Bury.[9]

The earliest prospectus had proposed the ambitious and somewhat surprising subtitle, *A Poem with Historical and Legendary notices, including some Observations upon the characteristic similarities discoverable between the countries and inhabitants of the Apeninnes and those of the Highlands of Scotland*.[10] In the preface to the published volume, she expanded: 'Not only in the sanctuaries did she become lifted, as it were, above the visual sphere of human life', but the routes there, mostly off the beaten track, had added to the novelty of experience, while the 'kindly disposition of the agricultural peasantry of the Casentino' reminded her of the 'similar characteristics of my native Highlanders', enabling her to feel that in the heart of the Apennines, 'I was not altogether in a foreign land', although this was followed by a tirade against the differences in their religions and love of letters.

The subtitle of the final volume of 1833 was different, but no less ambitious, *A Poem with Historical and Legendary Notices by the Right Honourable Lady Charlotte Bury. Illustrated by engravings of the scenery from original Drawings by the Late Reverend Edward Bury.*[11] The folio volume was fulsomely dedicated to Queen Adelaide by 'Her most respectful and loyal servant and subject, Charlotte Maria Bury'. This was the first of any of her publications to acknowledge authorship. The folio pages were expensively bound, some with tooled leather and marbled endpapers, others with silk effect on boards. In January 1834 one copy of the latter was inscribed to 'The Lady Tullamoore from her affectionate mother, the authoress'.[12] The British Library copy is inscribed as a gift to her friend, Lady Kirkwall, while another (ex-University of Aberdeen library) was given by her daughter Eliza at Christmas 1834 to 'B. Wilson'.

It may be hard to envisage the effort involved in venturing then to these remote and isolated spots, difficult of access by foot or horse, now centres of both tourism and pilgrimage. But, recounting the uplifting novelties of the first part of the journey from Florence to Assisi, Charlotte and her small party enjoyed 'the noble hospitality and ingenuous hospitality shewn to strangers (to ourselves particularly), together with the scorn of pecuniary reward for services rendered to us', comparing the close resemblance between her own 'northern mountaineers' and those 'southern mountaineers' of the Casentino province of Tuscany.[13]

Charlotte's antiquarian and legendary prose accounts and the poems for each of the sites were perhaps composed subsequently to their excursions. The historical and legendary accounts for each of the three sanctuaries occupy almost half of the volume, and although conventional, show evidence of considerable reading and observation, while remaining relentlessly anti-monastic. Supplementing her presumed commonplace entries Charlotte must have pored over her many named sources in private and public libraries. As tutor or bearleader to Charlotte's half brother, the Duke of Hamilton touring the continental mainland in the 1770s, John Moore had produced an account of their travels. Charlotte specifically mentions Joseph Forsyth's *Remarks* on his excursion in Italy in 1802 and 1803, which her brother Lord John may have taken on his travels, and she probably knew John Eustace's *Tour through Italy* (1815). Charlotte Waldie Eaton's *Rome in the Nineteenth century* (1820)—they had both been in Rome in the late 18teens—and Lady Morgan's *Italy* (1821) were also volumes that she probably knew well. Antiquarian French and Italian sources such as Dante and Machiavelli were consulted as well as the canon of Milton, Byron, Campbell and Scott. Using the words sanctuary, monastery and convent almost interchangeably, Charlotte provided biographical backgrounds for the founders of the three monasteries: San Giovanni Gualberto at Vallombrosa (Benedictine), San Romulaldo (Eremetic) at Camaldoli, and St Francis of Assisi at Laverna (Franciscan). The settings, historical and legendary accounts of each sanctuary were amplified with Charlotte's strongly expressed views on religion and monasticism, Napoleonic dispersion of artefacts, especially paintings of Michel Angelo and others, as well as eulogising Walter Scott, who, after all his efforts, had not lived to receive an inscribed copy of the *Three Great Sanctuaries* from Charlotte.

The 'poem' comprised three cantos, one composed for each of the three sanctuaries. As she put it in her preface:

> The feelings called forth by places on which nature has bestowed her most romantic forms, which Letters and Arts have hallowed as their favoured retreats, and which religion has consecrated for ages (however wide my dissent from the dogmas of the Roman Catholic Church) seemed spontaneously to resolve themselves into verse.[14]

Whereas her earlier poems had fashionably turned inwards to personal melancholy, it was the wider historical world that inspired her to move outwards here. It was ambitious poetry for a woman, even though she did not overtly compare herself to her quoted male poets. Charlotte asserted that she had varied her chosen and dominant Spenserian stanzas with rhymed tetrameter couplets 'to lighten the monotony'. Each long canto evoked the history, legends, surroundings and metaphysics for each setting, picking up the themes of the preceding 'Notice'; and each was interrupted by one on a different, more personal, often melancholic or religious theme. In Vallombrosa, this was a 'Sonnet to Mary' in which the charms of music, verse, painting and the fashionable poetry of the seasons were invoked, with seasonal fragrances summoning up the lament of an exile. For Camaldoli the main poem was more melancholy and introspective; in hindsight the insertion of 'The Wanderer' reflected Charlotte's stressfulness of youth and divulged the romantic and subsequent woes of her first marriage. The poem ended with a paean to Italy. The Laverna canto focussed on religion, the recurrent face in the inserted 'Haunted One' reflecting Charlotte's desire for, and consolation in, devotion. A monk from Camaldoli, Father Michele, was recalled in her novel *Conduct is Fate*. Laverna had also been the setting for vivid banditti scenes and an almighty thunderstorm and conflagration in the same novel.

Before his tour to Assisi and Laverna a few years later at the end of May 1837, William Wordsworth reported that Charlotte had sent him a copy of the volume and he turned to it again, for his poem 'The Cuckoo at Laverna'. Not only did he consult it for the biographical section of this poem, but there were verbal echoes between the two works.[15] Both drew parallels between Franciscan severity and the harshness of the surrounding landscape, while Charlotte's 'song of the vagrant bird' was, perhaps unsurprisingly, transmogrified by Wordsworth as 'that vagrant Voice'. Hearing the cuckoo on his arrival at Laverna his words also echoed Charlotte's depictions of St Francis of Assisi at the same spot under the shade of the great beech trees.

Edward Bury's engraved half-title and six plates of the Ponte della Santa Trinita in Florence and the three great sanctuaries, were presumably sketched during their excursion in 1818. Edward Bury himself etched the Camaldoli illustration, the rest being engraved by Thomas Lupton of 4 Leigh Street, Burton Crescent. *The Literary Gazette*'s review of the *Three Great Sanctuaries* deemed 'these fine landscapes' to be 'in that high and severe style of art which, with reference both to composition and to effect, rejects minor details, and retains only general forms and masses', continuing: 'Their solemnity of tone strongly reminds us of some of the noblest works of Annibal Caracci.' 'Great' credit was also given to 'Mr Lupton for the masterly manner in which he has transformed the drawings to copper'.[16] Despite his rejection of the project, Colburn's same notice deemed Murray's production a 'beautiful volume', and quoted excerpts to show that it was 'full both of poetic and good feeling, touched with a high tone of enthusiasm'. As well as praising Bury's fine illustrations, *The Literary Gazette* thought the volume 'altogether most honourable to the talents of this accomplished writer on account of its 'tenderness, grace and a high tone of religious feeling'. It was an expensive luxury production of fashionable drawing room poetry inspired by the likewise fashionable world of Italian touring. The author was characterised as 'high-born, singularly beautiful, admired and courted ... with a mind of no common order', perhaps suggesting that the volume was to grace the tops of tables as much as to be read.

Sir Walter Scott's faith in his long standing friend's worth was reflected in the literary reviews, which, it is hoped, helped to sell what was, after all, intended also as a gift book. *The New Monthly Magazine* positively gushed.[17] The historical and legendary notices were 'replete with intense interest; and the versification is so perfectly adapted to the subject, so graceful, so flowing, so easy, that we are at a loss what to admire most'. At last her union with Edward Bury was being recognised. 'It was a beautiful task for Lady Charlotte Bury and her husband to undertake together; his pencil and her pen were well calculated to illustrate each other.' While 'in design and execution' it was reckoned a 'book of beauty', the concluding view perhaps gilded it excessively: 'We recommend all who have dreamt of loveliness to look upon the Lady's Portrait, and their dream will be realised.' Probably related to the lack of sufficient wherewithal, the last known likeness of Charlotte had been about the time of the death of her first husband almost quarter of a century before. The preliminary pages to *The Three Great Sanctuaries* thus included a Posslewhite/Lupton etching of the portrait by George Hayter of a much younger Charlotte (see plate 24), when the dove resting on her left hand might have been more appropriate, presumably before all the family squalls subsequent upon her second marriage. In this late Romantic portrait Charlotte's long fair hair fell over her right shoulder: classically dressed, she had a soulful upward gaze and a butterfly hovered nearby. More appropriate and perhaps more seemly might have been a gracious likeness not exhibited at the Royal Academy until the following year, when H. Perronet Briggs portrayed a serene and gracious person looking much younger than someone in her sixtieth year.

Fraser's Magazine also waxed lyrical. After describing the 'fine engraving of Lady Charlotte' as 'a great likeness', it contended: 'Here indeed is a book of beauty! Lady Charlotte's Three Great Sanctuaries of Tuscany, a book splendid in execution, composition, decoration, poetry—in every thing which the genius of any author or the artist can produce.'[18] Dazzled perhaps by its being 'royally subscribed for by some couple of dozen of kings and queens, emperors and empresses, princes and princesses' (let alone dukes and duchesses), the editor gave a sample of some of the verses about Florence in the canto Valombrosa [*sic*]. 'How harmonious is the verse!—and the sentiment is as fine. Why does not Lady Charlotte Bury write more poetry?' *The Quarterly Review* compared Charlotte's work to that of William Beckford's account of his travels in Italy, Spain and Portugal. Beckford described how, in verse and prose, Charlotte had painted the 'beautiful gloom of Vallombrosa's towers with a skill and grace which must do honour to her name'.[19] He did, however, point out to readers of *The Quarterly Review* that 'this work, if published in a less expensive form, would, we have little doubt, be as popular as its whole execution is creditable to the fancy and feeling of the authoress'. He deemed the engravings 'exquisite'. The critic noted that, while engaged in reviewing Beckford's two volumes, 'another has been laid on our table, in which we find the same scenery described with hardly inferior power, and with a gentleness of feeling, to dwell on which for a moment ere we pass on, may soothe as well as interest our readers'. An extract was then used to illustrate this encomium.

The reviewer in *Fraser's Magazine* asked: 'Why does not Lady Charlotte Bury write more poetry?' This she had continued to do, sometimes for payment, in the women's magazines and annuals, in miscellanies such as her *Journal of the Heart*, more often to incorporate in her novels where and when appropriate. Like other aristocratic young women of the late-eighteenth century, Charlotte's first forays had been in poetry, her 1797 volume being published in Edinburgh both privately and anonymously. While some at least knew in 1822 of her authorship of *Conduct is Fate*, and a reviewer mentioned her by name in 1826 (the 1826 Prayers were 'By a Lady'), the 1833 volume was the first to which she attached her name, intentionally to attract subscribers. Her name was similarly printed in *The Divorced* in 1837; thereafter she often used her initials, CB or CMB for poems in novels, magazines and the like. In her correspondence the initials CMB were sometimes designed as a geometric logo. The reader may assume that unattributed poems in her novels and miscellanies (up to 1837) are those of Charlotte, since most other quotations were attributed. Perhaps at heart she always identified herself as a poet, rather than having to produce formulaic novels to meet demand and provide necessary income. Having just turned 30 in 1805, she confided in her journal: 'Sometimes I think my Poetry is Poetry at other times I am disgusted with and more with myself for writing it ... But the fit, the delirium returns and I relapse into rhyme as naturally as a Drunkard does into wine.'[20]

Her ineffably sad poems of 1809 and 1821 on the loss of her first husband and last child have already been mentioned, and she continued to read and write poetry as illustrated in her commonplace books. Her most ambitious poetic works were clearly the *Prayers* and *The Three Great Sanctuaries*. Understandably the negatives in her life not only made poetry composition more problematic, but resulted in its often dolorous tone. Apart from her 1797 volume, the rhymed *Prayers* and the Tuscan folio, almost one thousand lines are in archives or known to have been published, but unknown are the other verses which may never have found their way into archive or print. For instance, in her journal she mentions being asked to recite her dog poems.[21] Lengthy poems, many written long before publication, include that composed for Susan Ferrier's album in 1809, 'The Eagle' above Duniquaich at Inveraray,[22] 'Stanzas on Sydenham'[23] and 'On Leaving England',[24] 'To Azzarotti of Genoa', renowned instructor of the deaf and dumb there,[25] the 'Cascade of Chede in the Chamonix valley',[26] and the threnody on the death in 1821 of her last daughter, Beatrice, published in the 1835 *Journal of the Heart*, with the first verse recycled in her novel *Devoted*.[27] Most of the others, long and short, that have survived are to be found in her novels of the 1820s and 1830s, in her favoured pentameter style. However, as the exigencies of publishers and fashion changed, less poetry appeared in novels published later. As well as including others' poems and translations, often as epigraphs, many of her own compositions invoked the natural world and the seasons, often metaphorically. Other recurrent themes were in melancholy and religious vein or on topics such as passion, love and marriage.

Just as many of her novels can be interpreted as partly autobiographical, it is no surprise to find refrains echoing her own life experiences:

Yes! I have loved thee long and well,
How well thou dost not know;
For thou art stranger to the spell
Of my Impassioned woe:
But there's a time, that time is near,
When I may cease to feel;
The altered mien I see thee wear,
Has cased my heart with steel;
This numbing power, this deadly chill,
Is now a welcome guest.—
It is my wish, it is my will,
To nurse it in my breast.[28]

She had conjured up a romantic view of marriage in a supposed gravestone inscription in *The Exclusives*, a scene recalling Gray's *Elegy*:

They were so one, it never could be said
Which of them ruled, or which of them obeyed;
He ruled because she would obey, and she
BY him obeying, ruled as well as he.
There ne'er was known betwixt them a dispute,
Save which the other's will should execute[29]

This was, however, somewhat revised in the novel's second volume.

Never answer till her husband cools
And if she rules him, never show he rules.[30]

Published posthumously in *The Two Baronets* but presumably composed years before were quatrains:

How blest the maid whose bosom
No headstrong passion knows!
Her days are days or peace,
Her nights of calm repose.[31]

Love is not love
Which alters when it alteration finds,
Or bends with the remover to remove;
Oh, no! It is an everfixed mark
That looks on tempests, and is never shaken.[32]

At various times such as in 'The Wanderer' in *The Three Great Sanctuaries*[33], Charlotte found herself reflecting on exile, whether voluntary or involuntary, while admitting that travel rarely solves problems, as in *History of a Flirt*:

They bid me seek in change of scene
The charms that others see;
But were I in a foreign land
They'd find no change in me![34]

Her earlier poetry often evoked her West Highland background. One piece of Argyll lore which she used in both prose and poetry concerned the supernatural in a phantom army, for example in 'The Vision' in the 1830 *Journal of the Heart*, as well as a poem in *Conduct is Fate*.[35] A few pages earlier in the latter novel she had incorporated a song in Scots, before echoing the lore (as well as Campbell and Baillie) in her version of the Lady of the Rock, victim of Campbell-Maclean feuding, left to drown on the incoming tide and recited to her London characters sailing round the Isle of Mull.

The natural world was often invoked, whether in moonlight or for a rainbow:

Blest harbinger of sunny days,
Emblem of peace, good-will to men;
Shine forth with gay prismatic rays,
And chase the cheerless stormy train.
So hope shines forth in promise bright,
To hush the mental torment's strife;
But hideous gloom her beams benight,
And oft she cheats the views of life:
Not so the aerial rainbow's hue
Bends its light arch athwart the skies,
Although 'tis transient to the view.

With colours fading as they rise:
For though they fly, they leave impress'd
A boon on earth by mercy given,
A promise dear to every breast,
The covenant made with man by heaven.[36]

She reused parts of her own poems such as excerpts about the sea in *The Devoted*[37] and the sands in *The Devoted*[38] which resurfaced in a longer poem on the sea in *The Divorced*.

As on the ocean's vast expanse
The scintillating sunbeams glance,
So pleasure's beams upon the breast
Sparkle, but leave no warmth imprest.
And as the spirit of the air
Darts through the wave its shadows rare,
And changes to an iris hue
The ocean's own cerulean blue;
So many a varying thought that springs
From sad review of human things
Oft clouds the human face divine
With shade most exquisitely fine:
But not like those innocuous pass
Which shoot athwart the liquid glass,—
For these with many a heavy trace
Stamp rugged lines that ne'er efface.[39]

In the longer poem the first and last lines have been altered and improved to 'As on thy vast and dread expanse' and 'time can't efface'.

Sea shanties and Ligurian fishermen's songs were built around lighter, if hardly humorous, themes. There is even a banditti's drinking song.[40] However formulaic her silver fork novels were to become, the hundreds of lines composed or selected by Charlotte for her novels were not only highly appropriate, but added atmosphere and depth to her tales and their characters. She was still 'scribbling' poetry in the 1840s while in Italy.[41] Back in London in 1849, the appearance of Dr William Beattie's *Life and Times of Thomas Campbell* not only stirred in her some nostalgic longings for her youthful and 'then happy Family circle', but it also inspired her to produce a poem which her daughter Emma probably copied out and sent to Beattie. It celebrated Campbell's stance on behalf of Poland's independence as well as his place in the pantheon of poetry, culminating in his funeral and resting place in Poets' Corner in Westminster Abbey.[42]

As with her prose, Charlotte's stock has started to rise with another generation's re-evaluation and in 2001 when discussing her main volumes of poetry, Pamela Perkins averred that 'Bury's writing might well be of more interest now than at any other point since its original publication'.[43] She considered that both poetry and prose showed Charlotte to be the very embodiment of literary fashion, as she was prepared to experiment with tone and style throughout her career, with 'aristocratic raciness jostling with melancholy expressions of sensibility'.

18

The Professional

Charlotte and Blanche had returned to London later in 1832 to downsize house, or perhaps to leave memories behind. Furniture, silver, china, linen, books, pictures, prints and so on, must have been removed from 3 Park Square at Regent's Park. For the next couple of years and more, correspondence was addressed variously. On 19 October 1832 an agreement with Richard Bentley was signed in 16 Connaught Square.[1] To the address 128 Mount Street in October 1833 she added 'Messrs Clares Decorators',[2] while a month later she invited Tommy Moore to dine 'at her humble lodging over a grocer's shop'.[3] In May 1834 she borrowed 'the Paperhouse under her new apartments' for her Salle,[4] and she was still writing from 128 Mount Street at the start of the new year of 1835.[5] Sometimes she asked for her correspondence to be directed to the Tullamore home in St George's Place. Eventually the joys of Regent's Park were exchanged for Hyde Park, to apartments which Charlotte probably bought at 3 Connaught Place West, behind Marble Arch. Writing to Charles Kirkpatrick Sharpe in November 1836 she was able to claim: 'By some miracle or other, I am at present in a good house, half furnished and half lived in. I have saved something from a wreck; and I have still given to me a stout heart till a stone brae.'[6] Their four dogs could enjoy Hyde Park, as they had done Regent's Park; and Charlotte still had four 'birds'. She could also claim that she and her 'beautiful girl of seventeen—literally beautiful—' were often visited by 'all' of her surviving Campbell children who were not only all flourishing, but were now 'in perfect harmony, so that is a great sunshine ... other people I daresay think me old; but I think myself young, and am determined to do so as long as I live'.[7]

Richard Cockle Lucas was commissioned to execute busts of Charlotte's late husband and of Blanche (exhibited at the Royal Academy in 1833), and of herself (shown at the Royal Academy in 1835).[8] Perhaps she had by then recovered from Moore's somewhat harsh judgement of her two years before. They had been dining at the house of Sir Walter Scott's daughter and son-in-law, the Lockharts, on Saturday 9 November 1833 after which he recorded that 'poor Lady Charlotte Campbell [was] so aged and altered that I did not know her till she herself addressed me'.[9] He added, however: 'There was with her ... a young Bury—a girl about 14 and like all her other progeny stamped with her mother's loveliness—nor could I help exclaiming when she presented her to me "How you have strewed the land with beauty!"' Blanche was painted romantically by Charles Eastlake (see plate 25) and Charlotte responded enthusiastically in October 1833 to the request of publisher, S. C. Hall, to have this portrait engraved for his 'beautiful Amulet', a representative copy of which annual he had sent her.[10] Eastlake had given his consent, but wanted the painting returned from the engraver, Charles Rolls, by the end of the following March in time for the Somerset House exhibition of the Royal Academy.[11] The proud mother thought that 'as a work of Art' the picture was 'of such a sublime character' that she hoped it would 'obtain for the Artist all the Fame it Merits', although she added sardonically 'but she has to fear that like other sublime things it may not be understood at least not generally'. Appearing as the frontispiece of Hall's annual of 1835, it was embellished further by an encomium from the editor, the Countess of Blessington:

Meet emblem is that flower, fair girl, of thee,—
Fair and unspotted as thy face and mind;
Thy mother's beauty in thy face we see,—
O may we in thy soul her virtues find.

Eastlake had wanted Blanche dressed romantically, her long hair waved from plaiting, and holding a stem of white lilies. The description of Blanche's father almost twenty years earlier by her half-sister, Beaujolois, as 'long-nosed', appears to have exaggerated the Argyll nose of her mother and many of her half-sisters.

By May 1834 Royal Academician, Richard Westmacott, was writing to Mary Berry hoping that 'the change of air and variety of scene have completely re-established Lady Charlotte Bury's health'.[12] He reported that the latter's was one of the three rival establishments (the others being Mrs Chency and Lady M. Shephard) for the increasingly popular charades. 'If it goes on thus, there won't be a word capable of dismemberment left unatomized in the Dictionary.' He had heard that for one on 8 May

Charlotte had borrowed 'the Paperhouse under her new apartments for her Salle, and had covered herself with glory'. Charlotte introduced this 'new game that is started in the course of pleasure' into her novel *The Devoted*. 'Charades are all the rage' the narrator declared, characterising them as 'enacted enigmas'.[13] Lady Charlotte Guest described another evening in May 1834 when, after a dinner party, she and her company went along to Lady Charlotte Bury's, 'where there was a pleasant party of a very different description, but nearly over'. Charlotte became a habituée of the salon of the formidable Lady Charleville in Cavendish Square, along with Beaujolois, Eliza, Adelaide and Julia when they were in town. The soirées and conversations of Beaujolois' mother-in-law were 'hardly exceeded by any in London, for their agreeableness and the brilliancy of intellectual enjoyments',[14] presided over by the 'stately and imposing' countess with her 'magnificent grey eyes' in her huge wheeled chair to which she had been confined since about 30 years old, 'giving the appearance of a queen upon the throne'.[15] At one of the countess' later dinner parties, Charlotte was cruelly depicted by one guest as 'that famous beauty of bygone years ... looking most picturesque—like a splendid ruin in her purposely old-fashioned attire'.[16] On the last day of October, 1835, Lady Charleville became the dowager countess, while Beaujolois' husband entered the Lords, and like Uxbridge and the Argylls, served at court, especially that of Queen Victoria.

Another favoured salon was that of the Berrys in Curzon Street, while Charlotte's circle also encompassed a few female writers including Maria Edgeworth, Lady Morgan, Mrs Caroline Norton, Lady Catherine Stepney and many others. One of the 'literary lionesses' for whom 'she had a penchant' was 'Miss Mitford, whom she invited to one of her conversaziones', but Miss Mitford was averse to the 'vapoury aid of fashionable notoriety ... of the scribbling race', and contrived to be out of London on the day concerned.[17] Charlotte was 'among the most distinguished patrons of art' at the British Artists' Exhibition in Suffolk Street at its opening on Saturday 22 March 1834, when the Countess of Blessington was also an attendee.[18] The latter thereafter sent Charlotte a presentation copy of *The Confessions of an Elderly Gentleman*, which the recipient 'read throughout without being able to lay it down', esteeming both its 'distinguished talent and varied charm'.[19] Despite the infamous triangle of the Blessingtons and Count Alfred d'Orsay, Charlotte was one of the few who did venture to visit. As William Archer recollected: 'With the exception of Lady Charlotte Bury, the Countess of Guiccioli [Byron's mistress], her own sisters, Lady Canterbury and Madame san Marseau [and Louis Napoleon's Elizabeth Howard] one never meets any Ladies at Gore House.'[20]

Even in March 1813 when they had just met and she was reading many of Germaine de Staël's writings, with her own first novel recently published, Charlotte was aware of her ambitions in the authorial world. In her *Diary*, exploring the perception and reception of female authors she claimed 'there is not a man, perhaps, existing, who does not think that those women are wisest and happiest who do not attempt that bold and dangerous adventure, authorship'.[21] She quoted one of her writer friends whose view it was that 'men have the camp, the court, the senate, and the field; but we—we have nothing but thought and feeling left'. Eventually, however, these lofty sentiments gave way to more mundane ones. As she admitted to Charles Kirkpatrick Sharpe, 'It would be well enough if one lived to write for fame and fancy, and to try to do good, but to coin money is slavery to body and mind. I am that slave.'[22]

In what was almost the equivalent of Verdi's 'galley years' after the death of his first wife and two children in 1839, her second widowhood was to see Charlotte, in her late fifties and sixties, penning a score of novels and short stories, writing poems, editing other authors' works, as well as compiling a second *Journal of the Heart* in 1835; there were also translations and further editions of some of her novels, as well as two further editions of her cookbook. From the time of her first novel in 1812 Charlotte's publishers had ranged from Blackwood and Clarke in Edinburgh to Richard Bentley, James Cochrane, Thomas Cadell, Henry Colburn, Glaisher, Longman, John Murray, Routledge and Saunders and Otley in London, as well as editions being published in continental Europe (Baudry, Fourmestraux and Galignani in Paris) and by various publishers in Boston, Philadelphia and New York. Mostly triple deckers, the novels were written 'by a Lady', until 1837 when, for the first time, her name was attached to *The Divorced*, although her authorship had been attributed to novels long before.

Her dealings with publishers could be peremptory; John Murray, Henry Colburn and others all had to follow the path to Charlotte's door. On 2 January 1835 she requested Messrs Cochrane and Macrone to come and 'speak to Her tomorrow morning at Eleven O'clock' in 128 Mount Street, presumably to discuss the second *Journal of the Heart*, which they were to publish that year.[23] In the 1830s it was mostly Henry Colburn and Richard Bentley with whom she dealt. Henry Colburn was an opportunistic and usually financially overstretched publisher who had gone into partnership with Richard Bentley in 1829, when the latter had sold his interest in the publishing firm he had set up in 1810 as S. and R. Bentley to his older brother, Samuel.[24] Colburn brought his investments and copyrights to the new business and Bentley invested £2,500. The projected profits of £10,000 were to be split 60:40, although it took a couple of years to sort out Colburn's shambolic accounts. Of the four series of books which they intended to launch, only the Standard Novels became 'enormously successful'. The series comprised monthly one-volume reprints at 6s. each beginning in February 1831 and concluding with volume 126 in 1854. They still, however, continued to print new triple-deckers (although almost one-third of these may have been remaindered or pulped). Several periodicals were also successful, in which they puffed or advertised their other publications. But the debts mounted, the partners fell out in September 1832, and Colburn set up on his own again in 1836 at 13 Great Marlborough Street. Like all such works, Charlotte's novels were 'puffed' by the publishers, particularly stressing her thinly veiled aristocratic authorship. But they were also noticed or reviewed in the daily newspapers as well as the periodicals. The triple-deckers normally sold for one and a half guineas (£1 11*s.* 6*d.*) and cheaper editions followed, especially in France and America. The first-edition volumes were mostly well bound octavo pages, with large print, wide margins and relatively few lines per page. Notoriously this encouraged narrative padding with short-sentenced dialogue all filling up more space. Subsequent cheaper editions, often in one volume, such as the Bentley Standard novels and Colburn's Modern Standard novels, and especially the French and composite American ones, were much more cramped, with smaller print, slender margins, closer lines and more lines to the page. Likewise, bindings and covers varied from the earlier tooled leather ones to subsequent plain board.

Advertisements ran in *The Times* for remaindered copies or those from circulating libraries.[25] At the latter, for a subscription, a reader could borrow one volume at a time.[26] At the end of the first two volumes of the triple-decker novels, the (mostly female) readers might, hopefully, have been walking to the library in eager anticipation of the way in which the previous volume's cliffhanger would be resolved. But for Colburn's novelists, such niceties could not always be attained. Charlotte herself developed a formulaic approach: her advice to Harriet Pigott was that 'in order to sell the work to advantage it will be absolutely necessary that it should consist of three vols. of four hundred pages, each volume about 220 words in a page and that the whole three volumes be offered together ready to publish'.[27] After giving further counsel to Pigott, she observed somewhat gratuitously, perhaps thinking of her own manuscripts: 'The handwriting is of no consequence—the printers read every hand and the look is of no consequence. However that it should be plainly legible is certainly a great advantage to its being favourably judged.' She did not always manage to get the formula quite right, however, as she explained in 1837 to William Shoberl, then working for Colburn, when he asked for alterations to the third volume of *Love*.[28] Writing to him formally in the third person, she asked him to return

> the whole of the third volume of Love … she will in a few hours add in a chapter. But to lengthen out the last thirty pages would be to mar the Grace of the Book and render it wearisome … The fact is the first and 2d vols are too full. But that cannot now be remedied.

She was 'willing to make up the deficit of the 3d volume providing she does not spoil the work', and was anxious to see the proofs of the first and second volumes. According to Nathaniel Parker Willis:

> Lady Blessington's novels sell for a hundred pounds more than any other authors except Bulwer's [… who] gets fifteen hundred pounds, Lady B. *four* hundred, Honourable Mrs. Norton *two* hundred and fifty, Lady Charlotte Bury *two* hundred, Grattan *three* hundred, and most others below this. d'Israeli cannot sell a book at all, I hear.[29]

At Colburn's behest Charlotte also edited *Memoirs of a Peeress*, published on March 25, 1837,[30] normally assumed to be by Mrs Catherine Gore, then living in Paris, and who had, like Charlotte, resorted to writing to support an ailing husband and ten children, although Charlotte claimed in a letter to Harriet Pigott that 'Mrs Gore did not put her name to the Memoirs of a Peeress. Neither do I know for certain who wrote that book—or compiled it. I lent my name to Colburn in order to oblige Him that He might oblige me.'[31] Catherine Gore was one of the most prolific of the silver fork novelists and excelled 'in the portraiture of the upper section of the middle class, just at that point of contact with the aristocracy'.[32] Gore herself claimed that she was transferring the familiar narrative of Jane Austen to a 'higher sphere of Society'.[33] Although her work was often trenchant, the *Memoirs*, purporting to be those of the fictional Lady Mordaunt, were very well received by reviewers in many papers including *The Despatch* ('an Extraordinarily clever book'), *The Edinburgh Evening Courant* ('a work of great talent and originality'), *The Glasgow Courier* ('a Work of greatest interest and power'), and the *Scotchman* ('a most fascinating story').[34] *The Times* deemed it 'an extremely clever book. Colburn brought out a second edition the following year, with the words 'Memoirs of' omitted from the title. 'The writer paints what she saw and participated in with sense and judgment. She introduced us to the private lives of Fox, Burke, Sheridan, Lord Grey … galaxy of fashion.'[35] There was, however, at least one dissenting view when the American edition was published under the title *The Posthumous Memoirs of a Peeress*, and attributing its authorship to Charlotte.[36] Objecting to the frequently expressed opinions 'from which most readers, we are sure, in common with us, will at once dissent', the reviewer assessed 'the balance of credit as against the *Peeress*'.[37] Charlotte was also one of several translators of Godoy's *Memoir(s)* for which she was paid £5 on 5 December 1835.[38]

That she had become a professional writer by the 1830s is evinced not only in the content of her correspondence with publishers but also in her correspondence with, and hospitality to, Harriet Pigott.[39] When proposing to handle a manuscript of Pigott's in 1838 Charlotte told her that she could only lend her name to a work 'in consideration of sharing the profits', given that 'the responsibility of editing a work, is great, and the labor [*sic*] of bringing it through the press is not small'.[40] In a subsequent letter to a potential publisher she made it clear that 'when I said share the profits I meant half the profits',[41] at the same time explaining to Harriet Pigott that she depended 'for my existence on my literary gains'.[42] Emphasising that times in the late 1830s were once again hard for publishers, 'the trade of Books' having fallen to 'far less than a quarter of what it was', she claimed that 'every English novel that goes over to France and Holland is published for two pence and sold for half a crown. I leave you to judge of the consequence to us poor starving Authoresses.' Realising that memoirs 'were required by publishers',[43] Charlotte acted as agent for, and wrote the introduction to, Harriet Pigott's epistolary and supposedly autobiographical *Records of Real Life in the Palace and the Cottage* (1839). Pigott had already written the two-volume *The Private Correspondence of a Woman of Fashion* based on her continental travels in 1814-15, which had appeared in 1832.[44] She was now hoping to have her 'Records of Real Life' published. By this time a hardened professional in her dealings with publishers, Charlotte warned Pigott that it was imperative that the 'whole three volumes be offered together ready to publish'.[45] On sending manuscripts to publishers her advice was to give each publisher only a few days in which to decide whether to accept or reject, although in her own case, of the manuscripts which Colburn had had for six months in 1838 this did not ring true. While Colburn had 'hitherto taken all the Mss written by myself which I could give him', he was now offering her a lower price and she averred that 'if one could afford to print and publish it at one's own expense it would fetch four or five hundred pound'.[46] But in the same breath she was writing that she was 'so necessitous' that 'I must submit to whatever brings me a little money' and 'the fact is I am miserably poor and live entirely by contrivance' and 'am myself in very great distress'. At this stage she also thought that perhaps Colburn was unlikely to publish any more of her novels on account of the problems engendered by her notorious *Diary*, nevertheless she again claimed that he owed her favours and was 'the best and most liberal of all the publishing tribe and his Bills are good and secure and immediately negotiable', and he did subsequently publish more of her novels.

'The sale of a Work is a lottery' Charlotte had warned Pigott, and she had to admit after a few weeks that none of Colburn, Saunders and Otley or Longman would purchase 'our precious M.S. for precious it is in despite of all these stupid ignorant Publishers'.[47] In the spring and summer of 1838, after Colburn's rejection of Harriet Pigott's manuscript,[48] and conceding that her by then notoriety had perhaps not helped, Charlotte approached Theodore Hook and John Galt, Richard Bentley and John Murray. If 'all and every London Publisher' then failed, and rejecting the option of self-financing as not being feasible, she recommended going to 'Liverpool and Birmingham and Manchester where are respectable Booksellers'. She went further in recommending Pigott 'to try abroad with Galignani if at Home does not succeed'. Her opinions of publishers were frequently less than charitable and her letters to Pigott painstakingly evince all the ups and downs of high hopes and rejections involved in authorship. By April 1839 Charlotte was still trying: she hoped to use her influence with her new acquaintance, 'a literary Lady … who understands the whole trickery of the Trade of Authorship'. This was Mrs Cornwell Baron Wilson, who had just written the life of 'Monk' Lewis, published by Colburn that year.[49] In the end, however, it was Saunders and Otley who not only published Pigott's work in 1839 but also agreed to the fifty-fifty split between Charlotte and the author.[50] However, Charlotte was incensed that they had asked Pigott to revise and condense her manuscript: 'I think it is a mistake and an impertinence. I really cannot say what Publishers are about. There must be some strange change in the Literary World and I am convinced it will all end by Authors publishing at their own expense.'[51]

None of the cumbersome titles suggested by Charlotte had been taken up, and it was for *Records of Real Life* that she composed the introduction.[52] This turned into an encomium to the recently deceased John Galt, who had himself had a hand in revising the work 'with intense interest' beguiling 'much time in revising its pages', adding notes and an effusive preface.[53] Over two long columns, the *Times* reviewer liked 'the good humour, brisk, pleasant reading' in the letters purporting to be from the author's extensive European travels and experiences, while deploring the excessive and execrable use of French and italics, the French being, he suggested, even worse than that of Lady Charlotte, Lady Morgan or Lady Bulwer.[54] It may even have been John Galt who had brought the two women together. Harriet Pigott has often been taxed with having plagued Galt in his last years in Greenock, and she certainly started to write his biography but this was apparently forestalled. Whatever the reality, it would seem that John Galt was much involved in Colburn's *Diary* venture with Charlotte. As well as expressing the required or perhaps heartfelt pieties, she requested Pigott to ask Galt's widow if she could have his pen as a memento.[55] And it was with this rather scratchy implement 'which in abler hands discoursed so eloquently' that her thank you letters to 'Miss' Pigott and the widow were written.[56]

Although little appears to have come of some of her projects, for many years in the 1820s and 1830s Charlotte collected and solicited material for two miscellanies which did see the light of day. Both still supposedly anonymous, the first *Journal of the Heart*, 'edited by the authoress of "Flirtation"', was published in 1830 by Henry Colburn, by then in business with Richard Bentley; a second followed in 1835 from James Cochrane and Co. of Waterloo Place.[57] The first was dedicated to Mrs Hook, 'The friend of a Lifetime ... who in all the duties of a woman's existence, has preserved such a diary as must render her at once the most competent judge, and the most lenient of critics'. Anne Hook had supported Charlotte throughout the problems of her first marriage and its aftermath; and she and her husband remained intimates through the different complications engendered by Charlotte's second marriage. Colburn's hand is perhaps seen in her introduction:

> The heart is full at all times; and, were its various emotions, day by day, noted down as they occurred, a Journal of it would be endless; a source for the press more prolific, perhaps, than any other—once having a beginning, it would need have no end, till the heart itself ceased to beat: and so true is this, that the ink stamping the concluding feeling of these pages will scarcely be dry, before a thousand others shall have arisen from the same source, and be ready to follow in the form of a second, and it is hoped, of a more interesting volume.

The panegyric in the *Edinburgh Literary Journal* must have encouraged the author, although its premise started strangely.

> It is no inconsiderable achievement for any man or woman to make themselves known at all in their day and generation. How many millions live and die without being once heard of beyond the immediate circle of their own personal acquaintances! ... If literary reputation be worth having, better to be the author of a small poem, published in a small provincial periodical, and discussed at a small tea-party congregated in a small town, than for ever remain a shadow without a name.[58]

Admitting that 'hundreds of our living authors are pretty nearly in the former situation', it was claimed that 'Lady Charlotte Bury, the author of the book before us, is somebody. Apart from her novels, she has now published a "Journal of the Heart", with another novel, "Separation" in press.' This apparently entitled her to raise herself out of 'the class of stitchers of wristbands and knitters of silk purses', an image hard to conjure up for the person concerned, for whom there appear to be few references to such skills or activities. Again, it is strange to read: 'She has clothed thoughts in words, and these words have been set up in type, and printed in the best kind of paper, for the behoof of the reading public. We respect Lady Charlotte Bury for this.' The effect was somewhat diminished, however, although Charlotte herself would probably not have demurred, by adding 'though her works do not belong to the very highest order of mind, they are nevertheless, such as to entitle her to say to meet other Charlottes,—Here is something that it may do you good to peruse.'

Giving some idea of the feel of the *Journal of the Heart*, the review described 'the number of miscellaneous papers and remarks, mostly of a grave description, and is pretty nearly what it professes to be, an account of the different states of feeling which the ordinary events of life give birth to in an amiable, pious, and sensitive nature'. Poems and tales were mentioned, and a sample of one of the 'old letters' added to the highly readable volume, 'full of kindliness, pure morality, and lady like feeling'. Charlotte had included a handful of continental and other illustrations, perhaps those of her husband or even one of her daughters.

More like a Book of Days, it mostly comprised prose, with various thoughts on keeping a journal and themes of prayer and meditation (including 'How to pass the Sabbath delightfully'), but it also excoriated publishers and their desire for fashionable fiction, especially when not written by those of *ton*, and included pieces on the weather which evolved into moral—even socialist—diatribes on charity and the poor. She probably retrieved her journal entries to write of Italy with an illustrated account of Volterra where she had bought a 'copy of Benvenuto Cellini's autobiography for a mere trifle' to add to her library. She avowed: 'It is one of the best gifts of Heaven ... to love literature—to love it for its own dear sake. The very sight of books inspires me with reverential awe.'[59] Also utilised was 'an old letter' which told of 'The Vision' previously mentioned—'the best authenticated story of a supernatural occurrence that I know'—one of the tales sent to her of the spectral Jacobite army marching along Loch Fyne to Inveraray. Her threnody on the death of her daughter, Beatrice, was first put into print in the *Journal*, as was an affectionate poem from the hand of Charlotte's youngest Campbell daughter, Julia, in April 1830, addressed to her 10-year-old half-sister 'Biancha Augusta Romana Bury', extolling her name as 'an emblem of the blest in heaven', but also urging 'Dear Biancha, be *for ever dear*,/Nor cause one fruitless sigh or tear,/ Nor anxious hour, nor doubting fear,/To her whom we both fondly claim,/By that loved tie, a mother's name.' Some prose and poetry from Thomas Sheridan and Monk Lewis were added.

Already by 1831 Charlotte was soliciting material for a second volume. Writing in April to one of the 'Ladies of Llangollen', Sarah Ponsonby, for an original contribution 'to grace a Little Work of mine, entitled "Journal of the Heart"', she stressed her pedigree as 'the daughter of one of those Miss Gunnings of whose beauty you perhaps have heard, a Daughter too of the House of Argyll'.[60] She then claimed she 'would give anything to possess records of her Maternal ancestors to insert them in a projected Memoir of her ancestors'.[61] The outcome of this rather unclear request is not known, but Sarah Ponsonby was to die before the year was out. According to Richard Bentley, however, writing to Charlotte on 1 June 1831, the public had 'given so little encouragement to the first volume of the Journal of the Heart', that 'this discouraged him and Mr Colburn from printing a second volume' she had proposed.[62] Nevertheless, James Cochrane and Co. did publish a second *Journal of the Heart* in 1835. This was dedicated to another of Charlotte's friends, the Marchioness of Hastings and Baroness Grey de Ruthyn, Lord Moira's daughter-in-law, whose portrait includes her little lapdog gazing adorably up at her mistress.[63] The fulsome dedication informs the reader that Lady Grey's 'virtues and talents adorn the high station she holds and whose name confers lustre on the page which it graces'. Cochrane's advance publicity claimed the tales as of 'moderate lengths and extremely varied in their subjects'. Titles such as 'Highland Janet', 'The Countess of Essex', 'The House of Falkenstein' and 'Too Happy', were interspersed with poems of her own or others with initials. Inserted at the start was Charlotte's preface written in 1827 for a proposed second edition of a novel, *Belmore* or *Belmour*, by her cousin Anne Damer. Charlotte considered that the novel had 'never been so generally well known as it deserved to be', and that friends were then anxious to see a new edition. Anne Damer had died in 1828 and this second *Journal of the Heart* contained a twelve-page paean on her cousin's life. This was in part to counteract a 'lately published Life of Mrs Damer which 'gave me (and I must suppose will give all who loved her) great pain'.[64] Explaining its 'sneering deprecation of her character and talents', Charlotte was aware 'that all women who aspire to fame are subject to severe criticism. Happiest are those who, not being compelled by circumstances of a pecuniary nature, rest in the tranquil shade of domestic life'. As wife of a bounder, beloved daughter and benefactress ('and who can speak to his better than myself'), Anne Damer was 'noble and magnificent'.

This contrasted with the rest of the contents of this *Journal of the Heart* that Charlotte introduced to her readers in journal style of inner thoughts and outer social requirements, as well as of planting two cedars at the foot of her garden, or gazing at the Elgin marbles after they had arrived in the British Museum in 1816. She divulged her thoughts and poems on leaving England's shores in 1817, again perhaps mining her journal, travelling through 'Lewis the Fourteenth's France to Dijon, Besancon, Valorbe and Lausanne ... sublime scenery changing suddenly to the beautiful where the traveller descends into Italy creating almost a faintress'. She relived the cities of the Lombardy plain, especially Milan, and wondered over the manuscripts in the 'Ambrozian [*sic*] library' there, including those of Petrarch; she copied Pliny and delighted in the pictures, before continuing on to Gandolfo, Florence and Rome. She recounted being snowed up in Radicofani, six weeks of captivity telling stories, singing songs and reciting poetry, the result of which was 'the packet which accompanied this volume'. The *Sunday Times* deemed this second volume to be 'distinguished by the elegance and variety of its contents'.[65] Like other wordsmiths, Charlotte was no stranger to recycling.

Late in 1836 'after years of silence', she was soliciting from Charles Kirkpatrick Sharpe, without explanation, 'Anecdotes of Society—political or moral, or critical or immoral—of the years 1810 and 1811 down to 1820—any letters or opinions upon the times and the curious state of public affairs'.[65] At the start of 1837, she was asking him:

> Get for me some ancient MS. out of the Advocates' Lybrary ..., which never has been published or rifled. Get it copied; and send it to me, and tell me how to dress it up. If there was any book you would take in conjunction with me—especially if You would illustrate it with your most inimitable drawings—I could (I know I could) sell it for a good price, and you would be benefiting me and yourself. Your drawings if you have any by you cut and dry would, I am sure, with a very little letterpress from myself, fetch you a good price. Colburn is in the field again. C'est tout dire. Memoirs—real memoirs, and old Letters, original ones—are the rage. According to their bulk and magnitude, they would fetch large sums. Who so capable as yourself to dig these out of their hiding-places?[67]

By the end of 1837 she was writing to him about a project that had perhaps arisen out of the earlier enquiries. Prefacing the business part of the letter with the remarks:

> What a pity that agreeable people live so far asunder! ... Presently, when a railroad will be completed, and that I shall think it safe, I do intend to visit my friends in Scotland—but never can by water; and want of

> money hinders my doing so in a coach-and-four at easy stages—the only lady-like conveyance, after all is said and done. But my ideas are wholly obsolete.[68]

By this time she had acquired the 'Lord Buchan papers' for a 'considerable sum'. She expatiated on Lord Buchan's diary and correspondence which consisted of:

> About a thousand Letters many of the Letters from curious and distinguished persons; all interesting, more or less, and with notes would be exceedingly more so, which I propose to put to them. Now, do you think there is any publisher in Edinr who would undertake such a publication? And what would they give for this work? I tell you that I have bought this at a large price, and therefore expect a high price for it. Besides that, the notes on the one-half of the persons [*sic*] names in the diary, and respecting the letters, would take much research, and require to be written with spirit of which I conceive myself to be capable.[69]

She went on to explain her reasons for wanting an Edinburgh publisher, since she had 'so much going on here, that I cannot get all I want managed', continuing: 'Now, will you ask this question for me of Blackwood's successor, or any great man (if such there be in the publishing world, without naming me? ... answer me quickly; I am a dreadfully impatient person.' Another project that had apparently come to nought was an earlier hope of Sharpe's that 'Mr Bury would print what he has of the Stuart papers'.[70]

Poor Sharpe—she had yet another 'work on the stocks which I really think will be very amusing ... an essay upon letter-writing from the earliest known periods, illustrated by original letters'.

> Now, dear Mr Sharpe, how you could make my fortune by giving me some of your collection! But by no possible mode could you so secure my work success as by writing to me yourself, or giving me some of your own ... Now, be gracious ... oh what an Annual you might have got up!—drawings and writing ... friends ... and I would have been the editor, and we all shall have got rich! A speedy answer will prevent hopes making me sick.

She signed off, greeting him 'all in mince-pie wishes ... with the season'. Such requests for society anecdotes and letters were at the least disingenuous and illustrated the lengths to which Charlotte would go in writing for money.

On the question of collections, another correspondent in 1837 was William Upcott of 102 Upper Street, Islington, to whom she had apparently sent a copy of her *Three Sanctuaries*.[71] Charlotte had shown his catalogue to one of the trustees of the British Museum 'but I do not think there are any hopes of his forwarding your views'. She had concluded that there was little hope of any public body being interested in such times: 'If an ignoble love of money did not prevail over every other Sentiment, you would get your collection ... placed ... but that terrible if is bar to all things good or great.' She recommended instead selling the collection to some private rich individual, adding in parenthesis 'though I do not know of them'. She visited him on 30 September in her capacity as someone whose poetry he admired, not as a rich collector.

When retired, the American publisher, H. C. Carey, wrote scornfully of the London copyright system with its stranglehold of publishers on authors. He had heard from Captain Marryat that even 'in the zenith of her reputation, Lady Charlotte Bury received ... but £200 for the absolute copy-right of her novels'.[72] The interests of publishers and authors diverged sharply. There were three kinds of contract. The author or joint authors could sell the copyright to a publisher for a lump sum, the latter meeting all the costs of editing, printing and distribution, while the author had no further claim. If, however, the publisher bought the copyright to an edition of agreed size, usually about 750 copies (but varying from 500 to 1,000 or more), then another fee was supposed to be negotiated for subsequent editions, although publishers sometimes clandestinely printed extra numbers of copies first time around. A third route involved raising the finance required for publication by subscription. Only once did Charlotte spend the huge energy required to produce the 1833 folio volume *The Three Great Sanctuaries*.

After 1815 Paris and the United States of America became main centres of offshore publication. Even in the late 1820s Galignani and Baudry were printing in three-volume format within three days of London publication, bound in cloth and with a price only one-quarter of that in London. Wherever British travellers were to be found on the Continent, in real life and in fiction, Galignani's *Messenger* and his *Weekly Reporter and Literary Gazette* catalogued the latest fiction. If such triple-deckers were then transported or posted back to Britain, customs duty was supposed to be paid, but evasion and smuggling were rife. Publishers in Brussels, Frankfurt, Leipzig, Vienna and others elsewhere were to follow, sometimes in translation. *Marriage in High Life*, which Charlotte edited, was first published in two volumes in 1828 by Colburn, translated into French by 1832, printed along with Blessington's *Elderly Gentlemen* by Baudry in Paris in 1836, translated into German by Carl M. Bohm as *Eine Heirath in der grossen Welt* in Vienna in 1837, and finally published in a new English edition in 1857, as well as appearing over the years in various imprints and collections in America. *The Divorced* (1837) was translated into Dutch in 1839, and *Love* (1838) into Danish in 1843. Subsequent pirated editions of the three-deckers were usually reduced to two volumes (ignoring any satisfactory breaks), and finally to one in larger collected volumes of several novels by different authors. About half the price of English editions, with tightly packed small print and minuscule margins, they did not, and still don't, however, make for pleasurable reading; in 1846 Peterson, a recent publisher to appear in America, sold Charlotte's *The Divorced* at 25 cents (then about 2 shillings or 20 pence), the price was presumably some compensation for quality. Eventually such cheap editions were driven out of the market to a main extent by British ones such as the Routledge Railway Library.

Despite reprints, new editions, foreign editions and translations, it is unlikely that much extra was earned by Charlotte or any other author once the copyright had been given to publishers such as Colburn or Bentley. Some of the earlier editions of her works can still fetch up to three and four figure sums; but many can now also be read online, or increasingly purchased at modest cost using print on demand. But until early in the present century none has been cited, or perhaps even read, more often than the *Diary*, of which the early-twentieth-century partial edition is still often available and affordable.

19

Galley Years

Only one manuscript fragment survives of a novel which is attributed to Lady Charlotte; it is neither in her hand (not an obstacle in itself, since she employed copiers), nor of any work which subsequently appeared.[1] While this chapter discusses her novels in the order in which they were published, the available evidence raises a question mark over their creative chronology. 'I have two or three works coming out but when Heaven alone and Mr Colburn only knows', Charlotte complained to fellow author Harriet Pigott in April 1839.[2] By then Colburn had been sitting on her manuscripts for six months. She noted that while memoirs, letters and journals still fetched a good price, her *Rachel Countess of Peterborough* which she considered 'one of the most powerful novels' had not 'fetched the worth of a rotten apple' and was never published.[3] Others written during these years might have included *Roses* and *The Lady of Fashion* which finally appeared in 1853 and 1856 respectively,[4] while *The Two Baronets* appeared posthumously in 1864.[5]

There are few references to her sitting at her desk actually composing, except perhaps in Italy in the 1840s when she reported devoting the mornings to 'work'.[6] But in carriages, writing rooms and libraries in homes in Scotland, England and Italy, Charlotte penned over 5 million words in prose, poetry, diary and memoir, as well as her wide-ranging correspondence. As previously mentioned, she included her own poetry in many of her novels and inserted the words of songs, particularly Scots ones, but also those of fey characters or action songs of fishermen. Lallans Scots, French and Italian were selected when relevant to the locale, although one acidulous reviewer referred to the deplorable habit of women writers such as Bury and Pigott pointedly using French which he deemed execrable. In the earlier novels, others' poems had to be chosen, perhaps as her publishers demanded, either where apposite on title pages, as epigraphs at the head of each chapter, or within the text. Sometimes seemingly portentous, 'a password of intellectuality ... epigraphs perhaps work best when they are not entirely fitting, when incongruity is part of their meaning'[7]. Listings of her own libraries might have suggested sources for these hundreds of epigraphs and quotations, and the few existing commonplace books might have helped with these as well, perhaps, as including snippets or possible chronology of her writings. Only three survive; one in the British Library is uncharacteristically compiled in a small and closely written hand, containing items copied from her mother-in-law's own commonplace book.

In her partly autobiographical first miscellany, *Journal of the Heart*, Charlotte somewhat disingenuously elaborated:

> How I long for a well-written romance! It would be so refreshing to get off the beaten track of modern novels, away from the lords, and ladies, and fashionables, and would-be representatives of the beau monde, such as the rage for scandal, renders the idol, the Moloch idol [pagan god] of most publishers, and many novel readers of the day ... But I know *not of one publisher* who will withdraw the veil of obscurity from before such a work.[8]

Not content, however, with offering these comments she went on to disparage competitors:

> Of others, it may be said, the nonentity of their pages is their best claim to being a true portraiture of the most confined circles which they depict ... The fact is, that most of the things calling themselves pictures of *ton* and high life, have been either written by persons who never could have opportunities (a most fortunate circumstance for them) even of seeing or mixing, at whatever distance, and under whatever circumstances, with those they intend to represent; and others, again, by persons who have only *achieved their station* among *the race apart*, and are not of that indigenous stock which can alone enable anyone to write of the arcana of *ton*. Pitiful prerogative! if unsupported by better stuff.

That parenthetical phrase 'a most fortunate circumstance for them' underlay Charlotte's equivocation towards the mores and manners of her own class and her first novel in 1812 can be regarded as a very early novel of 'ton'. It was William Hazlitt in *The Examiner* of 18 November 1827, mocking Theodore Hook's excessive admiration for the aristocracy, who inadvertently coined the phrase 'Silver Fork' for the genre, since aristocrats ate their fish with a silver fork.[9] The words 'fashionable novel' and 'silver fork novel' were the culmination of Colburn's success in overcoming his financial difficulties and the book trade recessions in the aftermath of the regency. Colburn is estimated to have published about three-quarters of the 500 or so silver fork novels by aristocratic and other authors.

Silver fork novels mostly portrayed manners as they were in the regency, before the realism of the Victorian novel. But they were also being produced against the background and volatility of the reform movement and age. Edward Copeland claimed that silver fork novels of the 1820s and 1830s could hardly be imagined without 'the Italian opera and London's Italian Opera House, the King's Theatre, in Haymarket ... closely attached to the reform ideology of the Whig party', Haymarket being the centre of the political map of London, between the houses of parliament, the clubs of Mayfair and Marylebone. Citing, amongst others, Charlotte's (edited) *Marriage in High Life* (1828), *Flirtation* (1828), *The Exclusives* (1830), *Separation* (1830) and *The Devoted* (1834), Copeland expatiated on the use of opera boxes, with their public and private connotations, as one of the main arenas in which women could participate in public life. Generally, perhaps occasionally, interested in the political happenings of the time, they had to be bystanders, as is clearly brought out in Charlotte's *Ellen Glanville* (1839). Aristocrats' opera attendance and haut bourgeois opera aspirations were characteristic of the changing world of reform. For men and novels' heroes, the roles were clearer than for women and heroines who had to negotiate public duty and display as well as private duty and family. Many of the silver fork novels of the time therefore became more concerned with the externals of the characters rather than their inner lives—whether the occupants of a box on a particular night displayed the 'nonchalance' of the season's named owners, or the 'mauvaise honte' of the *arrivistes*. But an interesting feature of the use of the opera (and the integral ballet performances) was the knowledge that had to be assumed of the novels' readers. The shilling 'books of the opera with translations' may have helped, but the range of composers (and their works) mentioned or discussed in Charlotte's novels was eclectic, including Mozart, Bellini, Cimarosa, Paesnello, Rossini, Meyerbeer and Donizetti. Singers of the day were much sought after celebrities including Mara, Banti, Grassini, Catalini, Pasta, Sontag, Malibran and Grisi. The opera box in *Marriage in High Life*, *Flirtation*, *The Exclusives*, *Separation* and *The Devoted*, became 'a preaching box for Bury', when the old corrupt and aristocratic values gave way to reformed ones as the political alignment of the landed and the commercial classes, with gentry in the middle, accelerated.

Copeland deemed *The Devoted* as Charlotte's most ambitious attempt to link political reform to opera trope.

Her first two-volume novel of 1812, *Self-Indulgence*, was expanded into three volumes for Henry Colburn and Richard Bentley in 1830 with the fashionable *ton* more explicit, as *The Separation: A Novel* and also published, still anonymously, in New York. By then, chapter headings had been replaced with numbers and each chapter had an appropriate epigraph ranging from Burns to Shakespeare, Lallans Scots to French and Italian, and John Milton to Germaine de Staël; also included were some unattributed verses, presumably penned by the author herself. The title too had been turned into a moral: 'The foregoing is the real history of a Separation (the result of bigamy) which for a long time occupied the fashionable world.' The print run of the revamped 1812 novel now called *Separation* in 1830 was 'supposed to be 1,250'.[10] Colburn and Bentley, however, had perhaps overreached themselves in pufferies. A review in *The Court Journal* was the first to call attention to the book's literary history. 'It strikes us that we can trace a resemblance to a novel called *Self Indulgence*, published fifteen years ago, and attributed at the time to the same noble authoress.'[11] Perhaps this was not such a damning indictment as the plagiarism suggested by the reviewer of *Alla Giornata* years before. But *The Athenaeum* in turn pointed out: 'The real fraud practised, was upon the public … by not rewriting and improving an old novel.'[12] The same periodical then proceeded to quote *The Literary Gazette* (owned by Colburn) which had rushed to the defence of Colburn and Bentley, not by denying the facts, but by asserting that 'the firm was not aware of the deception', thereby putting the blame, squarely if somewhat ungallantly, on the author,[13] and not for the only time, as it subsequently transpired. It does, however, appear that right was on their side. Working on a Saturday, they wrote to Charlotte asking for an explanation and 'immediate statement calculated to remove from the public mind the disadvantageous impression now existing', inimical to the character of their publishing house,[14] but the outcome is not known.

Perhaps unjustifiably, Charlotte never considered herself 'political' and more probably viewed her novels as part of a continuing moral crusade against the fashionable world of 'ton', while profiting financially from writing about it. Here was her defence in *The Exclusives*:

> There is an indulgence in spleen, a silly, gossiping espionage, which delights in prying into the faults of others, without any motive but that of gratification of its own mean nature—but there is an investigation into the habits and manners of the actors in the scene of fashionable

> folly, which, by dispelling the illusion may preserve others from being heedlessly drawn unto the vortex of so dangerous a career. A sermon would not, could not, descend from its sacred dignity to affect this.[15]

As a title, *The Exclusives* of 1830 was the epitome of 'ton' (fashionable style or society). While a puff in 1828 had claimed that it was 'nearly ready for publication', it was 4 August 1829 before an advertisement for *The Exclusives* appeared in *The Star*, followed by reviews from late November onwards.

Subtitled in Bentley's list of publications from 28 November 1830 as 'A Satirical Novel of Fashionable Life',[16] the three volumes revolved around the characters drawn from the powerful, including and excluding patronesses of Almacks. Qualifications for inclusion in this select Wednesday evening gathering (despite only tea and bread being served) were stated explicitly. The first requisite was to 'cut all friends and relatives not deemed worthy of being of a certain coterie'; the second, to dress after a particular fashion, and thirdly to speak in a peculiar tone of voice and in a particular species of language. Two separate love intrigues were developed, despite separations by 'ton', with the characters rarely saying what they were thinking. Operatic references and singers and current bestsellers such as Thomas Moore's *Lalla Rookh*, were among the devices employed to illustrate the fashionable world, while the short epilogue tidied up loose ends and provided a happy ending for the 'goodies' as opposed to comeuppance of the 'baddies'. The author recorded:

> The unthinking and the hardened may ascribe all this to chance; but the wise and good know that *chance* is only another word for Providence; and that in every turn of our lives ... there is a mightier power to be acknowledged than any secondary cause can alone produce.[17]

Shortly after publication a pamphlet was issued entitled 'A Key to the Royal Novel "The Exclusives"', and in the British Library copy the majority of the initials in the key become names filled in by hand.[18] Despite *The Edinburgh Literary Journal* declaiming, 'We are tired of the whole class of works to which it belongs. We wish the writers in this department would try to strike out something new', three editions appeared over three months in London in 1830, followed by others in Albany, New York and Philadelphia.[19] Charlotte might have been forgiven some *schadenfreude*, the newspapers having reported that the patronesses had refused her admission when she had turned up ticketless that Wednesday evening in 1817.

About June 1830 a six-line letter had arrived at 3 Park Square West from Colburn and Bentley, rejecting Charlotte's proposal for a one-volume novel, *The Disinherited*.[20] Two years later, soon into her second widowhood, however, she signed an agreement with Richard Bentley alone on 9 October 1832.[21] She was to hand over 'a new Work to form three volumes post octavo, consisting of Two Tales, namely Seduction and The Disinherited'. £200 was the sum agreed for 750 copies 'payable by Promissory Note', with an advance payable at six months from the date of the agreement. The volume itself did not appear until 1834, as *The Disinherited and the Ensnared*, consisting of one novel, *The Disinherited,* which ran to page 57 of the second volume, while a longer novel, *The Ensnared*, filled the remainder of this volume and the third.[22] *The Court Journal* thought the first to be 'tenderly, touchingly, exquisitely told,'[23] while *The Times* deemed it 'entirely successful ... in its subject of difficulty and delicacy, requiring a skilful hand'.[24] Charlotte must have welcomed such reviews, for (even though the authorship was still anonymously 'by the authoress of "Flirtation"') she had dedicated these volumes to one of the most eminent naturalists of the day. To Aylmer Bourke Lambert she expressed her gratitude 'as an affectionate Cousin and Friend ... for having afforded me asylum at a time of distress and destitution'. At the very least the genial, if eccentric, Lambert and his charming wife appear to have offered hospitality to the Burys in their homes in London and Wiltshire and had also provided an interim home to the Burys on their return from the West Country in 1825. Lambert was widowed in 1828, and Charlotte and her daughter Blanche continued having him to dine, or dined with him during the 1830s. This particular three-decker, however, does not seem an especially apt choice for this (childless) dedicatee.

Although in the 'disinherited' genre of novels, the epigraph heading *The Disinherited*, 'Give me any plague but the plague of the heart; and wickedness but the wickedness of a woman', suggested the context for both novels. Set in London and Scotland, one of the serious themes it explored concerned the upbringing and education of both sons and daughters. The title of a chapter in the first volume was 'the Effects of Education' with the aphorism 'Train up a child in the way he should go'. The Edgeworths' interest in the education of daughters as well as sons followed in the next chapter. London's expansion was deplored for the first time: 'When Sydenham was in its glory, before the cruel grips of avarice appropriated every acre of ground to an increase of gain' was a very different refrain from her earlier long poem extolling Sydenham. The 'brick boxes, adorned with excrescences called verandahs', all in the name of 'improvement' nullified the healthiness of rural life in crammed suburbia.

In her preface to *The Ensnared* Charlotte advised the reader: 'The following tale was written to endeavour to show the ultimate misery and extended mischief which are the inevitable consequences of all attachments that are not founded on principle and sanctioned by virtue.' Citing 'that powerfully written book, Thomas de Quincey's *Confessions of an English Opium Eater*', she incorporated her family experience of the drug 'which intoxicates the victims of unhallowed love'.[25] It related the affair of 19-year-old Lord de Courcy and the married Lady Constance Percy, which developed in the romantic surroundings of the bay of Naples and its islands, began to falter in Sicily and fell apart on return to England, with the almost inevitable consequences for both, more especially the (female) ensnarer. Published more than a dozen years since she had been living in Italy, memory or perhaps a commonplace book contributed to the scene enrapturing the fated couple. They both watched

> the beauty of the peerless bay, with all its adjuncts of reflected interest, now illumined by a brilliant moonlight, the fiery mountain, that great magician, which presides over the scene, was in semi-action, and kept attention on the alert. Like a vase filled by an unseen hand, its burning fluid rose frequently to the very brim of the dark cup, and then sinking again emitted volumes of varied tinted vapours, which reared themselves for a moment in a straight column against the unclouded ether of the firmament, and then spread out in a vast canopy above the mouth of the crater: while at intervals some streams of ignited lava rushed over the sides of the mountain, and their red reflections danced in the long lines of fervid light across the cerulean bay.[26]

Perhaps the editor of *John Bull*, Theodore Hook, younger brother of her friend James Hook, was responsible for the fulsome review of The *Devoted* which Richard Bentley brought out at the end of February 1836. Deemed in *John Bull* 'this beautiful work', and esteemed 'the best novel of its class of the present season',[27] 1,000 copies had been printed for the first London edition, and it was also published in two volumes in Philadelphia that same year. The *Athenaeum* ignored the anonymity of the author, considering that it 'was the best of Lady Charlotte Bury's novels', and contained 'more interest, variety and vigour than any she has hitherto published'. Another critic, however, begged to differ, assessing it as at once 'more ambitious and more feeble than its predecessors, with more salient faults of character, thought and expression'.[28] This latter reviewer found disagreeable not only the 'devoted' heroine's brother, modelled on Lord Byron, down to the deformed foot, but also many of the other characters, from reverend swains, low villains and 'a Jew', to a brilliant and ambitious beauty, who sacrificed all for a marriage of pride to please her father. The language of this review is strong and disapproving to the end, although it then rather lamely concluded that 'it would be easy to select beauties from this novel ... there are in every page the traces of an elegant mind and refined taste, fancy and feeling, if not imagination and passion'. One particular cause for disapproval was that 'Lady Charlotte Bury is displeased with the state of politics at home and abroad'. She again expounded on London's growing too fast and too far: 'Life is too short, selfishness too ripe; it grasps at the present moment, it lives not in futurity', to cite one of her favourite nouns. She described the outskirts of London as 'that melancholy part of the town which is neither city nor country'.

> On one side of the path [along the Thames] were houses being built—those pretences to houses which spring up on all sides of London as fast as weeds. There was a for sale board on the other side of the path, Chelsea in the distance, with its old red-brick mansions and gardens, just visible.[29]

Reform was but 'the froth and scum of the would-be patriots'. Referring to one of her 'personages', she called him 'a monarch who rules over the regions of fashion, not as monarchs rule now-a-days, with no power at all, but virtually, despotically and effectively', before continuing: 'See the wickedness of those liberals and constitutionalists of Europe who would curtail the power of monarchs.' This while complaining also of the same revolutionary spirit in literature.

A 'Memorandum of Agreement' with Richard Bentley was signed on 6 November 1835 in which Charlotte promised 'a work of fiction ... the title of which is not yet determined, to consist of three stories, respectively named "The Divorced" [which was already in Richard Bentley's hands], "A Short Parenthesis in Life", and "The Male Coquet"'.[30] The three volumes of post octavo were to consist of 310 pages each, and for the entire copyright, Charlotte was to receive £300. In the memorandum she amended the advance from £200 to £250, with the remaining £50 to be paid 'on delivery of the entire manuscript'. There is some confusion as to whether the manuscripts were to be handed over ready for publication by the end of April 1836, or nine months from the date of the memorandum, i.e. 6 August. For her advance, moreover, she also had to resign to Bentley the copyright of *The Disinherited and Ensnared,* as well as that of *The Devoted*. But, in a later note at the foot of the memorandum, by 31 October the agreement had been cancelled, and it is not clear whether Charlotte had to return the £250 and still lose copyright.[31] Neither the 'Parenthesis' nor the 'Male Coquet' appeared: the publisher's note added 'abandoned'.

On 22 February 1837, however, on the title page of the three-volume *Divorced* Charlotte's name appeared for the first time on one of her works of fiction, but under the imprint of Henry Colburn: for £200 as of yore, or more?[32] *The Divorced* concerned the status and societal hypocrisies for women when separated or divorced, while there was little censure in fashionable life of the male divorcé or co-respondent. At the end of the third volume her polemic argued: 'let it not be imagined that this history is a fiction, or an exaggerated description of the consequences'. *The New Monthly Magazine* deemed it 'without question the best of all Lady Charlotte's fiction' (echoed a century and a half later by Janet Todd, who appraised it 'one of her best').[33] *The Monthly Review* was less kind. While praising her 'usual talent of cleverly drawing characters which ... are distinct', it denigrated both the subject and her approach to it.[34] Although several decades had passed, she had taken a risk in making the leading characters recall the Lady Holland scandal of the later 1790s, divorcing her first husband before remarriage to Lord Holland in 1797.

Meanwhile, in the autumn of 1836, Henry Colburn, 'having resumed general Publishing', had announced that Charlotte was now preparing a novel for publication to be titled *Love*.[35] Due perhaps to Shoberl's editorial reservations in 1837, however, the production did not appear until the start of 1838, to be reviewed sardonically by Thackeray in *The Times* and in *Fraser's Magazine* in his 'Yellowplush Correspondence'.[36] Thackeray had written his review of *Love* or *Eros and Anteros* after dining the evening before it appeared: 'If this be exclusive Love, it should be a lesson to all men never to marry a woman beyond the rank of a milkmaid, and *vice versa*.' He gave up reading after the second volume, considering the novel 'too dull to be dangerous, and too entirely vapid and insignificant to be efficiently immoral', but it did not deter him from composing further parody in *Fraser's Magazine*. This contrasted with the puff in the *New Monthly Magazine*. Writing of the 'rapidity, liveliness, and grace of her pen', her works were 'addressed to her own sex ... and continue these practical lessons which are required by so many, and could be conveyed by so few'. Despite his editorial strictures Shoberl's careless editing did not flatter Charlotte—the first volume ended at an appropriate point with reconciliation between the passionate heroine, Lady Herbert who 'had never had but one ambition ... living for Love', and her errant and drunken lord.[37] Volume Two finished with the latter's fatal duel, but halfway through, chapter titles disappeared, replaced by roman numerals. The third volume carried on several sub-plots in separate chapters and perhaps the curious epilogue, referring back to the start, was the response to Shoberl's requested 'extra'.[38] Spellings were also inconsistent—the *Zephyr* launched in the first volume had become *Zephir* in the third. Until this latter volume, *Love* was less overtly a fashionable novel of *ton*, but the same volume echoed *Conduct of Fate* (1822), with its autobiographical references to passion (all the poems chosen and written dilated on passion), religion (the epilogue was discursive on Quakers), drunken episodes, divorce, and health-related locations on the Rhône, at Nice and so on. There was even a drive to Sydenham Hill where the 'improvements' were noted.

The Glanville Family was produced by Henry Colburn in 1838 and published in Philadelphia in the same year under the title *Ellen Glanville*;[39] very few copies exist, but the novel is available online. The title page, 'By a Lady of Rank', sets the tone. Charlotte used the interesting device of setting the plot in the course of one social year; the novel's opposites were developed between the lives of the families on their country estates (Sussex, Hertfordshire and Lancashire) and in their London houses during the season (Grosvenor Square, Brook Street, Harley Street and Manchester Square). The Glanville family was aristocratic, the other families mercantile—the Howards/Rivers, Beaumonts and Harrisons. Much of the action revolves around the House of Commons, Mayfair clubs and country seat elections—Tory versus liberal and radical, reform, slavery, Irish and English churches, and rail-road Bills—this is one of the most politically charged of Charlotte's novels. In structure, the Glanville family echoed Charlotte's own Argyll family, with an ageing paterfamilias, Lord Mordaunt and his dysfunctional two sons and two daughters, although similarities perhaps ended there. The aloof heir, Lord Lindsay, niggardly guarded his potential inheritance. The overweening and sarcastic elder daughter, Lady Elizabeth, married the wearisome Charles Dalrymple, thanks to his £10,000 a year (his only employment was 'dropping in and visiting'), being the overawed son of the snobbish Lady Dalrymple. The younger and wild son, Captain Edward Glanville, was worshipped by his devoted sister, Lady Ellen Glanville, herself bound by duty to her father and to an early engagement with Frederick Percival, brought up in the Glanville family, and an up and coming politician. Another, besotted but undeclared suitor of Lady Ellen was Lord Raymond of Norland.

The narrative of this novel was mainly developed in free indirect speech and thoughts, mainly those of Ellen Glanville, with one foray into first-person narrative. The chapters were successfully separated into episodes of all the different sets of families; each headed by one, two or even three very appropriate epigraphs. The reader was encouraged to follow a particular scent, principally in the career of the younger son. The second volume was somewhat laboured, especially over the recurrent rejection by Lady Ellen of Lord Raymond, in dutiful favour of Frederick Percival. But the third volume took surprising turns of direction until in the last chapters after a quite unexpected event, the various 'lovers' were appropriately and happily reconciled in their aristocratic and mercantile couplings. The change of title between London and Philadelphia perhaps reflected the publisher's or author's attempts to focus the reader's sympathetic interest particularly in the eponymous heroine, even if she is not such a singular individual as Jane Austen's Emma.

Returning to flirtation and to the silver fork genre, the theme of one of her earlier novels of 1828 was revisited in *The History of a Flirt* and published by Colburn in 1840, with a second edition the following year.[40] It was only one of a few of her works of fiction written in the first person. The subtitle, set in upper case, informed the reader that the story is 'RELATED BY HERSELF'. Making extensive use of Charlotte's own sojourns, and starting with west country gentry in Clifton, Bath and the Malverns, the anti-heroine was exiled to Southampton and the Isle of Wight where her selfish behaviour continued. Eventually, after marriage to the wrong person, she found herself widowed in London, and underwent 'a complete revolution' in her character, which led to a happier ending than in some of Charlotte's moral tales.

Family Records, or the Two Sisters followed in 1841 from the Saunders and Otley stable, as well as coming out the same year in Philadelphia, with subsequent editions in London (1843), Paris (1848) and New York (1849).[41] Echoing Jane Austen, the two sisters were the serious Margaret and the frivolous and beautiful Susan. Margaret had 'light gold ringlets, a laughing blue eye and pearly teeth', while Susan was taller, with 'dark masses of brown hair ... plaited in wreaths'. Her features 'escaped the harshness of Roman contour' and her 'slight aquiline nose kept expression superior to the regularity of the Grecian', while her pale complexion was enlivened with 'ruby tints of her smiling and delicate mouth' and her 'large loving blue eyes' under their straightly pencilled eyebrows. Their affairs of the heart intermingled and unravelled in the Highlands of Scotland, London, Paris and Italy, incorporating the author's beloved former haunts in Lombardy and Tuscany, including Schneidorf's Hotel in Florence, the magical arches of the Ponte della Trinita over the Arno, with the marble-like stillness of a baby being buried at Leghorn. Equally evocative was a steamship journey from Blackwall, drinking brandy or beer to prevent seasickness, describing many of the fellow passengers, then reaching the sunny shores of the Firth of Forth past Bass Rock to reach 'Auld Reekie', and lodging in 'one of the hotels in the New Town'.[42] The 'loud roaring of evaporating steam' also portended the arrival in a highland bay of 'Low Country graziers on their way to purchase Highland cattle' for the Stirling and Doune markets, but also making their way to the inn, 'the only slated mansion in the village', its 'pompous appellation engraved in capital gilt letters above the door'.[43] The arrival of another 'smoking conveyance' paddler and the blast of its horn was 'an event of importance to all', bringing newspapers and the post, as well as visiting and returning passengers. Sitting in the bay, the sails were up one evening on *The Swallow* just about to raise anchor with emigrants for Canada; 'you get you sugar there for naething, just by gieing whin taps to the trees, it rins out like rain, and it's just as goode as we can get frae Glasgow'. Charlotte's keen ear and eye for the Highlands is likewise captured, describing one visitor whose 'double soled leather shoes gave notice of her approach', while the Provost of Pollockshaws kept roads well, unlike those in the Highlands. Of the latter incomer who had recently purchased the estate, the narrator opined: 'It is strange why vulgar people always prefer introducing their morning visitors to dining rooms rather than to any more commodious or habitable looking apartment.' His aesthetic taste was then excoriated—'walls painted red in imitation of brick', while he also had 'a fantastically liveried servant'. The two sisters eventually settle, older and wiser, in a somewhat hurried ending; indeed, to make up space in the third volume, two short stories were included. *The Promise*, set in Ireland and Highland Scotland revolved around another Lord de Courcy, and once more depicted drovers at an inn in Lapraog village, also with its ruined castle, an otter hunt with terriers, and fishermen with their Gaelic songs, all echoes of Islay; another sortie to Pisa and Leghorn was written in first person melancholy.[44] The fulcrum and denouement of *The Lovers*, moving between Matlock in Derbyshire and Ireland, also reflected Charlotte's background, using the device of a vivid and foretending dream.[45]

The Manoeuvring Mother from Colburn in 1842 also echoed a Jane Austen theme.[46] Sir John and Lady Wetheral had five daughters to marry off and between the border country of west England, Yorkshire and the Highlands, their very different life experiences, the result of their mother's social engineering, were recounted. As Lady Wetheral pithily expressed it, 'Marry your sons when you will but marry your daughters when you can.'[47] The oldest girl was groomed for a socially desirable marriage: 'Don't vulgarise her with nasty brown meats—dine upon chicken.' Only almond paste was to be used every evening on her hands. 'Manoeuvring' and 'manoeuverer' frequently appeared through the three volumes; the manoeuvring mother succeeds in marrying off all her daughters except the surprise fifth one, dispensing constant advice whether it be a leopard's claw to fasten a Tilbury cloak or telling another daughter not to nurse her child as it will ruin her figure: 'Give the child lettuce lozenges and make it sleep day and night.' The marriages have varying fortunes, the most splendid failing, another with four extremely disagreeable fighting and unruly children. Finally, her youngest daughter the mother thinks 'as Landscape Brown would have worded it' has 'great capability … with severe pruning and much preserving determination, would shine'. With her father's tutoring and encouragement, she resists all her mother's machinations and eventually marries for love and near equality of likemindedness. Her mother then 'dissolved into depression and camphor-julep', leaving the reader to ponder whether, if she recovers, she will 'be scheming for her grandchildren'. Again, the novel sort of fizzled out, although another edition was to appear from Routledge in London and New York in 1858.

The Wilfulness of Woman appeared in 1844 in three volumes from Colburn and was quickly produced in a highly economical but poorly edited version with the narrowest of margins and smallest of fonts, by New York's William Colyer.[48] It once again encompassed London and the Continent, but also embraced Cumbria. Only half of the six wilful women survived their entanglements with outrageous cads, involving coquetry and flirtation, marriage for money and status rather than love, or toyboy, elopement and a fatal duel, drug dependency, consumption and death. As the overdrawn doctor asserted, 'Laudanum is a very favourite and pernicious stimulant with the ladies', while reckoning gin to be 'less destructive of mind and body'.[50] The threads of 'methodistical' principles and 'northern wives and estates' wove through the volumes, along with familiar strictures from the authorial pen regarding the severity of Switzerland, the hissing steamboats on Lake Geneva and the haunting cries of the *rans des vaches*. In contrast to the view that Italy, with its climate, its music, and its luxuries, enervates the mind, due deference was paid to the ongoing Poor Law Bill passing through parliament.

Wilfulness of Woman may well have been the last of Charlotte's novels published during these galley years in the 1830s and early 1840s, although it was not the last to be published. In 1853 Henry Colburn sold his then thriving business at 13 Great Marlborough Street to Hurst and Blackett, who may have inherited the triple-decker *The Roses* which they published that very year, followed by *The Lady of Fashion* in 1856. It is impossible to know whether these were the work of Charlotte at this time or had been in Colburn's cupboard for almost twenty years, although they were treated as current novels by an enthusiastic press. New editions of *The History of a Flirt*, *Marriage in High Life, Family Records*, *The Manoeuvring Mother, The Divorced*, *Roses*, and *Love* also appeared in London, the Continent and the United States, the last when Charlotte was 85. Others had been published in Europe in English or translation. In 1839 Charlotte had mentioned *The Two Baronets*, then one of three of her works with Colburn. But it was not until after her death that this last tale came out in 1864, in Routledge's Railway Library Series (see plate 26), costing 2/- for the single volume, a far cry from the guinea and a half of her earlier triple-deckers. It had been 'found in an unfinished state' among her papers and edited by the publishers, who had republished her *Roses* a few years before.

Less than a score of her novellas and short stories have so far been mentioned in detail. Some were essentially short novels. Others were included in her miscellanies or in the annuals edited by the Countess of Blessington, as well as some of her poetry. In what has always been a difficult genre, Theodore Hook was one who successfully compiled his short stories into *Sayings and Doings,* condensing the narrative action and dispensing humour. But the latter is not an attribute that came easily to many women writers of the silver fork genre and Charlotte was no exception. Her tales were perhaps the result of her lore collecting from Argyll, and often graphically held the attention when evoking various manifestations of the supernatural.

While Colburn may have had a hand in suggesting some of the saleable titles for his novels, Charlotte's were quite specifically introduced as abstract or descriptive nouns, and elaborated on within the works, often for didactic and moral purposes. Only *Alla Giornata* used part of a quotation. The eye-catching 'or' between title and subtitle to indicate the author's real aim was only used in *Family Records or the Two Sisters*. The opening had to attract and hold the reader's attention as well as setting the tone or theme of the work. *Wilfulness of Woman* started satisfyingly: "Well, Sydney Harrington, I must acknowledge this to be a very lover-like composition. It is very proper, very clever, and very complimentary, considering it is tainted with Methodism." Formulaic writing produced the main defects of some of her tales. Some simply peter out, or end abruptly with a quick one-page resumé of what would have transpired had she not already reached the required page 330 of Volume III. Ideally each volume would end at an appropriate point to whet the appetites of library borrowers and other readers. The literary device of coincidence could be used perfunctorily or more obviously as in *Flirtation*, when Lord Mowbray arrived via Bristol to rescue the heroine.

Occasionally epistolary devices were inserted to give the reader descriptions of, for instance, the Fitzhammond family in *Flirtation*. Letters and post (or lack of) propelled the action, 'letters running down to the very turndowns of the paper'. The same novel contained nanny Macalpine's letter, written as she spoke, in Scots—'she has certainly not studied Madame de Sévigny's art in vain, although she has preserved her own originality'. Classical and literary allusions and phrases proliferated in some novels (*History of a Flirt* and *Roses*), while the reviewer of *Alla Giornata* had considered her similes 'original and highly poetical'. Favourite words were iterated: in *Roses* 'Futurity murdered sleep'. Superstition was often near at hand; in *The History of a Flirt*, 'three was ever an unlucky number'. Mountebanks and banditti were colourfully brought to life.

Hand-copying of successive drafts has almost been forgotten in today's electronic cut-and-paste. But it was the careless editing of many of her works that served Charlotte least well, suggesting haste. Early reviewers excoriated her for poor grammar in English, perhaps through living abroad, and poor proofreading in French and Italian. In some novels, chapters had headings while others did not; in *Love* they stopped halfway through. Epigraphs were similarly treated rather cavalierly—one incongruous epigraph chosen for a chapter on winter in *Love/History of a Flirt* was from James Thomson's 'Spring'. How important was it that the two Scottish Loch Levens were conflated or confused in *Manoeuvring Mother*?

A reader's satisfaction with a novel often depends on its ending, which should fulfil what has gone before and may even occur long before the final pages, yet still leaving the reader wanting to know more ('the Darcy effect'). While every novel ends, not every novel always has a resolution, though it is better if some kind of explanation can be provided sometimes by a postscript or an epilogue. Twists and false trails can be intriguing, as in the unexpected denouement in *Ellen Glanville*, or somewhat unsatisfactorily as in *Conduct is Fate* or *Love*.

While at times sentimental her novels demonstrated some vivid pictures of high society and court life, drawn from genuine experience rather than imagination or servants' gossip, and some spirited castigation of fashionable vices, particularly self-indulgence, illicit passion, flirtation ('the demon of coquetry') and the ambitious match-making of manoeuvring mothers. Charlotte's powers of observation and deft characterisation were already strong as a 14-year-old recording in her journal one of her fellow passengers on the fraxcoot on the canal between Bruges and Ghent. The characters of her stories themselves were often well drawn physically, their inner thoughts usually narrated rather than in dialogue. Secondary characters were usually treated seriously and did not just disappear after entry. In *Flirtation*, the nanny, Miss Macalpine, was tellingly described as an old maid who took snuff and not only spoke with a Scotch accent, but also wrote her letters in Scots. In *History of a Flirt* a group of three females destined for Van Diemen's Land were sitting in a bow window overlooking Southampton water. Some words were penned in the same novel to characterise the head gypsy, Corrie Lovel. The supernatural was introduced in her earlier works, whether as a spectre—Rosalind and Lillee—or in the haunted King Charles room at Montgomery Hall shared by Lady Frances and Lady Emily. There were also presentiments and occurrences of second sight. Graveyards recalled Thomas Gray's *Elegy* in *Roses* and *History of a Flirt*. Lively Gothic situations and persons were vividly created in the banditti haunted Tuscan hills, culminating in a spectacular inferno. Pirates on moonlit seas off the Isle of Wight were foiled in a kidnap attempt. What much of this added up to confirms the view of one of her earliest reviewers, if not exactly a critic, identifying the anonymous author and avowing that there was enough imagination and material to fill a hundred works instead of one, while there should be fewer avoidable coincidences or plot-filling secondary characters.

Her love of fashion and shopping, and her knowledge of manners and habits were evidenced in many of the novels of ton and fashionable regency life. Heroines met in an evening to 'curl'. Imbued with her critical voice, the narrator in *Devoted* opined that 'few women dance well, and still fewer men', while 'very few understand the secret of dress'. Riding habits and hats were considered ugly. Wedding gowns were ordered from Paris. By contrast she had a character in *The History of a Flirt* tell the reader that she wore simple white and borrowed a pearl comb to confine her ringlets. Jewels featured prominently when social distinctions were to be made. Railing against the fate of women to fill up the hours of the days, sewing and knitting likewise often cropped up in both letters and novels. Although many of the society male characters occasionally had some occupation such as being owner of an estate or serving in the military, most were usually employed in the masculine round of fashionable man about town visiting gambling clubs, such as Wattier's and Whites, in which they lost disproportionate sums of money. Other such as sailors, or male picaro protagonists were portrayed in vivid detail—and in *Conduct is Fate* the disguise of the *femme fatale* as one of the banditti was cleverly and colourfully drawn. Women drove in their carriages from all over London to listen to a handsome cleric preaching in a society church in *Devoted*.

A proto-travel writer aware of the difficulties involved in evoking scenes for her readers, Charlotte used her pen more than brush or crayon to evoke landscapes. She bewailed: 'How often had I, in imagination, traced the most beautiful landscapes, which when I actually endeavoured to place them on paper eluded my own power, and yet I returned to the attempt with a delight and a persuasion of success.' The scale of Switzerland's scenery oppressed her, but her verbal descriptions of landscape, from her earliest poems to the folio volume and through most of the novels were highly evocative and successful. With local colour and appreciation of regionalism at home and abroad she captured the essence of Highland Scotland or Snowdonian Wales; the softer southern and western England; London's Mayfair squares, the Strand's shops, Deptford's congested shipping, the Dulwich Gallery or Richmond Hill, as well as the pinnacles of Milan's Duomo, the enchanting Genoese harbour front or the Mediterranean islands. Such descriptions alone make reading her works interesting and enjoyable, especially in recognition. For the Rest and be

Thankful pass through the Argyll 'Alps' leading down to Inveraray, her description in *Conduct is Fate* remains vividly realistic to this day. Haunts and chases of smugglers along the south coast in *Flirtation* speak volumes of not only visits with her friends the Hooks, but of her eye for detail and her love of place from the sublime to her own garden. Gardening was another of Charlotte's passions and pastimes, and she was acutely aware of the names, sights and scents of most flowers and plants, whether in the wild or grown, on the Continent or in Scotland, while reference was made to many of their medicinal uses. Awareness and appreciation of climate and weather enhanced not only such landscapes but accompanied her characters' adventures therein.

The reviewers of her published works were likely to have been men but they considered that Charlotte's writings were well suited to the audience at which they were targeted. The reviewer of *Alla Giornata* vouchsafed that 'for the patrons and patronesses of the circulating libraries, it must have proved a complete "Godsend" for it is composed precisely of those materials which fill their thirsty souls with never-ending wonder and delight'. Writing before the infamous *Diary* appeared, and perhaps not wholly impartial, the *New Monthly Magazine* of 1837 was impressed by *The Divorced*, deeming it the best of her fictions.

> The great charm of Lady Charlotte Bury's writings is their essentially feminine character ... few persons have been more brilliantly gifted ... the fairies gathered around the cradle of the younger daughter of the house of Argyle [*sic*], to lavish upon her every grace and charm. Years passed in the world must have brought with them knowledge, and knowledge is never acquired without suffering, but the many benefit when the result is such pages as now be open whether for interest in the story, truth in the characters, and power in the moral so developed.[51]

Reviewing *The Roses* in 1856, *The Athenaeum* rejoiced in the 'cheerfulness of spirit' in its author, 'more than ordinarily welcome during the present day despotic reign of dismal imagination'. Attributing to her 'a nice sense of humour, and a fair command over pathos', the reviewer noted that Charlotte 'combined a certain twinge of romance which veins novels so full of prudential wisdom very gracefully', adding that 'the interest of the Roses is sustained to the last'.[52]

Virtually all of Charlotte's novels essentially revolved around women, their roles, experiences and moral values. Some of the circle in which she had grown up were from the *bas bleu* mould. Most of her closest female relatives and friends were strong women (many of them Anglo-Irish); her mother, paternal aunt, Lady Frederick, cousin Anne Damer, sister-in-law

Lady John Campbell, Mary and Agnes Berry, Anne Hook, the Dowager Countess of Charleville, Lady Grey and Lady Kirkwall, let alone Mlle de la Chaux, and several of her own daughters. Her female literary coterie of acquaintances included Germaine de Staël, Maria Edgeworth, Harriet Pigott, Marguerite Blessington, Catherine Gore, and Caroline Norton, among others, and she participated in the upper echelons of society, whether in Britain or Italy. Her circle and correspondence also encompassed longstanding male friends and acquaintances such as Thomas Campbell, Theodore Hook, Sir Walter Scott, and she was later on in visiting terms with figures such as the Disraelis and Eastlakes. It was unlikely that in her long life such varied interests would not clash with the establishment of whatever day. Not only being a court diarist, but also expressing critical views of her own society in its pretensions and women's restrictions within it, it is perhaps to be wondered that she did regain her place in society and retain so many of such friends and acquaintances. Her aspirations for her daughters, however, seem quite contrarian when endeavouring to arrange 'good' early marriages for them.

It is perhaps also strange that so few references to her readers survive in Charlotte's correspondence, except in a letter to her sister-in-law, Lady John Campbell, in which she asked whether the latter recognised herself in one of the chief characters in *Conduct is Fate*. This had been read before or on publication by relatives and friends including Charlotte Clavering, Susan Ferrier and Bessie Mure. She involved her readers when introducing the first *Journal of the Heart*, expressing the 'aching desire to be appreciated and understood, even though it may be by some being whom we shall never see in this world'. One such was Frances Allen, wife of rector William Bosherton in South Pembrokeshire between 1831 and 1871 and an intimate of Lord and Lady Cawdor of Stackpole Court, who noted in her Diary that she had read in the evening, '"Marriage in High Life" by I believe, Lady Charlotte Bury'. Apart from such scant references her letters, however, revealed her greater concerns with the demands of Colburn, Shoberl and other publishers than with her readers. Yet in her fiction most of her heroines are reading books, for good or ill, beside streams, in their boudoirs or in the libraries of their homes where tomes are often scattered over almost every surface. Her novels were read—or acquired—by men too. Inscriptions of volumes in libraries on both sides of the Atlantic usually belong to men such as Colonel By, perhaps for his wife to read while he was building the Rideau Canal through Ottawa, or Maxwell of Pollock. Dr Charles Meryon read aloud Charlotte's edited *Memoirs of a Peeress* to Hester Stanhope. Charlotte's son, Walter, wrote his name in two sets of *Alla Giornata* and in *Flirtation*, which are still on the shelves of his descendants' library in Islay, perhaps taken as presents by Charlotte in 1828; they do not, however, look well-used. Even though it had a policy of not accepting fiction for its deposit library status, Cambridge University Library has one of the most inclusive collections of Charlotte's fictions—the volumes are mostly well-worn (sometimes to the point of split spines) and well-read (see plate 27). Were they borrowed by the dons for their wives? It seems unlikely that generations of male undergraduates were reading the quarter million words, so the prosaic answer probably lies in the later acquisition of ex-circulating library copies from sale rooms. Almost, but not quite complete, collections, if not all editions, are also to be found in the British Library and the Bodleian Library in Oxford, while other libraries in the United Kingdom and Europe occasionally have other editions, particularly in translation. Those in North America have partial collections; and a copy of *The Disinherited and the Ensnared* is even ensconced in the library of the University of Sao Paulo in Brazil. The rarest of her works now comprise her *Cookbook*, *Prayers* and *Glanville*. Some fetch four figures depending on rarity and condition. Meanwhile, digitisation and online printing have increasingly made many of her works available or affordable. But up until the early twenty-first century none has been cited, or perhaps even read, more often than the *Diary*, of which late-nineteenth-century copies are still available for modest sums.

Although it is clear that in his *Silver Fork School* of 1936 based on his doctoral thesis he had not even opened some of her books on which he was not shy to venture his opinion, Matthew Rosa virtually wrote off Lady Charlotte. While not rated particularly highly by either Sadleir or Block, although they both found some positive attributes, Alison Adburgham similarly repeated many of Rosa's sentiments almost verbatim in her *Silver Fork Society* of 1983. Janet Todd thought in 1989 there were 'some vivid pictures of high society and court life drawn from genuine experience rather than imagination or servants' gossip and some spirited castigation of fashionable vices'.[53] She percipiently added that the genre of the silver fork novel did not easily allow its characters to fit into the scenario of wanting them to have a future life beyond the pages, especially from the pen of a critical aristocratic insider. But it is as an observant and trenchant insider that she can now be included towards the upper part of the pantheon of the minor fictional genre of the silver fork novel.

20

The Diary

In 1789, 14-year-old Charlotte had conscientiously and even laboriously written up her travel journey to Naples; in 1803-4 she copied it up, which may have stimulated her to continue 'keeping' a journal or diary. Her resulting manuscript journal from 1805 to 1810 is now in the Huntington Library in California.[1] Excerpts in the published *Diary* mainly concerned the following years 1810 to 1815. Sporadic portions relating to the 18teens also surfaced in her second *Journal of the Heart*. From a few scattered references Charlotte may have continued writing up a journal, although perhaps the events surrounding her second marriage in 1818 might have been too painful to record. A few entries when in Rome in 1819 were also included in the published *Diary* and there is reference elsewhere to a travel journey in Italy in 1842.[2] But there is sadly no trace of the two decades in between, nor of the two decades still to come. Women were also notoriously prolific and prolix letter-writers and in this Charlotte was no exception. It has been suggested that the two talents of diary- and letter-writing were 'rarely if ever combined in an individual', and that there might even be 'some antagonism between the two'.[3] Perhaps there was also a balance to be found in the time taken to write a journal, especially while also composing or churning out several hundred thousand words annually in prose and poetry. Diaries do not usually have endings; they normally just fade away.

Often incomprehensible to non-diarists, there may be many reasons why people pen diaries or journals, from being *aides-mémoires*, taking the place of a confidant, to consoling grief, or as a mode of escape or withdrawal. Others deliberately set out to record for the future, either for their own justification or with loftier ambitions. Some diarists may simply like putting pen to paper (or now in other ways, with the egocentric explosion of social media). Charlotte's justifications of a diary or journal became ambivalent. In 1811 she claimed that if nobody was ever to read what one wrote in a journal, there was 'no satisfaction in writing'.[4] But at the same time she considered that if anybody were to see it, 'mischief' would follow. While at Court in October 1813, Charlotte explained why she often failed to write a consecutive diary, 'not from idleness, which is not my besetting sin, but from the danger of telling all I think—all I know—that I have shrunk back into silence, and thought it better, wiser, perhaps to forget entirely the passing events of the day, than to record them'.[5] Yet at breakfast on the sunny terrace overlooking Genoa's harbour in 1815, in the service of the Princess of Wales, Charlotte mused:

> I am often ashamed when I read over what I have written, to see how I allow my mind to wander, and my pen to note down so many of its vagaries. Yet I never have resolution to amend the style of my diary. And why should I not indulge myself by giving way to my feelings? One must confide in some one, or in something; and though it is very melancholy to be obliged to have recourse to the latter, still it is a comfort to have no secrets from one's Journal. It is this entire confidence, and this alone, which renders it a pleasure to keep one.[6]

Almost twenty years later, and still before the appearance of what was to become her infamous *Diary*, she once more reverted to her earlier views:

> I have thought very often, that I would keep a journal ... but it is never kept, even if written; and then comes danger to oneself, or others ... to put a stop to this resolution. If I wrote of people, their pastimes and pursuits, or idlenesses, or wickednesses, I might amuse some, but I felt sure to give offence to others ... as to writing for no eye to see, no thought to commune with, that is a stretch of abstract delight beyond my material capabilities.[7]

She then pointed to the direction which her writings would henceforth take.

> When I write it is in the ardent hope that some eye will read, some mind will like, some feeling will vibrate in unison with mine. I determine therefore to write a Journal of the Heart ... from my own room, that persons Eutopia (far better than Sir Thomas More's, by the way) ... to the 'own rooms' of others I address my Journal.

Charlotte's daughter Beaujolois observed and recorded her early travels, but whether her mother would have encouraged her subsequently to publish, however, is doubtful.

Some even attributed the *Diary*'s appearance to Charlotte's late husband, Edward Bury, who was alleged to have secreted his wife's journal and prepared it for publication. While this is possible, not only did he die half a dozen years before publication, but no evidence has so far turned up in letters or anywhere else to suggest or confirm this course of events. Nor did any other person ever claim authorship. The two volumes that first caused such a fuss were published anonymously at the start of 1838, their probable authorship widely disseminated and none too subtly hinted at by the publisher, Henry Colburn, in his *Literary Gazette*. Not only did two further reprints quickly follow in London, with editions in Paris and Philadelphia, but in 1839 two extra volumes were added, 'edited by John Galt', as it then appeared on the title page.[8] Lewis Melville went as far as to opine:

> It is believed that John Galt ... who did a good deal of literary hack-work, was responsible for seeing the first two volumes of the *Diary* through the press. That he edited the third and fourth volumes ... there is no question, for he wrote the preface and an appendix of personal reminiscences.[9]

With links to Colburn and other London publishers, Galt's prolific output of novels, poems and other writings had been published in Edinburgh, London and Greenock where he was born, and to which he had retired after varied careers in Europe and Canada. By his late fifties, and in poor health, he was responsible in the late 1830s for revising Harriet Pigott's *Records of Real Life*, eventually published by Saunders and Otley after his death in 1839. Charlotte had been advising Pigott on the project and the latter's diaries in the Bodleian Library reveal that Pigott had stayed near Galt at Lord John Campbell's Ardencaple Castle. This may have been the link with the projected *Diary* while Charlotte wrote the fulsome obituary to Galt which prefaced *Records of Real Life*.

Colburn may even have been cashing in on the success of Lady Anne Hamilton's alleged *Court of England* which he had published five years before. Galt's preface to the 1839 edition of Charlotte's *Diary* was defensive, and he suggested that even Colburn was perhaps becoming sensitive to the criticism of his role in its publication, while still disingenuously disclaiming much involvement or having seen many of its contents before publication. Editions of the 1839 volumes were also produced in Paris by Fourmestraux and in Philadelphia by Carey, Lea and Carey. Later versions of *The Diary* were published in London in 1896[10] and 1908[11], the latter rearranged, footnotes often abbreviated, omitting Galt's vignettes and annual descriptions, but illustrated with eighteen full-page portraits. *The Daily Telegraph* deemed this last

> beautifully printed and elaborately illustrated, in two comely volumes, which will, no doubt, set the town talking again, as they talked seventy years ago ... with much that is painful and unprofitable, this frank and vivacious diary contains even more that is tender and true. Its rehabilitation, after many years of oblivion, is a task upon which editor and publisher are likely to be heartily congratulated.[12]

The Daily News opined 'that there was 'nothing of the mere "scandalous chronicle" about this book, and that it helps one vividly to realise the almost absurd tragedy of one of the most unfortunate of English Queens'.[13]

Until free digital copies of most editions of the *Diary* became available online, the 1908 edition was the best known, obtainable and affordable. Reading it now, more than 175 years after the *Diary* first emerged, it is difficult to understand the degree of outrage. The original two volumes of 1838 had referred to most personages by initials or blanks such as Lord S-----n (Sefton), although the society readers of the day would have been able to fill in most of them. In a copy in the British Library, "suppressed" for a time, many suggested names were pencilled in. These helped the 1908 editor, Francis Steuart, in identifying most names. However, although he included parts or all of the original 1838 footnotes, it is only by a close scrutiny of the original two volumes' footnotes and commentaries, that it is perhaps possible to start to comprehend the outrage. Some of these were several hundred words long, and while most can probably be attributed to Charlotte, others may have been added editorially by Galt.

However he came to be involved, Galt's defensive preface to the additional volumes added in 1839 claimed that the author had in fact done the Princess of Wales a favour. 'We repeat, therefore, that the publication of these private memoranda of a person or persons living with the Princess of Wales on terms of the greatest intimacy, is the strongest testimony ever yet given in her favour', he wrote, adding: 'In fine, although not held up as a faultless character, she is represented to have been far more sinned against than sinning.'[14] He pointed out that the gossip noted in the *Diary* had been 'the subject of table-talk in every society and every newspaper for the last forty years', before asking:

> What breach of private confidence is there in narrating the 'on dits' of the day? Of what does Sir Walter Scott's Diary consist,—published by his son-in-law,—in which all his personal and private affairs are discussed—what Moore's Life of Byron—and, in short, all the Diaries that ever were compiled, collected, or written,—but similar shreds and patches of the times?

Returning to the work itself, he considered that another grave charge against it had been 'that of indecency and impiety', but argued that 'this is so utterly and even ridiculously false, that it is best refuted by a perusal of the work itself'. His final justification was that although the style of the *Diary* had been termed coarse and trashy, he considered that it bore 'internal evidence of never having been intended for publication; it is careless and colloquial, but pungent and forceful'. He avowed that there were passages which probably the writers would have expunged,

> had they anticipated that their note-books were ever to come before the public: there are private feelings expressed, of no interest to the world in general, which evidently were not intended for its perusal; and yet this Diary, so decidedly a collection of private memoranda, has been judged of as though it had been a production expressly designed for the press!

He even considered that 'the present work ought not to have appeared for the next fifty years'. Another view ventured:

> The public doubtless has been less influenced by the opinions set forth in the periodicals and other publications, from knowing or suspecting that much of the virulent abuse lavished on the Diary has been the vengeance taken by persons whose vanity has been mortified by some unwelcome personal reference to themselves in the work. A future generation will, however, give to the Diary an impartial award and it will undoubtedly remain a standard work for historians to refer to, as 'notes' to future memoirs of the time of which it treats.

By the time these percipient words appeared in print, Colburn had on 9 May 1839 composed a 'POSTSCRIPT by the Publisher' explaining:

> In consequence of the lamented decease of the distinguished person who has edited these volumes, the publisher thinks it right to state, that the original preface, and other documents connected with Mr. Galt's share in the publication, are in the publisher's possession, and may be seen by any one interested in the subject.

On hearing of Galt's death on 12 March 1839, Charlotte had been most concerned to retrieve 'letters and papers' belonging to her which Galt had had in his possession, and she had asked Harriet Pigott to retrieve them from Galt's widow.[15] But maybe some at least may have been with Henry Colburn. It is perhaps a wonder that they had survived at all, given Charlotte's peripatetic life over the previous three decades.

The Philadelphia edition of 1839 inserted an 'Advertisement' at the start which claimed:

> The authenticity of the following Diary and letters is too apparent to be questioned. The reader, however, cannot fail to notice certain discrepancies which occur in the work, and more particularly in the earlier portions of it, by which it would appear to have been the intention of the editor who first undertook to prepare it for the press, to disguise—by assuming the masculine style in the Journal and substituting the feigned for the real sex of the personage addressed in the Letters—the evident fact of the former having been written by a female, and of the latter being communications to one of the same sex. The reader, by being made aware of this circumstance, will be the less surprised at the other discrepancies which occur, with regard to dates; some of the Letters being brought in at periods quite at variance with the dates of the Journal.[16]

Occasional references to Lady Charlotte Campbell were inserted to the same obfuscatory end. The *Diary*, especially the third volume, thus sometimes appears to be a patchwork of dated (and misdated, deliberately or otherwise) and jumbled entries, interspersed with letters from the Princess of Wales and others such as Anne Damer, Keppel Craven and William Gell (using a variety of noms de plume in the earlier, more lighthearted correspondence), 'Monk' Lewis, Charles Sharpe and Jean-Charles Sismondi, received by the author and linked sometimes by sententious writing. It is also a curious amalgam of journal (as Charlotte termed it), diary (Colburn) and memoir. Sometimes it is written in daily or periodic sequence, either at the time, or subsequently. At other times it is more like a narrative memoir, such entries perhaps having been composed specifically for insertion in the published *Diary*. Using the ever-helpful Cheney's *Handbook of Dates*,[17] supplemented by secondary references and online searches, part, though by no means all, of the dating problems can now be unravelled or resolved, along with some of the remaining blanks and internal references that would have been more easily recognised in the late 1830s.

There are some pages devoted to the start of Charlotte's life at this secondary court, and the first two volumes mainly relate to the years between 1810 and the middle of 1814, some entries clearly sequential and divided into chronological sections. 'Interspersed' through these first volumes are gossipy letters from the Princess of Wales and the mutual friends and acquaintances of Charlotte's who had already been introduced to the mini court. But instead of finishing at a natural break in the middle of 1814, when Charlotte considered that she had given up her position with the princess, the end of the first volume was given over to fifteen miscellaneous letters from the Princess of Wales to Charlotte, of mixed or unspecified dates between 1814 and 1819. They are prefaced with an editorial note:

> The following compositions betray a want of education which, in the present day, would be discreditable even to a person of the middle class. But many of the sentiments are kind, and an impartial judge would be apt to say, in reading them, 'This person was not intended by nature to be a bad character'.[18]

While it is perhaps surprising that these letters were not also interspersed in appropriate places, each of the fifteen was accompanied by a commentary, normally too long for a footnote. Thus while in her letter of 27 June 1813, the princess wrote that she was awaiting a visit from Madame de Staël that morning, the commentary explained that the said lady had not only gone 'with the torrent' to the other camp, but had made the prince visit her first, and never did descend on the princess. Other letters discussed Princess Charlotte's rejection of her father's manoeuvrings to get her to marry the Prince of Orange and so remove her from London, as well as the constant aggravations concerning mother and daughter being permitted to meet. 'The princess was perpetually balked in all the minor occurrences of daily life' was the comment:

> The constant irritation in which the princess and the regent contrived to keep each other, was a perfect game of battledore and shuttlecock; and if the latter fell to the ground, there was always some bystander ready to pick it up again, and thus the game of torment was renewed, and lasted to their lives' end.

The second volume took up the entries from the middle of June 1814, and included the celebrations in Hyde Park when much of the world came to a London celebrating Napoleon's downfall. After these few pages, and within a month, however, the longed for wish of Charlotte to escape to the Continent with her daughters became reality and the *Diary* relates the Campbell family sailing across the channel and skirting the outskirts of Paris before reaching what Charlotte deemed the small world of Geneva. The princess, however, followed her there, and much to everyone's consternation inveigled Charlotte into arranging a ball for her at which the princess appeared déshabillé and was roundly ridiculed. After enjoying the company of the English and Swiss literati of Geneva and Germaine de Staël at Coppet across the lake, the Campbells sailed down the Rhône in a wet autumn to enjoy overwintering in Nice. The princess continued her wanderings, but as her English courtiers discovered reasons to leave her, she implored Charlotte to rejoin her in Genoa. A naval frigate carried the Campbell family to 'transcendent Genoa'. For the month of April 1815 they were caught up in the small English colony trying to second-guess Napoleon's next moves in 'The Hundred Days' after he had evaded Sir Neil Campbell. From her descriptions it is still easy to envisage Charlotte's sightseeing and socialising in the grand palaces; there was even a wistful suggestion of a flirtatious fling. She and her two elder daughters followed the princess to Milan for a fortnight, but she was adamant that she would not serve the princess any further, refusing all entreaties for her elder daughter to take her place, and they headed for Simplon and Lausanne. After Eliza's marriage in Zurich in September, the rest of the family journeyed reluctantly to Sydenham in the autumn of 1815, to face the sunless year of 1816.

Letters from the princess and others were scattered in this second volume, strangely including a possible trio to Charlotte's as yet unsuspected second husband. But there was also another collection towards the end, of which the original prefatory note declared that they were 'evidently intended for publication':

> They bear in that respect a distinct character from the foregoing Diary and Letters, which ... carry the conviction of having been decidedly written without any view of their coming before the public, but these Supplementary Letters will be found to throw a light upon the previous pages, and to contain much amusing and novel matter; while the opinions expressed in them may excite matter of consideration for the page of future history.

Written perhaps by a Scot who daily attended the trumped up 'trial' of Queen Caroline in the late summer of 1820, and events subsequent to it, the finishing of the second volume would appear to have justified the later title of the diary of a lady-in-waiting whose service with the princess, not queen yet, had finally ended in 1815, although they kept in sporadic epistolary touch.

Successful perhaps beyond Colburn's dreams, two further editions of the first two volumes followed in 1838 in London and others in Paris. Two additional volumes appeared from Colburn in 1839, the whole now being titled *The Diary Illustrative of the Time of George the Fourth, Comprising the Secret History of the Court, During the Reigns of George III and George IV; Interspersed with Original Letters from Queen Caroline, the Princess Charlotte, and from Other Distinguished persons*, edited by John Galt. The third volume found Lady Charlotte in Rome in 1819, early in her second marriage, though still written in the first person singular. It provided a brief but colourful portrait of the socialising among the expatriate English in Rome. It is hard to make sense of any order or even theme in the rest of the third volume—it is a true gallimaufry with journal text and letters geographically and chronologically incoherent, darting between Italy and London, the letters from a wide variety of people, undated and misdated, named or unidentified.

After a few pages in the same vein, the fourth volume comprised various collections of heavily edited letters from the Princess of Wales, Princess Charlotte (with comments), Gell, Sismondi and others as well as further 'supplementary letters' which provided commentary on the proceedings in the House of Lords against the queen 'from one who was present', written to Lady Charlotte, still in Italy. Thereafter Galt added twenty 'Sketches of eminent men of the Regency'; most were somewhat disparaging in vein. Sir Robert Peel had 'no more genious [*sic*] than a slice of turnip has of the flavour of the pine-apple ... yet is one of the most respected men in all England at this time' and Canning was deemed 'not first class'. Galt did not think that Richard Sheridan 'deserved the great celebrity to which he attained in his day', although his very beautiful and greatly renowned cantatrice wife was deemed 'a feather in his cap'. While he thought that 'perhaps I should not attempt to say what I think of Wellington', Hume was dismissed as a 'busybody who thinks notoriety is fame'. He considered Byron 'not as great a poet as his infamy', denigrated Coleridge but praised Wordsworth. Francis Horner was put down as a 'demi-intellect'. These sardonic vignettes were followed by fifteen annual reviews of the main events and tenor of each year between 1816 and 1830 (it might have been more logical to include all the Regency years from 1811). It is little wonder—if the reader is still following this project—that Lea, Carey and Lea inserted their 'Advertisement' when publishing the four volumes in Philadelphia.

A strange episode then transpired. Presumably while John Galt was collating material at Colburn's behest for the additional two volumes, Charlotte—or someone—had been recycling, using bits perhaps left over, and scribbling tendentiously related stories, anecdotes and poems for another printer, W. Emans of 31 Cloth Fair in London. The title of this illustrated potboiler was *The Murdered Queen! Or Caroline of Brunswick.*[19] This episodic ramble has sometimes been attributed to Lady Anne Hamilton, one of the Princess of Wales's longest (and confessedly one of her most irritating) companions. However, sufficient of the entries echoed Charlotte's words in her own correspondence, let alone in her published *Diary* (which could possibly have been mined), while many of the insertions attributed to Matt Lewis, Lord Byron, Thomas Campbell and others do suggest the hand of Charlotte. But one has to wonder why all of this also saw the light of day in 1838, or whether it too was intended to shore up her finances.

About one third of the 230 letters interspersed or collected in the four volumes were written by the Princess of Wales, another third from named people, and the rest from others not always easy to identify even through internal references. Lewis admitted to hurt pride in having been deemed 'très inférieur' by Madame de Staël, as well as enclosing a scurrilous poem 'The Triumph of the Whales', from *The Examiner*.[20] About these early friends such as Lewis, Lady Charlotte's notes were ambivalent—perhaps it was as well he was no longer around to expostulate on reading some of her unrequited's views on him, having died on a sea voyage in 1818 returning from his inherited plantation estate in the West Indies. He had been welcomed for many years at Inveraray by the duke and his family, and Charlotte nevertheless claimed him as one of her most ardent supporters. Gell and Craven, antiquarian and dilettante, fared better, and in any case, Gell had died in 1836. The unidentified letters were sometimes concerned with literary matters, but often gossiped over marriages arranged or postponed, affairs and elopements, and especially in the third volume, it is hard to understand their relevance or inclusion. Indeed it is possible to envisage unsorted bundles being handed over to John Galt who was perhaps too preoccupied with his sardonic vignettes and annual reports to attempt any evaluation or arrangement.

Charles Kirkpatrick Sharpe perhaps had a legitimate grievance. He had been particularly horrified to find letters printed which he had written 'in confidence to a ducal daughter'.[21] His letters from Christ Church in Oxford comprised the most gossipy of any included in the *Diary*. The Princess of Wales had opined: 'Mr Sharpe would do very well if he was not a great gossip, and there are days and times that it would be very inconvenient to have him in society.'[22] His youthful letters included observations and titbits such as Shelley being expelled from Christ Church in Oxford 'on account of his atheistical pamphlet. Was ever such bad taste and barbarity known?' In the *Diary* owned by T. Gibson Craig, there are extensive marginalia signed by Sharpe on most pages of the first volume and on a score of pages in the second.[23] As Sharpe worded it when the *Diary* appeared in early 1838, 'a certain lady ... has put an everlasting disgrace upon me. For some days I ate little and slept less.'[24] The later compiler of his letters commented: 'He behaved like a hero.'[25] Perhaps he was not even mollified when reading another of Charlotte's footnotes that he was 'one of the most amusing persons in the world. And one whose wit was as harmless as it was light and bright.'

The majority of the more expansive footnotes and commentaries in both text and letters, however, showed a kindly disposition to friends and acquaintances. One footnote referring to Madame de Staël was over 800 words long; while mentioning a few negatives, much of it was concerned with justifying the use of the adjective 'Great' when applied to her.

> Very few persons of all those who write or spoke of Madame De Staël were at all competent to form any just judgment of her character—I would rather say, of her whole moral being—not from deficiency in point of talent on their parts, but because they applied squares and rules to that which was immeasurable, and beyond all received standards of estimation ... In all that pertained to mind she was of no sex; those qualities which are supposed by divine right to belong to men alone—vigour of understanding—abstract reasoning—vastness of conception—the power of overreaping or discarding all minor considerations to arrive at a conclusion—were peculiarly her attributes, and never did the epithet of *Great* pertain more justly to any human being than to herself ... It was impossible for any one to like Madame De Staël by halves: she was destined to be either loved or hated. No wonder Bonaparte did the latter: perhaps she was the only human being he feared, and could not conquer.[26]

Of a different caste, she described Madame de Staël's cousin, Madame Necker, whom she had visited at Coligny on the Savoy shore of Lake Geneva, as 'hiding her talents in contrast to her cousin ... but with more instruction, more depth of thought'.[27] Echoing her encomium on De Staël, and revealing some of her own frustrations, Charlotte avowed:

> Whoever wrote of the society of Geneva in deteriorating terms ... was little deserving of partaking of all the friendly hospitalities, still less the intellectual and scientific intercourse, of men whose talents have resounded throughout the civilised world, and who do not disdain to associate themselves, even in their graver studies, their wives, their daughters, and the fair objects of their admiration. If their gallantry is of a somewhat less polished kind, their esteem for an association with women is of the highest standard.[28]

Other strong women whose stimulating company she enjoyed in London and on the continent included Lady Westmorland, mother of Lord Burghersh. But Charlotte lamented her 'restlessness of spirit ... which allows her to find no peace or pleasure for any length of time, in the same place'. Was it really necessary to include a footnote explaining that her friend had been placed in a madhouse by *a very near relation*, and had only been released thanks to the intervention of an unnamed countess, otherwise 'she would have been probably detained there all her life'? Charlotte was fortunate in the company of the two courtier sisters with whom she had spent many hours and days as well as confidences and complaints, Lady Glenbervie and Lady Charlotte Lindsay.

> Concerning these two ladies there was never a dissient [*sic*] voice. Gay, brilliant, witty, well-informed, kindly in all their thoughts, words, and actions, they were the sunshine of every circle in which they appeared ... They form a rare instance in life, of having been universally liked ... Alas! That only one should now remain.[29]

(Lady Glenbervie had been in poor health in Genoa in 1815 and died in February 1817.) Referring to herself in one footnote as 'editor of this journal, looking over papers of years before', Charlotte could not resist quoting Harriet, Lady Granville's opinion in August 1816 of Charlotte's second daughter Eleanora, 'who is just come out, is decidedly, as far as one day's experience of a person can go, the Girl I should prefer Hart's marrying [her brother, the Duke of Devonshire]. She is beautiful and *dans le meilleur genre*, with the sweetest manners I ever met with. She is quite enchanting.'[30]

It was inevitable, however, that exception was frequently taken by erstwhile acquaintances to the more scandalous, occasionally scurrilous views, even relating to those more recently deceased, such as Sir Humphry Davy. While he had died in 1829, his formidable widow, Lady Jane, must have been upset by Charlotte's ambiguous views on her late husband, oddly written in the present tense. She had taken 'his superior abilities upon trust ... but his superior ugliness I know by ocular demonstration ... there is a peculiar degree of under breeding in Sir Humphry, which is indicative of inferiority of intellect.'[31] The original entry was written in the present tense in diary form when Sir Humphry and Charlotte were often in the same company in Geneva in the mid-18teens. However, the editorial note, written with hindsight, started with the admission that 'Sir Humphry is harshly judged in this paragraph'. By then he was claimed to be 'a man of exceeding refinement of mind and singular discrimination of character'. Another footnote was scathing about Byron's 'deadly venom in his most sublime strains' while even 'in his most ribald poems, the sneer of the comic mask but ill conceals the vulture that is praying on his heart'. Lady Byron was considered 'wholly unfitted to be the poet's wife ... It seems that two more ill-assorted persons never were bound together in one chain. And yet they loved—incomprehensively *loved* each other!'[32] Her view of Shelley was that 'his genius was an evil one, and his powers were directed to a bad end. Or ... to no end at all ... The best parts of his phrenzied compositions have all the deleterious qualities of alcohol.'[33] A footnote omitted by Steuart in 1908 was blunt about her old friend, Thomas Campbell.

> Why sleeps the muse of Campbell? Why does party politics usurp her rightful throne in his breast, and drag *him* down to earth? ... When I hear of him, immersed in dinners, and meetings, and popular assemblies, it is as of one not done honour to, but debased. To be made the penny trumpet of faction, instead of commanding the voice of Fame to sound her paeans with his name, is selling his birthright for a mess of potage.[34]

So much for his interests in education, tirelessly helping to set up the secular university of London, his support of Poland and her culture when threatened by Russia, along with other causes.

Devoted attendees at the Princess of Wales' dinners had included 'Mr Ward', afterwards Lord Dudley. Charlotte's long footnote traced his passage from being one of the merriest and most amusing of the princess' guests to his mental derangement, consequent upon a succession of the women attracted to him suffering 'a melancholy fate'.[35] He had died in 1833 but perhaps the vein of such a footnote was what was perceived so scandalously. On another occasion Charlotte had sat next to Richard Payne Knight during one dinner at Kensington Palace, but she dismissed his work on 'Taste' as 'more pompous and dictatorial, more factitious and learned, than gifted with the spirit of his subject'. He himself 'was a man whom too much learning had made not mad, but pompous, not wise, but artificial; a man of systems and nomenclatures, dates and dulness [*sic*]; whose boast was scepticism, and whose enjoyments were those of a bon viveur'. Yet she admitted that 'in his own family he was loved, for he was generous and kind-hearted', before exclaiming 'Oh! The mixed texture of human nature'.[36] Sir James Mackintosh had been another guest that evening; in her editorial note, Charlotte had nothing but praise for this polymathic fellow Scot, recently deceased in 1835:

> Some men perform more than is expected of them throughout life, whilst others never answer to the idea that is formed of their capacity, Sir

> James Mackintosh had considerable fascination and extreme suavity of manner. He impressed his hearers with the belief that a great deal more remained to be said than he actually expressed; and thus his credit was unlimited.[37]

It is also possible to see how some of those still living could have been offended. Although Charlotte and her daughters socialised in Italy and England with Sydney, Lady Morgan, what had so troubled Lady Morgan's husband was perhaps the Princess of Wales' views on the then Sydney Owenson, with whom she had also been a guest at the Priory. 'I defy any person of taste to admire [her]' she started, before continuing: 'she is very plain, and has an unpleasing expression in her countenance ... she sings ... like a crow ... I trust that we shall not meet again. And I can easily imagine, that all men, except the Marquess [of Abercorn, her host], hold her in abhorrence'.[38] More seriously, writing severely to Henry Colburn, Lady Morgan said that although her husband had asked the publisher to suppress a 'libellous' passage referring to herself in a future edition, she renounced this, as she had 'never in my life interfered with the printed expression of an opinion relative to myself, personal or literary'.[39] Nor was she assuaged by Colburn's confessional if slippery reply that 'unfortunately the work was never properly examined ... and was hastily published'. She went on to scold him about the then 'degradation of British literature' and 'the promptitude of publishers to produce such works as the one you have just brought out'. Colburn subsequently became 'her slave and blackamoor', and presented her with a 'beautiful mirror' for her drawing room. All this, however, ignored the other effusive references to this 'very extraordinary woman, with genius of a high stamp'.[40]

In her book on Lord William Russell and his wife, Georgina Blakiston rather unfairly took Charlotte to task and blamed her 'scandalous memoirs having a part in spreading knowledge' of the Russells' 'mauvais ménage'.[41] Both were involved in affairs that were public knowledge. Despite being a descendant of Lady William, Blakiston is quite hard on her forebear throughout. But Charlotte's 800-word footnote concerning Lady William was an attempt to explain, if not justify, some of the background to 'the accomplished and beautiful woman' who had been Bessie Rawdon, noting: 'A woman who has any pretence to intellectual power, has much to endure.' Another long footnote in the *Diary* concerned the fascinating Duchess of Devonshire, 'whose character was in many respects extraordinary'. It is difficult to know whether the repetition of the 'well-known story' of the exchange of Georgiana's baby girl with Elizabeth's son and all its future implications as heir was deemed more scandalous than Charlotte's view of the latter duchess's love for and influence over Cardinal Gonzalvi.

'Whenever she saw him approach her whole frame was in trepidation, and no girl of fifteen ever betrayed a more romantic passion for her lover than did this distinguished but antiquated lady for the Cardinal.'[42] Charlotte did, however, qualify her view: 'It is to be doubted whether he returned the tender passion; but his idea of the duchess's consequence at the English court induced him to "se laisser aimer".' Thirty years after, the effects this had on the Pope's reversal of his attention to the Princess of Wales, by then queen, and despite this note in the *Diary*, Charlotte and the second Duchess of Devonshire were making friendly excursions in and around Rome.[43]

In his study of English diaries, Lord Arthur Ponsonby averred that Charlotte 'seemingly kept her head in the presence of royalty and ... exercised her critical faculties in this connection far more skilfully than when she was surrounded by her society friends'. He considered that whenever she was writing about the princess, her style seemed 'entirely to alter'. She remained 'a loyal and helpful friend to the princess of Wales', producing 'trenchant phrases, acute observations and sound judgments and she certainly provides the most intimate information with regard to the extraordinary treatment of George IV's wife that has been furnished from any source'. He even went as far as to claim the *Diary* as 'Lady Charlotte Bury's striking portrait of Queen Caroline'.[44] The author herself was always on guard with royalty: 'There is no believing what these royal people say; and I verily believe they do not know what they believe themselves.' Although critical, and despite constraints of various kinds, Charlotte did try to support her royal mistress, and this comes through in the *Diary*, even as Caroline's behaviour understandably deteriorated, given the treatment she received from her estranged husband and his mother.

Not only were her longstanding financial difficulties of several decades known to many of her family and friends, but her lack of wherewithal had often been repeated in her correspondence. Charlotte may have sat in her writing room shuddering at the denunciation being poured upon her and the *Diary*, perhaps even surprised by its virulence. But it is possible that, by then in her sixties and a hardened writer of *ton*, having scandalised society twenty years before by marrying her son's tutor, she was probably at least inured to some of the notoriety and may not have been discombobulated, thinking that the fuss would pass. She may have had the last word when claiming to Harriet Pigott in June 1839, that she thought that her name was back 'in repute in the Publishers estimation, as a <u>marquetable article</u>'. Although Charlotte had characterised herself in 1814 as not 'an amusing person at any time', the rather naïve view of Susan Ferrier's biographer was that Charlotte would hardly have realised the effect the book would have, since her nature was 'blithe, careless and fun-loving. She was not over sensitive herself and had always lived among people like Jane

Austen's Mr Bennet.'[45] Colburn's £1,000 must have seemed not only desirable, but essential, even enough to betray the professions of morality which she expressed regarding the keeping of a diary or journal as well as her reputation, status and friends. In late middle age Charlotte's thoughts were focussed on money-making projects. With memoirs much in demand and Henry Colburn always on the ball and on the make, it may even have been the lady herself who broached the subject of her journal 'kept' of life at court.

It is hard to imagine that Charlotte saw beyond Colburn's £1,000 (not even guineas). The *Diary* illustrated Charlotte's increasing reluctance and unhappiness in serving this court. She did not subsequently disguise the increasing levity and coarseness of Caroline's conduct, or that of the prince, future regent and king. While early widowhood and financial worries contributed to and necessitated this period of her life, while socially satisfactory at the start, the personal cost to herself and family was not all edited out of the final version of the *Diary*—and there was a final bonus in the delights of 'transcendant Genoa', even though, as she had predicted, she never did see it again. While she had excoriated society in her fiction, the *Diary* would prove that she was not just a writer of fashionable novels but would also find her place in history at the hub of real events. It illustrated that when she exposed the morals of royalty and aristocracy she knew what she was writing about. She had endured over four years in an establishment of increasingly dubious reputation which emphasised her cynical views of such society. Despite its deficiencies the work has been cited and used by scores of writers of the Regency period right up to the present. Voices such as that of Fitzgerald in 1882 not only castigated Croker's hypocritical mauling of Charlotte's 'vivacious Diary … full of piquant incidents, traits of manners and "characteristical letters"', but added that it was 'extraordinary to what an extent the innumerable books of memoirs since published support all that is set out in it though it was so impugned at the time'.[46]

Unless written specifically with a view to publication, diaries usually remain private until the writer's death, or if there are no instructions for their subsequent destruction. The content of the Lady Charlotte Huntington Journal of 1805 to 1810 is much more personal and stylistically different from the entries in the published *Diary*. Especially in its later volumes, the latter now appears a misnomer with its near lack of organisation, its letters, anecdotes, observations and lengthy notes and commentaries, not to mention Galt's sardonic fillers. *The Chambers Dictionary* defines 'potboiler' as 'a work of art or literature produced merely with regard to saleability, to secure the necessities of life', while 'gallimaufry' is 'any inconsistent or absurd medley'. Whether either should be attributed to Henry Colburn, John Galt or Charlotte or all of them, the *Diary* was a very odd compilation, and in many ways an unsatisfactory one for which Charlotte was mainly to be remembered in posterity.

A letter was published in the *Morning Post* of 18 April 1838, regarding the claim in the *Edinburgh Review* as to the authorship of the *Diary*. Legally verbose, Thomas Nettleship claimed that he, as the former lady-in-waiting's solicitor, had been directed by her again, 'although the facts upon which that conclusion has been come to have already been contradicted', to 'deny the correctness of any of Lady Charlotte Bury's private papers or letters', which would seem to be at odds with Colburn's subsequent claim. Almost 100 years later the Nettleship letter was quoted by one William T. Whitely in a letter to the *Times* in February 1930; he ended 'nothing could be more authoritative than this contradiction which curiously appears to have escaped the notice of the commentators on the Diary and its supposed writer'. The cleverly crafted wording however seems to have eluded his understanding.

21

Ducal Rescue

One Saturday in late April 1835, Charlotte entertained 'a select party at dinner', followed by a reception for 'a large party of fashionables', as it was reported in *The Court Journal.*[1] The same gossip columnist noted: 'As one of the "highest stars of our contemporary female literature, Lady Charlotte Bury, like Mrs Norton, Mrs Hemans and others, had a quadrille named after her".'[2] An even more notable society event, however, was in the offing. Delayed by the deaths of the Duchess of Argyll and of Mr Carter of Edgcott,[3] eventually, on 1 July 1835 Adelaide married Lord Arthur Lennox, the sixth son of the 4th Duke of Richmond, in St James's Church, Piccadilly, like her sister Emma (see plate 28). The *Journal* correspondent left its readers in no doubt that this was one of the society weddings of the season, with Charlotte well restored in what she may have considered her due place in society. 'There have been few marriages distinguished by the assembly of so large a number of noble relatives ... the élite of London ... dukes and duchesses, lords and ladies, baronets and ladies, and many princes and other foreigners of distinction.'[4] What was most particularly flattering to the parties concerned was the presence of his Grace the Duke of Wellington who signed his name as one of the witnesses.[5] In trying to find a suitable profession for his youngest son, the Duke of Richmond had requested for assistance with finding a career for the young Lord Arthur. The bride was given away by her brother, Walter, who gave the 'splendid breakfast' in the Tullamore home at St George's Place, though sadly 'the health of Lady Tullamore did not permit her to take an active part in performing the honours of that day'. The newly-weds then left for Goodwood. Their next few years were spent on the move with his regiment in London, Scotland, Ireland, Canada and Malta.

From Montreal, for example, Adelaide wrote to Eliza in 1838 with news of Eliza's first born, Penrose or 'Pen', then under canvas on warm and sticky Montreal Island in the St Lawrence River. Adelaide's marble bust by Lucas was exhibited at the Royal Academy that summer.[6] Three daughters and an heir were born to the Lennoxes between 1839 and 1844; the family were to be seen growing up in the censuses from 1841 onwards, on which dates they seemed always to have been in London.

As previously mentioned, many of Charlotte's Campbell daughters appeared to have inherited more of the Argyll and Gunning looks than Shawfield ones. But it is almost uncanny to compare Eastlake's 1839 portrait of 19-year-old Blanche Bury with Briggs/Blaikley's portrait of Charlotte in 1834. While the latter is of a widow's demeanour, perhaps Moore's judgment of her the year before 'as so aged and altered' had been somewhat harsh.[7] An engraving which had been executed by W. Read in 1837 for Henry Colburn as a frontispiece for the infamous *Diary* shows a somewhat severe Charlotte in profile looking to our right, with her still long hair plaited and wound round the top of her head. A later one, of 1841, attributed to Buckner, but more likely to be Blaikley, is more sympathetic, more rounded, wrapped, perhaps unnecessarily in a gauzy mantilla/shawl, but still with beautiful eyes at 66 years old. Her life experiences and oft-repeated tendency to melancholy, when younger, are belied in such a portrait which exudes serenity. Charlotte still deemed marriage prospects for Blanche to be poor. As she had explained to Hariett Pigott in October 1838:

> I grieve to say that My Excellent and Dear Blanche has no prospect whatever of any marriage with any body Duke or not Duke. She is perfectly beautiful—perfectly good—excessively clever—but for all these reasons has the worst possible chance of marriage. I could tell you why but it would take too much time. Only pray unsay the report of her about to be married just is perfectly without foundation.[8]

To Pigott, she had confided: 'In my child Blanche I have a Gem of purest ray serene to live for.'[9] But she gave what was perhaps a more honest assessment when writing to her eldest daughter, Eliza: 'I wish I could marry Blanche but she is trop difficile and has no money.'[10]

In the spring of 1838 Charlotte mentioned the members of her family who visited her in London, although 'sadly' she never saw Julia. In November 1836 the minister of Kilarrow church of Scotland in Bowmore, Islay, had recorded in his parish register that on the sixth, Julia had become the wife of Peter Langford-Brooke of Mere Hall in the parish of Rostherne in Cheshire.[11] Perhaps it was because she was his second wife that they had chosen Islay and a very different kind of ceremony and wedding from the grand ones of Emma and Adelaide. Although her mother would have been highly unlikely to have travelled from London to Islay, especially in November, Walter's estates including Islay had often been home to Julia in the fourteen years since the family had broken up. Walter Campbell's remaining child, John Francis Campbell, had been joined by his young cousins Walter and Edith, the orphans of John George Campbell who had died in Madeira on 6 August 1830, and their mother 'little' Ellen, who, with another little daughter, had died in 1832. After Lady Eleanor's death in 1832, Adelaide and Julia were often in Islay helping with the young children. Walter remarried in Twickenham on 12 March 1837, to another cousin, Isabella Catherine Cole, the granddaughter of Lady Betty Hamilton, and they had a further son and three daughters. Charlotte liked Walter's second wife, whose new 'babe was the prettiest I ever beheld',[12] while she also enjoyed the company of Walter's heir and her grandson, Johnny, who had just turned 18.

After only three 'very happy' years of marriage, and still hoping to have children 'when my health got stronger' (though this is the first ever mention of Julia's poor health), Julia graphically described in a letter to Eliza how her husband had on the morning of 9 January 1840 taken her in his arms and called her a treasure before going off to skate on his mere.[13] She had watched him from her writing desk at the window and several hours later heard a cry go up. Everyone rushed round; they tried to get their boat through the ice. And eventually they tried to revive his body with brandy, hot blankets and hot salt bags, all to no avail. Her mother, whom she described as 'having so kindly hastened to me in the first moments of my deep distress' was one of the chief mourners, accompanied by Adelaide's husband, Lord Arthur, and Beau's husband, now Earl of Charleville, as he had become on 31 October 1835. While accepting that it was God's will, Julia was comforted by her equally religious sister, Adelaide and her husband, who stayed on after the funeral.

While Eliza and her eldest daughter, Seymour, sometimes came to London during the season, as in August 1838, staying at the Clarendon Hotel in Bond Street, Adelaide often visited her mother when in London. Emma Russell also often arrived from Lincoln's Inn with some of her four children. On 6 May 1840 Emma's father-in-law, Lord William Russell, was murdered in his home by his valet, Courvoisier. Adelaide and Beaujolois were present at the trial in the crowded Central Criminal Court on 18 June which resulted in the death sentence.[14] On a happier note, 20-year-old Blanche Bury described a pleasant dinner *en famille* which had taken place at her mother's on 13 June 1839 when the Langford-Brookes, Lennoxes and Russells had all been there, along with the in-law

Campbells of Sunderland, Aylmer Lambert, the Nugents (she was the sister of the Duchesse de Montebello) and the Lushingtons (Sir Stephen, Lady and two daughters). The only family of which nothing is heard of in the correspondence of Charlotte's extended family after Eleanora's death in 1828 are her three Uxbridge grandchildren ('Ux' remarried 17 August 1833 and had a further four children). While Charlotte had written on the birth of her first grandchild that, lacking maternal instinct, she would really only be interested in grandchildren as they grew up, it was perhaps fortunate that many of them, in time, became interesting young adults, correspondents and visitors.

Beaujolois continued to suffer bouts of ill health, as in May 1837, when Julia and her husband were visiting Charleville, with alternately glorious early summer weather or Irish drizzle.[15] Eliza's two youngest children succumbed to scarlet fever at this very time, and a new-born daughter, customarily named after one of the dead children, had to be removed for a time from Altyre. In October 1839 after visiting Eliza, Beaujolois experienced what could have been a very serious coach accident at Dalwhinnie. The Earl of Charleville had dismounted when the carriage was losing its grip on the road, but it had gone over a precipice, and rolled over four times before resting on the river bank. Writing to Sir William at Altyre, Charleville called the lack of any serious injuries a 'miraculous interposition of providence for which I humbly thank God', adding 'the carriage will need to be patched up'.[16]

Charlotte's elder brother, George, the 6th Duke of Argyll, had continued to move in royal circles, playing a major role in George IV's visit to Scotland in 1822 as Master of the Household, and along with Lord John and Walter Frederick Campbell, leading scores of kilted followers in various processions. He often spoke in the House of Lords on behalf of Highland Scotland; and in October 1831 had presented a petition from Campbeltown in favour of reform. He and his duchess were frequently reported as participants in London society events before she died in 1835. The duke and the Charlevilles, as the Tullamores were by then, watched a balloon ascent from tea-gardens in Bayswater, an enthusiasm he shared with his younger brother.[17] After 1837 he continued in the service of King William as Lord Steward of the Household, and was even more involved in that of Queen Victoria, frequently dining at her table. Suddenly, at Inveraray on 22 October 1839, shortly after his seventy-first birthday, 'He died at dinner; fell off his chair, supposed to be in a fit of apopexly. He was out and well before dinner, and had a ride up Glenary [*sic*].'[18] On All Souls Day his body lay in state at Inveraray in the 'principal drawing room … hung around with black cloth and lighted with wax candles'.[19] The next day the coffin was taken by the steamer *Vulcan* to lie in the main drawing room at Rosneath, 'fitted up in the same way', after which those of the public 'of respectable exterior' were able to pay their respects. The *Vulcan* was again to take the coffin to its final resting place in the family mausoleum at Kilmun, followed by two other steamers, most of the Argyll tenantry having been invited, and also fifty mourners from Islay, the weather being 'very tempestuous'.[20] Pallbearers included his nephews, the new Marquis of Lorne and Walter Frederick Campbell of Islay (with his son, John Francis), as well as his nephews-in-law, the Earl of Charleville (and his son, now Lord Tullamore), Lord Arthur Lennox, Sir William Gordon-Cumming, and several Argyll Campbells. The new duke and duchess and his two remaining children,[21] the new Lord Lorne and Lady Emma Campbell were the chief mourners, but perhaps others of his nieces and perhaps even his sister Charlotte were also present. The 6th Duke had had no legitimate issue (although his illegitimate progeny is scarcely likely to have reached the four hundred suggested by one of his successors).[22] His will was proved at 'Doctors' commons' at the start of the following year by 'Miss Campbell his daughter and sole executrix; she was the main beneficiary, mostly of debts due to considerable arrears of rent, arising from his Scottish estates'.[23]

The new 7th Duke was Lord John, who on 8 January 1831 had married for the third time, a widow, Anne Monteath.[24] The duke was a man of many parts, a Fellow of both the Royal Society and the Royal Society of Edinburgh, active in parliament (particularly trying, unsuccessfully, to avoid disruption in the Church of Scotland, and to alleviate Highland destitution) as well as continuing to improve the financial affairs of the Argyll estate and family. At the beginning of September 1842, it was reported that Inveraray burgh and its castle had been the scene of 'extensive alterations and improvements', 'likewise the whole of the apartments in the principal inn, all for the proposed visit of Queen Victoria'. She arrived in Loch Fyne in the royal yacht a few days later and was received by the duke at the entrance to the Castle.[25] On a somewhat different scale, early in the new year of 1840, the Bury household had been in a frenzy over the proposed visit of the new duke and his duchess. As Blanche reported to Harriet Pigott on 1 January1840, they had been living in a bustle for the last fortnight, 'with the house full of work people putting down carpets etc and Mamma assisting our little Household'.[26] This must all have added to the household expenditure, but the duke was not yet truly aware of the disarray and extent of Charlotte's finance and debts, or it could have made for a somewhat uncomfortable visit. While in hock to usurers, she was probably not herself wholly cognisant of, or perhaps even admitting to herself, the extent of the problems.

Her several protestations of poverty to Harriet Pigott were absolute, not relative, and Colburn's four-figure sum for *The Diary* can only have been of small consolation either to her status or her accounts, such as they were. The available evidence takes considerable disentanglement but it is yet again an Argyll brother who had to come to her aid, her son Walter having continued to refuse help with the escalating debts through the 1830s. Lord John spent considerable time and effort on behalf of his importunate brother, George, 6th Duke, as well as his sisters, the stress further impairing his health.[27] In respect of Charlotte, the debts of £7,000 to £10,000 that had been so laboriously detailed just before the death of Edward Bury appear to have been partly resolved by Argyll payments including one of at least £4,000 in 1837. Through the rest of the 1830s Charlotte's son, Walter, never did accept the basic premise of underfunding since his mother's first widowhood in 1809, having expected Edward Bury to cope with the glaring gap between income and relatively modest expenditure, continuing to give her at most £1,000 a year, while also continuing to spend lavishly on his estates, even during the increasingly difficult economic circumstances over the Highlands and Islands.

Letters and financial statements among Lord John, then later as duke, his aptly named agent, Alexander Moneypenny in Edinburgh, agent Robert MacGibbon in Inveraray, lawyer Thomas Nettleship in London, Charlotte and the Shawfield/Islay agent, the elderly James Macinnes in Edinburgh, gradually reveal much about expenditure, although the hard-earned income from her pen does not surface in the accounts. As Charlotte put it:

> I am perfectly aware of My Good brother John's opinion about women's writing. But as I differ from Him in toto on this head, I would rather never speak to Him on the subject ... I have no way of living as I like to live except by my Pen, and my pen is My all.[28]

It was April 1839, however, before she could gladly acknowledge that her brother at last 'had some feeling for ladies' writings'.[29] Despite all her 'scribbling' efforts, however, finances continued to deteriorate calamitously.

In November 1837 Charlotte had confirmed to Robert MacGibbon that Lord John had raised another £2,000 'which have half liquidated my debts', and that she had asked her son Walter to join her 'in a Bond for £2,500 in a life insurance policy' designed for 'extricating me from my difficulties ... I am in a very critical and anxious state.'[30] Not only did her son not agree to this, despite, or perhaps due to, all the expenses of Playfair's plans for extending Islay House at a time of great agricultural difficulties and rental arrears. But by 1840 the new duke was himself apparently having to fund Charlotte's Shawfield allowance of £750. Her crisis had by then escalated, and the new duke's letters to his Edinburgh agent were as factually horrifying as Charlotte's to various interlocutors were emotionally distraught. On 7 August 1840 the duke was writing to Alexander Moneypenny about the Argyll estate's continuing financial problems, adding: 'I have also a very melancholy and heavy Burden to be answerable for upon account of My Sister Lady Charlotte, which I will further explain tomorrow.'[31] True to his word, on 11 August he was reporting: 'My sister's affairs are still distressing, but I have not yet got at the whole and, the best method of relieving her. I have however found out that her new Debts amount to £6,500.' He had asked Nettleship in London to investigate thoroughly and come up with another insurance scheme for which he himself would pay the interest. Understandably somewhat bitter, he added: 'Islay [her son] has declined doing any thing except offering £300 to pay her passage abroad.' Her furniture was said to be worth £5,000, 'against which some of the money might be borrowable if it is not forestalled'. Despite the complexities, Nettleship managed to get back to the duke on 15 August, in a long letter from Harley Street. He had 'for several days past been engaged in endeavouring to ascertain the nature and extent of Lady Charlotte Bury's liabilities and have I believe succeeded as far as the enormous Debts for money borrowed is concerned'. He had also had a long interview with Charlotte herself on the previous day, the outcome of which, despite her being 'much affected' by her brother's 'extreme liberality and kindness', Nettleship had to disclose 'a Mass of Debt far greater than your Grace appears to have been aware of'. Three different solicitors were involved, as well as usurers and tradespeople. He had asked Charlotte for a detailed account of housekeeping expenses for the past three years but 'she was unable to comply in detail having kept no accounts which will shew what is required'.

Accounts of expenditure were kept more meticulously thereafter.[32] The annual salaries and wages for Guyot the butler (£50), her footman (£20), her lady's maid Annie MacLeod (£30), the cook (£32) and the other maids (£32) were itemised, along with fees for doctor and dentists, subscriptions for the circulating library, the *Morning Post* and so on. Another sum of about £50 or £60 was for household expenses and servants' board and wine. When Charlotte had first returned to London after Edward Bury's death, she had used hackney coaches. Then she had a fly ('less dangerous as to catching disease'), then flying in the face of her finances, a carriage and horses once more. But now she was again reduced to 'an occasional fly'. There were also necessities to be obtained from shoemakers, milliners, dressmakers, glove makers, watch repairers and others. Charlotte considered these sums modest, but had had to start borrowing to pay for furniture, silver plate and so on. However, by this time, all the furniture had had to be assigned to one lender who was owed £1,500 and who 'on 15 August had a person in the House at this Moment taking charge of it and he will probably exercise his Power of Sale' if the money owed were not to materialise 'by the day'. Nettleship sympathised with this more honest lender, although another earlier lender for £3,250 had also to be repaid under a warrant of attorney signed by Charlotte. Moneypenny suggested to the duke that if these debts could be covered by borrowing on her life it would be best for him then to purchase the furniture and grant a lease of the furnished house to his sister. These were the most urgent payments required immediately. But the biggest shock for the duke must have been Thomas Nettleship's list which showed that Charlotte's debts now stood, not at £6,500 'only', but at £10,696. As the first year's insurance money would have to be paid almost immediately, 'little less than £12,000 could be considered as requisite to be paid so as to clear off everything'. Nettleship cannily observed: 'I cannot presume to anticipate how this alarming Increase may operate upon your Grace.'

Charlotte once again made her way to Harley Street on the 21 August 1840. Nettleship had arranged two insurances on her life for £2,500 each on which the premiums would be £458 7*s.* 11*d.* The duke agreed to these proposals but 'the whole business appears to be so complicated' that he thought Moneypenny should go from Edinburgh to London to consult with Nettleship 'as to what can be done and what should be done', particularly to reduce the 'horrible mass of debts ... illegal interest and ... other exorbitant demands'. He again despaired of his nephew Walter's offer of £300 to send his mother to the Continent, saying that 'he could not suffer his sister to be disgraced by making a moonlight flitting abroad'.[33] Thomas Nettleship had been 'distinctly under the impression that the £4,000 raised in 1837 would have covered every debt' and managed to delay some of the lesser debtors for a year. But the house and furniture could be seized for the two major debts on 10 and 29 September. Nettleship had to go off to Worcester on the death of his father, and on 9 September Charlotte was desperately imploring Alexander Moneypenny in Edinburgh 'to hasten to London very speedily' as she had nobody to protect her from 'the most insolent person in the House'. Nettleship managed to delay the payment of the two major sums for a fortnight until the new insurances had been put into place. He and Moneypenny spent the rest of September busily trying to extricate Charlotte. But on 25 September, before a meeting with Nettleship, Charlotte asked Moneypenny to visit her, presenting him with a list of still further liabilities. Even after deduction of the main two debts from the first list, the new total had escalated to £16,414.

It was not long before a valuation of the effects was on its way to the duke, but there were worth a mere fraction of the debts. By this stage, the duke decided to sell off some lands in Argyll (with a right of redemption) so that he could purchase the house and furniture as surety for insurances to raise more capital, and it was proposed to lease back 3 Connaught Place and its contents to his sister, while she paid the insurance premiums. By the beginning of October he was asking Nettleship to give sufficient money to Charlotte 'for her journey down to this place [Ardencaple] per Railway to Preston, and Posting from thence to Glasgow and Ardencaple as soon as possible', accompanied by two servants. Also travelling north soon after, on October 5, was a relieved Alexander Moneypenny. Charlotte was looking forward to three months in Scotland to reflect 'what I had best do' in consultation with her brother to arrange payments towards the remaining smaller creditors during 1841 'when I may be suffered to bear the penalty of the Evil I have brought upon myself'.[34] The duke was clear that some of the creditors were more straightforward and he accordingly settled with them. The more uxurious ones were either reduced in their demands, or paid off, probably at the composition of five shillings in the pound.

But her stay in Scotland turned out to be more eventful than she had foreseen. One of her pursuers, though not listed, Adam Glen, a baker of 106 Regent Street in London, and his 'mandatory' or lawyer, pursued her to Inveraray Castle with a warrant for her arrest in November.[35] She had promised to pay him £450 in three months from 20 July 1840. It being Highland Argyll, the messenger, David Black, contrived to delay serving notice, allowing Charlotte to escape from Inveraray. She had been 'bundled out of bed' and had driven off in a post-chaise to Edinburgh. The Duke of Argyll, traditionally the State Master of the Royal Household at Holyrood had, as emolument, the use of a large set of rooms in the Palace. No creditor could arrest her as long as she remained in the precincts of the palace. Glen sued Black for negligence over the whole affair.[36] On 6 May 1841 a proclamation of outlawry, putting her beyond the protection of the law, was made against Charlotte by the Sheriffs at the county court in Red Lion Square in London, on behalf of yet another creditor.[37] In the end it was several years before all claims were settled.[38]

22

Italian Sojourn

By 12 December 1841 Charlotte was writing from the Hôtel des Bergues (no less) in Geneva, realising that it was somewhat late in the season to be venturing across the Alps. Accompanied by her 'good and charming companion', Blanche, she managed to reach what she deemed her Italian home, Rome; it seemed 'a miracle how we escaped' the winds and other hazards of transalpine and trans-Apennine travel in winter, as she wrote to her friend of long standing, Sismondi.[1] She extolled her 'raptures on beholding Rome once more ... this incomprehensible City of the World'. But it had not been an easy re-entry for it was by then, at the start of February 1842, carnival time and, as they had been delayed en route, their lodging had been taken up. They were three hours in the midst of the Piazza di Spagna before they could find 'any sort of shelter'. Meanwhile the 'puerile crowd and to me distasteful crowd of masks and noise and sugar plumbs and dirty scentless flowers—the bodily inconvenience of being pelted with these latter—the recent fatigue of our journey inspired me with a profound melancholy'. Other remembrances of twenty years before crowded in—'the ghosts of pleasures, the Consciousness of Mistakes, Errors [and] Follies'. After ten days, however, they had settled on the Corso at number 12 and things began to look up. Nevertheless she confessed to Sismondi:

> I became conscious of that uprooting of existence which an involuntary absence from Native Soil always produces—and the great distance from—Home—and the irregularity of letters and the uncertainty of when I should return, were so many little and big daggers stuck in my heart. But this too subsides, this aching smarting sense of strangeness,

> this restless dissatisfaction and distaste of surrounding comforts and pleasures gradually gives way to necessary resignation.

She was, however, soon deeming 'Rome the most delightful and wonderful place in the World'. A Mr Aubyn, 'a sort of intermediate political and private between the Holy See and Britain has provided for us a pretty general introduction into Society' and, despite it being Lent by then, she and Blanche were mixing almost every night with ambassadors and friends, both English and Roman. In the same letter she made reference to her hope of meeting Sismondi in Tuscany that year as illusory, adding: 'The great expense of so long a journey (seeing that I must return here next Winter) is alas out of the question.' Despite this strange and ambiguous reference to her 'exile', Charlotte and Blanche stayed on the Continent and wintered in Rome from 1842 to 1848, often summering south of Naples at Castellammare. To her (Shawfield or Argyll) income of £750 per annum she continued to add from her writings (although not from new editions). Staying right in the heart of Rome at 12 Corso Roma—on the desirable first floor piano nobile—she transmitted news of their activities in long letters to the formidable Dowager Lady Charleville, Beau's mother-in-law. While mother and daughter worked, drove and walked in the mornings,[2] the letters are interspersed with the names of the 'good and noble' English society whom they visited and entertained.[3]

Unexpected news arrived at the Corso on 6 May 1842, a fortnight after a great flurry of letters had been sent to Sir William Gordon-Cumming in Altyre from all the Campbell sisters and their spouses back home. Eliza had her thirteenth confinement on 28 March but died on 21 April aged 45. In an understandably shocked, emotional and religious letter to her son-in-law, Eliza's mother thought 'she had taken too much of that Drug already ... the dreadful habit which had fastened itself upon her Constitution'.[4] It later transpired that Eliza had been involved in capturing a bolting horse only a month before, which had contributed to her demise.[5] The large funeral was held on Monday 25 April in St Michael's Episcopal Church in Forres, after which her coffin was lowered into the tomb there.[6] She had been skilled in music and art, had developed the pleasure gardens of the estate, was an informed plant breeder and salmon fisher, as well as nurturing both her large family and the estate's people, not to ignore finding time to participate in London seasons. For several decades Eliza had also corresponded with many of the naturalists and other scientists of the day such as the botanist and plant collector, and first director of Kew Gardens, Sir William J. Hooker, and she organised geological fossil collections on several estates in the north-east. A collection of these fossils was sent to the Geological Society of London. Eliza's apparently sudden death came as a great shock to her mother, who wrote of her to Sismondi as being charming and gifted 'with talents of the highest order'.[7] Only a month after Eliza's death Charlotte was urging Sir William to come to Rome with his grieving daughters: 'I should say travel was the only worldly resource left to you for a time' and it had apparently been their intention to visit Italy.[8] Julia had immediately gone to Altyre to help with the bereft widower and the five children still at home, including the last born baby son, but was expected to join her mother in the autumn.[9]

The Burys were planning to leave Rome for Naples about the middle of June. Writing on 14 December 1842 to the Islay agent, James Macinnes, in Edinburgh on thin 'shabby paper to spare postage', Charlotte advised him, somewhat belatedly perhaps, that she was 'now in a Foreign land'.[10] She was daily expecting to see her nephew, George, now Lord Lorne. 'Were it not for the occasion which brings Him Here [Eliza's death] I should indeed be happy at the thought of seeing Him again.' She mentioned that it was a long time since she had heard any news from Islay, but proudly proclaimed that her grandson, John Francis Campbell of Islay, had come of age and was 'a very fine young man'. He was travelling extensively on the continent in the 1840s and he stayed in Rome and Naples during October and November of 1842. His atmospheric watercolours depicted the Campagna, and especially evoked the excursions on paddle steamers with their tall stacks and smoke plumes plying around and across the Bay of Naples to Castellammare, Sorrento, Capri and Ischia, while noting that 265 passengers were on one steamer alone. His close vista of the Bay of Naples was a serene evocation, perhaps even then unrealistically so, with Vesuvius smoking in cerulean skies. More detailed was his tripartite panorama of Naples from the shoreline Hotel Della Vittoria, measuring 38 by 110 centimetres (see plate 29).

Julia, 'a Dear and excellent Daughter', arrived to stay in Rome with her mother over the winter of 1842-3. Writing to Sir William on 29 December 1842 from the Hôtel de l'Europe in the Piazza di Spagna close to the Corso, Julia sadly told of seeing on her arrival 'my poor mother's face. Habit has now reconciled me to her appearance but I cannot hide from myself it is an altered one.'[11] However, she went on to admire the

> spring of life and cheerfulness in her which was always in your eyes so great a charm and those who have the good taste to cultivate her here, both among foreign and English appear always to enjoy her society and admire her in spite of years etc. There is a grace about her I see in No one else.

Julia also noted Charlotte's 'chief luxury'—a carriage—'in which we drove together every day'. One excursion on a glorious sunny day in November, reported by Harriet Countess Granville to the Duchess of Devonshire, had been 'down the Corso, by the Ruins of the Temple of Peace, the Coliseum, the Constantine Arch etc, to Mr Mills's garden, all full of roses, cape jessamines and heliotropes'.[12] Nephew and cousin, Lord Lorne, arrived in December with his tutor, 'our good friend Willy Cumming' and Mrs Howson.[13] The 'handsome and charming' Francis or Frank Charteris was another welcome visitor and Shawfield in-law Colin Campbell visited for several weeks. Rome being 'full of English', Julia dropped many of their names including the Cadogans, Chesterfields, Devonshires, Gores, Granville Levesons, and Lady Coventry, as well as Russian ambassador Ptomekin and the grand duke and duchess. Others had gone to Naples for the winter, but were to return for the carnival. There were dinners, 'evenings' and 'some tableaux' which Julia was helping to 'get up' and in which Blanche was to figure. Julia described her half-sister as 'in great beauty—not too fat now and is much admired when seen but she is as usual very lazy about going out'.[14] The studios of sculptors and artists were frequented, and Charlotte was even inspired to write a poem on suddenly coming across a white marble Madonna in a woodland glade.[15]

How much solace all this breathless end-of-year news was to Sir William and his family at Altyre is perhaps arguable, but Julia also described the 'great blessing of a regular place of worship established here just outside the Porta del Popolo'. Nonetheless, Julia ended by apologising for having no news and no scandal, and hoping to see the family at Altyre on her return the following summer. Apart from the slight snobbishness of the society names, her letter gives no hint of the fault Charlotte subsequently complained of when writing from south of Rome to Lady Charleville.

> Kind and excellent as Julia was in coming to me I am relieved to think she is safe at home again for her prejudices as to the whole of continental life were such as to render her séjour here quite a pain and not a pleasure: without her sister Adelaide's presence to take care of and protect her I could not wish her ever to undertake the thing again.[16]

Later she returned to the same theme:

> She always <u>means well</u>. But her nerves are so weakened and her prejudices so strong she was an anxiety to me all the time she was here and she often distress'd me in society. She is very injudicious in her Conduct and is often impertinent in taking upon herself to give advice and obtrude her Enthusiasm in those whose feelings she ought rather to respect in silence. But this is a monomania of hers, wh[ich] the indulgent who know her real merits may forgive but which others less kind will hate her for.[17]

Charlotte was particularly terrified by Julia's 'finding fault with the Established religion of the Country', and summed up her feelings, 'though I love her, I am certain she is far better for all our sakes and her own at home than on the Continent'.

More positively, Charlotte enthused about how easily and cheaply books of every kind could by then be obtained since 'the communication is now so constant and rapid with England and France that truly one hardly feels to be in a foreign Land'. She particularly enjoyed the prospect of everyday improvement of communication. From the Hôtel de la Ville de Paris south of Rome she described the new road 'at this moment in progress between [the hotel] and next Post to avoid the steep hill in and out of Lariccia which will be completed in two months'. She compared the countryside since her visits with Edward Bury over twenty years before, and marvelled at the magnificent new road which now meant a journey of only four days between Rome and Naples. Further, she enjoyed the even more attractive prospect that 'in two or three years it is hoped a rail road will be established between Rome and Naples'. The summer months of 1843 in Castellammare were intended as escape from a Roman summer but is was unfortunately 'infinitely hotter'.[18] Again, there were lots of English acquaintances—including her Jenkinson nieces and their husbands—the Duc and Duchesse of Montebello were particular favourites, along with the latter's sister and husband, Mrs and Mr Nugent. Since the King of Naples forbade carriages and the English mostly stayed at the top of a steep hill, Charlotte's options were to walk, be carried, or ride on a donkey, none of which appealed to her before and after dinner. As twenty years earlier, the great panorama of the Bay of Naples and the islands of Capri and Ischia still enchanted her.

From Castellammare she confided to the Dowager Countess of Charleville that, since there was 'little chance of ever returning to England', she preferred 'Rome as a Home to any other Place out of my own Country ... and Rome is now my Home'.[19] She was looking forward to another winter's family visitors. Charlotte's brother and his duchess (the latter, reluctantly) had decided to spend the winter of 1843-4 'at Rome with Lorne and me'. The prospect delighted her since 'I should be very happy here were it not for the far distance of many that I love, and the anxiety I entertain about some of them'.[20] This referred particularly to her last surviving brother with his still indifferent health, and to Beaujolois, although Charlotte confided to Lady Charleville that she found the accounts of Beau's ills 'incomprehensible'. Illness affected the temper and equanimity of her brother, John, so that he was often 'brusque in manner'.[21] Despite a cold winter ('an English one'), Charlotte thought that the stay in Rome did prove good for the duke's health, but his duchess had been underwhelmed by things Italian. She disliked being abroad and Charlotte felt 'disappointment in and from her'.[22] Despite this, the Argylls stayed until April and the sojourn did prove a relatively successful few months. Particularly enjoyable, perhaps especially for Blanche, had been the enthusiastic delight of both Lorne and his sister, Emma. Again the Roman winter society had been 'excellent', Charlotte naming those 'in whose Houses I have been and who have been in mine'.[23] The list was long, including the Angersteins, Brabizons, Dalmenys, Fitzclarences, Gainsboroughs, Lady Pellew, the Poltimores, Prideaux, Montagus, Osbornes, Riddells, Selwins, Lady Tollemache and her daughter. She noted that many were going to congregate at Castellammare for the summer, though Charlotte herself would 'greatly have preferred Venice from newness of interest as well as all its recollections'. After a delay due to a severe eye infection of Blanche's, they did in fact spend the rest of the summer of 1844 at Castellammare. A 'great loss' to Charlotte that October 1844 was the unexpected death of her 'friend of a lifetime in sunshine and gloom, always kind and faithfull', Mrs Hook.[24]

A happier piece of news had been the marriage on 31 July 1844 between Lorne and Lady Elizabeth Georgiana Sutherland Leveson-Gower, daughter of the 2nd Duke of Sutherland. The Venerable Archbishop of York conducted the ceremony in the Sutherland family chapel at the immensely grand and Italianate Trentham Park in Staffordshire, with Sir John Barry's recently designed spectacular main entrance and portico, gallery and state rooms, tower, stunning conservatory and extensive park and pleasure gardens. Charlotte's granddaughter, Edith Campbell, was one of the bridesmaids, and Adelaide and her husband attended, as did John Francis Campbell of Islay. Walter Frederick Campbell and John Francis took part in the subsequent celebrations at Inveraray, forming 'no inconsiderable ornament to the pageant of Highland retainers and clansmen'.[25] A year later there were further rejoicings when an Argyll heir arrived on 6 August 1845. In Victorian fashion he was given many family forenames, John George Edward Henry Douglas Sutherland Campbell.[26] Following on the 6th Duke's having had the wand of office break in his hand, with King William dying shortly after to satisfy the superstitious, the 7th Duke dropped the Crown at the proroguing of Parliament in August 1845, as Charlotte reported to the Dowager Lady Charleville.[27] This had led Charlotte into a long exposition on not only Queen Victoria as a monarch in modern times of 'steam and rail roads', but also of the grand duke and duchess who were 'much beloved' by their people. Back in London, *The Times* had reported the duke's stumble when walking backwards at the proroguing, the crown falling off its velvet cushion.[28] Several diamonds were knocked out, but as Queen Victoria was consoling the duke the gems were found. *The Times* had a tongue-in-the-cheek suggestion ten days later that either aristocrats had to be trained better to walk backwards, or a revolutionary change had to be made to walk forwards.[29]

Instead of summering in Castellammare in 1845 Charlotte and Blanche ventured to Florence, hoping to escape Rome's insalubrious heat. As to Blanche, she had 'always been very delicate and will never be robust ... the hotter the weather the better she is ... as long as she lives it will never be safe for her to pass a winter in Britain. She has much more of her father's Constitution than of Mine I grieve to say.'[30] While Charlotte thought Blanche had become much thinner than she had expected, she regarded her as being 'now very beautiful' and 'a really good girl ... and a perfect Daughter'. But her mother feared that, as Blanche was already 26, 'she will never marry indespight of my plain exposition of her state and beggary whenever I may die'. She added that 'no temporal advantage whatever shall make her marry any one she does not Love'. Charlotte herself remained ambivalent about the relationship between lack of wherewithal and living abroad.

> If it should so be that by some miracle I ever have it in My power with any degree of honor to return to England, I shall be blest beyond My Deserts—and to see some few whom I love and to feel that I am reinstated in the place I ought to hold in society and which I lost by My own imprudence would indeed afford me greater and more complete Happiness than I have a right to expect.

But immediately she added:

> In every Thing that regards a Continental Life I mean Manners Hours Customs Society I greatly prefer living Abroad to living at Home. Were I a person of Consequence ... of a great Estate, a member of Parliament or anything in short of Weight in My own Country (bodily weight excepted which by the bye I have no longer being very thin) I should deem it a duty to reside in my Native Land but as an insignificant Woman there is no comparison in the pleasures and advantages of all that constitutes Stirring Life Here to the dull Monotony and gloomy Fogs of an English sejour in some secondary Town or some antiquated Park.

Knowing her old friend the dowager countess would agree with her, she still averred that London was the only place she could bear—'I always so thought and felt and it would require to live there as I should like to live more money than ever I can have.' Travelling on their Tuscan tour with their Murray guidebook, at one point speeding by rail in twenty minutes from

Pisa to Leghorn, they had stayed in inns and hotels that were 'all excellent'. They returned to Rome earlier than planned on account of on-going illness, as Charlotte did not think 'Florence has agreed with me, but it is perhaps that I have not agreed with Florence', as she put it to Jacques Galiffe.[31] They then rented accommodation in the Palazzo Buffalo.

Despite lifelong indifferent health, Charlotte's brother John, the 7th Duke, was in his seventieth year when he died on 25 April 1847 at home in Ardencaple, to be succeeded as 8th Duke by the 25-year-old Lorne. It is not known when the news reached them, but this must have proved very sad tidings for Charlotte, by then 72. She was now the sole survivor of all her siblings and half-siblings.

A different kind of loss had been hinted at in a letter to the Dowager Countess of Charleville in October 1844—Charleville's bankruptcy, about which she knew 'only the fact and I am quite in ignorance of all particulars'.[32] Perhaps he had not been such a good manager as Mlle de la Chaux had foreseen, although, to be fair, he had inherited a vastly encumbered estate, heavily in debt, from his father in October 1835. Even allowing for the lavish lifestyle of himself and Beau, not to speak of their heir, now Lord Tullamore. Charleville and his mother were at pains to point out in letters to Sir William Gordon-Cumming that Tullamore would be a most unsuitable prospect for one of the Gordon-Cumming daughters on the grounds both of his financial situation and of his being a first cousin.[33] It is also likely that the problems with rental income from an extended Irish estate in the 1840s were fundamental. Charleville Castle was mothballed, the London establishment dismantled, and the Charlevilles were reported as 'being on their way to the continent, heading for Berlin'. On 26 September 1845 Charlotte reported to the dowager countess that Beaujolois had 'suddenly arrived' in Rome. But little more is known of her until her death from her 'serious malady' (consumption) in Naples on 1 February 1848, in her forty-fifth year. She was buried in the Protestant Cemetery at Santa Maria della Fede in Naples. Afterwards, her children, Lord Tullamore and Lady Beaujolois, stayed with their grandmother in Rome, leaving at the beginning of April and heading for England 'in these Equinoctial gales'.[34] Twenty-three-year-old 'Little' Beau had apparently wanted to make her home with her paternal grandmother, the dowager countess. But it had been arranged that she was to 'live with Adelaide', which Charlotte regretted 'for Her sake (and I believe she does so for her own)'. Never slow to criticise her offspring, Charlotte opined that although Adelaide was 'an excellently <u>intentioned</u> Creature and a perfectly chaste wife', she thought her 'injudicious in many respects, and where the Husband and Wife are at variance there can be no peace, or real advantage to any one resident with them'. The Lennoxes were based in London during most of the 1840s and had four surviving young children. Every August they were part of the house party at Goodwood during the races, and Adelaide, as Lady Arthur, was also much involved in charitable institutions. Their niece, Beau, was listed in their household at 21 Ovington Square at the time of the 1851 Census, along with her cousins, Constance (12), Ada (10) and Ethel (6); Arthur, 9, was a scholar at school on Wimbledon Common.

Unexpected, if happier, news, though clouded by Beau's death, had been relayed in the same letter to the dowager countess by Charlotte: 'Blanche was married on the 6th [April 1848] as privately as possible on account of my mourning which I only put off for that Day'.[35] The ambassador's brother, the secretary of the Legation, Coll Bowen and Coll Crawfurd were 'the only four persons besides the Parties present' at the ceremony in Rome. 'It was impossible to be more composed than Blanche and the Ceremony was performed with all due reverence', her mother adding rather sagely, 'we had no demonstrations of any sort'. Twenty-eight-year-old Blanche had married 53-year-old David Lyon of Goring Park in Sussex. When young he was a scion of the wealthy Lyons of Auldbar branch of the Bowes-Lyon family; the man about town had been captured by Lawrence in one of his 'swaggering' portraits. He had inherited three sugar plantations in Jamaica from his wealthy eponymous father; and with the £6 million compensation awarded on the abolition of the slave trade, had in 1834 bought the Sussex estate as well as a London house in South Street, Park Lane. He had built Goring Hall on the estate in 1840, the approach to which was an avenue planted with Ilex which still stand. Charlotte verged on the ecstatic:

> I had the happiness of seeing Her really Happy—perfectly Her own Mistress—He declaring there will only be one Danger for her, that of Her being completely free to do all the things as she pleases. And I firmly believe from all I have observed of his Character that so it will be. But I apprehend no danger for Her, because she is so singularly gifted with purity and good Sense. All that this Worlds wealth can give will be Hers, and I firmly believe she will make a good and kind use of it.

This was Easter 1848 and the continent was in turmoil. Instead of their projected honeymoon in Germany, Vienna and elsewhere, the Lyons had gone Post by voiturier to Pisa 'whither I followed them the next day ... finding all my rooms and fires prepared for me by their kind care and attention'. Blanche then chose to stop in Turin 'till I joined them not liking to be so long absent from Me'. They then continued through northern Italy 'where they met with no molestation on our route what ever', and travelled from Geneva to Brussels, Calais and Dover by 'Voiturier, Rail road, Steam boat etc etc'. Charlotte did not feel 'as if Blanche were parted from me—an inexpressible Happiness so long as I live—for all our tastes and habits and modes of living are entirely similar'.

The events of 1848 had propelled Charlotte into leaving Italy, to return to Britain's grey skies. She was also returning to a country in crisis. Many had been financially ruined that year, including her son, Walter. Susan Ferrier had noted on 8 November 1847: 'The Islay crisis is come, and I fear poor Lady Charlotte must suffer, with many others.'[36] While the Lanarkshire estate of Woodhall with its coal and iron mines was profitable, the rental income from the Islay estate (whose population had risen to 15,000 in the 1830s) had been affected by poor harvests, and the extravagant costs involved in replanning an economy and landscape with an overpopulated society had been mounting. By the time he was sequestrated in December 1847, Walter's debts were almost £900,000—on a somewhat different scale from his mother's.[37] But there was no one to bail him out, and the estates had to be sold. In such times this was difficult, particularly in the Highlands and Islands of Scotland, and the estates were run by trustees. Islay was eventually sold for £453,000 to Mr James Morrison, a Liberal MP, of Basildon Park in Berkshire. The latter was reputed to be one of the richest and most cultivated men in Britain, whose family fortune had taken off in 1821 when he cornered the market in the black crêpe ordered in his Fore Street wholesale business and draper's shop in London for the funeral of Queen Caroline. Woodhall was sold later. Meanwhile Walter and his wife (by now blind) removed to Normandy where they already had a property at Avranches looking over to Mont St Michel. From sketches by their son, John Francis, and from his father's two-volume *Sketches of Life in Normandy* published in Edinburgh in 1863, the family seemed to resume the style and kind of lairdship he had pursued in Scotland.[38]

Walter's heir, John Francis, or Iain Og Ìle, had desperately wanted to buy part of the Islay estate but could not raise the capital. An 1846 list detailed the large amount of new and old silver and plate then in Islay House; it included 'breakfast' silver, sideboard ornaments, candlesticks, gilt dessert and tea sets and crystal.[39] A small amount of this was 'taken with Mr Campbell' in October the following year. With the sale of Islay House, as part of the attempt to recoup for creditors, a two-day sale of Walter's remaining plate, paintings, books, china, articles of vertu, wines and so on was held by the auctioneers Dowells and Lyon in Edinburgh on 29 and 30 November 1854.[40] The plate alone weighed 'over 3000 ounces' (about 8.5 kilograms), including a 'magnificent Dessert Service of 90 pieces' of Silver Gilt. As late as the 1880s the Campbell and Bury statues still remained in Islay House; the factor was asking what should be done with them. Perhaps satisfactorily, the link with the Campbells of Shawfield and Islay was to be re-established in 1892 when Walter's granddaughter and Charlotte's great-granddaughter, Lady Mary Leveson-Gower, married James Morrison's grandson, Hugh Morrison; their descendants still own the main estate on the island.

Walter died aged 55 on 8 February 1855 and was buried at Avranches, not after all in the other half of the sarcophagus in the Round Church at Bowmore in Islay. To his aunt, Emma Russell, John Francis Campbell sent the introduction and encomium given in a mixture of English and French at his father's funeral service on 11 April, with internment on the following day.[41] Referring to the 'inexhaustible benevolence' of the 'kilted Highlander', it was averred that he 'counted his days by his good deeds', dying surrounded by most of his children.

23

London Finale

Aged 73, Charlotte was back in Britain living mostly with her youngest daughter, Blanche Lyon, and presumably delighted to be enjoying London society again. On 1 June 1849, Benjamin Disraeli was sitting opposite 'a lady whose countenance haunted me all dinner as one I had at any rate seen in another world. She turned out to be Mrs Lyon, wife of the celebrated yachter, née Blanche Bury.'[1] Noting that Lyon was very rich, and that Charlotte lived with them in South Street, it is somewhat surprising that he divulged that David Lyon had 'paid or settled all her debts. They are very happy, and as for Lady Charlotte I think she is the most lucky woman in the world.'

In 1851, Adelaide, Julia and Blanche all appear to have been in Scotland during the summer and early autumn. The Lyons had taken Castle Menzies in Perthshire for the shooting season. When in Edinburgh with the Lyons Charlotte visited Susan Ferrier who described her as 'soft and caressing as ever' so that she began to feel 'the old glamour coming over me'.[2] The by now rather curmudgeonly Ferrier, however, spoke of Charlotte 'talking all the time ... about her affairs, her happiness with the Lyons, etc etc etc'. Another time Ferrier described Julia calling on her in Edinburgh and she was also visited by Adelaide whom she was glad to see was 'looking well and happy'. The Lyons were then off to Italy and the Lennoxes to Malta with his regiment. In 1853, Julia remarried; she and her husband, Stuart Ker of Liverpool, 'kindly placed her house in London' at Charlotte's disposal. As Ferrier acidly put it, however, 'I believe she is no more fit to manage a house in London than one of her own pugs or parakeets.'[3] Lady Eastlake, journalist and writer on art and wife of Sir Charles Eastlake, then president of the Royal Academy, painted a more sympathetic picture.

She described her erstwhile Roman friend's coming to visit for an hour at 7 Fitzroy Square on 22 July 1850, 'still a beautiful woman, and having lived in the world all her life—and tolerably fast too—her commonest reminiscences are interesting'.[4]

Aged only 50, Beaujolois' widower, the Earl of Charleville, died in London on 14 July 1851.[5] As his son and heir's letters graphically described, he had been seriously afflicted after a seizure in May 1850, which they kept from his mother, the dowager countess, prior to her own death on 24 February 1851. There had been 'no chance whatsoever of his recovering', as his son informed their agent back at Charleville. It was a sad end to Sydney, Lady Morgan's young hero, so highly esteemed by Mlle de la Chaux. He had inherited a hugely encumbered estate in 1835, moved from assiduously attending the Commons to the Lords, but on his bankruptcy in 1844, had not one shilling of income from the properties, the rental income going straight to creditors. His agent had often wondered 'how he had existed at all'. His son arranged that his father's body was taken from London via Dublin for his funeral and burial at Tullamore. The new 3rd Earl and his wife, Arabella Case, whom he had married on 7 March 1850, reopened the castle, but in turn he himself succumbed on 19 January 1859 at the age of only 36.

When Henry Colburn sold his business in 1853 to Hurst and Blackett, Charlotte may not still have been 'scribbling' for lucre, but Hurst and Blackett may have inherited *The Roses* which they published that very year. The novel echoed *Sense and Sensibility* with two young women friends, Alice the serious minded, and Frances, the more giddy one. Written in the first person as autobiography, Snowdonia and Anglesey were metaphors for the two different kinds of friend or 'roses'. The action started near Snowdon, then moved from Gloucestershire to Downsfield in south-eastern England, London and Dublin. Alice married out of familial duty but found mature love in the end, while Frances broke a few hearts including her own. The reader had to be content with a large time-gap between the second and third volumes. But in what was termed 'the present despotic reign of dismal imagination', *The Athenaeum* enjoyed Charlotte's 'healthy cheerfulness of spirit ... With a nice sense of humour, and a fair command over pathos, is combined a certain tinge of romance which veins novels so full of prudential wisdom very gracefully.' At least the interest of *The Roses* was 'thoroughly well sustained to the last'. *The Morning Post* complimented the author on 'the delicate delineation and clever contrast of female character', adding 'we know of few modern stories that will endure comparison with *The Roses*', while *John Bull* deemed it 'a charming tale', and *The Daily News* called it 'one of the most readable novels of the season', *The Observer* opining that 'it cannot fail to charm'.[6] Perhaps if he had foreseen such favourable reviews in the spring of 1839, Colburn might have decided to publish these volumes instead of consigning them to languish forgotten in a drawer or cupboard.

Charlotte had reached the age of 81 in 1856 when the same publishers also produced *The Lady of Fashion* which again might have been one of the novels written long before and set aside by Colburn. Set in the Regency England of almost half a century earlier, but still apparently in demand by publishers and readers alike, and vividly delineating the new town and old county families of regency Brighton, it convincingly set new money against old, as in her first novel, and new style against old. The setting was the then fashionably modern and busy resort of Brighton and its downs, in contrast to the old Barnadiston House in rural Sussex. Befitting the seaside, much of this novel was expressed in nautical terms. The new Lady Caroline Barnardiston's view was that 'The Lady of Fashion cannot always be sparkling in diamonds. I must have emeralds for one style of dress, and sapphires for another, and no leader of 'ton' can get on without all sorts and sizes of pretty gems.'[7] The wedding dress and trousseau were ordered from Paris, 'there being no English term that could express the elegant airiness and crispiness of the materials ... the sit and sweep of the fantastic sleeve was something to dream about for weeks.' The fashionable Steyne expected superlative carriages, dogs had names like Gingerpop—and, rarely for Charlotte, kittens were introduced as Kittykoo and YellowBoy.

The appearance in 1849 of Dr William Beattie's *Life and Letters of Thomas Campbell* had caused Charlotte some nostalgic longings for her youthful and 'then happy Family circle', but it also inspired her to produce what may have been one of her last poems, which her daughter Emma probably copied out and sent to Beattie. It particularly celebrated Campbell's stance on Poland's behalf, as well as his place in the pantheon of poetry, culminating in his tomb in Westminster Abbey.

The Mallalue v. Lyon case concerned a debt of £362 for clothes purchased by Blanche between April 1857 and the end of June 1858. In his summing up for the jury on the third day of 'this very painful case', the judge lamented pointedly that 'some arrangement had not been made to render the inquiry unnecessary'. A chronological rearrangement of answers to the seemingly random examination of the defence and prosecution witnesses reveals the forlorn changes in the expectations of Charlotte and her youngest daughter. Blanche Lyon and other witnesses testified to Charlotte's having lived happily with the newly-wed Lyons from the time of their return from Italy in the early summer of 1848. One of their several homes which must have mightily suited Charlotte was at South Street off Park Lane in Mayfair. According to Blanche 'we had a large establishment there—17 or 18 servants'. Goring Park near Worthing comprised another home, built in 1840 by David Lyon which Blanche declared was 'a good house, and a large establishment there also'. At times, there was a Scottish base for the shooting season, and particularly during northern winters, there was a Roman apartment. While Blanche never exactly knew her husband's income, various witnesses thought he probably lived at the rate of 'at least £10,000 a year'. The marriage settlement gave Blanche £300 pin money per annum, but she also had free rein for 'ornamenting and getting objects of *vertu* for the handsomely furnished houses'. The carriage must also have been a great joy to Charlotte.

All testified to the early happiness of the marriage. David Lyon's brother, William, lived at 28 Park Lane, and often visited them in town, at Goring (where he still had a room) and in Scotland. However, he 'first noticed a change in Mrs Lyon in the early part of 1851', adding: 'It continued to increase. She was constantly in a state of great excitement. I could only conjecture the cause. I observed she took a considerable quantity of wine at dinner. I attributed the excitement to exciting liquors.' This had even caused him to stop visiting his brother's homes. But another witness, whose family had long 'been close to Lady Charlotte's family' was more concerned. Robert Hook, the younger son of the 'late dean of Worcester' told the court that he had known Blanche since childhood, that the Lyons had lived very happily together till 1852, but that she had been very ill 'with a Lady's case'. This may have been a reference to two miscarriages which Blanche endured. She herself also talked of 'pains in her limbs' for which she had taken wine, opium and brandy. Her physician had ordered the opiates and stimulants and 'everything which would strengthen me and do me good'. But she also admitted that she had taken 'more than was good for me, leading to a quarrel with my husband upon the subject in October 1852'. By this time, according to David Lyon's counsel, 'her unhappy propensity for opiates and stimulants ... had increased to such a degree that it became utterly beyond control, and rendered her incapable of managing her establishment'. She had even pawned plate and jewellery for £3,514 as well as borrowing a further £1,500 'from a Lady'.

As of wont, the Lyons went to Rome, arriving there early in December 1852. But by April of the following year, after only five years of marriage, David Lyon appears to have had enough. He brought her back to England, along with a Mr Richard Deakin who had been attending her in Rome. Blanche was deposited in Torquay in May 1853, her husband travelling on immediately to Paris. The arrangement was described by Blanche as being 'placed under restraint [by Deakin] to a certain extent corporally, and entirely so morally'. Although Deakin did not have 'an English diploma', she told the court that she was 'controlled by Mr Deakin, acting under

Mr Lyon's authority'. A physician in Exeter, Dr Shapter, was, however, responsible for her medical care from 17 May until 18 September. He allowed her no stimulants 'except a glass or two of sherry', although she suspected Deakin of surreptitiously plying her with drugs. Descriptions of her incarceration varied by witness. She herself had thought in London in mid-May that she was going to Torquay 'to be treated as a lunatic' and even David Lyon's counsel was unsure whether or not Deakin's was a 'private asylum'. Lyon's longest-standing friend, Mr James, implied that she was in 'Dr Deakin's house, in her own apartments with a most respectable maid and woman as attendants'. But he also prevaricated: 'I do not think they had her at a lunatic asylum, but they had her at a hospital for the cure of insane persons.'

By August Dr Shapter thought Blanche substantially recovered, sufficiently so to live with 'some supervision, such as her mother'. It is almost impossible to imagine the heartbreak and dashed expectations that the 78-year-old Charlotte must have been enduring over her youngest, perhaps favourite, daughter. She had taken apartments in Torquay, and there they stayed until the end of September, Dr Shapter relieved that Blanche 'still maintained her recovered state of mind'. This in itself seems quite a remarkable feat given the events divulged in the law report. In late July or early August Blanche had asked Dr Shapter to write to her husband to 'ask in what probable time, provided she abstained from drink, she might return to him'. David Lyon's reply was apparently long premeditated. Not only had he 'broken up his establishment' in South Street in 1852, letting the house to the Dowager Duchess of Norfolk, but he had also run down his staff at Goring Park. Instructions had also been sent from Rome in early 1853 to his lawyer's chambers in Lincoln's Inn to draw up a deed of separation. Although he signed it on return on 19 April 1853, his trustee brother, William Lyon, apparently did not. David Lyon's reply to Dr Shapter from the Hotel Belle Vue at Aix-la-Chapelle on 7 August was brutal: 'I wish Mrs Lyon not to live in any fool's paradise: whatever takes place, I am resolved not to communicate with Mrs Lyon, nor to live with her again.' He emphasised his determination, adding that 'she was never contradicted till she married', and also maintained that 'she cannot bear the sight of me', which might appear in direct contradiction to Blanche's request to him a few days earlier. He continued to Dr Shapter: 'When she is recovered she must either separate from me, or I must take precautions that she do not again demean me or herself. By "demean" I mean "degrade".'

Blanche's first reaction was to complain to Dr Shapter 'in the strongest possible terms'. A clerk to Lyon's lawyer travelled to Torquay to deliver the deed and a copy. Mr James entered on the scene suggesting that unless she agreed to the separation Mr Lyon 'would not allow her anything'. Additionally there was an implied threat that unless she complied she would be kept under asylum. Given her lifetime of experience, it seems odd, if not rather reckless, but perhaps in character, that Charlotte and Blanche did not involve a lawyer on her behalf. Instead they over-relied on medical advice. Dr Shapter thought Blanche was of mind sound enough to sign such a deed, making an entry in his medical journal to that effect on 18 or 25 September (though later in court he 'wished to retract the words'). He had been much impressed with a person 'of such an age' as Charlotte 'thoroughly understanding the deed, though she had also expressed her strong conviction against her "daughters" separations from their husbands'. Blanche later claimed that both she and her mother had thought the deed was for a temporary separation, and that under coercion and the threat of renewed incarceration, they were, in the end, obliged to sign. In Charlotte's apartments, on 30 September 1853, Blanche 'brought the inkstand from a side table' and with her mother attesting, signed the deed which allowed her ten monthly payments of £130, and pin money of £300 payable in the other two months of January and July. Her husband's solicitor told her 'she would be in the position of a widow ... but could not marry again and would be answerable for her own debts like an unmarried lady'.

The very next day, Saturday 1 October, Charlotte and Blanche left Torquay and in less than a fortnight, Blanche 'took a house at 9 South Audley Street. My mother lived with me.' After this they went to Paris for the winter of 1854, remaining there for four months, apparently hoping to see Lyon. Portraits, prints, books and other of Charlotte's possessions must have been arranged in the various homes which her remaining four daughters (Adelaide, Emma, Julia and Blanche) helped to organise for her. She no longer had any siblings, many of her friends had passed away, as had many of her children, so fewer letters existed or have survived to provide news of her whereabouts and activities. The last letter in her hand and the last occasion on which she may have been abroad, in her eightieth year, may have been that written in November 1854 from 23 Rue Royale in Paris to her first grandson, Pen, on the death of his father, her beloved son-in-law, Sir William Gordon-Cumming.[8] One wonders if perchance she ventured to Avranches to see her son Walter and his wife. Why she was in Paris in 1854 was suddenly explained in a rather unexpected source, a 10,000 word law report about the Mallalue v. Lyon case which appeared in *The Times* in London in February 1859.[9] On return, another house was taken at 5 Audley Square, but Charlotte and Blanche subsequently moved once more to apartments above a tailor's at 81 South Audley Street. Alimony payments were paid regularly through the bankers, Farquhar and

Co., until 10 April 1858. Both mother and daughter probably continued to live beyond their means. Blanche went to Sir James Clark and Dr Bird 'and they gave me certificates that I was sound in body and sane in mind, and had been so for the last five years'. This was the precursor to her bizarrely instituting a suit in the Divorce Court for the restitution of conjugal rights. A decree to that effect was pronounced on 19 May 1853, and an even more bizarre sequence of events ensued, as revealed by various witnesses, including David Lyon's housekeeper and other domestic staff.

Lyon had taken a furnished house at 46 Gloucester Place off Baker Street for one month from 1 May. In accordance with the decree for restitution of conjugal rights, he arranged for Blanche to meet him there at 2 o'clock on Wednesday 26 May. As Blanche described it, the start was inauspicious. He 'opened the door very violently ... was very rude and pushed my little dog off the steps ... pushed me into the house, shut the door, locked it, chained it', and her maid was not allowed to enter. She found the housekeeper and six other women in the drawing room assembled to hear the strange arrangements David Lyon was about to read to them.

Blanche went back, accompanied, to her mother's to pick up some items, and that night and for the next days, returned to Gloucester Place each evening, had coffee in her room in the morning and then left. For his part, David Lyon also returned to his room between 10 and 11 in the evening (for legal reasons, to make out that this was his home) and left before breakfasting next morning in his old home at South Street where his friend Mr James was staying in the short term with his own staff. Her family friend, Robert Hook, had been anxious on her behalf when he heard of her staying at Gloucester Place and promised to call on her the first morning. But on doing so he found that she had already left, leaving a note saying she was going to the home of a friend. He overtook her in Portman Square, accompanied by 'a tall woman, who owned to me that she had been a keeper in a madhouse in the country'. They managed to dissuade her from accompanying them further, but Hook was still anxious. The two nurses themselves thought their attendance was unnecessary and they soon left No 46. Understandably, Blanche also left No 46 on 1 June, never to return. She heard that Lyon had then taken a house at 57 Gloucester Place, and finally, another, at 1 York Place near Regent's Park.

While David Lyon averred that she was free to live in any of these homes, the judge questioned not only whether Lyon had any *bona fide* intention of resuming his marriage, but also whether Blanche 'could with safety or propriety remain in any house, without the apprehension of personal restraint'. This absentee defendant to whom the judges remarks were aimed was David Lyon, Sheriff of Sussex, then aged 58. Towards the end of the court case in February 1859, Blanche had described her mother by then as 'childish from great age'. Perhaps it was as well Charlotte may have understood little of the court revelations and proceedings. While the unpaid goods that had been involved in the court case had been delivered for Blanche at her mother's house in South Audley Street and Blanche was still living there in July 1858, Charlotte's final home was at 91 Sloane Street. In February 1859 Blanche told the court that she could 'no longer live with my mother, because I can no longer afford to meet her expenses, which I have done for the last eleven years'. Whether this was because she was receiving no further funds from her husband or not, David Lyon was ordered to pay part of the cost of the claimant's goods ordered by Blanche. Strangely, Blanche disappears from the record of her mother's life at this point.

In the 1850s, Charlotte's likeness was still being captured several times. Her granddaughter, the traveller and writer, Constance Frederica Gordon-Cumming, 'Eka', tantalised posterity by writing of her grandmother in old age always keeping 'a lovely portrait of herself standing on an easle [*sic*] beside her, of which the dear old lady used complacently to say "It is the only picture that ever did me justice"'. She went on: 'It was just head and shoulders, with the strikingly picturesque fluffy lace and satin cap which so well became her. I think it was by Swinton, and that it was in crayon.'[10] Eka then reported: 'Shortly before her death it disappeared and none of the family have ever been able to trace it. It is thought possible that her daughter by Mr Bury Blanche Lyon may have disposed of it.' To the last, Charlotte was never forgiven for her Bury marriage. Scottish James Rannie Swinton had portrayed almost 'every reigning beauty' in his time 'in crayon drawings the size of life with singular grace'.[11] His obituarist noted: 'Nor were his female sitters all youthful or all still beautiful ... that of Lady Charlotte Bury, daughter of a Gunning, the faded lineaments of the most beautiful woman of her day' (see plate 30). Though effected in 1855, it was not exhibited at the Royal Academy until 1872 when *The Times* described it as 'a graceful picture of one of the most beautiful old ladies of her time, who transmitted to our generation the hereditary charm of the Gunnings'.[12] Eka jotted down for posterity that, even in old age, Charlotte was 'stately and fair to see, notwithstanding the lamentably free use of red and white paint'.[13]

Buckner's last picture, now seemingly mislaid, closely resembles Catherine Read's painting of her mother in a similar dormeuse. According to her great-grand nephew, the 9th Duke of Argyll, Charlotte's last home was a 'very small house [that] had to be taken for her'.[14] He recalled visiting her in his youth: 'She just managed to have room enough, among her Italian books and Maltese dogs, to give a little tea-party now and then ... you looked at her and thought her like a pretty piece of Dresden china. There she sat, with a high cap on her head.' He compared the 'delicate nose, her blue eyes, the regular little mouth', while noting that the wonderful carmine bloom on the cheeks [still visible], was alas! Not that of youth.' The duke continued:

> Here was the beauty for whom Walter Scott had laboured to write out in his best handwriting his finest ballads. Here was the loveliness that Hoppner so adored ... But alas! Voice and memory were changed, and only her art books, which she still loved to handle, told of her old tastes, and may have made her feel again in Italy, buying prints or rare bindings in Florence or Rome.[15]

Charlotte died, aged 86, at her home 91 Sloane Street on the night of March 31 and 1 April 1861.[16] The obituary in the *Annual Register* in 1861 claimed that in her youth Charlotte was 'remarkable for her personal beauty, and throughout her life for the charm of her manners'.[17] The obituarist however was not only dismissive of her writings but also observed 'she had long retired from the world', and was as much forgotten as her books. The writer of the *DNB* went further by claiming she had died alone. Julia had died on 8 September 1858 and was buried in the same grave as Anne MacLeod, the faithful family servant of sixty years who had died just three weeks before on 15 August at the age of 77, and for whom the grave in Brompton Cemetery had been organised by the Lennoxes. In one of London's finest cemeteries, it was in the same grave that Charlotte herself was then placed, today commemorated with a newer headstone erected in 1937 beside that of Lord Arthur Lennox.

Of her eleven or twelve children, all sources report that only Adelaide (56) and Emma (55) survived her. To Adelaide and Emma fell the task of settling their mother's affairs—which took a further four and a half years—and her debts, which should not perhaps come as such a surprise. Emma wrote to her nephew, Penrose Gordon-Cumming, saying she wished him to have 'an inkstand which belonged to my dearest Mother. I think you will value it for that reason, and it is one which will look well on a man's table.'[18] She also wanted to send him some pieces of music which had been given to his mother, Eliza, by Princess Charlotte, and hoped that his daughter, Isa, would 'like to try her grandmother's music'. It seems somewhat fitting that in the same letter she had to respond to his request for a picture 'that had been Mamma's' with the explanation: 'Alas we are compelled to sell the few that remain for one must endeavour to pay her debts and as yet have not the prospect of paying more than half.' Before sending eight or nine pictures for sale, she offered Penrose one of Lord Frederick Campbell, his great-grand uncle (as well as others) for £10 each. Colnaghi had valued the pictures and several were still unsold. Adelaide would be glad, two years on, to get even £10 towards her mother's debts. 'The little head by Buckner, with a red cap, Penrose was given for 5 guineas.' By September 1863 he had sent £15 for Lord Frederick's portrait, which sum Adelaide was going to use to pay one of her mother's tradesmen 'who are continually worrying me'. In 1865, when she herself was giving up her house, Adelaide offered Penrose a bust of George, 6th Duke of Argyll, his grand uncle, for £35.

Perhaps the need to raise money was also the reason behind the posthumous appearance of one of the novels Charlotte had mentioned giving to Colburn over thirty years before. In 1839 Charlotte had written that *The Two Baronets* was one of three of her works with Colburn. But is was not until after her death that this last tale appeared in 1864 in London and New York, in Routledge's Railway Library Series. It had been 'found in an unfinished state' among her papers and edited by the publishers (who had re-published her *Roses* a few years before). They characterised her oeuvre as that of

> a prolific writer dealing with the faults and foibles of the fashionable world in which she lived, and that not leniently ... very low estimate at which she treated the morals of her own class ... she had a sagacious insight into motives ... whimsical mixture of morality and scandal characterises most of her fictions.

With its subtitle, *A Novel of Fashionable Life,* the word 'ton' appears already in the first chapter. The 'yellow-back' was the sobriquet given to the cheap two shilling editions displayed for sale in railway bookstalls—Charlotte might even have liked that. With a picture on the front, decorative titling on the spine, coloured advertisements on the back cover and good clear text within, they included good-value reissues of novels by some of Charlotte's contemporaries such as the Countess of Blessington.

Adelaide, returning 'from the Rhine' in October 1862 had visited Mlle de la Chaux, then '93 and in full possession of all her faculties except her sight'.[19] She was to die at Yverdon on 20 April 1864 within six weeks of her ninety-fifth birthday. Emma was 81 when she died on 14 January 1886, her husband, William, having predeceased her on 5 September 1884. Adelaide, a widow from 1864, died aged 84 on 14 August 1888 and was buried at Swallowfield in Berkshire, the home of her daughter, Lady Constance Charlotte Elisa Russell, the author of *Three Generations of Fascinating Women* and *Swallowfield and its Owners*. But although in Lady Charlotte's extended Campbell family and in all other accounts, there is never any mention of her youngest daughter, ten years after her mother's death an entry in the Census of England and Wales on 2 April 1871 reveals that Blanche Augusta Lyon 'of independent means' was visiting Bury St Edmunds; and she was still designated 'married'.[20] Almost five years later, on 21 March 1876, Blanche was described as the widow of 'David Lyon Gentleman', having herself died aged 55 at 14 St Marys Road in Upper Westbourne Park.[21] It was just over a century since her beautiful mother had erupted into such a very different world.

Lady Charlotte had craved a life far beyond the limited confines and conditioning of her time, place and context, although her identity as a ducal daughter of the House of Argyll never wavered. Charlotte had grown up in impressive surroundings in Scotland and the south but she also travelled and encountered many different people and absorbed different cultures. She became widely, if somewhat earnestly, read, well-informed and an astute observer of character. Despite inherent passions and ambivalences, greater freedom, even rebellion (as in her marriages) and questioning of stereotypes, became her holy grail, evident in her eyes and mouth in the Opie portrait of 1784. John Opie's Charlotte became beautiful, was healthy despite frequently repeated child-bearing, and she developed wider circles of artistic, literary and society friends and acquaintances than might perhaps have been her trajectory as an aristocratic bride. While she may not have been fulfilled in longlasting happy marriages, she not only bequeathed her beauty in portraits and descendants' genes, but writing for money was a bold, if ambivalent choice for a ducal daughter, and satisfied her aspirations to leave the printed word for posterity. It is time for the latter to re-evaluate her role as a major novelist in a minor genre and not to remember her solely as a notorious diarist. As the Argyll motto, *Ne Obliviscaris*, urges, 'Forget Not'.

Charlotte Bury's Œuvre

Novels

Self-Indulgence. A Tale of the Nineteenth Century, 2 vols, 12° (Edinburgh: T. Allan, 1812)
Conduct is Fate, 3 vols, 12° (Edinburgh: William Blackwood, 1822)
Alla Giornata: or To the Day, 3 vols, 12° (London: Saunders and Otley, 1826)
Flirtation, 3 vols, 12° (London: Henry Colburn, 1828)
The Separation: A Novel, 3 vols 12° (London: Henry Colburn and Richard Bentley, 1830)
The Exclusives, 3 vols, 12° (London: Henry Colburn and Richard Bentley, 1830)
The Disinherited and The Ensnared, 3 vols, 12° (London: Richard Bentley, 1834)
The Devoted, 3 vols, 12° (London: Richard Bentley, 1834)
Love, 3 vols, 8° (London: Henry Colburn, 1837)
The Divorced, 2 vols, 12° (London: Henry Colburn, 1837)
Ellen Glanville/The Glanville Family, 3 vols, 8° (London: Henry Colburn; Philadelphia, E. L. Carey and A. Hart, 1838)
The History of a Flirt; Related by Herself, 2 vols, 8° (London: Henry Colburn, 1840)
Family Records; or the Two Sisters, 2 vols, 12° (London: Saunders and Otley; Philadelphia: Lea and Blanchard, 1841)
The Manoeuvring Mother, 3 vols, 8° (London: Henry Colburn, 1842)
The Wilfulness of Woman, 3 vols, 8° (London: Henry Colburn, 1844)
The Roses; A Novel, 3 vols, 12° (London: Hurst and Blackett, 1853)
The Lady of Fashion, 3 vols, 8° (London: Hurst and Blackett, 1856)
The Two Baronets; A Novel of Fashionable Life, 1 vol, 8° (London; New York: Routledge, Warne, & Routledge, 1864)

Edited Novels

Scott, Lady Lucy Caroline, *A Marriage in High Life*, 2 vols, 12° (London: Henry Colburn, 1828)
Gore, Catherine Grace Frances, *Memoirs of a Peeress; or the days of Fox*, 3 vols, 12° (London: Henry Colburn, 1837)

Poems

Poems on Several Occasions. By a Lady., 1 vol, 12° (Edinburgh, 1797)

'Stanzas Written at Sydenham' in *Journal of the Heart*, 1 vol, 12° (London: James Cochrane and Co., 1835)
'On the Cascade of Chede' in Marguerite, Countess of Blessington, *Heath's Book of Beauty* (London: Longman, Brown, Green, and Longmans, 1837)
Suspirium Sanctorum, 1 vol (London: Saunders and Otley, 1826)
Suspirium Sanctorum, 2 vols (London: Saunders and Otley, 1830)
The Three Great Sanctuaries of Tuscany, Valombrosa, Camaldoli, Laverna: A Poem, with Historical and Legendary Notices, 1 vol, folio (London: John Murray, 1833)

Miscellaneous

Journal of the Heart, 1 vol, 12° (London: Henry Colburn and Richard Bentley, 1830)
Journal of the Heart, 1 vol, 12° (London: James Cochrane and Co., 1835)
The Lady's Own Cookery Book, 1 vol (London: Henry Colburn, 1835)
Diary illustrative of the Times of George IV, 2 vols (London: Henry Colburn, 1838)
Diary illustrative of the Times of George IV, 4 vols (London: Henry Colburn, 1839)
The Murdered Queen! Or Caroline of Brunswick, 1 vol, 8° (London: W. Emans, 1838)
The Court of England under George IV, 2 vols (London: John MacQueen, 1896)
Diary of a Lady-in-Waiting, ed. A F Steuart, 2 vols (London: John Lane, The Bodley Head, 1908)

Endnotes

PROLOGUE

1 *The Times* (8 January 2005).
2 Lady Sydney Morgan, *Memoirs*, 2 vols (London: W. H. Allen, 1862), vol. 2, p. 431.
3 Anon, *Diary illustrative of the times of George the Fourth, interspersed with original letters from the late Queen Caroline, and from various other distinguished persons*, 2 vols (London: Henry Colburn, 1838). Hereafter referred to as Bury, *Diary* (1838).
4 *The Athenæum* (6 January 1838).
5 *The Times* (11 January 1838).
6 P. W. Wilson, *The Greville Diary*, 2 vols (London: W. Heinemann, 1927), vol. 1, p. 7.
7 *The Quarterly Review* (1838), pp. 150-164.
8 J. Greig, *The Farington Diary*, 8 vols (London: Hutchinson, 1922-8), 1, note p. 141.
9 M. Rosa, *The Silver Fork School* (New York: Columbia University Press, 1936), p. 154.
10 *The Idler, and Breakfast-Table Companion* (20 January 1838), p. 18.
11 *The Morning Post*, 18 April 1838.
12 *The Times*, 26 February 1930, Letter of 19 February 1930 from William T. Whitley.
13 T. Wright, *Historical and Descriptive Account of the Caricatures of James Gillray* (London: H. G. Bohn, 1851), p. 419.
14 L. Melville, *Regency Ladies* (London: Hutchinson, 1926), p. 120.
15 Hereafter referred to as Lady Charlotte 1789 Journal. (NLS Acc. 8110), Lady Charlotte Memoir (also NLS Acc. 8110) and Lady Charlotte Huntington Journal (The Huntington Library, San Marino, California).
16 L. Melville, *Regency Ladies*, p. 115.
17 Sir Herbert Maxwell (ed.), *The Creevey Papers. A Selection from the Correspondence & Diaries of the late Thomas Creevey, M.P.*, 2 vols (John Murray, London, 1903), vol. 2, p. 333.
18 Quoted in *The Times,* 3 March 1930. Thomas Hood, *Hood's Own: or Laughter from Year to Year* (London: Bailey & Co., 1839), p. 240.
19 Bodleian Library, Pigott Mss., d.16, f. 12, Lady Charlotte Bury to Harriet Pigott, 24 July 1838.
20 NLS, Dep. 175, 164, 1, Lady Charlotte Bury to Lady Gordon-Cumming, 4 March 1838.

21 Plymouth and West Devon Record Office, Parker of Saltram Correspondence, 1259/3/8, Theresa Villiers to Frances Countess of Morley, 17 April 1838.
22 Bury, *Diary* (1908), vol. 1, p. 33.
23 *The Corsair* (1839), p. 345.
24 University of Oxford, Bodleian Library, Pigott Mss., d.16, f. 18, Lady Charlotte Bury to Harriet Pigott, 15 June 1839.
25 A. Grant, *Susan Ferrier of Edinburgh* (Denver: A. Swallow, 1957), pp. 159-60.
26 P. H. Fitzgerald, *The Life and Times of William IV*, 2 vols (London, 1884), vol. 2, pp. 214-22.
27 The Bury of her second marriage was pronounced as in 'berry', according to the 1828 reviewer of one of her novels; confusingly, the family name of the Charlevilles in Ireland into which one of her daughters married, was also Bury, but pronounced as in 'fury'.

Chapter 1: Aristocratic Mobility

1 British Museum, Crace portfolio XXIX. 32 (leaf 13).
2 *The Times*, 2 February 1802, advertisement of freehold sale of Argyll House.
3 Royal Academy of Arts, *Catalogue* of the Reynolds exhibition (1986).
4 *The Times* 27 April 1775; Birth of a daughter to Lady Campbell; born 28 January; baptised 18 February; *Complete Peerage; Scots Peerage; Scots Magazine.*
5 Born 1732, married George, 6th Earl of Coventry, died 1 October 1760; Francis Cotes, National Gallery of Ireland.
6 W. Wassyng Roworth (ed.), *Angelica Kauffman, A Continental Artist in Georgian England* (London: Reaktion Books, 1992), p. 110. A. Goodden, *Miss Angel: The Art and World of Angelica Kauffman* (London: Pimlico, 2005).
7 Later, Anne Seymour Damer (1749-1828), sculptress.
8 M. Archer, *India and British Portraiture 1770-1825* (Oxford: Oxford University Press, 1979) p. 118. Lady Victoria Manners, 'Catherine Read: the English "Rosalba"', *The Connoisseur* (New York, 1931), pp. 376-86; (1932), pp. 35-40 and pp. 171-8. Read had been born into a wealthy and ultra-Jacobite family at Dundee, lived in France and Italy after 1745 and, on return in 1754, set up in St James's in London working chiefly as a portrait painter. Between 1760 and 1772 she exhibited 32 portraits at the Society of Artists and four at the Royal Academy between 1773 and 1776. Her pastel work was especially acclaimed, and a crayon portrait of the duchess had been delivered with difficulty to Inveraray in 1771. Although seemingly a difficult character, she became extremely fashionable in aristocratic circles during the sixties, painting Queen Caroline and her sons, being especially popular for her portraits of ladies and children. She sailed for India in February 1777 and died on voyage to Cape of Good Hope on 15 December 1778.
9 It has sometimes been thought of as being of her elder sister, Lady Augusta.
10 I. Gantz, *The Pastel Portrait. The Gunnings of Castle Coote and Howards of Hampstead* (London: Cresset Press, 1963), p. 71.
11 Royal Academy of Arts, *British Portraits* Winter Exhibition, (London, 1956-7), no. 358.
12 J. J. Rogers, '*Opie and his Works: being a Catalogue of 760 Pictures by John Opie, R.A., preceded by a Biographical Sketch* (London: P. and D. Colnaghi and co., 1878); A. Earland, *John Opie and his Circle* (London: Hutchinson & Co., 1911), pp. 267-8. Reynolds was much impressed, likening Opie to 'Caravaggio, but finer'. While Opie enjoyed a remarkable reputation in his lifetime, his own (and his second wife's) 'high estimation of his achievement' did not last, although his portraits of children have continued to be well thought of.
13 Later suggested, amongst others, as the 'Lord Nevil' of Madame de Stael's 'Corinne' (*Corinne ou l'Italie*, 1807).

14 H. Bleackley, *The Story of a Beautiful Duchess: being an Account of the Life and Times of Elizabeth Gunning, Duchess of Hamilton and Argyll* (London: A. Constable & co., 1907), p. 295.
15 Rosneath on the Gareloch peninsula on the Clyde belonged to the 5th Duke of Argyll; Ardencaple on the opposite bank of the Clyde at Rhu was owned by his brother, Lord Frederick Campbell, who subsequently bequeathed it to the duke's younger son, Lord John Campbell. It was then pronounced as 'Aryngapple'.
16 Argyll, J. D. S. Campbell, *Intimate Society Letters of the Eighteenth Century*, 2 vols (London: S. Paul & Co., 1910), vol. 1, p. 212.
17 NLS, Acc. 8110, Lady Charlotte Campbell, Memoir [hereafter referred to as Lady Charlotte Memoir]. Begun 'Thursday the 21st Nov 1799' at Woodhall (the Campbell of Shawfield house near Bothwell in Lanarkshire) and not finished till Thursday the 8th July 1800 at Woodburn (near Dalkeith), ff. 20v-21v.
18 Bleackley, *op. cit.*, p. 291.
19 *Ibid.*, p. 292.
20 Youngest daughter of John, 3rd Earl of Bute.
21 Lady Louisa Stuart, *Gleanings from an old portfolio*, (ed.) Mrs G. Clarke, 3 vols (Edinburgh: privately printed for David Douglas, 1895-8), vol. 2, p. 281.
22 Bleackley, *op. cit.*, p. 293.
23 Lady Charlotte Memoir, f. 19v.
24 J. Cradock, *The Literary and Miscellaneous Memoirs*, 4 vols (London: J. B. Nichols, 1826-8), vol. 2, pp. 155-6.
25 Bleackley, *op. cit.*, p. 296.
26 Cradock, *op. cit.*, 1, 252.
27 Lady Constance Russell, *Three Generations of Fascinating Women* (London, New York, 1905), p. 184.
28 Cradock, *op. cit.*, vol. 2, p. 184.
29 Bleackley, *op. cit.*, p. 296.
30 D. Lysons, *Environs of London*, 5 vols (London, 1795-1800), vol. 2, (1795), p. 228.
31 A. E. Jackson, *Annals of Ealing* (London: Phillimore & Co., 1898), p. 214.
32 H. Baring (ed.), *Diary of the Rt. Hon. William Windham 1784-1810* (London: Longmans, Green, and co., 1866), p. 61; BL, Hardwicke Mss. 35535, f. 170.
33 Bleackley, *op. cit.*, pp. 290-1.
34 F. McK. Bladon (ed.), *The Diaries of Col. The Hon. Robert Fulke Greville* (London: John Lane, 1930), p. 25.
35 *Ibid.*, p. 28.
36 H. B. Wheatley (ed.), 'Reminiscences of Royal and Noble Personages', in *The Historical and Posthumous Memoirs of Sir Nathaniel William Wraxall,* 5 vols (London: Bickers & son, 1884), vol. 5, pp. 369-70.
37 The Nisbets of Dirleton: Mary Nisbet would become Lady Charlotte's new mother-in-law, as the second wife of Walter Campbell of Shawfield and Islay.
38 Lady Charlotte Memoir, f. 23v.
39 C. Barrett (ed.), *The Diaries and Letters of Madame D'Arblay (1778-1840)*, 6 vols (London: Macmillan, 1905), vol. 3, p. 405.
40 Countess Castalia Granville (ed.), *The Private Correspondence of Granville Leveson-Gower First Earl Granville*, 2 vols (London: J. Murray, 1916), vol. 1, p. 22.
41 Lady Charlotte Memoir, f. 35r.
42 Lady Charlotte Memoir, ff. 11r to 18r; P. Toynbee (ed.), *The Letters of Horace Walpole*, 4 vols (Oxford: Clarendon Press, 1905), vol. 1, p. 76.
43 Lady Elizabeth Hamilton had been born to the Duchess of Hamilton on 26 January 1753 and died on 1 April 1797.

44 Lady Charlotte Memoir, ff.11r to 18r.
45 Mrs Campbell was to become Lady Charlotte's mother-in-law.
46 This daughter became Lady Charlotte's daughter-in-law.
47 V. di Sermoneta, *The Locks of Norbury* (London: J. Murray, 1940), p. 105. Less than seven weeks after Lady Betty's death, Lord Derby married the actress, Elizabeth Farren. In 1795, Lady Betty's daughter had married Stephen Thomas Cole, a brewer in Twickenham.
48 Lady Charlotte Memoir, ff. 37v to 39r.
49 *Ibid.*, ff. 27v and 28r.
50 Lady C. Granville, *The Private Correspondence of Lord Granville Leveson-Gower*, 1.
51 Lady Charlotte Memoir, f. 28r.
52 *Letter from Mrs Gunning: addressed to His Grace the Duke of Argyll.* Printed for the author: and sold by Mr. Ridgway and Mr. Beyter (1791).
53 *The Seige of Blenhem or the new system of gunning, discovered* (5 March 1791); *Margaret's Ghost* (25 March 1791) and *Betty Canning revived* (25 March 1791). See also P. Perkins, 'Gunning, Susannah (1739/40-1800)', *ODNB*.
54 Betsey married Major James Plunkett from Kinnaird in Roscommon in 1804; she died on 20 July 1823. See I. Grundy, 'Gunning, Elizabeth (1769-1823)', *DNB* (Oxford, 2004).
55 Lady Charlotte Memoir, ff. 34v-35r.
56 Bleackley, *op. cit.*, pp. 290-1.
57 *The Public Advertiser*, 5 June 1789; Lady Theresa Lewis (ed.), *Extracts of the Journals and Correspondence of Miss [Mary] Berry from 1783 to* 1852, 3 vols (London: L. Green & Co., 1865), vol. 1, p. 185.
58 Bleackley, *op. cit.*, p. 307.
59 Toynbee,*The Letters of Horace Walpole*, p. 182.
60 Lady Charlotte Memoir, f. 35r. George Clavering was reported as 'dying' in April 1806.

Chapter 2: Neapolitan Adventure

1 *The Edinburgh Advertiser,* 11 September 1789.
2 NLS, Acc. 8110, Lady Charlotte Campbell, 'Journal ... begun Saturday the 12th September 1789' [hereafter Lady Charlotte 1789 Journal].
3 Russell, *Three Generations of Fascinating Women,* p. 184.
4 When spending the winter of 1790-91 in Naples, Lord Minto denounced 'the thick fog and rain ... the climate [is] detestable ... What Rain!' Countess of Minto (ed.), *The Life and Letters of Sir Gilbert Elliot, First Earl of Minto*, 3 vols (London: Longmans, Green & Co.,1874), vol. 1, p. 398.
5 Coombe Park, Sundridge, Kent.
6 R. Brookes, *The General Gazetteer: or Compendious Geographical Dictionary*, 6th edition (London, 1786), in which the phrase 'celebrated university' appears.
7 Daughter of Lord William Campbell (brother of the 5th Duke of Argyll) and subsequently to become the wife of Sir Alexander Johnston, Chief Justice of Ceylon, and later of Carnsalloch, Dumfriesshire.
8 F. Fraser, *Beloved Emma. The Life of Emma, Lady Hamilton* (New York: Anchor Books, 2004), p. 76 et seq. See also S. Sontag, *The Volcano Lover. A Romance* (London: Macmillan, 1992).
9 The Royal Society of London, Log books 1779-1794, 8 vols; Geoffrey V. Morson, 'Hamilton, Sir William (1731-1803), *ODNB*. See also various *Transactions of the Royal Society of London for illustrations of vases.*
10 Fraser, *Beloved Emma.*, p. 141 et seq.
11 Toynbee, *The Letters of Horace Walpole.*

12 Russell, *Three Generations of Fascinating Women*, p. 184.
13 Scottish National Portrait Gallery, *Great Scots* (Edinburgh, n.d.), p. 40. Also caption to hung picture.
14 Royal Academy of Arts, *Catalogue of Italian Art and Britain*: catalogue, 1960, p. 90, no. 225; Wilhelm Tischbein *Aus meinem Leben* (1922), pp. 248 et seq.
15 S. Lloyd, *Raeburn's Rival: Archibald Skirving 1745-1819* (Edinburgh: Scottish National Portrait Gallery, 1999), p. 67.
16 Russell, *Three Generations of Fascinating Women*, pp. 184-5.
17 The home of her brother, George, by then 6th Duke of Argyll.
18 Bleackley, *op. cit.*, p. 311.
19 Toynbee, *Letters of Horace Walpole*, vol. 14, p. 277; Campbell, *Intimate Society Letters of the Eighteenth Century*, vol. 1, p. 125.
20 Bleackley, *op. cit.*, p. 312.
21 Lady Mary Coke, *Letters and Journal*, 4 vols, (Edinburgh: David Douglas, 1889-96), 20 November 1790. J. A. Home (ed.), *The Letters and Journals of Lady Mary Coke* (Bath, 1970).
22 Bleackley, *op. cit.*, p. 315.
23 *Scots Peerage; Scots Magazine*; Toynbee, *Letters of Horace Walpole* Index; Marylebone OPR.
24 Lady Mary Coke, *op. cit.*, 29 December 1790; *cf.* Toynbee, *Letters of Horace Walpole*, 15, 17. The duke shortly after this gave up Ealing Grove (Lysons, *op. cit.*, 2, 228).
25 *The Edinburgh Evening Courant*, 6 January 1791.
26 F. A. Walker, *The Buildings of Scotland. Argyll and Bute* (London: Penguin, 2000). Until the late-eighteenth century the Argyll Campbells were buried in a small vault attached to the north-east end of the choir of the medieval church at Kilmun. In 1794 this was demolished and a new mausoleum was built in 1795-6, subsequently remodelled and re-roofed between 1891and 1893. The entrance into the square building leads into a short north-south aisle running between arcaded platforms, within which are the coffins of the dukes and duchesses of Argyll, their names recorded on marble panels.
27 *The Caledonian Mercury*, 13 January 1791; *The Edinburgh Advertiser*, 14-18 January 1791; *The Glasgow Mercury* 11-18 January 1791.
28 Lady Charlotte Memoir, f. 19r.
29 Lady Charlotte Memoir, f. 18v.
30 For the Gunning family, see Bleakley, *op. cit.*, and I. Gantz, *op. cit.* The first decade of the 21st century saw the total renovation of Castle Coote on the river Suck.
31 Lady Charlotte Memoir, ff. 4v-5r.
32 A. Sisman, *Boswell's Presumptuous Task: Writing the Life of Dr Johnson* (London: Harper Perennial, 2006).

Chapter 3: Celebrated Beauty

1 I. G. Lindsay and M. Cosh, *Inverary and the Dukes of Argyll* (Edinburgh: Edinburgh University Press, 1973) p. 279.
2 Russell, *Three Generations of Fascinating Women*, p. 184.
3 L. Melville (ed.), *The Berry Papers: Being the Correspondence Hitherto Unpublished, of Mary and Agnes Berry 1763-1852* (London: John Lane, 1904/1914), p. 50.
4 *Ibid.*, p. 64.
5 Russell, *Three Generations of Fascinating Women*, p. 185.
6 C. L. Meryon, *The Memoirs of Lady Hester Stanhope as related by herself, in Conversations with her Physician, comprising her Opinions and Anecdotes of some of the Most remarkable persons of her Time*, 3 vols (London: Colburn, 1846), vol. 3, p. 68.
7 NLS exhibition catalogue, *Susan Ferrier 1782-1854* (Edinburgh, 1982).

8 G. C. Williamson, *John Russell RA* (London: George Bell & Sons, 1894).

9 H. Osborne, *Oxford Companion to Art* (Oxford: Oxford University Press, 1981). Russell developed a large clientele, being generally regarded as 'the first man of his time for "crayons"'. Regularly exhibiting at the Royal Academy from 1769 to 1806, he became an Associate in 1772, and was appointed Crayon Painter to the Prince of Wales 1785, and a Royal Academician in 1788. His pastel portraits have been deemed 'technically and aesthetically brilliant, easily surpassing those of his friend and mentor, Francis Cotes. They are usually on blue paper, his self-made pastel colours vivid, a striking *sfumato* [gradual transition] of colour or tone from light to dark, blending them by rubbing in gently with his finger'. Hundreds of portraits were produced, including those of many royals, but although he charged and earned much the same as Reynolds, he never became quite so fashionable.

10 Anna Tonelli, née Nistri, exhibited at the Royal Academy in 1794 and 1797.

11 M. Levey, *Sir Thomas Lawrence* (New Haven and London: Yale University Press, 2005).

12 T. Wright (ed.), *The Works of James Gillray* (London: Chatto and Windus, 1873), p. 196; *Modern Elegance—A Portrait*, published 22 May 1795 by H. Humphry, No. 37 New Bond St.; Russell, *Three Generations of Fascinating Women*, p. 186 note.

13 T. Wright, *Historical and Descriptive Account of the Caricatures of James Gillray* (London: Henry G. Bone, 1851), p. 418.

14 *Ibid*., p. 179.

15 V. di Sermoneta, *op. cit*., p. 105.

16 H. Bate Dudley Sir, *Passages selected by Distinguished Personages on the Great Literary Trial of Vortigern and Rowena; a Comi-Tragedy* (London Printed by H. Brown, for J. Ridgway, York-Street, St. James's-Square, [1796?]).

17 Lady C. Granville, *The Private Correspondence of Lord Granville Leveson-Gower*, vol. 1, p. 79.

18 *Ibid*., p. 22.

19 *Ibid*., p. 65.

20 W. E. and R. E. Auckland, *The Journal and Correspondence of William Lord Auckland*, 4 vols (London: R Bentley, 1861), 2, 511. Letter from Miss Chowne to Lady Auckland, 21 May 1793.

21 T. Wright, H*istorical and Descriptive Account of the caricatures of James Gillray* (1851), p. 219, Lady Termagant Tingleburn the lovely flagellation (303). *Ladies dress, as it soon will be* [No. 8896/ 8720] *20 January 1796*.

22 *The Morning Chronicle*, 26 February 1794.

23 D. M. George, *Catalogue of Political and Personal Satires*, 11 vols (1793-1800), (London: British Museum, 1942), 7, No. 8388. 1 May 1793, S W Fores No 3? Piccadilly.

24 F. Reynolds, 'How to Grow Rich'; R.Woodbridge, 'The Pad' (1793). 'Lady Charlotte Campbell last seen with cushion so placed as to appear with child'.

25 M. Beacock Fryer, *Elizabeth Postuma Simcoe (1762-1850): A Biography* (Toronto: Dundurn Press, 1989), p. 99.

26 *Too much and too little or summer cloathing for 1556 & 1796*, published by Fores on 8 February 1796, No. 8904.

27 *Savoyards of Fashion*, or *the Musical Mania*, 1799, No. 9459.

28 Royal Academy Exhibition 1796, No. 117; W. McKay and W. Roberts *John Hoppner* (1909) calls it 'Aurora'—p. 40. Article in *The Graphic* (20 Aug 1910). p. 290, [check title] 'The Quality in the Eighteenth Century'. In centre of article is—The Beautiful Lady Charlotte Campbell (1755-1861), as painted by Hoppner. John Hoppner was born of German Roman Catholic parents, perhaps at St James Palace, and spent his childhood

at court, becoming a chorister in the Chapel Royal (he may even have been a son of George III). His earliest portraits were of the gentry, followed by the nobility, and by the middle of the 1780s he was painting the youngest princesses of George III. After the Royal Academy schools, he began exhibiting at the academy in 1780 (and continued until 1809, apart from ill health in 1801 and 1808). By 1787 he was widely considered as successor to Reynolds and Gainsborough as a most respected portraitist, and became an Associate by 1792, and Academician in 1795. On Reynolds' death he was appointed portrait painter to the prince of Wales (Thomas Lawrence was the king's) and was patronised by all sectors of society (£2,000 was the price for a full length portrait in 1798, rising to £3,000 by 1801). He was considered handsome and a brilliant conversationalist, amusing and animating his sitters. Some thought he tried too hard to emulate other artists and never quite matured into a style of his own. Nevertheless, his portraits were frequently thought to be very good likenesses, even when the composition as a whole was less satisfactory. His style was less flamboyant than that of Lawrence, and while some deemed his male portraits best, those of beautiful young women were particularly esteemed for their sweetness and tenderness.

29 This portrait was sold from the collection of Captain T. A. Tatton MC of Cuervon Hall Preston. in 1928.

30 Greig, *op. cit.*, vol. 1, p. 141 and note.

31 *Ibid.*

32 *Ibid.*

33 A. Pasquin, *Critical Guide to the Exhibition of the Royal Academy* (London, 1796), pp. 10-41.

34 *The Times*, 5 May 1796.

35 A.W. Tuer, *A Select Series of Ten Portraits of Ladies of Rank and Fashion from paintings by John Hoppner engraved by C. Wilkin* (London, New York: Leadenhall Press, Scribner, 1883).

36 Burke, *La Belle Assemblée* of 1 June 1809; Richard and Hart; T. Wright (1830).

37 *The Times*, 30 January 1796.

38 National Records of Scotland, Scotland's People, Old Parish Register 534/1, Inveraray Marriages Register 1796. Ch. *Scots Peerage*, vol. 1, p. 387 and *Scots Magazine* (1796); Burke says 21 June. *Gentlemen's Magazine* 11 (1796), p. 611.

39 NLS, Dep. 175, 63, 2, Copy of Contract of Marriage between John Campbell Esq. and Lady Charlotte Campbell 15 June 1795; Inveraray, Argyll Papers, 3144, Copy of Bond of Provision his Grace the Duke of Argyll to Lady Charlotte Campbell his Daughter, 20 June 1796.

40 Russell, *Three Generations of Fascinating Women*, p. 187.

41 J. B. Aliquis and J. Pagan, *Glasgow Past and Present: Illustrated in Dean of Guild Court Reports and in the Reminiscences of Scorex, Aliquis, J.B., etc.* (Glasgow: D. Robertson, 1884), p. 482.

42 J. Foster, *Members of Parliament, Scotland* (London: Privately printed, Hazell, Watson & Viney, 1882), p. 60; R. G. Thorne, *History of Parliament*, 5 vols (1986), *The House of Commons 1790-1820.*

43 C. Campbell, *Vitruvius Britannicus*, 2 vols (London: printed and sold by the author, 1715-25), vol. 2.

44 K. Cruft, 'The Enigma of Woodhall House', *Architectural History* 27 (1984), p. 211.

45 M. MacCulloch, 'Parish of Bothwell', *The Statistical Account of Scotland*, 21 vols (1795), 16, 316. William Aiton had trained as a gardener on the estate before leaving for London, eventually becoming the superintendent of Kew and publishing three volumes of *Hortus Kewensis* (1789).

46 Russell, *Three Generations of Fascinating Women*, p. 178.

47 M. Storrie, *Islay. Biography of an Island*, (Islay: Oa Press, 2011), p. 76.
48 P. McGowan with M. Storrie, Islay House designed landscape management plan, (Islay Estate Company and Scottish Natural Heritage, Islay, 2001), p. 224. M. Storrie, 'Recovering the Historic Designed Landscape of Islay Estate', *Scottish Archives* (2001), pp. 59-77.
49 Russell, *Three Generations of Fascinating Women*, p. 186.
50 J. B. Aliquis and James Pagan, *op. cit.*, pp. 483-4.
51 P. Mackenzie, *Old Reminiscence of Glasgow and the West of Scotland*, 3 vols (Glasgow: John Tweed, 1865-6), vol. 1, p. 447.
52 Stuart, *Gleanings from an old Portfolio*, vol. 3, p. 86. Woodhall is described in 1802 as being 'at that time the residence of ... Colonel John Campbell of Shawfield' in Russell, *Three Generations of Fascinating Women*, p. 186.

Chapter 4: Salonnière

1 M. Rosa wrote off this volume with the comment 'it helps us to understand the basic tendency in Lady Charlotte's character towards an incurable sentimentality'. Rosa, *op. cit.*, p. 147.
2 P. Perkins has viewed it more sympathetically. P. Perkins, 'Scottish Women Poets of the Romantic Period', http://www.Alexanderstreet2.com.
3 Now in Cambridge University Library.
4 Inscribed in his hand 'Walter Scott from the Author' from 'R. H. Lady Charlotte Campbell—now Lady Charlotte Bury', the copy is in the Library at Abbotsford.
5 This volume is in the British Library.
6 P. Perkins, *op. cit.*
7 A. Allardyce (ed.), *Letters to and from Charles Kirkpatrick Sharpe*, 2 vols (Edinburgh: William Blackwood and Sons, 1888).
8 Argyll, G. D. Campbell, *Autobiography and Memoirs*, (ed.) Ina, Dowager Duchess of Argyll, 2 vols (London: John Murray, 1906), vol. 1, p. 30. Introduction to *The Two Baronets*—Glenfinlas, Eve of St John.
9 W. Scott, *Heart of Midlothian*, 4 vols (Edinburgh, 1818), vol. 4, ch. 11, p. 222; Greig, *op. cit.*, 5, note p. 141.
10 Verses addressed by Sir Walter Scott to Lady Charlotte Campbell, Castle Street, 1 November 1799. Argyll, J. D. S. Campbell, *Intimate Society Letters of the Eighteenth Century*, vol. 2, p. 653.
11 NLS, Acc. 11772, 'House of Aspen', *c.* 1800, not published till thirty years later as *The House of Aspen. A Tragedy* (1830).
12 *The Times*, 3 May 1859, auction included 'Songs by Sir Walter Scott sent to Lady Charlotte Campbell, January 16 1801 ... 2 gns'.
13 H. J. C. Grierson, *The Letters of Sir Walter Scott*, 12 vols (London: Constable: 1932-7), p. 129.
14 J. G. Lockhart, *Memoirs of Sir Walter Scott*, 5 vols (London, 1900), vol. 1, p. 296. Letter to Ellis, 2 March 1802.
15 Lockhart, *Narrative of the Life of Sir Walter Scott*, 10 vols (Edinburgh, 1902), vol. 1, p. 324.
16 The copy of *The Lady of the Lake* (1810) is now in New York Public Library. Bury, *Diary* (1908), vol. 1.
17 E. Grant, *Memoirs of a Highland Lady* (London: John Murray, 1898 and Edinburgh: Canongate, 1988), p. 2.
18 MacCunn, Florence A., *Sir Walter Scott's Friends* (London: William Blackwood, 1909), p. 116.
19 J. Russell (ed.), *Memoirs, Journals and Correspondence of Thomas Moore*, 8 vols (London: L. B. Green and Longman's, 1853-6), vol. 8, p. 49.

20 MacCunn, *op. cit.*, p. 116.
21 W. Scott, *Border Minstrelsy of the Scottish Minstrelsy*, 4 vols (Edinburgh, 1802) 3, 334.
22 'Significant Scots', the Scottish Studies Foundation, http://www. Electric Scotland.com.
23 V. Glendinning, *Raffles and the Golden Opportunity* (London: Profile Books, 2012).
24 Russell, *Three Generations of Fascinating Women*, note, p. 185.
25 Lockhart, *Narrative of the Life of Sir Walter Scott*, vol. 1, p. 88.
26 Russell, *Three Generations of Fascinating Women*, note, p. 185.
27 J. G. Lockhart, *Memoirs of the Life of Sir Walter Scott*, vol. 1, p. 255.
28 Russell, *Three Generations of Fascinating Women*, note, p. 185.
29 M. Harries (Mrs C. Baron-Wilson) (ed.), *The Life and Correspondence of M. Gregory Lewis, 1787-1818, with many pieces in prose and verse never before published*, 2 vols (London: H. Colburn, 1839), vol. 1, p. 186.
30 M. G. Lewis, *The Monk*, ed. Howard Anderson (London: Oxford University Press, 1981), pp. v and vi.
31 Simon Brett, 'Lewis, Matthew Gregory (1775-1818)', *Oxford Dictionary of National Biography* (Oxford: Oxford University Press, 2004).
32 M. G. Lewis, *Romantic Tales*, 4 vols (London: Longman, Hurst, Rees & Orme, 1799).
33 M. G. Lewis, *Poems* (London: Hatchard, 1812).
34 *Ibid.*, pp. 41-4.
35 C. Baron-Wilson, *op. cit.*, vol. 2, p. 302.
36 M. Lewis and H. Abrams, *Crazy Jane: written by G. M. Lewis Esq., in consequence of a lady having, in her walks, during her residence in Scotland, met with a poor mad woman, known by the above appellation, at whose appearance the Lady was much alarmed* (London: J. Davenport, 1800).
37 Bury, *Diary* (1838), vol. 2, p. 103.
38 C. Bury, *Conduct is Fate,* 3 vols (Edinburgh, 1822), 2, chapters 16 and 17.
39 I. G. Lindsay and M. Cosh, *op. cit.*, p. 296.
40 NLS, Acc. 12610. Peter Mark Roget 'Touring the Highlands with Uncle Samuel' (1795).
41 G. Peacock, *Life of Thomas Young MD FRS* (London: John Murray, 1855), p. 72.
42 Grant, *Susan Ferrier of Edinburgh*, pp. 26-9. The Mures of Caldwell, see *ODNB*.
43 Scotts Shipbuilders, *Two Hundred Years of Shipbuilding by the Scotts at Greenock* (Greenock: Scotts, 1906 and 1951), p. 63.
44 J. A. Home (ed.), *Letters of Lady Louisa Stuart to Miss Louisa Clinton*, 2 vols (Edinburgh: David Douglas, 1903), vol. 2, p. 221.
45 NLS, Acc.11538, Scottish Mountaineering Club deposit, item 97, ff. 4r-8r.
46 Bury, *Conduct is Fate*, vol. 15, p. 227.
47 Mabell, Countess of Airlie, *In Whig Society 1775—1818* (London: Holder & Stoughton, 1921) p. 64 et seq.
48 J. Hogg, *The Ettrick Shepherd's travels in the Scottish Highlands and Western Isles, 1802, 1803, and 1804*, (ed.) William F. Lughlan (Hawick: Byways, 1981).
49 D. Wordsworth, *Recollection of a Tour Made in Scotland AD 1803*, (ed.) J. C. Shairp, (Edinburgh: Edmonston and Douglas, 1874), pp. 127-9.
50 Ms. journal of Lachlan Macquarie, 28 and 29 August. Public Library of New South Wales, MS A70 online.
51 Marie-Charlotte de la Chaux—Tiranna or Mamie—the Swiss governess, H. C. B. Campbell, *A Journey to Florence in 1817*, (ed.) G. R. de Beer (London: Geoffrey Bles, 1951), p. 15.
52 J. Grierson, *Letters of Sir Walter Scott*, vol. 2, p. 16.
53 William Campbell was a lieutenant in the Royal Navy, and the son of the 5th Duke of Argyll's brother, Lord William Campbell, governor of New South Wales and South Carolina.

54 Lindsay and Cosh, *op. cit.*, p. 397.
55 Argyll and Bute Archives.
56 C. Baron-Wilson, *op. cit.*, vol. 1, pp. 197-9.
57 Lindsay and Cosh, *op. cit.*, p. 301.
58 Mabel, Countess of Airlie, *op. cit.*.
59 Walpole, quoted in Russell, *Three Generations of Fascinating Women*.
60 Lord John Russell, *Memoirs, Journals and Correspondence of Thomas Moore*, p. 3.
61 Lindsay and Cosh, *op. cit.*, p. 296 et seq. John Henry Manners (5th Duke of Rutland) *Journal of a Tour to the Northern Parts of Great Britain*, (London: privately printed, 1813) pp. 224 *et seq.*.
62 Russell, *Three Generations of Fascinating Women*, p. 184.
63 *Ibid.*
64 John Hamilton was 'the proprietor' of 'Lady Charlotte Campbell's Medley' and 'Lady Charlotte Campbell's Strathspey' in Niel Gow and Son's *Part Second of the Complete Repository of original Scots Tunes, Strathspeys Jigs and Dances* (1802); while 'Lady Charlotte Campbell's New Reel' was composed, selected and published by I. Copper at Banff and published in *A Collection of Strathspeys Reels and Jigs*. These have subsequently been published in various collections and tutors, arranged for harp, piano, fiddle, flute and as dance music. They have been recorded as 'the wonderful Strathspey of Lady Charlotte Campbell's New Strathspey', which transforms into 'Lady Charlotte Campbell's Reel, the notes cascading out like a fountain'. Alasdair Fraser, *Legacy of the Scottish Fiddle* (2001, CD).
65 Finch, *Marches* (1805).
66 J. Patterson, *The Contemporaries of Burns* (Edinburgh: Hugh Paton, 1840), p. 382. Charles Rogers, *Modern Scottish minstrel,* 2 vols (Edinburgh: A. & C. Black, 1855-8), vol. 2, p. 120.
67 R. Ford, *Harp of Perthshire* (Paisley: A. Gardner, 1893), pp. 406-7.
68 Stuart, *Gleanings from an old Portfolio*, pp. 124-32.
69 Lady Charlotte Memoir.
70 Lindsay and Cosh, *op. cit.*, p. 279.
71 Argyll, J. D. S. Campbell, *Intimate Society Letters*, vol. 2, p. 455.
72 *Ibid.*, vol. 2, p. 520.
73 *Ibid.*, pp. 454-5.

Chapter 5: Peregrinations

1 Lady Charlotte Huntington Journal.
2 *The Times*, 27 April 1797, 'Lady Charlotte Campbell ... of a daughter'.
3 NLS, Acc. 8110, Lady Charlotte Campbell, Memoir 'begun at Woodhall Thursday 21st Novr 1799 not finish'd till Tuesday 8th July 1800 at Woodhall'.
4 NLS, Ms. 6294, 7 December 1805 'seven children, Eliza, Walter Frederick, Eleanora, John George, Beaujolois, Adelaide, Emma'.
5 Stuart, *Gleanings from an old Portfolio*, vol. 3, p. 86.
6 H. C. B. Campbell, *A Journey to Florence*, p. 14. Cf. also M. Price, *The Perilous Crown. France between the Revolutions 1814-1848* (London: Pan Macmillan, 2007).
7 NLS, Dep. 175, 164, 3, Beaujolois Campbell to Lady Gordon-Cumming, 30 September 1820.
8 Dalkeith House is now a campus of the University of Wisconsin. Woodburn House was demolished in 1934 to make way for council housing.
9 LS, Dep. 175, 164, 1, Lady Charlotte Campbell to Miss Eliza Campbell, 27 March 1803.

10 Argyll, Duke of, J. D. S. Campbell, *Passages from the Past*, 2 vols (London: Hutchinson and Co., 1907), vol. 2, p. 468.
11 Nearby Newbattle Abbey also belonged to the Marquis of Lothian's family.
12 Argyll, J. D. S. Campbell, *Passages from the Past*, vol. 2, p. 453.
13 J. Greig, *op. cit.*, 1, n. on p. 141; NLS, Mss. 10102.a-b; J. Clubbe (ed.), *Two Reminiscences of Thomas Carlyle* (Durham, North Carolina: Duke University Press, 1974), p. 133, n. 14.
14 G. Cleghorn, *Remarks on Ancient and Modern Art: historical and critical* (Edinburgh: Blackwood, 1848), p. 204.
15 S. Lloyd, *op. cit.*, p. 67.
16 *Ibid.*
17 This portrait was exhibited in Edinburgh in 1863 along with that of Colonel John Campbell. Between 1979 and 1997 it was, however, cut down to its present size while Colonel John Campbell's profile portrait was reportedly destroyed in the early 1980s (*Ibid.*, pp. 25-6 and p. 67).
18 T. J. Pettigrew, *Memoirs of the Life of Vice Admiral Lord Viscount Nelson*, 2 vols (London: T. and W. Boone, 1849), vol. 1, p. xvii.
19 *The Annual Biographer and Obituarist* (1831) p. 272; obituary of Sir Thomas Lawrence, p. viii.
20 J. Russell (ed.), *Memoirs, Journals and Correspondence of Thomas Moore*, vol. 4, p. 1570.
21 A C. Albinson, P. Funnell and L. Peltz, *Thomas Lawrence. Regency Power and Brilliance* (New Haven and London: Yale University Press, 2011), pp. 37-9.
22 L. J. Jennings (ed.), *The Correspondence and Diaries of the late Rt. Hon. John Wilson Croker 1809-1830*, 3 vols (London: John Murray, 1885), vol. 1, p. 428.
23 A. Allardyce (ed.), *op. cit.*, vol. 2, p. 441.
24 J. Greig, *op. cit.*, vol. 2, pp. 93-95.
25 A. B. Jameson, *Memoirs of the Beauties of the Court of Charles II* (London: Henry Colburn, 1835), p. 50.
26 Half-length of The Rt. Hon. Lady Charlotte Bury, Drawn and Engraved by Richard J. Lane and Thomas Wright from a painting by Sir Thos. Lawrence, *La Belle Assemblée*, 66 (new series), June 1830.
27 'Born in Scotland', according to the Census of 1851.
28 NLS, Mss 6294, f. 17, Lord John Campbell to Anne Damer, 14 January 1806.
29 NLS, Mss 6294, ff. 19-21. Lady Charlotte Campbell to Anne Damer. Lord John subsequently told Anne Damer that her cast of Lady Charlotte was adorning his room in Holyroodhouse [or Queen Street] and 'everybody knows it directly who comes here to see me' (f. 24).
30 Joanna Baillie was born in 1762 in Bothwell parish manse; an elaborate memorial to her stands at the approach to the parish church.
31 Teignmouth, Baron, (John Shore), *Memoirs of the Life, Writings and Correspondence of Sir William Jones* (London: J. W. Parker, 1835).
32 NLS, Mss 6294, Lady Charlotte.
33 *Gentleman's Magazine* (1806) 1, 385. NLS Acc. 8168, 1. 215.
34 F. A.Walker, *op. cit.*.
35 See A. Campbell, *A History of Clan Campbell from the Restoration to the Present Day* (Edinburgh: Edinburgh University Press, 2004). See also James Fergusson, *Argyll in the Forty Five* (London: Faber & Faber, 1951).

Chapter 6: Accumulating Problems

1 A. Fremantle (ed.), *The Wynne Diaries*, 3 vols (Oxford: Oxford University Press, 1935-40), vol. 3. These were the journals of Elizabeth Wynne, daughter of

Richard Wynne of Swanbourne, who in 1797 married Admiral Thomas Fremantle (1765-1819), and her younger sisters, Eugenia and Harriet.

2 Jack Campbell of Shawfield's sister, Katherine, had married Charles Jenkinson; Theodore Hook was the brother of Lady Charlotte's friend, Anne; another of Jack's sisters, Glencairn was later to marry Mr Thomas Carter; Lady Elizabeth Cole was by now the married daughter of Lady Charlotte's half-sister, Lady Betty Derby.

3 Of the Wemyss family.

4 Fremantle, *op. cit.*, 3, 297, Tuesday 26 August 1806.

5 *Ibid.*

6 NLS, Mss. 3875, f. 238, Lady Charlotte Campbell to Walter Scott, 9 November 1806.

7 Now a hotel.

8 Russell, *Three Generations of Fascinating Women*, pp. 187-8.

9 Lady Charlotte Huntington Journal 33v and 34 r.

10 NLS, Mss. 3875, f. 238, Lady Charlotte Campbell to Walter Scott, 9 November 1806.

11 Grierson, *Letters of Sir Walter Scott*, p. 327.

12 Perth and Kinross Council Archives, MS 169/2/3/11, Thriepland Papers. Memorial by Sir Patrick Murray Thriepland of Fungask, 1849.

13 Jack Campbell entered parliament with the backing of his brother-in-law, the 6th Duke of Argyll but was in opposition to the Portland ministry, voting against it on four important divisions (Thorne).

14 Perth and Kinross Council Archives, Thriepland Papers, 169/2/3/(16v), (19 et seq.).

15 *Ibid.*, Ms. 169/2/3 (37).

16 *Ibid.*, Ms. 169/2/3(19).

17 *Ibid.*, Ms 169/2/3 (44-9).

18 *Ibid.*, Ms.169/2/3 (32).

19 *Ibid.*, Ms. 169/2/3 (20).

20 *Ibid.*, Ms. 169/2/3 (20-7).

21 *Ibid.*, Ms. 169/2/3 (27).

22 *Ibid.*, Ms. 169/2/3 (22-6).

23 A. Grant, *Susan Ferrier of Edinburgh*, p. 64.

24 Stuart, *Gleanings from an old portfolio*, 3. Lady Louisa Stuart to the Duchess of Buccleuch, 4 March 1809.

25 *The Times*, 31 March 1809, Major Campbell.

26 National Records of Scotland, Scotlands People, Old Parish Register.

27 Perth and Kinross Council Archives, Ms. 169/2/3(37). Sworn at Mansion House 6 March 1817.

28 *Ibid.*, 169/2/3 (50).

29 J. Grierson, *Letters of Sir Walter Scott*, vol. 2, pp. 232-3.

30 NLS Dep. 175, 164, 1, Lady Charlotte Campbell to Lady Gordon-Cumming, 10 February 1818.

31 A. Prucher *Figure Europee del Primo '1800 nel Diary di Lady Charlotte Campbell Bury con documentie inediti* (Florence: Leo S. Olschki, Editorie, 1961), p. 30.

32 Bury, *Devoted*, 3 vols (1836), vol. 2, p. 272.

33 A. Grant, *Susan Ferrier of Edinburgh*, p. 87.

34 NLS, Acc. 8585, Mf. MS 414 XI 8.

35 Lambeth Palace Library, MS 3273 f. 111.

36 NLS Dep. 175, 164-1 Lady Charlotte Campbell to Lady Eliza Gordon-Cumming. 5 February 1818.

37 Inveraray, Argyll Papers, goods and chattels.

38 Perth and Kinross Council Archives, Thriepland Papers, Ms.169/2/3 (16).

39 *Ibid.*

40 NLS 6294, f. 56, This was sometimes augmented voluntarily to £1,000.
41 I. G. Lindsay and M. Cosh, *op. cit.*
42 NLS, Mss. 6294, f. 56, Lady Charlotte's credit when she left England.
43 Bodleian Library, Harriet Pigott Mss., Lady Charlotte Bury to Harriet Pigott.
44 A. Fremantle, *op. cit.*, 10 October 1806; H. C. B. Campbell, *A Journey to Florence*, p. 16.
45 NLS, Dep. 175, 165, 2.
46 J. Doyle, *Memoir and Correspondence of Susan Ferrier 1782-1854*. (London: John Murray, 1898), p. 64. Susan Ferrier to Charlotte Clavering, 26 July 1809.
47 L. Melville, *Regency Ladies*, p. 114; British Library, Add. Mss 37726, f. 68, Lady Charlotte Campbell to Mary Berry, 21 January 1810.

Chapter 7: Reluctant Courtier

1 Lady Charlotte Huntington Journal.
2 Bury, *Diary* (1908), vol. 1.
3 F. Bickley (ed.), *Diaries of Sylvester Douglas, Lord Glenbervie*, 2 vols (London: Constable and Co, 1928). The manuscript diaries are in the NLS, Mss. 5987.
4 L. Melville, *Regency Ladies*, p. 114. Bury, *Diary*, vol. 1, pp. 397-9.
5 British Library, Add. Mss. 37726, f. 68, Lady Charlotte Maria Campbell to Mary Berry, 21 January 1810.
6 NLS, Acc. 10505, 9, Sylvester Douglas Mss Diaries, 30 October 1810.
7 A. Somerset, *Ladies in Waiting from the Tudors to the Present Day* (London: George Weidenfeld and Nicolson, 1984), p. 241.
8 *Ibid.*, p. 259.
9 Margaret Morris Cloake (ed.), *A Persian Ambassador at the Court of King George III 1809-10: the journal of Mirza Abul Hassan Khan 1809-10* (London: Barrie and Jenkins, 1988).
10 Bury, *Diary*, vol. 2, p. 398.
11 *Ibid.*, vol. 1, p. 14.
12 *Ibid.*, vol. 1, p. 402.
13 A. Allardyce (ed.), *op. cit.*, vol. 2, p. 93.
14 *Bury*, *Diary*, vol. 1, p. 19.
15 *Ibid.*, vol. 1, p. 220.
16 *Ibid.*, vol. 1, p. 110.
17 *Ibid.*, vol. 1, p. 128.
18 *Ibid.*, vol. 1, p. 25.
19 Bury, *Love*, 3 vols (1837), vol. 1, p. 193.
20 Bury, *Diary*, vol. 1, p. 27.
21 P. Noble, *Anne Seymour Damer. A Woman of Art and Fashion 1748-1828* (London: Kegan Paul, Trench, Turner & Co. Ltd., 1908), p. 198.
22 L. Melville, The *Berry Papers*, pp. 306-7. Lady Charlotte to Mary Berry, 18 August 1812; British Library, Add. Mss. 37726, f. 99.
23 *Ibid.*, p. 307-8, Lady Charlotte Maria Campbell to Mary Berry, 21 August 1812; British Library, Add. Mss. 37726, f. 101.
24 J. Russell, *Memoirs, Journals and Correspondence of Thomas Moore*, 8, 118, Lady Donegal to Thomas Moore, 28 August 1812.
25 B. Fitzgerald, *Emily, Duchess of Leinster* (London: Staple Press, 1949), p. 282.
26 Scott had dedicated the work to Lord Abercorn; this presentation copy is now in New York Public Library and is inscribed to 'Lady Charlotte Campbell from her Ladyship's Most Obedient and very Faithful humble servant The Author' Todd and Bowden, *Sir Walter Scott*, (1998).
27 W. Partington, *Sir Walter's Postbag* (London: John Murray, 1932), p. 95.

28 NLS, Mss. 3879, f. 207, Lady Charlotte Campbell to Walter Scott, 8 October 1810.
29 H. J. C. Grierson (ed.), *The Letters of Sir Walter Scott*, 2, 432, 11 Jan 1811.
30 E. Castle (ed.), *The Jerningham Letters, 1780-1843. Being excerpts from the correspondence and diaries of the Honourable Lady Frances Jerningham*, 2 vols (London: R. Bentley and Son, 1896), vol. 1, p. 379.
31 NRS, CC8/5 and CC8/6. Papers relating to divorce. Lady Paget agt Lord Paget 1810.
32 Lady C. Granville, *The Private Correspondence of Lord Granville Leveson-Gower*, vol. 2, p. 366.
33 D. Douglas (ed.), *Scott's Familiar Letters*, 2 vols (Edinburgh: David Douglas, 1894), 1, 208. Walter Scott to Lady Abercorn, 11 January 1811. Damer encomium by Lady Charlotte in *Journal of the Heart* (1835), pp. 1-12. Inveraray, Argyll Papers, 3144, Appendix 3, Edward John Bury to Walter Frederick Campbell. Westwood was a' 'residence which the affection of as near relative of her own family had bestowed upon her'.
34 C. E. Knight, *Autobiography of Miss Cornelia Knight, Companion to Princess Charlotte of Wales*, ed. J .W. Kaye, 2 vols (London: W. H. Allen, 1861), vol. 1, p. 180.
35 *Ibid.*, vol. 1, p. 206.
36 British Library, Add. Mss. 37726, f. 99, Lady Charlotte Campbell to Mary Berry, 18 August 1812.
37 British Library, Add. Mss. 37726, f. 98, Lady Charlotte Campbell to Mary Berry, 12 May 1812.
38 Bury, *Diary*, vol. 1, pp. 24-5.
39 Bury, *Diary*, vol. 1, p. 155.
40 K. Jameson-Cempter, *Selected Correspondence by Georges Solovieff* (Dordrecht, Boston: Kluwer Academic, 2000), p. 312.
41 Roundel, *Lady Blessington* 2 vols (London, 1860), vol. 2, p. 30.
42 *Ibid.*, 1, 151, 143-4. G. de Staël, *Corinne ou L'Italie* (1807); *Essai sur les Fictions* and *Petits Romans* (1795); *Essai sur les Passions* (1796).
43 Bury, *Diary*, vol. 1, pp. 143-4.
44 *Ibid.*, vol. 1, p. 119.
45 J. Doyle, *op. cit.*, p. 111, Charlotte Clavering to Susan Ferrier, 2 April 1811.
46 The British Library, Add. Mss. 37726, f. 101, Lady Charlotte Campbell to Mary Berry, 21 August 1812.
47 A. Allardyce, *op. cit.*, 1, 444, Lady Charlotte to Charles Kirkpatrick Sharpe, 17 March 1811.
48 *Ibid.*, vol. 1, p. 34.
49 A. Grant, *Susan Ferrier of Edinburgh*, p. 88.
50 Edinburgh University Library Special Collections, MSS La.II.509, Lady Charlotte Campbell to James Hamilton Esq, 28 June 1811.
51 British Library, Add. Mss. 39929, f. 97, Lady Charlotte Maria Campbell to Mary Berry, 22 April 1812.
52 A. Allardyce, *op. cit.*, 1, 450, Lady Charlotte Campbell to Charles Kirkpatrick Sharpe, 15 July 1811.
53 Bury, *Diary* (1908), vol. 1, p. 50.
54 *Ibid.*, vol. 1, pp. 124-5.
55 Damer obituary. Edward John Bury letter 183x. Inveraray Argyll Mss 3144, appendix 3. Westwood was a 'residence which the affection of a near relative of her own family had bestowed upon her'.
56 Doyle, *op. cit.*, p. 120, Susan Ferrier to Mrs Connell, 5 December 1812.
57 NLS, Dep. 175, 164, 1.
58 G. Carnell, 'Campbell, Thomas (1777-1844)', *ODNB*.

59 W. Beattie (ed.), *Life and Letters of Thomas Campbell*, 3 vols (London: E. Moxon, 1849), vol. 2, p. 213, 16 April, 1812.
60 *Ibid.*, 2, 215.
61 NLS, Mss. 3884, f. 14, Lady Charlotte Campbell to Walter Scott, 11 January 1813.
62 Beattie, *op. cit.*, vol. 2, p. 217.
63 *Ibid.*, vol. 1, p. 134.
64 Doyle, *op. cit.*, pp. 105-6, Charlotte Clavering to Susan Ferrier, 10 December 1810.
65 *Ibid.*, p. 112, Charlotte Clavering to Susan Ferrier 20 December 1810.
66 *Ibid.*, pp. 93-4.
67 Footnote by John Ferrier, grand nephew of Susan Ferrier: 'one would infer from this that the book under discussion was one in which Miss Clavering was engaged with her aunt, Lady Charlotte. Probably it was *Self-Indulgence*. Perhaps it was more likely to be Charlotte Clavering's one chapter in *Marriage*.
68 Doyle, *op. cit.*, p. 113.
69 Bury, *Self Indulgence*, 2 vols (1812), vol. 1, p. 53.
70 Doyle, *op. cit.*, pp. 112-3.
71 Bury, *Diary*, vol. 1, p. 40.
72 A. Allardyce, *op. cit.*, vol. 2, p. 14, Charles Kirkpatrick Sharpe to Henry Adams, 13 September 1812.
73 Now in University of Pennsylvania Library.
74 Bury, *Diary*, vol. 1, p. 20.
75 *Ibid.*, vol. 1, p. 94.
76 *Ibid.*, vol. 1, p. 219.

Chapter 8: Continental Escape

1 Bury, *Diary* (1908), vol. 1, p. 239.
2 NLS, Dep. 175, 165, 6, Mary Maguire to Eliza Campbell, 18 July 1814.
3 Bury, *Diary*, vol. 1, p. 244.
4 Second wife of John Fane, 10th Earl of Westmorland, and stepmother of Lord Burghersh (1784-1859).
5 M. Price, *The Perilous Crown. France Between Revolutions, 1814-1848* (London: Pan Macmillan, 2007), p. 13.
6 Russell, *Three Generations of Fascinating Women*, p. 189.
7 *Ibid.*, p. 195.
8 Petite and vivacious, she had been a wealthy, well-connected and sophisticated widow, Mrs. Jane Apreece, who hosted an intellectual Edinburgh salon; she was married to Humphry Davy in 1812 by the Bishop of Carlisle at her mother's London home in Portland Street. S. Forgan, 'Davy, Lady Jane, 1780-1855', *ODNB*.
9 University of Cambridge, Scott Polar Research Institute, MS 248/19 vol. 4.
10 Charles Richard Sumner was the clergyman tutor travelling with Lord Mountjoy, eldest son of Lady Conyngham. In Berne, Lord Mountjoy had fallen in love with a Swiss girl, whom his mother considered unsuitable, so she told Sumner 'to marry her yourself'. He later became bishop of Winchester at the age of 36. Rosa, 42.
11 Bury, *Diary*, vol. 1, p. 275.
12 J. M. Colles (ed.), *Journal of John Mayne of Dumfries during a tour of the Continent, 1814*, (London: John Lane, 1909), p. 94.
13 Bury, *Diary*, vol. 1, p. 280.
14 *Ibid.*, vol. 1, p. 275.
15 *Ibid.*, vol. 1, p. 280.
16 A. Prucher, *op. cit.*, p. 94, Lady Charlotte Campbell to Jean-Charles Sismondi, 16 October 1814.

17 Bury, *Diary*, vol. 1, pp. 293-4.
18 H. C. B. Campbell, *A Journey to Florence*, p. 122: 'All Saints Day—this day three years ago we were just arrived at Nice.'
19 Prucher, *op. cit.*, p. 94, Lady Charlotte Campbell to Sismondi, 16 October 1814.
20 C. Redding, *Fifty Years' Recollections, literary and personal with observations on men and things*, 3 vols (London, 1858), p. 318.
21 Doyle, *op. cit.*, p. 107.
22 NLS, Acc. 8508, Eliza Campbell, Ardpatrick, to Eliza Campbell, Nice, 28 October 1814.
23 NLS, Dep. 175, 165, 6, Mary Maguire to Eliza Campbell, 18 July 1814.
24 Bury, *Diary*, vol. 1, p. 303.
25 Redding, *op. cit.*, p. 318.
26 Prucher, *op. cit.*, pp. 95-6.
27 H. Lowe, *Unprotected Females in Sicily, Calabria and on the Top of Mount Aetna* (London, New York: Routledge, Warne and Routledge, 1859), pp. 117-8.
28 Bury, *Diary*, vol. 1, p. 306.
29 *Ibid.*, vol. 1, p. 303. Anne Damer to Lady Charlotte Campbell, 10 January 1815.
30 *Ibid.*, vol. 1, p. 330.
31 See F. Fraser, *The Unruly Queen. The Life of Queen Caroline* (London: Macmillan, 1996).
32 Bury, *Diary*, vol. 1, p. 334.

Chapter 9: 'Transcendent Genoa'

1 Bury, *Diary*, vol. 1, p. 342.
2 Captain Samuel J. B. Pechell, (1785-1849) and his brother George R. B. Pechell (1789-1860) went on to become rear-admiral and admiral respectively, as well as becoming 3rd and 4th baronets. They were nephews by marriage of Lady Augusta Clavering.
3 Anonymous, *The Legislative Trial of her Majesty Caroline Amelia Elizabeth, Queen of England, consort of George the Fourth, for the Alleged Crime of Adultery with Bartolomeo Bergami* (London: H. Rowe, 1820), pp. 31-4.
4 Bury, *Diary*, vol. 1, p. 350.
5 Madame de Boigne, abridged by Charles Nicouillaud, *Memoirs of the Comtesse de Boigne*, 2 vols (London: William Heinemann, 2002) vol. 2, pp. 39-40.
6 F. Bickley (ed.), *op. cit.*, vol. 1, p. 137.
7 Bury, *Diary*, vol. 1, p. 353.
8 *Ibid.*, vol. 1, p. 346.
9 NLS, Dep. 175, 165, 6, Captain S. J. B. Pechell to Mlle de la Chaux, 28 May 1815.
10 J. Nightingale, *Memoirs of the Public and Private Life of Queen Caroline*, ed. C. Hibbert (London: The Folio Society, 1958), p. 143.
11 Lord William Bentinck, second son of the 3rd Duke of Portland had been at Dr Samuel Goodenough's school in Ealing before going on to Westminster at the same time as Lady Charlotte's brothers. Military by training, by 1811 he had been appointed envoy to the Court of the Two Sicilies, in 1814 replacing Murat with his son.
12 A. J. C. Hall, *Life and Letters of Maria Edgeworth*, 1767-1849, 2 vols (London: Edward Arnold, 1894) vol. 1, p. 248.
13 A. M. Maxwell, *My Adventures*, 2 vols (London: Henry Colburn, 1845), 2, 108-9.
14 *The Legislative Trial of her Majesty Caroline Amelia Elizabeth, Queen of England*, p. 25.
15 Bury, *Diary*, vol. 1, pp. 377-8.
16 *Ibid.*, vol. 1, p. 375.
17 *Ibid.*, vol. 1, pp. 391-2.

18 *Ibid.*, vol. 1, p. 395.
19 Russell, *Three Generations of Fascinating Women*, pp. 197-8.
20 NLS, Dep. 175, 165, 1, Walter Frederick Campbell to Eliza Campbell, 4 July 1815; NLS, Mss. 6294, f. 56, loss of rent was over £100 per annum.
21 NLS, Dep. 175, 165, 1, Lord John Campbell to Miss Campbell, 17 June 1815.
22 NLS, Dep. 175, 164, 1, Lady Charlotte Bury, to Lady Gordon-Cumming, 4 November 1815.
23 NLS, Dep. 175, 165, 1, John George Campbell to Eliza Campbell, 4 July 1815.
24 J. Nightingale, *op. cit.*, p. 144.
25 C. F. Gordon-Cumming, *Memories* (Edinburgh and London: Wm. Blackwood and Sons, 1904), p. 15.
26 NLS, Dep. 175, 64, 4, Memories of Constance Frederica Gordon-Cumming.
27 H. C. B. Campbell, *A Journey to Florence*, introduction and pp. 173-4. He adopted the surname of Bruce on his marriage to Mary Bruce of Kinnaird.
28 A lock of his hair is amongst the passports in the Gordon-Cumming Papers, NLS, Dep. 175.
29 H. C. B. Campbell, *A Journey to Florence*, introduction and note 52, pp. 173-4.
30 E. Grant, *Memoirs of a Highland Lady*, p. 163.
31 NLS, Dep. 175. 164, 1.
32 NLS, Dep. 175, 164, 1, Beaujolois Campbell and Lady Charlotte Campbell to Lady Gordon-Cumming, 25 September 1815.
33 *Ibid.*
34 NLS, Dep. 175, 164, 1, Lady Charlotte Campbell to Lady Gordon-Cumming, 25 September 1815.
35 *Ibid.*, Lady Charlotte Campbell to Lady Gordon-Cumming, 21 October 1815.
36 *Ibid.*, Eleonora Campbell to Lady Gordon-Cumming, 21 October 1815.
37 *Ibid.*, John Campbell to Sir William Gordon-Cumming, undated.
38 *Ibid.*, Eleonora Campbell to Lady Gordon-Cumming, 21 October 1815.
39 *Ibid.*, Lady Charlotte Campbell to Lady Gordon-Cumming, 4 November 1815.
40 NLS, Dep.175, 164, 4, Eleonora Campbell to Lady Gordon Campbell, 14 November 1815.

Chapter 10: Sunless Sydenham

1 W. Beattie, *op. cit.*, 2, 61.
2 NLS, Dep. 175, 164, 1, Lady Charlotte Campbell to Lady Gordon-Cumming, 22 August 1816.
3 J. Coulter, *Sydenham and Forest Hill Past* (London: Historical Publications, 1999), pp. 58, 60.
4 Heath's *Book of Beauty* (London: Longman et al., 1835), pp. 79-82.
5 Bury, *Journal of the Heart* (1835), 'Stanzas written at Sydenham'.
6 Geneva, Bibliothèque Publique et Universitaire, Galiffe.
7 H. C. B. Campbell, *A Journey to Florence*, p. 15, 'as Mary Frampton related'.
8 A. Prucher, *op. cit.*, p. 99, Lady Charlotte Campbell to Jean Charles Sismondi, 14 February 1816.
9 NLS, Dep. 175, 165, 1, Walter Campbell, to Lady Gordon-Cumming, 1 January 1816.
10 *Ibid.*, John Campbell to Lady Gordon-Cumming, 28 [January] 1816.
11 NLS, Dep. 175, 165, 5, Douglas Clavering to Lady Gordon-Cumming, 15 August 1816.
12 NLS, Dep. 175, 164, 3, Beaujolois Campbell to Lady Gordon-Cumming, 12 September 1816.
13 E. Grant, *Memoirs of a Highland Lady 1816-1817*, vol. 2, p. 44.

14 NLS, Dep. 175, 164, 1, Lady Charlotte Campbell to Lady Gordon-Cumming, 29 June 1816.
15 *Ibid.*, Lady Charlotte Campbell to Lady Gordon-Cumming, 30 August 1816.
16 *The Times*, 23 July 2007.
17 NLS, Dep. 175, 164, 1, Lady Charlotte Campbell to Lady Gordon-Cumming, 22 August 1816.
18 *Ibid.*
19 NLS, Dep. 175, 165, 2, Mlle de la Chaux to Lady Gordon-Cumming.
20 *Ibid.*, Lady Charlotte Campbell to Sir William Gordon-Cumming, 22 August 1816.
21 *Ibid.*, Lady Charlotte Campbell to Lady Gordon-Cumming, 28 August 1816.
22 *Ibid.*, Lady Charlotte Campbell to Lady Gordon-Cumming, 30 August 1816.
23 *Ibid.*, Eleonora Campbell to Lady Gordon-Cumming, 22 August 1816.
24 NLS, Dep. 175, 164, 3, Beaujolois Campbell to Lady Gordon-Cumming, 12 September 1816.
25 NLS, Dep. 175, 164, 1, Lady Charlotte Campbell to Lady Gordon-Cumming, n.d., but before 22 August 1816.
26 *Ibid.*, Lady Charlotte Campbell to Lady Gordon-Cumming 22 August 1816.
27 NLS, Dep. 175, 164, 3, Beaujolois Campbell to Lady Gordon-Cumming 12 September 1816.
28 NLS, Dep. 175, 164, 1, Lady Charlotte Campbell to Lady Gordon-Cumming, 28 August 1816.
29 NLS, Dep. 175, 165, 5, Alexander Baillie to Lady Gordon-Cumming, 24 October 1816. Alexander Baillie of the Dochfour family had been a schoolfellow of Lord John's at Ealing, and travelled on the continent. He was one of the Campbell family's favourite escorts in London 1816-17 and was often in their company at the Priory, along with a Norwegian friend,Yorgen, with whom he frequently travelled when on the content. Baillie's name was inscribed on the same headstone as that of Beaujolois in the old protestant cemetery in Naples, five years after she died in 1848.
30 NLS Dep. 175, 165, 6, Lady Charlotte Campbell to Lady Gordon-Cumming.
31 D. Thomson *The Art of Sir Henry Raeburn 1756-1823* (Edinburgh: Scottish National Portrait Gallery, 1997), p. 27.
32 NLS, Dep. 175, 164, 1, Lady Charlotte Campbell to Lady Gordon-Cumming, 6 May 1817.
33 NLS, Dep. 175, 164, 4, Eleanora Campbell to Lady Gordon-Cumming, 25 April 1817.
34 'National Maritime Museum', *Scottish Historical Review* 19 (Edinburgh: Edinburgh University Press, 1922), pp. 273-82.
35 'Journal of a Homewardbound voyage in the *General Hewitt* (East Indiaman) from the mouth of the Pei-Ho (or White River) in the Gulf of Petch-e-Lee, Empire of China, to England'. *Scottish Historical Review* (Edinburgh: Edinburgh University Press, 1923).
36 NLS, Dep. 175.
37 British Library, Add. Mss. 37727, f. 82, Mary Berry to Agnes Berry.
38 NLS, Dep. 175, 164, 1, Lady Charlotte Bury to Lady Gordon-Cumming, nd August 1816.
39 *Ibid.*, Eleanora Campbell to Lady Gordon-Cumming, 28 August 1816.
40 *Ibid.*, Beaujolois Campbell to Lady Gordon-Cumming, 12 September 1816.
41 *Ibid.*, Lady Charlotte Campbell to Lady Gordon-Cumming, 29 June 1816.
42 *Ibid.*, Lady Charlotte Campbell to Lady Gordon-Cumming, August 1816.
43 *Ibid.*, Lady Charlotte Campbell to Lady Gordon-Cumming, July 1816.
44 *Ibid.*, Eleanora Campbell to Lady Gordon-Cumming, 9 January 1816.

45 *Ibid.*, Eleanora Campbell to Lady Gordon-Cumming, 28 August 1816.
46 J. Doyle, *op. cit.*, p. 131.
47 E. Grant, *Memoirs of a Highland Lady*, p. 285.
48 NLS, Dep. 175, 165, 5, Charlotte Clavering to Lady Gordon-Cumming, 24 October 1816.
49 J. Doyle, *op. cit.*, pp. 130-2.
50 Andrew Geddes (1783-1844).
51 NLS, Dep. 175, 164, 4, Eleanora Campbell to Lady Gordon-Cumming, 25 April 1817.
52 *Ibid.*
53 NLS, Dep. 175, 164, 1, Eleanora Campbell to Lady Gordon-Cumming, 6 May 1817.
54 NLS, Dep. 175, 164, 4, Eleanora Campbell to Lady Gordon-Cumming, 25 April 1817.
55 NLS, Dep. 175, 164, 1, Lady Charlotte Campbell to Lady Gordon-Cumming, 6 May 1817.
56 NLS, Dep. 175, Bessie Mure to Lady Gordon-Cumming, 24 June 1817.
57 NLS, Dep. 175, 164, 1, Eleanora Campbell to Lady Gordon-Cumming.
58 *Ibid.*, Lady Charlotte Campbell to Lady Gordon-Cumming, 22 August 1816.
59 *Ibid.*, Lady Charlotte Campbell to Lady Gordon-Cumming, 2 July 1817.
60 *Ibid.*, Lady Charlotte Campbell to Lady Gordon-Cumming, 6 May 1817.
61 *Ibid.*, Lady Charlotte Campbell to Lady Gordon-Cumming, 2 July 1817.
62 *Ibid.*, Eleanora Campbell to Lady Gordon-Cumming, 6 May 1817.
63 NLS, Dep. 175, 164, 4, Eleonora Campbell to Lady Gordon-Cumming, 5 July 1817.
64 NLS, Dec. 175, Bessie Mure to Lady Gordon-Cumming, 24 June 1817.
65 *Ibid.*
66 NLS, Dep. 175, 164, 1, Lady Charlotte Campbell to Lady Gordon-Cumming, 2 July 1817.
67 *Ibid.*
68 NLS, Dep. 175, 164, 1, Eleonora Campbell to Lady Gordon-Cumming, 7 July 1817.
69 A marble monument sculpted by J. Marshall was erected in 1819 in the entrance to Kilarrow Church in Bowmore, Isle of Islay.
70 NLS, Dep. 175, 165, 5, Elizabeth Campbell, Ardpatrick to Eliza Campbell, Nice, 28 October 1814.
71 Rome was the intended destination for two years' stay. NLS, Dep. 175, 164, 1, Lady Charlotte Campbell to Lady Gordon-Cumming and Eleanora Campbell to same, 6 May 1817.
72 NLS, Dep. 175, 164, 1, Lady Charlotte Campbell to Lady Gordon-Cumming, 2 July 1817.
73 H. C. B. Campbell, *A Journey to Florence*, p. 44.
74 NLS, Dep. 175, 164, 4, Eleonora Campbell to Lady Gordon-Cumming, 14 July 1817.
75 NLS, Dep. 175, 164, 1, Lady Charlotte Campbell to Lady Gordon-Cumming, 24 July 1817.
76 NLS, Dep. 175, 164, 3, Beaujolois Campbell to Lady Gordon-Cumming, 27 July 1817.
77 NLS, Dep. 175, Mlle de la Chaux to Lady Gordon-Cumming, 24 June 1817.

Chapter 11: Florentine Intrigue

1 H. C. B. Campbell, *A Journey to Florence in 1817* (London: Geoffrey Bles, 1951). Hereafter, Campbell, *Florence Journey*.
2 *Ibid.*, p. 19.
3 Bury, *Journal of the Heart* (1835), p. 24.

4 *Ibid.*
5 Campbell, *Florence Journey*, p. 43.
6 *Ibid.*, p. 66.
7 H. Matthews, *Diary of an Invalid being the Journal of a tour in pursuit of health in Portugal Italy Switzerland and France* (London: John Murray, 1820), p. 39.
8 E. R.Vincent, *Ugo Foscolo in English Society. An Italian in Regency England* (Cambridge: Cambridge University Press, 1953), p. 55.
9 Campbell, *Florence Journey*, pp. 143-4.
10 NLS, Dep. 175. Bessie Mure to Lady Gordon-Cumming, 26 June 1817.
11 Campbell, *Florence Journey*, p. 34.
12 Lady Theresa Lewis, *op. cit.*, vol. 3, p. 155.
13 Campbell, *Florence Journey*, p. 99.
14 *Ibid.*
15 H. Matthews, *op. cit.*, pp. 39-40.
16 Campbell, *Florence Journey*, p. 37.
17 *Ibid.*
18 Obituary in *The Quarterly Review* (1834).
19 J. Greig, *op. cit.*, vol. 7, p. 58. The date given is 9 November 1811, but Bury would only have been eleven at that time.
20 Campbell, *Florence Journey*, p. 124.
21 'Esse ci sono conservate in tre letter poste in fondo al primo volume del *Diary* come indirizzate a lei da altri, ma evidentemente suee, senza ombra di dubbio, dirette all'uomo che essa doveva sposare alcuni nesi dopo, e cioè al Rev. Edward Bury che si trovava allora in Svizzera con Walter, il di lei figlio maggiore, di cui egli era precettore.'; 'These are conserved in three letters at the end of the first volume of the Diary, as tho' addressed to her from another, but clearly hers, and without shadow of doubt, addressed to the man whom she was later to marry, and that is the Rev. E. Bury, who at that time was to be found in Switzerland with Walter, her eldest son, to whom he was tutor.', A. Prucher, *op. cit.* There is also a letter in Bury, *Diary* (1908), 2, in all probability attributable to Lady Charlotte seemingly addressed to the same person and belonging to the same period in which the other three were written.
22 Campbell, *Florence Journey*, p. 134.
23 NLS, Dep. 175, Beaujolois Campbell to Lady Gordon-Cumming.
24 NLS, Dep. 175, 164, 1, Lady Charlotte Campbell to Lady Gordon-Cumming, 5 February 1818.
25 Geneva, Bibliothèque Publique et Universitaire, Galiffe letter 1 June 1819: 'I am sorry to say Eleanor is not married nor do I hear of any Marriage at present—the one which was in contemplation is entirely at an end'.
26 NLS, Dep. 175, 164, 1, Lady Charlotte Campbell to Lady Gordon-Cumming, 10 February 1818.
27 NLS, Dep. 175, 165, 6, Anne Damer to Lady Gordon-Cumming, 15 October 1821. Anne Damer was 'sorry she [Mlle de la Chaux] has decided to settle in Switzerland as I much doubt her being happy there', but she was to live on in her Swiss birthplace of Yverdon until she died in 1864 aged 95. She kept in touch with copious letters and visited many members of the family.
28 NLS, Dep. 175, 165, 2, Mlle de la Chaux to Lady Gordon-Cumming, 12 February 1818.
29 NLS, Dep. 175, 165, 2, Mlle de la Chaux to Lady Gordon-Cumming, 23 February 1818.
30 Sydney, Lady Morgan, *Italy*, 2 vols (London: H. Colburn, 1821), vol. 2, p. 111.
31 Lady Theresa Lewis, *op. cit.*, vol. 3, p. 157.

32 The Certificate of Marriage is in the London Metropolitan Archive.
33 B. Burke, *A Genealogical and Heraldic Dictionary of the Landed Gentry of Great Britain and Ireland for 1853*, 3 vols (London: Henry Colburn, 1853), vol. 3, p. 69.
34 E. Castle, *op. cit.*, vol. 2, p. 119.
35 NLS, Mss. 6294, f. 38, Lord John Campbell to Anne Damer.
36 L. Melville, *The Berry Papers*, pp. 394-5. British Library, Add. Mss. 37726, f. 144, John Playfair to Mary Berry, 5 August 1818.
37 D. Douglas, *Scott's Familiar Letters*, vol. 2, p. 63, Walter Scott to Lady Abercorn, 25 November 1819.
38 Geneva, Bibliothèque Publique et Universitaire, Galiffe letters 7 April and 1 June 1819. By 7 April a new governess, Miss le Grand, arrived in Geneva, however by 1 June it was no longer Miss le Grand but Miss Despard.
39 Campbell, *Florence Journey*, epilogue, p. 137.
40 NLS Dep. 175, 64, 4, Certificate of Baptism of Anne Conway Gordon-Cumming at the Albergo della Villa di Londra, Naples, 5 April 1818, born 5 March 1818. The witnesses/godparents were William Hamilton-Campbell of Winton and Pencaitland and Lady Ruthven.

Chapter 12: Lady Charlotte Maria Bury

1 Bury, *Three Great Sanctuaries*, Preface, p. vii.
2 Campbell, *Florence Journey*, p. 137.
3 Bury, *Diary* (1908), vol. 2, p. 26 *et seq.*
4 Lady Sydney Morgan, *Italy*, vol. 2, p. 227.
5 H. Matthews, *op. cit.*, p. 133.
6 Joan Glassel's journal is in NLS, Acc. 8508. Lord John's first wife died on 9 December 1818 and he married Joan Glassel on 31 March 1820 (NLS, Dep. 175, 165/6).
7 W. C. Maughan, *Roseneath Past and Present* (Paisley: Gardner, 1896), p. 258. Mr James Smith FRS (1782-1867) of Jordanhill tenanted Roseneath until 1823.
8 Lady Sydney Morgan, *Italy*, vol. 2, p. 228.
9 *Ibid.*, vol. 2, p. 304.
10 NLS, Dep. 175, 164, 3, Lady Charlotte Bury to Lady Gordon-Cumming, 28 February 1820.
11 *Ibid.*, Beaujolois Campbell to Lady Gordon-Cumming, 28 February 1820.
12 NLS, Acc. 8508, 24, Lord John Campbell to Joan Glassel, 14 October 1819.
13 *Ibid.*, Lord John Campbell to Joan Glassel, 5 October 1819.
14 *Ibid.*, Lord John Campbell to Joan Glassel, 15 October 1819.
15 Bury, *Diary*, vol. 2, pp. 210-3.
16 Lord John Russell, *Memoirs, Journals and Correspondence of Thomas Moore*, 1, 257, 16 November 1819.
17 NLS, Dep. 175, 165, 5, Mlle de la Chaux to Lady Gordon-Cumming, 16 March 1820.
18 NLS, Dep. 175, 64, 1, Memories of Frederica Constance Gordon-Cumming.
19 NLS, Dep. 175, 164, 4, Lady Uxbridge to Lady Gordon-Cumming, 12 December 1819.
20 *Ibid.*, Lady Uxbridge to Lady Gordon-Cumming, 17 April 1820.
21 NRS, Scotlands People, Old Parish Register 683/5, Parish of Aberlady, 6 January 1820.
22 NLS, Dep. 175, 165, 2, Mlle de la Chaux to Lady Gordon-Cumming, 18 February 1820.
23 NLS, Dep. 175, 164, 3, Beaujolois Campbell to Lady Gordon-Cumming, 28 February 1820.
24 NLS, Dep. 175, 165, 5, Mlle de la Chaux to Lady Gordon-Cumming, 16 March 1820.

25 *Ibid.*, Anne Damer to Lady Gordon-Cumming, 12 April 1820.
26 NLS, Dep. 175, 164, 3, Beaujolois Campbell to Lady Gordon-Cumming, 28 February 1820.
27 *Ibid.*, Beaujolois Campbell to Lady Gordon-Cumming, 3 June 1820.
28 NLS, Dep. 175, 165, 6, Charlotte Clavering/Fletcher to Lady Gordon-Cumming, 31 March 1820.
29 NLS, Dep. 175, 165, 5, Anne Damer to Lady Gordon-Cumming, 12 April 1820.
30 *Ibid.*, 5, Mlle de la Chaux to Lady Gordon-Cumming, 15 March 1820.
31 NLS, Dep. 175, 165, 2, Mlle de la Chaux to Lady Gordon-Cumming, 8 January 1820.
32 NLS, Dep. 175, 164, 3, Beaujolois Campbell to Lady Gordon-Cumming, 11 March 1820.
33 *Ibid.*, Beaujolois Campbell to Lady Gordon-Cumming, 3 June 1820.
34 *Ibid.*
35 NLS, Dep. 175, 165, 2, Adelaide Campbell to Mlle de la Chaux, 9 July 1820.
36 NLS, Dep. 175, 165, 5, Anne Damer to Lady Gordon-Cumming, 12 July 1820.
37 NLS, Dep. 175, 164, 4, Lady Uxbridge to Lady Gordon-Cumming, 17 July 1820.
38 NLS, Acc. 5987, Lady Charlotte Bury to Captain Bosville, 23 July 1820.
39 NLS, Dep. 175, 164, 3, Beaujolois Campbell to Lady Gordon-Cumming, 30 September 1820.
40 The Wilsons were siblings of John Wilson or Christopher North, and would soon marry Sir John McNeill of Colonsay as his second wife, then move to diplomatic life in Persia.
41 NRS, GD 371/70, The Private Journal of Eliza Wilson, later McNeill, of a journey from Greenock, to Liverpool . . . Genoa, Leghorn, Pisa and Florence, 1820-1. Later published, with variations, by F. McAllister, *Memoir of the Rt. Hon. Sir John McNeill . . . and of his second wife, Elizabeth Wilson* (London: John Murray, 1910).
42 NLS Dep. 175, 164, 4, Beaujolois Campbell to Lady Gordon-Cumming, 17 July 1820.
43 Lady Sydney Morgan, *Italy*, p. 58.
44 T. W. Bond, *The Marlay Letters 1778-1820* (London: Constable and Company Ltd, 1937), p. 395.
45 NLS, Dep. 175, 164, 3, Beaujolois Campbell to Lady Gordon-Cumming, 30 September 1820.
46 *Ibid.*, Beaujolois Campbell to Lady Gordon-Cumming, 16 January 1821.
47 Westmeath Library, Mullingar, Howard-Bury Papers, Finance B15, Earl Charleville to agent, 6 May 1821.
48 NLS, Dep. 175, 165, 2, Lady Tullamore to Mlle de la Chaux, 10 April 1821.
49 NLS, Dep. 175, 64,1, C. F. Gordon-Cumming, Memoirs.
50 Lady Sydney Morgan, *Italy*, vol. 2, p. 59.
51 Islay Estate Papers, Letter from Charles Morrison to John Heatley Dickson, 18 November 1886—discussion about two full-length statues in Islay House . . . given to John Francis Campbell but pedestals kept.
52 NLS, Dep. 175, 165, 5. Anne Damer to Lady Gordon-Cumming, 24 February 1821.
53 NLS, Dep. 175, 165, 5, Anne Damer to Lady Gordon-Cumming, 24 February 1821.
54 M. Rosa, *op. cit.*, p. 148.
55 Argyll, J. D. S. Campbell, *Intimate Society Letters*, 2, 660, Lady John Campbell to 'Francis'.
56 NLS, Dep. 175, 165, 5, Anne Damer to Lady Gordon-Cumming, 12 July 1820.
57 NLS, Dep. 175, 165, 4, Lady Uxbridge to Lady Gordon-Cumming 14 Aug 1821.
58 NLS, Mss. 8508, 35, Lady Charlotte Bury to Lady John Campbell, 11 February 1822.
59 *Ibid.*, Lady Charlotte Bury to Lady John Campbell, 13 November 1821.
60 NLS, Dep. 175, 165, 5, Anne Damer to Lady Gordon-Cumming, 15 October 1821.

61 L. J. Jennings, *op. cit.*

Chapter 13: Crises

1 NLS, Acc. 8508, 35, Lady Charlotte Bury to Lady John Campbell, 11 February 1821.
2 NLS, Dep. 175, 165, 5, Anne Damer to Lady Gordon-Cumming, 15 October 1821.
3 NLS, Acc. 8508, 35, Lady Charlotte Bury to Lord John Campbell, 13 November 1821.
4 NLS, Dep. 175, 165, 5, Anne Damer to Lady Gordon-Cumming, 15 October 1821.
5 NLS, Acc. 8508, 3, Mlle de la Chaux to Lady John Campbell, 14 January 1822.
6 NLS, Acc. 8508, 35, Bessie Mure to Lady John Campbell, n.d. [February 1822].
7 NLS, Dep. 175, 161, 2, Lady Charlotte Bury to Sir William Gordon-Cumming, 26 November 1821.
8 NLS, Dep. 175, 161, 2, Lady Charlotte Bury to Lady Gordon-Cumming, 26 November 1821.
9 NLS, Acc. 8508, 5, Mlle de la Chaux to Lady John Campbell, 5 August 1822.
10 *Ibid.*
11 NLS, Acc. 8508, 5, Mlle de la Chaux to Lady John Campbell, 5 August 1822.
12 NLS, Acc. 8508, 35, Lady Charlotte Bury to Lady John Campbell, 13 April 1822.
13 NLS, Acc. 8508, 1, Bessie Mure to Lord John Campbell, 15 April 1822.
14 NLS, Dep. 175, 161, 2, Lady Charlotte Bury to Sir William Gordon-Cumming, 20 June 1822.
15 NLS, Dep. 175, 164, 1, Edward J. Bury to Lady Gordon-Cumming, n.d.
16 NLS, Dep. 175, 161, 2, Lady Charlotte Bury to Sir William Gordon-Cumming, n.d.
17 *Ibid.*
18 NLS Dep. 175, 161, 2, Sir William Gordon-Cumming to Lady Charlotte Campbell to, n.d.
19 NLS Acc. 8508, 35, Bessie Mure to Lady John Campbell, n.d. [June 1822].
20 *Ibid.*, 18 July 1822.
21 NRS, Old Parish Register 683/5, Parish of Aberlady, 6 January 1820.
22 NLS, Dep. 175, Lady Uxbridge to Lady Gordon-Cumming.
23 NLS, Acc. 8508, 1, Bessie Mure to Lord John Campbell 15 April 1822.
24 NLS, Dep. 175, 165, 5, Emma Campbell to Lady Gordon-Cumming, n.d.
25 NLS, Acc. 8508, 35, Bessie Mure to Lady John, n.d.
26 NLS, Dep. 175, 164, 4, Lady Uxbridge to Lady Gordon-Cumming, November 1821.
27 NLS, Acc. 8508, 35, Lady Charlotte Bury to Lady John Campbell, 15 July 1822.
28 *Ibid.*, Lady Charlotte Bury to Lady John Campbell, 13 April 1821. Walter was M.P. for Argyllshire from 1822 to 1832, and from 1835 to 1841.
29 *Ibid.*, mid July 1822.
30 *Ibid.*
31 NLS, Acc. 8505, 35, Lady Charlotte Bury to Lady John Campbell, 15 July 1822.
32 NLS, Acc. 8059, 3 Lady Charlotte Bury to Lord Glenbervie, 26 June 1822 and other dates.
33 NLS, Acc. 8059, 5, Lord Glenbervie to Lady Charlotte Bury, 18 August 1822.
34 H. C. B. Campbell, *Florence Journey*, p. 37.
35 Bury, *Conduct is Fate* (1822).
36 J. Doyle, *op. cit.*, p. 156.
37 John Wilson (1785-1854), professor of moral philosophy and political economy in Edinburgh University from 1820; alias Christopher North.
38 Cardiff University, CEIR (Centre for Editorial and Intertextual Research), William Blackwood to Thomas Cadell Jr, 5 March 1822.
39 NLS, Acc. 8058, 35, Lady Charlotte Bury to Lady John Campbell, 13 April 1822.

40 NLS, Acc. 8058, 35, Bessie Mure to Lady John Campbell, mid-May 1822.
41 Doyle, *op. cit.*, pp. 156-7.
42 Cardiff University, CEIR, Theodore Hook to William Blackwood, 27 March and 2 April 1822.
43 *Ibid.*, John Galt to William Blackwood, 4 April 1822.
44 *Blackwood's Edinburgh Magazine* (April 1822), pp. 430-2.
45 NLS, Acc. 8058, 35, Lady Charlotte Bury to Lady John Campbell, 20 December 1822.
46 Chatsworth. Devonshire Mss., Chatsworth 6th Dukes Group, 656, Lady Charlotte Bury to the Duke of Devonshire, 22 July 1822.
47 NLS, Mss. 3900, f. 172, E. J. Bury recorded that 'The affection of a near relative of her own family had bestowed' Westwood House on her. Inveraray, Argyll Papers, Appendix.
48 Inveraray, Argyll Papers, 3180 or 3144, Memorandum, 24 May 1832.
49 *Ibid.*
50 NLS, Dep. 175, 165, 1, Lady Charlotte Bury to Julia Campbell, 3 February 1823.

Chapter 14: Aftermath

1 Inveraray, Argyll Papers, 3144, 6 July 1824.
2 A. Prucher, *op. cit.*, 9 October 1824.
3 NLS, Dep. 175, 164, 4, Lady Uxbridge to Lady Gordon-Cumming, 23 July 1824.
4 NLS, Dep. 175, 164, 3, Lady Tullamore to Lady Gordon-Cumming, 10 October 1824.
5 NLS, Acc. 8508, 35, Bessie Mure to Lady John Campbell, 20 July 1825.
6 NLS, Mss. 3900, f. 172, Lady Charlotte Bury to Sir Walter Scott, 16 April 1825.
7 J. A. Home (ed.), *Letters of Lady Louisa Stuart to Miss Louisa Clinton*, p. 2.
8 'Aylmer Bourke Lambert, 1761-1842', William B. Stearn, *ONDB* (Oxford: Oxford University Press, 2004-5).
9 'William Scrope, 1772-1852.', *Ibid.*
10 NLS, marriage John George Campbell, 16 May 1824, Isle of Wight Record Office.
11 NLS, Dep. 175, 164, 4, Lady Tullamore to Lady Gordon-Cumming, 28 April 1824.
12 NLS, Acc. 8508, 36, Emma Campbell to Lady John Campbell, 20 April 1825.
13 *Ibid.*
14 NLS, Acc. 8508, 36, Emma Campbell to Lady John Campbell, 3 May 1825.
15 Argyll, J. D. S. Campbell, *Intimate Society Letters*, vol. 2, pp. 665-6.
16 NLS, Acc. 8508, 36 Emma Campbell to Lady John Campbell, 17 August, 1825.
17 NLS, Dep. 175, 62, 3, Ms. Plan of Ardimersay, 1821.
18 NLS, Acc. 8508, 36, Emma Campbell to Lady John Campbell, 2 December 1825.
19 NLS, Dep. 175, 165, 1, Emma Campbell to Lady Gordon-Cumming, 10 August 1822.
20 NLS, Acc. 8508, 36, Adelaide Campbell to Lady John Campbell, 12 September 1825.
21 NLS, Acc. 8508, 36, Emma Campbell to Lady John Campbell, 18 October 1825.
22 *Ibid.*
23 NLS, Dep. 175, 165, 1, Julia Campbell to Lady Gordon-Cumming, 19 May 1824.
24 NLS, Dep. 175, 164, 1, Lady Charlotte Bury to Sir William Gordon-Cumming, 22 August 1816.
25 NLS, Dep. 175, Mlle de la Chaux to Lady Gordon-Cumming, n.d.
26 E. Haldane, *Scots Gardens in Old Times* (London: Alexander Maclehose, 1934), p. 131.
27 NLS, Acc. 8508, 35, Bessie Mure to Lady John Campbell, 11 February 1823.
28 NLS, Acc. 8508, 35, Bessie Mure to Lady John Campbell, 13 February 1823.
29 NLS, Acc. 8508, 5, Mlle de la Chaux to Lady Gordon-Cumming, 27 March 1823.
30 NLS, Acc. 8508, 3, Mlle de la Chaux, 14 January 1822.
31 Westmeath Library, Mullingar, Howard-Bury Papers, P1, 27, Earl of Charleville to Francis B... 28 March 1822.

32 Ibid., P1/27, 28, 1822.
33 NLS, Dep. 175, 164, 3, Lady Tullamore to Lady Gordon-Cumming 19 June 1824 and 10 October 1824.
34 NLS, Dep. 175, 164, 3, Lady Tullamore to Lady Gordon-Cumming, 10 October 1824.
35 NLS, Acc. 8508, 5, Mlle de la Chaux to Lady John Campbell, 10 September 1822.
36 R. W. Bond, *op. cit.*
37 NLS Dep. 175, 165, 2, Mlle de la Chaux to Lady Gordon-Cumming, 24 January 1821.
38 NLS Dep. 175, 164, 4, Lady Uxbridge to Lady Gordon-Cumming, 17 July 1820.
39 NLS Dep. 175, 165, 5, Anne Damer to Lady Gordon-Cumming, 12 April 1820.
40 NLS Dep. 175, 165, 5, Lady Uxbridge to Lady Gordon-Cumming, 20 May 1820.
41 NLS, Dep. 175, 164, 3, Lady Tullamore to Lady Gordon-Cumming, 19 June 1824.
42 NLS, Dep. 175, Lady Uxbridge to Lady Gordon-Cumming, 16 June 1824.
43 NLS, Acc. 8508, 35, Bessie Mure to Lady John Campbell, 25 September 1825.
44 NLS, Dep. 175, 164, 3, Lady Tullamore to Lady Gordon-Cumming, 19 June 1824.
45 NLS, Acc. 8508, 35, Bessie Mure to Lady John Campbell 25 September 1825.
46 NLS, Dep. 175, 164, 4, [ch] Adelaide Campbell to Lady Uxbridge, 1 December 1825.
47 NLS, Dep. 175, 164, 3, Lady Tullamore to Lady Gordon-Cumming, 10 December 1825.
48 *Ibid.*
49 NLS, Dep. 175, 164, 4, Lord Uxbridge to Lady Uxbridge, 18 December 1825.
50 NLS, Acc. 8508, 35, Bessie Mure to Lady John Campbell, 25 September 1825.
51 NLS, Acc. 8508, 1, Bessie Mure to Lord John Campbell, 12 December 1825.
52 NLS, Dep. 164, 4, Lord Uxbridge to Lady Uxbridge, 13 December 1825.
53 NLS, Acc. 8508, 35, Bessie Mure to Lady John Campbell, 20 October 1825.
54 NLS, Dep. 175, 164, 4, Lord Uxbridge to Lady Gordon-Cumming, 5 December 1825.
55 NLS, Dep. 175, 161, 3, Hoper to Sir William Gordon-Cumming, 29 December 1825.
56 NLS, Dep. 175, 161, 4, Tupper to Sir William Gordon-Cumming, 4 January 1826.
57 NLS, Dep. 175, 164, 4, Lord Uxbridge to Lady Gordon-Cumming, 2 January 1826.
58 NLS, Dep. 175, 161, 3, Tupper to Sir William Gordon-Cumming, 4 January 1826.
59 NLS, Dep. 175, 164, 4, Lord Uxbridge to Lady Uxbridge, 19 January 1826.
60 NLS, Dep. 175, 161, 4, Hoper to Sir William Gordon-Cumming, 3 May 1826.
61 NLS, Dep. 175, 161, 4, Lord Uxbridge to Sir William Gordon-Cumming, 3 June 1826.
62 Houghton Library, Yale University, HM 19704, Lady Charlotte Bury, 4 January 1827.
63 NLS, Dep. 175, 165, 1, Adelaide Campbell to Lady Gordon-Cumming, 12 January 1827.
64 *Ibid.*, Lady Tullamore to Lady Gordon-Cumming, 22 January 1827.
65 *Ibid.*, Lady Tullamore to Lady Gordon-Cumming, 25 January 1827.
66 *Ibid.*, Lady Tullamore to Sir William Gordon-Cumming.
67 Joan Glassel, Lady John Campbell, died on 21 January 1828, shortly after giving birth to a daughter, born on 8 January, but who also died a month after her mother on 19 February 1828.
68 NLS, Dep. 175, 165, 5, Mr Croker to Lady Gordon-Cumming, 13 February 1828.
69 D. C. Clavering, 'Journal of a Voyage to Spitzbergen and the East Coast of Greenland in His Majesty's ship *Griper*', *Edinburgh Literary Journal*, 28 August 1830.
70 Headstones in Sundridge parish church graveyard also include Anne Damer's mother.
71 Bury, *Journal of the Heart* (1830), pp. 3-5.
72 Bury, *Journal of the Heart* (1835), pp. 1-12.
73 NLS, Acc. 8508, 36, Emma Campbell to Lady John Campbell, 14 June 1825.
74 G. Blakiston, *Lord William Russell and his wife* (London: John Murray, 1972), p. 150.
75 *The Times*, 21 May 1828.
76 Blakiston, *op. cit.*, p. 165.
77 *The Times*, 21 May 1828.
78 NLS Dep. 175, 165, 1 Julia Campbell to Lady Gordon-Cumming 12 May 1829.

Chapter 15: Prayers and Projects

1 NLS, Acc. 8508, 36, Emma Campbell to Lady John Campbell, 14 June 1825.
2 NLS, Acc. 8508, 35, Bessie Mure to Lady John Campbell, 20 July 1825.
3 *Ibid.*
4 Lady Exeter divorced the 8th Duke of Hamilton, Lady Charlotte's half brother. She subsequently married the 1st Marquis of Exeter as his third wife and he died in 1804.
5 Lord John Russell, *Memoirs, Journals and Correspondence of Thomas Moore*, vol. 2, p. 831. Lydia White was a 'blue' of large fortune, handsome, witty and with a hospitable salon.
6 NLS, Acc.8508, 35, Bessie Mure to Lady John Campbell, 20 July 1825.
7 NLS, Acc.8508, 1, Bessie Mure to Lord John Campbell, 12 December 1825.
8 Bury, *Suspirium Sanctorum or Holy Breathings* (1826).
9 NLS, Acc. 8508, 35, Bessie Mure to Lady John Campbell, 20 October 1825.
10 J. H. Price, 'Samuel Goodenough' (1743-1827), *ODNB*.
11 J. Doyle, *op. cit.*, p. 168, Susan Ferrier to Mrs Connell, n.d.
12 M. Rosa, *op. cit.* (1936), p. 150.
13 NLS, Acc. 8508, 35, Bessie Mure to Lady John Campbell, 20 October 1825.
14 *Ibid.*, Bessie Mure to Lady John Campbell, 20 October 1835.
15 *The Times*, 18 January 1839. 'Two small vols. "Holy Breathings: a Series of Morning Prayers".'
16 Bury, *Alla Giornata*, 3 vols (1826).
17 NLS, The Murray Archive.
18 Earl of Ilchester (ed.), *Lady Holland to her son 1791-1811* (London: John Murray, 1846), p. 44.
19 *The Monthly Review* 3 (1826), pp. 191-202.
20 Bury, *Alla Giornata*, vol. 2, p. 59.
21 *Ibid.*, vol. 1, pp. 324-6.
22 Bury, *Flirtation*, 3 vols (1827).
23 E. Copeland, *The Silver Fork Novel: Fashionable Fiction in the Age of Reform* (Cambridge: Cambridge University Press, 2012).
24 Rosa, *op. cit.*, p. 150. Rosa was more critical of his selected women authors than of men.
25 N. P. Willis, *Pencillings by the Way*, 3 vols (London: John Macrone, 1835), 1, 30.
26 C. Thoresby, 'Romanticism and Flirtation', *Literature Compass* 1 (Oxford: Wiley-Blackwell Publishing, 2004), pp. 1-4.
27 Lady Lucy C. Scott, (ed.), Lady Charlotte Bury, *Marriage in High Life*, 2 vols (1828), vol. 1, p. 302.
28 *Ibid.*, vol. 1, pp. iii-iv.
29 A. Adburgham, *Silver Fork Society. Fashionable Life and Literature from 1814 to 1840* (London: Constable, 1983), p. 122.
30 G. Jones, *Anecdotal Reminiscences of Distinguished Literary and Political Characters* (London: R. and A. Bielefeld, 1830), p. 273.
31 L. Melville, *The Berry Papers*, p. 407, Lady Charlotte Lindsay to Mary Berry, 25 April 1828.
32 M. Edgeworth, *Letters from England* (Oxford: Clarendon Press, 1971), p. 485.
33 Bury, *The Lady's Own Cookery Book and New Dinner-Table Directory*; the subtitle continued, *in which will be found a large collection of original receipts including not only the result of the authoress's many years observation, experience and research, but also the Contributions of an extensive circle of acquaintance; adapted to the use of persons living in the highest style, as well as those of moderate fortune* (1844).
34 G. Paston, *Little Memoirs of the Nineteenth Century* (London, 1902), p. 279.

35 *The Journals of Sir Walter Scott 1825-1832: from the original manuscript at Abbotsford*, 2 vols (Edinburgh: D. Douglas,1890-91), vol. 1, p. 277, 18 October 1826.
36 Bury, *Journal of the Heart* (1835), pp. 142-44.
37 San Marino, California, The Huntington Library, SY17, Lady Charlotte Bury to Mr Sotheby, 14 September 1826.

Chapter 16: Public and Private Lives

1 A. MacV. Grant, *Memoir and Correspondence of Mrs Grant of Laggan*, 3 vols (London: Longman, Brown, Green & Longmans, 1844), vol. 3, p. 136.
2 NLS, Dep. 175, 161, 2, Edward John Bury to Sir William Gordon-Cumming, 3 October 1828.
3 Islay Estate Papers, Islay Estate Ledger 1828-9, 12 December 1828.
4 M. Storrie, 'Recovering the Historic Designed Landscape of Islay Estate, *Scottish Archives* (Edinburgh: Scottish Records Association, 2001), pp. 59-77.
5 M. Storrie, *Islay. Biography of an Island* (Islay, 2011), pp. 153-55.
6 V. Glendinning, *Raffles and the Golden Opportunity*. See also *ODNB* articles on these Crawfurds.
7 NRS, Scotlands People, Old Parish Register 536 (Kilarrow), 2, 4 September 1828.
8 Shore, C. J. (Baron Teignmouth), *Sketches of the Coasts and Islands of Scotland, and the Isle of Man descriptive of the scenery and illustrative of the progressive revolution in the . . . social condition of the inhabitants of those regions*, 2 vols (London: J. W. Parker, 1836), vol. 2, p. 311.
9 Bury, *The Separation: a Novel* (1830).
10 University of Glasgow Library Special Collections, Ms. Murray 502-97, Letter, Julia Campbell to Lady Charlotte Bury, n.d.
11 A. Allardyce, *op. cit.*, vol. 2, p. 462.
12 University of Glasgow Library Special Collections, Ms. Murray 502-98, 23 February 18xx.
13 NLS, Acc. 5987, bundle 283.
14 NLS, Acc. 5987, Robert MacGibbon to Lady Charlotte Bury, 8 November 1828.
15 NRS, GD46/15/36, Seaforth Muniments, Lady Charlotte Bury to Mary Stewart Mackenzie, 6 January 1829.
16 NLS, Acc. 5987, Robert MacGibbon to Lady Charlotte Bury, 18 December 1828.
17 NLS, Acc. 5987, Robert MacGibbon to Lady Charlotte Bury, 26 December 1828.
18 Bury, 'The Vision', *Journal of the Heart* (1830), pp. 102-12.
19 A. MacV. Grant, *op. cit.*, vol. 3, p. 148.
20 NLS, Dep. 175, 165, 1, Julia Campbell to Lady Gordon-Cumming, 12 May 1829.
21 *The Journals of Sir Walter Scott*, 2, 289, 27 May 1829.
22 *Ibid.*, 2, 299, 8 June 1829.
23 *The London Weekly Review*, 8 March 1828. Advertisement in *The Times*, 6 March 1828, 7E.
24 J. Burke, *The Portrait Gallery of Distinguished Females: Including Beauties of the Courts of George IV and William IV / With Memoirs*, 2 vols (London: E. Bull, 1833), vol. 1, p. 103.
25 M. Edgeworth, *Letters from England*, pp. 447-9.
26 D. Thomson, *The Art of Sir Henry Raeburn 1756-1823* (Scottish National Portrait Gallery, Edinburgh, 1997).
27 Ross miniature engraved by Thomson for *La Belle Assemblée* no. 76 (new series), April 1831.
28 *The Times* 25 March 1831 and 25 June 1831.

29 Francis W. Wilkin, John Cochran; after a drawing, 1841, published in W. Finden's *Female Aristocracy of the Court of Queen Victoria* (1849).
30 Sir Herbert Maxwell (ed.), *op cit.*, T. Creevey, October 1834.
31 M. Sadleir, *The Strange Life of Lady Blessington* (London: Constable & Co., 1947), p. 141.
32 M. Blessington, *Grace Cassidy; or, The Repealers*, 3 vols (London, 1833).
33 NLS, Murray Archive.
34 *Ibid.*
35 University of Dundee, Archive, Records Management and Museum Services, MS 25/1/3 vol. 2 (16). Lady Charlotte Bury to Thomas Campbell, 13 March 1830.
36 University of Glasgow Library, Special Collections, Gen. 1662/15, f.6, Lady Charlotte Bury to Thomas Campbell, 18 March 1830.
37 W. Partington, *op.cit.*, p. 286, Lady Charlotte Bury to Sir Walter Scott, 12 March 1830.
38 J. Doyle, *op. cit.*, p. 223, Mrs Kinloch to Susan Ferrier, 30 April 1831.
39 NLS, Mss. 3918, f. 115, Lady Charlotte Bury to Sir Walter Scott, 15 June 1831.
40 NLS, Murray Archive.
41 University of Nottingham Library, Marley Papers, Cellar Book. This relates to St George's Place, London, not to Charleville Castle, as listed.
42 NLS, Mss. 3081, 11 February 1831.
43 NLS, Mss. 3081, 25 February 1831.
44 NLS, Mss. 3081, 21 April 1831.
45 A. Fremantle, *op. cit.*, vol. 3, p. 303.
46 NLS, Dep. 175, 165. 1. Adelaide Campbell to Lady Gordon-Cumming, 16 April 1830.
47 W. C. Maughan, *op. cit.*
48 A daughter had died before the time of Lady Charlotte's memoir; another son, George, was described as 'dying' in 1809.
49 Lady Mary Richardson (ed.), *Autobiography of Mrs Fletcher of Edinburgh with selections from her Letters and other Family Memorials* (Edinburgh: Edmonton and Douglas, 1875).
50 NLS, Dep. 175, 64, 3, Lady Tullamore to Lady Gordon-Cumming. They were buried in Brighton old church cemetery; the two remaining children, Walter and Edith being subsequently brought up in Islay by co-guardian, Walter Campbell.
51 University of Nottingham, Marley Papers, 598, 1, Lady Charlotte Bury to the Countess of Charleville, 9 November 1831.
52 Anna Maria de Blaquière, daughter of the 1st Baron de Blaquière of Ardkill, Co. Londonderry, had married Viscount Kirkwall on 11 August 1802.
53 The Duchess of Richmond had been Eleonora's sister-in-law, and would become Adelaide's.
54 NLS, Dep. 175, 165, 1, Adelaide Campbell to Lady Gordon-Cumming, 13 April 1832.
55 British Library, Add. Mss. 5103, f. 21r. Lady Charlotte Bury to the Rev. J. D. Lille, n.d.
56 NLS, Dep. 175, 165, 1, Lady Charlotte Bury to Lord Tullamore, 10 May 1832.
57 NLS, Dep. 175, 64, 3, Lady Tullamore to Lady Gordon-Cumming, 14 May 1832.
58 NLS, Dep. 175, 165, 1, Adelaide Campbell to Lady Gordon-Cumming, 13 April 1842.
59 NLS, Dep. 175, 165, 1, Adelaide Campbell to Lady Tullamore, 7 May 1832.
60 Islay Estate Papers, Ledger 1832-3. Almost £38 of the £80 cost of the funeral was for 'aqua' (whisky).
61 The other half of the sarcophagus remained unoccupied. Walter remarried five years later, but was to die and be buried in 1855 at Avranches in Normandy.
62 W. C. Maughan, *op. cit.*, pp. 168-9.
63 NLS, Dep. 175, 165, 5, Anne Damer to Lady Gordon-Cumming, 12 April 1820.
64 NLS, Acc. 8508, 35, Lady Charlotte Bury to Lady John Campbell, 11 February 1822.

65 Russell, *Three Generations of Fascinating Women*, p. 199.
66 University of Nottingham Library, Marley Papers, 598-1, Lady Charlotte Bury to the Countess of Charleville, 9 November 1831.
67 *Quarterly Review* 51 (1834).

Chapter 17: The Three Great Sanctuaries

1 NLS, Mss. 3134, f. 48, T. Wilson Craig.
2 *Ibid.*, Lady Charlotte Bury to T. Thomson, 6 July 1831.
3 J. Doyle, *op. cit.*, John Ferrier to Susan Ferrier, 21 July 1831, p. 224.
4 NRS, GD 170/2261, Lady Charlotte Bury to Sir Duncan Campbell, 1831.
5 University of Manchester, John Rylands Library, Eng Mss 363/85 Lady Charlotte Bury to Lady Winterton, 15 June 1831.
6 *The Royal Lady's Magazine, and Archives of the Court of St. James's*, 5 vols (London: W. Sams, 1832), vol. 3, p. 205.
7 JRUL, Eng Mss 344/89, Lady Charlotte Bury to James Moyse, n.d.
8 Harvard University, Houghton Library, Lady Charlotte Bury (Campbell) to Rev. Edward Scobell, 30 May 1833.
9 Bury, *The Three Great Sanctuaries* (1833), Preface.
10 NLS, Mss 3134, f. 49, *Prospectus* for 'The Three Great Sanctuaries'.
11 Bury, *The Three Great Sanctuaries* (1833).
12 Advertised for sale at £350 online in late 2012.
13 Bury, *The Three Great Sanctuaries*, p. viii.
14 *Ibid.*, p. xii.
15 B. E. Graver, 'Wordsworth, St. Francis, and Lady Charlotte Bury', *Philological Quarterly*, 65 (1986), pp. 371-80.
16 *The Literary Gazette and Journal of Belles Lettres, Arts, Sciences, Etc.* (London: H. Colburn, 1834), p. 62.
17 *New Monthly Magazine*, vol. 40 (London: H. Colburn, 1834), p. 381.
18 *Fraser's Magazine for Town and Country*, vol. 10 (London: James Fraser, 1834), pp. 350-2, 449, 751-2.
19 *The Quarterly Review*, vol. 51 (London: John Murray, 1834), p. 439.
20 Lady Charlotte Huntington Journal.
21 *Ibid.*
22 Heath's *Book of Beauty*, pp. 79-82 and pp. 161-3.
23 *Ibid.*, pp. 161-3.
24 Bury, *Journal of the Heart* (1835), pp. 25-7.
25 Bury, *Diary* (1908), vol. 1, p. 377.
26 Heath's *Book of Beauty*, pp. 116-8.
27 Bury, *The Devoted* (1836), ch. 17.
28 *Ibid.*
29 Bury, *The Exclusives* (1830), vol. 1, ch.12.
30 *Ibid.*, vol. 1, ch. 8.
31 Bury, *The Two Baronets* (1864), ch. 12.
32 *Ibid.*
33 Bury, *The Three Great Sanctuaries*, pp. 77-87.
34 Bury, *The History of a Flirt* (1840), vol. 3, ch.1.
35 Bury, *Conduct is Fate* (1822), vol. 2, ch. 16, pp. 237-9.
36 *Ibid.*, vol. 3, ch. 122.
37 Bury, *The Devoted*, vol. 3, p. 107.
38 *Ibid.*, vol. 2, p. 272.
39 Bury, *The Divorced* (1837), p. 52.

40 Bury, *Conduct is Fate*, vol. 3, pp. 234-6.
41 The British Library, Add. Mss. 32151, f. 119. Ms. Holland poem; rainbow CF 3; Scots song CF 122; sea *The Devoted*, 3, 107;*The Divorced*, 1, 140-8; Grave *The Exclusives*, vol. 1, ch. 12, vol. 2, ch 8.
42 Glasgow City Archives, The Mitchell Library, Ms. 75/210 and 210a.
43 Perkins, P., 'Scottish Women Poets of the Romantic period', https://www.proquest.com/books/lady-charlotte-susan-maria-campbell-bury-1775/docview/2352938251/se-2, accessed 28 October 2024.

Chapter 18: The Professional

1 Richard Bentley Archives.
2 Birmingham Library, Archives and Heritage, MS 135, Letter from Lady Charlotte Bury to Mr [S. C.] Hall, 21 October 1833.
3 Lord John Russell, *Memoirs, Journals and Correspondence of Thomas Moore*, 4, 1570, 9 November 1833.
4 L. Melville, *The Berry Papers*, pp. 415-6; British Library, Add. Mss. 37726, f. 195.
5 Edinburgh University Library, Mss. LaIII, f. 217r, Lady Charlotte Bury to Messrs Cochrane and McCrone, 2 January 1835.
6 A. Allardyce, *op. cit.*, vol. 2, p. 486.
7 *Ibid.*, vol. 2, p. 496.
8 It may have been the bust mentioned as still being in Islay House in 1886, when the commissioner/factor asked John Francis Campbell about its future, Islay Estate Papers. Again, in January 1825 Lady Granville noted that the bust of Blanche Bury was 'at present in Islay House', Islay Estate Papers, Family Box 2.
9 Lord John Russell, *Memoirs, Journals and Correspondence of Thomas Moore*, vol. 4, p. 1570.
10 Birmingham Library, Archives and Heritage, MS 135, Letter from Lady Charlotte Bury to Mr Hall, 21 October 1833.
11 Exhibited at the Royal Academy, 1834, No. 341.
12 Melville, *The Berry Papers*, p. 415.
13 Bury, *The Devoted*, vol. 2, ch. 7.
14 R. R. Madden, *The Literary Life and Correspondence of the Countess of Blessington*, 3 vols (London, 1855), vol. 3, p. 449.
15 Sydney, Lady Morgan, *Lady Morgan's Memoirs: Autobiography, Diaries and Correspondence*, eds Miss Jewsbury and W. Hepworth Dixon, 2 vols (London: W. H. Allen & Co., 1862) vol. 2, pp. 68-70.
16 E. H. Dering (ed.), *Memoirs of Georgiana, Lady Chatterton. With some passages from her diary* (London: Hurst and Blackett, 1878), p. 309.
17 G. Jones, *op. cit.*, pp. 95-6.
18 *The Times*, 24 March 1834.
19 R. R. Madden, *op. cit.*, vol. 2, p. 89.
20 W. A. Shee, *My Contemporaries, 1830-1870* (London: Hurst & Blackett, 1893), p. 97.
21 Bury, *Diary* (1908), vol. 1, pp. 143-4.
22 A. Allardyce, *op. cit.*, vol. 2, p. 496, Lady Charlotte Bury to Charles Kirkpatrick Sharpe, 13 January 1837.
23 University of Edinburgh Library, Special Collections, LaIII, f. 366, Lady Charlotte Bury to Messrs Cochrane and Macrone, 2 January 1835.
24 R. L. Patten, 'Bentley, Richard (1794-1871)' and 'Bentley, Samuel (1785-1868)', *ODNB* (2004); 'Colburn, Henry (1784-1855)', *ODNB* (2004).
25 'Cheap editions of celebrated works at only 4s. per volume bound' included Lady Charlotte's *Flirtation*, *The Times* 10 April 1835. 'Cheap Novels and Romances. The

Stock of a circulating library, including works by Lady Charlotte Bury . . . is to be sold at the low price of 1s. per volume. Carvalho's Cheap book warehouse, 147 Fleet Street', *The Times*, 3 December 1836. Lady Charlotte Bury's works were included in the catalogues of 'Ten Thousand Volumes of Novels and Romances' advertised for sale in June 1840 at A. K. Newman's in Leadenhall, *The Times*, 29 June 1840, while 100 novels and romances for £10 were offered in April the following year, *The Times* 24 April 1841.

26 W. St Clair, *The Reading Nation in the Romantic Period* (Cambridge: Cambridge University Press, 2004).

27 With lots of space on all sides of the page round the fairly large font of the text and well spaced lines.

28 Edinburgh University Library, Special Collections, La. III, f. 218, Lady Charlotte Bury to W. Schoberl Esq[r], 31 August 1837.

29 N. P. Willis, *Pencillings by the Way*, p. 191.

30 *The Times*, 20 March 1837.

31 The Bodleian Library, Pigott Mss., d.16, f. 67, Ms. Preface by J. Galt to 'Records of Real Life'.

32 R. H. Horne, *The New Spirit of the Age*, 2 vols (London: Smith, Elder and Co., 1844), vol. 1, p. 236.

33 C. Gore, Preface to *Pin Money. A Novel* (London, 1831).

34 *The Times*, 23 June 1837.

35 *The Times*, 23 June and 14 December 1837 (from *The Dispatch*).

36 Bury, *The Posthumous Memoirs of a Peeress* (1837).

37 *The Knickerbocker: or New Monthly Magazine* (New York, 1837), p. 527.

38 Richard Bentley Archives, reel 43, vol. 90, p. 83.

39 Pam Perkins, 'Pigott, Harriet, (1775-1846)', *ONDB* (2004).

40 The Bodleian Library. Pigott Mss, d.16, f. 3, Lady Charlotte Bury to Harriet Pigott, 26 March 1838.

41 *Ibid.*, f. 35, Lady Charlotte Bury to Harriet Pigott, 12 April 1838.

42 *Ibid.*, f. 5, Lady Charlotte Bury to unnamed publisher, 6 April 1838.

43 *Ibid.*

44 Anon. (Harriet Pigott), *The Private Correspondence of a Woman of Fashion*, 2 vols (London: Henry Colburn and Richard Bentley, 1832).

45 The Bodleian Library, Harriet Pigott Mss., d.16, f. 3, Lady Charlotte Bury to Harriet Pigott, 26 March 1838.

46 *Ibid.*, f. 46, Lady Charlotte Bury to Harriet Pigott, 23 May 1838.

47 *Ibid.*

48 *Ibid.*, d.16, f. 5, Lady Charlotte Bury to Harriet Pigott, 6 April, 1838.

49 Mrs Cornwell Baron-Wilson, *The Life and Correspondence of M. Gregory Lewis, 1787-1818, with many pieces in prose and verse never before published*, 2 vols (London: H. Colburn, 1839).

50 It was Colburn's rivals, Saunders and Otley, who had published Lady Charlotte's *Alla Giornata* in 1826, as well as her prayers in 1826 and 1830.

51 Bodleian Library, Pigott Mss., d.16, f. 94, Lady Charlotte Bury to Harriet Pigott, n.d.

52 *Ibid.*, f. 3, Lady Charlotte Bury to Harriet Pigott, 26 March 1838. One suggestion had been 'Diary of a Woman of Fashion, interspersed with original letters to the present time'. Another, which Lady Charlotte favoured less, was the cumbersome 'Anecdotes and Opinions of Men Manners and Things of the last century and the present interspersed with original letters'.

53 H. Pigott, *Records of Real Life in the Palace and the Cottage*, 3 vols (London: Saunders and Otley, 1839), vol. 1, p. xi.

54 *The Times*, 18 April 1840.

55 Bodleian Library Pigott Mss., d.16, f. 54, Lady Charlotte Bury to Harriet Pigott, 12 April 1839.
56 *Ibid.*, f. 60, Lady Charlotte Bury to Harriet Pigott, 25 April 1839.
57 Bury, *Journal of the Heart* (1830) and *Journal of the Heart* (1835).
58 *The Edinburgh Literary Journal or Weekly Register of Criticism and Belles Lettres* (Edinburgh: Constable and Co., July-December 1830), p. 323.
59 Bury, *Journal of the Heart* (1830), p. 113.
60 National Library of Wales, MS 229777D, ff. 23-4, Lady Charlotte Bury to Sarah Ponsonby, 8 April 1831.
61 Sarah Ponsonby was a sister of the 6th Duchess of Argyll.
62 Richard Bentley Archive.
63 Heath's *Book of Beauty*, pp. 44-5.
64 Bury, *Journal of the Heart* (1835), pp. 1-12.
65 *The Sunday Times*, 25 May 1835.
66 A. Allardyce., *op. cit.*, vol. 2, p. 487, Lady Charlotte Bury to Charles Kirkpatrick Sharpe, 11 November 1836.
67 *Ibid.*, p. 496, Lady Charlotte Bury to Charles Kirkpatrick Sharpe, 13 January 1837.
68 *Ibid.*, pp. 501-3, Lady Charlotte Bury to Charles Kirkpatrick Sharpe, 4 December 1837.
69 *Ibid.*
70 *Ibid.*, vol. 2, p. 441.
71 San Marino, California,The Huntington Library, UP 118, Lady Charlotte Bury to William Upcott, 5 September 1837; UP 119, same to same, 29 September 1837; and UP 719, William Upcott to Lady Charlotte Bury, 7 September 1837.
72 H. C. Carey and A. Hart, *Letters on International Copyright* (Philadelphia: A. Hart, Late Carey and Hart, 1853), p. 38.

Chapter 19: Galley Years

1 University of Manchester, John Rylands University Library.
2 Bodleian Library, Pigott Mss., d.16, f. 52, Lady Charlotte Bury to Harriet Pigott, 7 April 1839.
3 Bodleian Library, Pigott Mss., d.16, f. 16, Lady Charlotte Bury to Harriet Pigott, 28 November 1838.
4 Bury, *The Roses* (London: Hurst and Blackett, 1853); *The Lady of Fashion* (London: Hurst and Blackett, 1856).
5 Bury, *The Two Baronets. A Novel of Fashionable Life* (London: New York: Routledge, Warne, & Routledge, 1864).
6 University of Nottingham Library, Marley Papers, Lady Charlotte Bury to Dowager Lady Charleville.
7 J. Mullen, *How Novels Work* (Oxford: Oxford University Press, 2006), p. 26.
8 Bury, *Journal of the Heart* (1830), pp. 89-93.
9 W. Hazlitt, *The Examiner*, 18 November 1827.
10 W. St Clair, *op. cit.*, p. 564.
11 *The Court Journal*, 18 September 1830, p. 198.
12 *The Athenaeum*, 30 October 1831, p. 680.
13 M. Rosa, *op. cit.*, p. 197.
14 Richard Bentley Archives, reel 39, vol. 80, p. 4.
15 Bury, *The Exclusives* (London, 1830) p. 17.
16 Richard Bentley Archives, reel 39, vol. 78, p. 5.
17 Bury, *The Exclusives*, vol. 3, p. 528.
18 The British Library, N.737; *Key to the Royal Novel* (1830).

19 *BP*, 28 November 29; *The Star*, 27 November 1829; *ECB*, November 1829, 195 and *ER*, April 1830 51:294.
20 Richard Bentley Archives, reel 39, vol. 81, p. 56.
21 *Ibid.*, reel 25, vol. 52, p. 317.
22 Bury, *The Disinherited and The Ensnared*, 3 vols (1834).
23 *The Literary Gazette and Journal of Belles Lettres, Arts, Sciences, Etc*, vol. 36 (London: H. Colburn, 1834), p. 534.
24 *The Times*, 6 August 1834.
25 Bury, *The Disinherited and The Ensnared*, vol. 2, p. 65.
26 *Ibid.*, vol. 2, pp. 74-5.
27 Quoted in *The Times*, 30 June 1836.
28 *The British and Foreign Review: or European Quarterly Journal*, (London: J. Ridgeway and Sons, 1836), p. 506.
29 Bury, *The Devoted*, vol. 1, ch. 8, and vol. 3, ch. 14.
30 Richard Bentley Archives, reel 26, vol. 53, pp. 194-6.
31 Richard Bentley Archives, reel 54, vol. 117A, p. 4.
32 Bury, *The Divorced* (London: H. Colburn, 1837).
33 J. Todd (ed.), *A Dictionary of British and American Women Writers, 1600-1800* (London: Methuen, 1987).
34 *The Monthly Review*, vol. 1 (London: G. Henderson, 1837), pp. 603-6.
35 Bury, *Love* (1837).
36 *The Times*, 11 January 1838.
37 Bury, *Love*, vol. 1, p. 142.
38 *Ibid.*, 3, 75. EUL, Special collections, La.III, 218, Lady Charlotte Bury to W. Schoberl, 31 August 1837.
39 Bury, *The Glanville Family* (London: H. Colburn, 1839); *Ellen Glanville*, 2 vols (Philadelphia, 1839).
40 Bury, *The History of a Flirt* (London: H. Colburn, 1840).
41 Bury, *Family Records: or the Two Sisters* (London: Saunders and Otley, 1841).
42 *Ibid.*, vol. 2, p. 138.
43 *Ibid.*, vol. 1, p. 157.
44 Bury, 'The Promise' in Bury, *Family Records*, vol. 2.
45 Bury, 'The Lovers', in Bury, *Family Records*, vol. 2.
46 Bury, *The Manoeuvring Mother* (London: H. Colburn, 1842).
47 *Ibid.*
48 Bury, *The Wilfulness of Woman* (London: H. Colburn, 1844).
49 *Ibid.*
50 *Ibid.*
51 *The New Monthly Magazine and Humorist*, vol. 49 (London: H. Colburn, 1837), p. 443.
52 *The Athenaeum*, 19 November 1853.
53 J. Todd, *British Women Writers: A Critical Reference Guide* (New York: Continuum, 1989), p. 116.

Chapter 20: The Diary

1 San Marino, California, Huntington Library, Lady Charlotte Huntington Journal.
2 A. Prucher, *op. cit.*, Lady Charlotte Bury to Jean-Charles Sismondi, March 1842.
3 P. A. Spalding, *Self Harvest. A Study of Diaries and the Diarist* (London: Independent Press, 1949), p. 12.
4 Bury, *Diary*, vol. 1, p. 350.
5 *Ibid.*
6 *Ibid.*, vol. 1, p. 32.

7 Bury, *Journal of the Heart* (1830), p. 1.
8 Bury, *Diary*, 4 vols (London: H. Colburn, 1839).
9 L. Melville, *Regency Ladies*, p. 115.
10 Lady Charlotte Bury, *The Court of England under George IV. Founded on a Diary Interspersed with Letters written by Queen Caroline and various other Distinguished Persons*, 2 vols (London: Macqueen, 1896).
11 Lady Charlotte Bury, *The Diary of a Lady-in-Waiting being the Diary illustrative of the times of George the Fourth interpersed with original Letters from the late Queen Caroline and from other Distinguished Persons*, (ed.), with an introduction by A. Francis Steuart, 2 vols (London and New York: J. Lane, 1908).
12 Advertisement at back of second volume of Bury, *Diary* (1908).
13 *Ibid.*
14 Bury, *Diary* (1839), Preface.
15 The Bodleian Library, Pigott Mss., d.16, f.60, Lady Charlotte Bury to Harriet Pigott, 25 April 1839.
16 Bury, *Diary*, 2 vol. (Philadelphia: Carey, Lea and Blanchard, 1839), vol. 1, p. 3.
17 C. R. Cheney (ed.) and M. Jones (rev. ed.), *A Handbook of Dates For Students of British History* (Cambridge: Cambridge University Press, 2000).
18 Bury, *Diary* (1839), vol. 1, preface to 15 letters from the Princess of Wales.
19 The title after the plaque on the Princess of Wales' coffin taken to Brunswick.
20 Bury, *Diary* (1839), vol. 1, p. 71.
21 A. Allardyce, *op. cit.*, vol. 2.
22 Bury, *Diary* (1839), vol. 1, p. 125.
23 These volumes are in the National Library of Scotland, Dur. 1602-1603.
24 A. Allardyce, *op. cit.*, vol. 2, p. 519.
25 *Ibid.*, vol. 1, p. 483.
26 Bury, *Diary* (1839), footnote, vol. 1, pp. 69-71.
27 *Ibid.*, vol. 2, p. 83.
28 *Ibid.*, vol. 2, p. 70.
29 *Ibid.*, vol. 2, p. 270.
30 Bury, *Diary* (1908), vol. 1, p. 224.
31 *Ibid.*, vol. 1, p. 54.
32 Bury, *Diary* (1838), vol. 3, p. 399.
33 *Ibid.*, vol. 1, p. 99.
34 *Ibid.*, vol. 1, p. 202.
35 *Ibid.*, vol. 2, p. 117.
36 *Ibid.*, vol. 1, p. 105.
37 *Ibid.*, vol. 1, pp. 105-106.
38 *Literary Gazette and Journal of Belles Lettres* (1838), p. 7.
39 Sydney, Lady Morgan, *Lady Morgan's Memoirs*, vol. 2, p. 436.
40 Bury, *Diary* (1839), vol. 1, p. 87.
41 G. Blakiston, *op. cit.*, p. 376.
42 Bury, *Diary* (1838), vol. 2, p. 179.
43 University of Nottingham Library, Marlay Papers.
44 Lord Arthur Ponsonby, *English Diaries. A Review of English Diaries from the Sixteenth to the Twentieth Centuries, with an Introduction to Diary Writing* (London: Methuen, 1923), p. 17.
45 Grant, *Susan Ferrier of Edinburgh*, p. 160.
46 *Belgravia: An Illustrated London Magazine*, vol. XLVII (London: Chatto and Windus, 1882), p. 228.

Chapter 21: Ducal Rescue

1 *The Court Journal*, 1835, p. 261.
2 *Ibid.*, p. 315.
3 *Ibid.*, p. 390.
4 *Ibid.*, p. 420.
5 Copy of Marriage certificate, West Sussex Record Office.
6 Royal Academy Exhibition 1838, No. 1366.
7 Lord J. Russell, *Memoirs, Journals and Correspondence of Thomas Moore*, vol. 4, p. 1570, Saturday 9 November 1833.
8 Bodleian Library, Pigott Mss., d.16, f. 14, Lady Charlotte Bury to Harriet Pigott, 17 October 1838.
9 *Ibid.*, f. 50, Lady Charlotte Bury to Harriet Pigott, 5 April 1839.
10 NLS, Dep. 175, 164, 1, Lady Charlotte Bury to Lady Gordon-Cumming, 4 March 1818.
11 NRS, Old Parish Records, (Kilarrow, 536): notice 6 November 1836; marriage 8 November 1836.
12 Bodleian Library, Pigott Mss., d.16, f. 14, Lady Charlotte Bury to Harriet Pigott, 17 October 1838.
13 NLS, Dep. 175, 165, 1, Julia Langford Brooke to Lady Gordon-Cumming, 21 January 1840.
14 T. Dunphy and T. J. Cummins, *Remarkable Trials of All Countries* (New York: Diossy and Cockcroft, 1870), p. 311.
15 NLS, Dep. 175, 164, 1, Julia Langford Brooke to Sir William Gordon-Cumming, 27 May, 1837.
16 NLS, Dep. 175, 161, 4, Lord Tullamore to Sir William Gordon-Cumming, 15 October 1839.
17 *The Times*, 23 August 1836.
18 *The Times*, 26 October 1839.
19 *The Times*, 1 November 1839.
20 *The Times*, 6 November 1839.
21 An infant daughter, Elizabeth, had died in 1828, while their elder son John Henry, had died aged only sixteen, in 1837.
22 A. Campbell, *A History of Clan Campbell*, 3, 294.
23 *The Times*, 28 January 1840.
24 *The Times*, 1 September 1842.
25 *The Times*, 6 September 1842, 'from *The Glasgow Chronicle*'.
26 Bodleian Library, Pigott Mss., d.16, f. 88, Blanch Bury to Harriet Pigott, 1 January 1840.
27 NLS, Acc. 8508, Bessie Mure to Lady John Campbell.
28 Bodleian Library, Pigott Mss., d.16, f. 52, Lady Charlotte Bury to Harriet Pigott, 7 April 1839.
29 Bodleian Library, Pigott Mss., d.16, f. 61, Lady Charlotte Bury to Harriet Pigott, 25 April 1839.
30 Inveraray, Argyll Papers, 3144; NLS/NAS, Campbell Gibson, Lady Charlotte Bury to Robert McGibbon, 16 November 1837.
31 Inveraray, Argyll Papers, 3022.
32 *Ibid.*, 3180.
33 *Ibid.*, 3180, 15 August 1840.
34 *Ibid.*, 3022, 3 October 1840.
35 *Ibid.*, 3023, 11 November 1840.
36 *The Scottish Jurist* (1842), pp. 12-15. Reports of cases decided 19 November 1841, First Division. Adam Glen Pursuer v. David Black and his cautioners, Defenders.

37 *The Times*, 7 May 1841.
38 Inveraray, Argyll Papers, 1842, 1844, list 273, 8 February 1842 and 10 June 1843.

Chapter 22: Italian Sojourn

1 A. Prucher, *op. cit.*, p. 104, Lady Charlotte Bury to Jean-Charles Sismondi, 27 December 1841.
2 Nottingham University, Marley Papers, 602, Lady Charlotte Bury to Dowager Countess of Charleville, 24 June 1843.
3 Marley Papers, 607, Lady Charlotte Bury to Dowager Countess of Charleville, 23 July 1844.
4 NLS, Dep. 175, 160, 4, Lady Charlotte Bury to Sir William Gordon-Cumming, 27 May 1842.
5 C. F. Gordon-Cumming, *Memories*, p. 43.
6 NLS, Dep. 175, 165, 5, Notice prepared for *The Forres Gazette*, 4 May 1842.
7 A. Prucher, *op. cit.*, p. 106, Lady Charlotte Bury to Jean-Charles Sismondi, 25 May 1842.
8 NLS, Dep. 175, 160, 4, Lady Charlotte Bury to Sir William Gordon-Cumming, 27 May 1842.
9 Sir William remarried in 1846 and had further issue.
10 NLS, Acc. 5987, Lady Charlotte Bury to James Macinnes, 14 December 1842.
11 NLS, Dep. 175, 161, 4, Julia Langford-Brooke to Sir William Gordon-Cumming, 29 December 1842.
12 F. Leveson-Gower (ed.), *Letters of Harriet, Countess Granville 1810-1845*, 2 vols (London: Longmans and Co, 1894), vol. 2, pp. 338-9.
13 NLS, Acc. 5987.
14 NLS, Dep. 175, 161, 4, Julia Langford-Brooke to Sir William Gordon-Cumming, 29 December 1842.
15 BL, Add. Mss. 52151, f. 119, Poem by Lady Charlotte Bury 1843, given perhaps to her distant kinswoman Lady Coventry, or her son.
16 University of Nottingham Library, Marley Papers, 605, Lady Charlotte Bury to Dowager Countess of Charleville, 24 June 1843.
17 Marley Papers, 603, Lady Charlotte Bury to Dowager Countess of Charleville, 21 Oct 1843.
18 Marley Papers, 602, Lady Charlotte Bury to Dowager Countess of Charleville, 27 Aug 1843.
19 Marley Papers, 603, Lady Charlotte Bury to Dowager Countess of Charleville, 27 August 1843 and 17 April 1844.
20 Marley Papers, 607, Lady Charlotte Bury to Dowager Countess of Charleville, 24 June 1843.
21 *Ibid.*, Lady Charlotte Bury to Dowager Countess of Charleville, 23 July1844.
22 Marley Papers, 607, Lady Charlotte Bury to Dowager Countess of Charleville, 23 July 1844.
23 Marley Papers, 606, Lady Charlotte Bury to Dowager Countess of Charleville, 17 April 1844.
24 Marley Papers, 608, Lady Charlotte Bury to Dowager Countess of Charleville, October 1844.
25 *Ibid.*, Lady Charlotte Bury to Dowager Countess of Charleville, October 1844.
26 Marley Papers, 609, Lady Charlotte Bury to Dowager Countess of Charleville, 31 August 1845.
27 *Ibid.*, Lady Charlotte Bury to Dowager Countess of Charleville, 31 August 1845.
28 *The Times*, 11 August 1845.

29 *The Times*, 21 August 1845.
30 University of Nottingham Library, Marley Papers, 606 and 609, Lady Charlotte Bury to Dowager Countess of Charleville, 17 April 1844 and 31 August 1845.
31 Geneva, Bibliothèque Universitaire et Publique, Galiffe, 25 September 1845.
32 Marley Papers, 608, Lady Charlotte Bury to Dowager Countess of Charleville, October 1844.
33 Buried in the same lair thereafter were Dominique Loridan (1780-1853) 'in memory of 55 years of service', and family friend, Alexander Baillie (1777-1855) of Dochfour, Inverness.
34 Marley Papers, 601, 1, Lady Charlotte Bury to Dowager Countess of Charleville, 23 April 1848.
35 Marley Papers, 601, Lady Charlotte Bury to Dowager Countess of Charleville, 23 April 1848.
36 J. Doyle, *op. cit.*, p. 297, Susan Ferrier to Mrs Tennent, 8 November 1847.
37 M. Storrie, *Islay: A Biography*, p. 153.
38 W. F. Campbell, (ed.), J. F. Campbell, *Life in Normandy; Sketches of French fishing, farming, cooking, natural history and politics, drawn from nature*, 2 vols (Edinburgh: Edmonston and Douglas, 1863).
39 Glasgow City Archives, Mitchell Library, TD 1284/4/1.
40 NLS, Sale catalogues, 16, f.2 (12). 29, 30 November 1852.
41 Glasgow University Library, Special Collections, MU 43, c.17, Introduction to sermon preached by Revd. Edward Penny to the protestant congregation at Avranches, 11 February 1855; and Discours de M. le Dr Thenbault at burial of Walter Frederick Campbell, 12 February 1855.

Chapter 23: London Finale

1 J. A. W. Gunn, *Benjamin Disraeli Letters* (Toronto: University of Toronto Letters, 1982), pp. 187-8.
2 J. Doyle, *op. cit.*, p. 323.
3 *Ibid.*, p. 326.
4 *The Journals and Correspondence of Lady Eastlake,* (ed.), C. E. Smith, 2 vols (London, 1895), vol. 1, p. 256.
5 Westmeath Library, Mullingar, Howard-Bury Papers.
6 Advertisement in Bury, *The Lady of Fashion* (1856).
7 *Ibid.*, vol. 1, ch. 6.
8 NLS, Dep. 175, 166, 6, Lady Charlotte Bury to Penrose Gordon-Cumming, November 1854.
9 *The Times*, February 1859.
10 Swinton 1855 chalk/pastel; 1972 the late Lady Charlotte Bury.
11 *The Times*, 28 December 1888.
12 *The Times*, 5 June 1872.
13 NLS, Dep. 175, 164, 4, Ms. Memoirs.
14 Argyll, J. D. S. Campbell, *Passages from the Past*, vol. 1, p. 65.
15 *Ibid.*, vol. 1, p. 64.
16 *The Times*, 2 April 1861.
17 *The Annual Register—or a View of the History and Politics of the Year 1861* (1862), p. 410.
18 NLS, Dep. 175, 166, 6, Emma Russell to Penrose Gordon-Cumming, 3rd bart, n.d.
19 H. C. B. Campbell, *Florence Journey*, p. 17.
20 Census 1871, Bury St Edmunds.
21 David Lyon MP died in Nice in 1872.

Bibliography

Albinson, A. Cassandra, Funnell, Peter and Peltz, Lucy (eds), *Thomas Lawrence. Regency Power & Brilliance* (New Haven and London: Yale University Press, 2011).

Aliquis, J. B. and Pagan, James, (eds), *Glasgow Past and Present: Illustrated in Dean of Guild Court Reports and in the Reminiscences of Scorex, Aliquis, J.B., etc.* (Glasgow: D. Robertson, 1884).

Adburgham Alison, *Shopping in Style: London from the Restoration to Edwardian Elegance 1800-1891* (London: Allen and Unwin, 1981); *Shops and Shopping: Where, and in What Manner the Well-Dressed Englishwoman Bought Her Clothes* (London: Allen and Unwin, 1989); *Silver Fork Society. Fashionable Life and Literature from 1814 to 1840* (London: Constable, 1983); *Women in Print. Writing Women and Women's Magazines from the Restoration to the Accession of Victoria* (London: Allen and Unwin, 1972).

Airlie, Mabel, Countess of, *In Whig Society 1775-1818. Compiled from the Hitherto Unpublished Correspondence of Elizabeth Viscountess Melbourne, and Emily Lamb, Countess Cowper, Afterwards Viscountess Palmerston* (London: Hodder & Stoughton, 1921).

Allardyce, Alexander, *Letters to and from Charles Kirkpatrick Sharpe, with a memoir by W. K. R. Bedford*, 2 vols (Edinburgh: William Blackwood and Sons, 1888).

Altick, Richard D., *The Shows of London [Diorama]. A Panoramic History of Exhibitions* (Cambridge, Massachusetts: Harvard University Press, 1978).

D'Andlau, B., transl. Georges Solovieff, *Madame de Stael* (Coppet: Éditions de l'Institut Coppet, 1975).

Anglesey, Marquis of (ed.), *The Capel Letters 1814-1817* (London: Jonathan Cape, 1955).

Anonymous, *The Legislative Trial of her Majesty Caroline Amelia Elizabeth, Queen of England, consort of George the Fourth, for the Alleged Crime of Adultery with Bartolomeo Bergami* (London: H. Rowe, 1820).

Anson, Elizabeth and Ansdon, Florence (eds), *Mary Hamilton, afterwards Mrs John Dickenson. At Court and at Home from Letters and Diaries 1756-1816* (London: John Murray, 1925).

Arbuthnot, Harriet, *Journal 1820-1832*, eds F. Bamford and the Duchess of Wellington, 2 vols (London: Macmillan, 1950).

Archer, Mildred, *India and British Portraiture 1770-1825* (London: Philip Wilson Publishers, 1979).

Argyll, Duke of (Campbell, George Douglas, 8th Duke) *Autobiography and Memoirs*, ed. Ina, Dowager Duchess of Argyll, 2 vols (London: John Murray, 1906).

Argyll, Duke of (Campbell J. D. S.), *Passages from the Past*, 2 vols (London: Hutchinson and Co., 1907); *Intimate Society Letters of the Eighteenth Century*, 2 vols (London: S. Paul and Co., 1910).

Armstrong, John, *The Secret Power of Beauty. Why Happiness Is in the Eye of the Beholder* (London: Penguin, 2004).

Askwith, Betty, *Piety and Wit. A Biography of Harriet Countess Granville 1785-1862* (London: Collins, 1982).

Aspinall, Arthur (ed.), *The Correspondence of George, Prince of Wales 1770-1812*, 8 vols (London: Cassell, 1963-71); *The Letters of King George IV with an introduction by C. K. Webster*, 3 vols (Cambridge: Cambridge University Press, 1938).

Atkinson, Diane, *The Criminal Conversation of Mrs Norton* (London: Random House Group, 2012).

Auckland, William E. and Robert E., *The Journal and Correspondence of William Lord Auckland; With a Preface and Introduction by the Bishop of Bath and Wells*, 4 vols (London: R. Bentley, 1861-2).

Bailey, F. E., *Lady Beaconsfield and her Times* (London: Hutchinson and Co. Ltd., 1935).

Baird, Rosemary, *Mistress of the House: Great ladies and Grand Houses, 1670-1830* (London: Weidenfeld and Nicolson, 2003).

Balfour, Sir James Paul, *The Scots Peerage, Founded in Wood's Edition of Sir Robert Douglas's Peerage of Scotland*, 9 vols (Edinburgh: David Douglas, 1904-14).

Baring, Mrs Henry (ed.), *The Diary of Rt Hon William Wyndham 1784-1810* (London: Longmans, 1866).

Baron-Wilson, Mrs Cornwell (Margaret Harries) (ed.), *The Life and Correspondence of M. Gregory Lewis, 1787-1818; With Many Pieces in Prose and Verse Never Before Published*, 2 vols (London: H. Colburn, 1839).

Barrett, Charlotte (ed.), D'Arblay, Fanny (Fanny Burney), *The Diaries and Letters of Madame d'Arblay 1778-1840*, 6 vols (London: Macmillan, 1904-5).

Barron, E., *The Legislatorial Trial of Her Majesty Caroline Amelia Elizabeth, Queen of England, Consort of George the Fourth, for the Alleged Crime of Adultery with Bartolomeo Bergami* (London: H. Rowe, 1820).

Bate Dudley, Henry, Sir, *Passages Selected by Distinguished Personages on the Great Literary Trial of Vortigern and Rowena; a Comi-Tragedy* (London: Printed by H. Brown, for J. Ridgway, York-Street, St. James's-Square, [1796?]).

Beacock Fryer, Mary, *Elizabeth Postuma Simcoe (1762-1850): A Biography* (Toronto: Dundurn Press, 1989).

Beattie, William (ed.), *The Life and Times Letters of Thomas Campbell*, 3 vols (London: E. Moxon, 1849).

Bentley, Richard, *Index to the Archives of Richard Bentley & Son 1829-1898*, Compiler and ed. Alison Ingram (Cambridge: Chadwyck Healey, 1975).

Berridge, Virginia and Edwards, Griffith, *Opium and the People; Opiate use in Nineteenth-Century England* (London: Allen Lane, 1981).

Di Bias, Carolina, *Strada Balbi a Genova. Residenza Aristocratica E Città* (Genova: Sagep Editrice, n.d.).

Black, Jeremy, *The British and the Grand Tour* (London: Croom Helm, 1985).

Bladon, F. McKno (ed.), *The Diaries of Col. the Hon. Robert Fulke Greville, 1751-1824, Equerry to His Majesty King George III* (London: John Lane, 1930).

Blakey, Dorothy, *The Minerva Press 1790-1820* (Oxford: Oxford University Press, 1939).

Blakiston, Georgiana, *Lord William Russell and His Wife, 1815-1846* (London: John Murray, 1972).

Blanch, Lesley, *Harriette Wilson's Memoirs 1786-1846; Selected and Edited, With Introduction* (London: Phoenix, 2003).

Blessington, Marguerite, Countess of, *Grace Cassidy; or The Repealers*, 3 vols (London, 1833).

Bleackley, Horace, *The Story of a Beautiful Duchess. Being an Account of the Life and Times of Elizabeth Gunning, Duchess of Hamilton and Argyll* (New York: E. P. Dutton and Company, 1907).

Blodgett, Harriet (ed.), *Centuries of Female Days. Englishwomen's Private Diaries* (Gloucester: Alan Sutton, 1989); *Capacious Hold All* (Charlotteville and London: University Press of Virginia, 1991).

De Boigne, *Memoirs of the Comtesse de Boigne*, ed. Charles Nicouillaud, 4 vols (London: William Heinemann, 1907).

Bond, T. Warwick, *The Marlay Letters 1778-1820* (London: Constable and Company Ltd, 1937).

Bowman, Peter James. *The First Celebrities: Five Regency Portraits* (Stroud: Amberley Publishing, 2023).

Bowron, Edgar Peters et al., *Best in the Show: The Dog in Art from the Renaissance to Today* (New Haven and London: Yale University Press, 2006).

Brewer, John, *The Pleasures of the Imagination. English Culture in the Eighteenth Century* (London: Harper Collins, 1997).

Brissenden, R. F., *Virtue in Distress. Studies in the Novel of Sentiment from Richardson to Sade* (London: Macmillan, 1974).

Brookes, Richard, *The General Gazetteer: or Compendious Geographical Dictionary*, 6th edn., (London: printed for J. F. C. Rivington, T. Carnan, and J. Johnson, in St. Paul's Church-Yard; G. G. J. J. Robinson, R. Baldwin, and J. Bent, in Pater-Noster-Row; B. Law, in Ave-Mary-Lane; T. Lowndes, and J. Murray, in Fleet-Street; C. Dilly, in the Poultry; T. Vernor, in Birchin-Lane; and S. Hayes, in Oxford-Street, 1786).

Brown, Philip A. H., *London Publishers and Printers c. 1800-1870* (London: The British Library, 1982).

Bryant, Arthur, *Years of Endurance and of Victory 1802-1812* (London: Collins, 1944); *The Age of Elegance 1812-1822* (London: Collins, 1975).

Burford, E. J., *Royal St James's: Being a Story of Kings, Clubmen and Courtesans* (London: Robert Hale, 1988).

Burke, Bernard. *A Genealogical and Heraldic Dictionary of the Landed Gentry of Great Britain and Ireland for 1853*, 3 vols (London: Henry Colburn, 1853); *The Romance of the Aristocracy, or, Anecdotes and Records of Distinguished Families*, new and rev. ed. (London: Published for H. Colburn, by his successors, Hurst and Blackett, 1855).

Burke, John. *The Portrait Gallery of Distinguished Females: Including Beauties of the Courts of George IV and William IV / With Memoirs*, 2 vols (London: E. Bull, 1833); *A Genealogical and Heraldic History of the Commoners of Great Britain and Ireland, Enjoying Territorial Possessions or High Official Rank: But Uninvested With Heritable Honours*, 4 vols (London: Published for Henry Colburn, by R. Bentley, New Burlington Street, 1834-1838).

Burney, Fanny (Mrs D'Arblay), *Diaries and Letters 1778-1840*, 6 vols (London: Macmillan, 1904-5).

Bushnell, Nelson S., 'Susan Ferrier's Marriage as a Novel of Manners', *Studies in Scottish Literature*, (Columbia, South Carolina: University of South Carolina Press, 1968), pp. 216-28.

Byrde, Penelope, *A Frivolous Distinction: Fashion and Needlework in the Works of Jane Austen* (Ludlow: Excellent Press, 1999).

Byron, George Gordon Byron, *Letters and Journals (The Works of Lord Byron)*, ed. R.E. Prothero, 2 vols (London, 1903).

Campbell, Alastair, *A History of Clan Campbell*, 3 vols (Edinburgh: Edinburgh University Press, 2000-4).

Campbell, H. C. Beaujolois, *A Journey to Florence in 1817*, ed. G. R. de Beer (London: Geoffrey Bles, 1951).

Campbell, Colen, *Vitruvius Britannicus, or the British architect, Containing the Plans, Elevations, and Sections of the Regular Buildings, Both Publick and Private, in Great Britain, With Variety of New Designs*, 2 vols (London: printed and sold by the author, 1715-25).

Campbell, Walter Frederick, *Life in Normandy. Sketches of French Fishing, Farming, Cooking, Natural History and Politics, Drawn from Nature*, ed. J. F Campbell, 2 vols (Edinburgh: Edmonston and Douglas, 1863).

Carey, H. C., *Letters on International Copyright* (Philadelphia: A. Hart, Late Carey and Hart, 1853).

Castle, Egerton (ed. and notes), *The Jerningham Letters, 1780-1945. Being Excerpts from the Correspondence and Diaries of the Honourable Lady Frances Jerningham and of Her Daughter, Lady Bedingfeld* (London: R. Bentley and Son, 1896).

Chancellor, Edwin B., *The History of the Squares of London* (London: Kegan Paul, 1907).

Cheney, C. R. (ed.) and Jones, M. (rev. ed.), *A Handbook of Dates For Students of British History* (Cambridge: Cambridge University Press, 2000).

Christianson, Rupert, *Romantic Affinities. Portraits from an Age 1780-1830* (London: The Bodley Head Ltd., 1988).

Clarke, Mrs Godfrey (ed.), *Gleanings from an Old Portfolio Containing Some Correspondence Between Lady Louisa Stuart and Her Sister Caroline, Countess of Portarlington, and Other Friends and Relations* (Edinburgh: privately printed for David Douglas, 1895).

Clavering, Douglas C. 'Journal of a Voyage to Spitzbergen and the East Coast of Greenland in His Majesty's ship *Griper*', *Edinburgh Literary Journal* (Edinburgh: Constable, 1830).

Clay, Edith, *Lady Blessington at Naples* (London: Hamish Hamilton, 1979).

Cleghorn, George, *Remarks on Ancient and Modern Art: Historical and Critical* (Edinburgh: Blackwood, 1848).

Clerici, Graziano Paolo, trans. Frederic Chapman, *Queen of Indiscretions; The Tragedy of Caroline of Brunswick, Queen of England* (London: John Lane, 1907).

Clifford, Brendon, *Life and Times of Thomas Moore* (Belfast: Athol Books, 1993).

Climenson, Emily J. (ed.), *Passages from the Diaries of Mrs Philip Lybbe-Powys* (London: Longmans, Green & Co., 1899).

Cloake, Margaret Morris (transl. and ed.), *A Persian Ambassador at the Court of King George III: the Journal of Mirza Abul Hassan Khan 1809-10* (London: Barrie and Jenkins, 1988).

Clubbe, John (ed.), *Two Reminiscences of Thomas Carlyle Now First Published* (Durham, North Carolina: Duke University Press, 1974).

Coke, Lady Mary, *Letters and Journals of Lady Mary Coke*, ed. J. A. Home, 4 vols (Edinburgh: David Douglas, Edinburgh 1889-1896).

Colles, John Mayne (ed.),*The Journal of John Mayne [of Dumfries] During a Tour on the Continent Upon Its Re-opening after the Fall of Napoleon, 1814* (London: John Lane, 1909).

Colvin, Christina (ed.), *Maria Edgeworth in France and Switzerland: Selections from the Edgeworth Family Letters* (Oxford: Clarendon Press, 1979).

Condon, Richard, *The Abandoned Woman* (London: Hutchinson Arrow Books, 1978).

Constantine, D., *Fields of Fire: A Life of William Hamilton* (London: Weidenfeld and Nicolson, 2001).

Copeland, Edward, *Women Writing About Money: Women's Fiction in England 1790-1820* (Cambridge: Cambridge University Press, 1995); *The Silver Fork Novel: Fashionable Fiction in the Age of Reform* (Cambridge: Cambridge University Press, 2012); 'Crossing Oxford Street: Silverfork Geopolitics', *Eighteenth-century Life* 25 (2001) pp. 116-34; 'Opera and Nineteenth-Century literature', *Romanticism on the Net* 345 (May–August, 2004).

Copeland, Edward and McMaster, Juliet, *The Cambridge Companion to Jane Austen* (Cambridge: Cambridge University Press, 1997).

Copley, Stephen and Garside, Peter (eds), *The Politics of the Picturesque: Literature, Landscape and Aesthetics Since 1770* (Cambridge: Cambridge University Press, 2010).

Coulson, Mavis, *Southwards to Geneva. 200 years of English Travellers* (Gloucester: Alan Sutton, 1988).

Coulter, John, *Sydenham and Forest Hill Past* (London: Historical Publications, 1999).

Craciun, Adriana, *Fatal Women of Romanticism* (Cambridge: Cambridge University Press, 2003).

Cradock, Joseph, *Literary and Miscellaneous Memoirs*, 4 vols (London: Privately printed, 1826-8).

Creston, Dormer, *The Regent and his Daughter* (London: Eyre & Spottiswood, 1943).

Cruft, K, 'The Enigma of Woodhall House', *Architectural History* 27 (1984), pp. 210-13.

Cumming, Frederica Constance Gordon, *Memories* (Edinburgh and London: Wm. Blackwood and Sons, 1904).

Curran, Stuart (ed.), *The Cambridge Companion to British Romanticism* (Cambridge: Cambridge University Press, 1993).

Dacres, Caroline, *The Holland Park Circle: Artists and Victorian Society* (New Haven and London: Yale University Press, 1999).

Damer, Anne S., *Belmour: A Novel* (London: S Johnson, 1801); New edition *Belmour*, ed. with introduction by J. D. Gross (Evanston: North Western Press, 2011).

Davidoff, Leonore, *The Best Circle* (London: Century Hutchinson, 1986).

Davies, Hunter, *The Grand Tour* (London: Hamish Hamilton, 1986).

Dering, Edward Heneage (ed.), *Memoirs of Georgiana, Lady Chatterton. With Some Passages From Her Diary* (London: Hurst and Blackett, 1878).

Dixon, W. Hepworth, *Lady Morgan's Memoirs: Autobiography, Diaries and Correspondence*, 2 vols (London: W. H. Allen and Co., 1863).

Dixon, W. Wilmott, *Queens of Beauty*, 2 vols (London: Hutchinson and Co., 1907).

Dolan, Brian, *Exploring European Frontiers: British Travellers in the Age of Enlightenment* (Basingstoke: Macmillan, 2000); *Ladies of the Grand Tour* (London: Harper Collins, 2001).

Douglas, David (ed.), *Scott's Familiar Letters*, 2 vols (Edinburgh: David Douglas, 1894).

Douglas, Paul, *Lady Caroline Lamb. A Biography* (Basingstoke: Palgrave Macmillan, 2004).

Douglas, Sylvester (Lord Glenbervie), *The Diaries of Sylvester Douglas, Lord Glenbervie*, ed. Francis Bickley, 2 vols (London: Constable and Co., 1928).

Dowden, Wilfred S. et al. (eds), *The Journal of Thomas Moore*, 6 vols (Newark: University of Delaware Press; London: Associated University Presses, *c.* 1983-*c.* 1991).

Doyle, John, *Memoir and Correspondence of Susan Ferrier 1782-1854. Based on Her Private Correspondence . . . Collected By Her Grand-Nephew, John Ferrier* (London: John Murray, 1898); *Works of Susan Ferrier* (London: Evelyn Nash and Grayson, 1929).

Duffy, Michael, *The English Satirical Print 1600-1832. The Englishman and the Foreigner*, 7 vols (Cambridge: Chadwyck Healey, 1986).

Dunphy, Thomas and Cummins, Thomas J. (compilers), *Remarkable Trials of All Countries* (New York: Diossy and Cockcroft, 1870).

Earland, Ada, *John Opie and his Circle* (London: Hutchinson and Co., 1911).

Earle, Rebecca (ed.), *Epistolary Selves: Letters and Letter-Writers 1600-1945* (Aldershot: Ashgate, 1999)

Eastlake, Lady (Elizabeth Rigby), *Journals and Correspondence of Lady Eastlake*, ed. C. E. Smith, 2 vols (London: John Murray, 1895); *The Letters of Elizabeth Rigby, Lady Eastlake*, ed. Julie Sheldon (Liverpool: Liverpool University Press, 2009).

Edgeworth, Maria, *Castle Rackrent* (Oxford: Oxford University Press, 1964); *Letters from England 1813-1844*, ed. Christian Colvin (Oxford: Clarendon Press, 1971); *Letters for Literary Ladies* (London: J. M. Dent, 1993).

Elliot-Drake, Lady (ed.), *Lady [Philippina] Knight's Letters from France and Italy 1776-1795* (London: Arthur L. Humphreys, 1905).

Ellis, Sir Henry, *Original Letters Illustrative of English History: Including Royal Letters From Autographs . . .*, 3 vols (London: Dawsons, 1969).

Eustace, John Chetwode, *A Tour Through Italy Exhibiting a View of Its Scenery, Its Antiquities and Its Monuments* (London, 1815).

Fairweather, Maria, *Madame de Stael* (London: Constable, 2005).

Farington, Joseph, *The Farington Diary by Joseph Farington*, ed. James Greig, 8 vols (London: Hutchinson, 1922-8).

Favret, Mary, *Romantic Correspondence: Women, Politics and the Fiction of Letters* (Cambridge: Cambridge University Press, 1993).

Le Faye, Deirdre, *Jane Austen's Letters* (Oxford: Oxford University Press, 1997); *Jane Austen: A Family Record* (Cambridge: Cambridge University Press, 2003).

Feldman, Paula R. and Kelly Theresa M., *Romantic Women Writers* (Hanover, New Hampshire: University Press of New England, 1995).

Fergusson, Sir James, *Argyll in the Forty-Five* (London: Faber and Faber, 1951).

Ferrier, Susan M., *Marriage*, 3 vols (Edinburgh: Blackwood, 1818).

De Figueiredo, Peter and Treuherz, Julian, *Cheshire Country Houses* (Chichester: Phillimore, 1988).

Fitzgerald, Brian, *Emily, Duchess of Leinster, 1731-1841* (London: Staple Press, 1949).

Fitzgerald, Percy H. *The Life and Times of William IV. Including a view of Social Life and Manners During His Reign*, 2 vols (London: Tinsley Bros., 1884).

Fletcher, Eliza (née Dawson), *Autobiography of Mrs Fletcher of Edinburgh With Selections From Her Letters and Other Family Memorials*, ed. by the survivor of her family, Lady Mary Richardson (Edinburgh: Edmonston and Douglas, 1875).

Fontana, Biancamara, *Rethinking the politics of Commercial Society. The Edinburgh Review 1802-32* (Cambridge: Cambridge University Press,1985).

Ford, Robert, *Harp of Perthshire* (Paisley: A. Gardner, 1893).

Foreman, Amanda, *Georgiana Duchess of Devonshire* (London: Harper Collins, 1998); *Georgiana's World. The Illustrated Georgiana, Duchess of Devonshire* (London: Harper Collins, 2001).

Foster, Joseph, *Members of Parliament, Scotland ... 1357-1882* (London: Privately printed, Hazell, Watson & Viney, 1882).

Foster, Shirley, *Victorian Women's Fiction: Marriage, Freedom and the Individual* (London: Croom Helm,1986).

Fothergill, B., *The Strawberry Hill Set. Horace Walpole and his Circle* (London: Faber & Faber, 1983).

Foulkes, Nick, *Last of the Dandies: The Scandalous Life and Escapades of Count d'Orsay* (London: Little Brown, 2003); *Scandalous Society: Passion and Celebrity in the Nineteenth Century* (London: Abacus, 2004).

Franzero, Carlo Maria, *A Life in Exile: Ugo Foscolo in London 1816-27* (London: W. H. Allen, 1977).

Fraser, Flora, *Beloved Emma; The Life of Emma, Lady Hamilton* (New York: Anchor Books, 2004); *The Unruly Queen. The Life of Queen Caroline* (London: Macmillan, 1996).

Fraser's Magazine for Town and Country, vol. 10 (London: James Fraser, 1834).

Fremantle, Anne, née Wynne (ed.), *The Wynne Diaries 1789-1820*, 3 of 4 vols (Oxford: Oxford University Press, 1935-40).

Fulford, Roger (ed.), *The Autobiography of Miss Knight, Lady Companion to Princess Charlotte* (London: William Kimber, 1960); *The Trial of Queen Caroline* (London: B. T. Batsford, 1967).

Galt, John, *The literary life, and Miscellanies, of John Galt*, 3 vols (London: William Blackwood, 1834); *The Autobiography of John Galt*, 2 vols (London: Cochrane & McCrone, 1883); *The Letters of John Galt from the Blackwood Papers in the National Library of Scotland (John Galt 1779-1839)* (Lexington: University of Kentucky Press, 1957); *The Earthquake*, 3 vols (Edinburgh, 1820).

Gantz, Ida, *The Pastel Portrait: The Gunnings of Castle Coote and Howards of Hampstead* (London: Cresset Press, 1963).

Garlick, Kenneth. *A Catalogue of the Paintings and Pastels of Sir Thomas Lawrence* (Glasgow: Glasgow University Press; Printed for the Walpole Society by R. Maclehose, 1964); *Sir Thomas Lawrence: a Complete Catalogue of the Oil Paintings* (Oxford: Phaidon,1989).

Garlick, Kenneth and Macintyre, Angus (eds), *The Diary of Joseph Farington*, Index compiled by Evelyn Newby, 4 vols (New Haven and London: Yale University Press, 1998).

Garside, P. J. Raven, and Schöwerling R. (eds),*The English Novel 1770-1829; A Bibliographic Survey of Prose Fiction published in the British Isles*, 2 vols (Oxford: Oxford University Press, 2000).

Gaylin, Anne, *Eavesdropping in the Novel from Austen to Proust* (Cambridge: Cambridge University Press, 2002).

George, Dorothy Mary, *Catalogue of Political and Personal Satires Preserved in the Department of Prints and Drawings in the British Museum*, 11 vols (1793-1800), (London: British Museum, 1942).

Gibb, Lorna, *Lady Hester; Queen of the East* (London: Faber and Faber, 2006).

Gibbs-Smith, Charles Harvard, *The Fashionable Lady in the Nineteenth Century* (London: HMSO, 1960).

Glenbervie, Lord Sylvester Douglas, *Diaries of Sylvester Douglas, Lord Glenbervie*, ed. Francis Bickley, 2 vols (London: Constable and Co., 1928); *The Glenbervie Journals*, ed. Walter Sichel (London: Constable and Vo., 1910).

Glendinning, Victoria, *Raffles and the Golden Opportunity* (London: Profile Books, 2012).

Goldsmith, Elizabeth, *Writing the Female Voice; Essays in Epistolary Literature* (London: Pinter, 1989).

Gonda, Caroline, *Reading Daughters' Fictions 1709–1834: Novels and Society from Manley to Edgeworth* (Cambridge: Cambridge University Press, 1996).

Goodden, Angelica, *Miss Angel; The Art and World of Angelika Kauffman* (London: Pimlico, 2005).

Gordon, Ian A. *John Galt: The Life of a Writer* (Edinburgh: Oliver and Boyd, 1972).

Gordon, Robert K., *John Galt* (Toronto: University of Toronto Library, 1920).

Gordon-Cumming, Frederica Constance, *Memories* (Edinburgh and London, 1924).

Gore, Catherine, *Pin Money. A Novel* (London, 1831).

Gottmann, Royal Alfred, *A Victorian Publisher: A Study of the Bentley Papers* (Cambridge: Cambridge University Press, 1960).

Gould, Warwick and Staley, Thomas F. (eds), *Writing the Lives of Writers* (Basingstoke: Macmillan Press, 1998).

Gow, Niel, and Son, *Part Second of the Complete Repository of Original Scots Tunes Strathspeys Jigs and Dances* (Edinburgh: Niel Gow, 1822).

Grant, Aline, *Susan Ferrier of Edinburgh: A Biography* (Denver: Allan Swallow, 1957).

Grant, Anne MacVicar, *Memoir and Correspondence of Mrs Anne Grant of Laggan*, ed. J. P. Grant, 3 vols (London: Longman, Brown, Green & Longmans, 1844).

Grant, Elizabeth, *Memoirs of a Highland Lady* (London: John Murray, 1898; Edinburgh: Canongate, 1988).

Leveson-Gower, Lady Castalia Granville (ed.), *The Private Correspondence of Lord Granville Leveson-Gower (First Earl Granville) 1781-1821*, 2 vols (London: John Murray, 1916).

Leveson-Gower, Lady Harriet Granville, *Letters of Harriet, Countess Granville 1810-1845*, ed. F. Leveson-Gower, 2 vols (London: Longmans and Co., 1894).

Graver, Bruce E., 'Wordsworth, St. Francis and Lady Charlotte Bury', *Philological Quarterly* 65 (1986), pp. 371-80.

Gray, Robert, *The King's Wife: Five Queen Consorts* (London: Secker and Warburg, 1990).

Green, Katherine, *The Courtship Novel 1740-1820: A Feminised Genre* (Lexington: University of Kentucky Press, 1991).

Greig, James (ed.), *The Farington Diary by Joseph Farington*, 2nd edn, 8 vols (London: Hutchinson, 1922-8).

Greville, Charles, *The Diaries of Colonel the Hon. Robert Fulke Greville 1751-1824 Equerry to His Majesty King George III*, ed. F. McKno Bladon (London: Bodley Head/ John Lane, 1830); *The Greville Diaries, Including Passages Hitherto Withheld From Publications*, ed. P. W. Wilson, 2 vols (London: William Heinemann, 1927); *The Greville Memoirs 1814-1860*, eds Lytton Strachey and Roger Fulford, 3 vols (London: Macmillan, 1938).

Gribble, Francis, *Madame de Stael and Her Lovers* (London: Eveleigh Nash, 1907).

Gronow, Captain, Rees Havel, *Reminiscences: the Last Recollections of Captain Gronow, Formerly of the Grenadier Guards and MP for Stafford: Being Anecdotes of the Camp, the Court and the Clubs at the Close of the Last War with France* (London: Smith, Elder, 1862).

Guinness, Desmond and Ryan, William, *Great Irish Houses and Castles* (London: Weidenfeld and Nicolson, 1992).

Gunn, John A. W., *Benjamin Disraeli Letters* (Toronto: University of Toronto Press, 1982).

Gunning, Mrs (Susannah), *A Letter from Mrs Gunning: Addressed to His Grace the Duke of Argyll* (London: printed for the author and sold by Mr. Ridgway and Mr. Boyter, 1791).

Haldane, Elizabeth, *Scots Gardens in Old Times 1200-1800* (London: Alexander Maclehose, 1934).

Hall, Augustus J. C., *The Life and Letters of Maria Edgeworth, 1767-1849*, 2 vols (London: Edward Arnold, 1894).

Hamilton, Lady Anne, *Epics of Ton or Glories of the Great World: A Poem* (London: C. and R. Baldwin, 1807); *Secret History of the Court of England from the Accession of George III to the Seath of George IV, Including . . . the Mysterious Death of the Princess Charlotte*, 2 vols (London: W. H. Stevenson, 1832).

Hanover, Lady, *The Autobiography and Correspondence of Mary Granville, Mrs Delany*, 6 vols (London: Bentley, 1862).

Hare, Augustus J. C. (ed.), *The Life and Letters of Maria Edgeworth*, 2 vols (London: Edward Arnold, 1894).

Håusermann, H. W., *The Genevese Background. Studies of Some English Writers in Geneva* (London: Routledge and Kegan Paul Ltd., 1952).

Heath's *Book of Beauty* (London: Longman et al., 1833-1847).

Hemlow, Joyce, *The Journals and Letters of Fanny Burney (Madame d'Arbay)*, 12 vols (Oxford: Oxford University Press, 1973).

Herold, J. Christopher, *Mistress to an Age: The Life and Times of Madame de Stael* (London: Hamish Hamilton, 1986).

Hibbert, Christopher, *The Court at Windsor* (London: Longmans, 1964); *London the Biography of a City* (Harmondsworth: Penguin, 1969); *George IV: Regent and King, 1811-1830* (London: Allen Lane, 1973); *The Grand Tour* (London: Thames Methuen, 1974); *The Court of St James* (London: Weidenfeld and Nicolson, 1979); *George IV* (London: Penguin, 1988).

Hickman, Katie, *Courtesans* (London: Harper Collins, 2003).

Hill, Draper (ed.), *The Satirical Etchings of James Gillray* (London: Constable, 1976).

Hoare, Sir Richard C., *The History of Modern Wiltshire* (Wakefield: EP Publishing, 1975).

Hodge, Jane A., *Passion and Principle. The Loves and Lives of Regency Women* (London: John Murray, 1996)

Hogg, James, *The Ettrick Shepherd's Travels in the Scottish Highlands and Islands, 1802 1803 and 1804*, ed. William F. Lughlan (Hawick: Byways, 1981).

Holme, Thea, *Caroline: A Biography of Caroline of Brunswick* (London: Hamish Hamilton, 1979).

Home, James A. (ed.), *Lady Louisa Stuart: Selections From Her Manuscripts* (Edinburgh: David Douglas, 1899); *Letters of Lady Louisa Stuart to Miss Louise Clinton* (Edinburgh: David Douglas, 1901-3).

Hook, Theodore E., *Sayings and Doings*, 3 vols (London: Henry Colburn, 1824 and subsequent).

Hopkirk, Mary, *Queen Adelaide* (London: John Murray, 1946).

Horne, R. H., *A New Spirit of the Age*, 2 vols (London: Smith, Elder and Co., 1844).

Hughes, Clair, *Dressed in Fiction* (Oxford: Berg, 2005).

Hughes, Winifred, 'Silver Fork Writers and Readers: Social Contexts of a Best Seller', *Novel* 25 (1991-2), pp. 328-47; 'Elegies for the Regency; Catherine Gore's Dandy Novels', *Nineteenth Century Fiction*, 50 (1995), pp.189-209.

Hylton, Lord (ed.), *The Paget Brothers 1790-1840* (London: John Murray, 1918).

Ilchester, Countess of, and Stavordale, Viscount (eds), *The Life and Letters of Sarah Lennox*, 2 vols (London: John Murray, 1901).

Ilchester, Earl of (ed.), *Elizabeth Lady Holland to Her Son 1821-1845* (London: John Murray, 1946).

Ishbell, John, *The Birth of European Romanticism* (Cambridge: Cambridge University Press, 1994).

Jackson, A. Edith, *Annals of Ealing From the Twelfth Century to the Present Time* (London: Phillimore & Co., 1898).

Jameson, Anna Bronwell, *Memoirs of the Beauties of the Court of Charles the Second, with Their Portraits, After Sir Peter Lely and Other Eminent Painters: Illustrating The Diaries of Pepys, Evelyn, Clarendon, and other Contemporary Writers* (London: Henry Colburn, 1835).

Jameson-Cempter, Kathleen, *Selected Correspondence by Georges Solovieff* (Dordrecht, Boston: Kluwer Academic, 2000).

Janner, Greville, *The Art of Letter Writing* (Aldershot: Gower, 1989).

Jefferies, Neil, *Dictionary of Pastellists before 1800* (London: Unicorn Press, 2006).

Jennings, Louis J. (ed.), *The Correspondence and Diaries of the late Rt. Hon. John Wilson Croker LLD, FRS, Secretary to the Admiralty from1809-1830*, 3 vols (London: John Murray, 1885).

Jewsbury, Miss and Dixon, W. Hepworth, *Lady Morgan's Memoirs: Autobiography, Diaries and Correspondence*, 2nd revised edition, 2 vols (London: W H Allen & Co. 1863).

Johnson, Charles, *The Complete Art of Writing Letters Adapted to All Classes and Conditions of Life ... Containing a Collection of Entertaining and Instructive Letters ...* (London: T Lowndes, 1779).

Johnson, Edgar, *Sir Walter Scot: The Great Unknown*, 2 vols (London: Hamilton, 1970).

Johnson, Jane, *Works Exhibited at the Royal Society of British Artists, 1824-1893 and the New English Art Club 1888-1917: An Antique Collectors' Club Research Project* (Woodbridge, Suffolk: Antique Collectors' Club, 1975).

Jones, George, *Anecdotal Reminiscences of Distinguished Literary and Political Characters* (London: R. and A. Bielefeld, 1830).

Kavenagh, Julia, *English Women of Letters: Biographical Sketches*, 2 vols (London: Hurst and Blackett, 1863).

Kelly, Gary, *Women, Writing and the Reviews 1790-1827* (Oxford: Clarendon, 1993); *English Fiction of the Romantic Period* (London: Longman, 1989).

Kelly, Ronan, *Bard of Erin: The Life of Thomas Moore* (Dublin: Penguin Ireland, 2008).

Kenworthy-Browne, J., 'Sculptor and Revolutionary Portraits by Bartolini', *Country Life*, 8 June 1978, pp.1655-6.

Kirby, Paul F., *The Grand Tour in Italy 1700-1800* (New York: S. F Vanni, 1952).

Knight, Ellis Cornelia, *Autobiography of Miss Ellis Cornelia Knight, Companion to Princess Charlotte of Wales with Extracts from her Journals and Anecdote Books*, ed. J. W. Kaye, 2 vols (London: W. H. Allen, 1861).

Lang, Andrew, 'Fashionable Novels', *Essays in Little*, 8 vols (London: Henry and Co., 1891).

de Langlade, Jacques, *Lady Blessington et le Comte d'Orsay* (Paris: Tallandier, 1987).

Laver, James, *A Concise History of Costume* (London: Thames and Hudson, 1972).

Layard, George S., *Sir Thomas Lawrence's Letterbag* (London: E. Allen, 1906).

Leslie, C. R. and Taylor, T. *Life and Times of Sir Joshua Reynolds*, 2 vols (London: John Murray, 1865).

Leslie, Doris, *Notorious Lady: The Countess of Blessington* (London: Book Club, 1970).

Lewis, Judith, *In the Family Way: Childbearing in the British Aristocracy 1760-1860* (New Brunswick, New Jersey: Rutgers University Press, 1986).

Levey, Michael, *Sir Thomas Lawrence* (New Haven and London: Yale University Press, 2005).

Lewis, Matthew G., *Crazy Jane: Written by G. M. Lewis Esq., in Consequence of a Lady Having, in Her Walks, During Her Residence in Scotland, Met With a Poor Mad Woman, Known by the Above Appellation, at Whose Appearance the Lady Was Much Alarmed* (London: J. Davenport, 1800); *The Monk. A Romance,* 3 vols (Waterford: J. Saunders, 1796); *The Monk*, ed. Howard Anderson (London: Oxford University Press, 1981); *Romantic Tales,* 4 vols (London: Longman, Hurst, Rees & Orme, 1808); *Poems* (London: sold Hatchards, 1812); *The Life and Correspondence of Matthew Gregory Lewis; With Many Pieces in Prose and Verse, Never Before Published* (London: Henry Colburn, 1839).

Lewis, Lady Theresa (Lister, afterwards Lewis) (ed.), *Extracts of the Journals and Correspondence of Miss [Mary] Berry from 1783 to* 1852, 3 vols (London: L. Green & Co., 1865).

Lewis, W. S. (ed.), *Horace Walpole Correspondence*, 48 vols (Oxford and New Haven: OUP and YUP, 1937-1983).

Leyden, John, *Journal of a Tour in the Highlands and Western Isles of Scotland in 1800*, ed. James Smith (London: William Blackwood and Son, 1903).

Lindsay, Ian G. and Cosh, Mary, *Inveraray and the Dukes of Argyll* (Edinburgh: Edinburgh University Press, 1973).

The Literary Gazette and Journal of Belles Lettres, Arts, Sciences, Etc. (London: H. Colburn, 1834).

Lloyd, Stephen, *Raeburn's Rival: Archibald Skirving 1745-1819* (Edinburgh: Scottish National Portrait Gallery, 1999).

Lockhart, J. G., *Memoirs of the Life of Sir Walter Scott*, 5 vols (London: Macmillan, 1900); *Narrative of the Life of Sir Walter Scott*, 10 vols (Edinburgh: Robert Cadell; London: John Murray and Whittaker and Co., 1837-1838).

Lowe, Helen, *Unprotected Females in Sicily, Calabria and on the Top of Mount Aetna* (London, New York: Routledge, Warne and Routledge, 1859).

Lysons, Daniel, *Environs of London Being an Historical Account of the Towns, Villages, and Hamlets, Within Twelve Miles of That Capital*, 4 vols (London: T. Cadell, Jun. and W. Davies, 1795-1800).

MacCulloch, Michael, 'Parish of Bothwell', *The Statistical Account of Scotland*, 21 vols (Edinburgh, 1795), 16, pp. 299-337.

MacCunn, Florence A., *Sir Walter Scott's Friends* (London: William Blackwood, 1909).

MacDonagh, Oliver, *Jane Austen: Real and Imagined Worlds* (New Haven and London: Yale University Press, 1991).

Mackenzie, Peter, *Old Reminiscence of Glasgow and the West of Scotland*, 3 vols (Glasgow: John Tweed, 1865-6).

Macmillan Dictionary of Women's Biography, ed. J. Uglow (Basingstoke: Palgrave Macmillan, 1989).

Madden, Richard Robert, *The Literary Life and Correspondence of the Countess of Blessington*, 3 vols (London, 1855).

Malcomson, A. P. W., *The Pursuit of the Heiress: Aristocratic Marriage in Ireland 1750-1820* (Belfast: Ulster Historical Foundation, 1982).

Manners, John Henry (5th Duke of Rutland), *Journal of a Tour to the Northern Parts of Great Britain* (London: Privately printed, 1813).

Manners, Lady Victoria, 'Catherine Read—The English "Rosalba"', *The Connoisseur* 88 (New York, 1931), pp. 376-86 and 89 (New York, 1932), pp. 35-40 and 171-8.

Markman, Ellis, *The Politics of Sensibility. Race, Gender and Commerce in the Sentimental Novel* (Cambridge: Cambridge University Press, 1996).

Marshall, Roderick, *Italy in English Literature 1775-1815* (New York: Columbia University Press, 1934).

Marshall, Rosalind, *The Days of Duchess Anne: Life in the Household of the Duchess of Hamilton, 1656-1716* (East Linton: Tuckwell Press, 2000); *Women in Scotland 1660-1780* (Edinburgh: Trustees of the National Gallery of Scotland, 1979).

Arthur Marwick, Arthur, *Beauty in History: Society, Politics and Personal Appearance c.1500 to the Present* (London: Thames and Hudson, 1988); *IT: A History of Human Beauty* (London: Hambledon, 2004).

Masters, Brian, *The Dukes. The Origins, Ennoblement and History of Twenty Twenty-Six Families*, Rev. & updated ed. (London: Pimlico, 2001).

Matthews, Henry, *Diary of an Invalid; Being the Journal of a Tour in Pursuit of Health and Happiness in Portugal, Italy, Switzerland and France—The Years 1817, 1818 and 1819* (London: John Murray, 1820).

Maughan, William C., *Roseneath Past and Present* (Paisley: Gardner, 1896); *Annals of Garelochside, Being an Account Historical and Topographical of the Parishes of Row, Rosneath and Cardross* (Paisley: Gardner, 1897).

Mavor, Elizabeth, *The Ladies of Llangollen; A study in Romantic Friendship* (London: Michael Joseph, 1971).

Maxwell, Sir Herbert (ed.), *The Creevey Papers; A Selection from the Correspondence & Diaries of the Late Thomas Creevey, M.P.*, 2 vols (London: John Murray, 1903).

Maxwell, Archibald Montgomery, *My Adventures*, 2 vols (London: Henry Colburn, 1845).

May, Keith M., *Characters of Women in Narrative Literature* (London: Macmillan,1981).

McAllister, Florence, *Memoir of the Right Hon. Sir John McNeill GCB and of His Second Wife Elizabeth Wilson by Their Grand-Daughter* (London: John Murray, 1910).

McKay, W and Roberts, W., *John Hoppner*, P & D. Colnaghi and Co., Supplement and index (London: John Lane, the Bodley Head, 1914).

McMillan, Dorothy, *The Scotswoman at Home and Abroad: Non-Fictional Writing 1700-1900* (Glasgow: Association of Scottish Literary Studies, 1999).

Melville, Lewis (ed.),*The Berry Papers: Being the Correspondence Hitherto Unpublished, of Mary and Agnes Berry 17623-1852* (London: John Lane, 1904/1914); *An Injured Queen: Caroline of Brunswick*, 2 vols (London: Hutchinson, and Co., 1917); *Maids of Honour* (London: Hutchinson & Co., 1927); *Regency Ladies* (London: Hutchinson & Co., 1926); *Horace Walpole 1717-1797. A Biographical Study* (London: Hutchinson, 1930).

Meryon, Charles L., *The Memoirs of Lady Hester Stanhope as Related by Herself, in Conversations With Her Physician, Comprising Her Opinions and Anecdotes of Some of the Most Remarkable Persons of her Time*, 3 vols (London: Colburn, 1846).

Mews, Hazel, *Frail Vessels: Woman's Role in Women's Novels from Fanny Burney to George Eliot* (London: Athlone Press, 1969).

Miller, Jane, *Women Writing about Men* (London: Virago, 1986).

Minto, Countess of (ed.), *The Life and Letters of Sir Gilbert Elliot, First Earl of Minto 1751-1806*, 3 vols (London: Longmans, Green & Co., 1814).

Mitchell, Leslie G., *Holland House* (London: Duckworth,1980); *Charles James Fox* (Oxford: Oxford University Press, 1992).

Moore, Thomas, *The Journal of Thomas Moore*, ed. Wilfred S. Dowden, 6 vols (London: London Association of University Presses, 1983-91); *Memoirs, Journals and Correspondence of Thomas Moore*, ed. John Russell, 8 vols (London: L. B. Green and Longman's, 1853-6).

Morgan, Lady Sydney (formerly Owenson), *Italy*, 2 vols (London: H. Colburn, 1821); *Lady Morgan's Memoirs: Autobiography, Diaries and Correspondence*, eds Miss Jewsbury and W. Hepworth Dixon, 2nd revised edition, 2 vols (London: W. H. Allen & Co., 1863); *Passages in my Autobiography* (London: Richard Bentley, 1859).

Mowl, Timothy, *Horace Walpole: The Great Outsider* (London: John Murray, 1996).

Mullen, John, *How Novels Work* (Oxford: Oxford University Press, 2006); *Anonymity: A Secret History of English Literature* (London: Faber, 2007); *What Matters in Jane Austen? Twenty Crucial Puzzles Solved* (London: Bloomsbury, 2012).

Mundy, Harriet Georgiana (ed.), *The Journal of Mary Frampton From the Year 1779 Until the Year 1846* (London: S. Low, Marston, Searly & Rivington, 1885).

Munson, James, *Maria Fitzherbert; The Secret Wife of George IV* (London: Constable & Robinson Ltd., 2002).

Murray, Amelia, *Recollections from 1803 to 1837: With a Conclusion in 1868* (London: Longmans, Green, 1868).

Murray, Venetia, *High Society: A Social History of the Regency Period* (London: Viking, 1998).

Nightingale, Joseph, *Memoirs of the Public and Private Life of Queen Caroline,* ed. and introduction Christopher Hibbert (London: The Folio Society, 1978).

Noble, Percy, *Anne Seymour Damer: A Woman of Art and Fashion 1748-1828* (London: Kegan Paul, Trench, Turner & Co. Ltd., 1908).

O'Connor, Maura, *The Romance of Italy and the English Political Imagination* (Basingstoke: Macmillan, 1998).

Oliphant, Mrs., *William Blackwood and his Sons: Their Magazines and Friends*, 2 vols (Edinburgh and London: William Blackwood, 1897).

Opie, John, *Opie and his Works* (London: P. and D. Colnaghi and Co., 1878).

Osborne, Harold, *Oxford Companion to Art* (Oxford: Oxford University Press, 1981).

Oxford Dictionary of National Biography, ed. H. C. G. Matthew and Brian Harrison (Oxford: Oxford University Press, 2004).

Paget, Sir Augustus B. , *The Paget Paper. Diplomatic and Other Correspondence of the Rt. Hon. Sir Arthur Paget,* 2 vols (London: W. Heinemann, 1896).

Palmer, Alan, *Encyclopaedia of Napoleon's Europe* (London: G. Weidenfeld and Nicolson, 1984).

Parissien, Steven, *George IV: The Grand Entertainment* (London: John Murray, 2001).

Parker, William M., *Susan Ferrier and John Galt* (London: Longman, 1965).

Parry, Sir Edward, *Queen Caroline* (London: Ernest Benn, 1930).

Partington, Wilfrid, *Sir Walter's Postbag: More Stories and Sidelights From His Unpublished Letter-Books Written and Selected by Sir Wilfrid Partington . . . With a Record of Scott's Correspondents* (London: John Murray, 1932).

Pasquin, Anthony, *Critical Guide to the Exhibition of the Royal Academy* (London, 1796).

Paston, George (pseudo. Emily Moore Symonds), *Little Memoirs of the Nineteenth Century* (London, 1902).

Patterson, James, *The Contemporaries of Burns and the More Recent Poets of Ayrshire, With Selections From Their Writings* (Edinburgh: Hugh Paton, 1840).

Patmore, P. G., *My Friends and Acquaintance; Being Memorials, Mind-Portraits, Personal Recollections of Deceased Celebrities of the Nineteenth Century*, 3 vols (London: Saunders and Otley, 1854); *Sir Thomas Lawrence's Cabinet of Gems, With Biographical and Descriptive Memorials* (London: Ackerman & Co, 1837); (ed.) *Finden's Gallery of Beauty: or the Court of Queen Victoria* (London: J. Hogarth, 1841).

Peacock, George, *Life of Thomas Young MD FRS* (London: John Murray, 1855).

Pearce, Edward (ed.), *Diaries of Charles Greville* (London: Pimlico, 2006).

Pearson, Jaqueline, *Women's Reading in Britain 1750-1835: A Dangerous Recreation* (Cambridge: Cambridge University Press, 1999).

Peck, Louis F., *A Life of Matthew G. Lewis* (Cambridge, Mass.: Harvard University Press, 1961).

Perkins, P., 'Scottish Women Poets of the Romantic period', https://www.proquest.com/books/lady-charlotte-susan-maria-campbell-bury-1775/docview/2352938251/se-2, accessed 28 October 2024.

Pettigrew, Thomas J., *Memoirs of the Life of Vice-Admiral Lord Viscount Nelson*, 2 vols (London: T. and W. Boone, 1849).

Phillips, Adam, *On Flirtation* (London: Faber and Faber, 1994).

Pigott, Harriet, *The Private Correspondence of a Woman of Fashion,* 2 vols (London: Henry Colburn and Richard Bentley, 1832); *Records of Real Life in the Palace and the Cottage*, revised by the late John Galt, 3 vols (London: Saunders and Otley, 1839).

Plowden, A., *Caroline and Charlotte: The Regent's Wife and Daughter 1795-1821* (London: Sidgwick & Jackson, 1989).

Plumb, J. H., *The First Four Georges* (London: B. T. Batsford Ltd., 1956).

Pocock, Tom, *Sailor King: The Life of King William IV* (London: Sinclair-Stevenson, 1991).

Ponsonby, Arthur, *English Diaries; A Review of English Diaries from the Sixteenth to the Twentieth Centuries, with an Introduction to Diary Writing* (London: Methuen, 1923).

Prebble, John, *The King's Jaunt George IV in Scotland, August 1822: 'One and Twenty Daft Days'* (London: Collins, 1988).

Price, Munro, *The Perilous Crown, France Between the Revolutions 1814-1848* (London: Macmillan, 2007).

Prucher, Auda, *Figure europee del Primo '1800 nel "Diary" di Lady Charlotte Campbell Bury con documenti inediti* (Florence: Leo S. Olschki, Editorie, 1961).

Quennell, Marjorie and Quennell, C. H. B., *A History of Everyday Things in England* (London: Putnam, 1961).

Quennell, Peter (ed.), *Genius in the Drawing Room. The Literary Salon in the Nineteenth and Twentieth Centuries* (London: George Weidenfeld and Nicolson, 1980).

De Quincey, *Thomas Confessions of an Opium-Eater* (Ware, Herts: Wordsworth Editions, 1994).

Ray, Gordon N., *The Letters and Papers of William M Thackeray* (Cambridge, Mass.: Harvard University Press, 1946).

Raymond, John, *Reminiscences and Recollections of Captain Gronow* (London: Bodley Head, 1964).

Redding, Cyrus, *Fifty Years' Recollections, Literary and Personal with Observations on Men and Things*, 3 vols (London, 1858).

Reed, M., *The Georgian Triumph 1700-1830* (London: Paladin, 1983).

Rees, Nigel, *Bloomsbury Guide to Letter Writing* (London: Bloomsbury Publishing, 1994).

Reeve, H. (ed.), *The Greville Memoirs: A Journal of the Reigns of King George IV, King William and Queen Victoria*, 3 vols (London: Longmans, Green, 1874-5).

Ribeiro, Aileen, *The Art of Dress: Fashion in England and France, 1750-1820* (London: Yale, 1995).

Robins, Jane, *Rebel Queen: How the Trial of Queen Caroline Brought England to the Brink of Revolution* (London: Simon Pocket, 2006).

Rogers, John Jope, *Opie and his Works: Being a Catalogue of 760 Pictures by John Opie, R.A., Preceded by a Biographical Sketch* (London and Truro: P, and D. Colnaghi & Co., 1878).

Rogers, Charles, *The Modern Scottish Minstrel; or The Songs of Scotland of the Past Half Xentury*, 2 vols (Edinburgh: A. & C. Black, 1855-6).

Rogers, Pat, *Literature and Popular Culture in Eighteenth-Century England* (Brighton: Harvester, 1985); *Eighteenth-Century Encounters: Studies in Literature and Society in the Age of Walpole* (Brighton: Harvester, 1985).

Rosa Matthew W., *The Silver Fork School: Novels of Fashion Preceding Vanity Fair* (New York: Columbia University, 1936).

Roundel, *Lady Blessington*, 2 vols (London, 1860).

Roworth, Wendy W. (ed.), *Angelica Kauffman. A Continental Artist in Georgian England* (London: Reaktion Books, 1992).

The Royal Lady's Magazine, and Archives of the Court of St. James's, 5 vols (London: W. Sams, 1832).

Russell, Lady Constance C. E., *Swallowfield and its Owners* (London: Longman, Green & Co., 1901); *Three Generations of Fascinating Women and Other Sketches from Family History*, 2nd edition (London: Longman, Green & Co., 1905).

Russell, Gillian and Tuite, Clare (eds), *Romantic Sociability: Social Networks and Literary Culture in Britain, 1770-1840* (Cambridge: Cambridge University Press, 2002).

Russell, Lord, of Liverpool, *Caroline. The Unhappy Queen* (London: Robert Hale, 1967).

Russell, Lord John (ed.), *The Memoir, Journals and Correspondence of Thomas Moore*, 8 vols (London: Longman, Brown, Green & Longmans, 1856).

Sadleir, Michael, *XIX Century Fiction: A Bibliographical Record Based on His Own Collection*, 2 vols (London: Constable, 1951); *The Strange Life of Lady Blessington* (London: Constable & Co., 1947); *Bulwer and his Wife: A Panorama 1803-1836* (London: Deutsch, 1955).

Sadleir, Thomas U. and Dickinson, Page L., *Georgian Mansions in Ireland* (Dublin: Dublin University Press, 1915).

Sanders, Lloyd, *The Holland House Circle* (London: Methuen & Co., 1908).

Saul, David, *Prince of Pleasure* (London: Little, Brown, 1998).

Saxon, A. H., *The London Pleasure Gardens of the 18th Century* (London: Macmillan, 1896).

Schofield, Mary Anne and Macheski, Cecilia, *Fetter'd or Free? British Women Novelists 1670-1815* (Athens, Ohio: Ohio University Press, 1986).

Scott, Lady Lucy Caroline, *Marriage in High Life*, ed. Lady Charlotte Bury (London: Henry Colburn, 1828).

Scott, Walter, *Minstrelsy of the Scottish Border*, 4 vols (Edinburgh, 1802); *Heart of Midlothian*, 4 vols (Edinburgh: Archibald Constable and Co., 1818); *The House of Aspen. A Tragedy* (Philadelphia: C. Alexander, 1830); *The Journals of Sir Walter Scott 1825-1832: From the Original Manuscript at Abbotsford*, 2 vols (Edinburgh: D. Douglas,1890-91); *The Lady of the Lake* (Edinburgh, 1816); *The Letters of Sir Walter Scott 1787-1807*, eds H. J. C. Grierson, et al., 12 vols (London: Constable, 1828-31;1832-7).

Scotts Shipbuilders, *Two Hundred years of Shipbuilding by the Scotts at Greenock* (Greenock: Scotts, 1906 and 1951).

di Sermoneta, Vittoria, duchessa., *The Locks of Norbury. A story of a Remarkable Family in the XVIIIth and XIXth Centuries* (London: John Murray, 1940).

Sharpe, Charles Kirkpatrick, *Letters to and from Charles Kirkpatrick Sharpe with a Memoir by W. K. R. Bedford*, ed. Alexander Allardyce, 2 vols (Edinburgh: William Blackwood & Sons, 1888).

Shattock, Joanne, *Politics and Reviewers. The 'Edinburgh' and the 'Quarterly' in the Early Victorian Age* (Leicester: Leicester University Press, 1989).

Shee, William A., *My Contemporaries, 1830-1870* (London: Hurst & Blackett, 1893).

Shevelow, Kathryn, *Women and Print Culture; The Construction of Femininity in the Early Periodical* (London: Routledge, 1989).

Simmel, Georg, *On Women, Sexuality and Love*, tr. Guy Oakes (New Haven, Conn.: Yale University Press, 1984).

Sisman, Adam, *Boswell's Presumptuous Task: Writing the Life of Dr Johnson* (London: Harper Perennial, 2006).

Smith, Charles Eastlake (ed.), *The Journals and Correspondence of Lady Eastlake 1809-1893*, 2 vols (London: John Murray, 1895).

Smith, E. A., *A Queen on Trial: The Affair of Queen Caroline* (Stroud: Sutton,1993/4).

Smith, R. A., *Late Georgian and Regency England 1760-1837* (Cambridge: Cambridge University Press, 1984).

Soames, Mary, *The Profligate Duke: George Spencer-Churchill, Fifth Duke of Marlborough and His Duchess* (London: Collins, 1987).

Solkin, David (ed.), *Art on the Line. The Royal Academy Exhibitions at Somerset House 1780-1836* (London: Courtauld Inst., 2001).

Somerset, Anne, *Ladies-in-Waiting from the Tudors to the Present Day* (London: George Weidenfeld and Nicolson, 1984).

Sontag, Susan, *The Volcano Lover: a Romance* (London: Vintage, 1992).

Spalding, Philip, *Self-Harvest: A Study of Diaries and the Diarist* (London: Independent Press, 1949).

Spencer, Jane, *The Rise of the Woman Novelist from Aphra Behn to Jane Austen* (Oxford: Blackwell, 1986).

Spender, Dale, *Mothers of the Novel: 100 Good Women Novelists Before Jane Austen* (London: Pandora, 1986).

St Clair, William, *The Reading Nation in the Romantic Period* (Cambridge: Cambridge University Press, 2004).

de Stael, Germaine, *Corinne, or Italy*, transl. and ed. Sylvia Raphael, with introduction by John Isbell (Oxford: Oxford University Press, 1998).

Stanhope, Hester and Meryon, Charles Lewis, *Memoirs of the Lady Hester Stanhope, As Related by Herself in Conversation with her Physician*, 3 vols (London: Henry Colburn, 1845).

Stark, Mariana, *Travels in Italy*, 2 vols (London, 1802).

Stirling, A. M. W. (compiler), *The Letterbag of Lady Elizabeth Spencer Stanhope* (London, 1913).

Stone, Laurence, *The Crisis of the Aristocracy* (Oxford: Oxford University Press, 1963).

Storrie, Margaret, *Islay: Biography of an Island* (Islay: Oa Press, 2011); 'Recovering the Historic Designed Landscape of Islay Estate', *Scottish Archives* 9 (2001), pp. 59-77.

Strachey, Lytton and Fulford, Roger (eds), *The Greville Memoirs,* 2 vols (London: Macmillan, 1938)

Stuart, Lady Louisa, *Some Account of John Duke of Argyll and his Family, Written in 1827 (privately printed 1863), Reprinted in Introduction to Letters and Journals of Lady Mary Coke*, (Edinburgh: Privately printed, 1889); *Gleanings from an Old Portfolio Containing Some Correspondence Between Lady Louisa Stuart and her Sister Caroline, Countess of Portarlington, and Other Friends and Relations*, ed. Mrs Godfrey Clarke, 3 vols (Edinburgh: Privately printed for David Douglas, 1895); *Letters of Lady Louisa Stuart to Miss Louisa Clinton*, ed. James A. Home, 2 vols (Edinburgh: D. Douglas, 1903).

Surtees, Virginia (ed.), *The Grace of Friendship* (Norwich: Michael Russell Publishing, 1995).

Swann, Elsie, *Christopher North: John Wilson* (Edinburgh: Oliver and Boyd, 1934).

Swinburn, Henry, *Travels in the Two Sicilies . . . in the Years 1777, 1778, 1799 and 1780* (London: T. Cadell, 1790).

Teignmouth, Baron (Shore, Charles J.), *Memoirs of the Life, Writings and Correspondence of Sir William Jones* (London: J. W. Parker, 1835); *Sketches of the Coasts and Islands of Scotland, and the Isle of Man Descriptive of the Scenery and Illustrative of the Progressive Revolution in the . . . Social Condition of the Inhabitants of those Regions*, 2 vols (London: J. W. Parker, 1836).

Thackeray, William M., *The Four Georges* (London: Smith, Elder & Co., 1861).

Thiher, Allan, *Revels in Madness: Insanity in Medicine and Literature* (Ann Arbor, Michigan: University of Michigan, 2005).

Thomson, Duncan, *The Art of Sir Henry Raeburn 1756-1823* (Edinburgh: Scottish National Portrait Gallery, 1997).

Thomson, Mrs, *Recollections of Literary Characters and Celebrated Places*, 2 vols (London: Richard Bentley, 1854).

Thoresby, Colin, 'Romanticism and Flirtation', *Literature Compass* 1 (Oxford: Wiley-Blackwell Publishing, 2004), pp. 1-4.

Thorne, R. G., *The House of Commons, 1790-1820*, 5 vols (London: Secker & Warburg, 1986).

Ticknor, George, *Life, Letters and Journals of George Ticknor 1791-1871*, ed. G. S. Hilliard (London: Sampson Low, Marston, Searle & Rivington, 1876).

Tillyard, Stella, *Aristocrats: Caroline, Emily, Louisa and Sarah Lennox, 1740-1832* (London: Chatto & Windus, 1994).

Tisdall, Ernest P., *The Wanton Queen: the story of Britain's strangest queen* (London: Stanley Paul & Co., 1939).

Tod, Andrew (ed. and introduction), *Memoirs of a Highland Lady. Elizabeth Grant of Rothiemurchus*, 2 vols (Edinburgh: Canongate, 1988).

Todd, Janet (ed.), *British Women Writers: A Critical Reference Guide* (New York: Continuum, 1989); *A Dictionary of British and American Women Writers, 1600-1800* (London: Methuen, 1987); *Jane Austen in Context* (Cambridge: Cambridge University Press, 2005).

Tomalin, Claire, *Mrs Jordan's Profession: The Story of a great actress and a future King* (London: Viking Books, 1995).

Trethewey, Rachel, *Mistress of the Arts: The Passionate Life of Georgiana, Duchess of Bedford* (London: Hodder Headline, 2002).

Tuer, Andrew W. (annotated), *A Select Series of Ten Portraits of Ladies of Rank and Fashion from Paintings by John Hoppner Engraved by C. Wilkin* (London, New York: Leadenhall Press, Scribner,1883).

Turquan, Joseph and d'Auriac, Jules, *A Great Adventuress: Lady Hester and the Revolution in Naples (1753-1815)* (London: Herbert Jenkins Ltd, 1914).

van der Kiste, *John, George III's Children* (Stroud: Alan Sutton, 1992).

Varey, Simon, *Space and the Eighteenth-Century English Novel* (Cambridge: Cambridge University Press, 1990).

Vickery, Amanda, *The Gentleman's Daughter: Women's Lives in Georgian England* (New Haven and London: Yale University Press, 1998).

Vincent, E. R. P., *Ugo Foscolo in English Society: An Italian in Regency England* (Cambridge: Cambridge University Press, 1953).

Vincenti, Caroline et al., *Palaces of Rome* (London: Thames and Hudson, 1997).

Walden, Sarah, *Whistler and His Mother; An Unexpected Relationship: Secrets of an American Masterpiece* (London: Gibson Square, 2003).

Walker, Frank Arneil, *The Buildings of Scotland, Argyll and Bute* (London: Penguin, 2000).

Walpole, Horace, *Horace Walpole's Correspondence*, ed. Edwine M Martz (Oxford: OUP; New Haven and London: Yale,University Press, 1983); *The Last Journals of Horace Walpole 1771-1783*, with notes by Dr Doran, ed. A. Francis Stewart, 2 vols (London: John Lane Bodley Head, 1910); *The Letters of Horace Walpole fourth Earl of Oxford*, ed. Mrs Paget Toynbee, 19 vols (Oxford: Clarendon Press, 1903-28); *Reminiscences Written in 1788 for the Amusement of Miss Mary and Miss Agnes Berry* (London: John Sharpe, 1818).

Watkins, David, *The Royal Interiors of Regency England from Watercolours, First Published by W. H. Pyne in 1817-1820* (London: Dent, 1984).

Weedon, A.,*Victorian Publishing: the Economics of Book Production for a Mass Market 1836-1916* (Aldershot: Ashgate, 2003).

Weigall, Lady Rose (ed. and daughter),*The Correspondence of Lady Burghersh with the Duke of Wellington* (London: John Murray, 1903); *The Correspondence of Lord Burghersh afterwards eleventh Earl of Westmoreland 1808-1840*, 2 vols (London: John Murray, 1912).

Wharton, G. and P., *The Queens of Society* (London: J. W. Jarvis & Son, 1890).

Wheatley, Henry B. (ed.), *The Historical and Posthumous Memoirs of Sir Nathaniel William Wraxall, 1772-1784*, 5 vols (London: Bickers & Son, 1884).

Wilkes, Roger, *Scandal. A Scurrilous History of Gossip* (London: Atlanta Books, 2003).

Wheeler, Michael, *English Fiction of the Victorian Period: 1830-1890* (London; New York: Longman, 1985).

White, Cynthia Leslie, *Women's Magazines 1693-1968 (London: Michael Joseph, 1970).*

Williams, D. E., *The Life and Correspondence of Sir Thomas Lawrence*, 2 vols (London: Henry Colburn and Richard Bentley, 1831).

Williamson, George C., *John Russell, RA* (London: George Bell & Sons, 1894).

Willis, Nathaniel Parker, *Pencillings by the Way*, 3 vols (London: John Macrone, 1835); *People I Have Met, or Pictures of Society and People of Mark, Drawn Under a Thin Veil of Fiction* (New York: Baker & Scribner, 1850).

Wilson, Francis, *The Courtesan's Revenge* (London: Faber and Faber, 2003).

Wilson. Hariette, *Memoir of Hariette Wilson Written by Herself*, 2 vols (London: Eveleigh Nash, 1909).

Wilton, Andrew and Bignamini, Flaria (eds), *Grand Tour: The Lure of Italy in the Eighteenth Century* (London: Tate Gallery Publications, 1996).

Wright, Thomas (ed.), *The Works of James Gillray. The Caricaturist with the Story of his Life and Times* (London: Chatto and Windus, 1873); *Historical and Descriptive Account of the Caricatures of James Gillray Comprising a Political and Humorous History of the Latter Part of the Reign of George the Third* (London: Henry G. Bone, 1851).

Wrigley, Richard and Revill, George (eds), *Pathologies of Travel* (Amsterdam: Rodopi, 2000).

Wyndham, William, *Diary of Rt. Hon. William Wyndham 1784-1810*, ed. Mrs Henry Baring (London: Longmans, 1866).

Wolff, Robert Lee (compiler), *Nineteenth-Century Fiction* (New York; London: Garland, 1981-1986).

Wordsworth, Dorothy, *Recollection of a Tour Made in Scotland AD 1803*, ed. J. C. Shairp, (Edinburgh: Edmonston and Douglas, 1874).

Wynne, Elizabeth, *The Wynne Diaries 1789-1820*, ed. Anne Freemantle, third edition, 3 vols (Oxford: Oxford University Press, 1982).

Wynn, Miss Frances Williams, (ed.), *Diaries of a Lady of Quality from 1797 to 1844*, ed. A. Hayward (London: Longmans, 1864).

Index